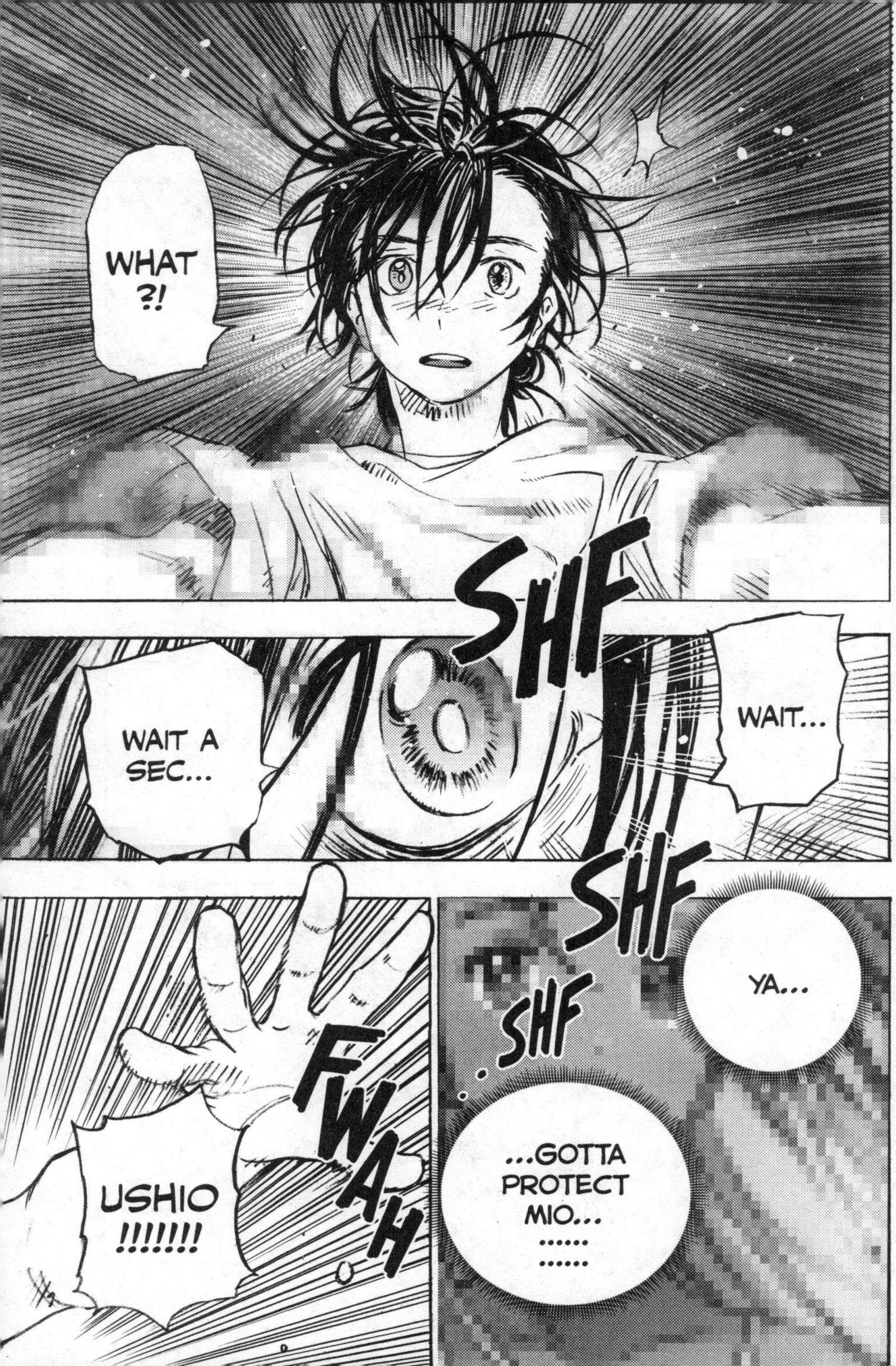
WHAT ?!
SHF
WAIT...
WAIT A SEC...
SHF
SHF
YA...
...GOTTA PROTECT MIO... ....
FWAH
USHIO !!!!!!!

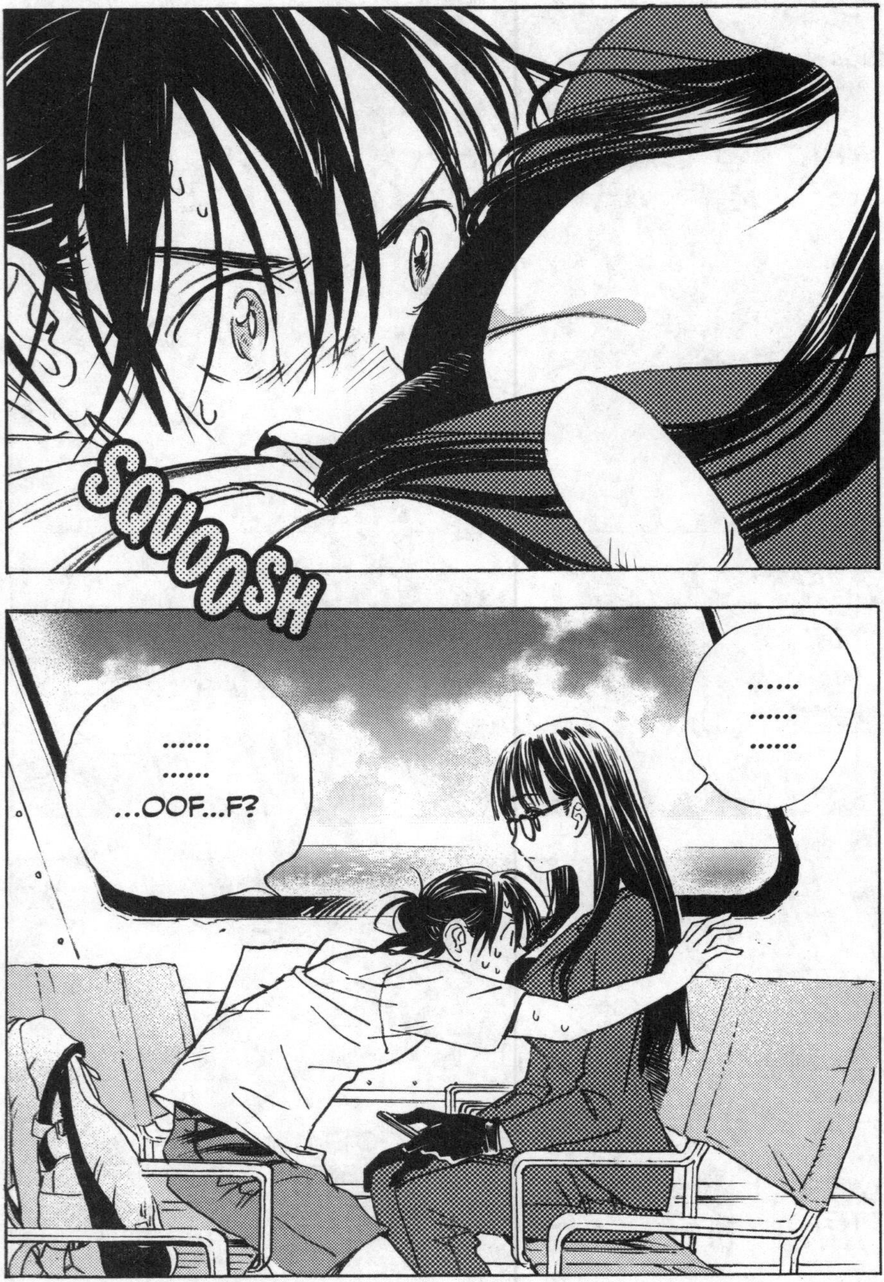
SQUOOSH
....
....OOF...F?

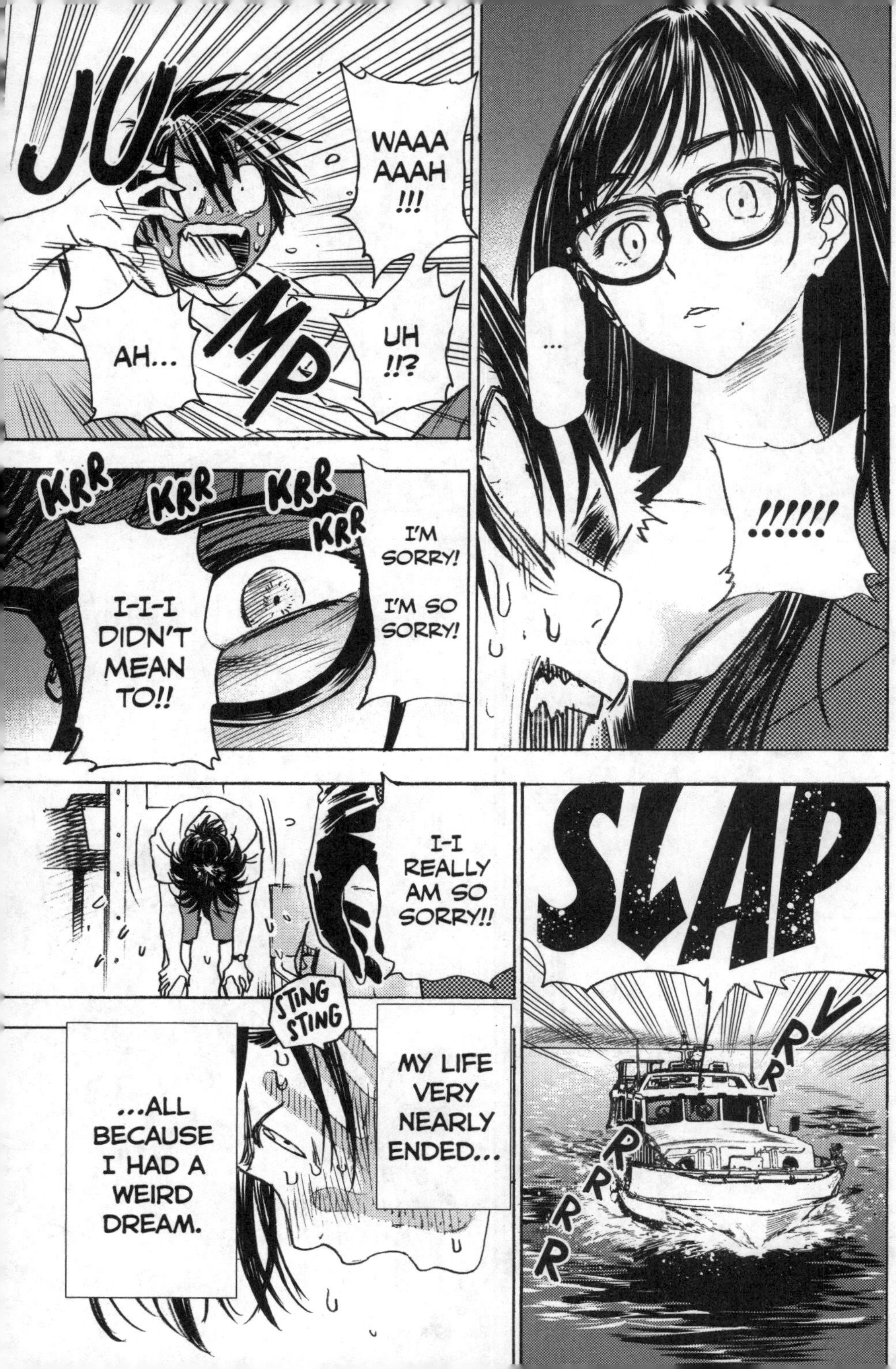
...
!!!!!!
WAAA AAAH !!!
JU
MP
UH !!?
AH...
KRR KRR KRR KRR
I'M SORRY!
I'M SO SORRY!
I-I-I DIDN'T MEAN TO!!
SLAP
RRRRRRRV
I-I REALLY AM SO SORRY!!
STING STING
MY LIFE VERY NEARLY ENDED...
...ALL BECAUSE I HAD A WEIRD DREAM.

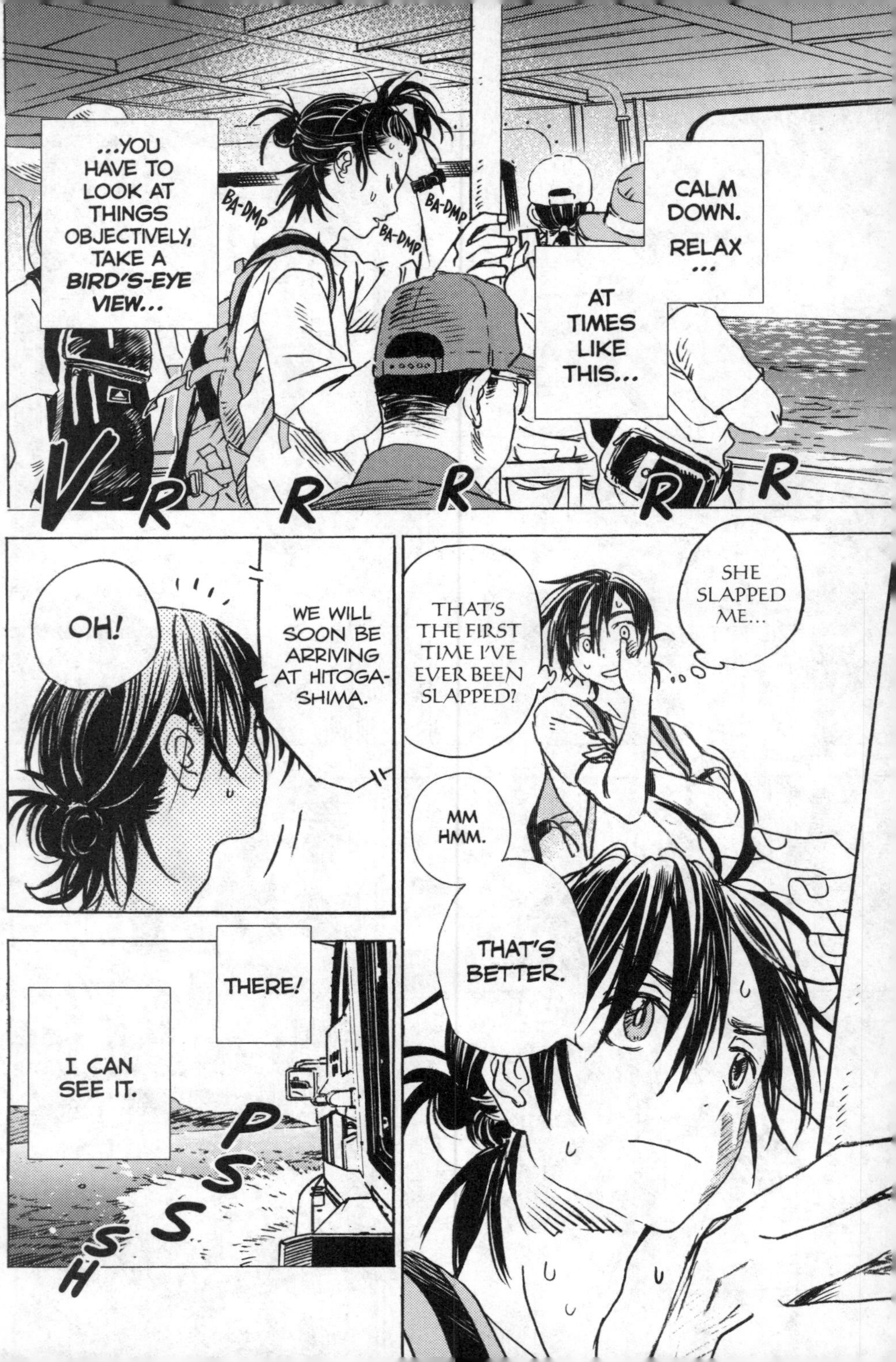
CALM DOWN.
RELAX ...
AT TIMES LIKE THIS...
...YOU HAVE TO LOOK AT THINGS OBJECTIVELY, TAKE A BIRD'S-EYE VIEW...
BA-DMP
BA-DMP
BA-DMP
V-RRRRR
SHE SLAPPED ME...
THAT'S THE FIRST TIME I'VE EVER BEEN SLAPPED?
MM HMM.
THAT'S BETTER.
WE WILL SOON BE ARRIVING AT HITOGA-SHIMA.
OH!
THERE!
I CAN SEE IT.
PSSSHH

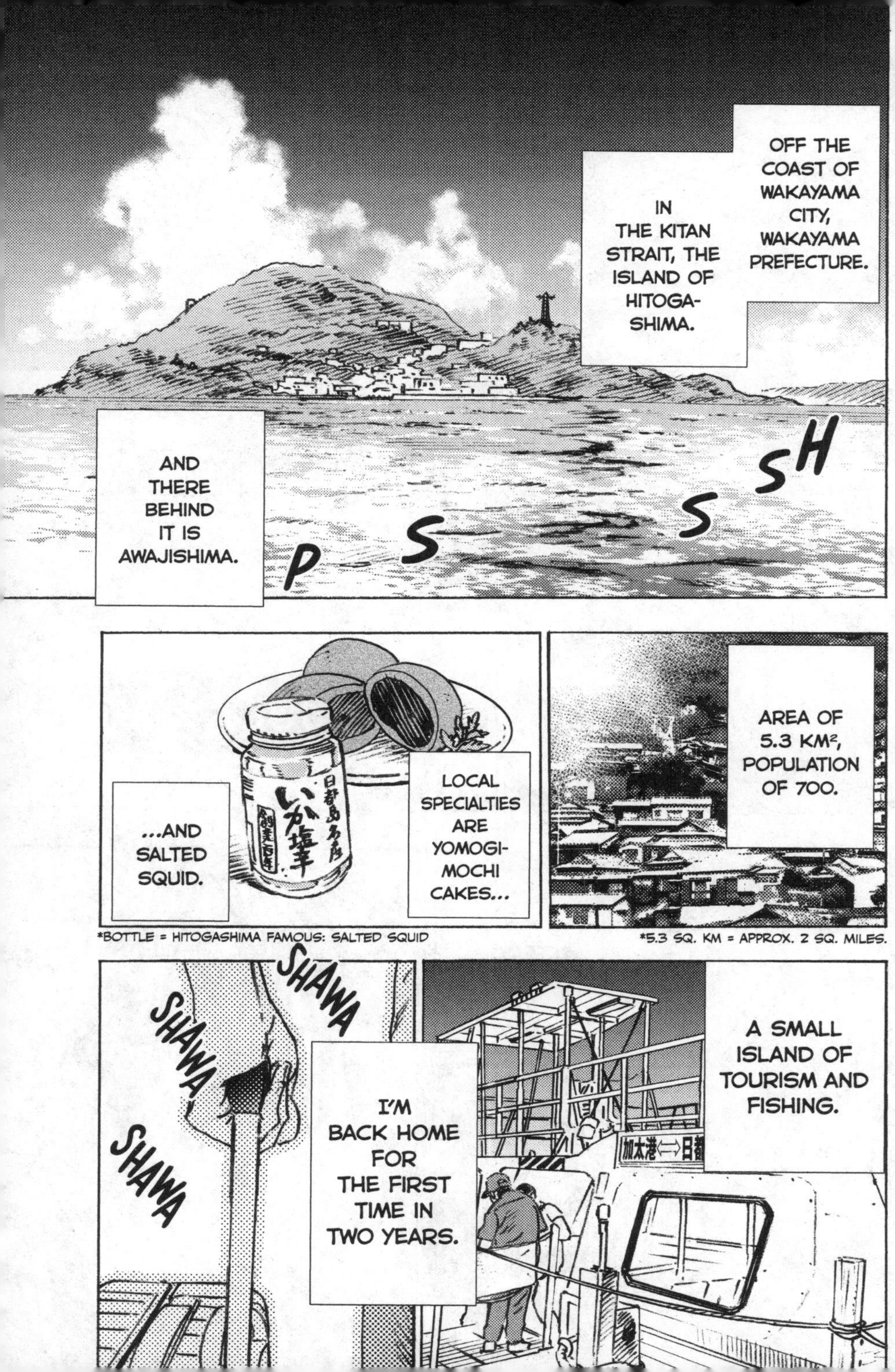
OFF THE COAST OF WAKAYAMA CITY, WAKAYAMA PREFECTURE.
IN THE KITAN STRAIT, THE ISLAND OF HITOGA-SHIMA.
PSSSH
AND THERE BEHIND IT IS AWAJISHIMA.
AREA OF 5.3 KM^2, POPULATION OF 700.
*5.3 SQ. KM = APPROX. 2 SQ. MILES.
LOCAL SPECIALTIES ARE YOMOGI-MOCHI CAKES...
日都島名産
いか塩辛
...AND SALTED SQUID.
*BOTTLE = HITOGASHIMA FAMOUS: SALTED SQUID
A SMALL ISLAND OF TOURISM AND FISHING.
加太港⇔日都
I'M BACK HOME FOR THE FIRST TIME IN TWO YEARS.
SHAWA
SHAWA
SHAWA
SHAWA

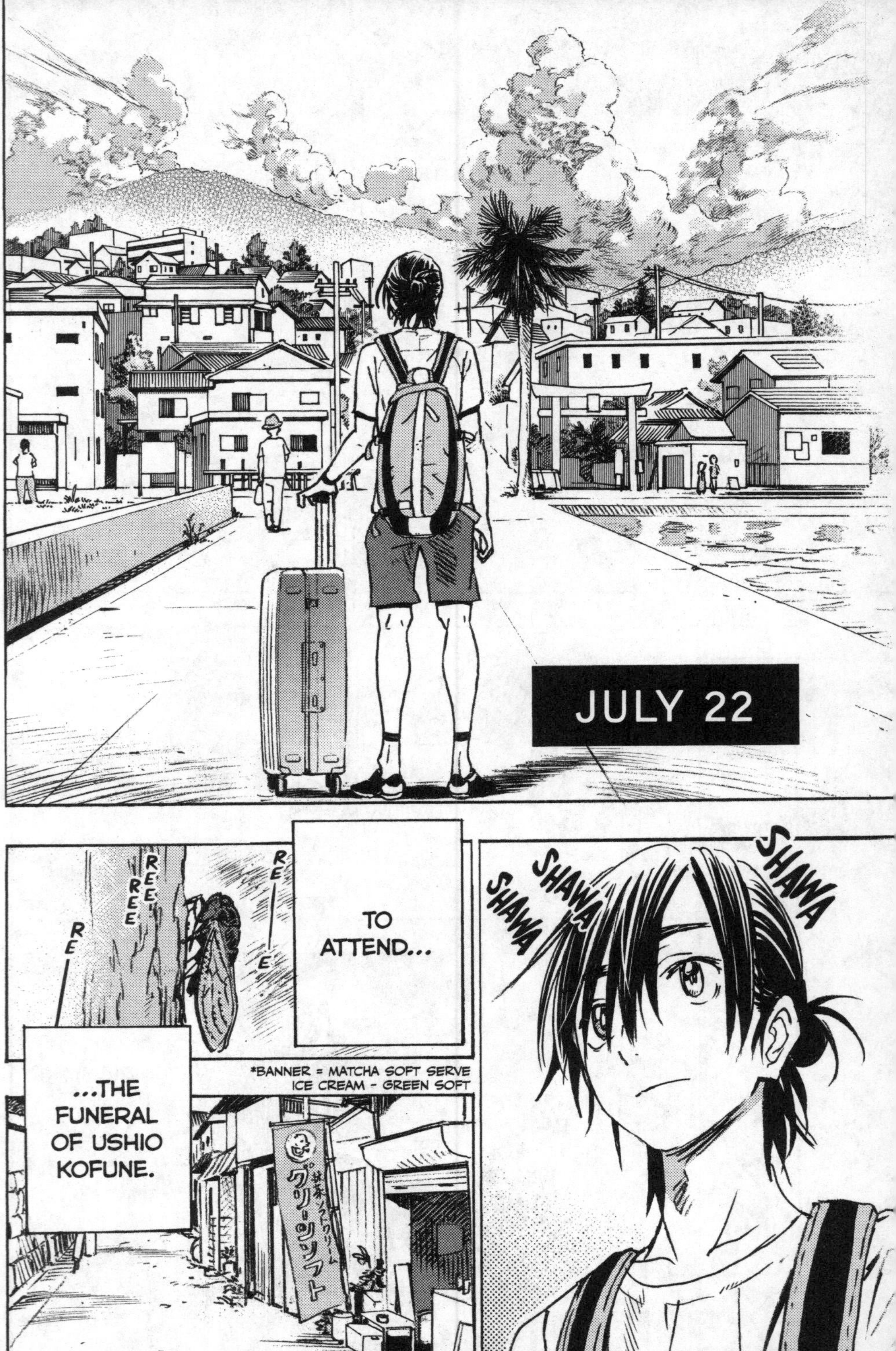
JULY 22
SHAWA
SHAWA
SHAWA
SHAWA
TO ATTEND...
RE— E
REE REE
RE—
...THE FUNERAL OF USHIO KOFUNE.
*BANNER = MATCHA SOFT SERVE ICE CREAM - GREEN SOFT
抹茶ソフトクリーム
グリーンソフト

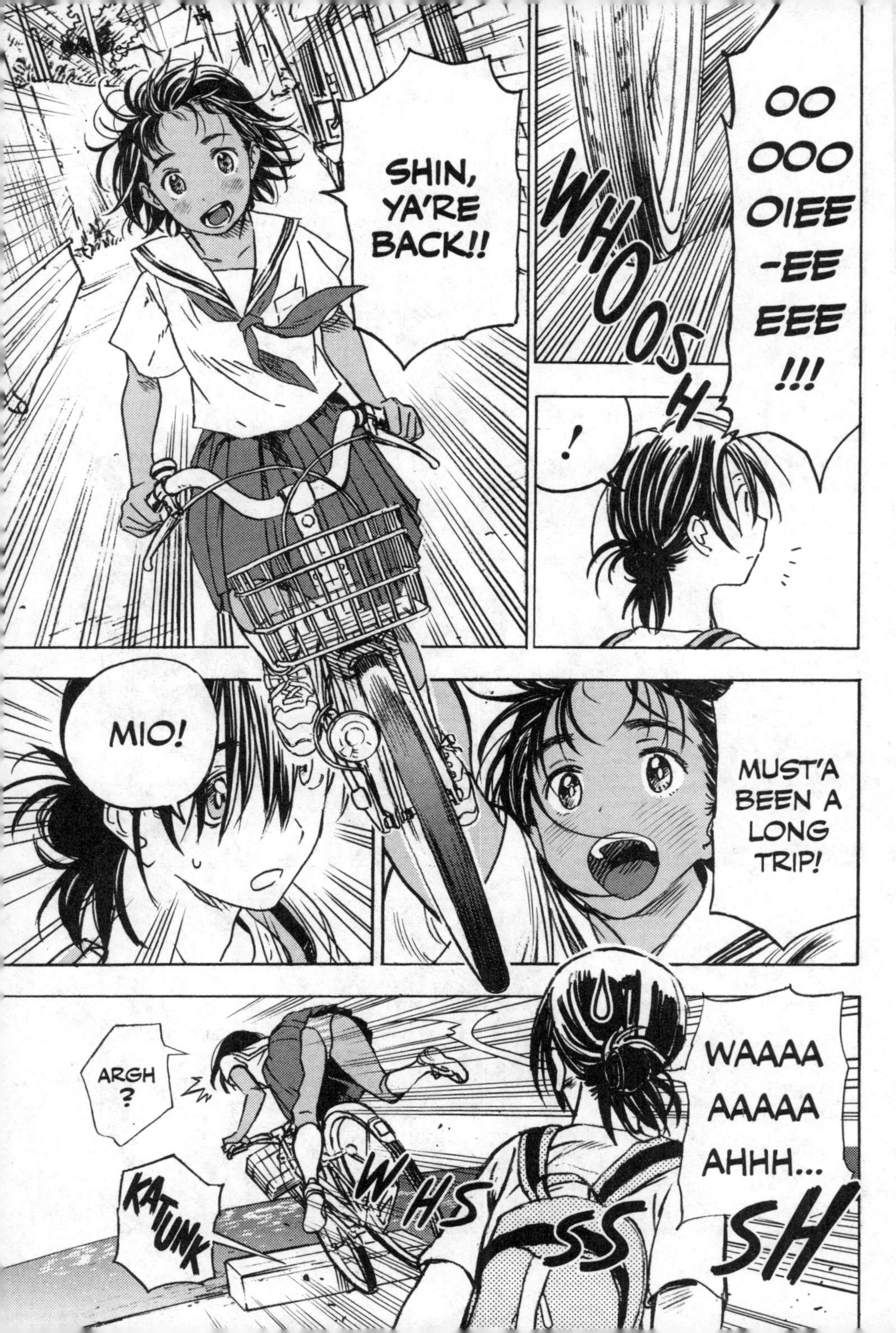
OO OOO OIEE -EE EEE !!!
WHOOSH
!
SHIN, YA'RE BACK!!
MUST'A BEEN A LONG TRIP!
MIO!
WAAAA AAAAA AHHH...
WHSSSSH
ARGH ?
KATUNK

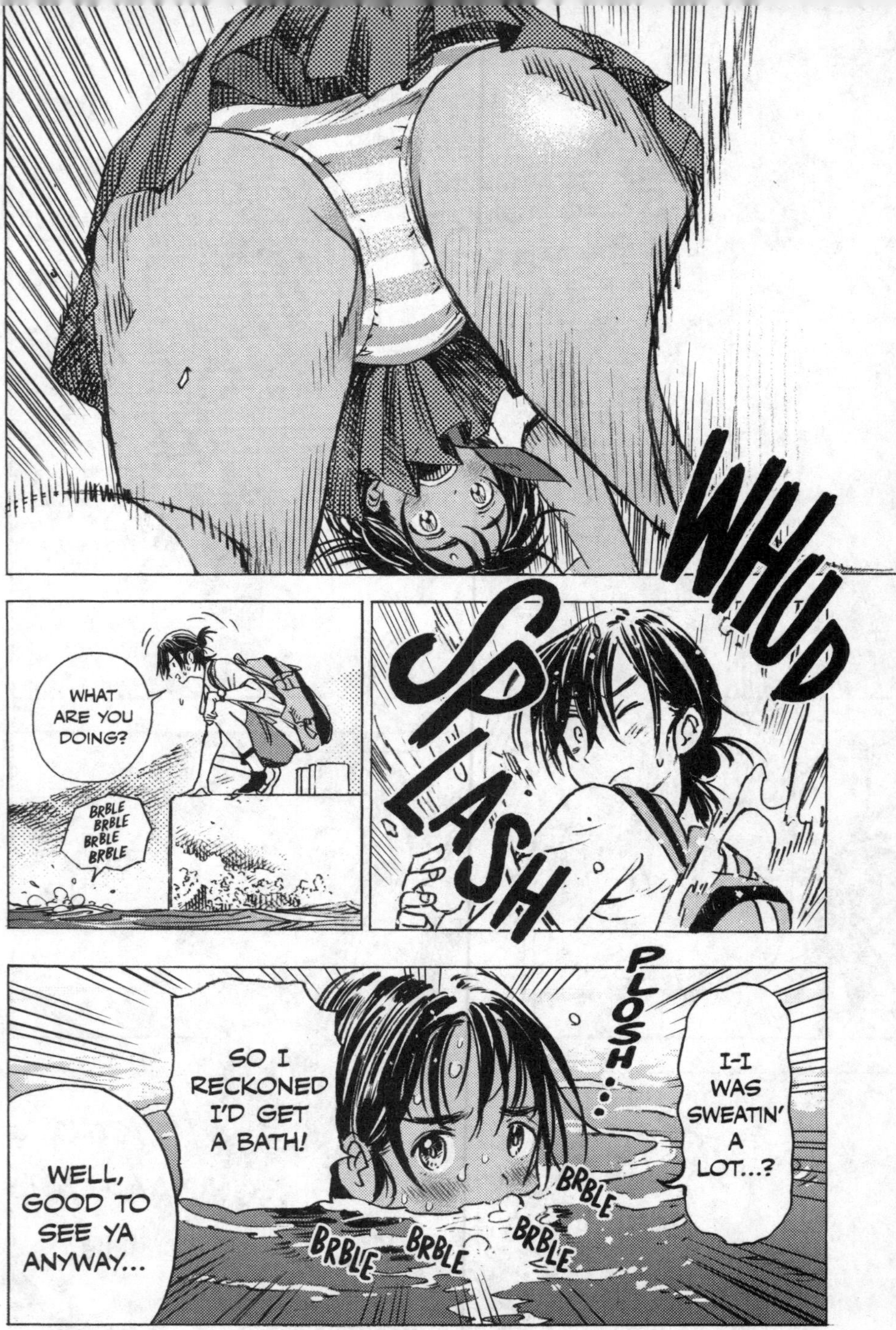
WHUD
SPLASH
WHAT ARE YOU DOING?
BRBLE BRBLE BRBLE BRBLE
PLOSH...
I-I WAS SWEATIN' A LOT...?
BRBLE
BRBLE
SO I RECKONED I'D GET A BATH!
BRBLE
BRBLE
WELL, GOOD TO SEE YA ANYWAY...

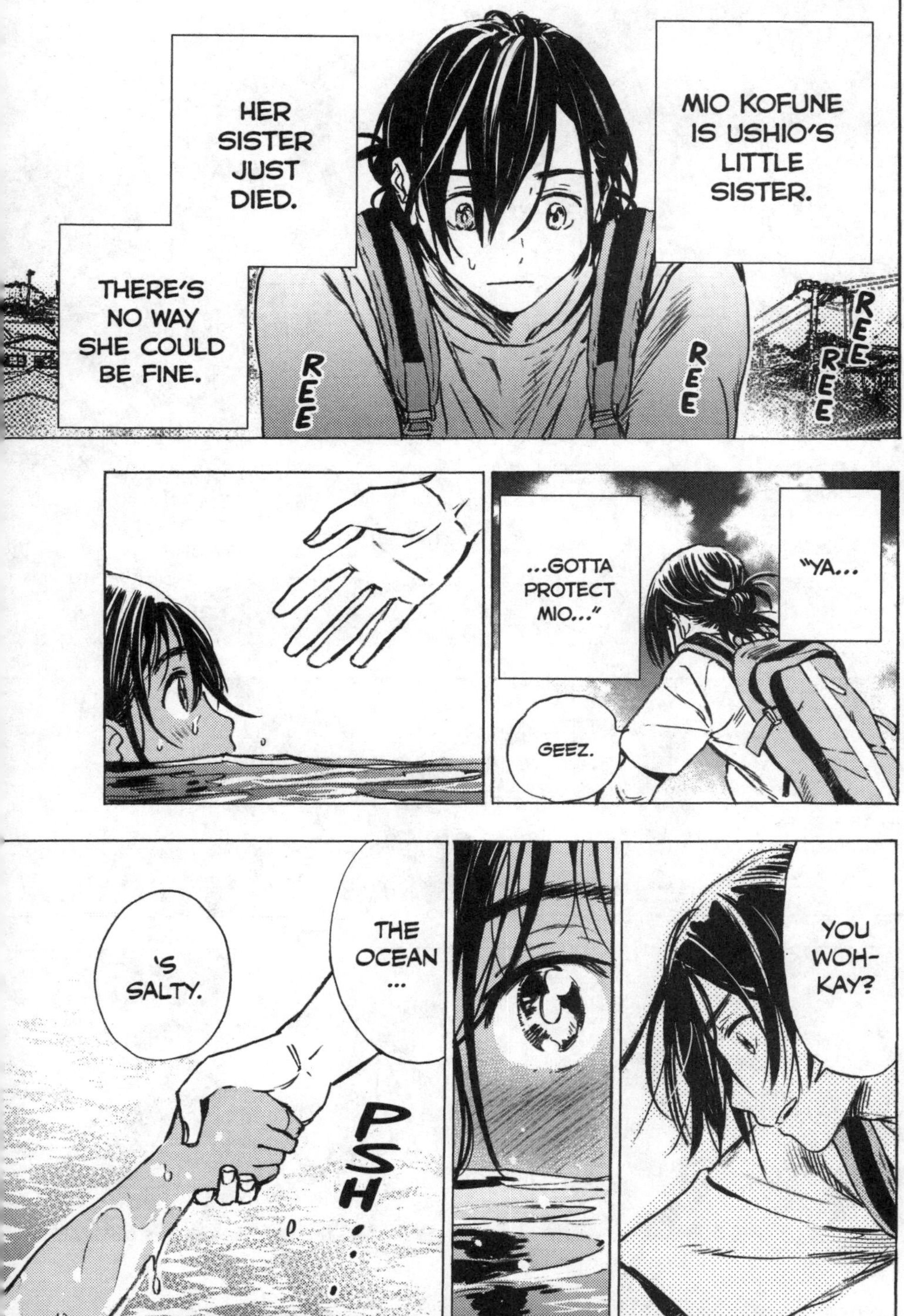
MIO KOFUNE IS USHIO'S LITTLE SISTER.
REE
REE
REE
HER SISTER JUST DIED.
THERE'S NO WAY SHE COULD BE FINE.
REE
"YA...
...GOTTA PROTECT MIO..."
GEEZ.
YOU WOH-KAY?
PSH...
THE OCEAN ...
'S SALTY.

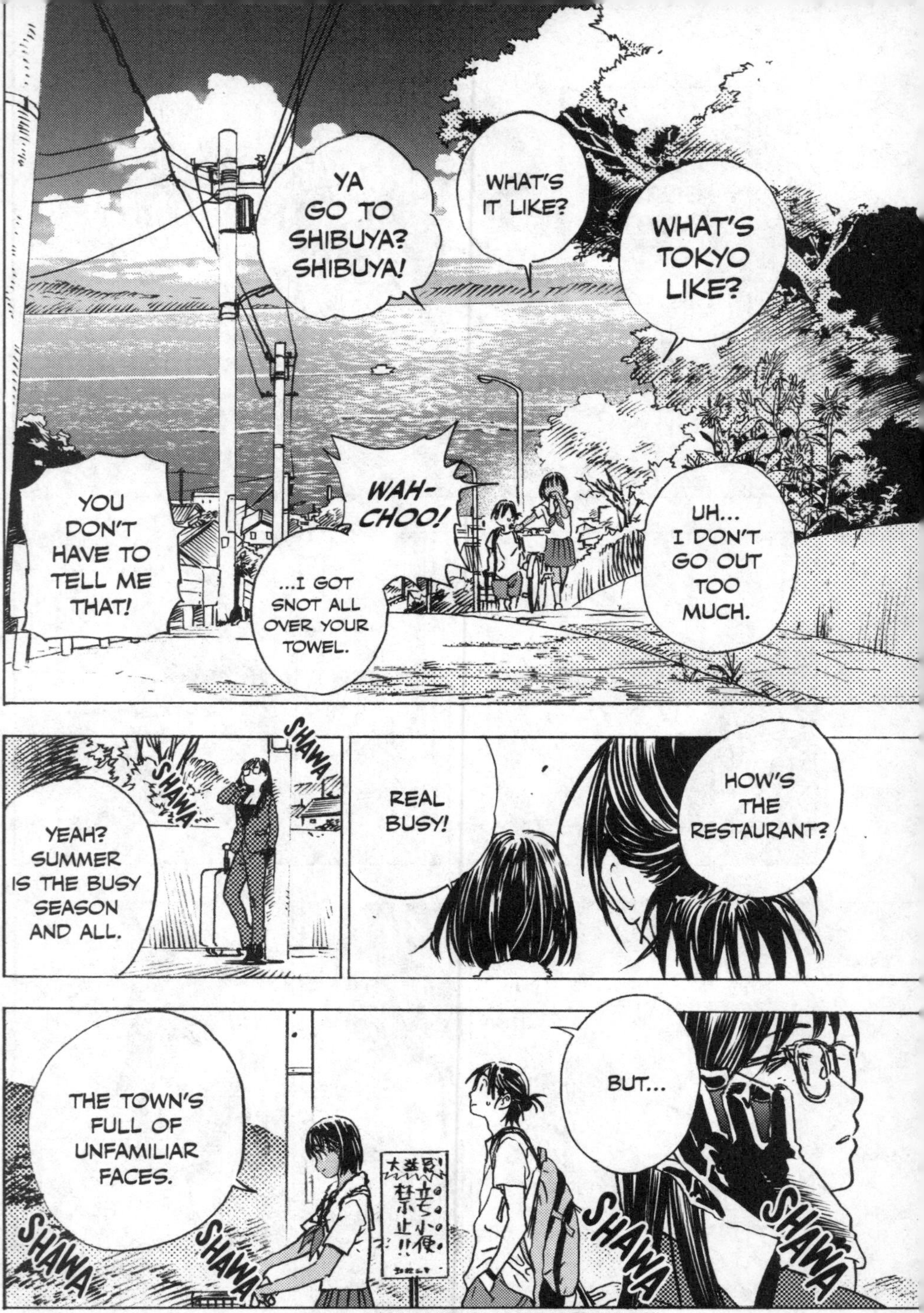
WHAT'S TOKYO LIKE?
WHAT'S IT LIKE?
YA GO TO SHIBUYA? SHIBUYA!
UH... I DON'T GO OUT TOO MUCH.
WAH-CHOO!
...I GOT SNOT ALL OVER YOUR TOWEL.
YOU DON'T HAVE TO TELL ME THAT!
HOW'S THE RESTAURANT?
REAL BUSY!
SHAWA
SHAWA
SHAWA
YEAH? SUMMER IS THE BUSY SEASON AND ALL.
BUT...
SHAWA
SHAWA
THE TOWN'S FULL OF UNFAMILIAR FACES.
SHAWA
SHAWA

*SIGN = DON'T DO IT! PEEING PROHIBITED!!

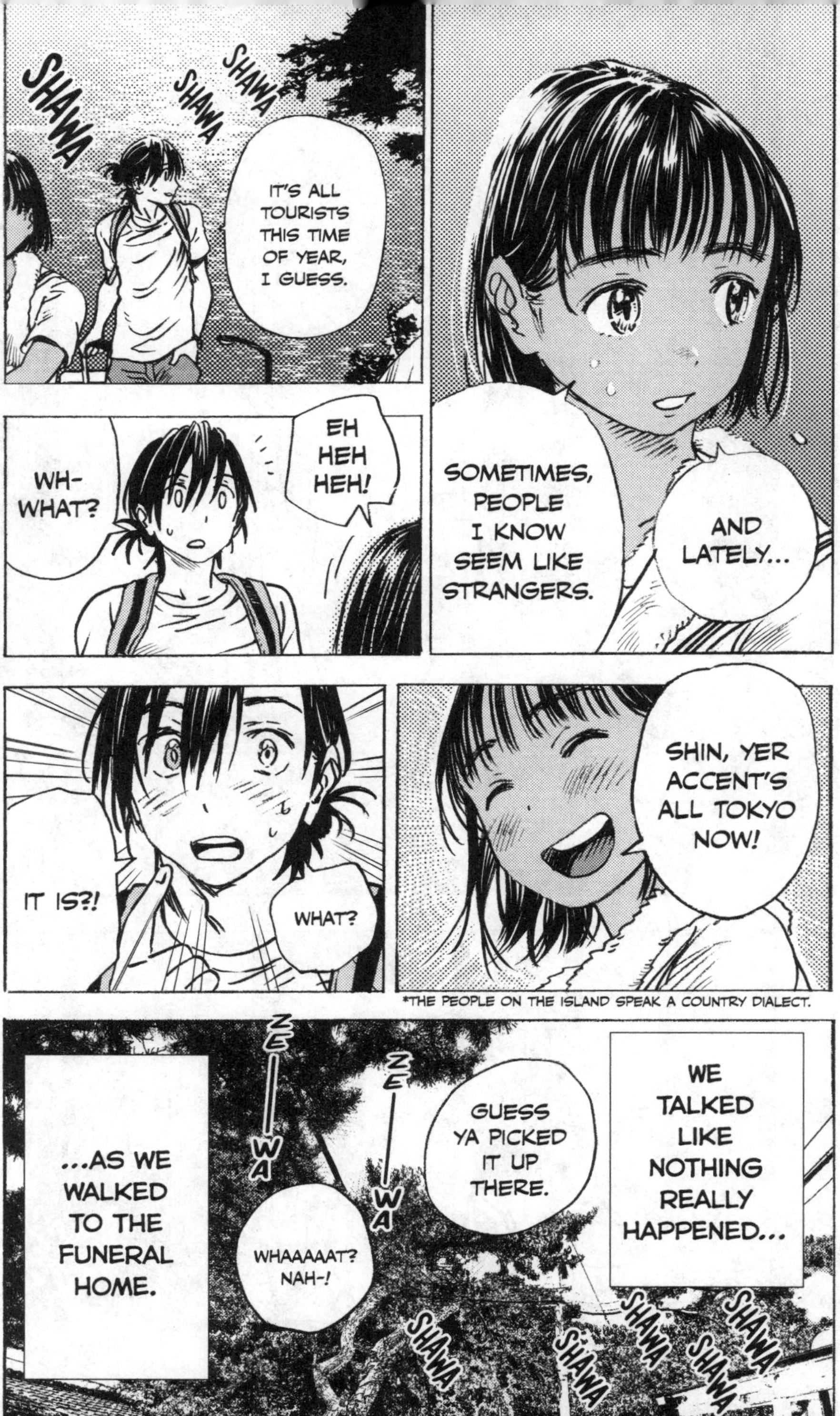
SOMETIMES, PEOPLE I KNOW SEEM LIKE STRANGERS.
AND LATELY...
SHAWA
SHAWA
SHAWA
SHAWA
IT'S ALL TOURISTS THIS TIME OF YEAR, I GUESS.
EH HEH HEH!
WH- WHAT?
SHIN, YER ACCENT'S ALL TOKYO NOW!
WHAT?
IT IS?!
WE TALKED LIKE NOTHING REALLY HAPPENED...
GUESS YA PICKED IT UP THERE.
ZE-WA
ZE-WA
WHAAAAAT? NAH-!
...AS WE WALKED TO THE FUNERAL HOME.
SHAWA
SHAWA
SHAWA
SHAWA
SHAWA
SHAWA

*THE PEOPLE ON THE ISLAND SPEAK A COUNTRY DIALECT.

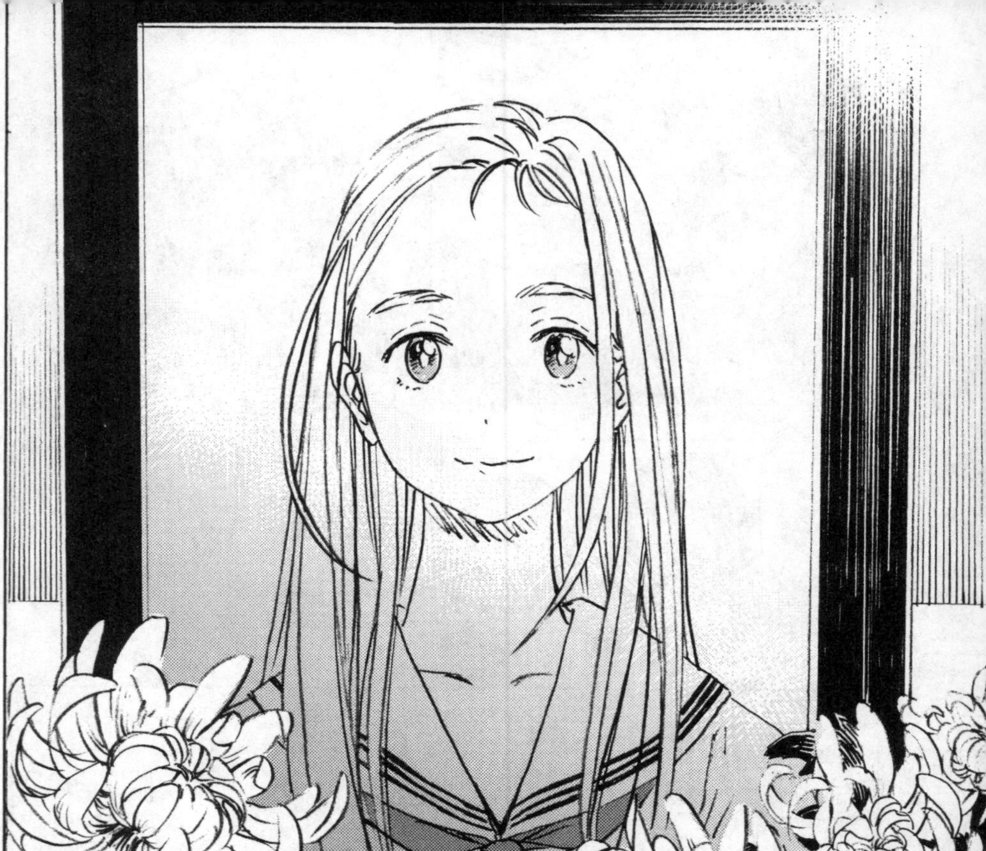
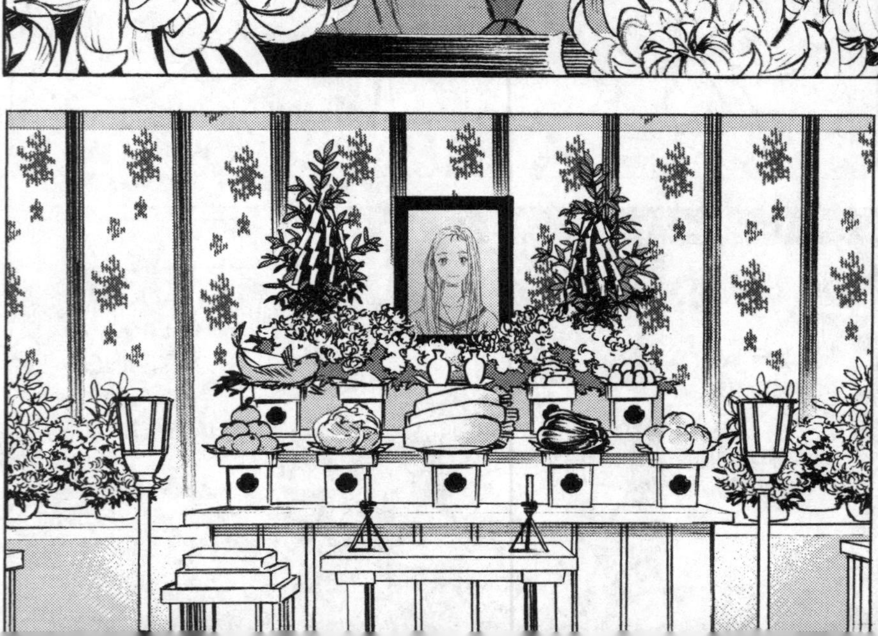

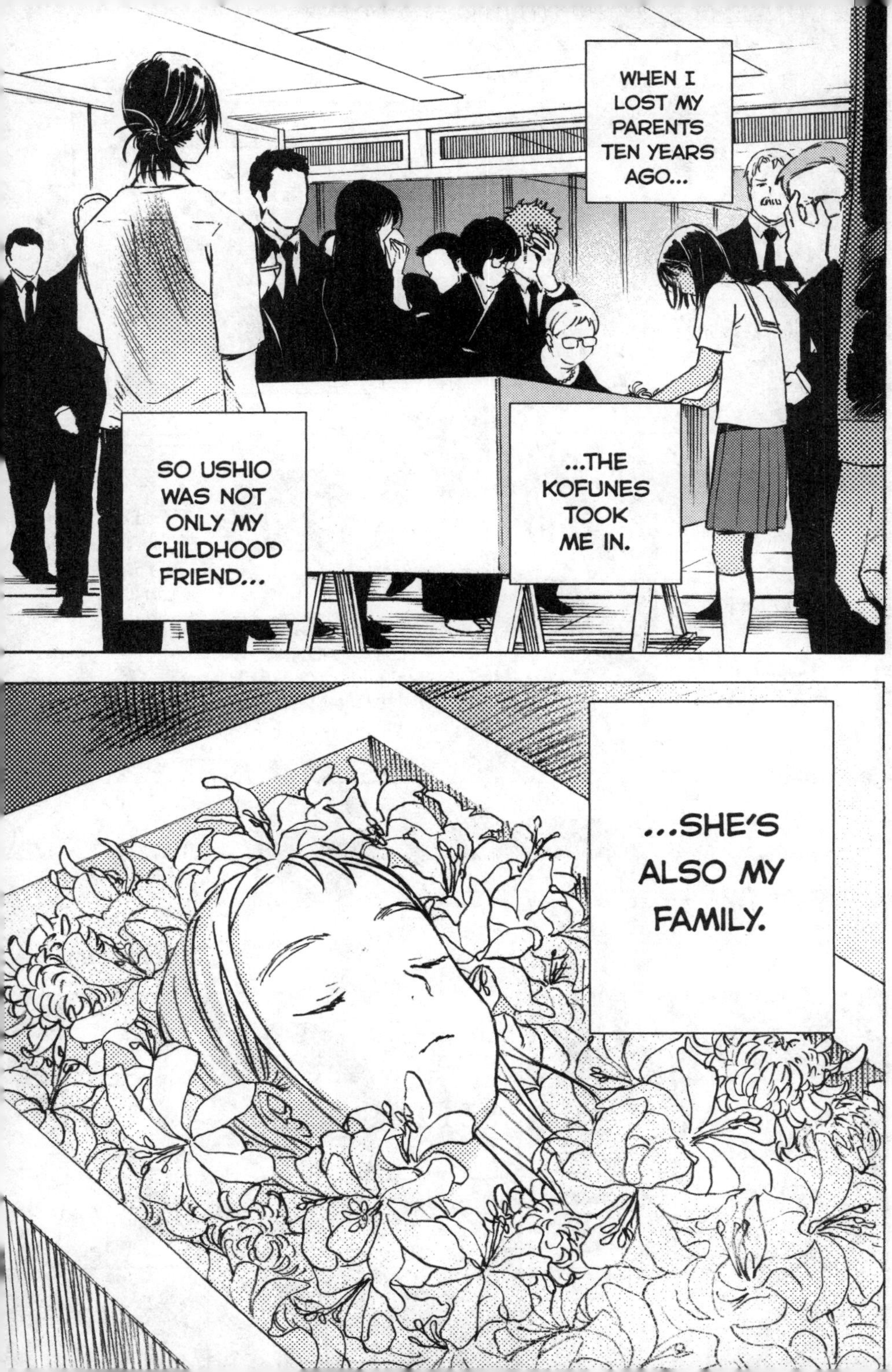
WHEN I LOST MY PARENTS TEN YEARS AGO...
...THE KOFUNES TOOK ME IN.
SO USHIO WAS NOT ONLY MY CHILDHOOD FRIEND...
...SHE'S ALSO MY FAMILY.

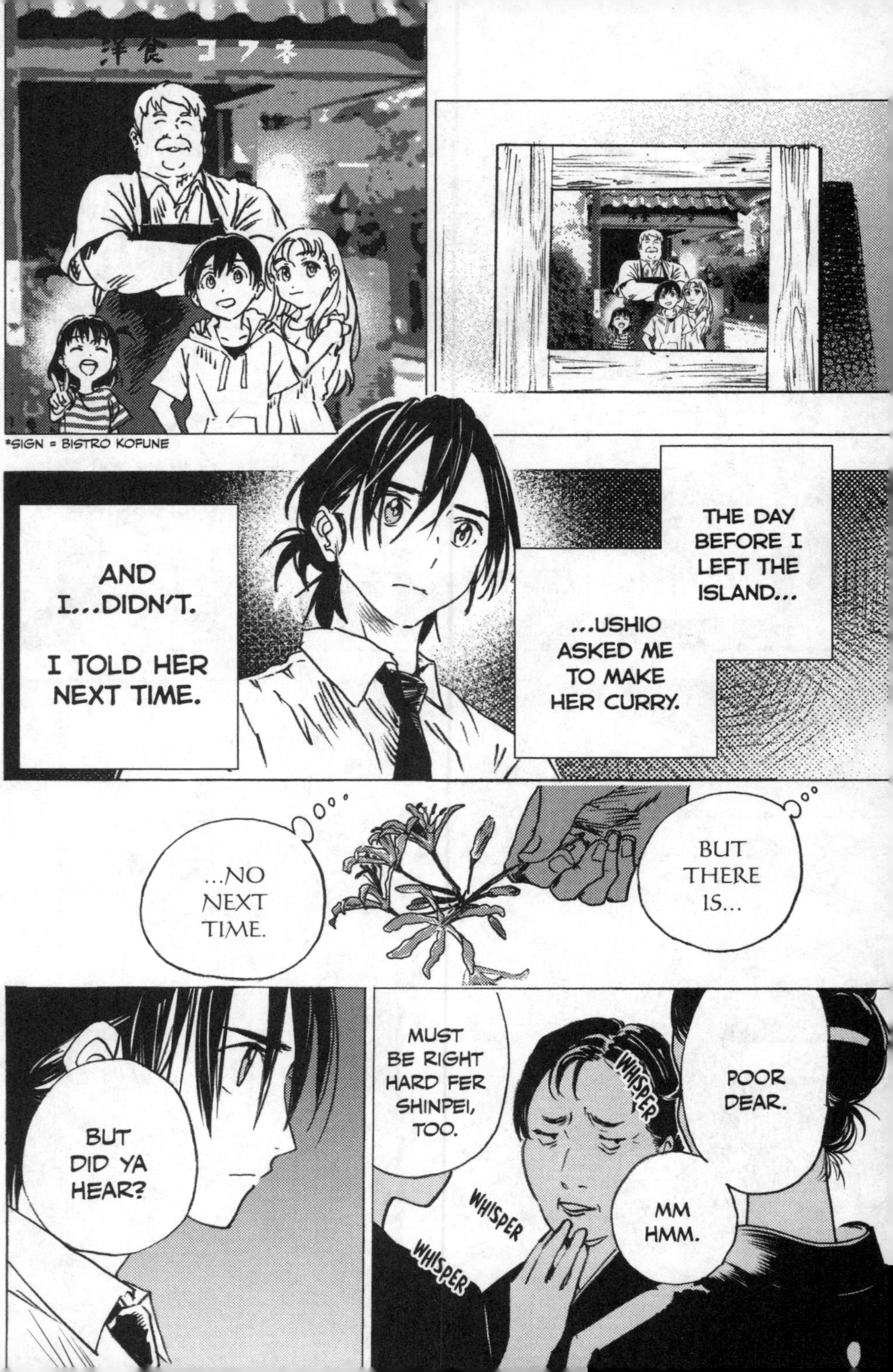
洋食 コフネ
*SIGN = BISTRO KOFUNE
THE DAY BEFORE I LEFT THE ISLAND...
...USHIO ASKED ME TO MAKE HER CURRY.
AND I...DIDN'T.
I TOLD HER NEXT TIME.
BUT THERE IS...
...NO NEXT TIME.
POOR DEAR.
MUST BE RIGHT HARD FER SHINPEI, TOO.
WHISPER
MM HMM.
WHISPER
WHISPER
BUT DID YA HEAR?

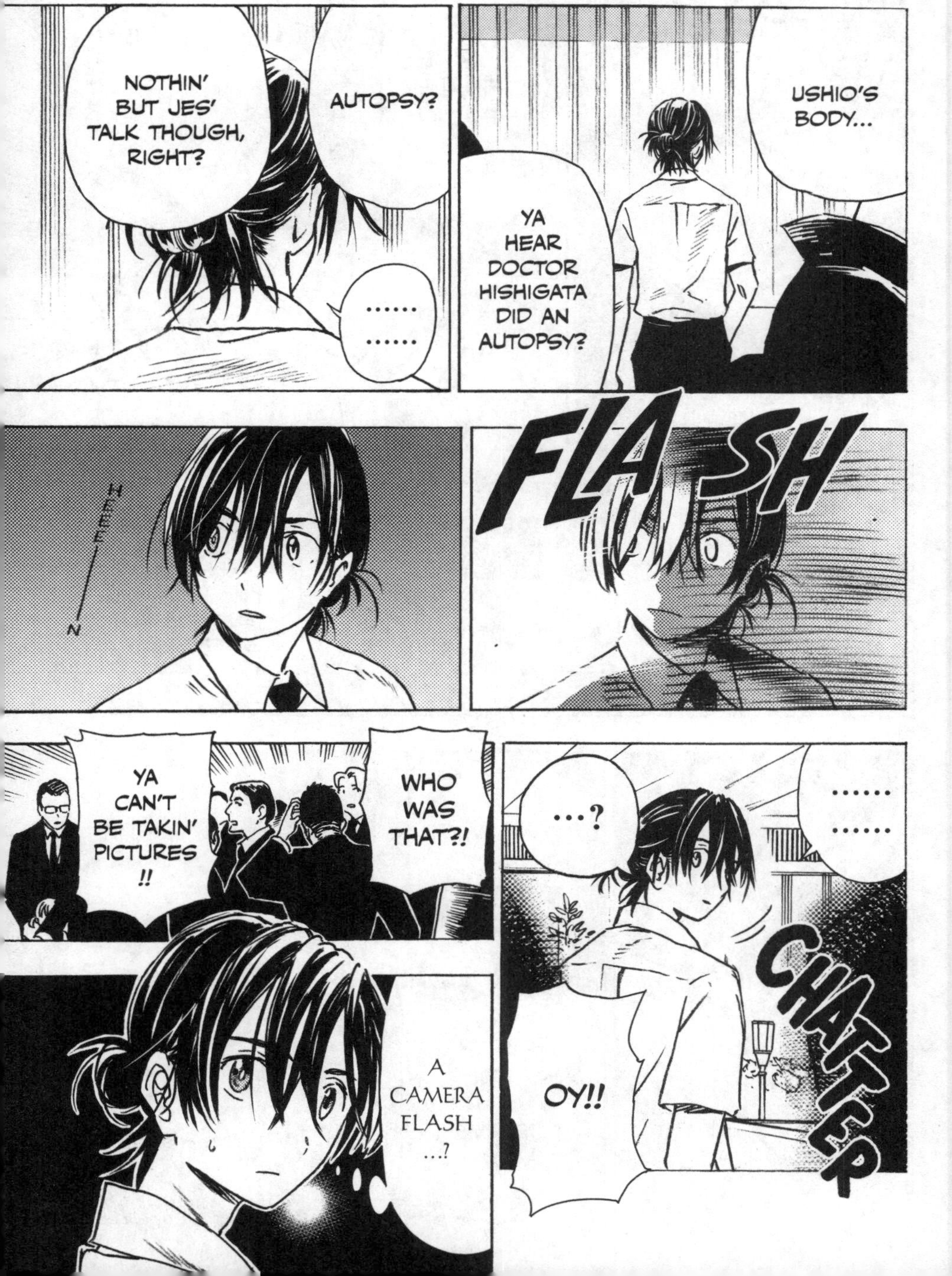
USHIO'S BODY...
YA HEAR DOCTOR HISHIGATA DID AN AUTOPSY?
AUTOPSY?
NOTHIN' BUT JES' TALK THOUGH, RIGHT?
…… ……
FLASH
HEEEN
…… ……
…?
CHATTER
OY!!
WHO WAS THAT?!
YA CAN'T BE TAKIN' PICTURES !!
A CAMERA FLASH …?

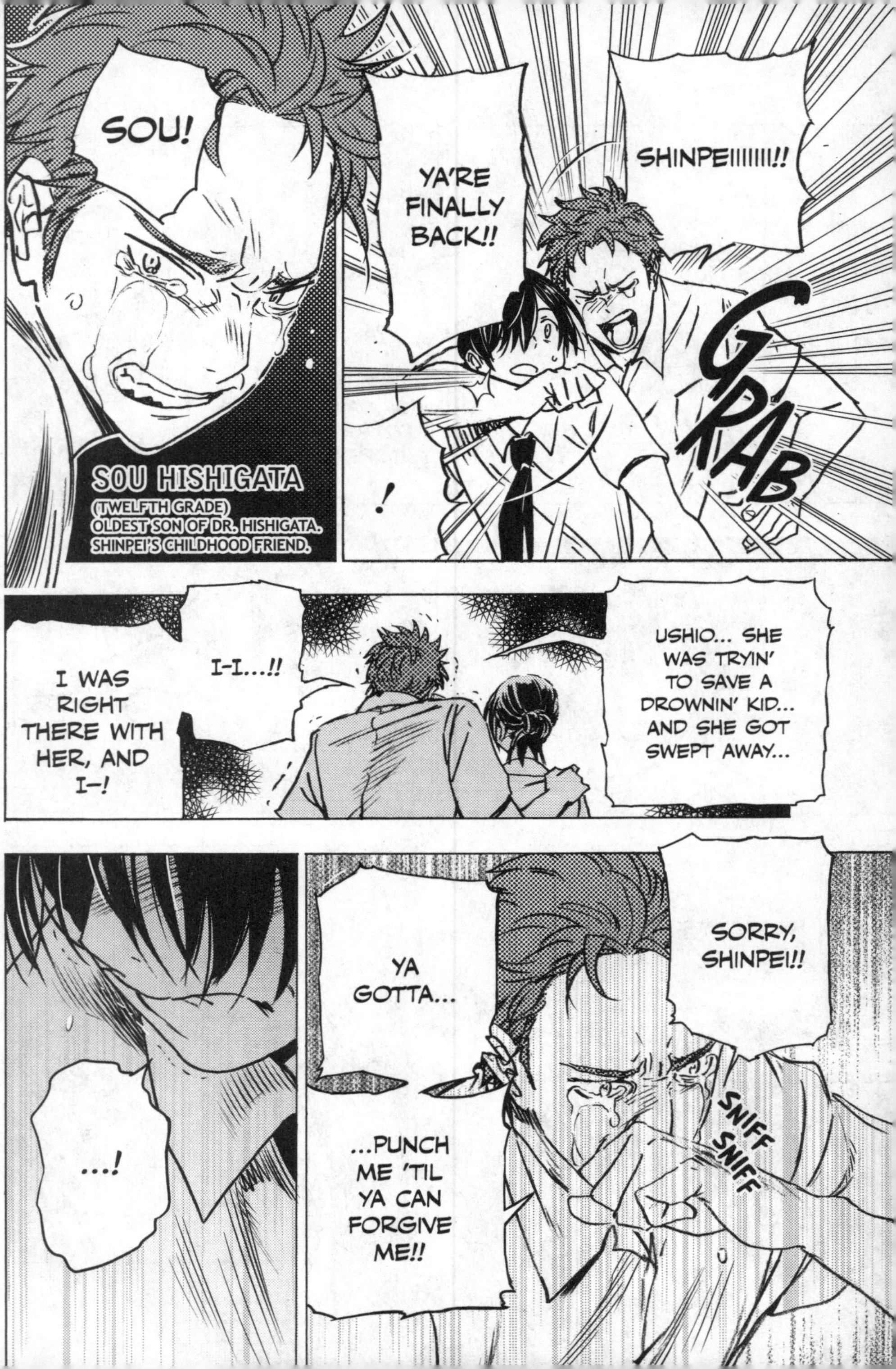
SHINPEIIIIIIIII!!
YA'RE FINALLY BACK!!
GRAB
!
SOU!
SOU HISHIGATA
(TWELFTH GRADE)
OLDEST SON OF DR. HISHIGATA.
SHINPEI'S CHILDHOOD FRIEND.
USHIO... SHE WAS TRYIN' TO SAVE A DROWNIN' KID... AND SHE GOT SWEPT AWAY...
I-I...!!
I WAS RIGHT THERE WITH HER, AND I-!
SORRY, SHINPEI!!
YA GOTTA...
...PUNCH ME 'TIL YA CAN FORGIVE ME!!
SNIFF SNIFF
...!

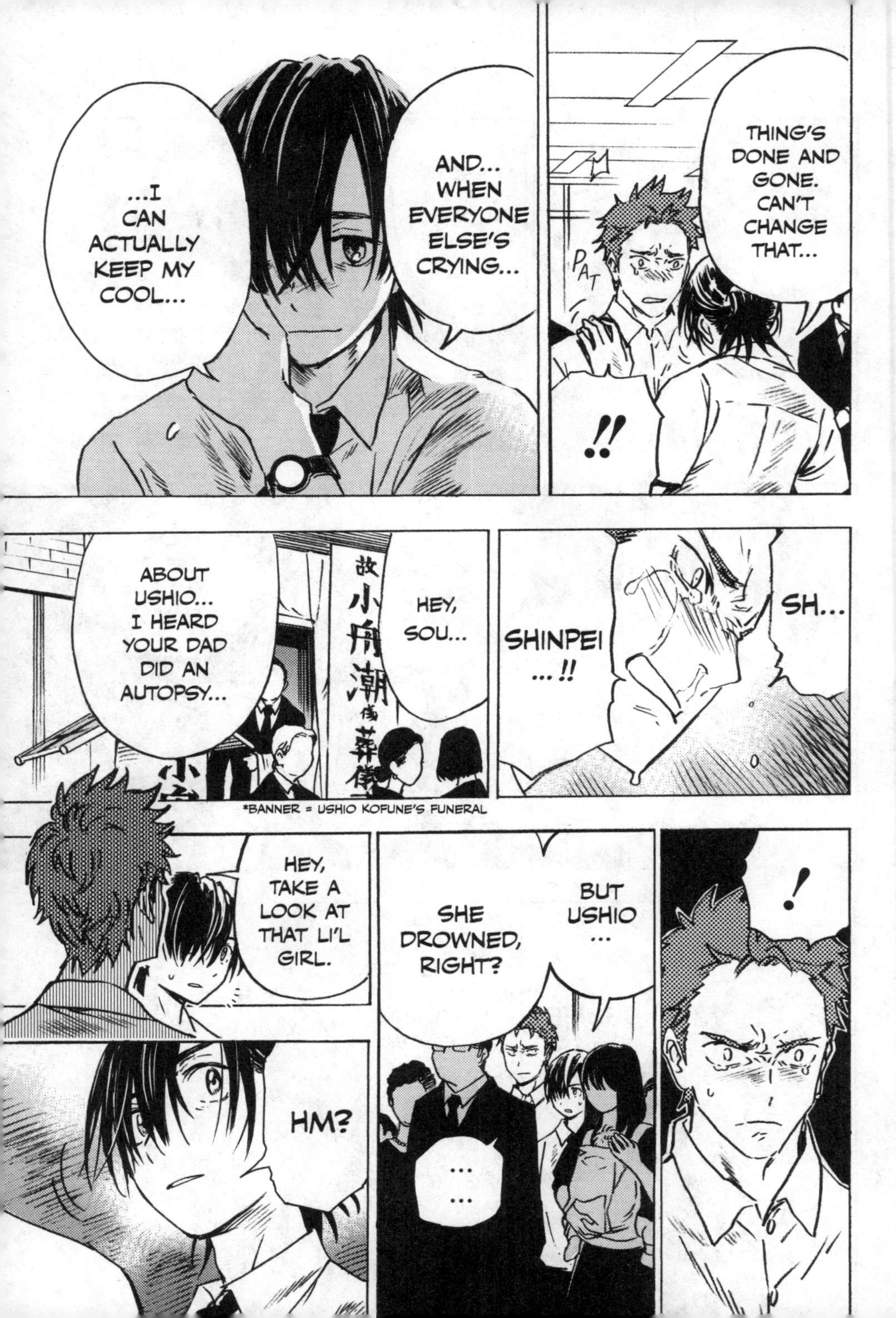
THING'S DONE AND GONE. CAN'T CHANGE THAT...
PAT
!!
AND... WHEN EVERYONE ELSE'S CRYING...
...I CAN ACTUALLY KEEP MY COOL...
SH...
SHINPEI ...!!
HEY, SOU...
故小舟潮
葬儀
ABOUT USHIO... I HEARD YOUR DAD DID AN AUTOPSY...
!
BUT USHIO ...
SHE DROWNED, RIGHT?
... ...
HEY, TAKE A LOOK AT THAT LI'L GIRL.
HM?

*BANNER = USHIO KOFUNE'S FUNERAL

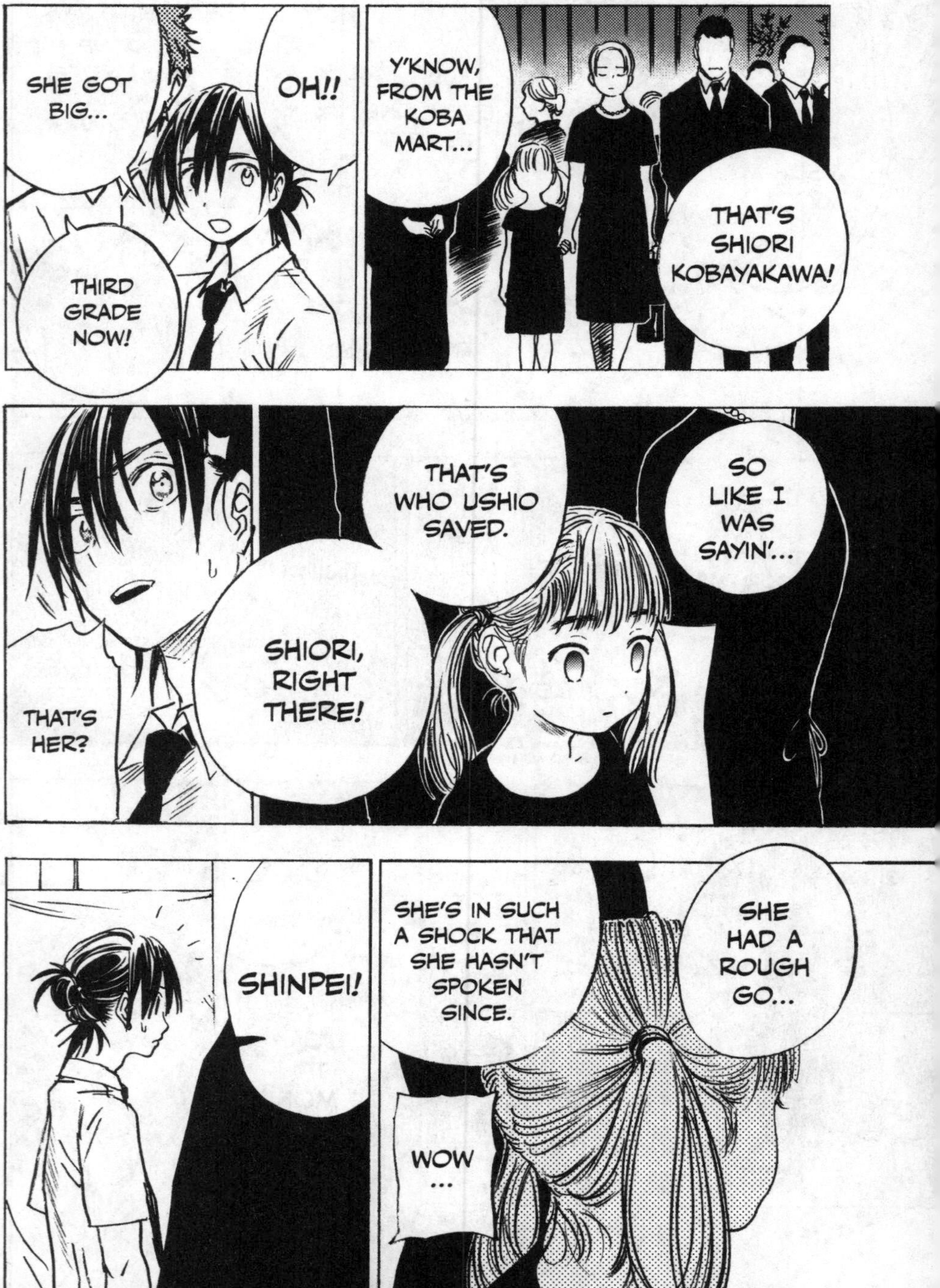
Y'KNOW, FROM THE KOBA MART...
THAT'S SHIORI KOBAYAKAWA!
OH!!
SHE GOT BIG...
THIRD GRADE NOW!
SO LIKE I WAS SAYIN'...
THAT'S WHO USHIO SAVED.
SHIORI, RIGHT THERE!
THAT'S HER?
SHE HAD A ROUGH GO...
SHE'S IN SUCH A SHOCK THAT SHE HASN'T SPOKEN SINCE.
WOW ...
SHINPEI!

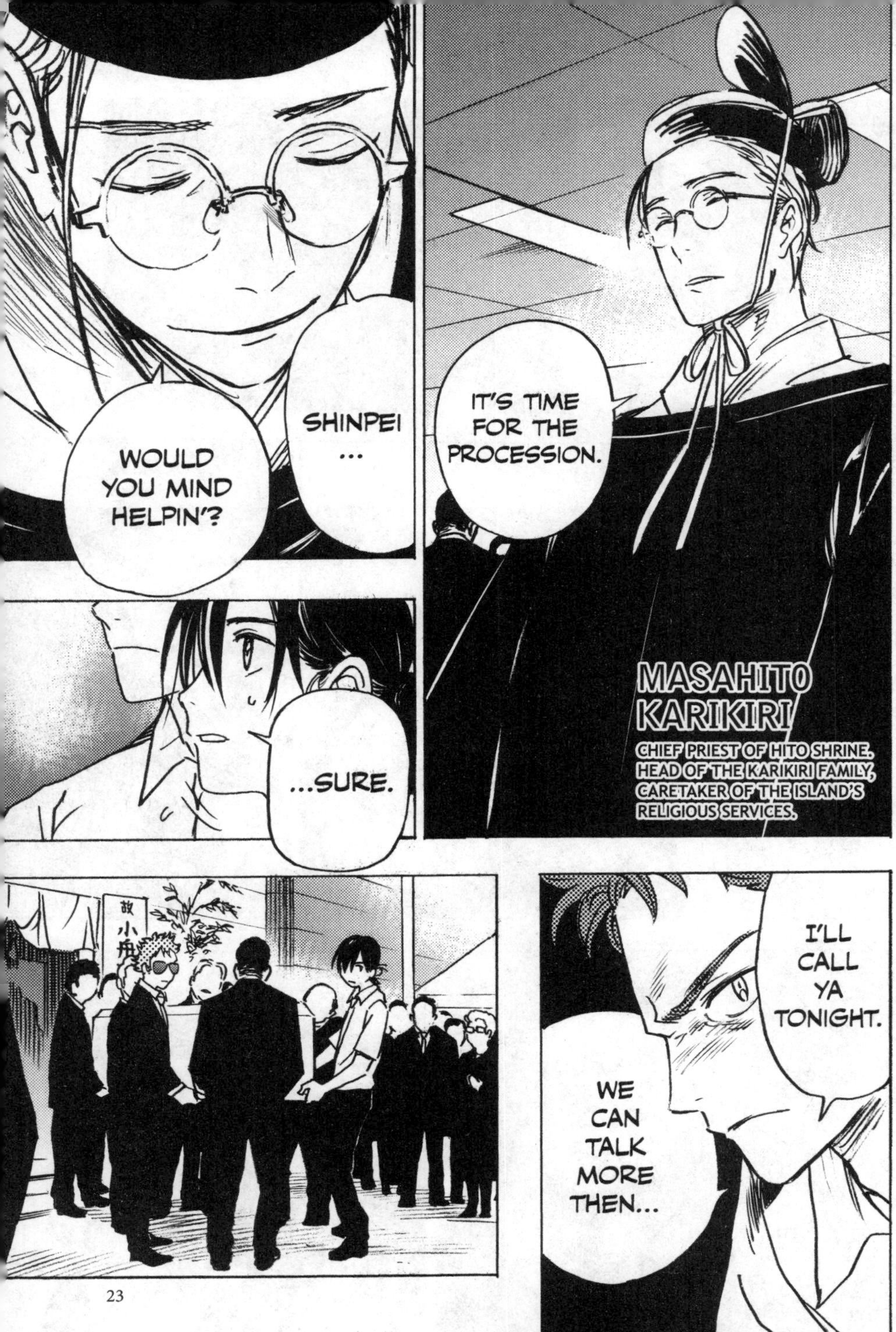
IT'S TIME FOR THE PROCESSION.
MASAHITO KARIKIRI
CHIEF PRIEST OF HITO SHRINE. HEAD OF THE KARIKIRI FAMILY, CARETAKER OF THE ISLAND'S RELIGIOUS SERVICES.
SHINPEI ...
WOULD YOU MIND HELPIN'?
...SURE.
I'LL CALL YA TONIGHT.
WE CAN TALK MORE THEN...

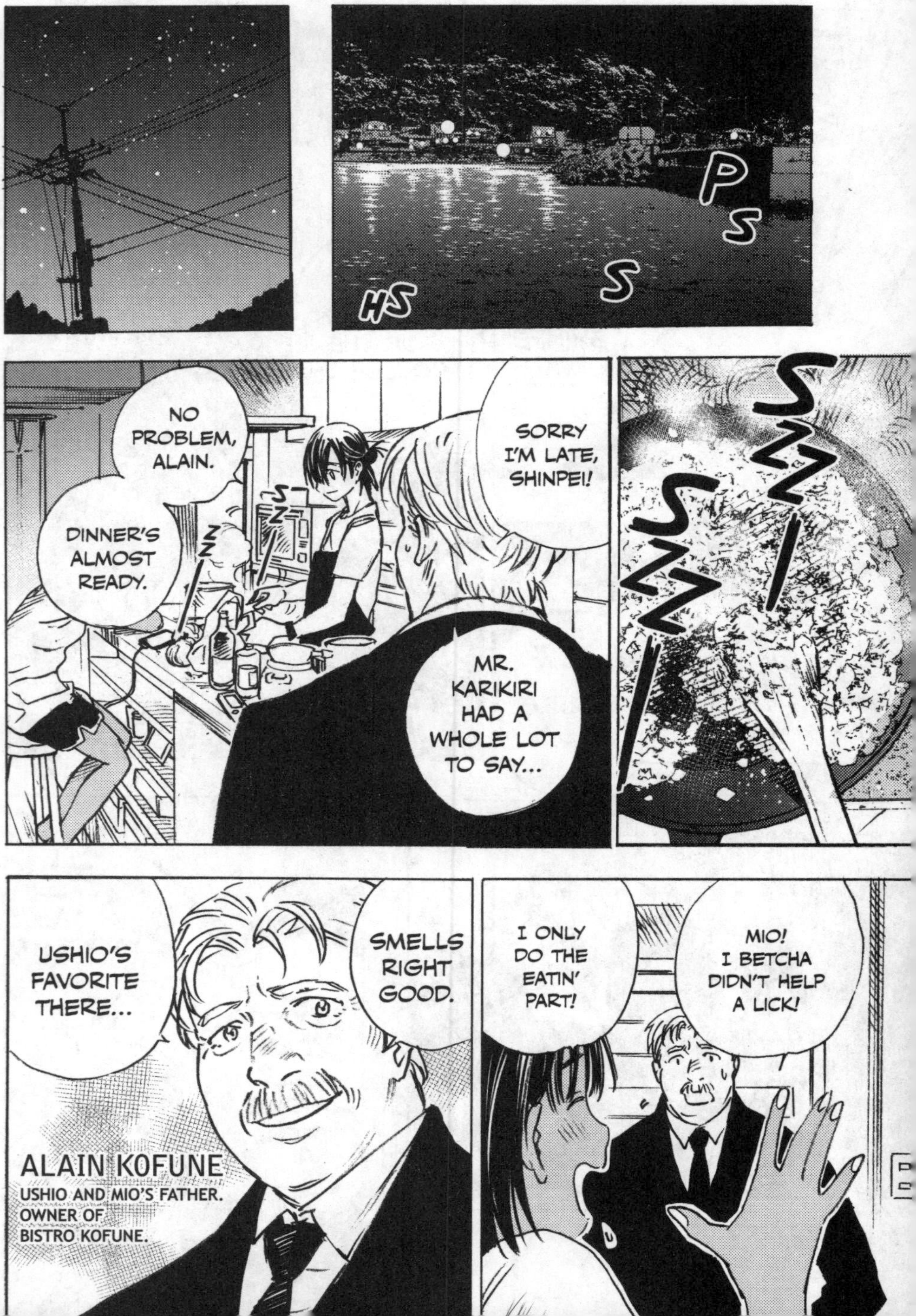
PS
PS
S
SH
SZZZ
SZZZ
SORRY I'M LATE, SHINPEI!
MR. KARIKIRI HAD A WHOLE LOT TO SAY...
NO PROBLEM, ALAIN.
DINNER'S ALMOST READY.
SZZ
MIO! I BETCHA DIDN'T HELP A LICK!
I ONLY DO THE EATIN' PART!
SMELLS RIGHT GOOD.
USHIO'S FAVORITE THERE...
ALAIN KOFUNE
USHIO AND MIO'S FATHER. OWNER OF BISTRO KOFUNE.

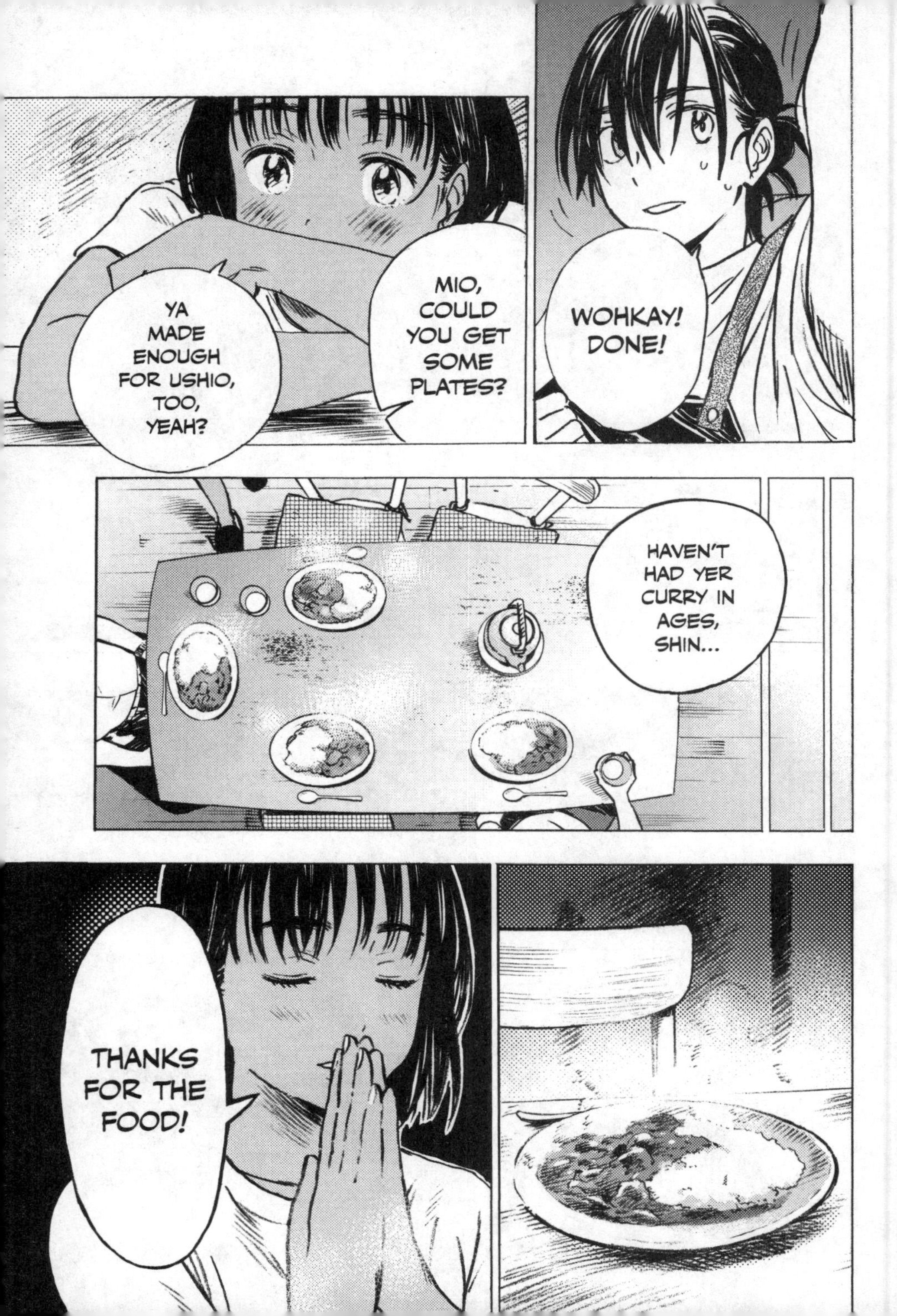
WOHKAY! DONE!
MIO, COULD YOU GET SOME PLATES?
YA MADE ENOUGH FOR USHIO, TOO, YEAH?
HAVEN'T HAD YER CURRY IN AGES, SHIN...
THANKS FOR THE FOOD!

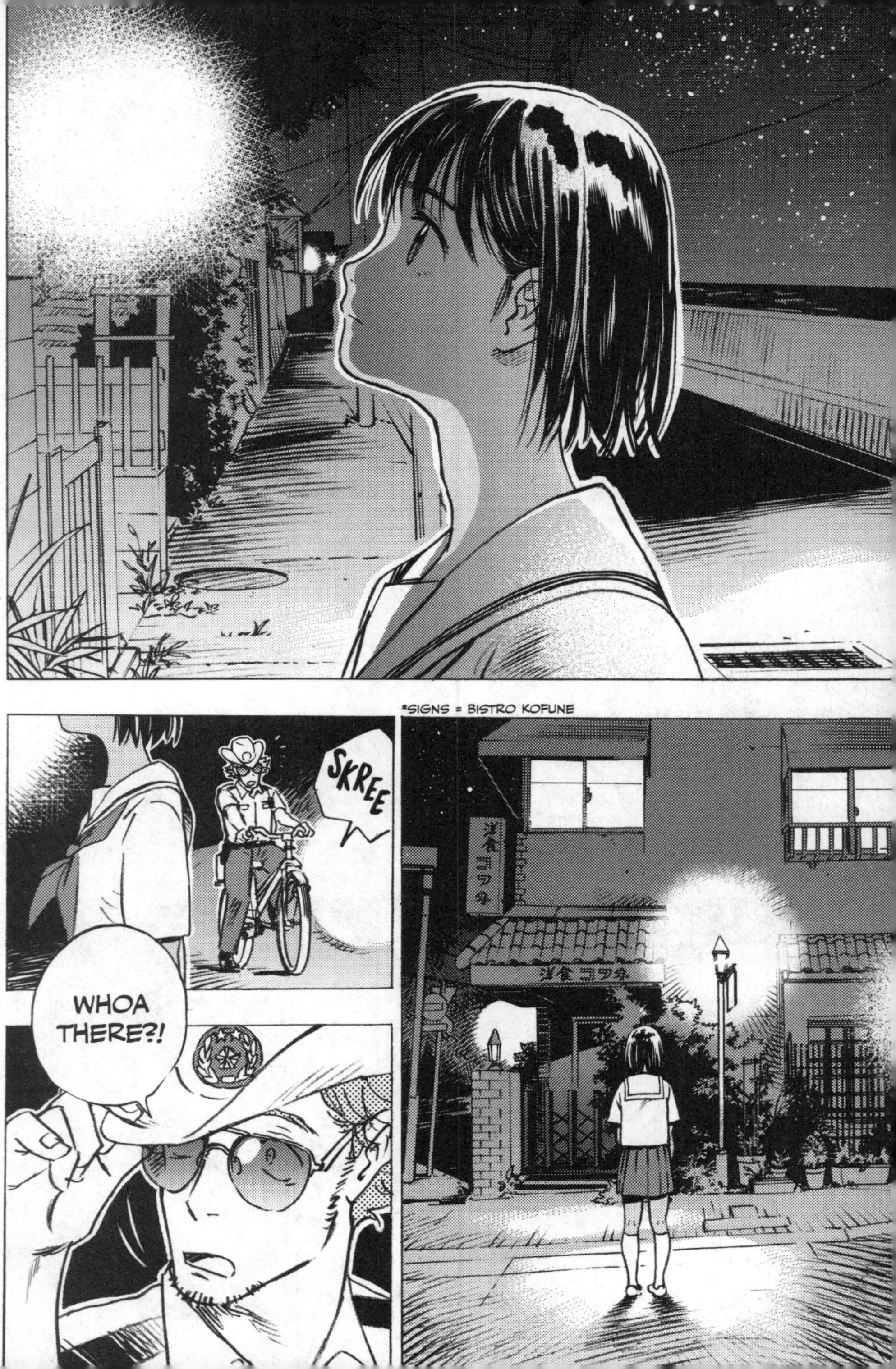
*SIGNS = BISTRO KOFUNE
SKREE
WHOA THERE?!

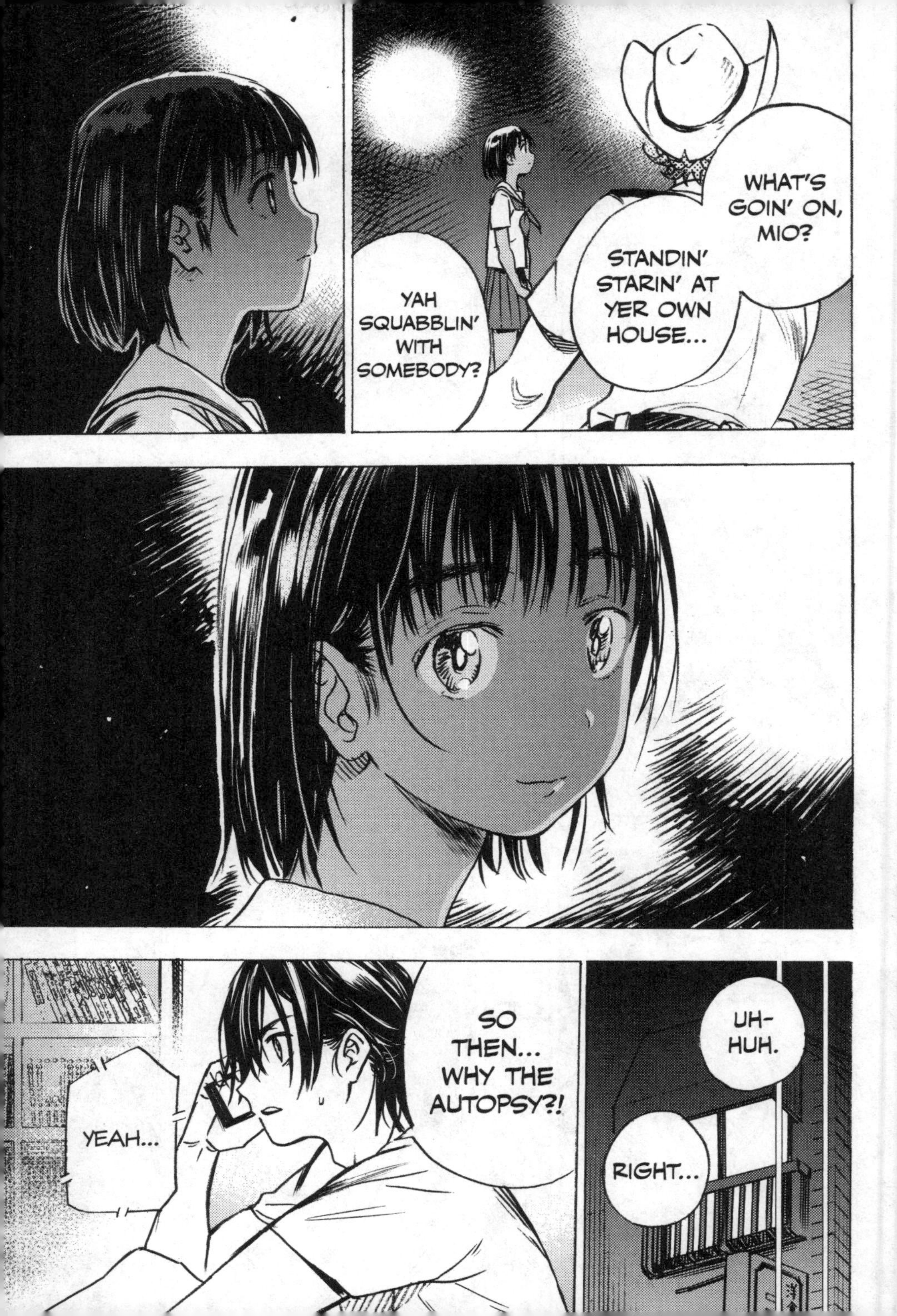
WHAT'S GOIN' ON, MIO?
STANDIN' STARIN' AT YER OWN HOUSE...
YAH SQUABBLIN' WITH SOMEBODY?
UH-HUH.
RIGHT...
SO THEN... WHY THE AUTOPSY?!
YEAH...

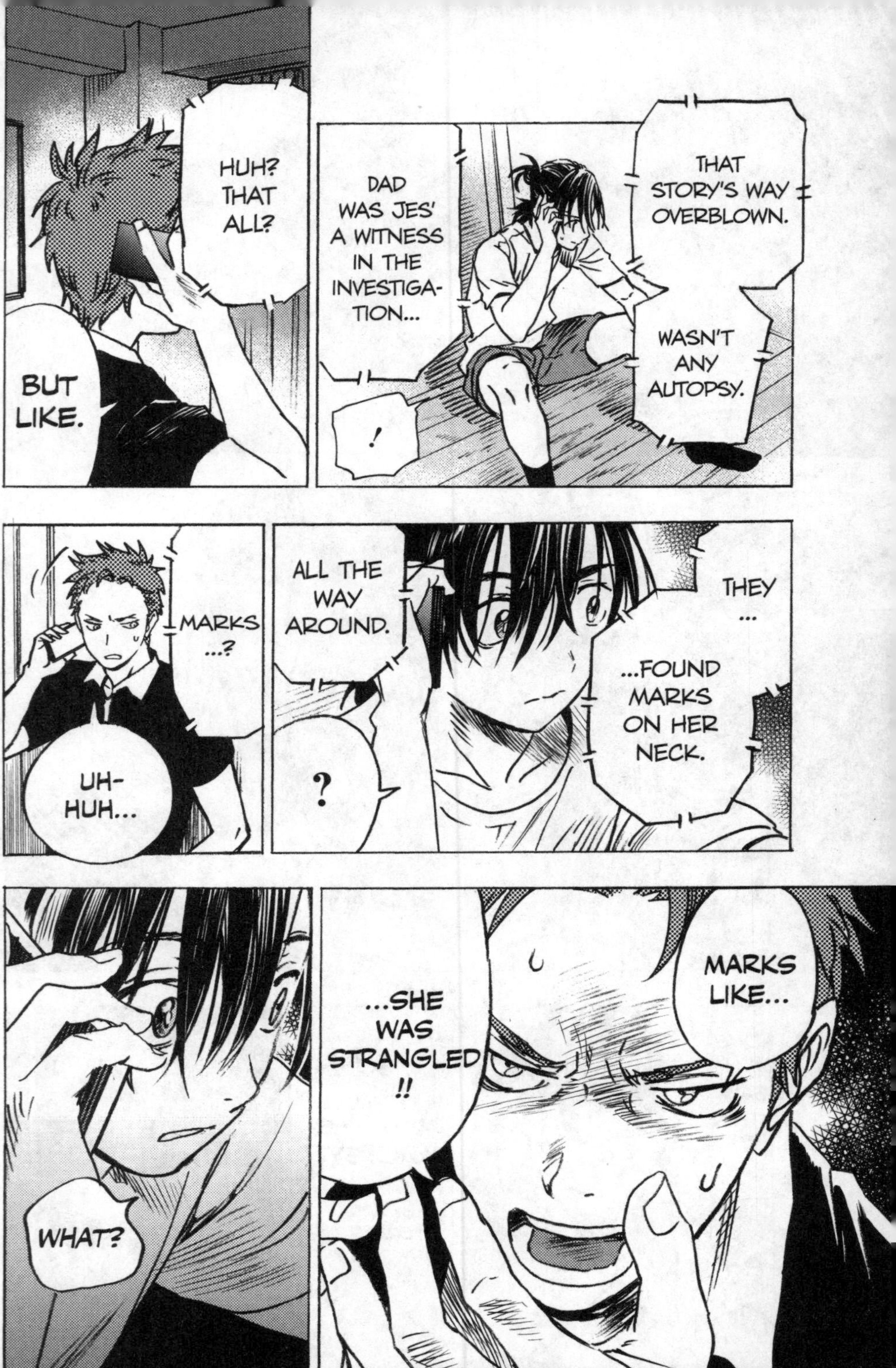
THAT STORY'S WAY OVERBLOWN.
WASN'T ANY AUTOPSY.
DAD WAS JES' A WITNESS IN THE INVESTIGA-TION...
!
HUH? THAT ALL?
BUT LIKE.
THEY ...
...FOUND MARKS ON HER NECK.
ALL THE WAY AROUND.
?
MARKS ...?
UH-HUH...
MARKS LIKE...
...SHE WAS STRANGLED !!
WHAT?

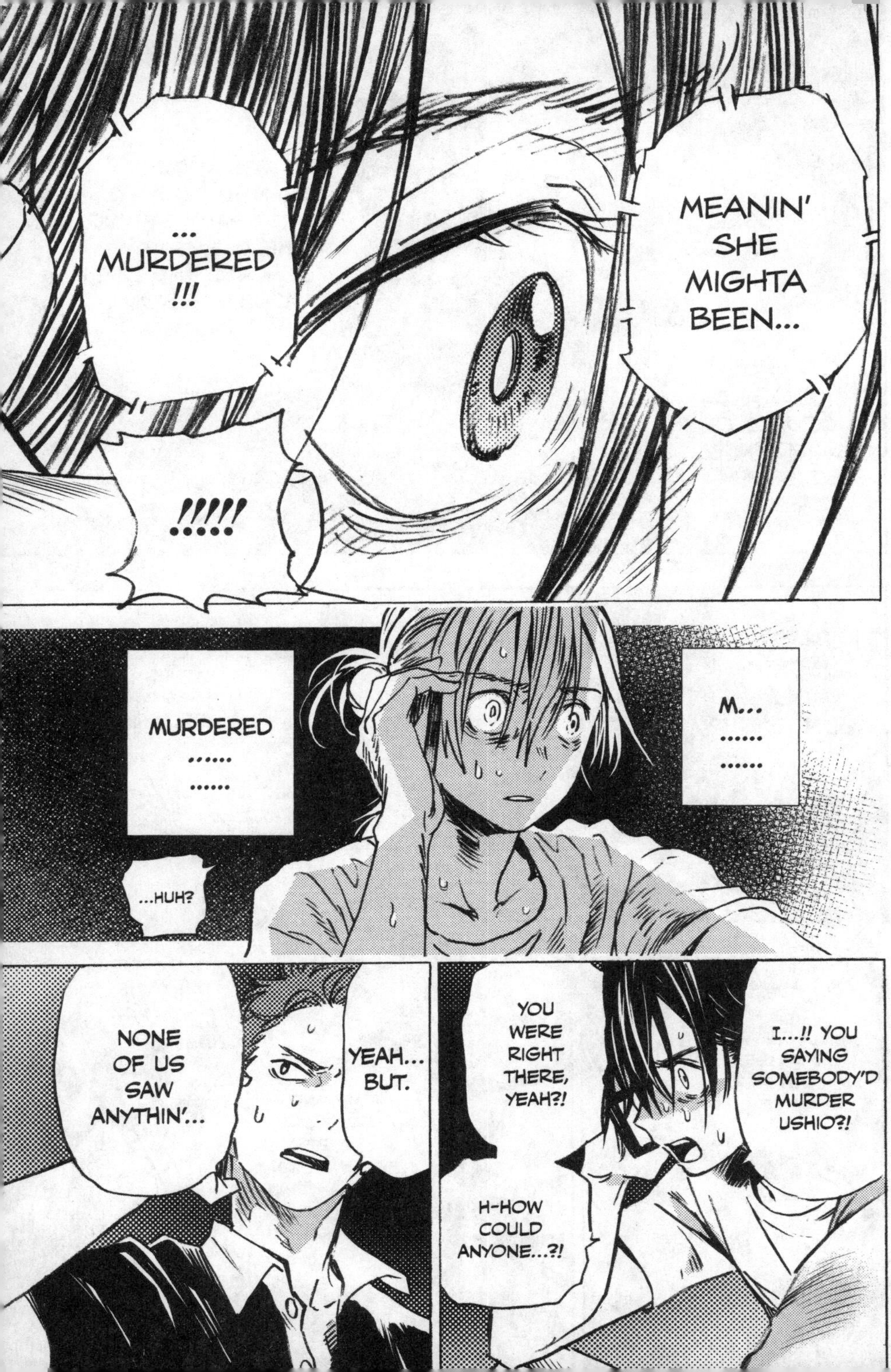
MEANIN' SHE MIGHTA BEEN...
... MURDERED !!!
!!!!!
M... ....
MURDERED ....
...HUH?
I...!! YOU SAYING SOMEBODY'D MURDER USHIO?!
YOU WERE RIGHT THERE, YEAH?!
H-HOW COULD ANYONE...?!
YEAH... BUT.
NONE OF US SAW ANYTHIN'...

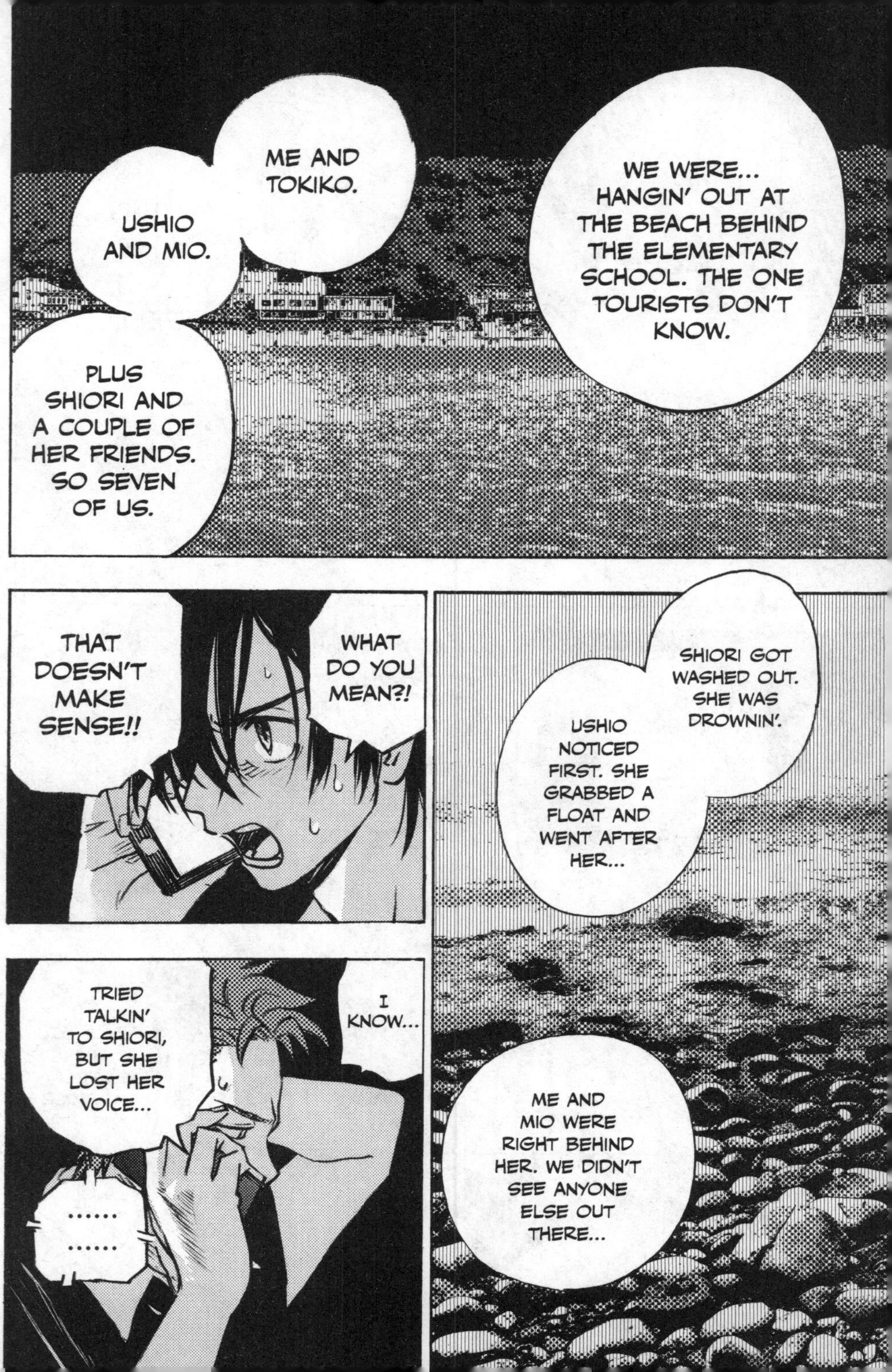
WE WERE... HANGIN' OUT AT THE BEACH BEHIND THE ELEMENTARY SCHOOL. THE ONE TOURISTS DON'T KNOW.
ME AND TOKIKO.
USHIO AND MIO.
PLUS SHIORI AND A COUPLE OF HER FRIENDS. SO SEVEN OF US.
SHIORI GOT WASHED OUT. SHE WAS DROWNIN'.
USHIO NOTICED FIRST. SHE GRABBED A FLOAT AND WENT AFTER HER...
ME AND MIO WERE RIGHT BEHIND HER. WE DIDN'T SEE ANYONE ELSE OUT THERE...
WHAT DO YOU MEAN?!
THAT DOESN'T MAKE SENSE!!
I KNOW...
TRIED TALKIN' TO SHIORI, BUT SHE LOST HER VOICE...
......
......

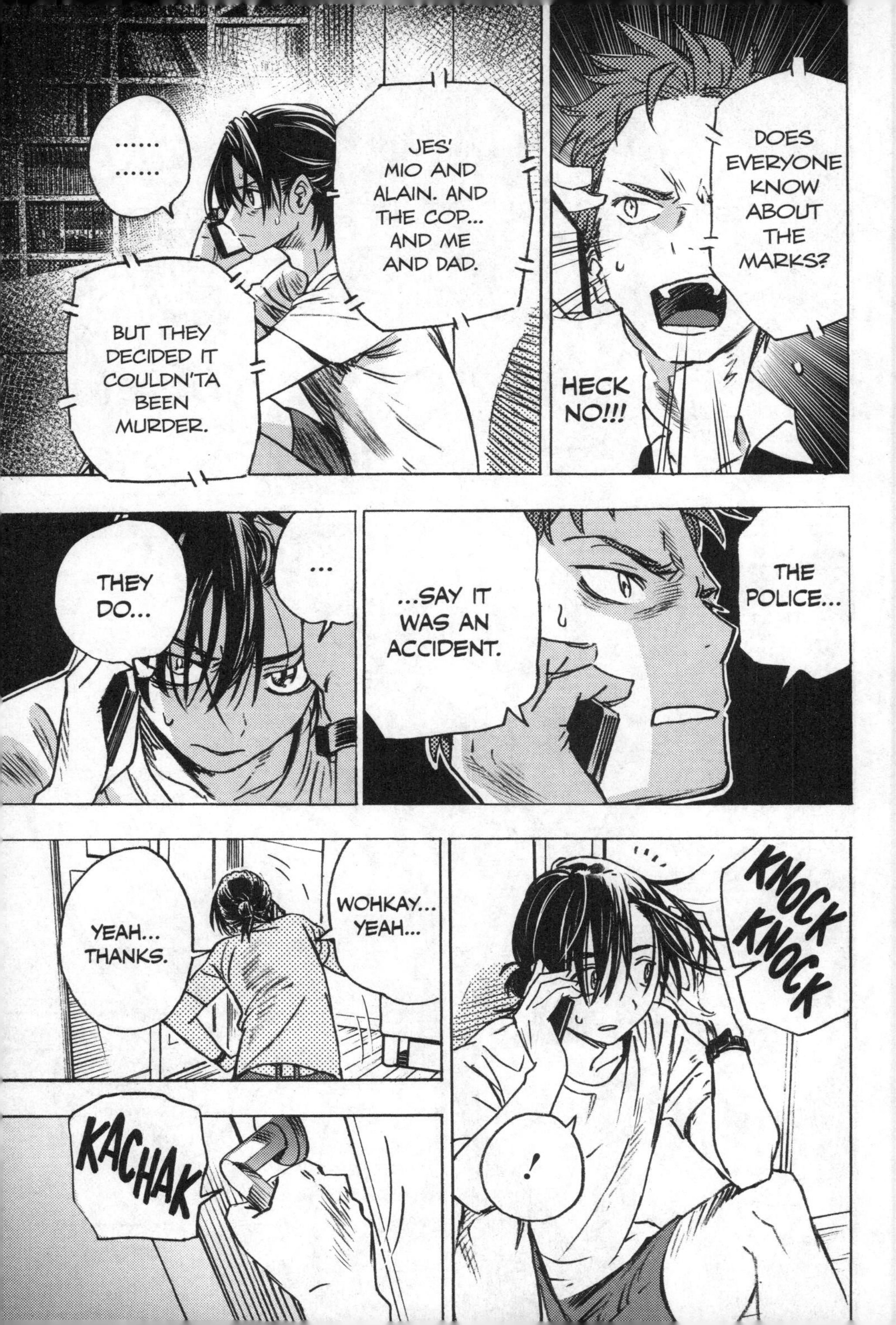
DOES EVERYONE KNOW ABOUT THE MARKS?
HECK NO!!!
JES' MIO AND ALAIN. AND THE COP... AND ME AND DAD.
....
BUT THEY DECIDED IT COULDN'TA BEEN MURDER.
THE POLICE...
...SAY IT WAS AN ACCIDENT.
...
THEY DO...
...
KNOCK KNOCK
!
WOHKAY... YEAH...
YEAH... THANKS.
KACHAK

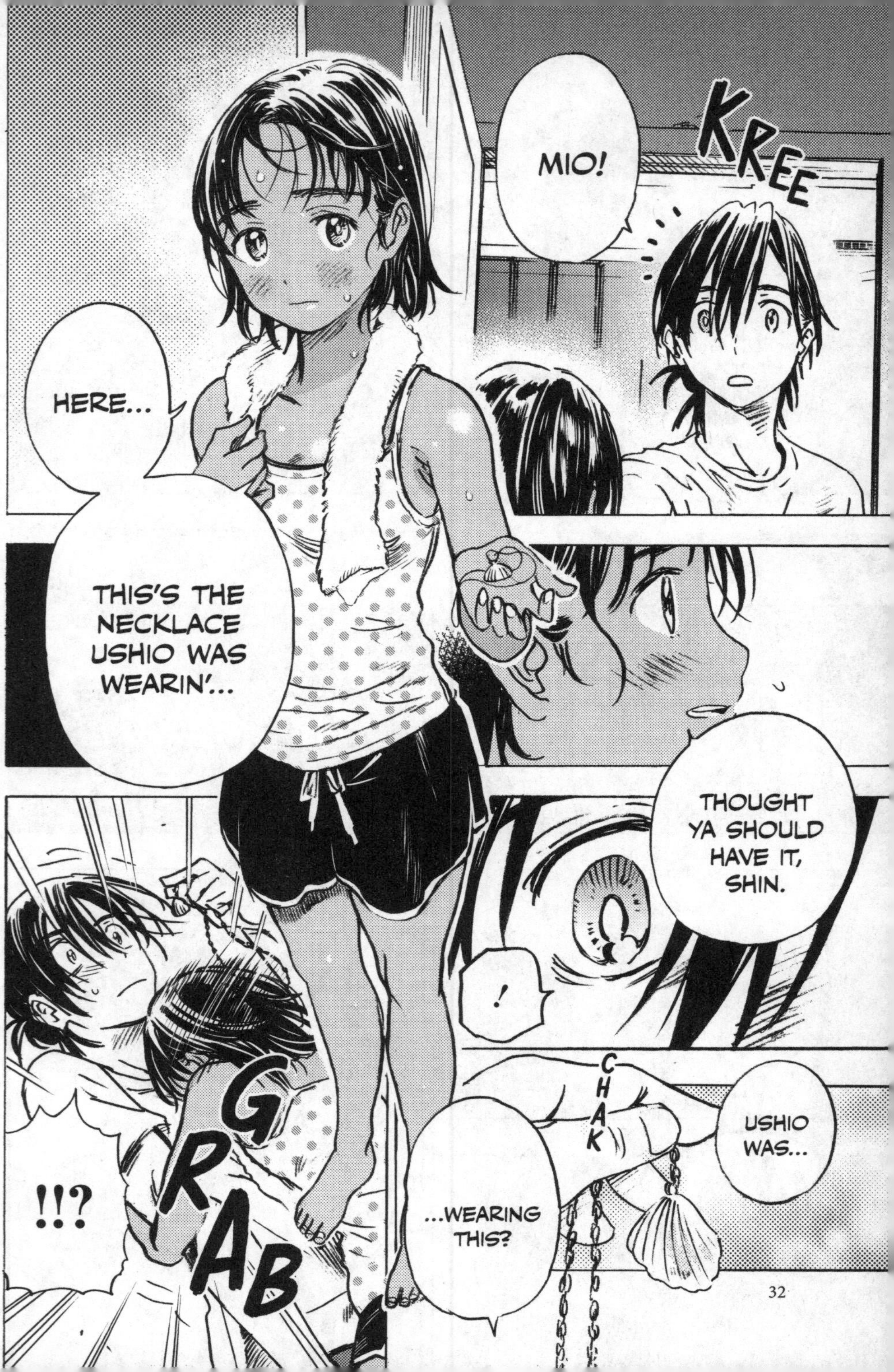
KREE
MIO!
HERE...
THIS'S THE NECKLACE USHIO WAS WEARIN'...
THOUGHT YA SHOULD HAVE IT, SHIN.
!
CHAK
USHIO WAS...
...WEARING THIS?
GRAB
!!?

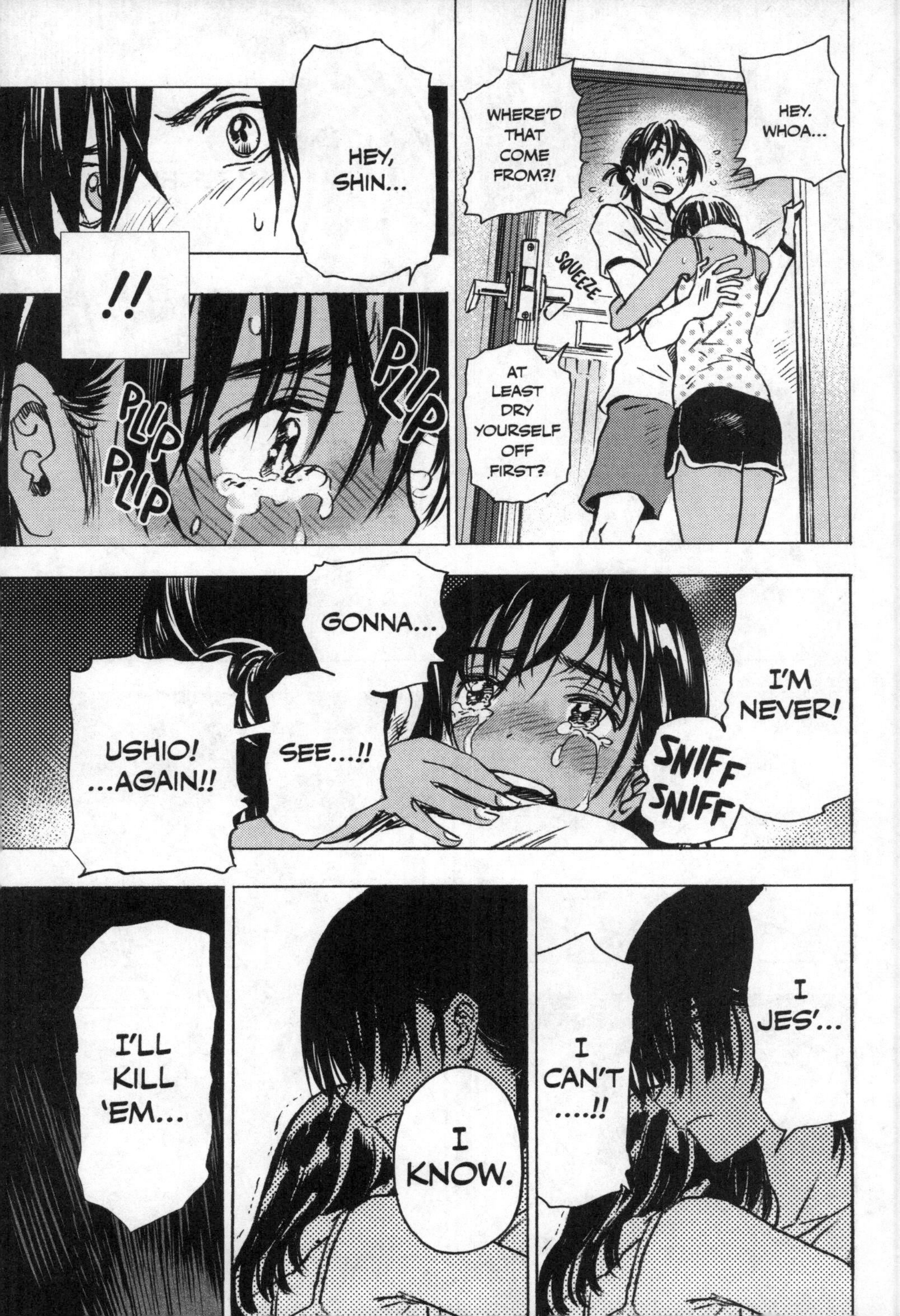
HEY. WHOA...
WHERE'D THAT COME FROM?!
SQUEEZE
AT LEAST DRY YOURSELF OFF FIRST?
HEY, SHIN...
!!
PLIP
PLIP
PLIP
PLIP
I'M NEVER!
SNIFF SNIFF
GONNA...
SEE...!!
USHIO! ...AGAIN!!
I JES'...
I CAN'T ....!!
I KNOW.
I'LL KILL 'EM...

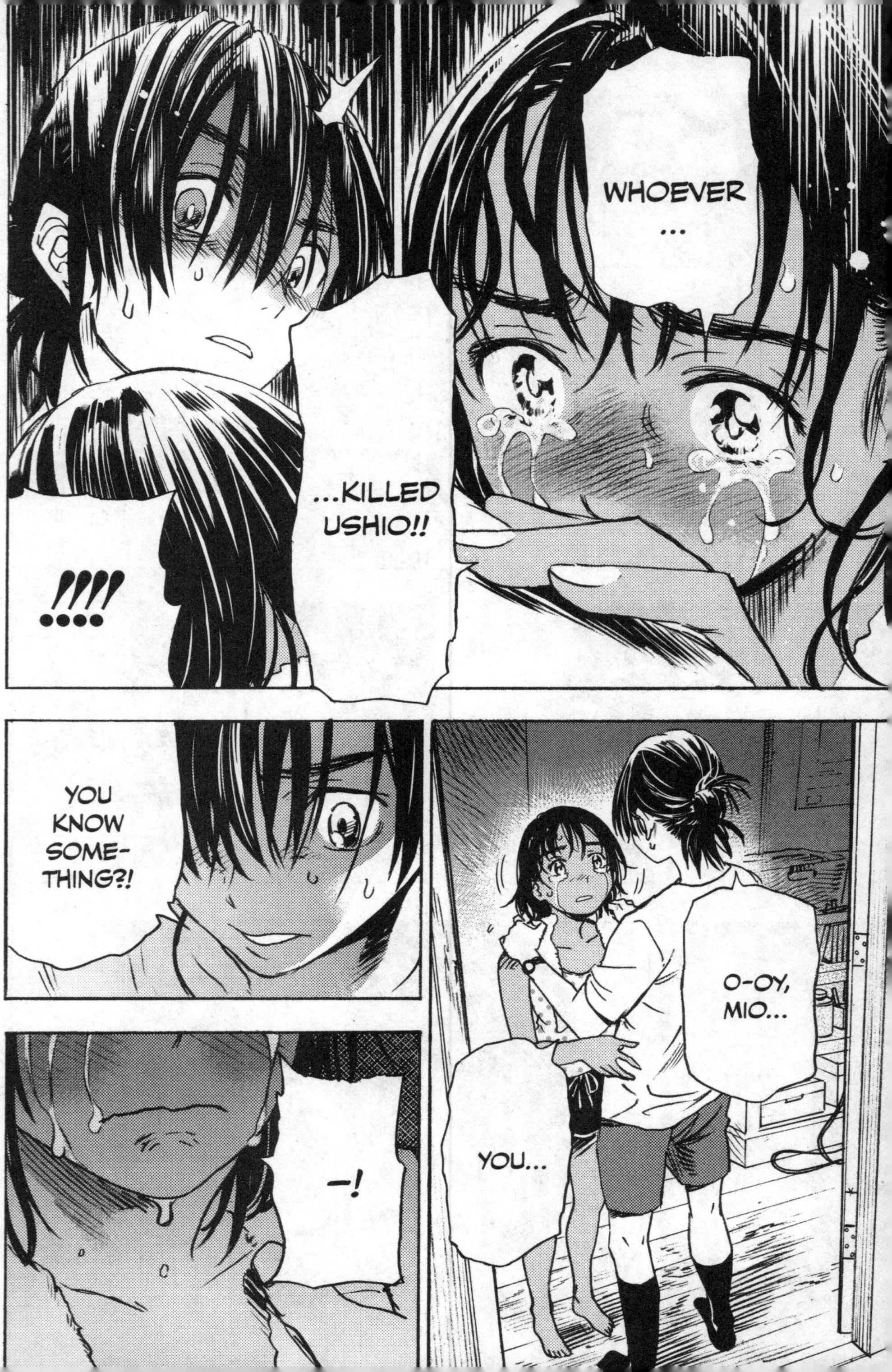
WHOEVER ...
...KILLED USHIO!!
!!!!
O-OY, MIO...
YOU...
YOU KNOW SOME-THING?!
—!

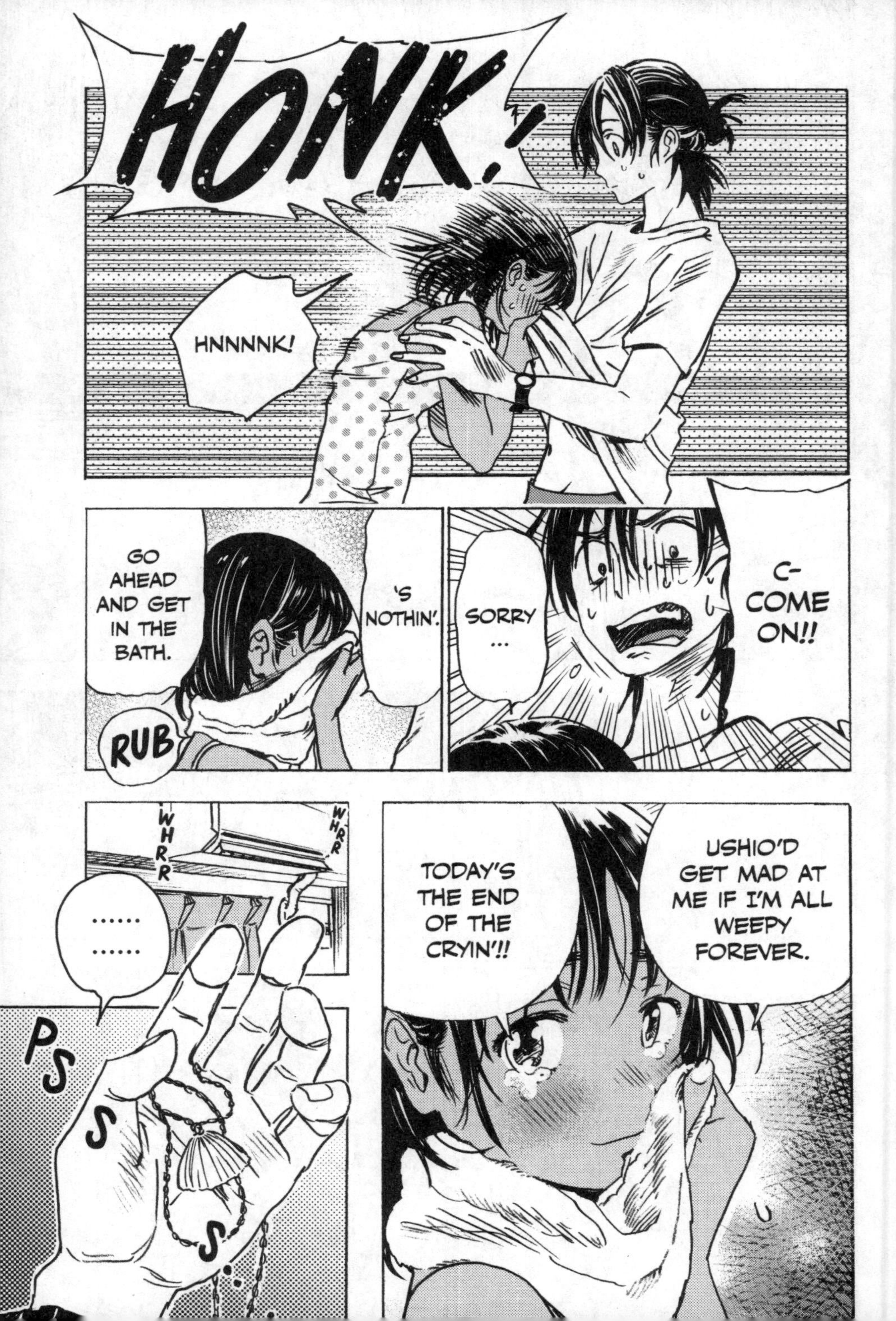
HONK!
HNNNNK!
C-
COME ON!!
SORRY ...
'S NOTHIN'.
GO AHEAD AND GET IN THE BATH.
RUB
USHIO'D GET MAD AT ME IF I'M ALL WEEPY FOREVER.
TODAY'S THE END OF THE CRYIN'!!
WHRR
WHRR
....
PSSS

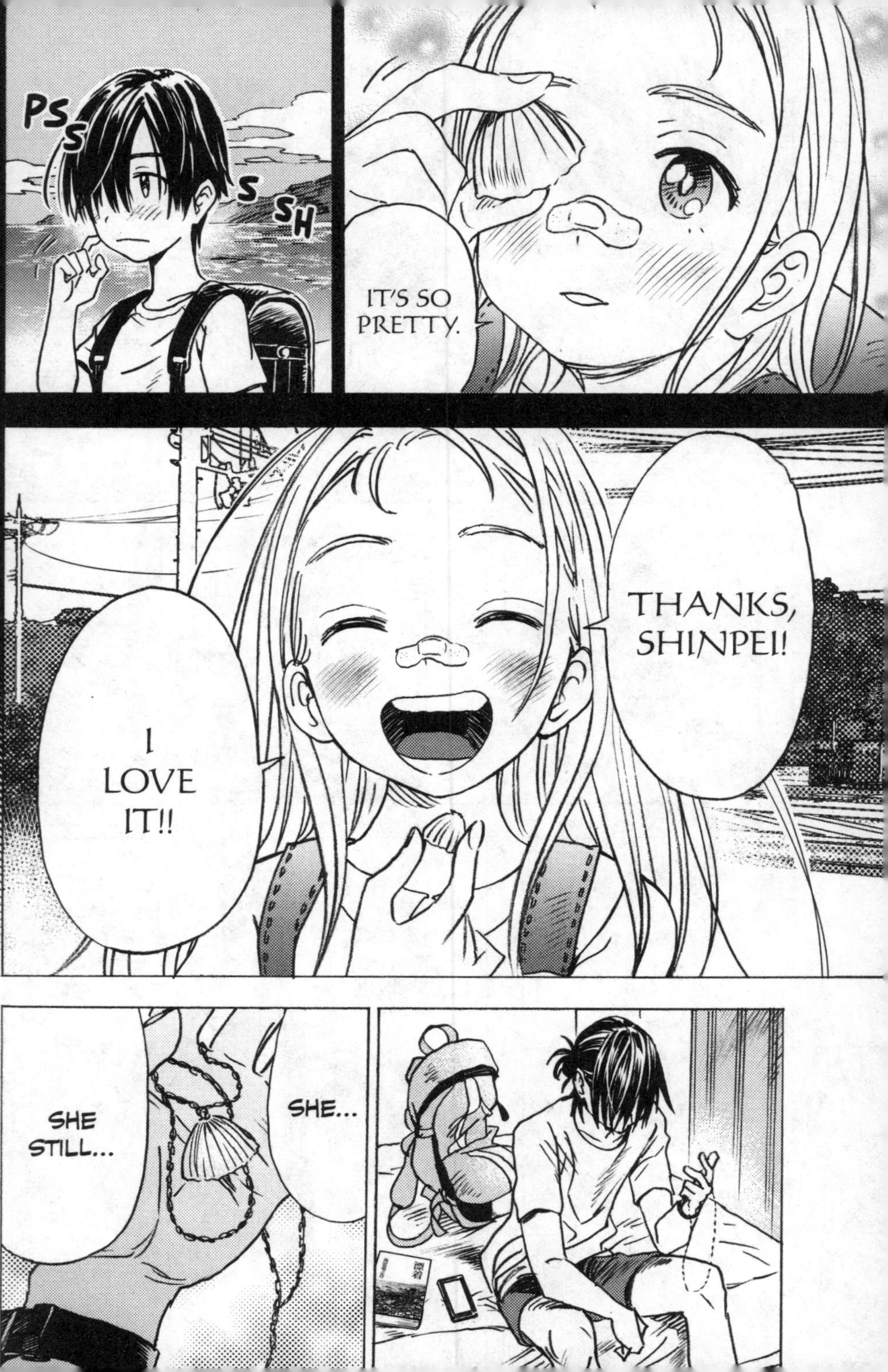
IT'S SO PRETTY.
PSSSSSH
THANKS, SHINPEI!
I LOVE IT!!
SHE...
SHE STILL...

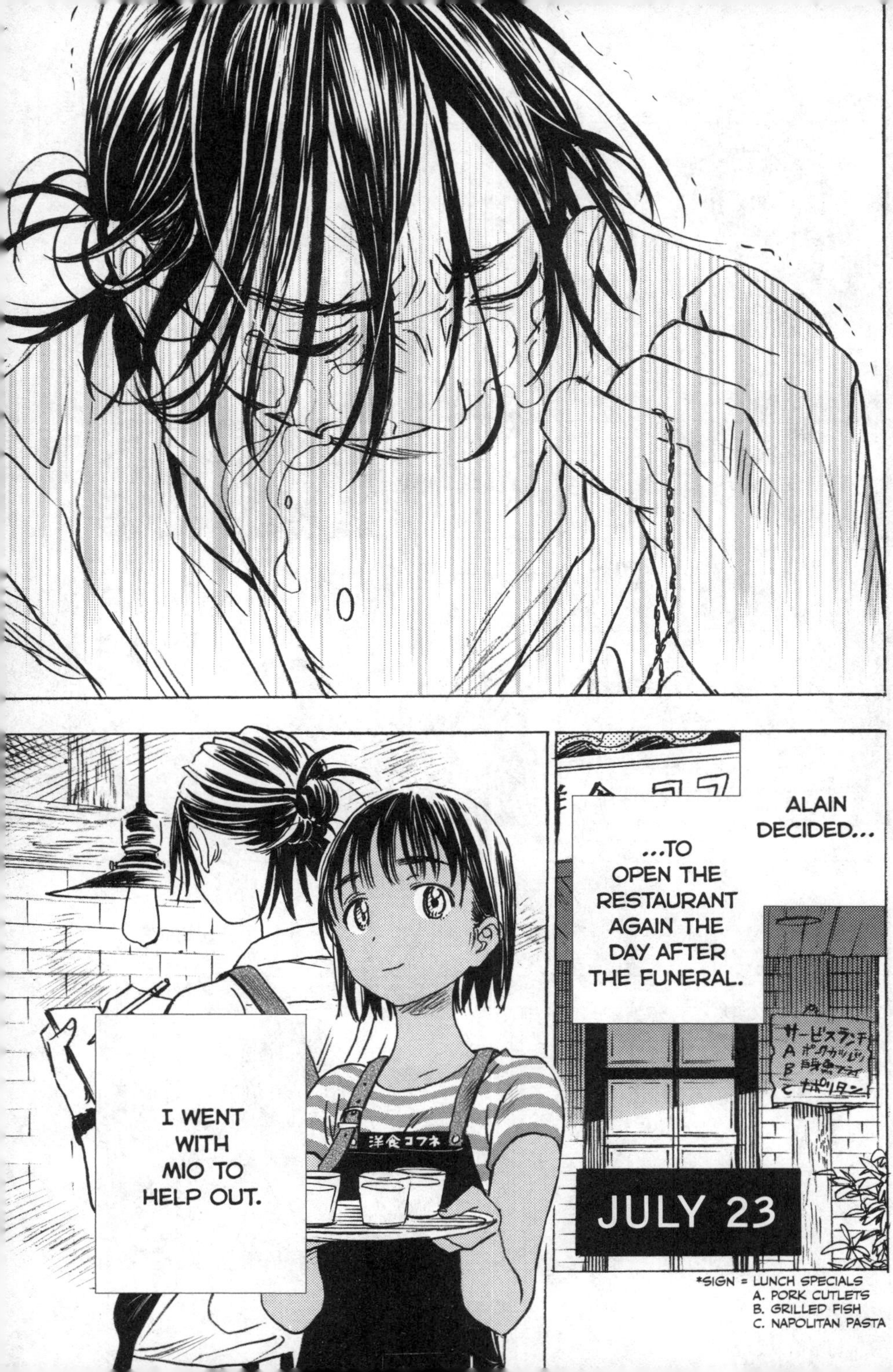
ALAIN DECIDED...
...TO OPEN THE RESTAURANT AGAIN THE DAY AFTER THE FUNERAL.
サービスランチ
JULY 23
*SIGN = LUNCH SPECIALS
A. PORK CUTLETS
B. GRILLED FISH
C. NAPOLITAN PASTA
I WENT WITH MIO TO HELP OUT.
洋食コフネ

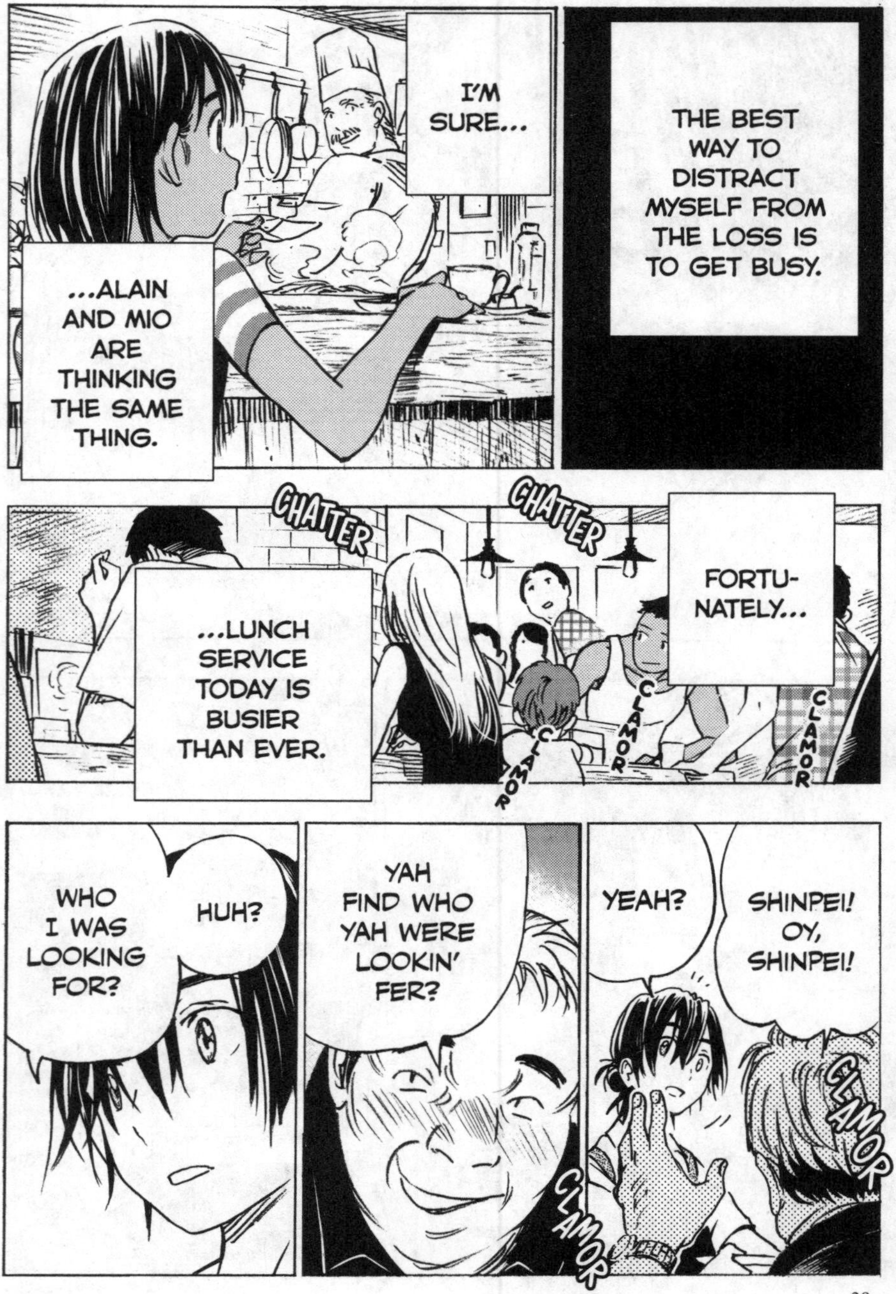
THE BEST WAY TO DISTRACT MYSELF FROM THE LOSS IS TO GET BUSY.
I'M SURE...
...ALAIN AND MIO ARE THINKING THE SAME THING.
FORTU-NATELY...
CLAMOR
CLAMOR
CHATTER
CHATTER
CLAMOR
...LUNCH SERVICE TODAY IS BUSIER THAN EVER.
SHINPEI! OY, SHINPEI!
YEAH?
CLAMOR
CLAMOR
YAH FIND WHO YAH WERE LOOKIN' FER?
HUH?
WHO I WAS LOOKING FOR?

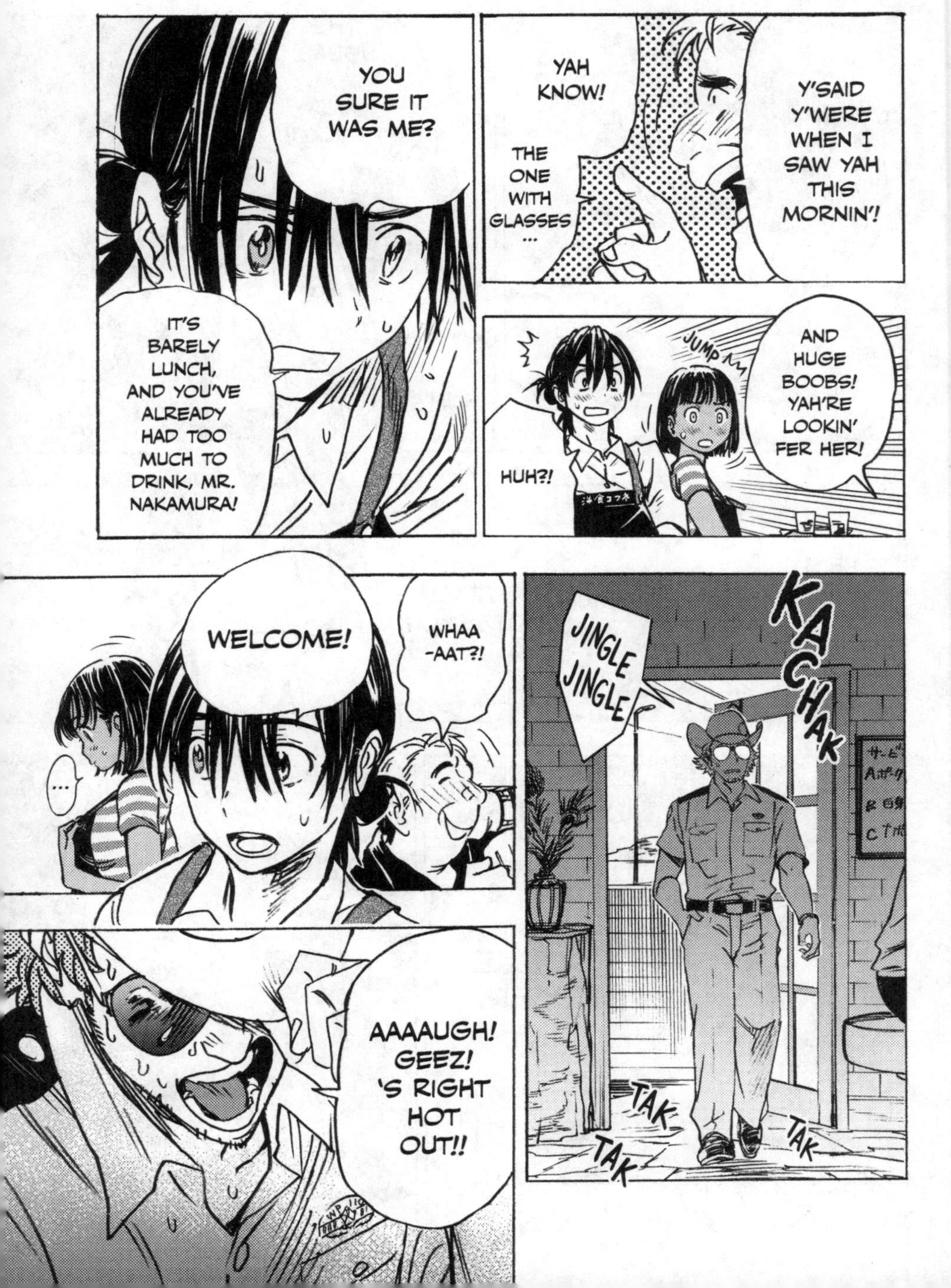

Y'SAID Y'WERE WHEN I SAW YAH THIS MORNIN'!
YAH KNOW!
THE ONE WITH GLASSES ...
AND HUGE BOOBS! YAH'RE LOOKIN' FER HER!
JUMP
HUH?!
YOU SURE IT WAS ME?
IT'S BARELY LUNCH, AND YOU'VE ALREADY HAD TOO MUCH TO DRINK, MR. NAKAMURA!
KACHAK
JINGLE JINGLE
TAK
TAK
TAK
WELCOME!
WHAA -AAT?!
...
AAAAUGH! GEEZ! 'S RIGHT HOT OUT!!

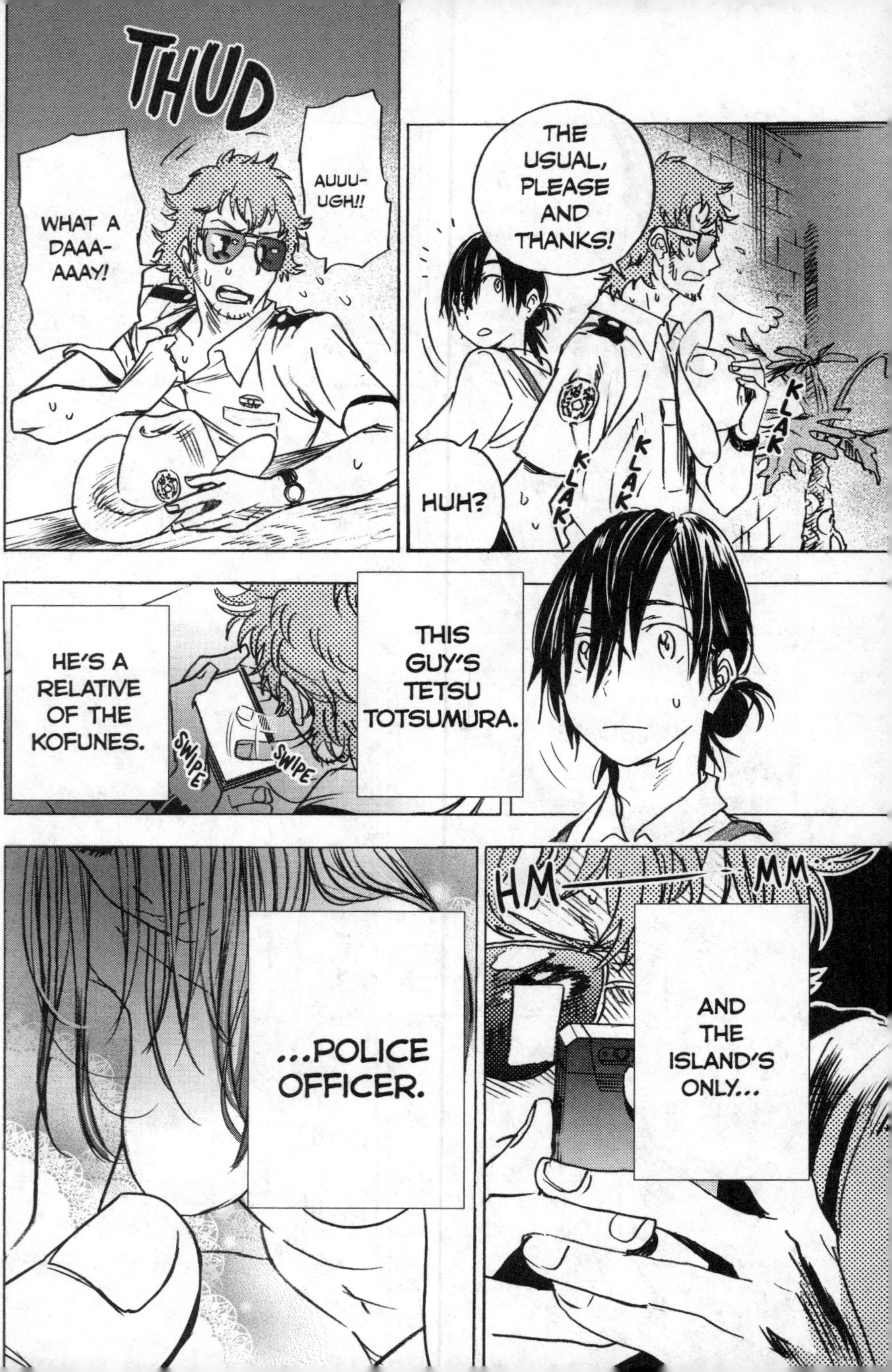
THE USUAL, PLEASE AND THANKS!
HUH?
KLAK KLAK KLAK
THUD
AUUU-UGH!!
WHAT A DAAAA-AAAY!
THIS GUY'S TETSU TOTSUMURA.
HE'S A RELATIVE OF THE KOFUNES.
SWIPE SWIPE
HM-MM
AND THE ISLAND'S ONLY...
...POLICE OFFICER.

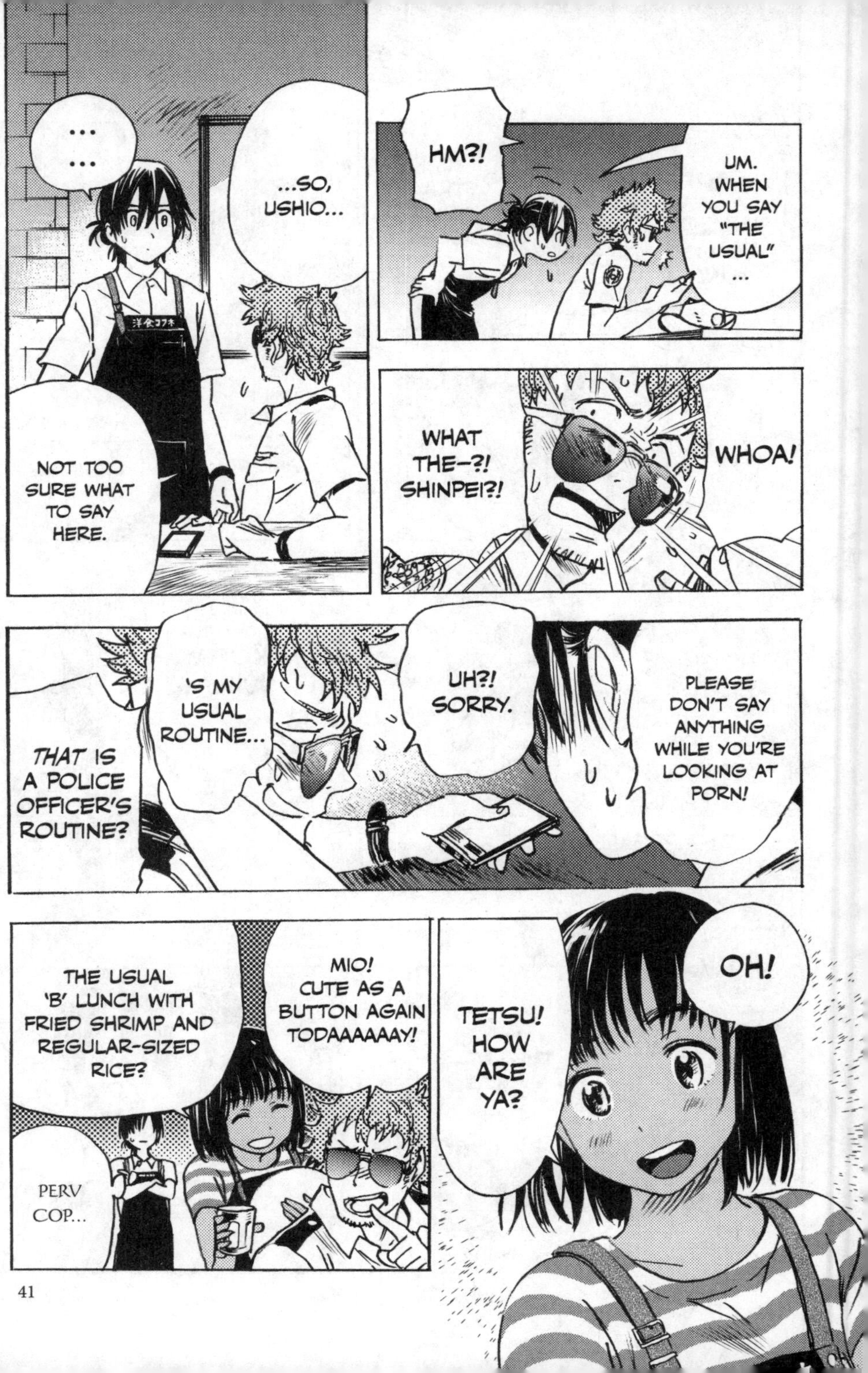
UM. WHEN YOU SAY "THE USUAL" ...
HM?!
WHOA!
WHAT THE–?! SHINPEI?!
...SO, USHIO...
… …
NOT TOO SURE WHAT TO SAY HERE.
PLEASE DON'T SAY ANYTHING WHILE YOU'RE LOOKING AT PORN!
UH?! SORRY.
'S MY USUAL ROUTINE...
THAT IS A POLICE OFFICER'S ROUTINE?
OH!
TETSU! HOW ARE YA?
MIO! CUTE AS A BUTTON AGAIN TODAAAAAAY!
THE USUAL 'B' LUNCH WITH FRIED SHRIMP AND REGULAR-SIZED RICE?
PERV COP...

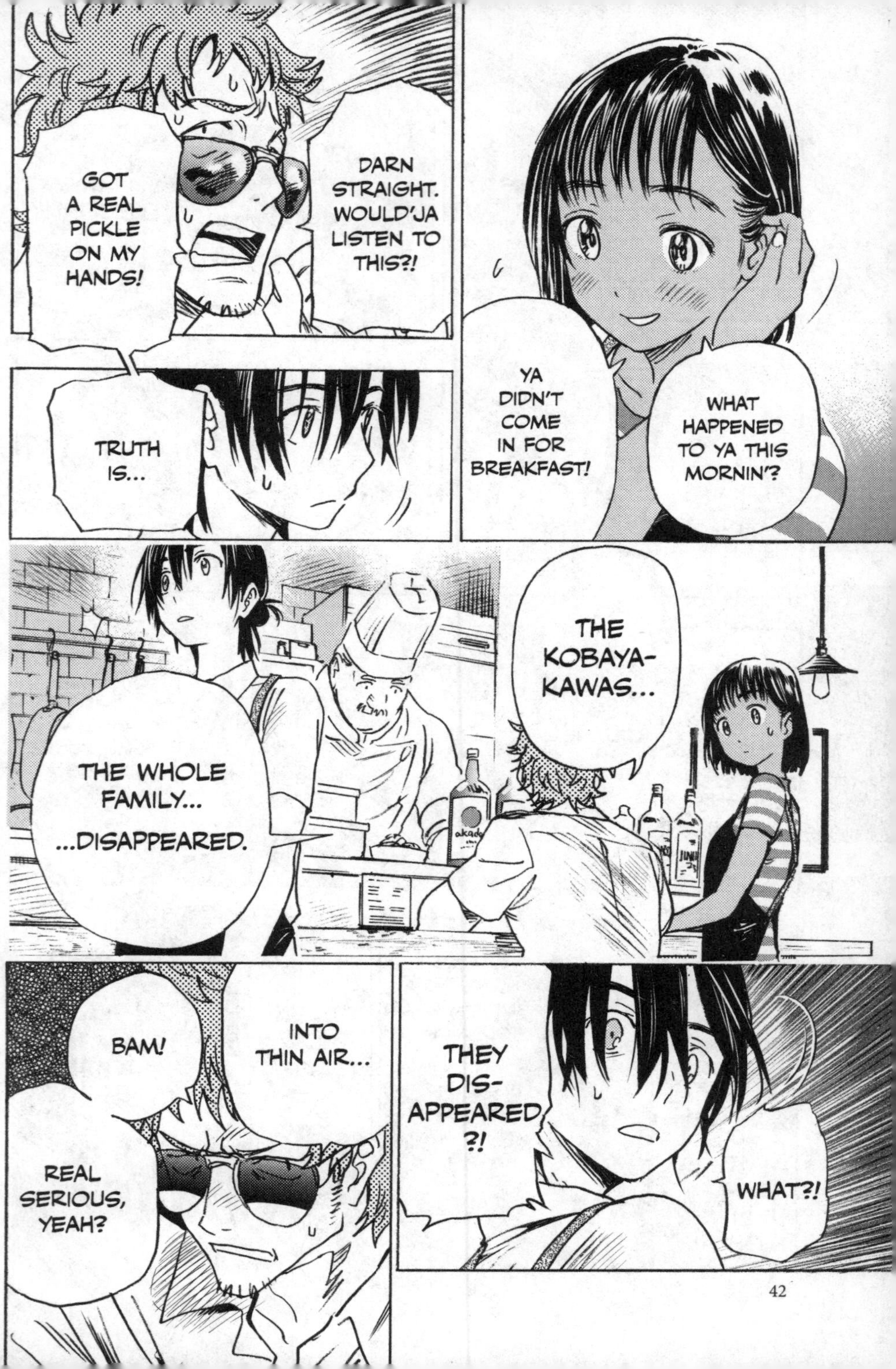
WHAT HAPPENED TO YA THIS MORNIN'?
YA DIDN'T COME IN FOR BREAKFAST!
DARN STRAIGHT. WOULD'JA LISTEN TO THIS?!
GOT A REAL PICKLE ON MY HANDS!
TRUTH IS...
THE KOBAYA-KAWAS...
THE WHOLE FAMILY...
...DISAPPEARED.
THEY DIS-APPEARED?!
WHAT?!
INTO THIN AIR...
BAM!
REAL SERIOUS, YEAH?

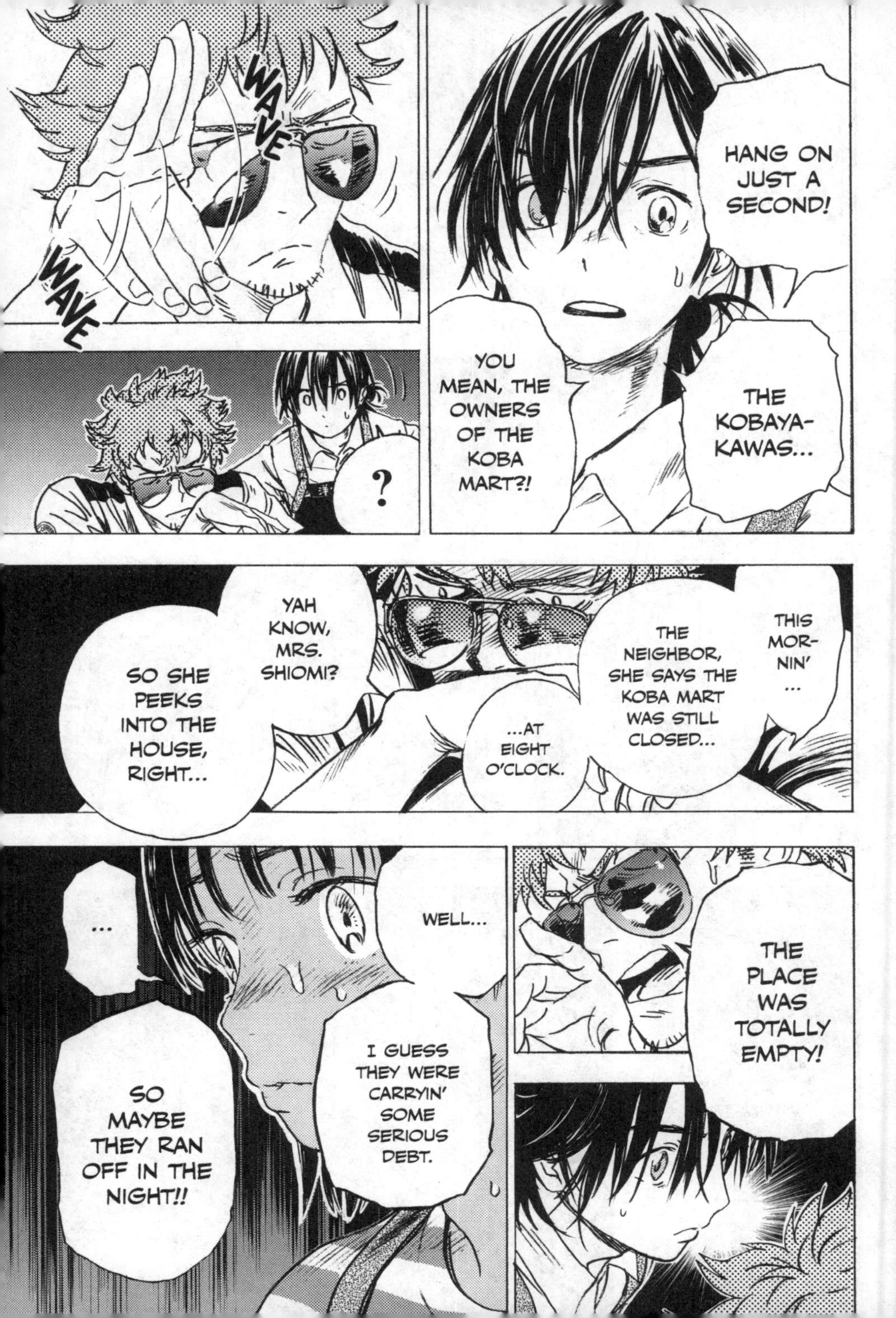
HANG ON JUST A SECOND!
THE KOBAYA-KAWAS...
YOU MEAN, THE OWNERS OF THE KOBA MART?!
WAVE
WAVE
?
THIS MOR-NIN' ...
THE NEIGHBOR, SHE SAYS THE KOBA MART WAS STILL CLOSED...
...AT EIGHT O'CLOCK.
YAH KNOW, MRS. SHIOMI?
SO SHE PEEKS INTO THE HOUSE, RIGHT...
THE PLACE WAS TOTALLY EMPTY!
WELL...
I GUESS THEY WERE CARRYIN' SOME SERIOUS DEBT.
SO MAYBE THEY RAN OFF IN THE NIGHT!!
...

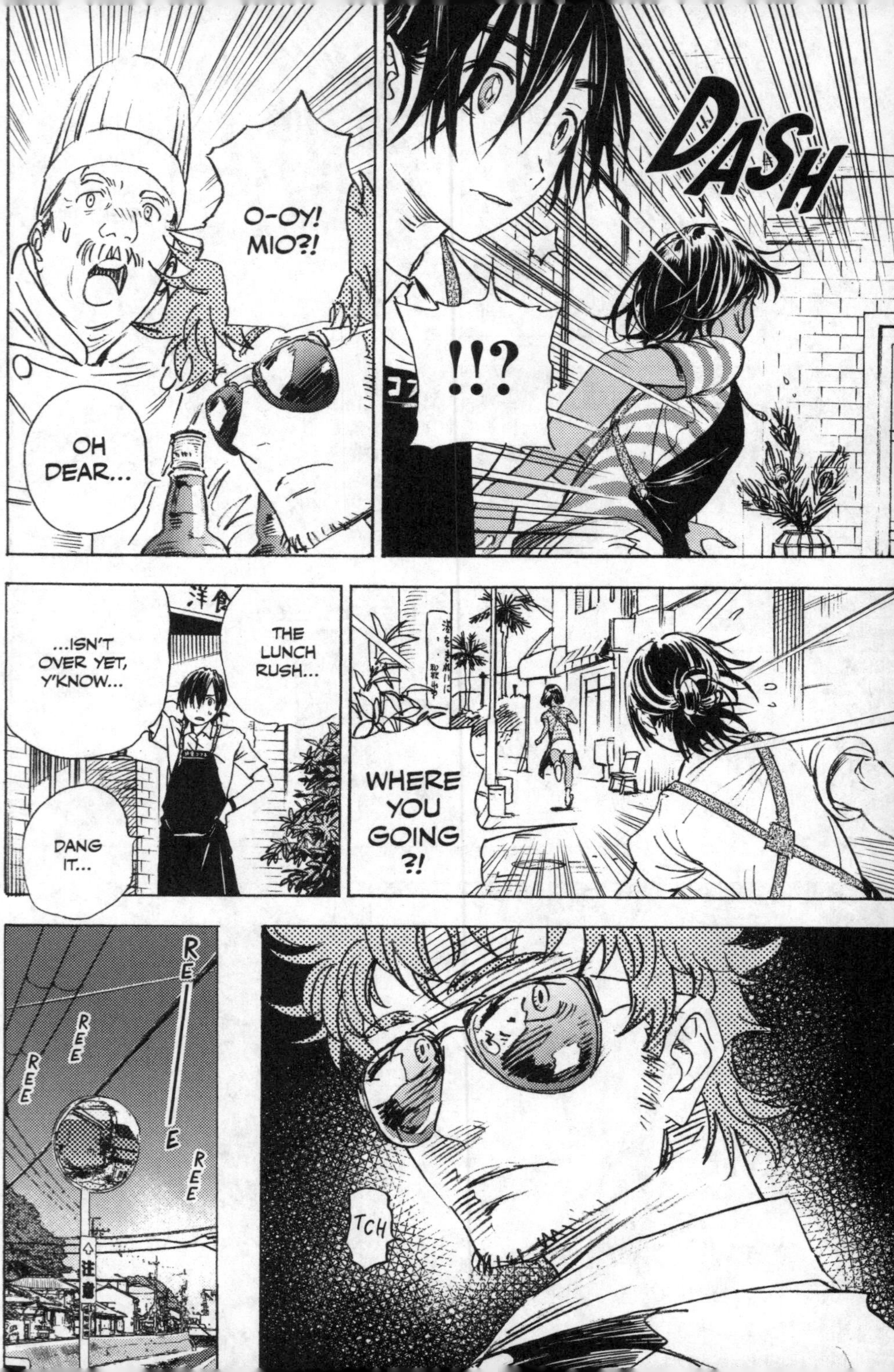
DASH
!!?
O-OY! MIO?!
OH DEAR...
WHERE YOU GOING ?!
THE LUNCH RUSH...
...ISN'T OVER YET, Y'KNOW...
DANG IT...
TCH
REE—E
REE
REE
REE

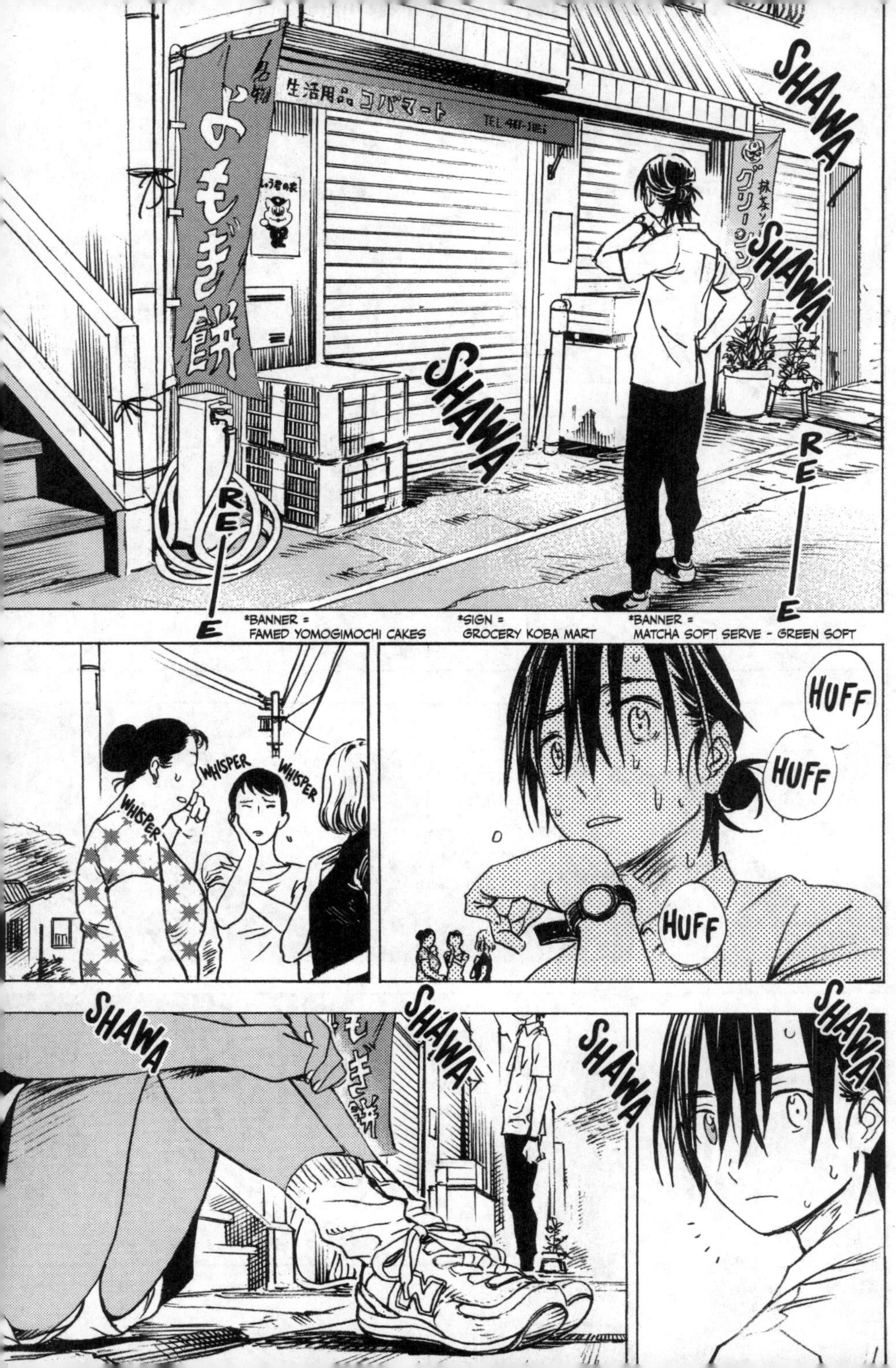
SHAWA
SHAWA
SHAWA
RE-E
RE-E
*BANNER = FAMED YOMOGIMOCHI CAKES
*SIGN = GROCERY KOBA MART
*BANNER = MATCHA SOFT SERVE - GREEN SOFT
HUFF
HUFF
HUFF
WHISPER
WHISPER
WHISPER
SHAWA
SHAWA
SHAWA
SHAWA

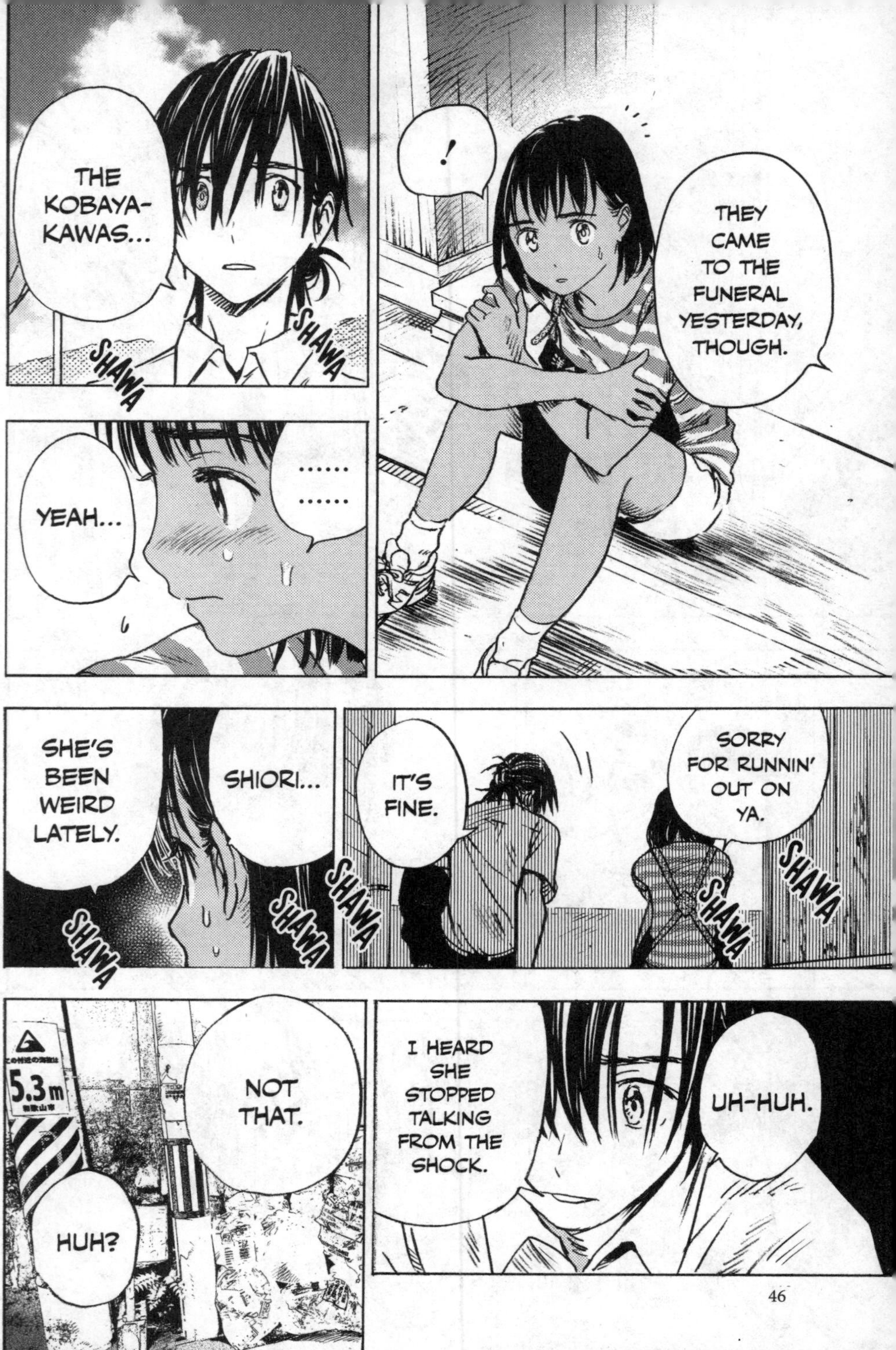
!
THEY CAME TO THE FUNERAL YESTERDAY, THOUGH.
THE KOBAYA-KAWAS...
SHAWA
SHAWA
......
......
YEAH...
SORRY FOR RUNNIN' OUT ON YA.
SHAWA
SHAWA
IT'S FINE.
SHIORI...
SHAWA
SHAWA
SHE'S BEEN WEIRD LATELY.
SHAWA
UH-HUH.
I HEARD SHE STOPPED TALKING FROM THE SHOCK.
NOT THAT.
HUH?
5.3m

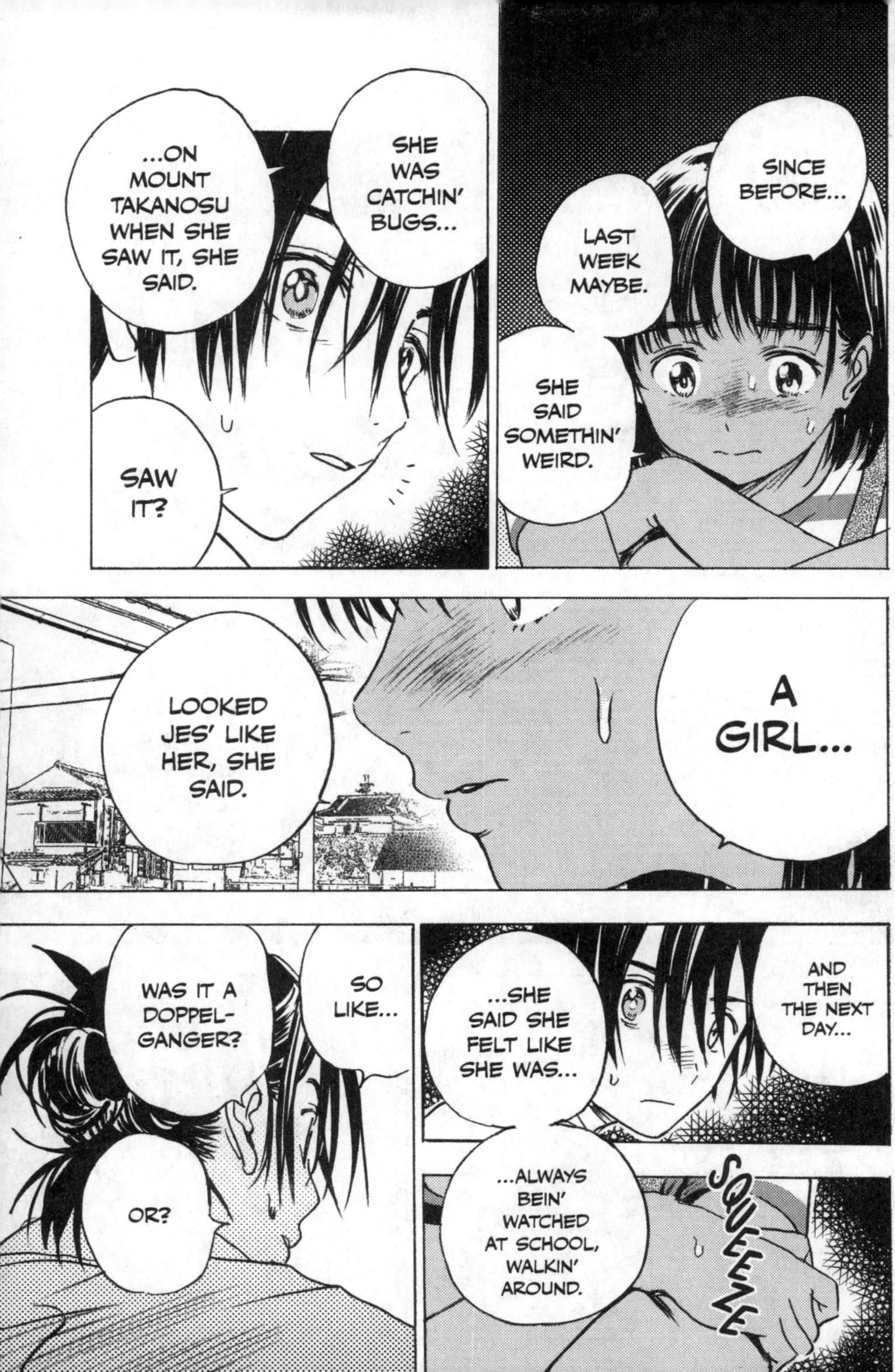
SINCE BEFORE...
LAST WEEK MAYBE.
SHE SAID SOMETHIN' WEIRD.
SHE WAS CATCHIN' BUGS...
...ON MOUNT TAKANOSU WHEN SHE SAW IT, SHE SAID.
SAW IT?
A GIRL...
LOOKED JES' LIKE HER, SHE SAID.
AND THEN THE NEXT DAY...
...SHE SAID SHE FELT LIKE SHE WAS...
...ALWAYS BEIN' WATCHED AT SCHOOL, WALKIN' AROUND.
SQUEEZE
SO LIKE...
WAS IT A DOPPEL-GANGER?
OR?

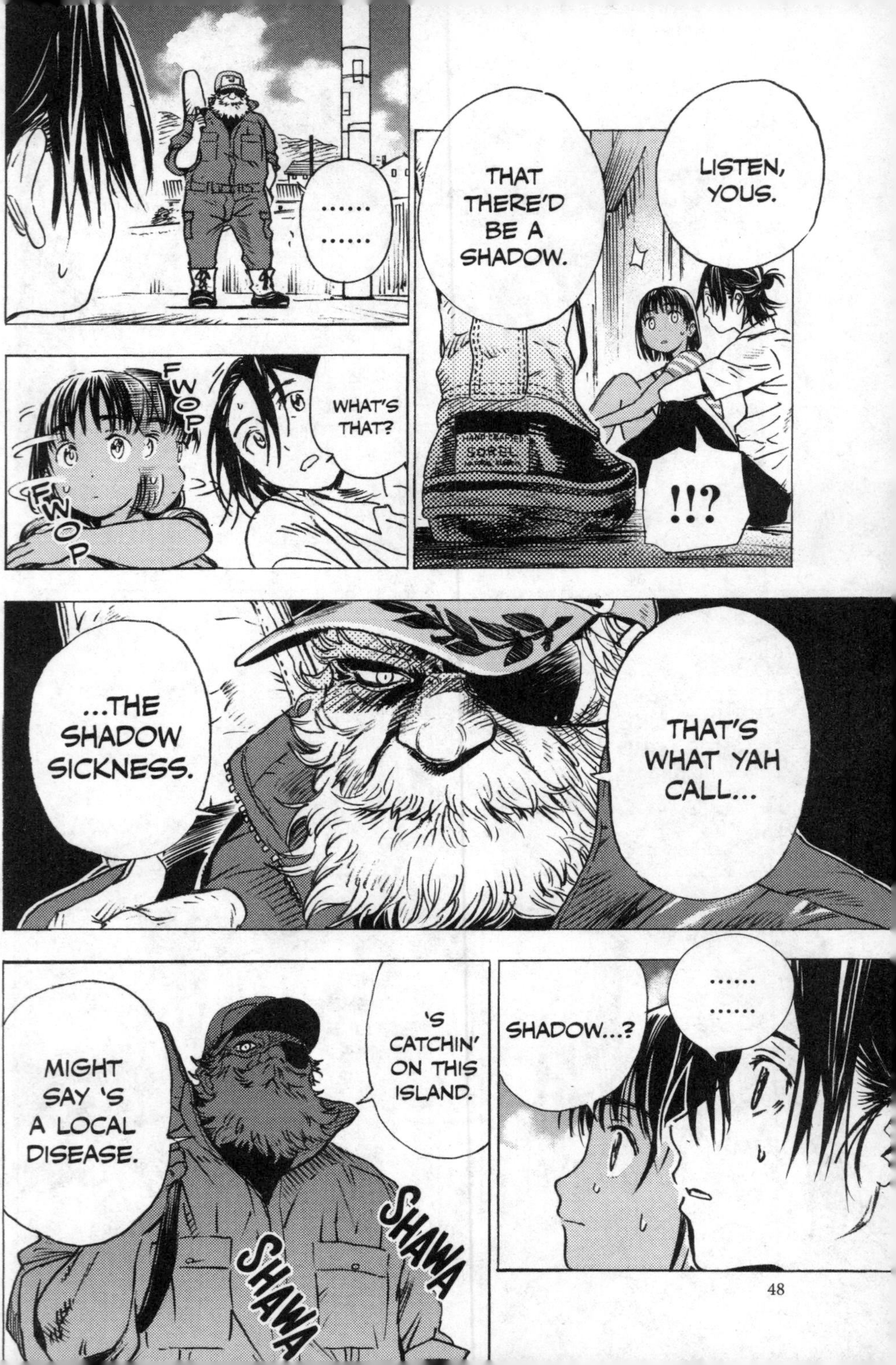
LISTEN, YOUS.
THAT THERE'D BE A SHADOW.
!!?
......
......
WHAT'S THAT?
FWOP
FWOP
THAT'S WHAT YAH CALL...
...THE SHADOW SICKNESS.
......
......
SHADOW...?
'S CATCHIN' ON THIS ISLAND.
MIGHT SAY 'S A LOCAL DISEASE.
SHAWA
SHAWA

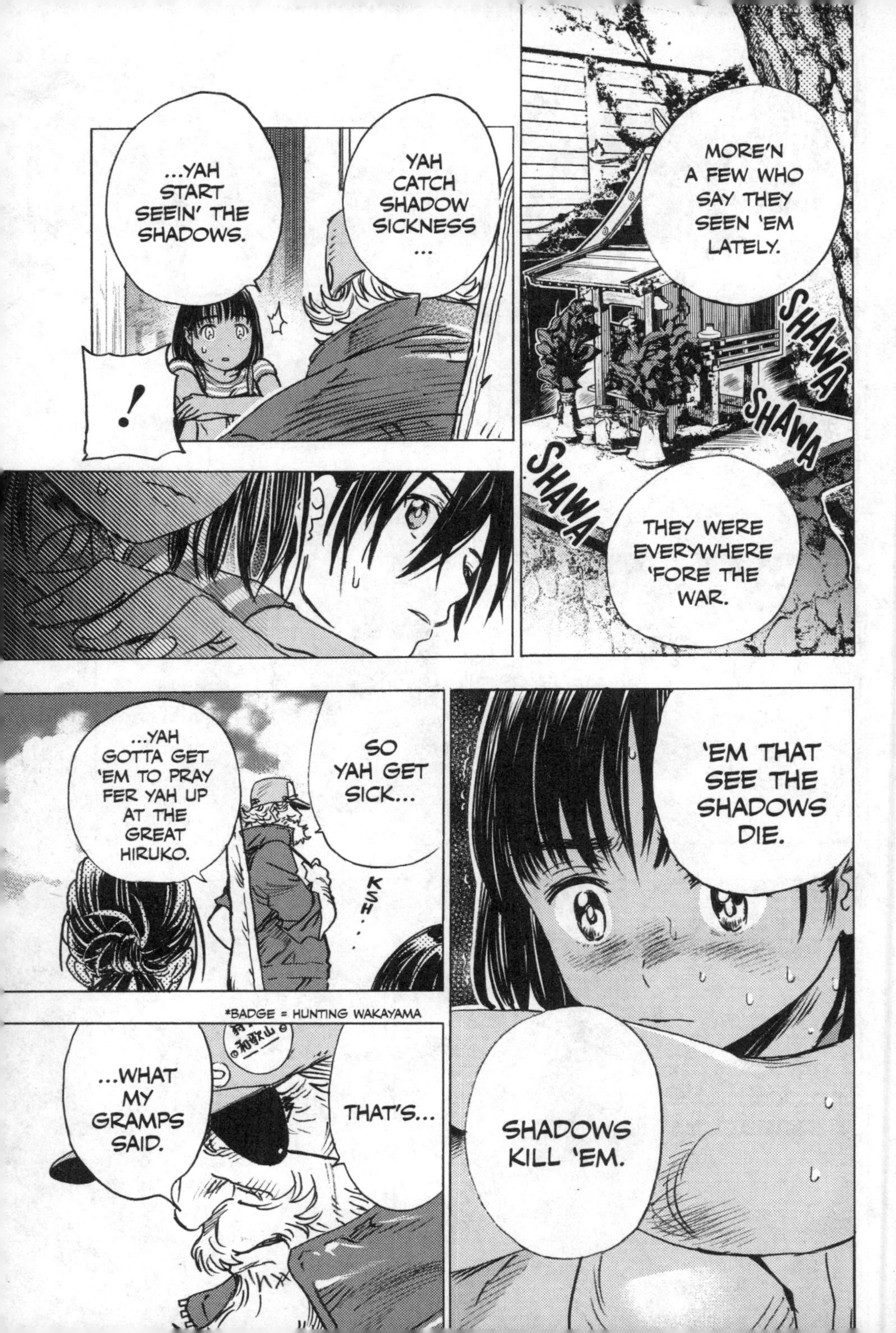
MORE'N A FEW WHO SAY THEY SEEN 'EM LATELY.
SHAWA
SHAWA
SHAWA
THEY WERE EVERYWHERE 'FORE THE WAR.
YAH CATCH SHADOW SICKNESS ...
...YAH START SEEIN' THE SHADOWS.
!
'EM THAT SEE THE SHADOWS DIE.
SHADOWS KILL 'EM.
SO YAH GET SICK...
...YAH GOTTA GET 'EM TO PRAY FER YAH UP AT THE GREAT HIRUKO.
KSH..
*BADGE = HUNTING WAKAYAMA
THAT'S...
...WHAT MY GRAMPS SAID.

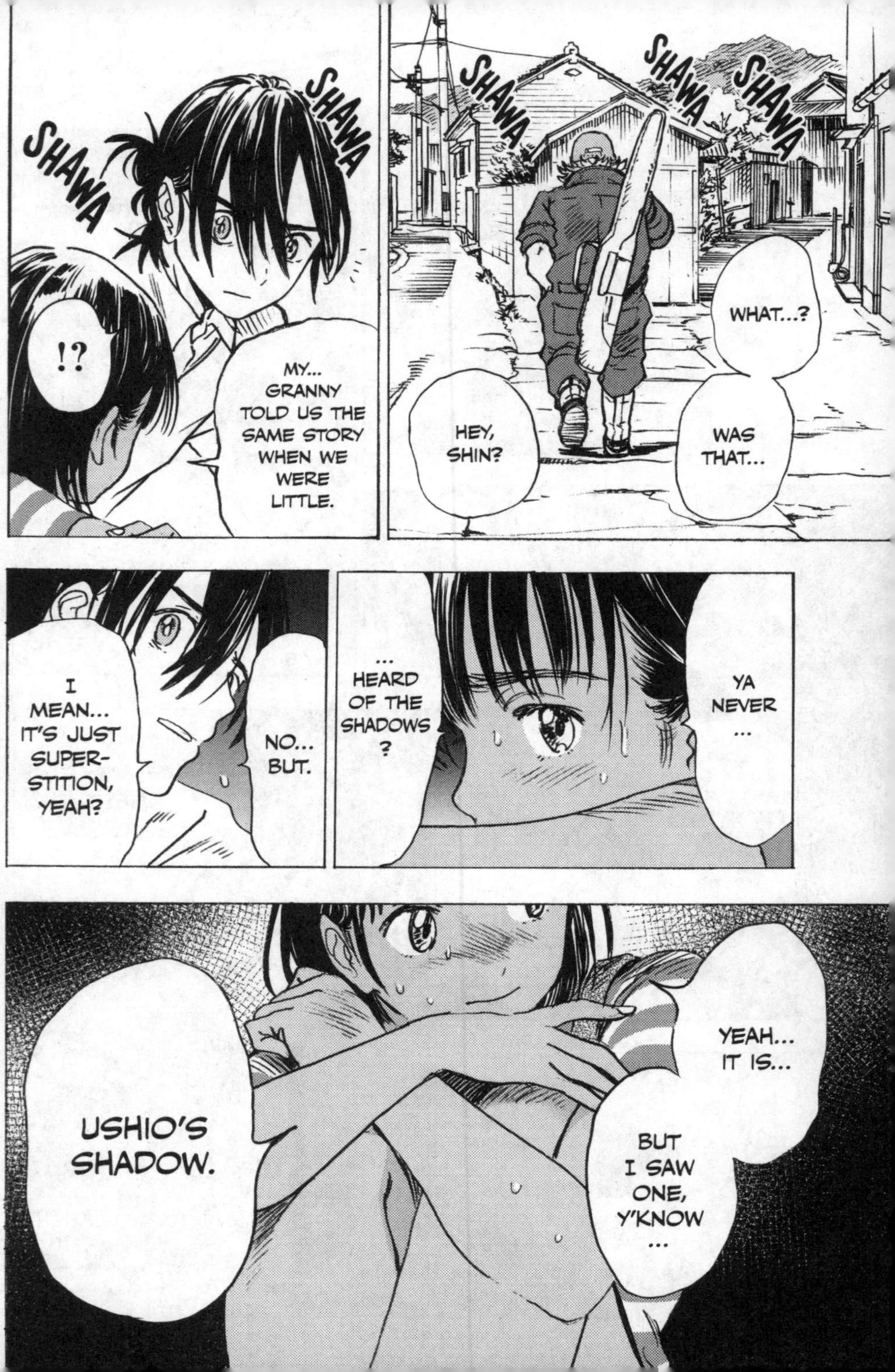
SHAWA
SHAWA
SHAWA
WHAT...?
WAS THAT...
HEY, SHIN?
SHAWA
SHAWA
!?
MY... GRANNY TOLD US THE SAME STORY WHEN WE WERE LITTLE.
YA NEVER ...
... HEARD OF THE SHADOWS ?
NO... BUT.
I MEAN... IT'S JUST SUPER-STITION, YEAH?
YEAH... IT IS...
BUT I SAW ONE, Y'KNOW ...
USHIO'S SHADOW.

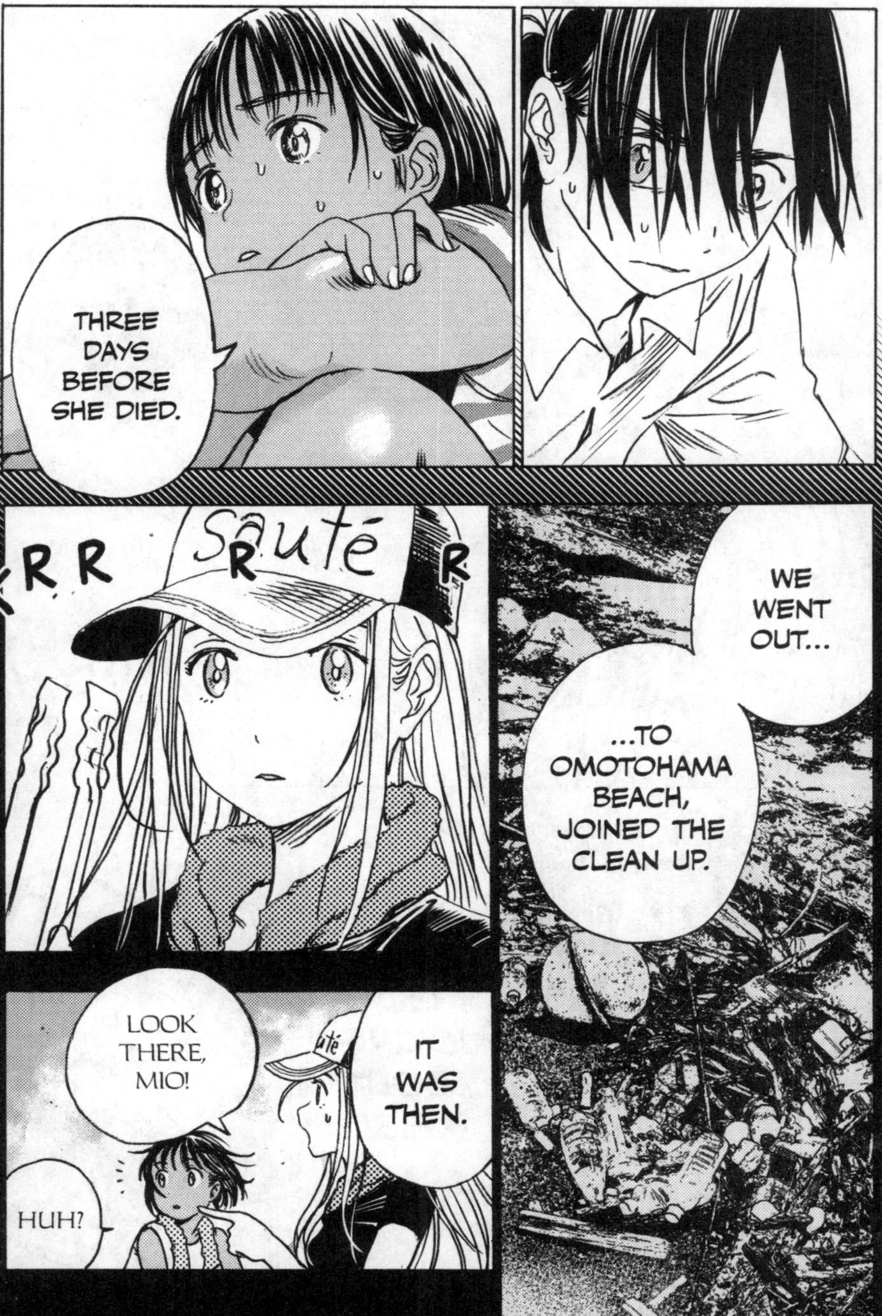
THREE DAYS BEFORE SHE DIED.
WE WENT OUT...
...TO OMOTOHAMA BEACH, JOINED THE CLEAN UP.
KRRRR
Sauté
IT WAS THEN.
LOOK THERE, MIO!
HUH?

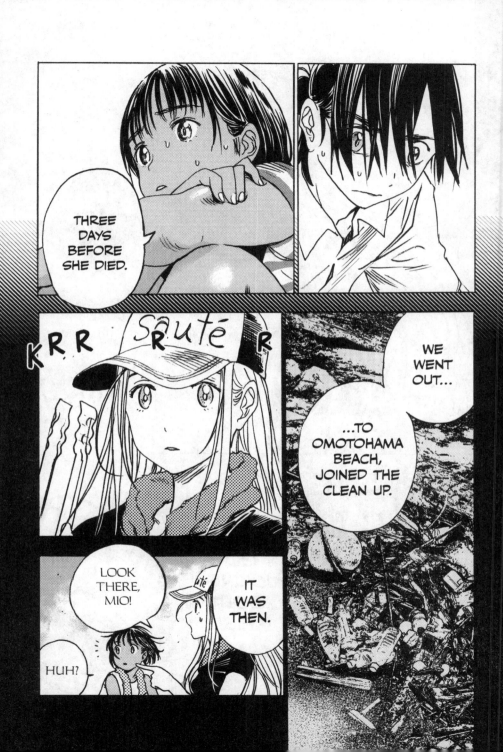

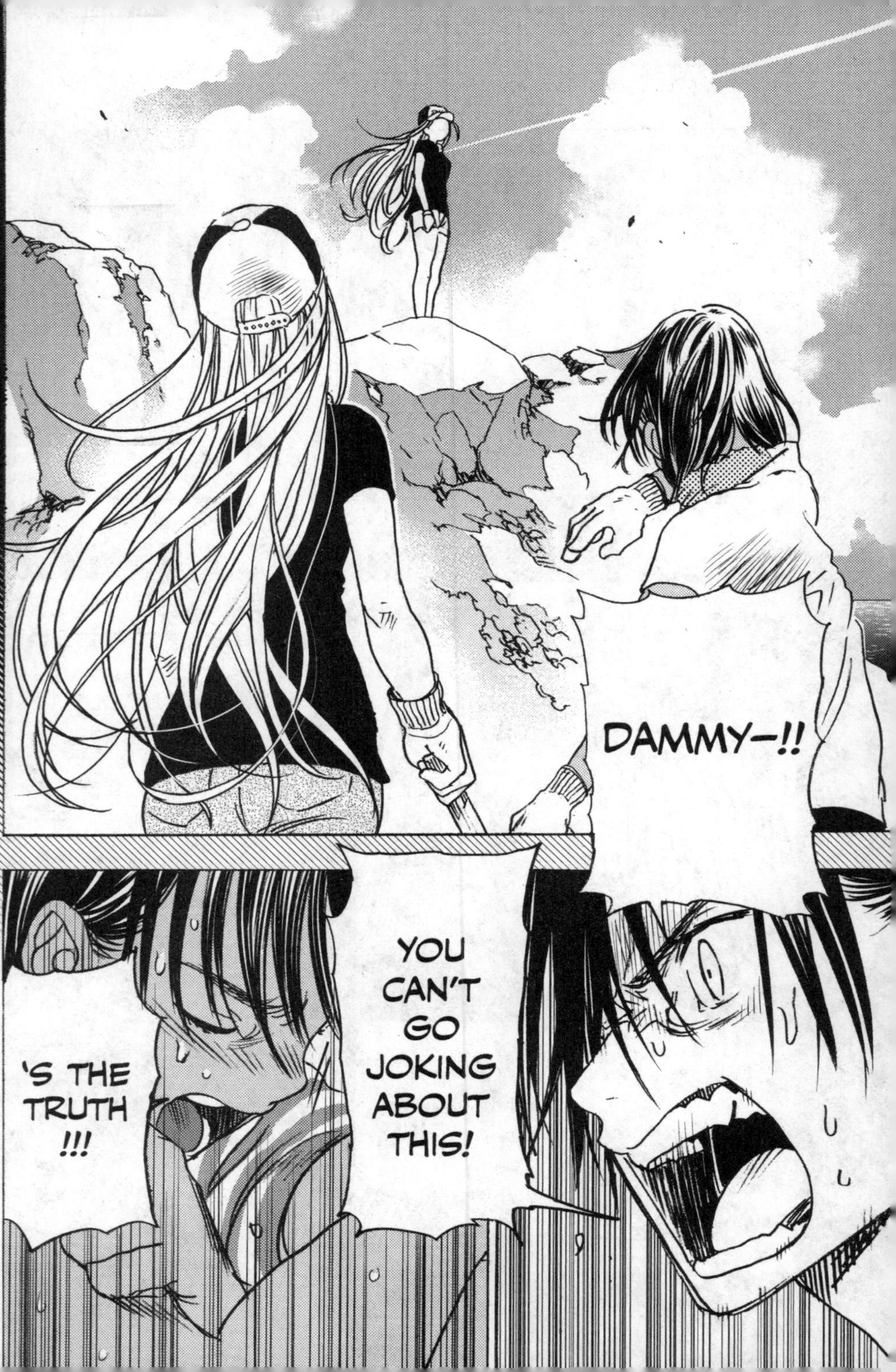
DAMMY–!!
YOU CAN'T GO JOKING ABOUT THIS!
'S THE TRUTH !!!

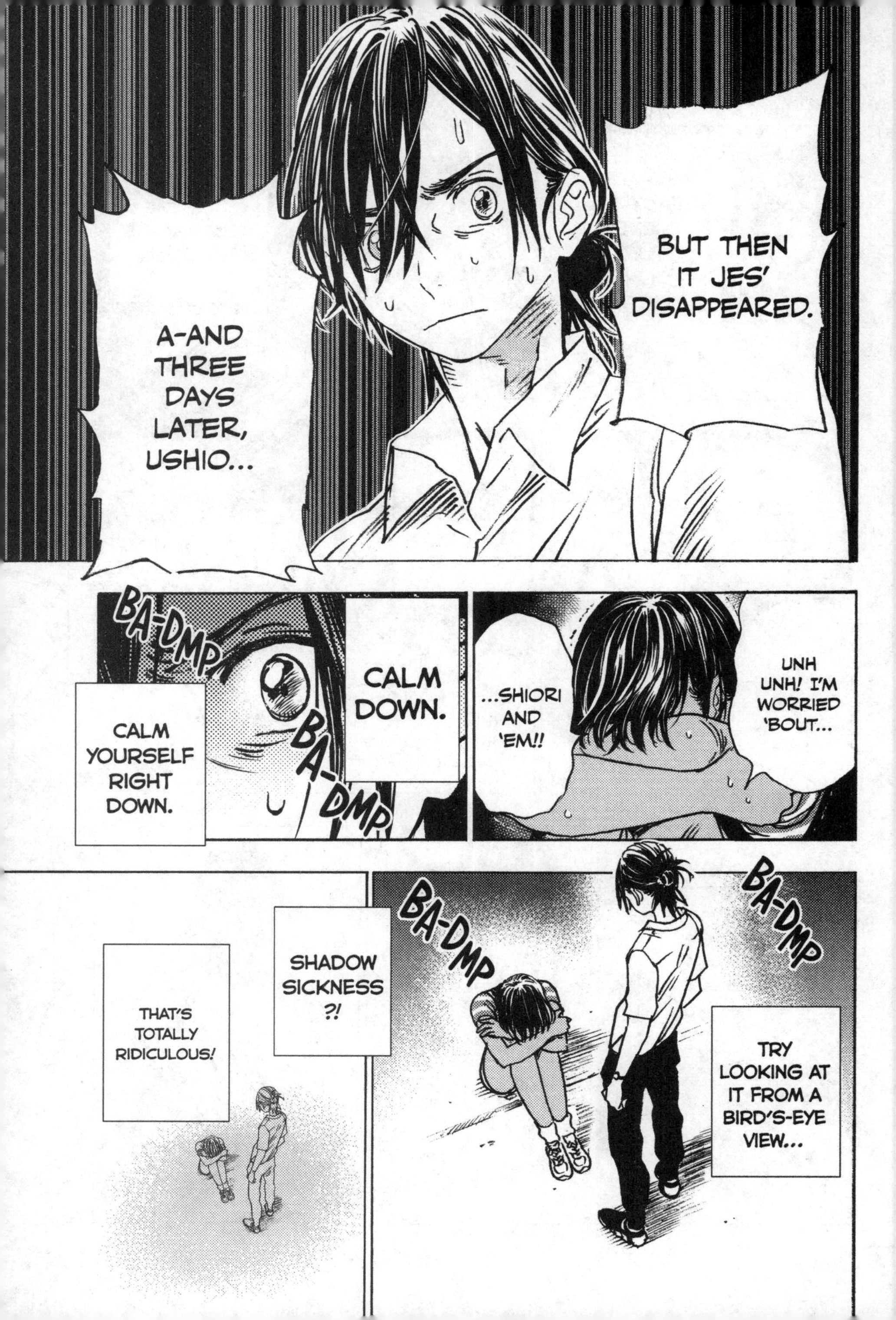
BUT THEN IT JES' DISAPPEARED.
A-AND THREE DAYS LATER, USHIO...
UNH UNH! I'M WORRIED 'BOUT...
...SHIORI AND 'EM!!
BA-DMP
CALM DOWN.
BA-DMP
CALM YOURSELF RIGHT DOWN.
BA-DMP
BA-DMP
TRY LOOKING AT IT FROM A BIRD'S-EYE VIEW...
SHADOW SICKNESS?!
THAT'S TOTALLY RIDICULOUS!

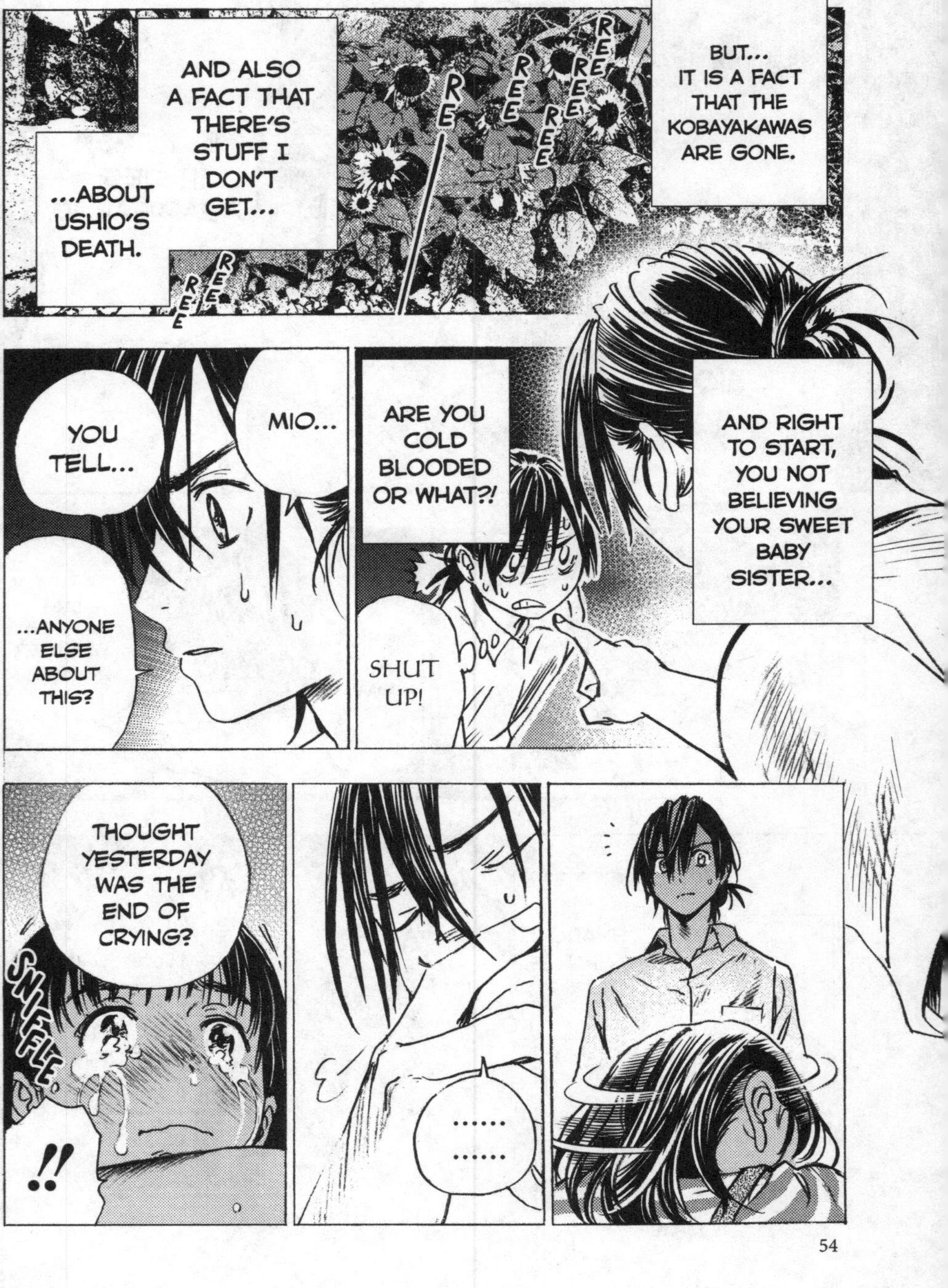
BUT... IT IS A FACT THAT THE KOBAYAKAWAS ARE GONE.
REE
REEE
REEE
REE
AND ALSO A FACT THAT THERE'S STUFF I DON'T GET...
...ABOUT USHIO'S DEATH.
REE
REE
AND RIGHT TO START, YOU NOT BELIEVING YOUR SWEET BABY SISTER...
ARE YOU COLD BLOODED OR WHAT?!
SHUT UP!
MIO...
YOU TELL...
...ANYONE ELSE ABOUT THIS?
......
......
THOUGHT YESTERDAY WAS THE END OF CRYING?
SNIFFLE
!!

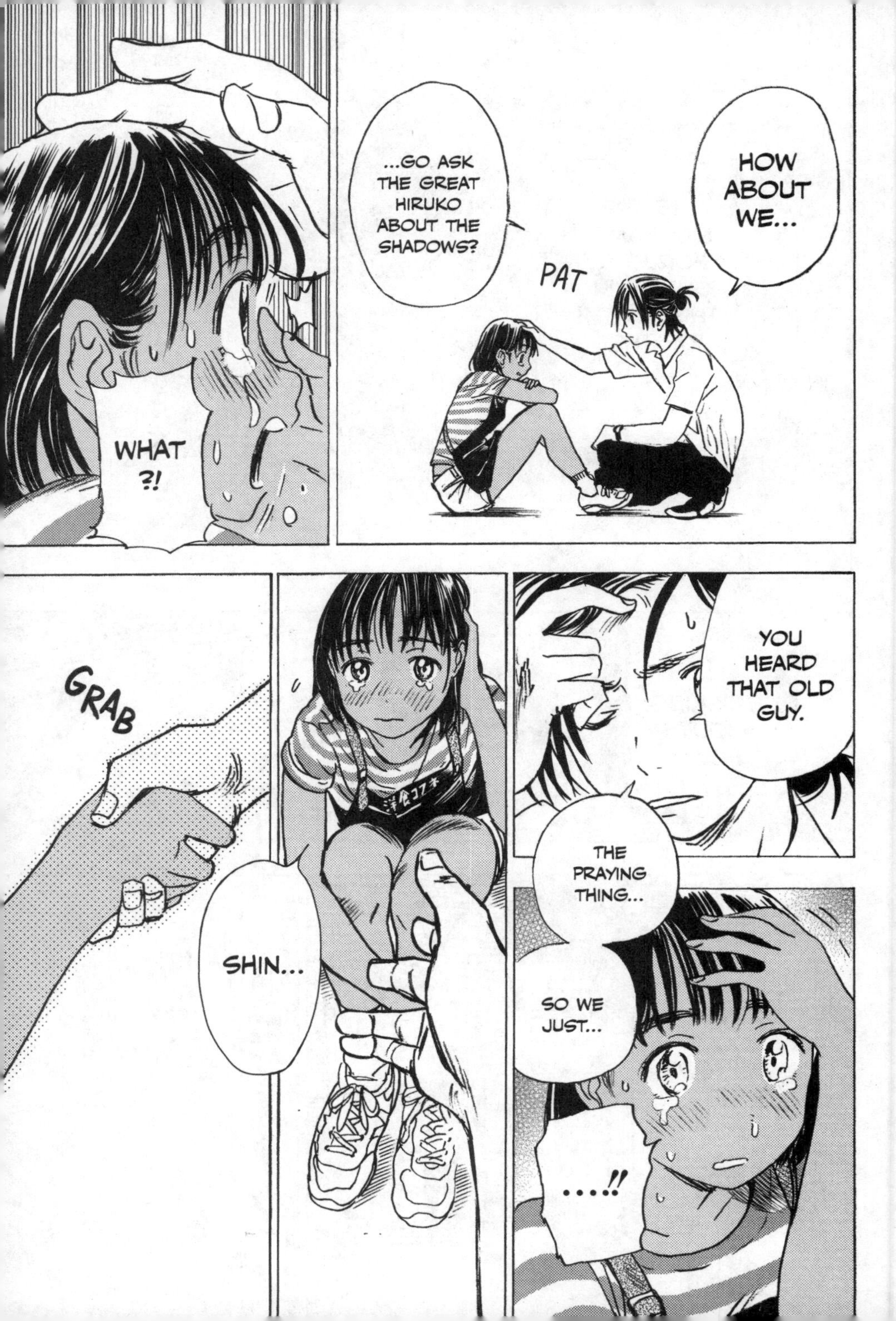
HOW ABOUT WE...
...GO ASK THE GREAT HIRUKO ABOUT THE SHADOWS?
PAT
WHAT ?!
YOU HEARD THAT OLD GUY.
THE PRAYING THING...
SO WE JUST...
....!!
SHIN...
GRAB

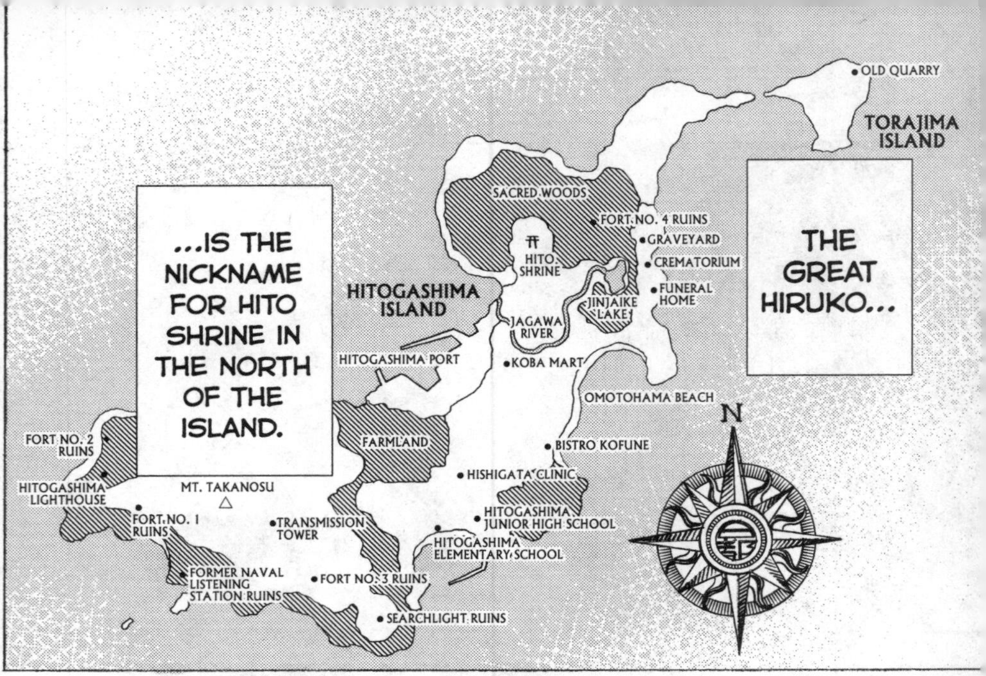
THE GREAT HIRUKO...
...IS THE NICKNAME FOR HITO SHRINE IN THE NORTH OF THE ISLAND.
OLD QUARRY
TORAJIMA ISLAND
SACRED WOODS
FORT NO. 4 RUINS
GRAVEYARD
CREMATORIUM
FUNERAL HOME
HITO SHRINE
JINJAIKE LAKE
JAGAWA RIVER
HITOGASHIMA ISLAND
HITOGASHIMA PORT
KOBA MART
OMOTOHAMA BEACH
N
FARMLAND
BISTRO KOFUNE
FORT NO. 2 RUINS
HITOGASHIMA LIGHTHOUSE
MT. TAKANOSU
HISHIGATA CLINIC
FORT NO. 1 RUINS
TRANSMISSION TOWER
HITOGASHIMA JUNIOR HIGH SCHOOL
HITOGASHIMA ELEMENTARY SCHOOL
FORMER NAVAL LISTENING STATION RUINS
FORT NO. 3 RUINS
SEARCHLIGHT RUINS

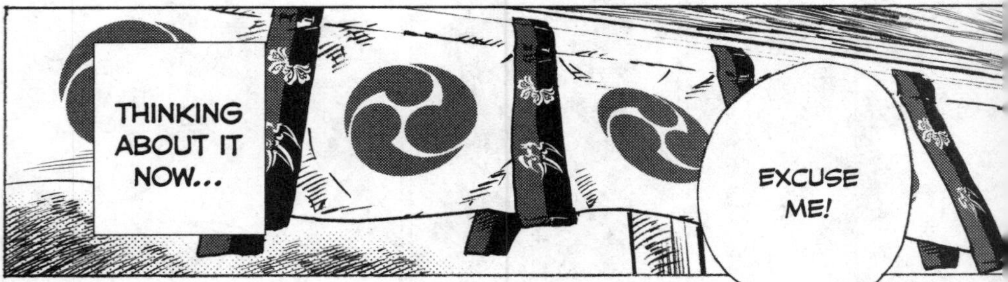
EXCUSE ME!
THINKING ABOUT IT NOW...

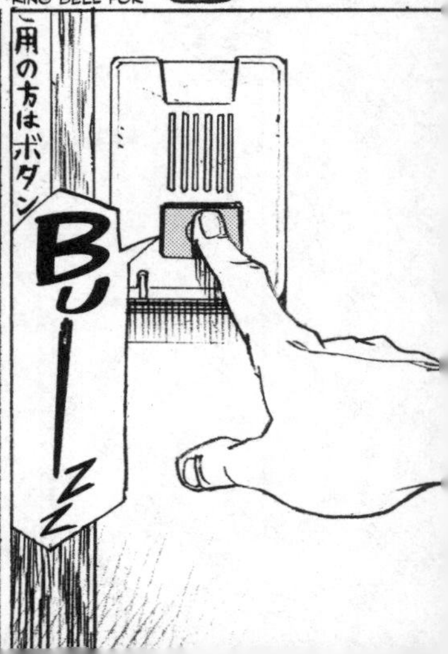
*RING BELL FOR
ご用の方はボタン
BUIIZZ

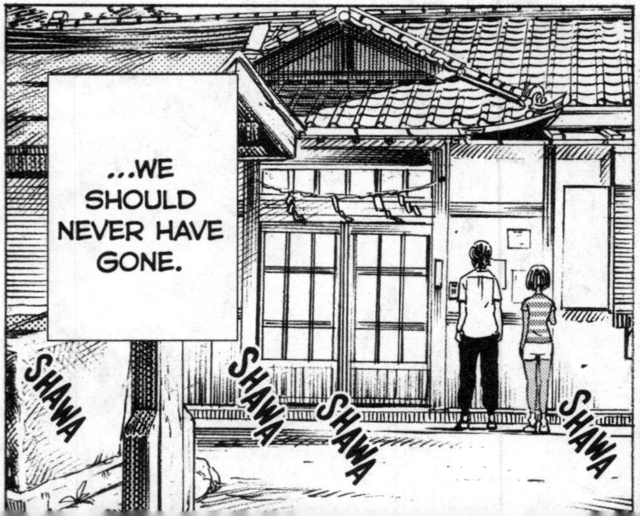
...WE SHOULD NEVER HAVE GONE.
SHAWA
SHAWA
SHAWA
SHAWA

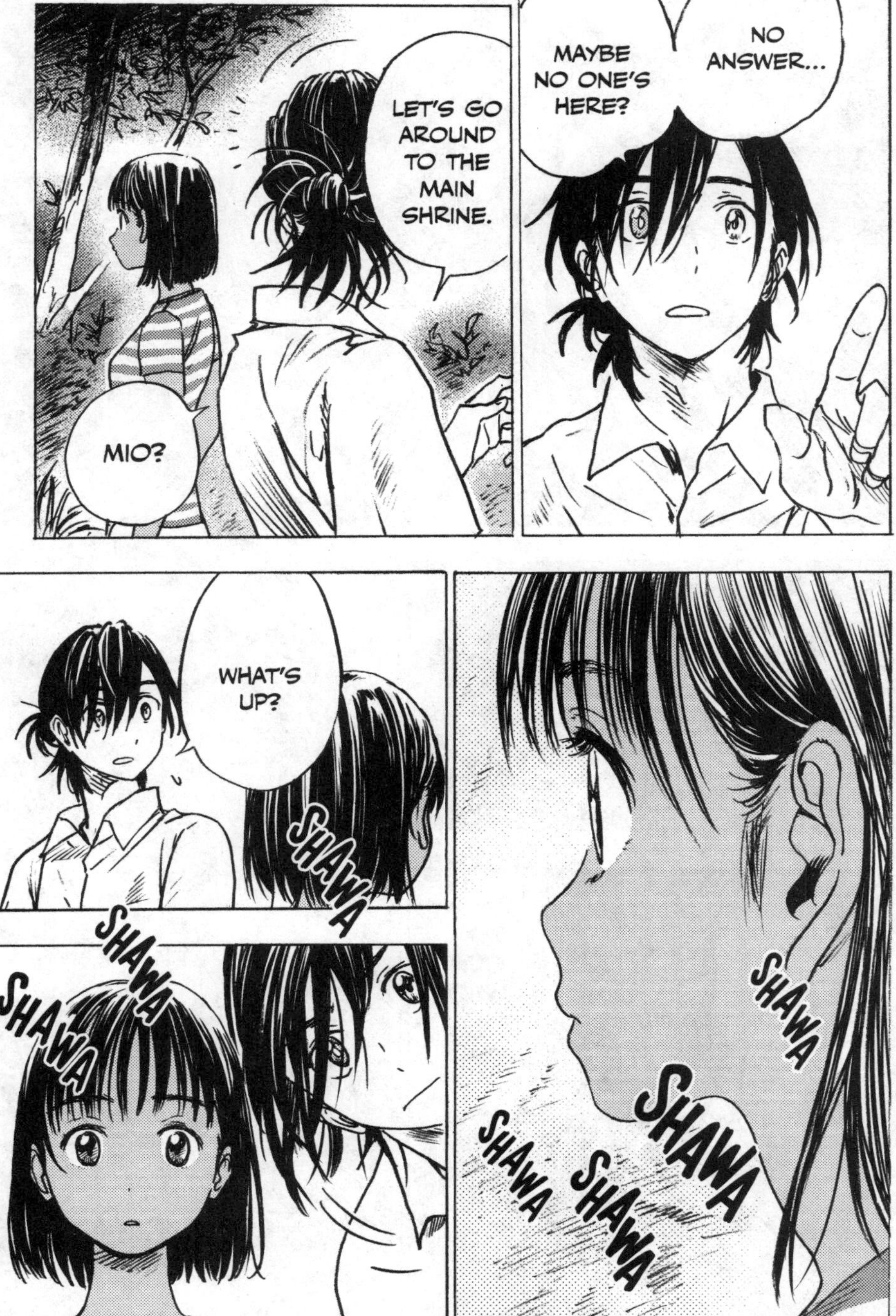
NO ANSWER...
MAYBE NO ONE'S HERE?
LET'S GO AROUND TO THE MAIN SHRINE.
MIO?
SHAWA
SHAWA
SHAWA
SHAWA
SHAWA
WHAT'S UP?
SHAWA
SHAWA
SHAWA

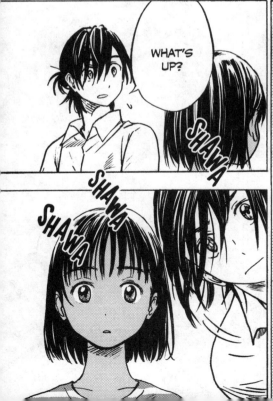

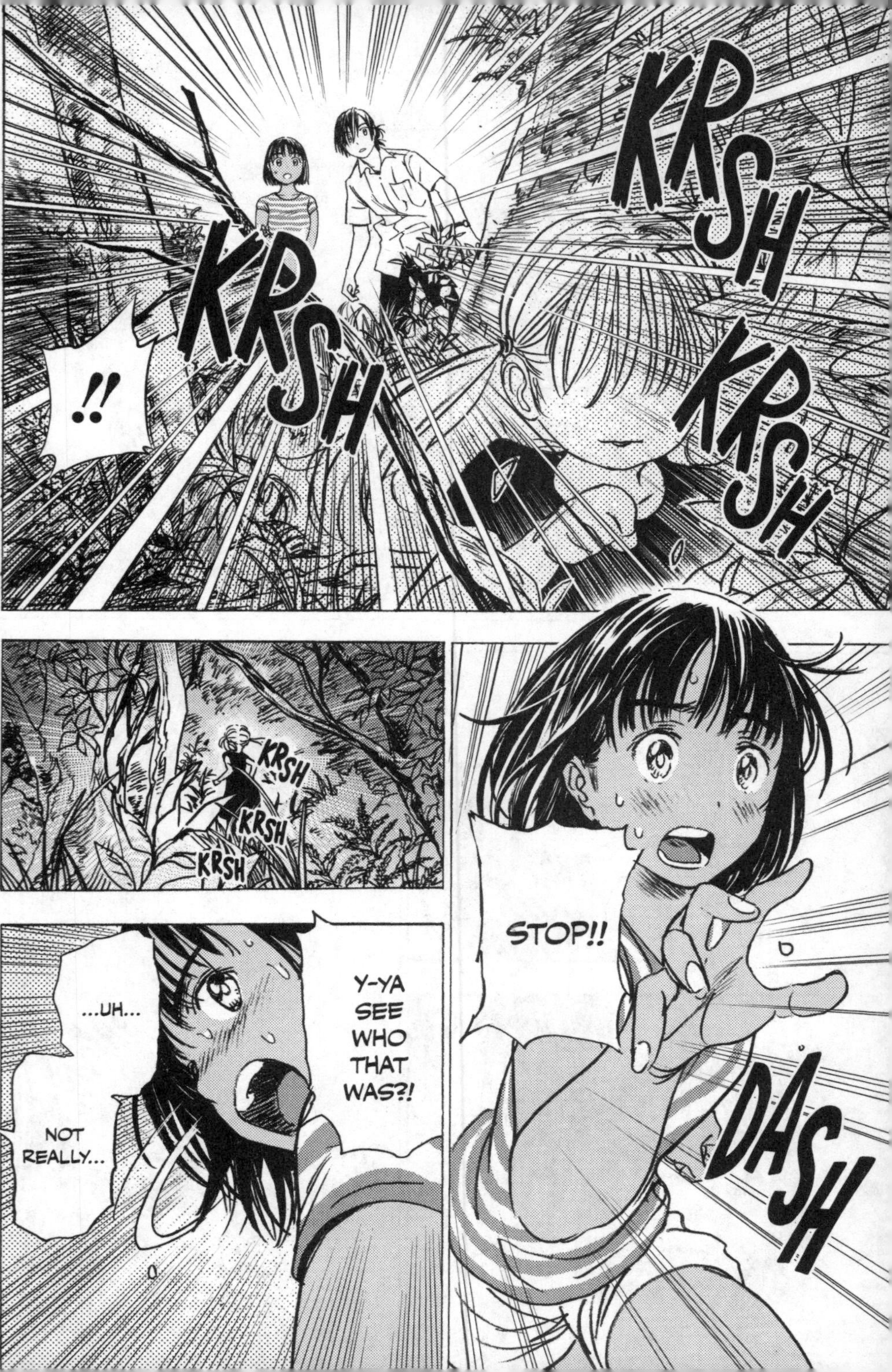
KRSH
KRSH
KRSH
KRSH
!!
STOP!!
DASH
KRSH
KRSH
KRSH
Y-YA SEE WHO THAT WAS?!
...UH...
NOT REALLY...

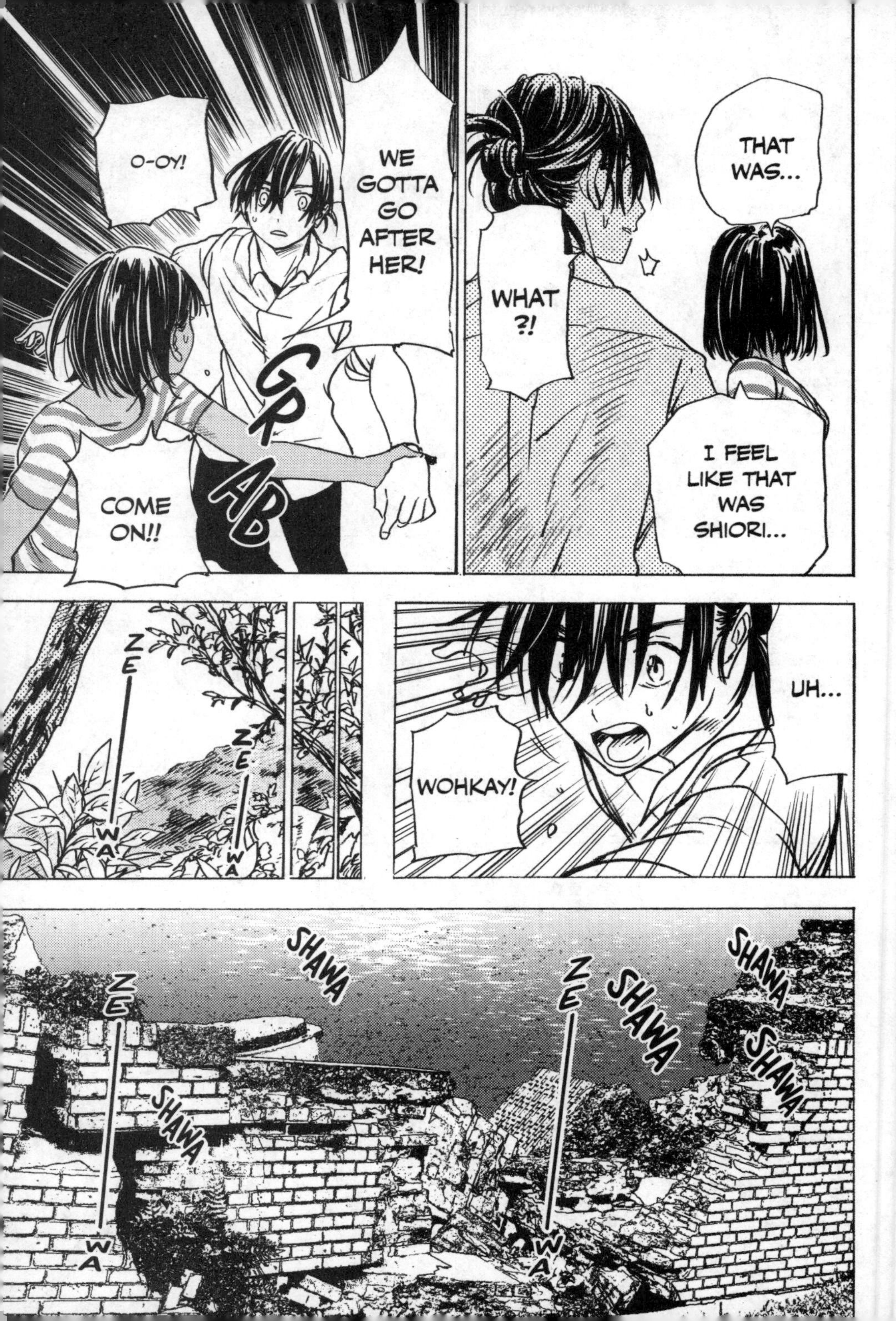
THAT WAS...
WHAT?!
I FEEL LIKE THAT WAS SHIORI...
WE GOTTA GO AFTER HER!
O-OY!
GRAB
COME ON!!
UH...
WOHKAY!
ZE
ZE
WA
WA
SHAWA
SHAWA
SHAWA
ZE
SHAWA
SHAWA
ZE
SHAWA
WA
WA

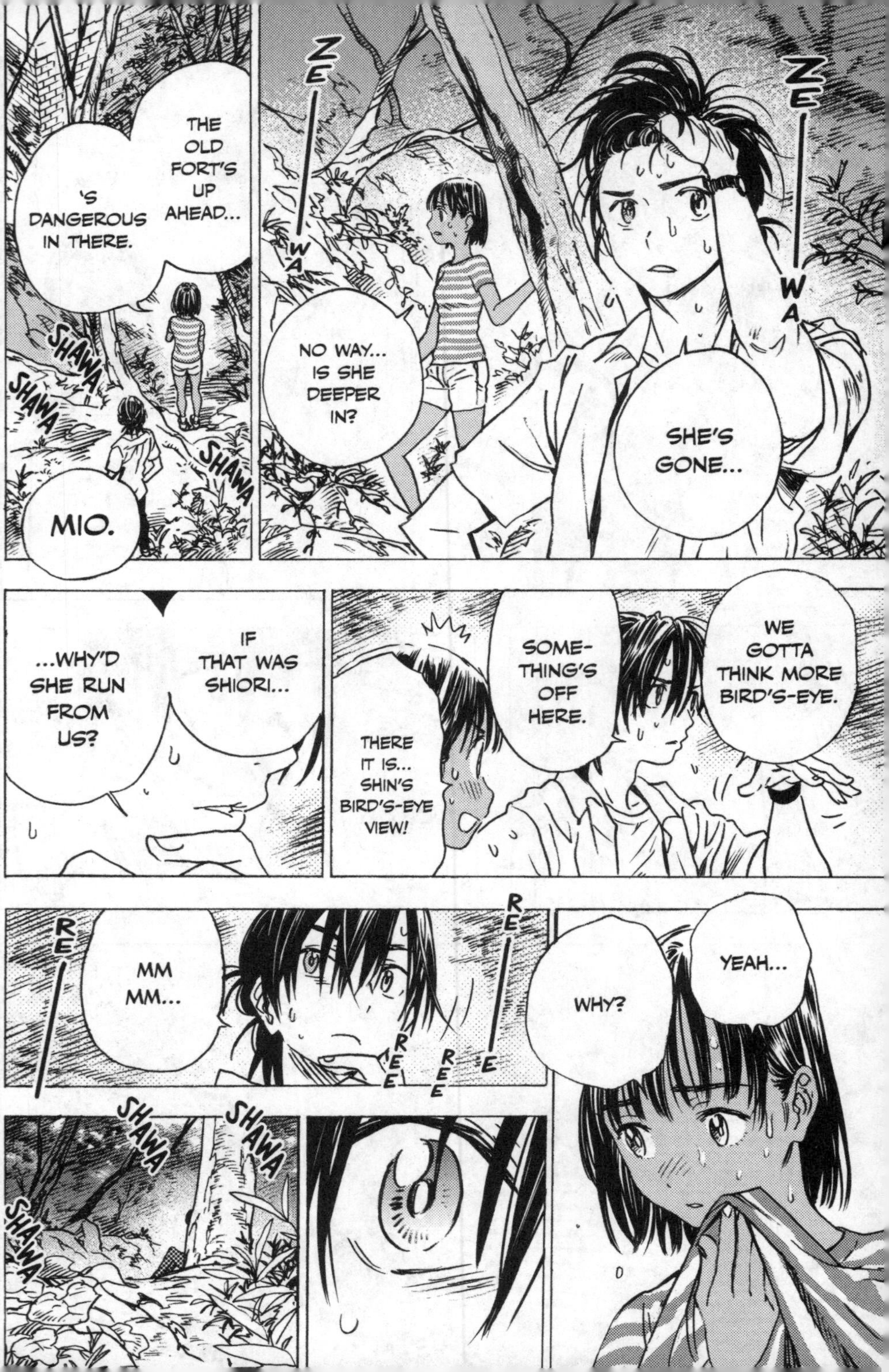
ZE-WA
SHE'S GONE...
ZE-WA
NO WAY... IS SHE DEEPER IN?
THE OLD FORT'S UP AHEAD...
'S DANGEROUS IN THERE.
SHAWA
SHAWA
SHAWA
MIO.
WE GOTTA THINK MORE BIRD'S-EYE.
SOME-THING'S OFF HERE.
THERE IT IS... SHIN'S BIRD'S-EYE VIEW!
IF THAT WAS SHIORI...
...WHY'D SHE RUN FROM US?
YEAH...
WHY?
RE-E
REE
REE
MM MM...
RE-
SHAWA
SHAWA
SHAWA

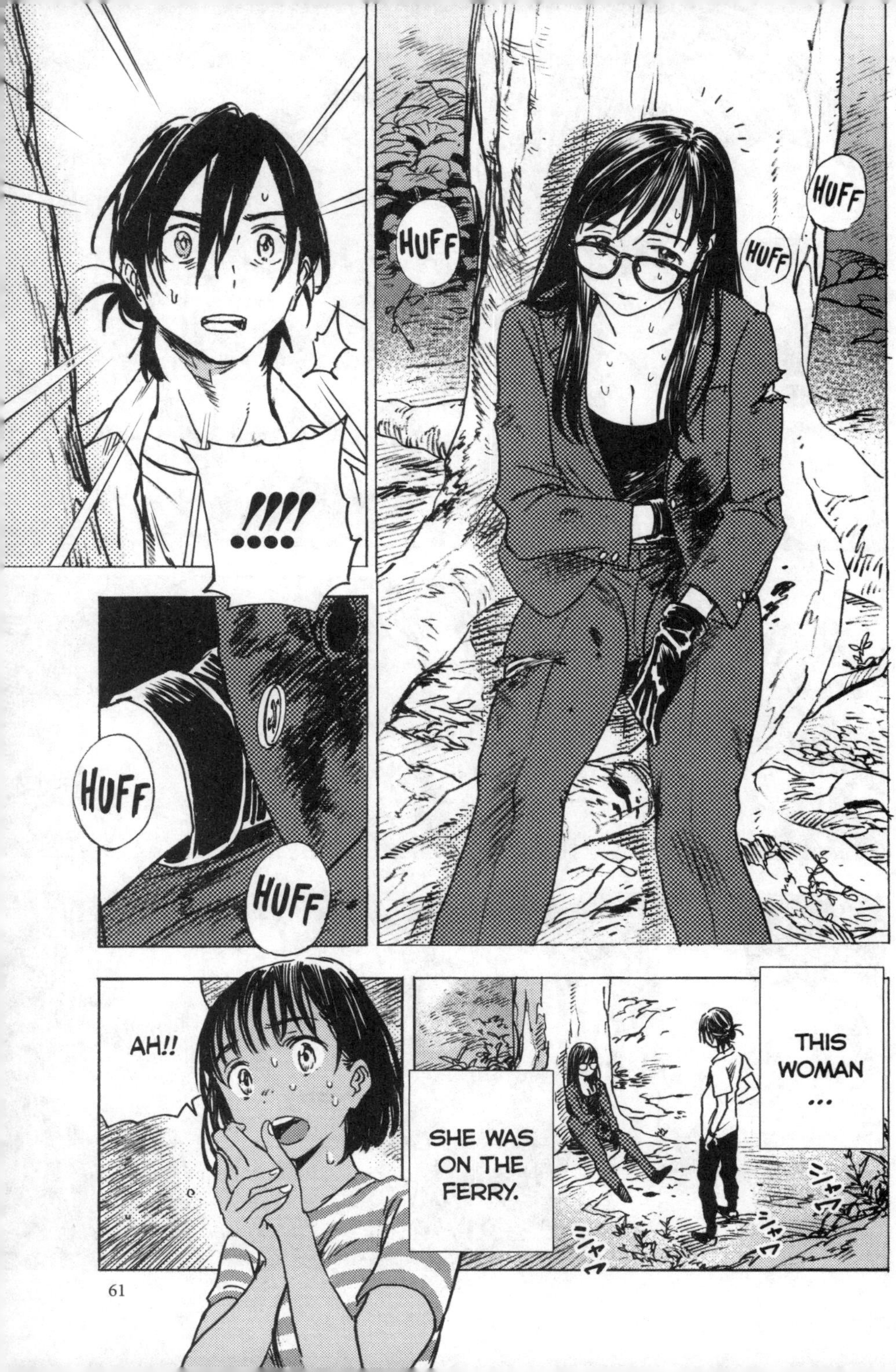
HUFF
HUFF
HUFF
!!!!
....
HUFF
HUFF
THIS WOMAN ...
SHE WAS ON THE FERRY.
AH!!

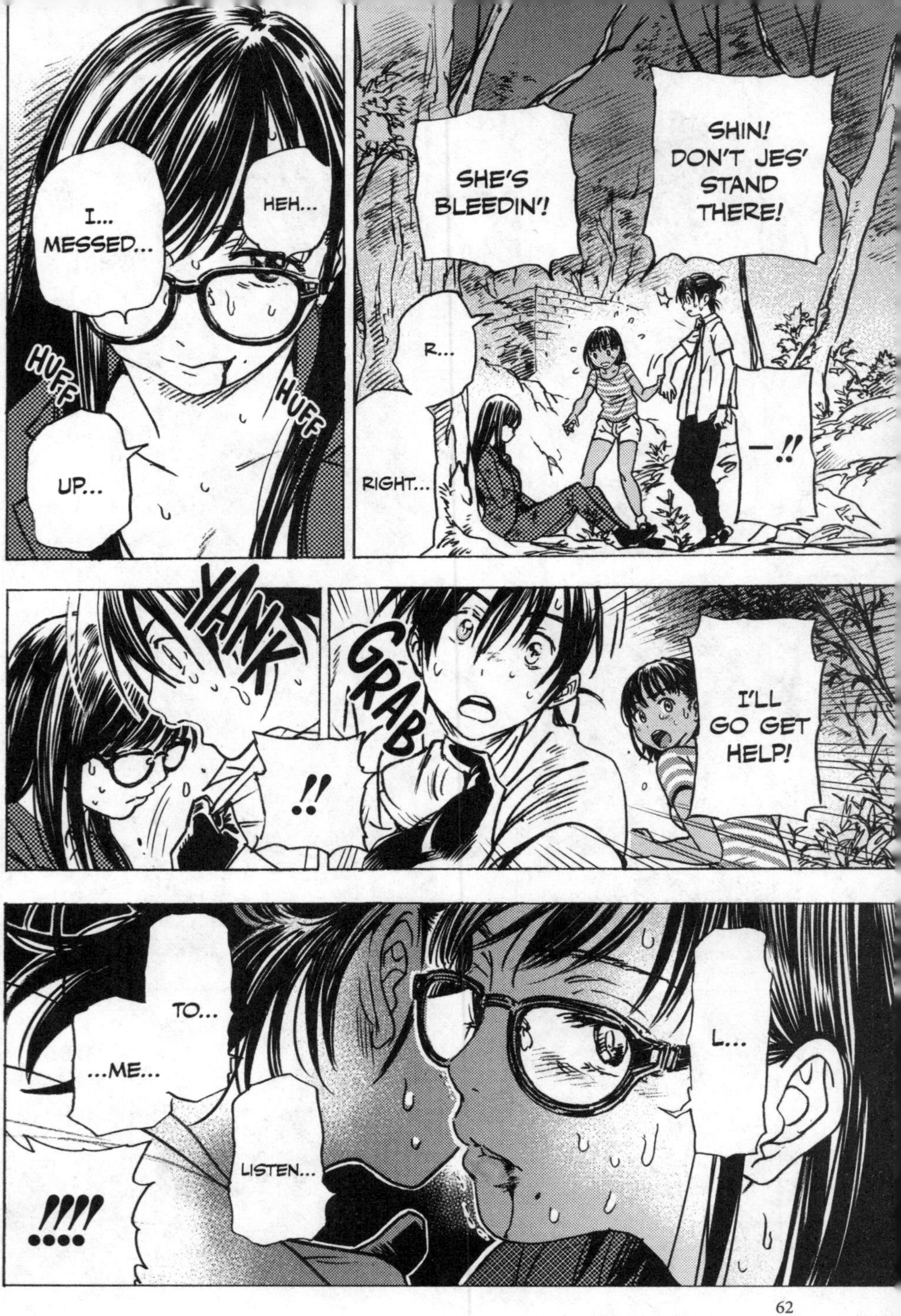
SHIN! DON'T JES' STAND THERE!
SHE'S BLEEDIN'!
—!!
R...
RIGHT...
HEH...
I... MESSED...
HUFF
HUFF
UP...
I'LL GO GET HELP!
GRAB
!!
YANK
L...
TO...
...ME...
LISTEN...
!!!!

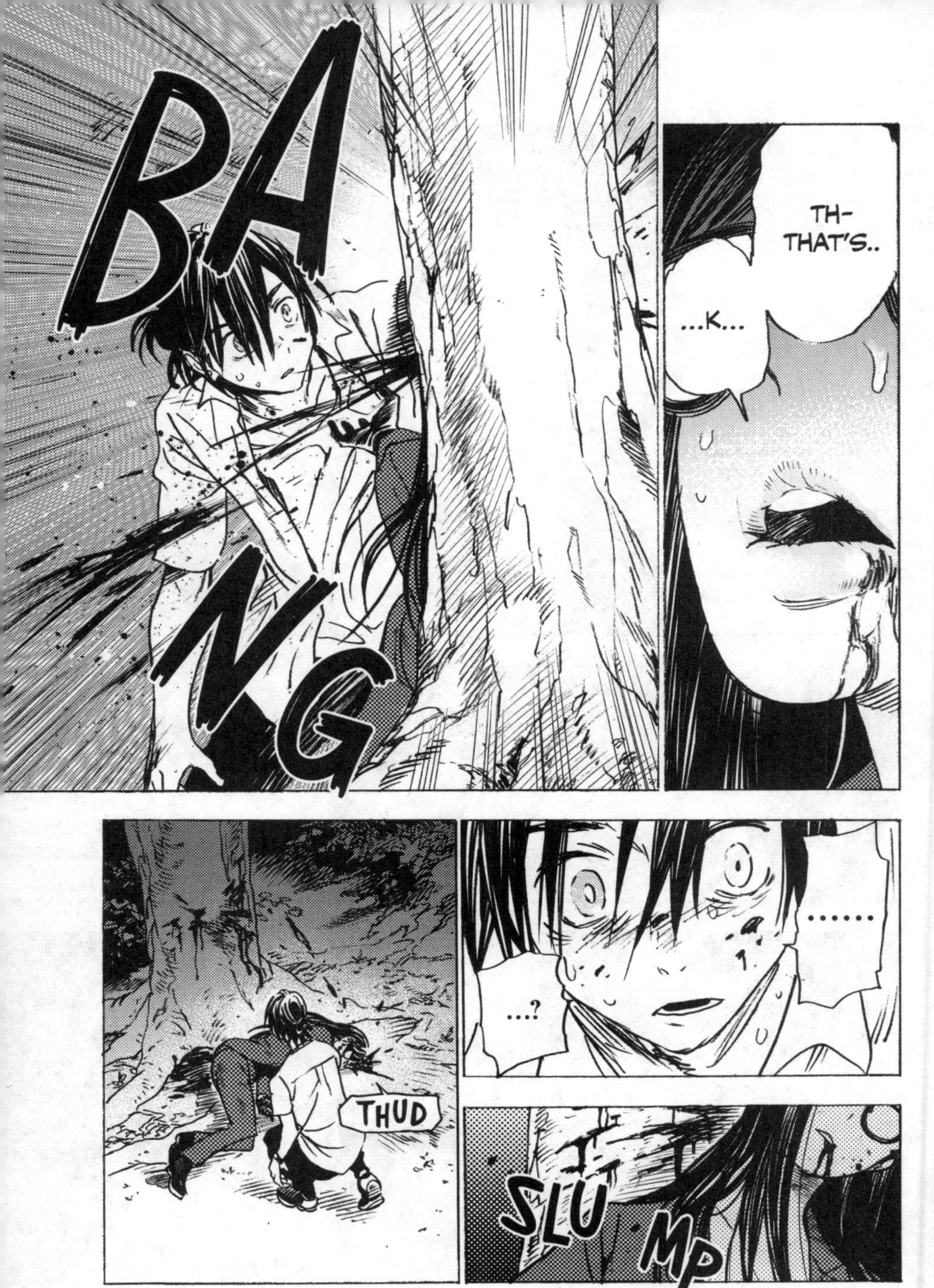
TH- THAT'S..
...K...
BANG
......
...?
SLUMP
THUD

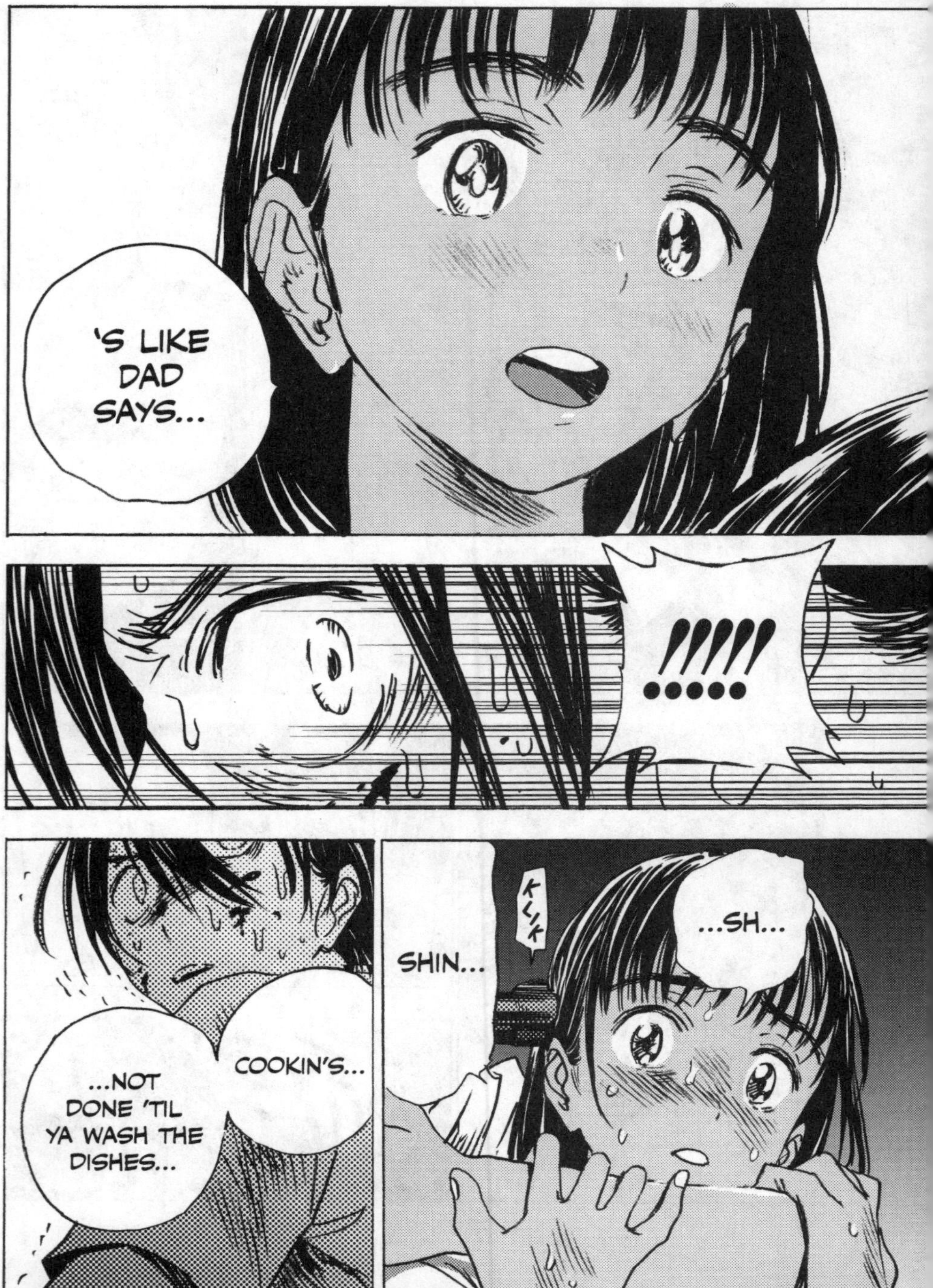
'S LIKE DAD SAYS...
!!!!!
...SH...
KLIK
SHIN...
COOKIN'S...
...NOT DONE 'TIL YA WASH THE DISHES...

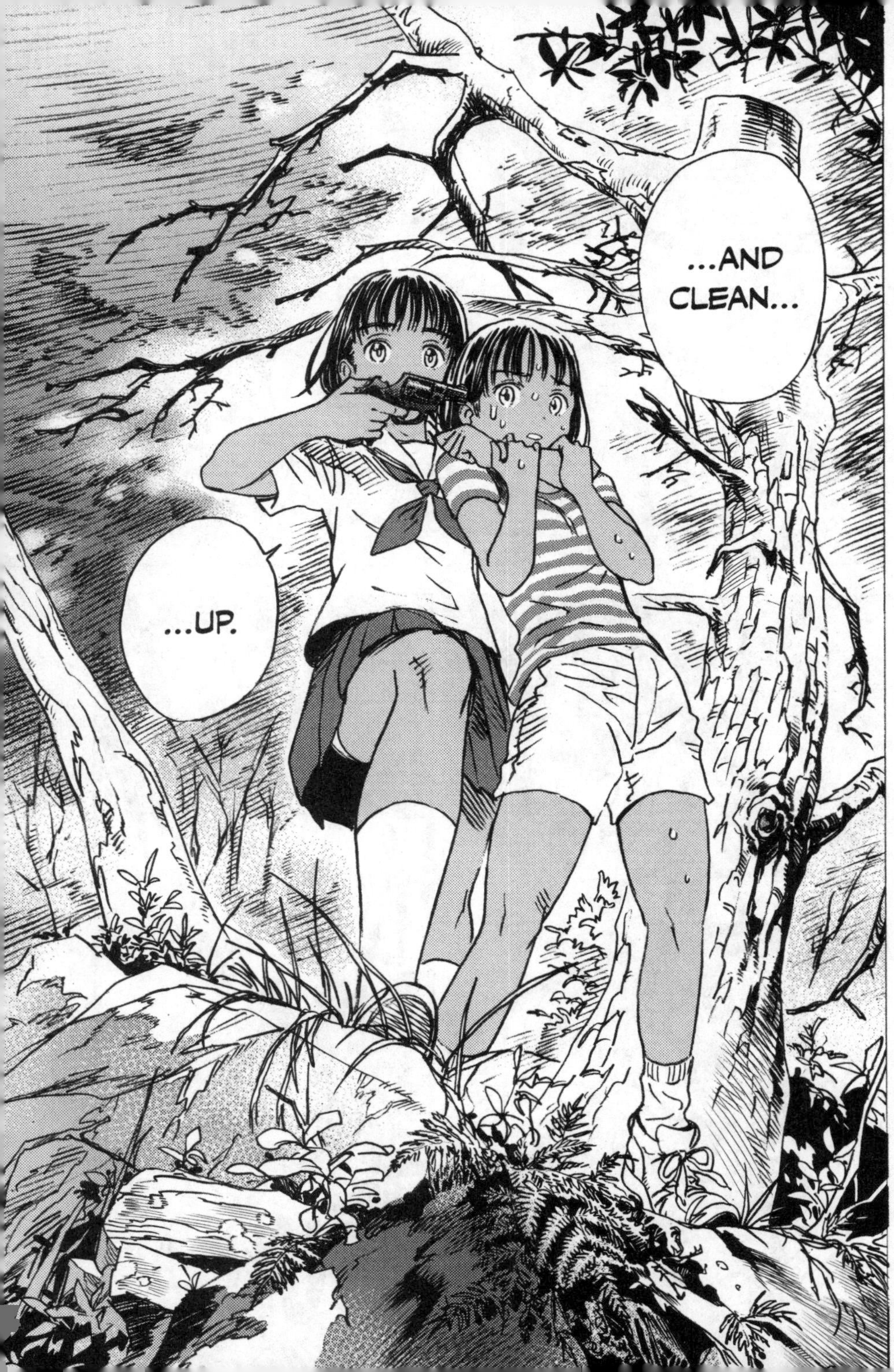
...AND CLEAN...
...UP.

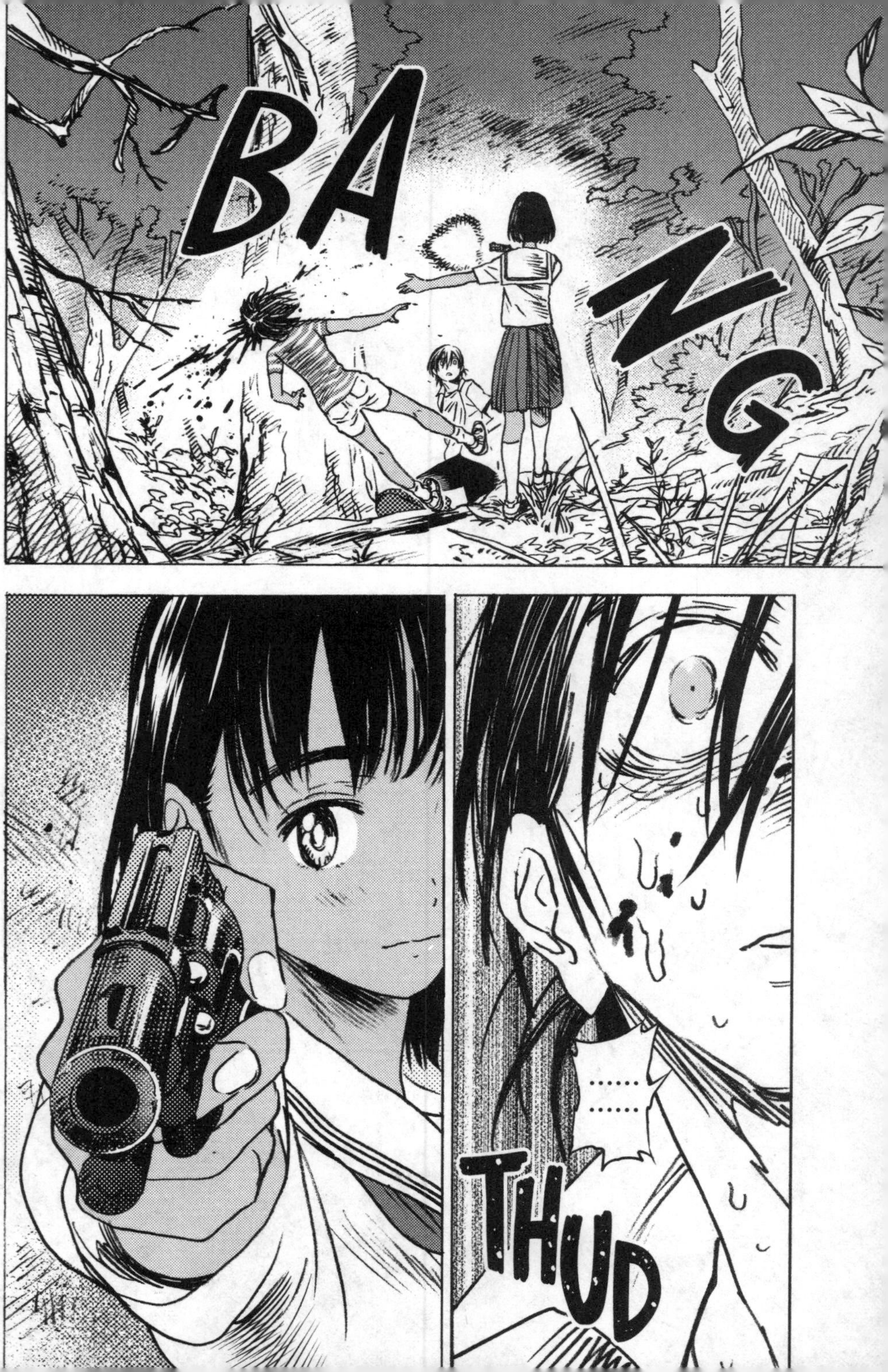
BANG
......
......
THUD

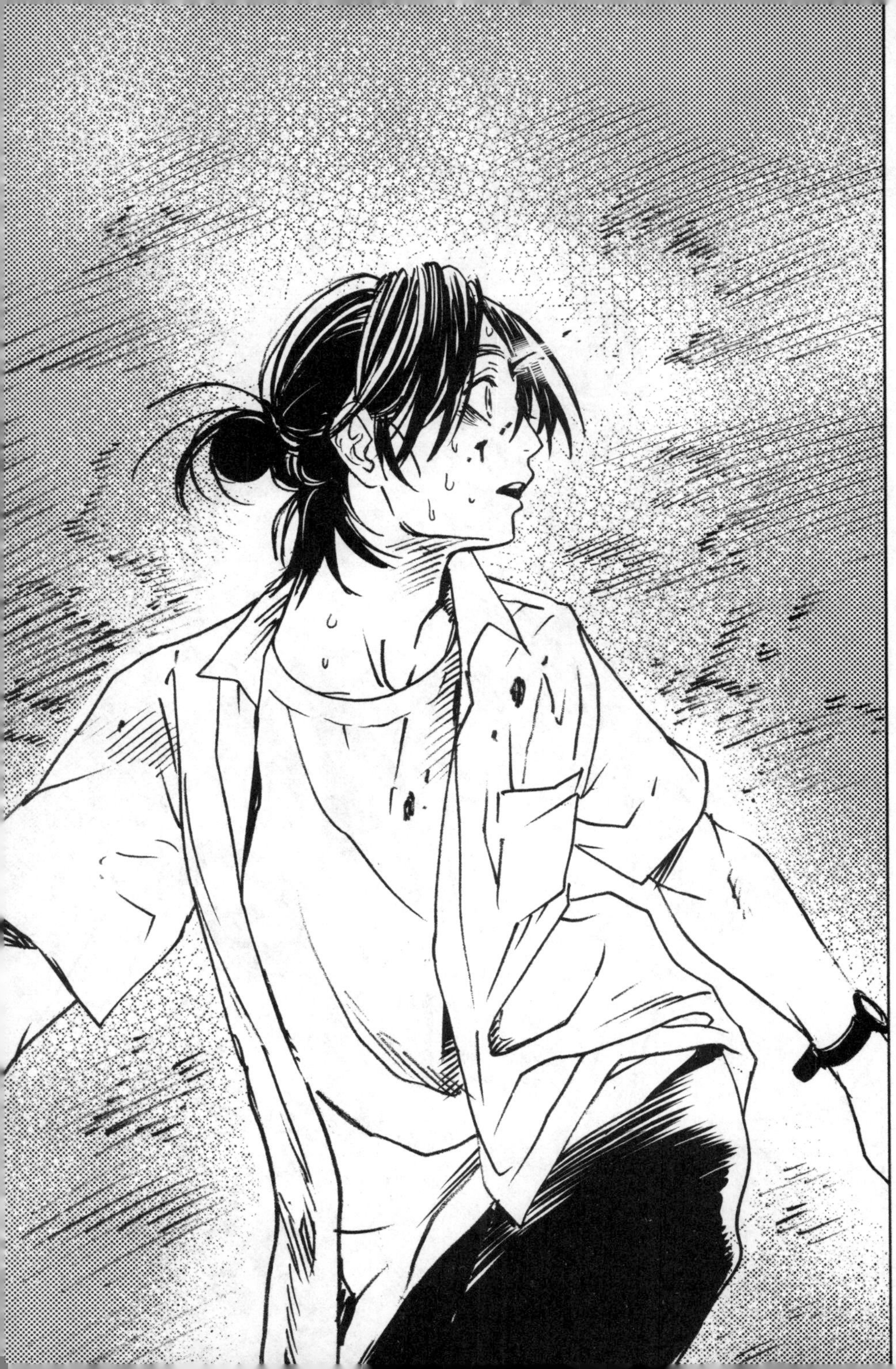

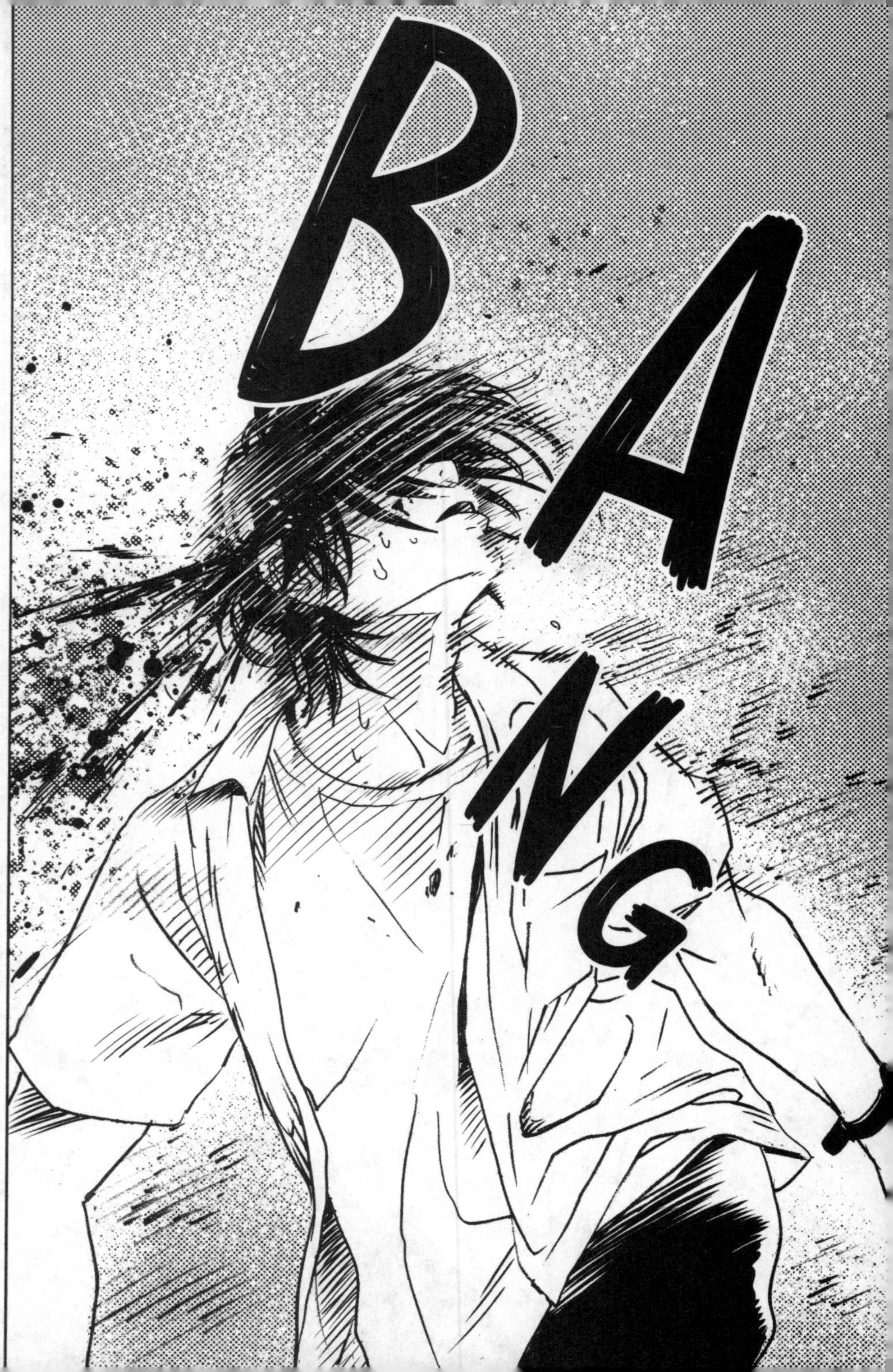
BANG

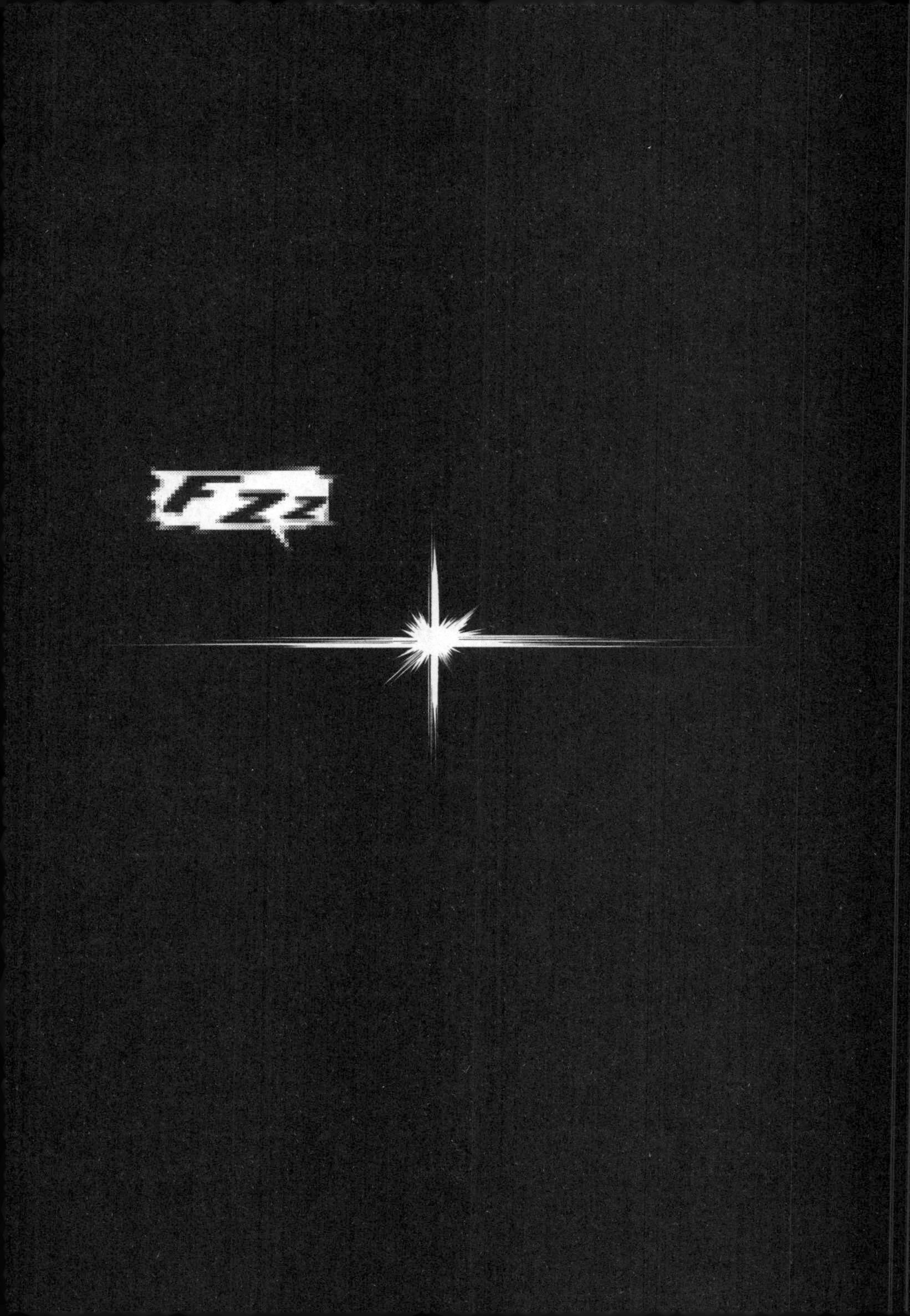
Fzz

サマータイムレンダ

Summer time rendering

[Drifting ashore]

田中 靖規
TANAKA YASUKI

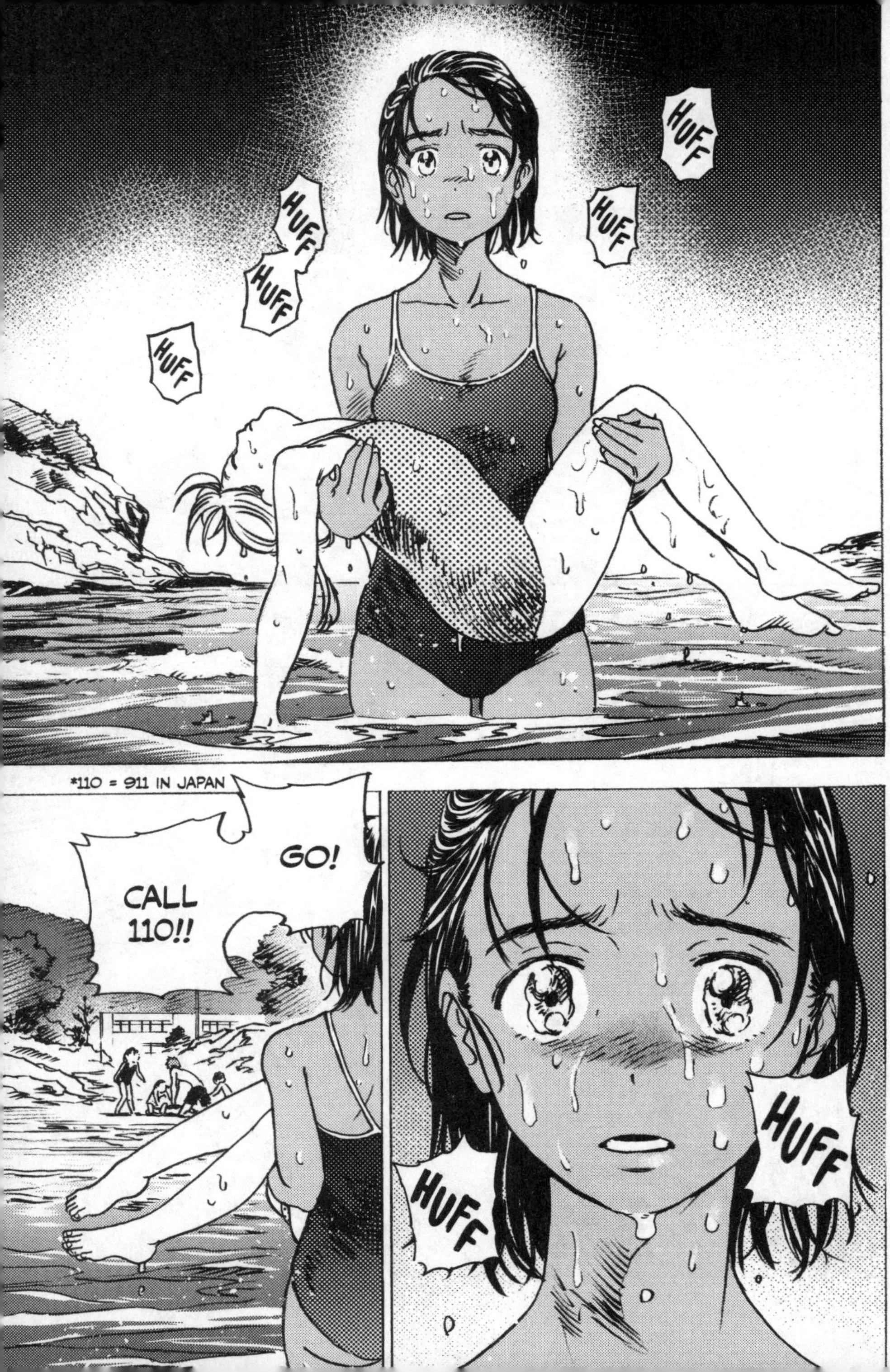
HUFF
HUFF
HUFF
HUFF
HUFF
HUFF
HUFF
GO!
CALL 110!!
*110 = 911 IN JAPAN

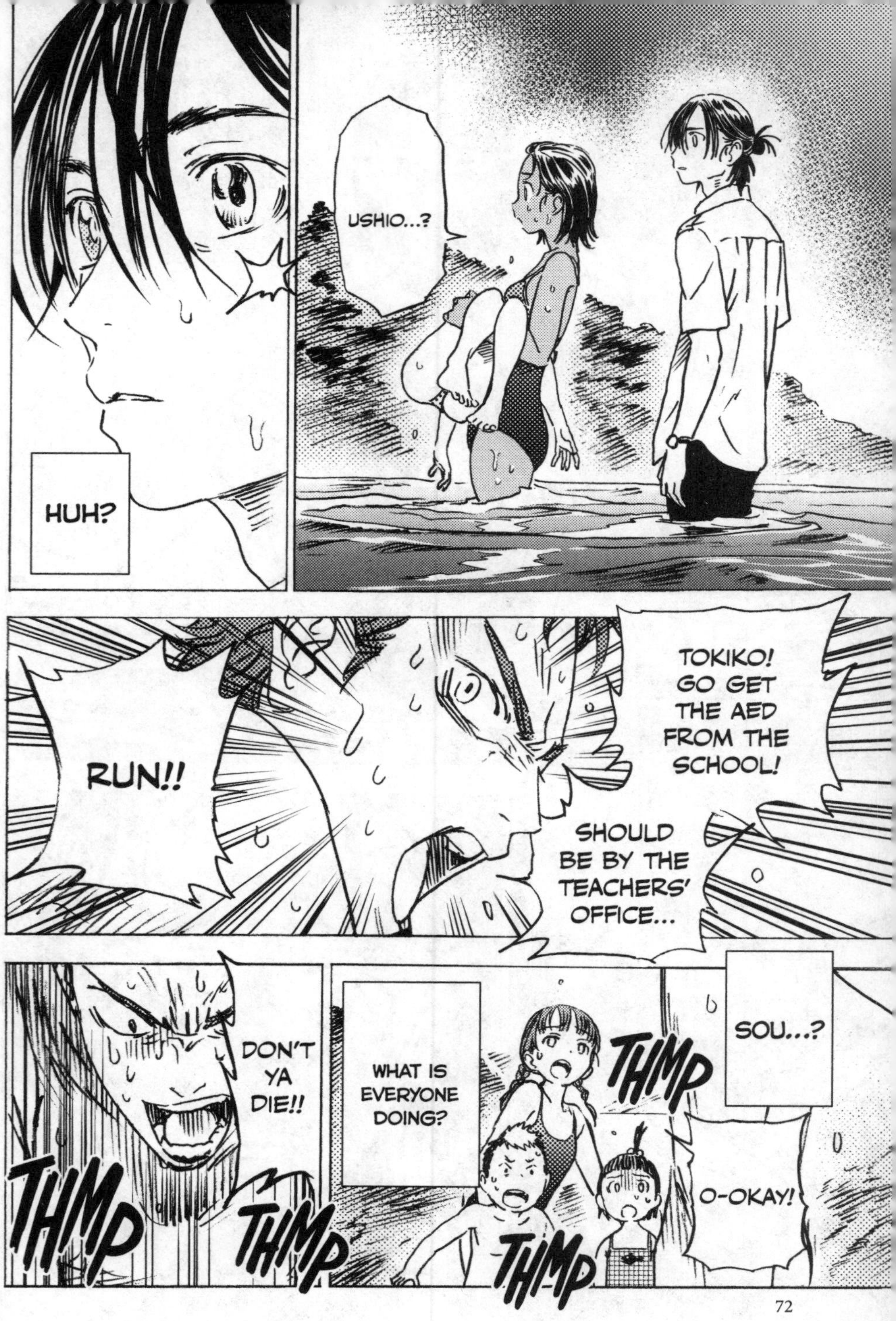
USHIO...?
HUH?
TOKIKO! GO GET THE AED FROM THE SCHOOL!
SHOULD BE BY THE TEACHERS' OFFICE...
RUN!!
SOU...?
O-OKAY!
THMP
WHAT IS EVERYONE DOING?
THMP
DON'T YA DIE!!
THMP
THMP

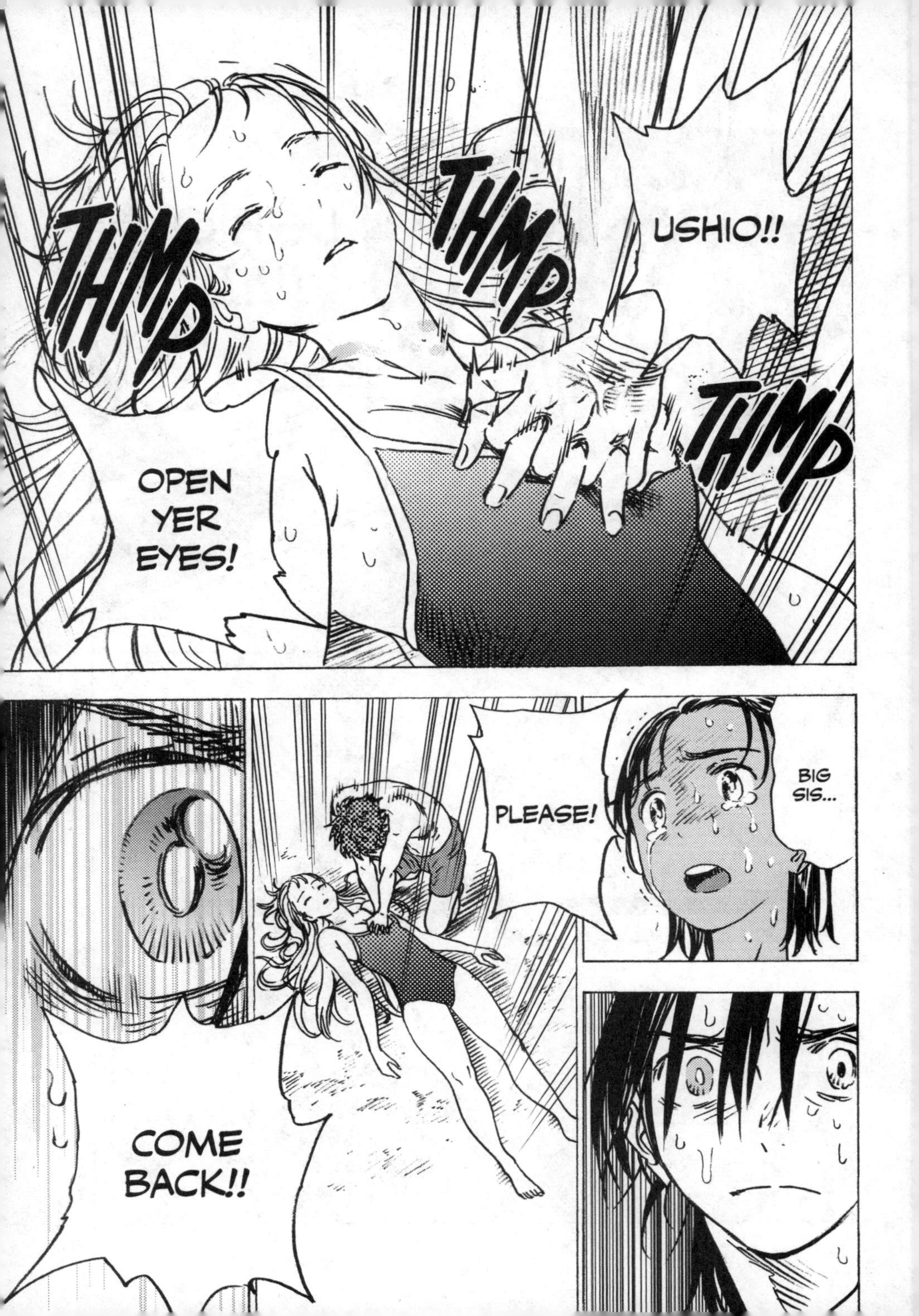

USHIO!!
THMP
THMP
THMP
OPEN YER EYES!
BIG SIS...
PLEASE!
COME BACK!!

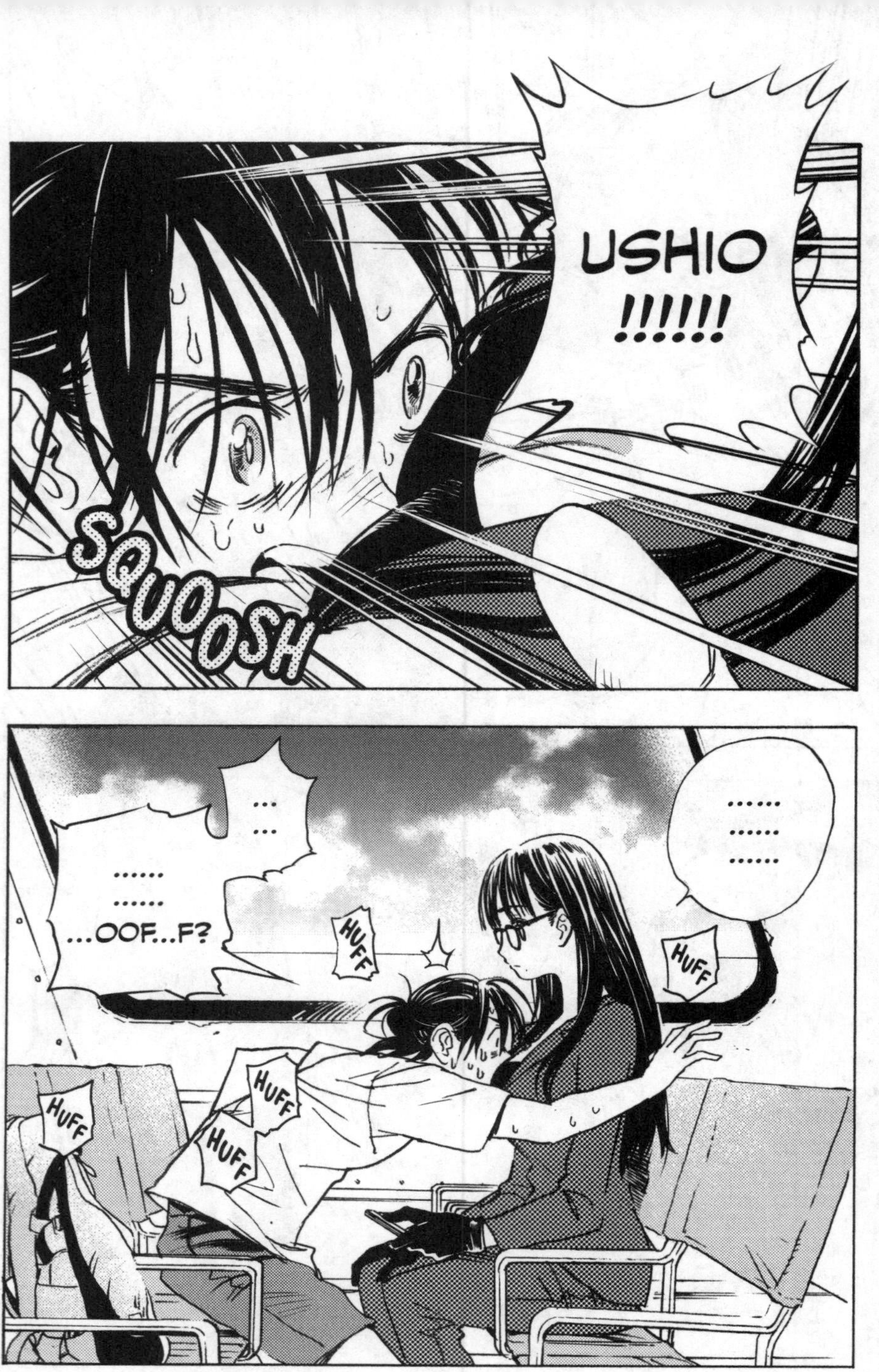
USHIO !!!!!!
SQUOOSH
......
......
......
HUFF
HUFF
...
...
......
......
...OOF...F?
HUFF
HUFF
HUFF
HUFF

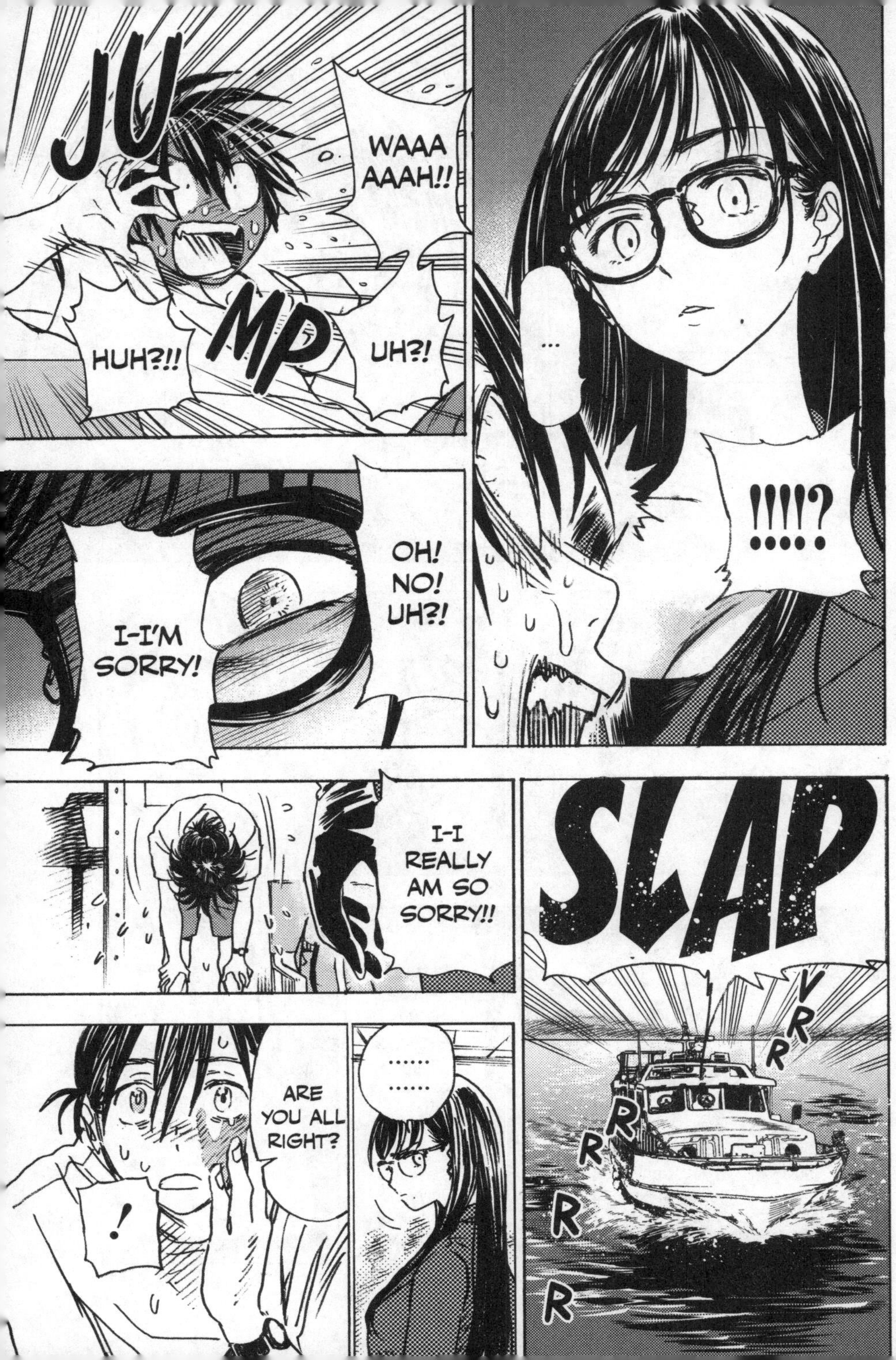
...
!!!!?
WAAA AAAH!!
JU
MP
UH?!
HUH?!!
OH! NO! UH?!
I-I'M SORRY!
SLAP
VRRRRRRRR
I-I REALLY AM SO SORRY!!
......
......
ARE YOU ALL RIGHT?
!

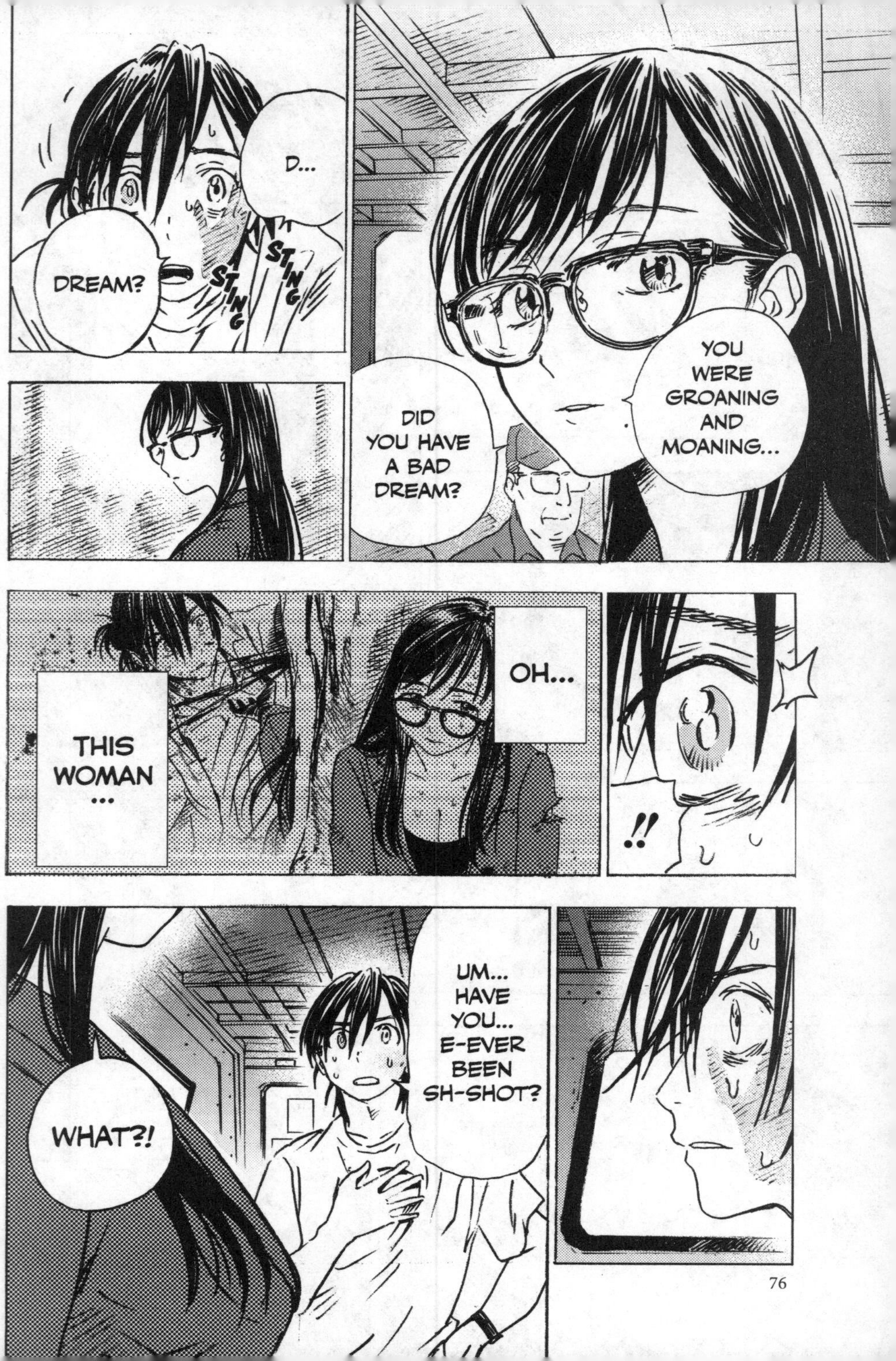
YOU WERE GROANING AND MOANING...
DID YOU HAVE A BAD DREAM?
D...
DREAM?
STING
STING
!!
OH...
THIS WOMAN ...
UM... HAVE YOU... E-EVER BEEN SH-SHOT?
WHAT?!

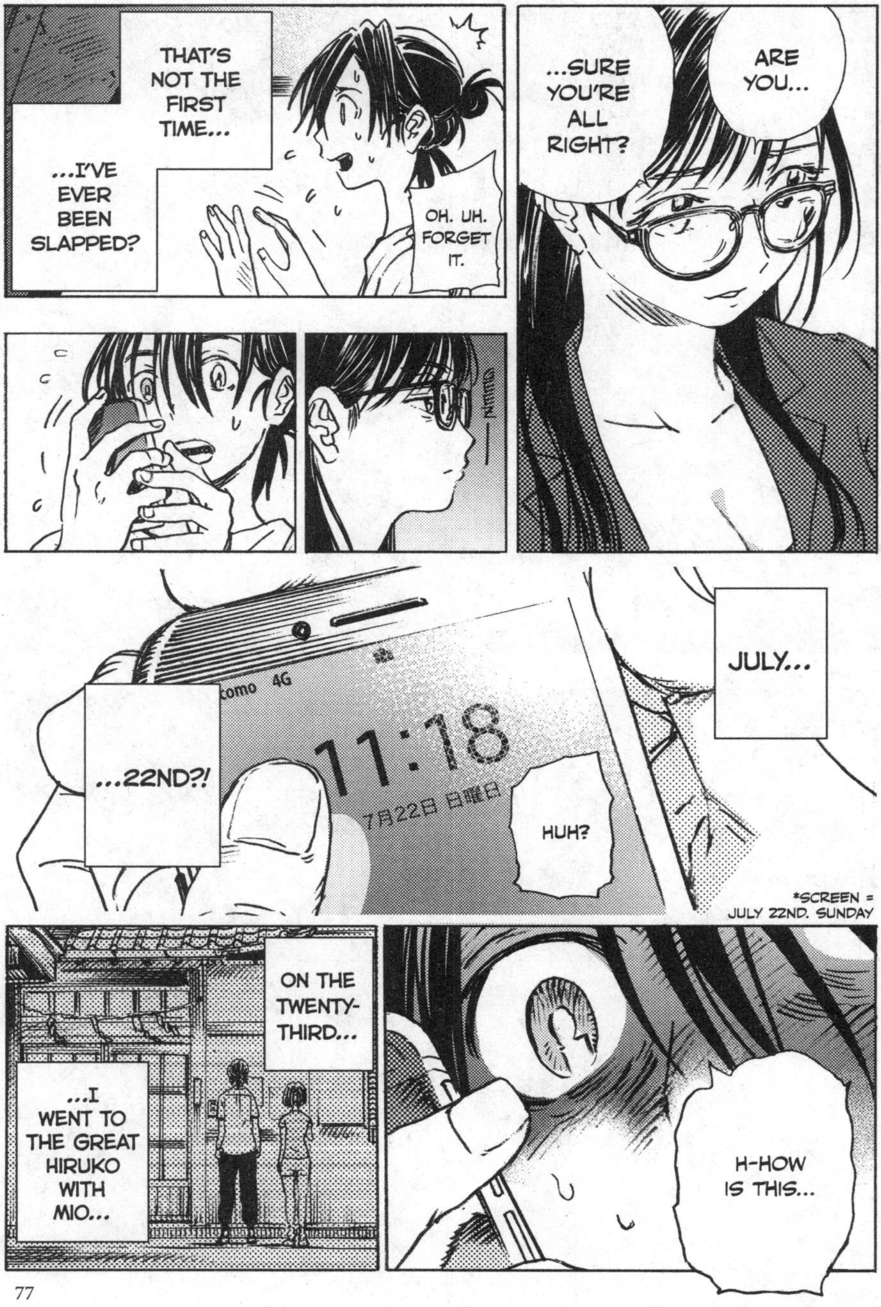
ARE YOU...
...SURE YOU'RE ALL RIGHT?
THAT'S NOT THE FIRST TIME...
...I'VE EVER BEEN SLAPPED?
OH. UH. FORGET IT.
JULY...
HUH?
...22ND?!
como 4G
11:18
7月22日 日曜日
*SCREEN = JULY 22ND. SUNDAY
H-HOW IS THIS...
ON THE TWENTY-THIRD...
...I WENT TO THE GREAT HIRUKO WITH MIO...

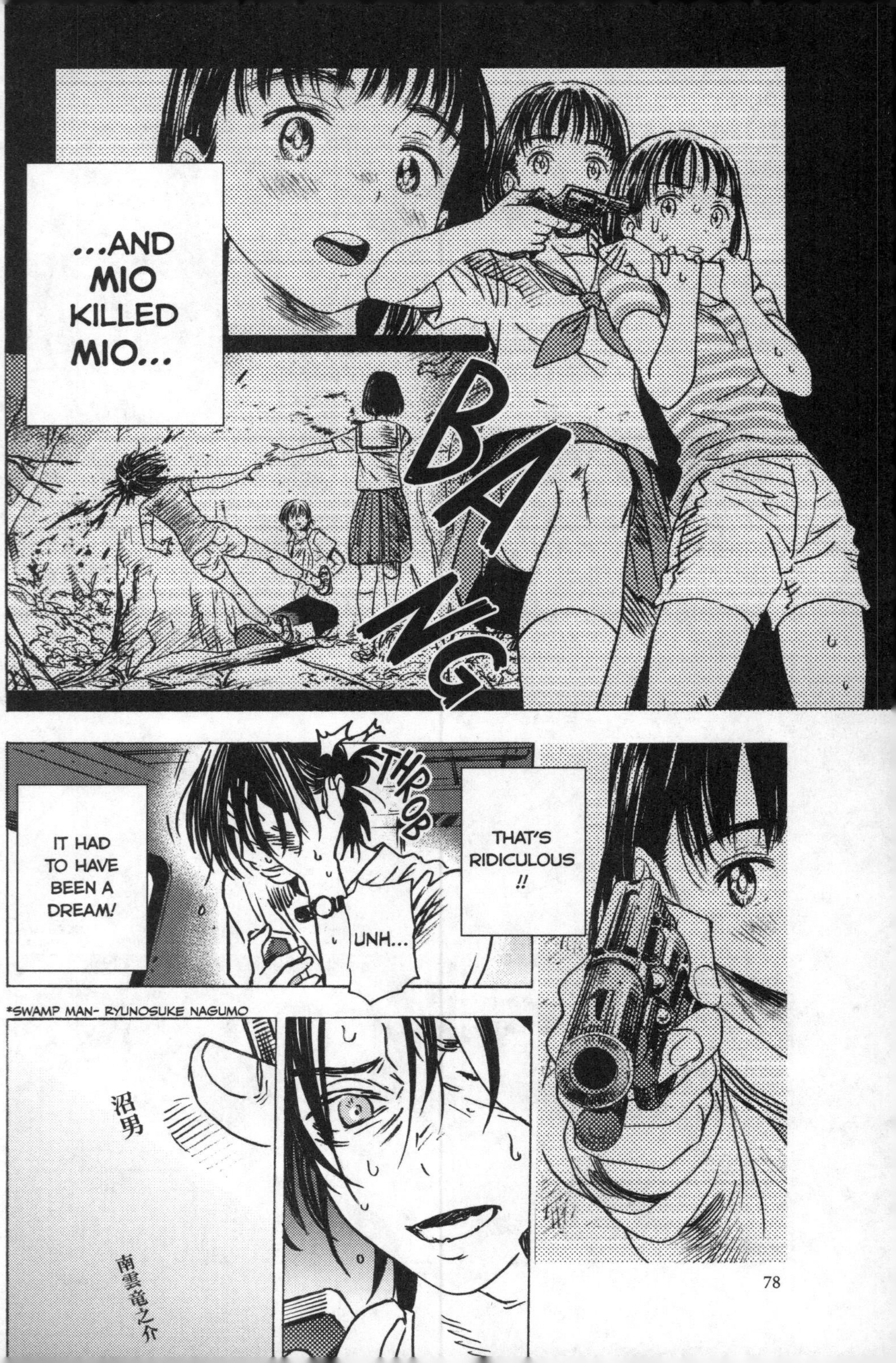
...AND MIO KILLED MIO...
BANG
THAT'S RIDICULOUS !!
THROB
IT HAD TO HAVE BEEN A DREAM!
UNH...
*SWAMP MAN- RYUNOSUKE NAGUMO
沼男
南雲竜之介

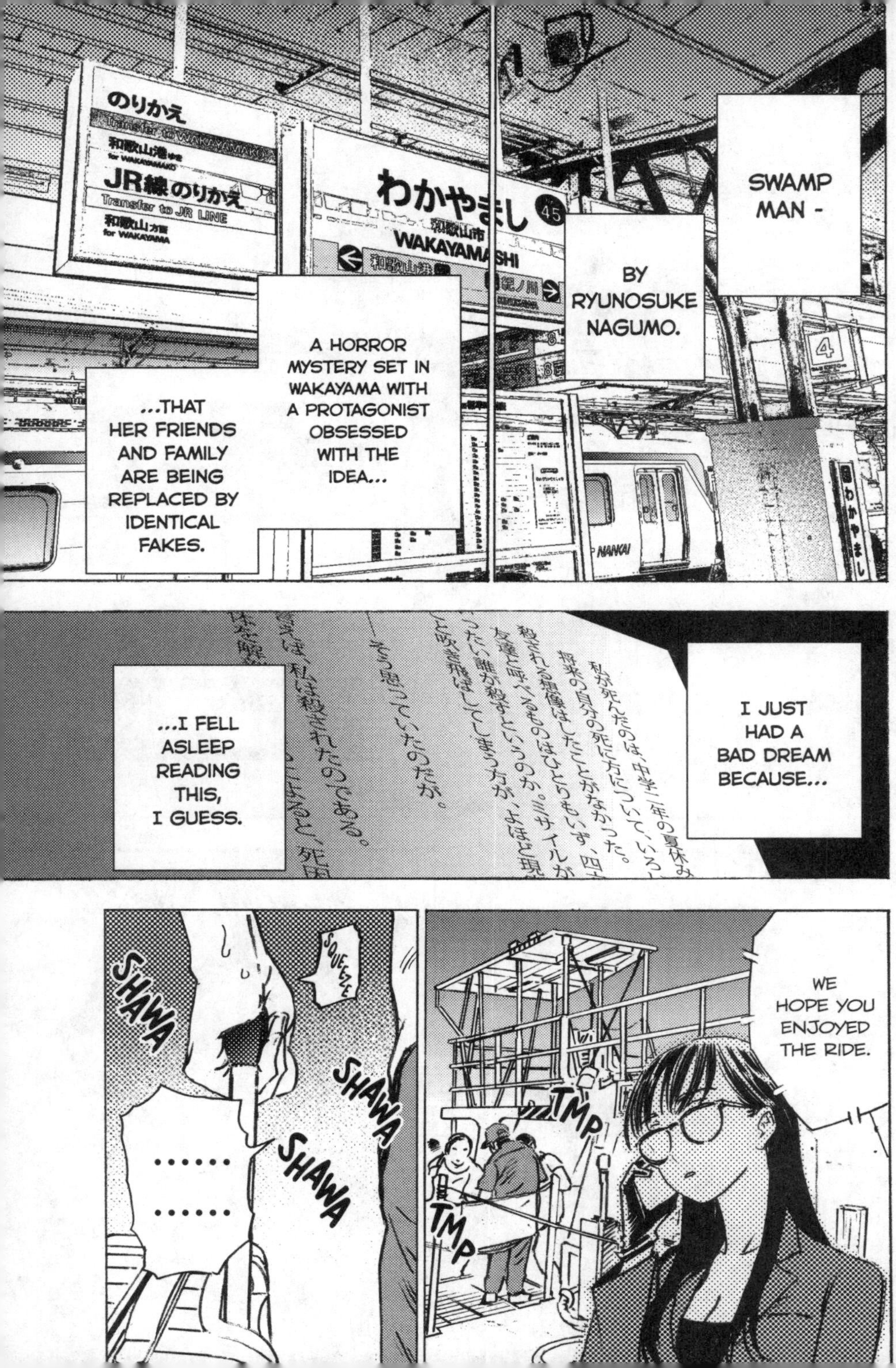

SWAMP MAN -
BY RYUNOSUKE NAGUMO.
A HORROR MYSTERY SET IN WAKAYAMA WITH A PROTAGONIST OBSESSED WITH THE IDEA...
...THAT HER FRIENDS AND FAMILY ARE BEING REPLACED BY IDENTICAL FAKES.
のりかえ
和歌山港
JR線のりかえ
Transfer to JR LINE
和歌山方面
for WAKAYAMA
わかやまし
和歌山市
WAKAYAMASHI
紀ノ川
NANKAI
I JUST HAD A BAD DREAM BECAUSE...
私が死んだのは、中学二年の夏休み
将来の自分の死に方について、いろ
殺される想像はしたことがなかった。
友達と呼べるものはひとりもいず、四
ったい誰が殺すというのか。ミサイルが
と吹き飛ばしてしまう方が、よほど現
——そう思っていたのだが。
実は、私は殺されたのである。
...I FELL ASLEEP READING THIS, I GUESS.
WE HOPE YOU ENJOYED THE RIDE.
TMP
TMP
SQUEEZE
SHAWA
SHAWA
SHAWA
SHAWA
......
......

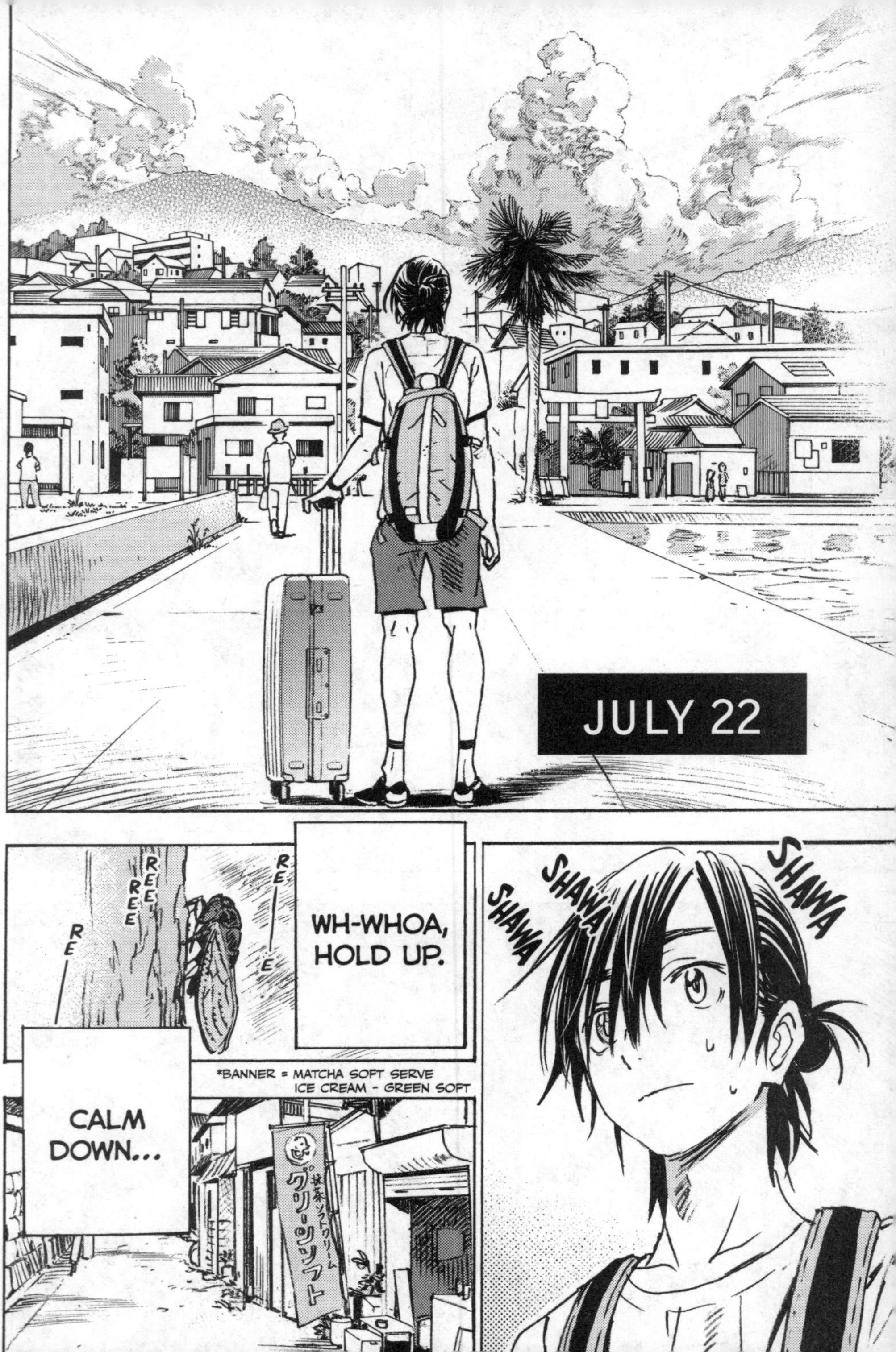
JULY 22
SHAWA
SHAWA
SHAWA
SHAWA
WH-WHOA, HOLD UP.
REE
REE
RE—E
RE—
CALM DOWN...
*BANNER = MATCHA SOFT SERVE ICE CREAM - GREEN SOFT
抹茶ソフトクリーム
グリーンソフト

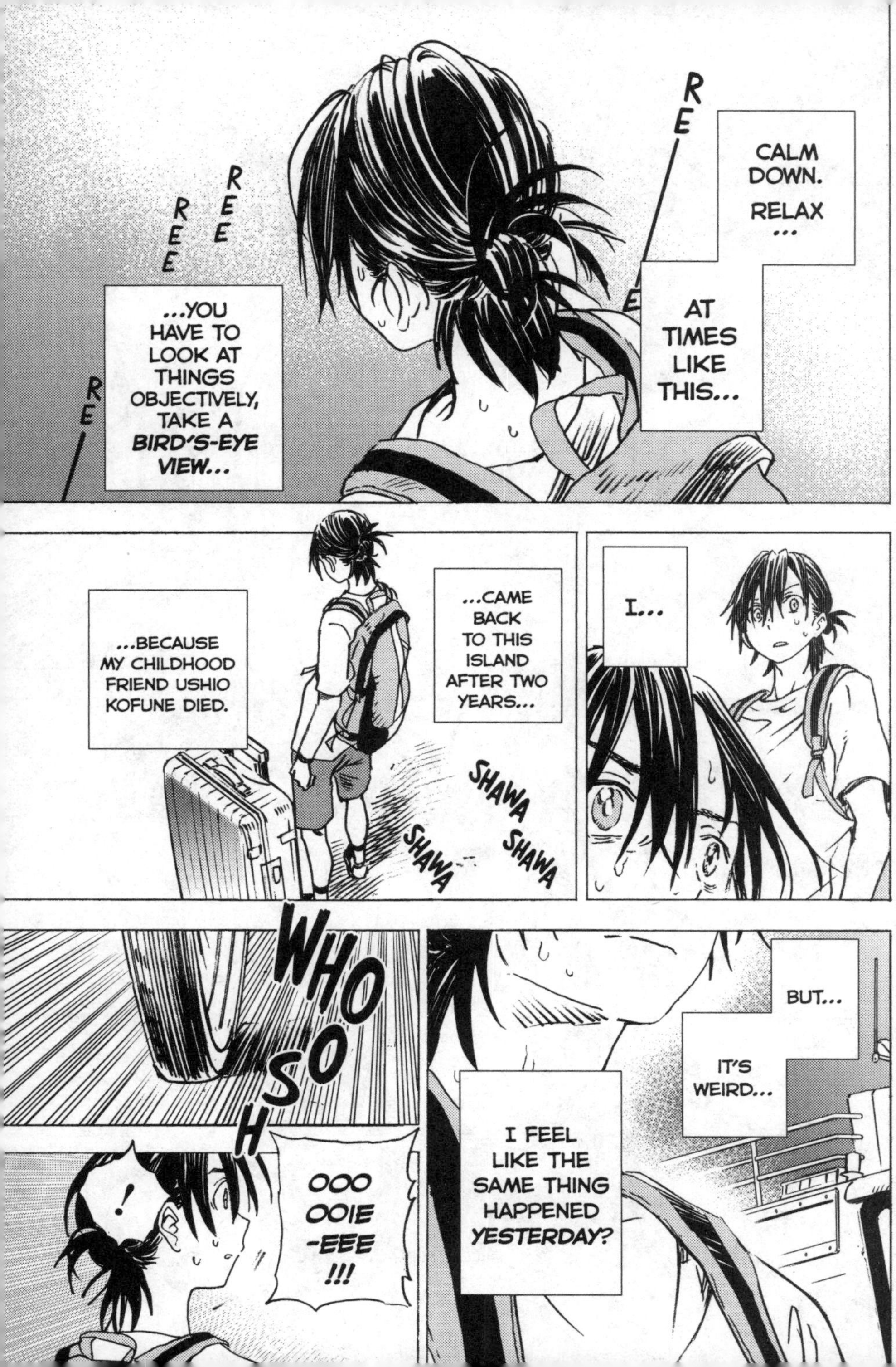
RE
E
CALM DOWN.
RELAX ...
AT TIMES LIKE THIS...
REE
REE
...YOU HAVE TO LOOK AT THINGS OBJECTIVELY, TAKE A BIRD'S-EYE VIEW...
RE
I...
...CAME BACK TO THIS ISLAND AFTER TWO YEARS...
...BECAUSE MY CHILDHOOD FRIEND USHIO KOFUNE DIED.
SHAWA
SHAWA
SHAWA
SHAWA
BUT...
IT'S WEIRD...
I FEEL LIKE THE SAME THING HAPPENED YESTERDAY?
WHOOSH
!
OOOOOIE-EEE!!!

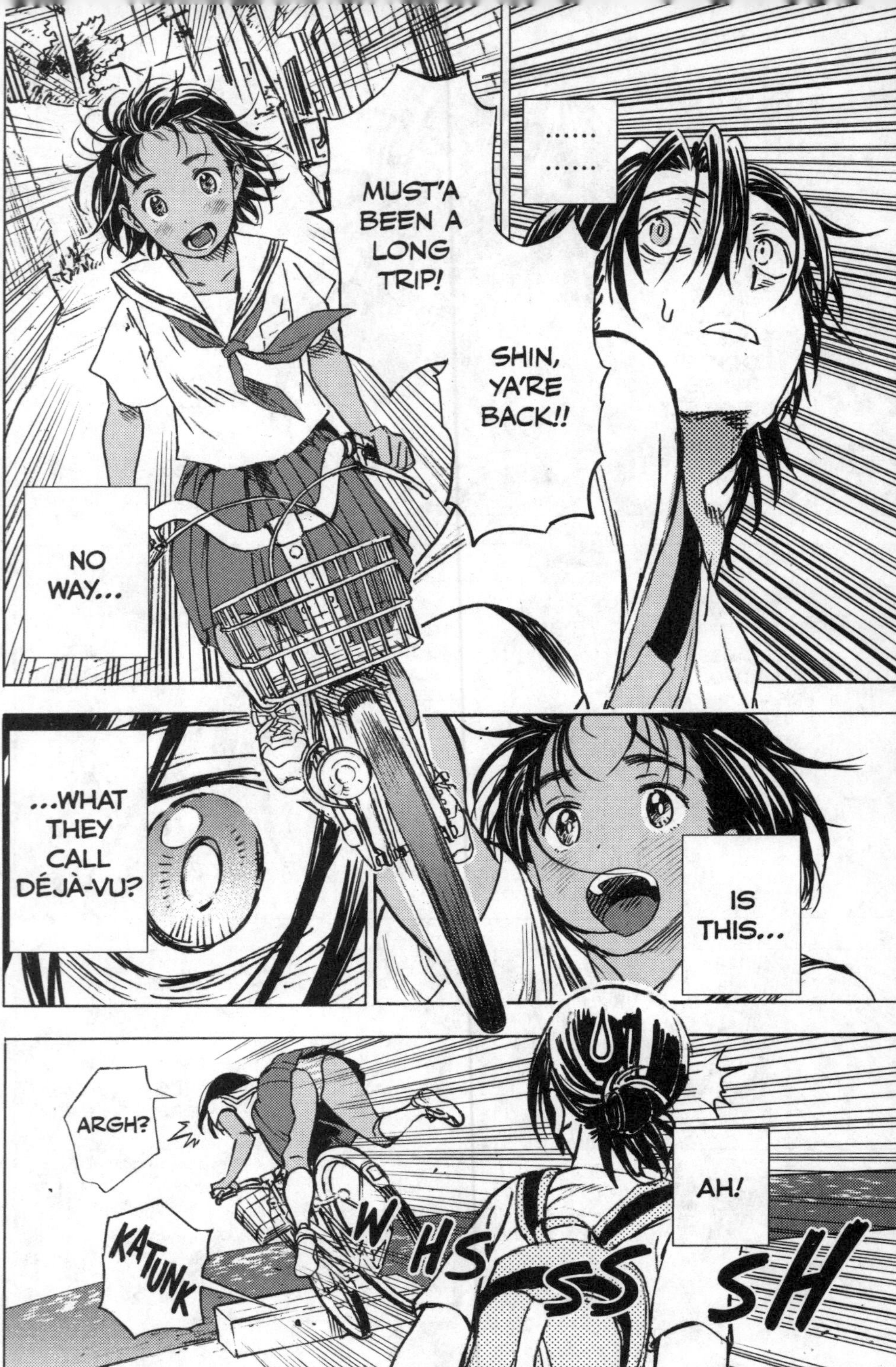
......
......
SHIN, YA'RE BACK!!
MUST'A BEEN A LONG TRIP!
NO WAY...
IS THIS...
...WHAT THEY CALL DÉJÀ-VU?
AH!
WHSSSSH
ARGH?
KATUNK

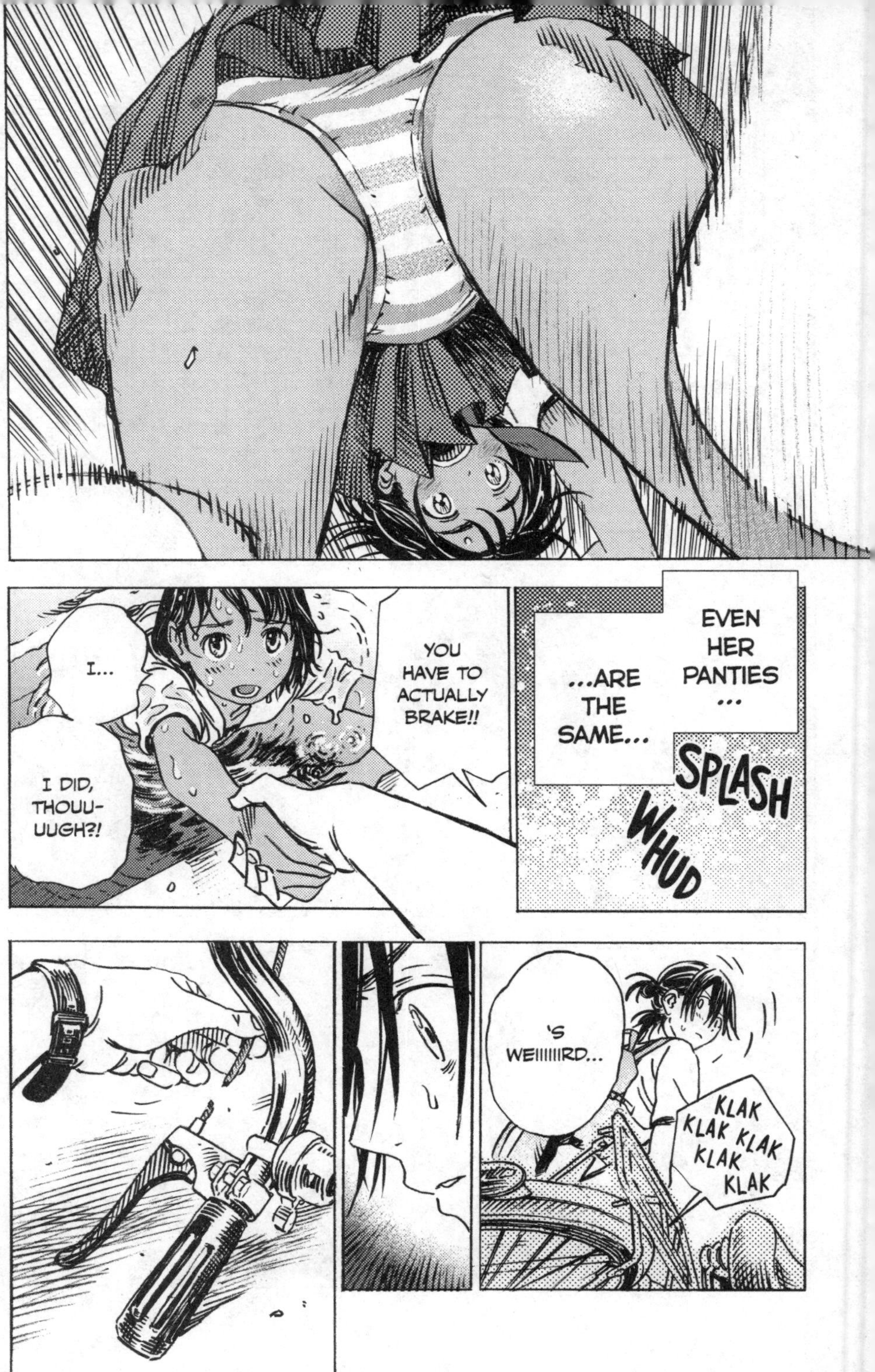
EVEN HER PANTIES...
...ARE THE SAME...
SPLASH
WHUD
YOU HAVE TO ACTUALLY BRAKE!!
I...
I DID, THOUUU-UUGH?!
'S WEIIIIIIRD...
KLAK KLAK KLAK KLAK KLAK

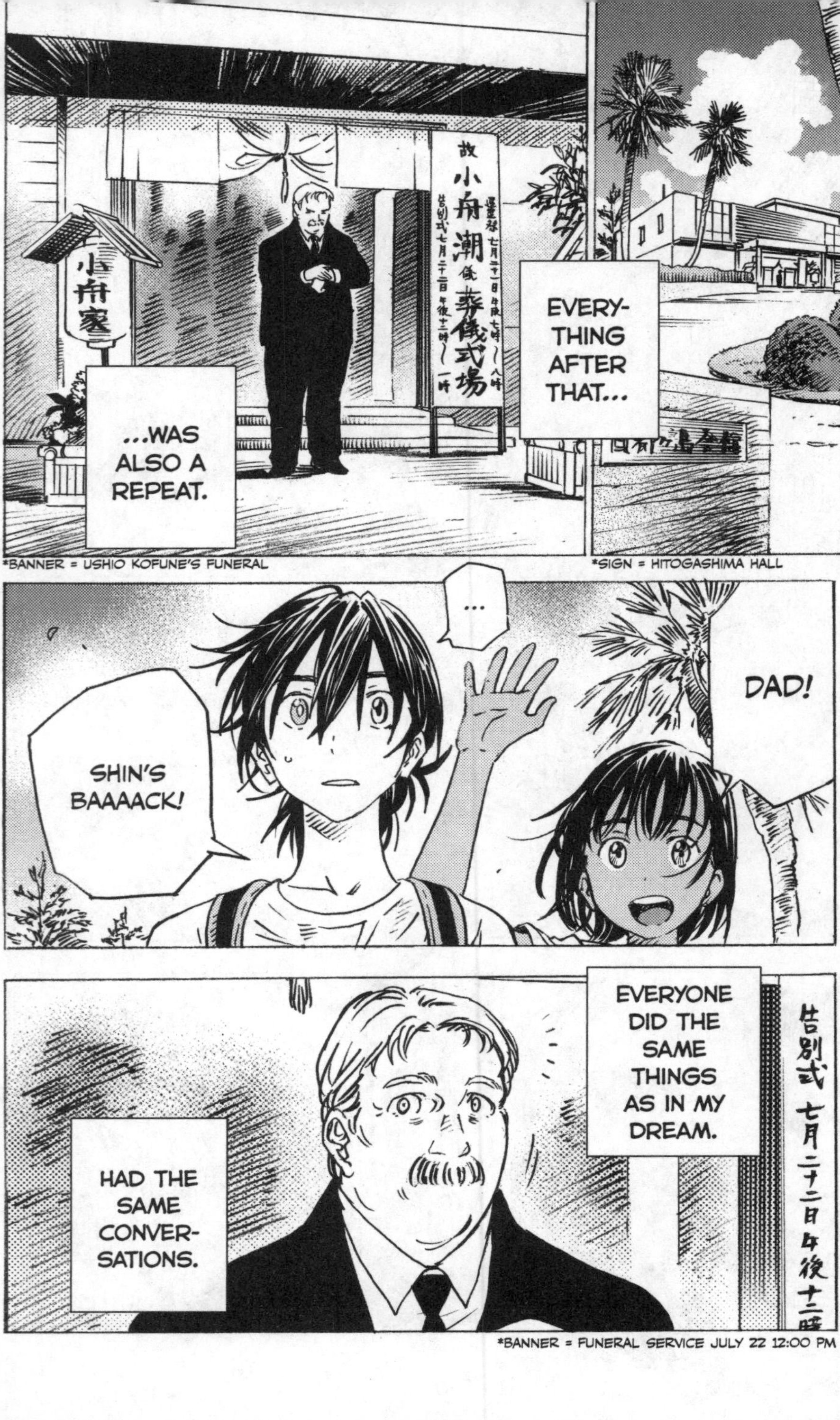
EVERY-THING AFTER THAT...
*SIGN = HITOGASHIMA HALL
...WAS ALSO A REPEAT.
*BANNER = USHIO KOFUNE'S FUNERAL
DAD!
...
SHIN'S BAAAACK!
EVERYONE DID THE SAME THINGS AS IN MY DREAM.
HAD THE SAME CONVER-SATIONS.
*BANNER = FUNERAL SERVICE JULY 22 12:00 PM

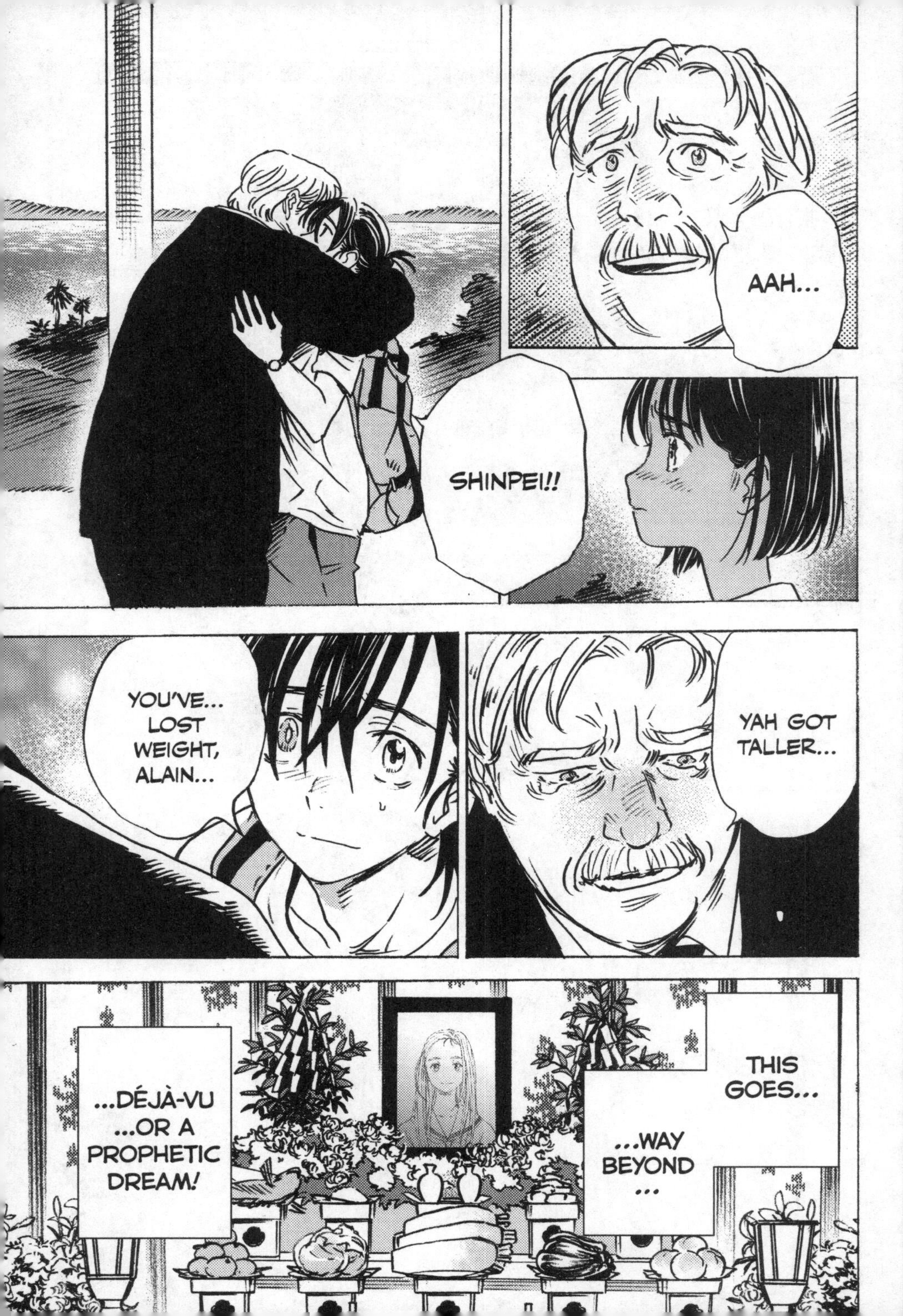
AAH...
SHINPEI!!
YAH GOT TALLER...
YOU'VE... LOST WEIGHT, ALAIN...
THIS GOES...
...WAY BEYOND ...
...DÉJÀ-VU ...OR A PROPHETIC DREAM!

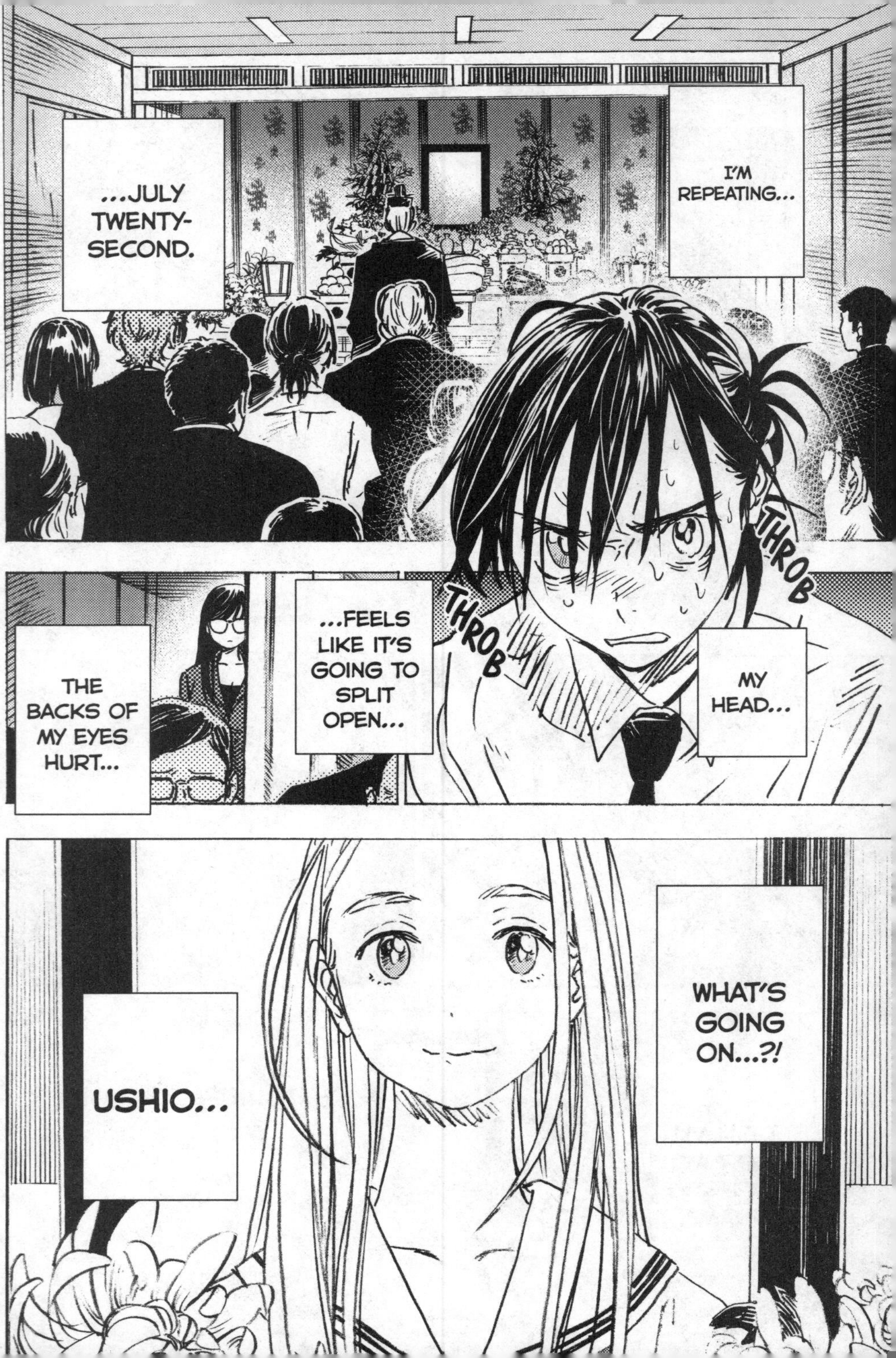
I'M REPEATING...
...JULY TWENTY-SECOND.
THROB
THROB
MY HEAD...
...FEELS LIKE IT'S GOING TO SPLIT OPEN...
THE BACKS OF MY EYES HURT...
WHAT'S GOING ON...?!
USHIO...

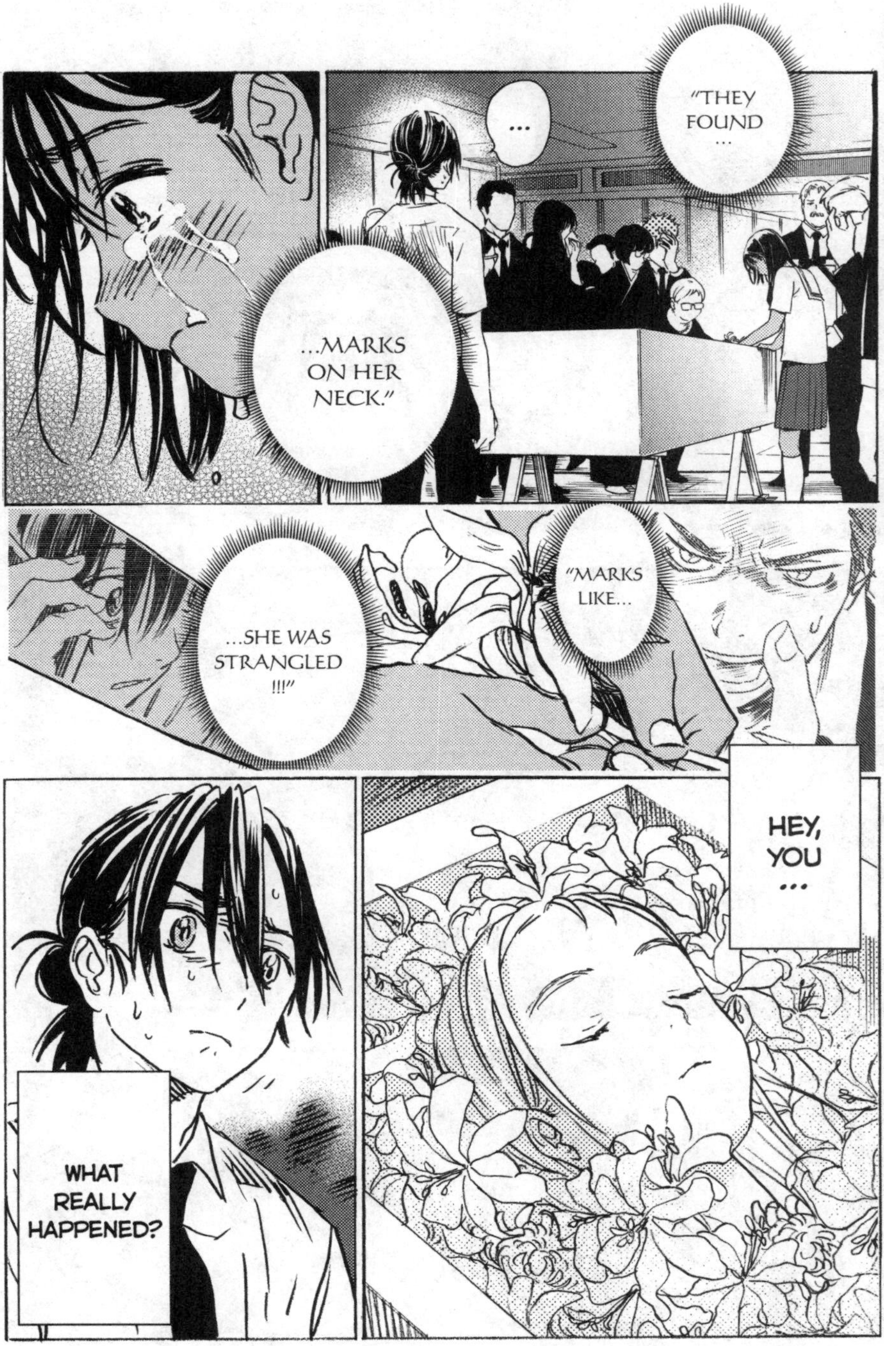
"THEY FOUND ...
...
...MARKS ON HER NECK."
"MARKS LIKE...
...SHE WAS STRANGLED !!!"
HEY, YOU ...
WHAT REALLY HAPPENED?

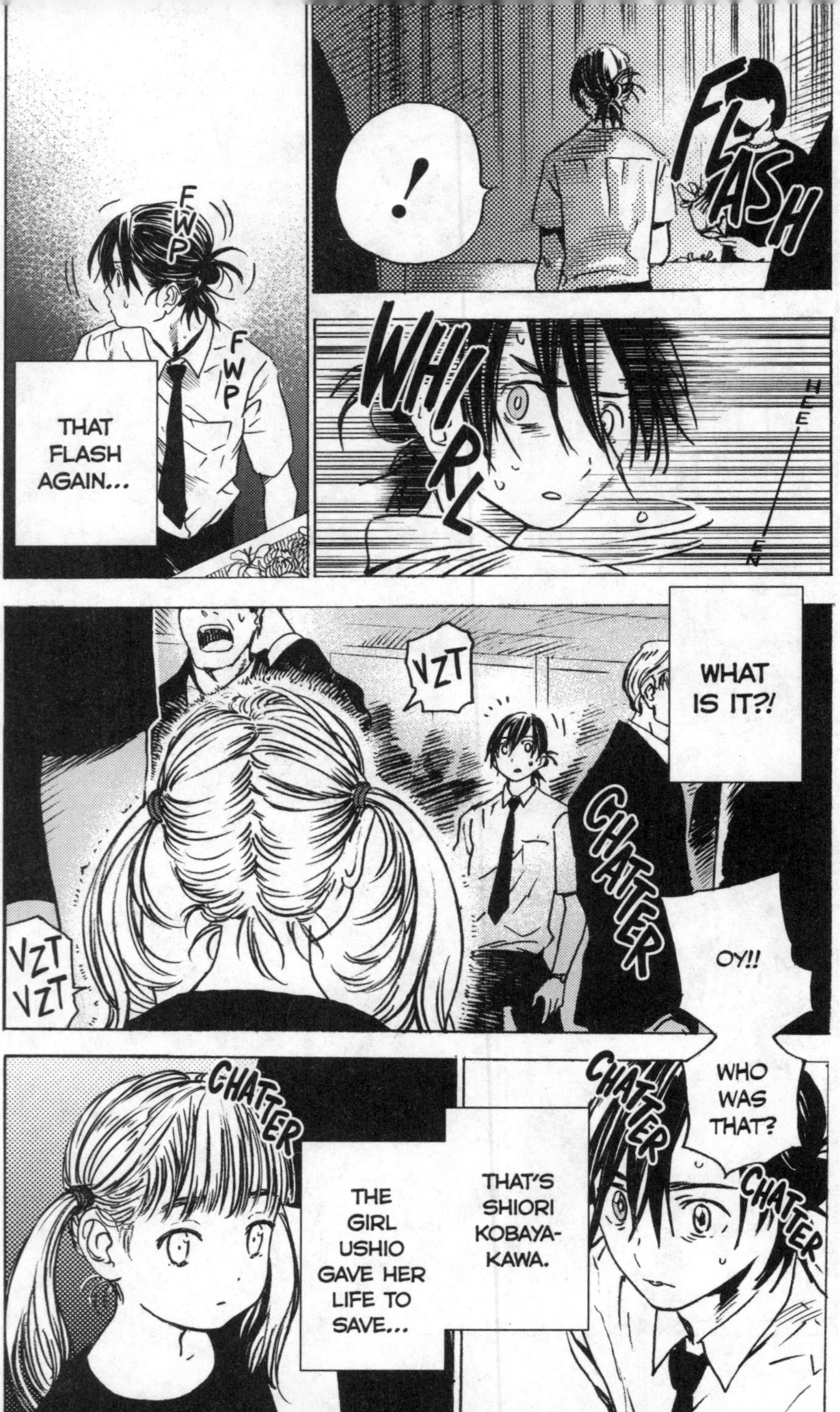

FLASH
!
WHIRL
HEEEN
FWP
FWP
THAT FLASH AGAIN...
WHAT IS IT?!
VZT
CHATTER
OY!!
VZT VZT
WHO WAS THAT?
CHATTER
CHATTER
CHATTER
THAT'S SHIORI KOBAYAKAWA.
THE GIRL USHIO GAVE HER LIFE TO SAVE...
CHATTER

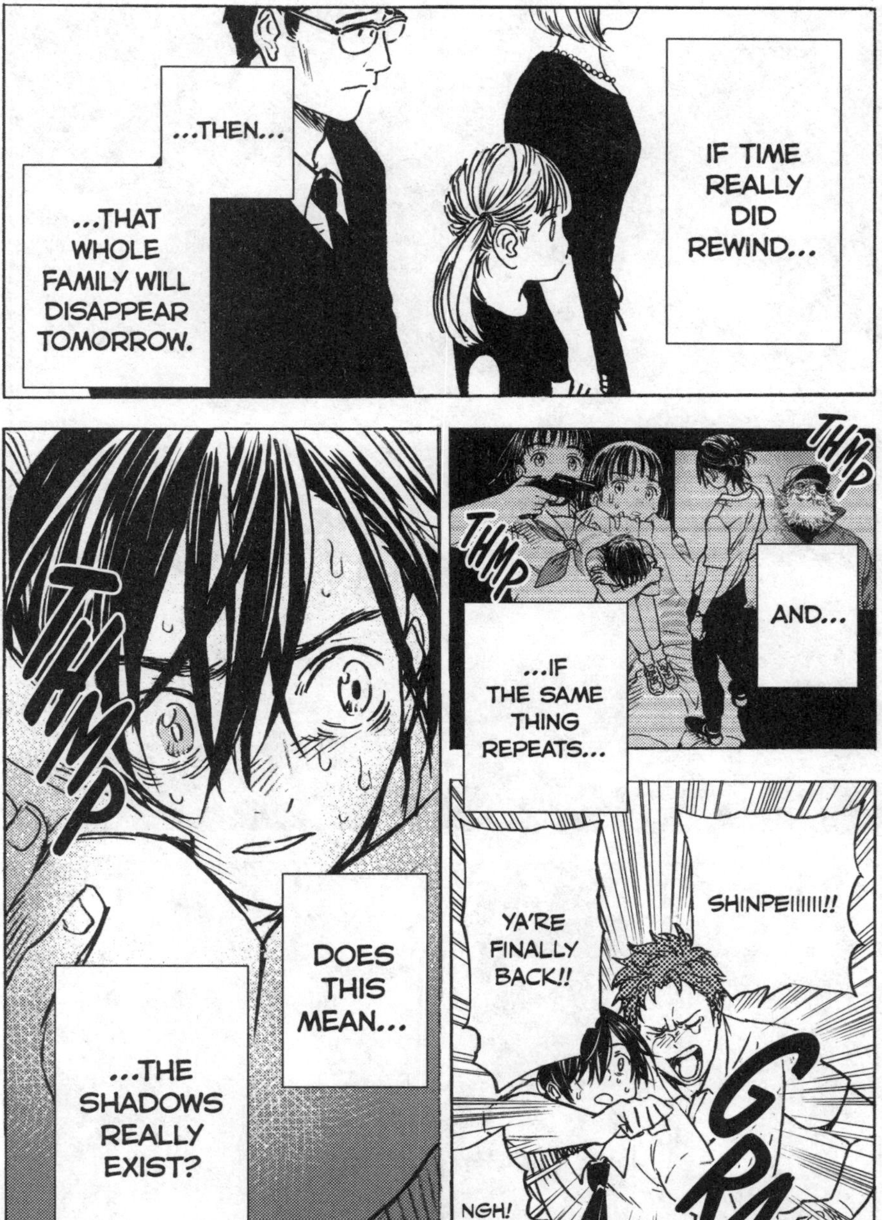
IF TIME REALLY DID REWIND...
...THEN...
...THAT WHOLE FAMILY WILL DISAPPEAR TOMORROW.
THMP
THMP
AND...
...IF THE SAME THING REPEATS...
SHINPEI!!!!!!!
YA'RE FINALLY BACK!!
GRAB
NGH!
THMP
DOES THIS MEAN...
...THE SHADOWS REALLY EXIST?

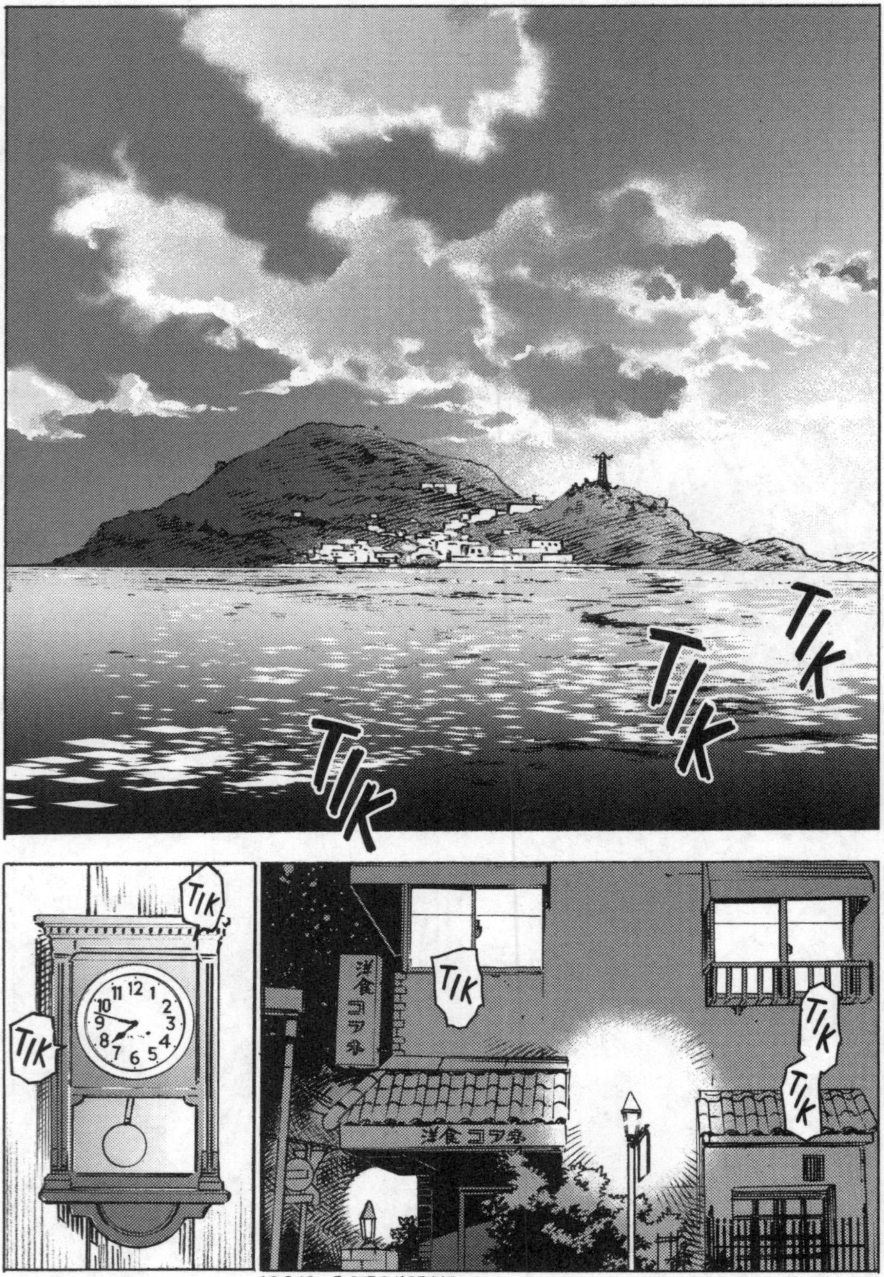
TIK
TIK
TIK
TIK
TIK
TIK
TIK
TIK

*SIGNS = BISTRO KOFUNE

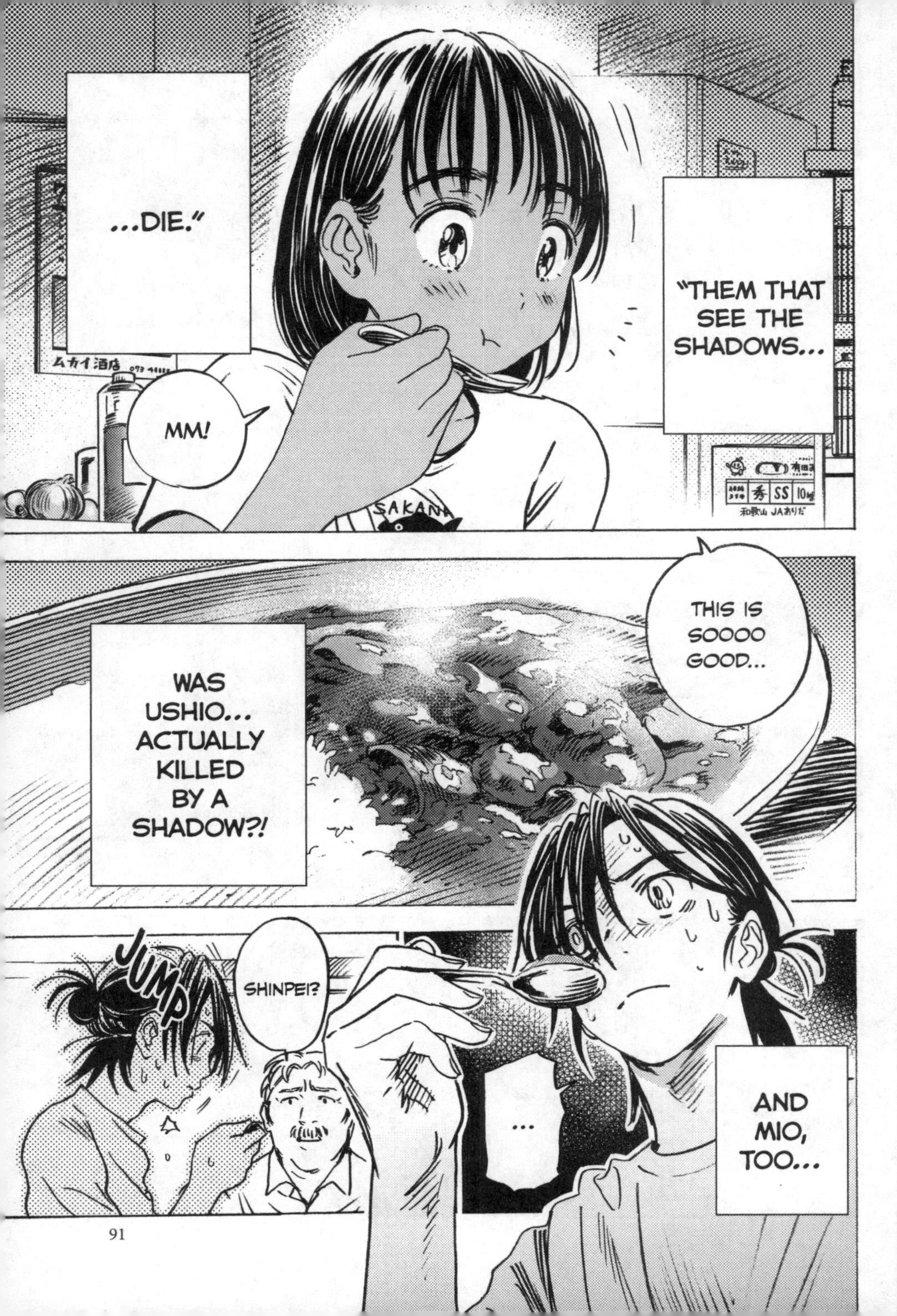
"THEM THAT SEE THE SHADOWS...
...DIE."
MM!
ムカイ酒店
和歌山 JAありだ
THIS IS SOOOO GOOD...
WAS USHIO... ACTUALLY KILLED BY A SHADOW?!
AND MIO, TOO...
...
SHINPEI?
JUMP

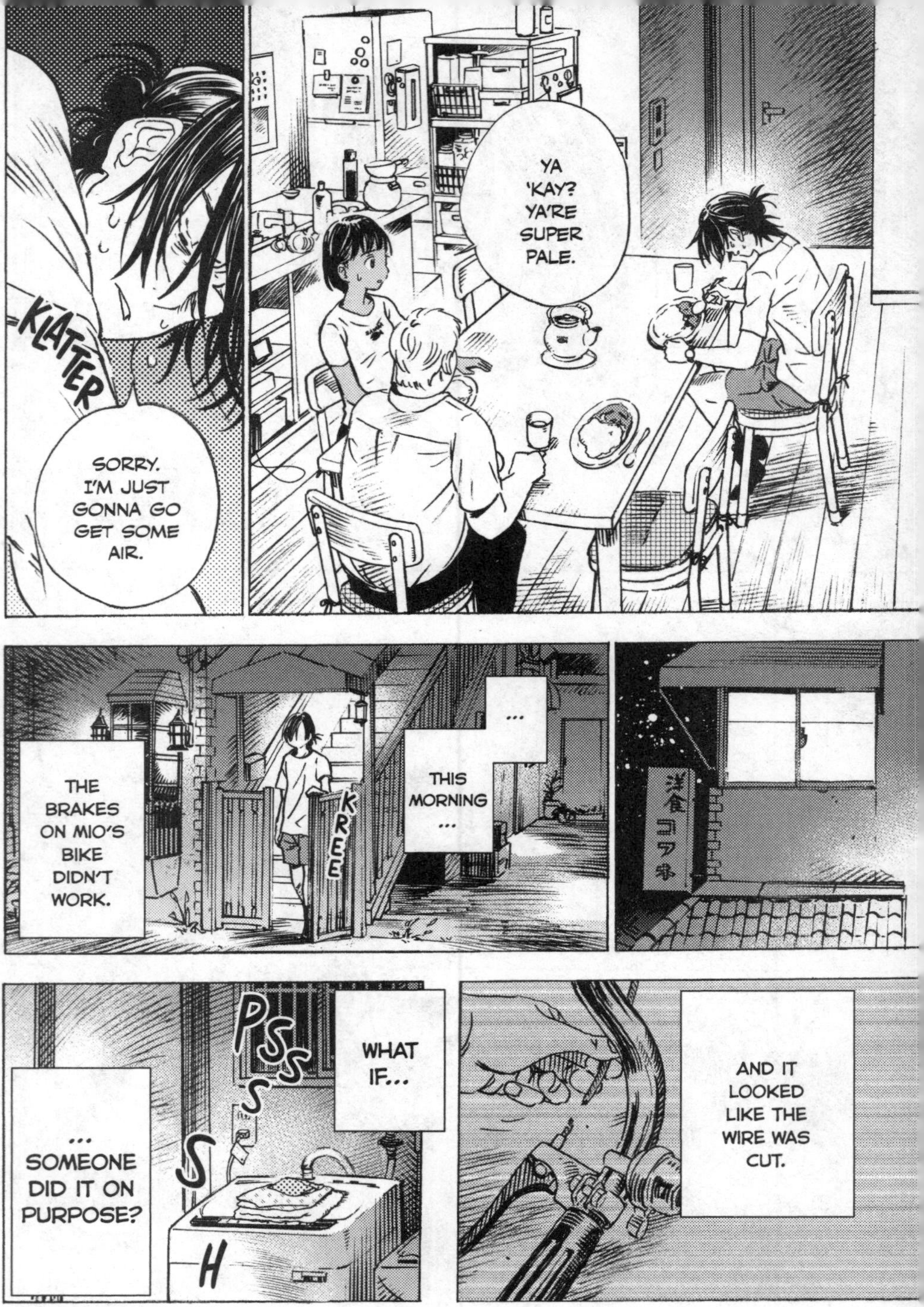
YA 'KAY? YA'RE SUPER PALE.
KLATTER
SORRY. I'M JUST GONNA GO GET SOME AIR.
...
THIS MORNING ...
KREE
THE BRAKES ON MIO'S BIKE DIDN'T WORK.
AND IT LOOKED LIKE THE WIRE WAS CUT.
WHAT IF...
PSSSSH
... SOMEONE DID IT ON PURPOSE?

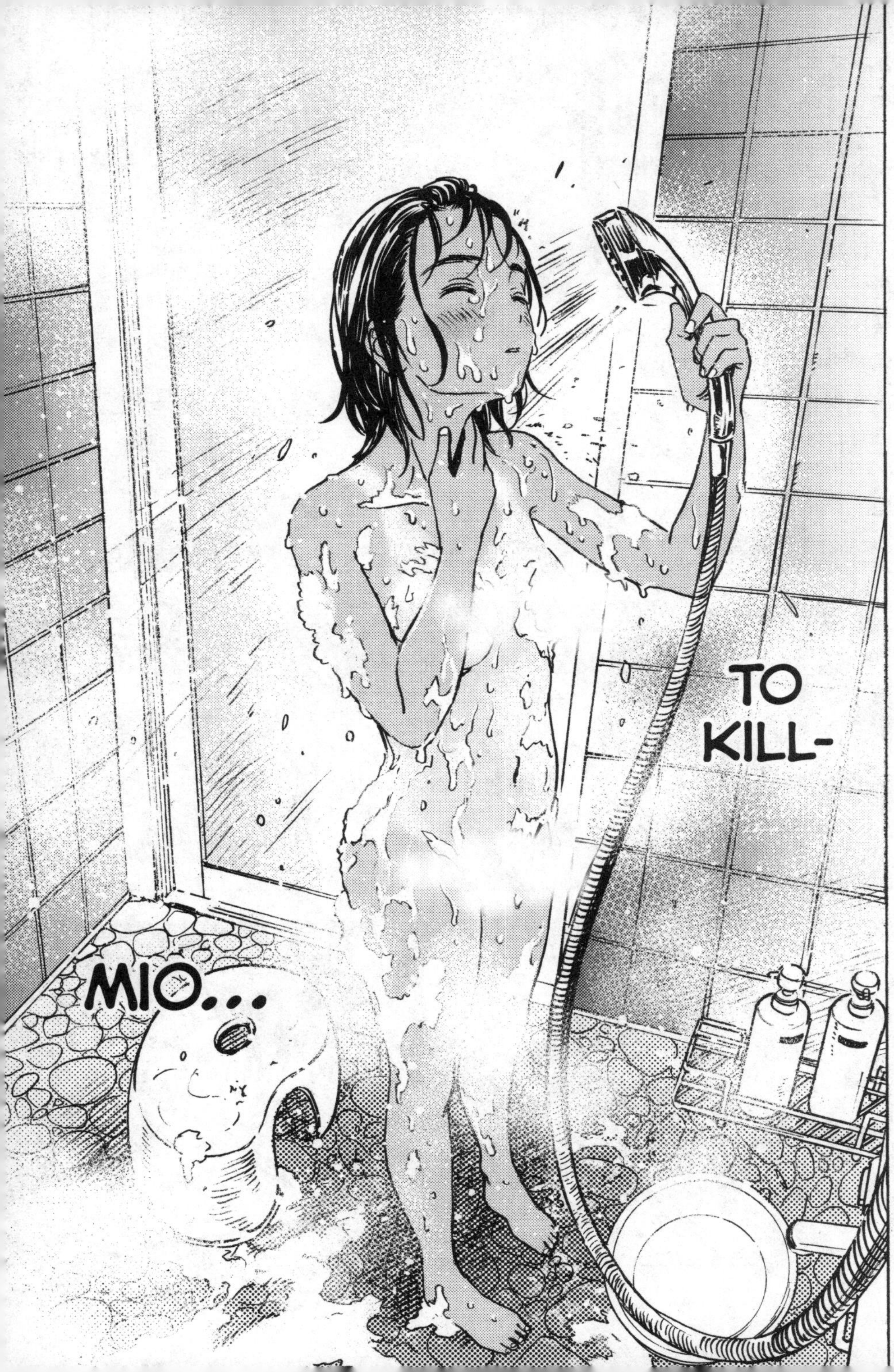
TO KILL-
MIO...

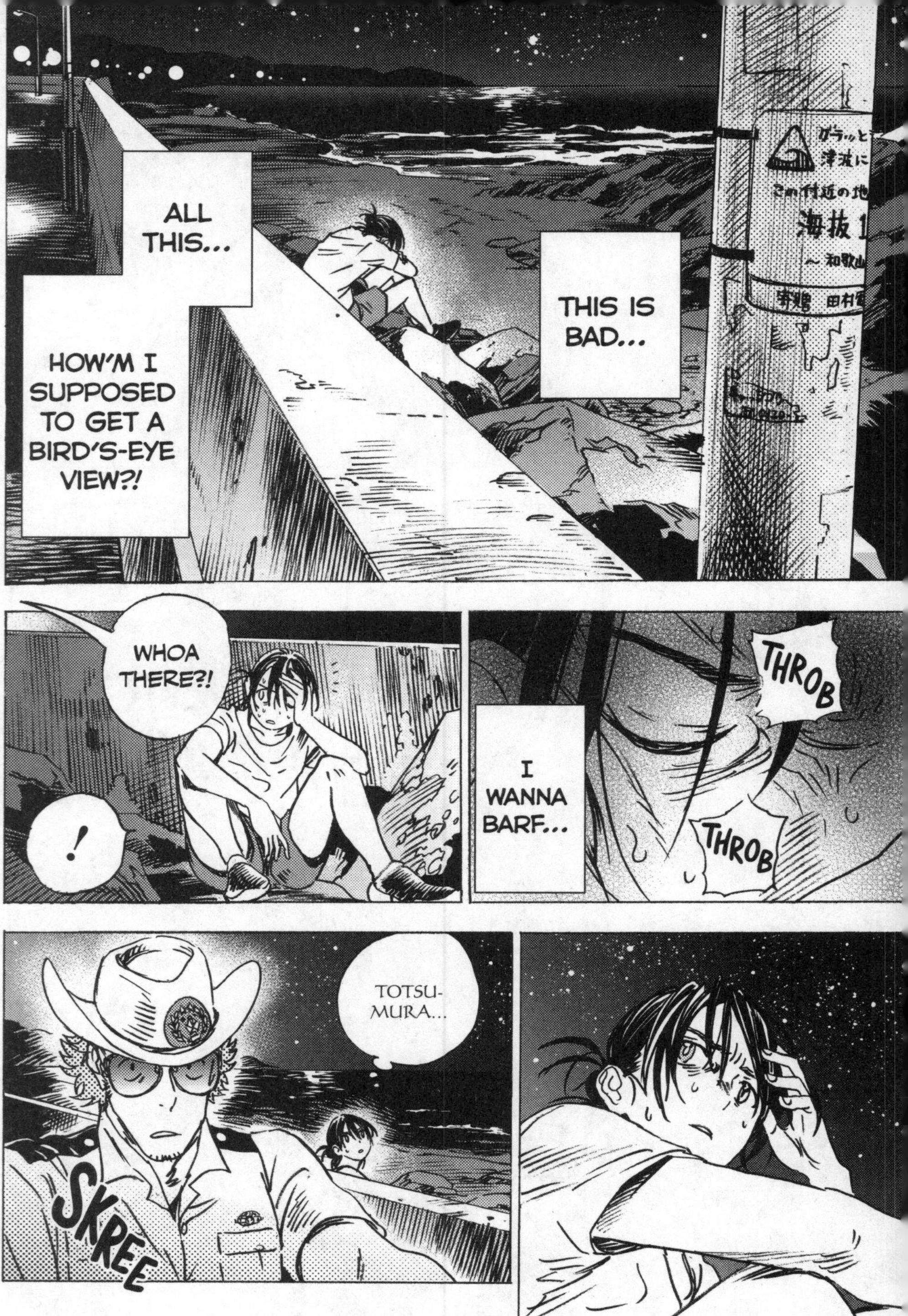
THIS IS BAD...
ALL THIS...
HOW'M I SUPPOSED TO GET A BIRD'S-EYE VIEW?!
THROB
I WANNA BARF...
THROB
WHOA THERE?!
!
TOTSU-MURA...
SKREE

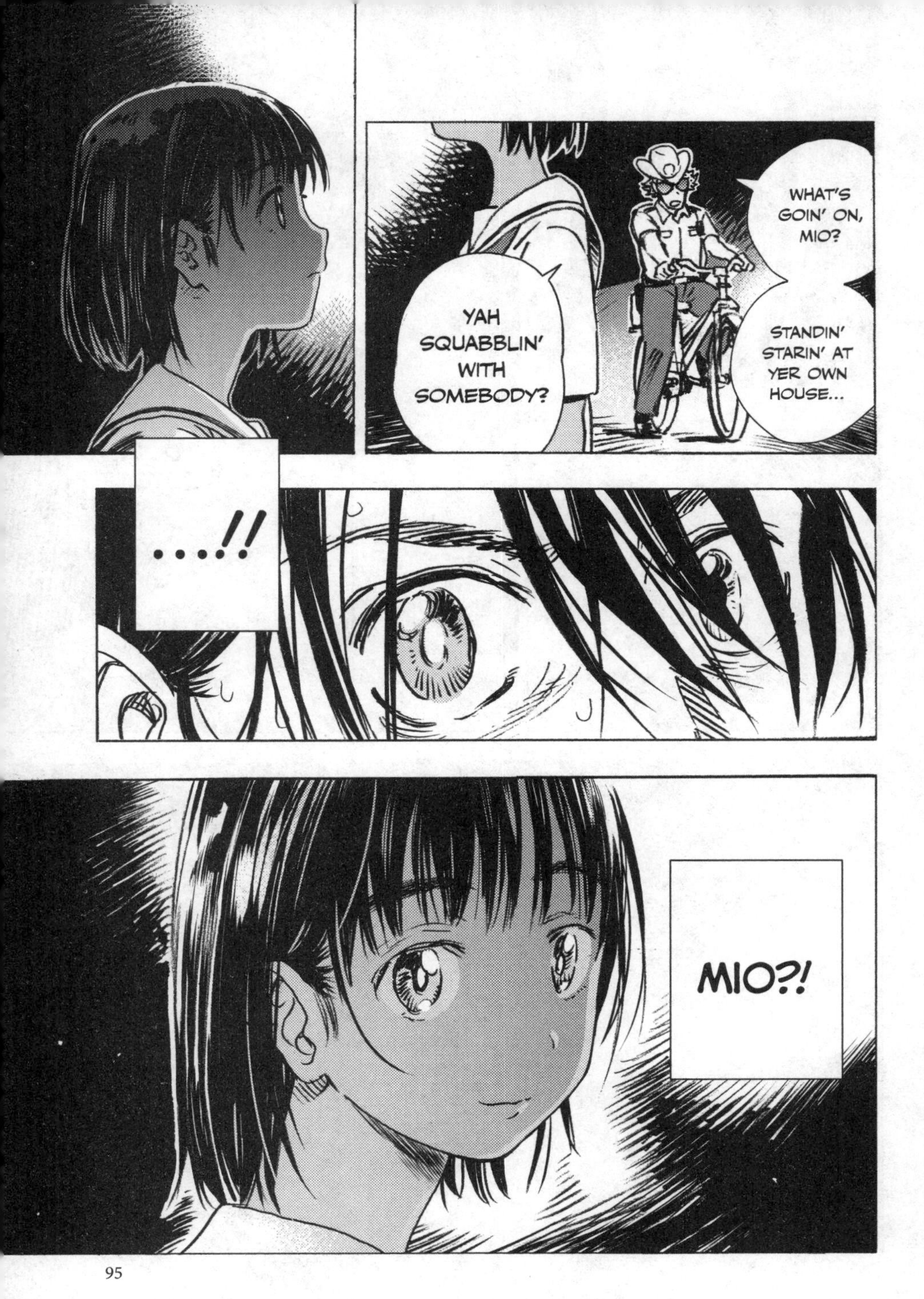
WHAT'S GOIN' ON, MIO?
STANDIN' STARIN' AT YER OWN HOUSE...
YAH SQUABBLIN' WITH SOMEBODY?
....!!
MIO?!

....?

WHAT'S SHE DOING OUTSIDE?

AND WEARING HER UNIFORM?

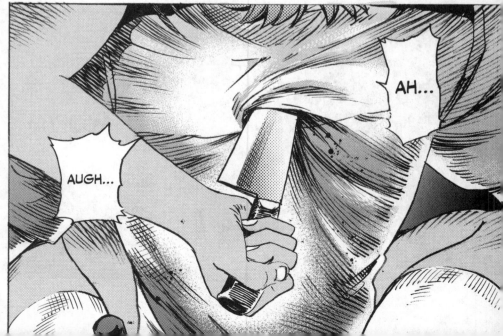

AH...

AUGH...

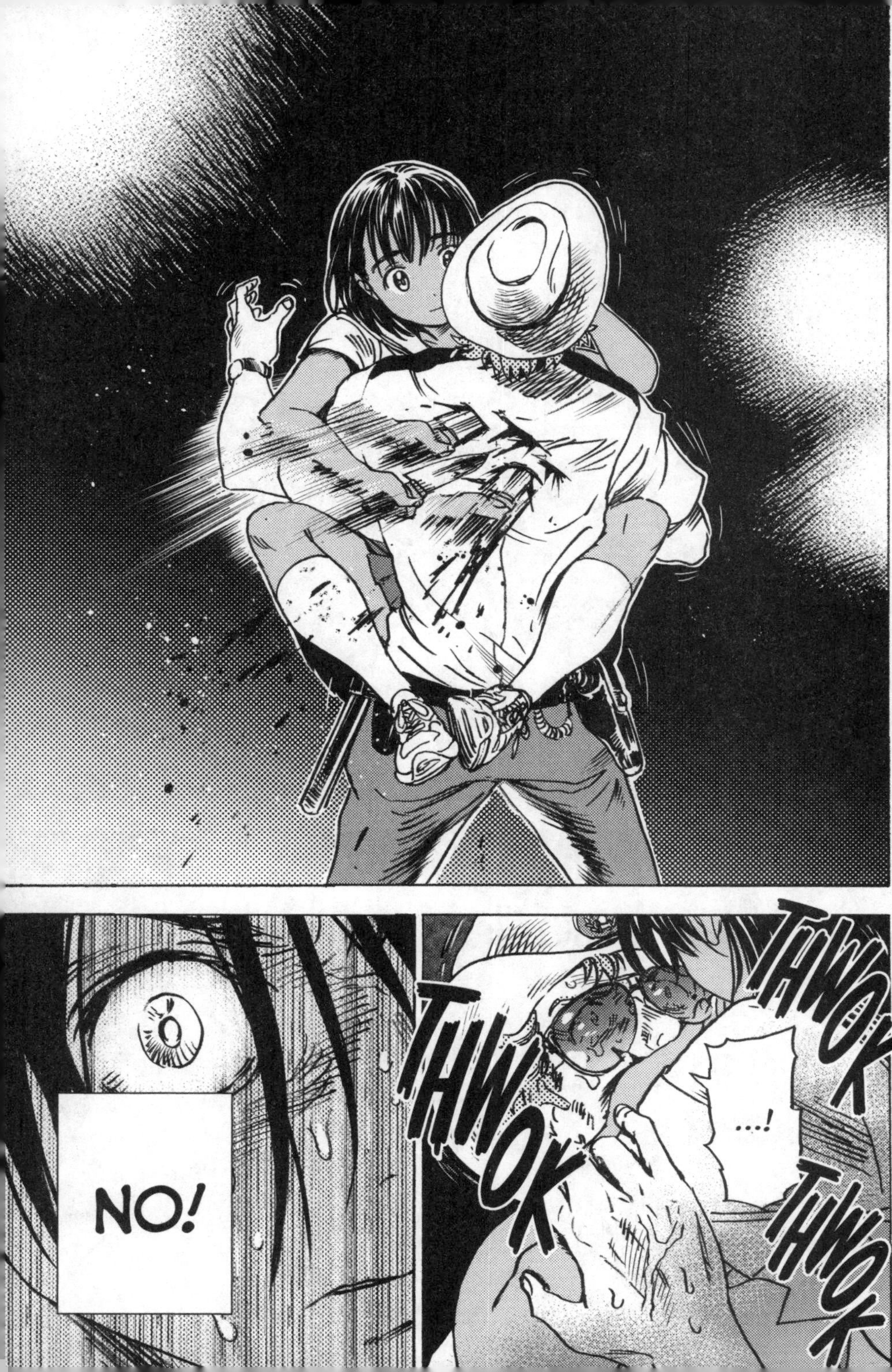
THWOK
...!
THWOK
THWOK
NO!

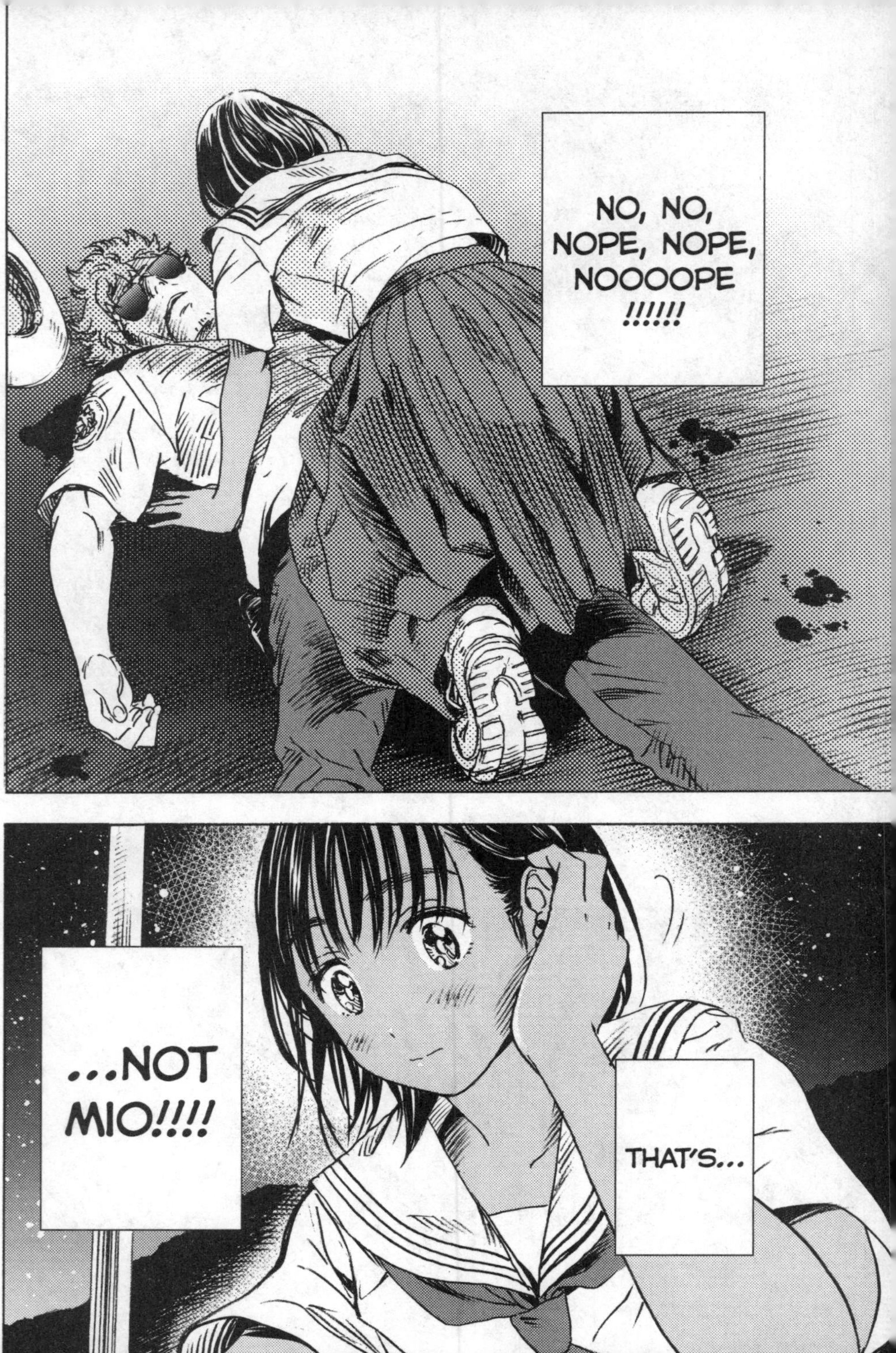
NO, NO, NOPE, NOPE, NOOOOPE !!!!!!
THAT'S...
...NOT MIO!!!!

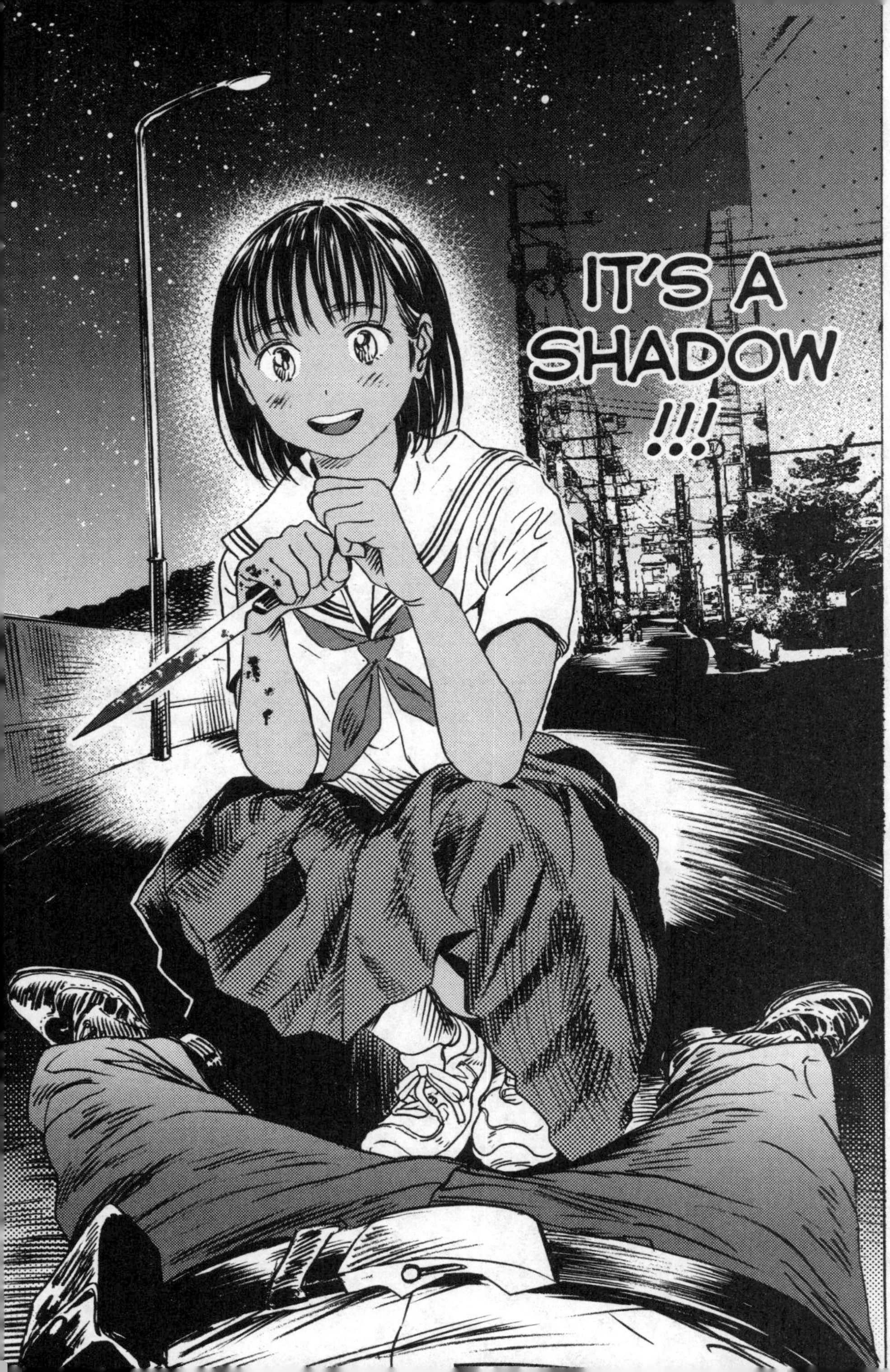
IT'S A SHADOW !!!

Summertime rendering

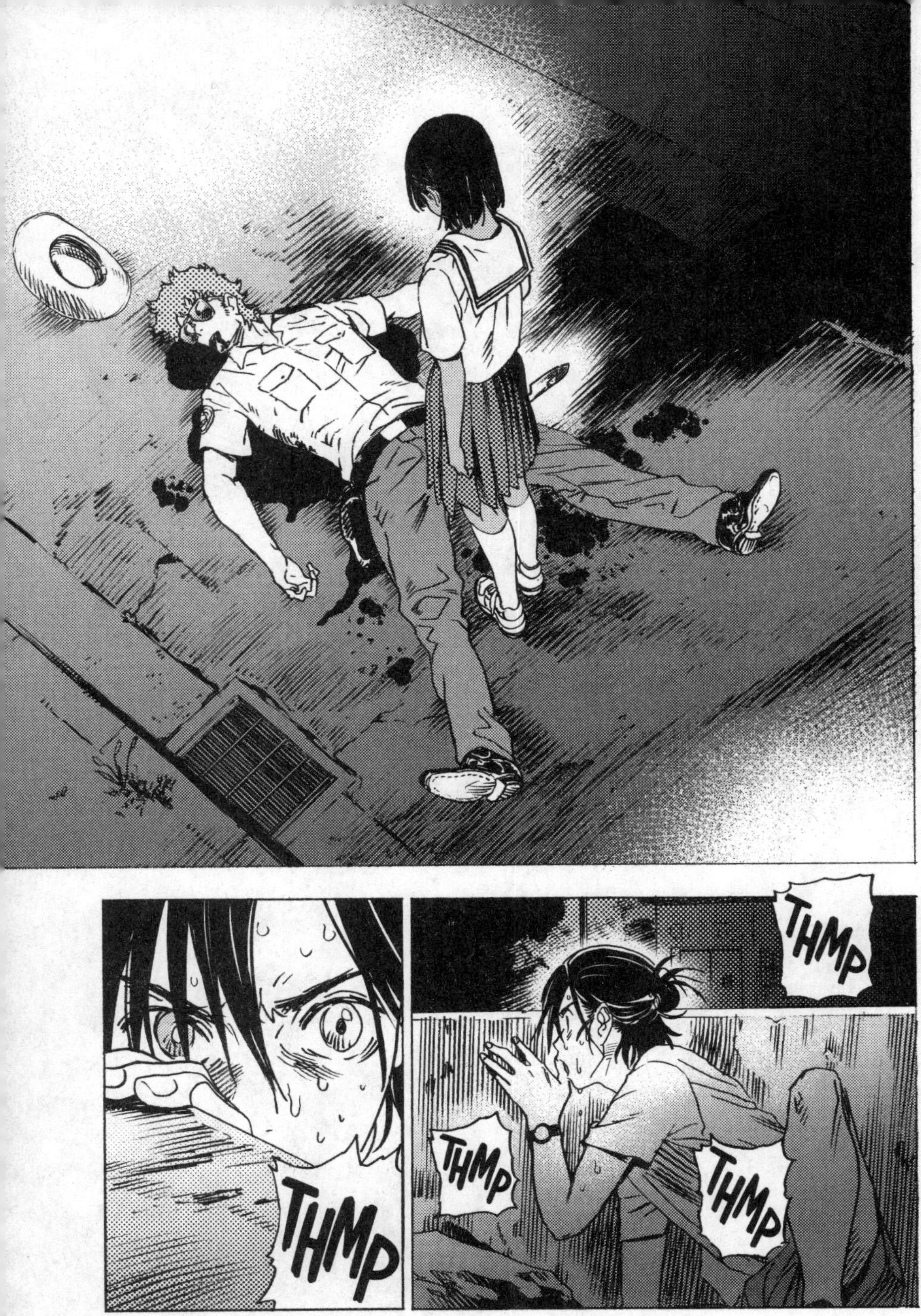
THMP
THMP
THMP
THMP

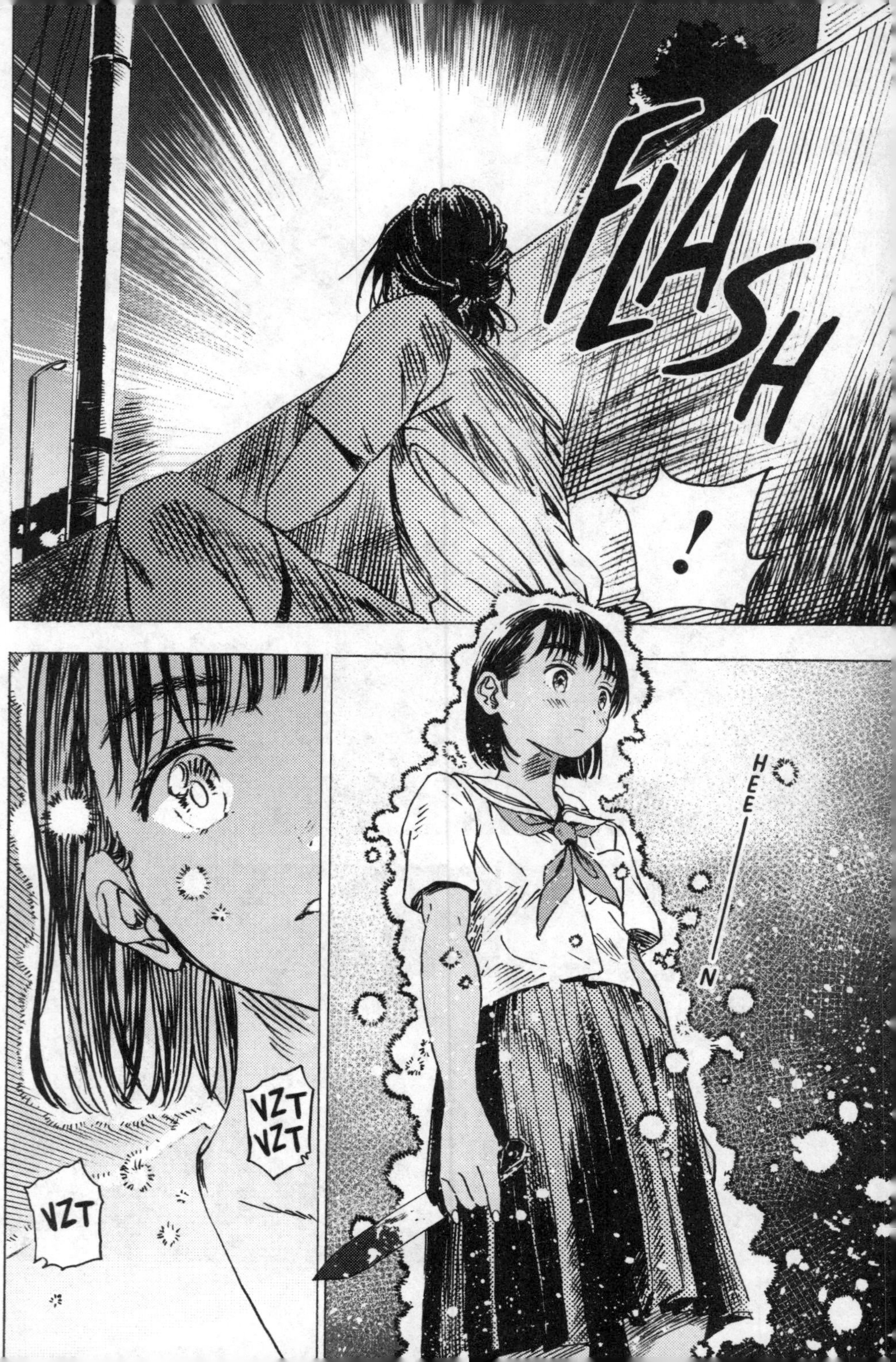
FLASH
!
HEEEN
VZT VZT
VZT

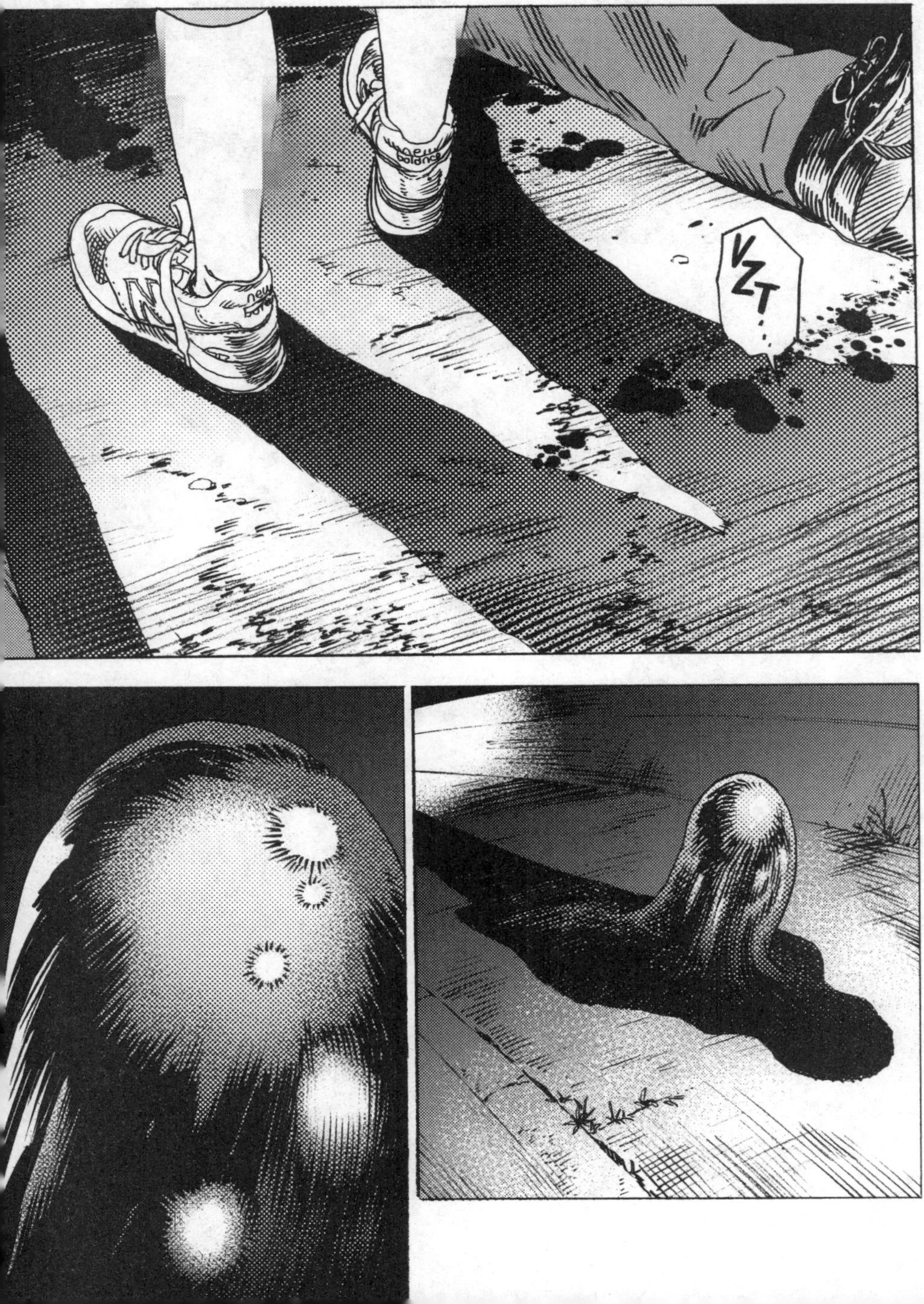
VZT

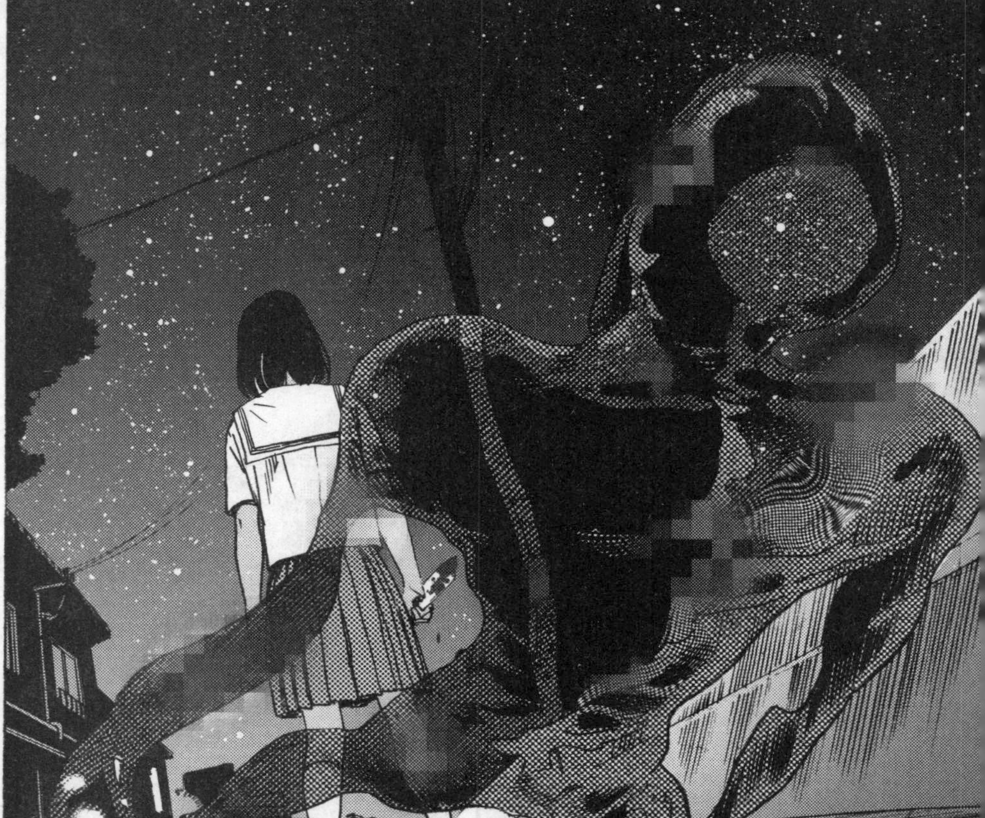

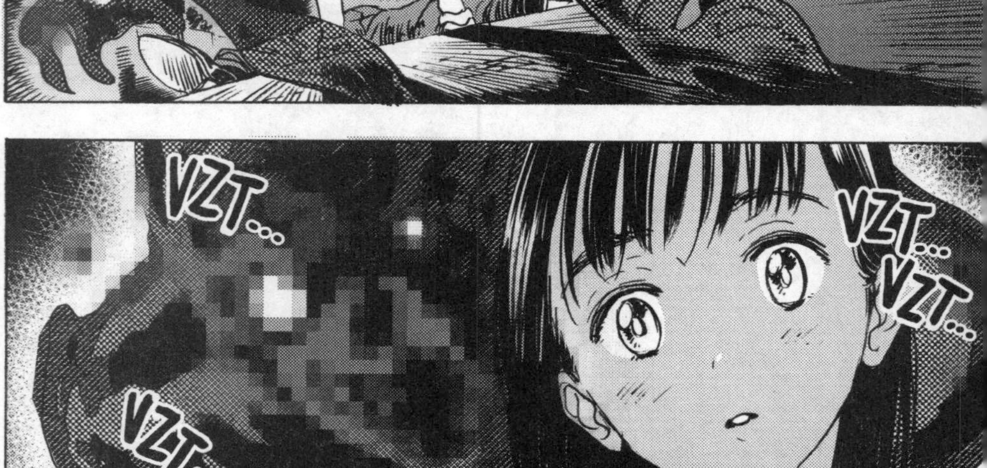
VZT...
VZT...
VZT...
VZT...

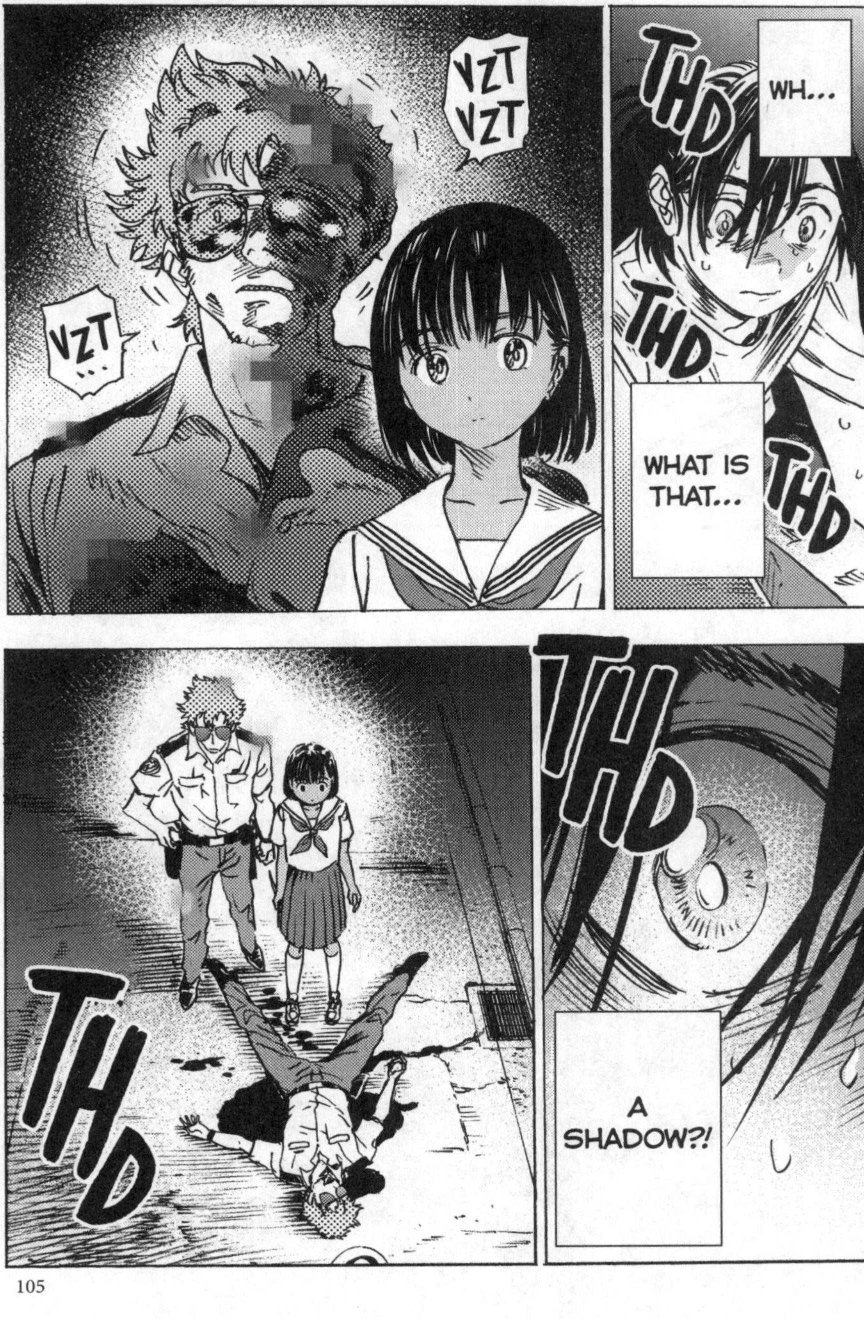
THD
WH...
THD
WHAT IS THAT...
THD
VZT VZT
VZT...
THD
A SHADOW?!
THD

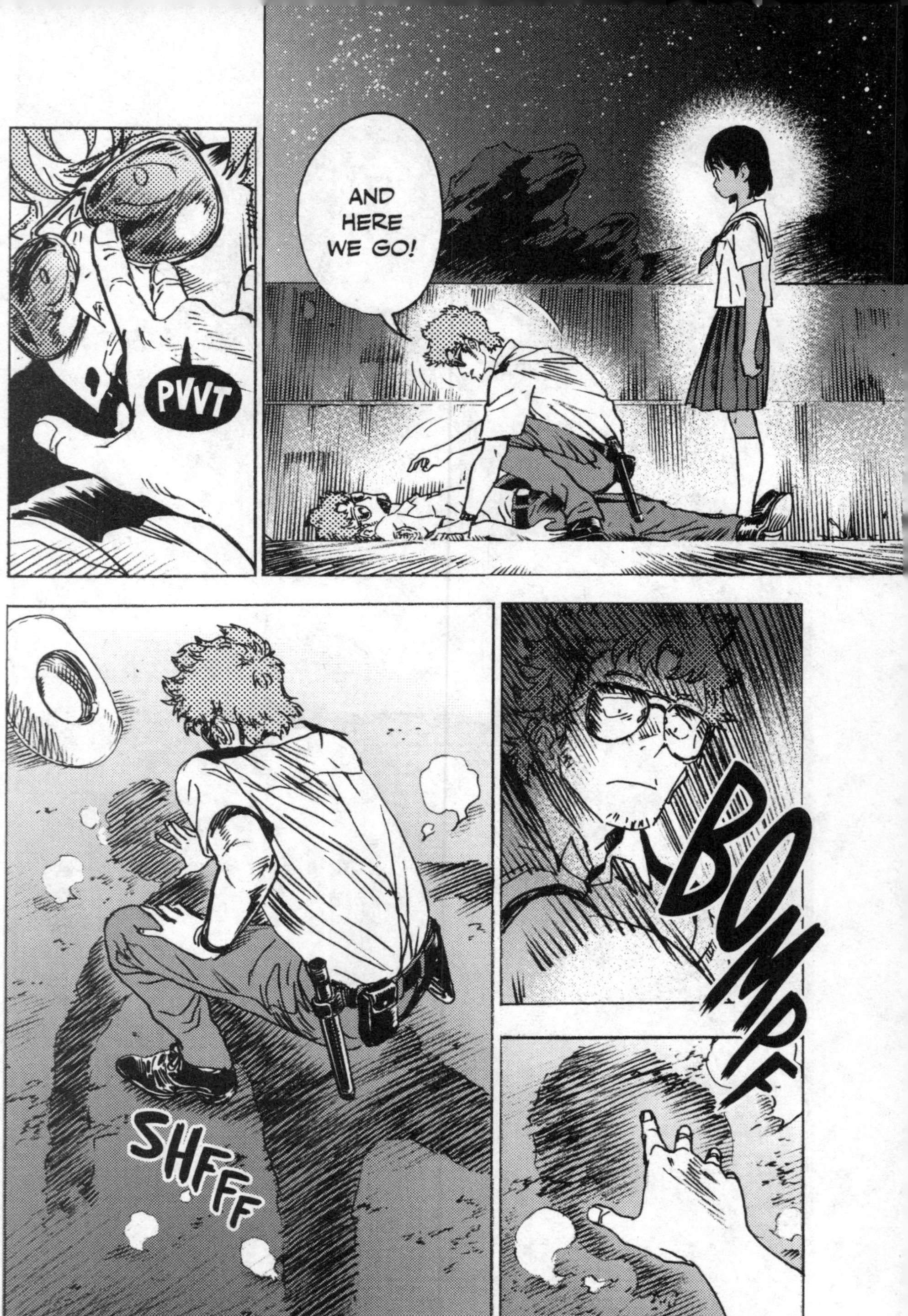
AND HERE WE GO!
PVVT
BOMPF
SHFFF

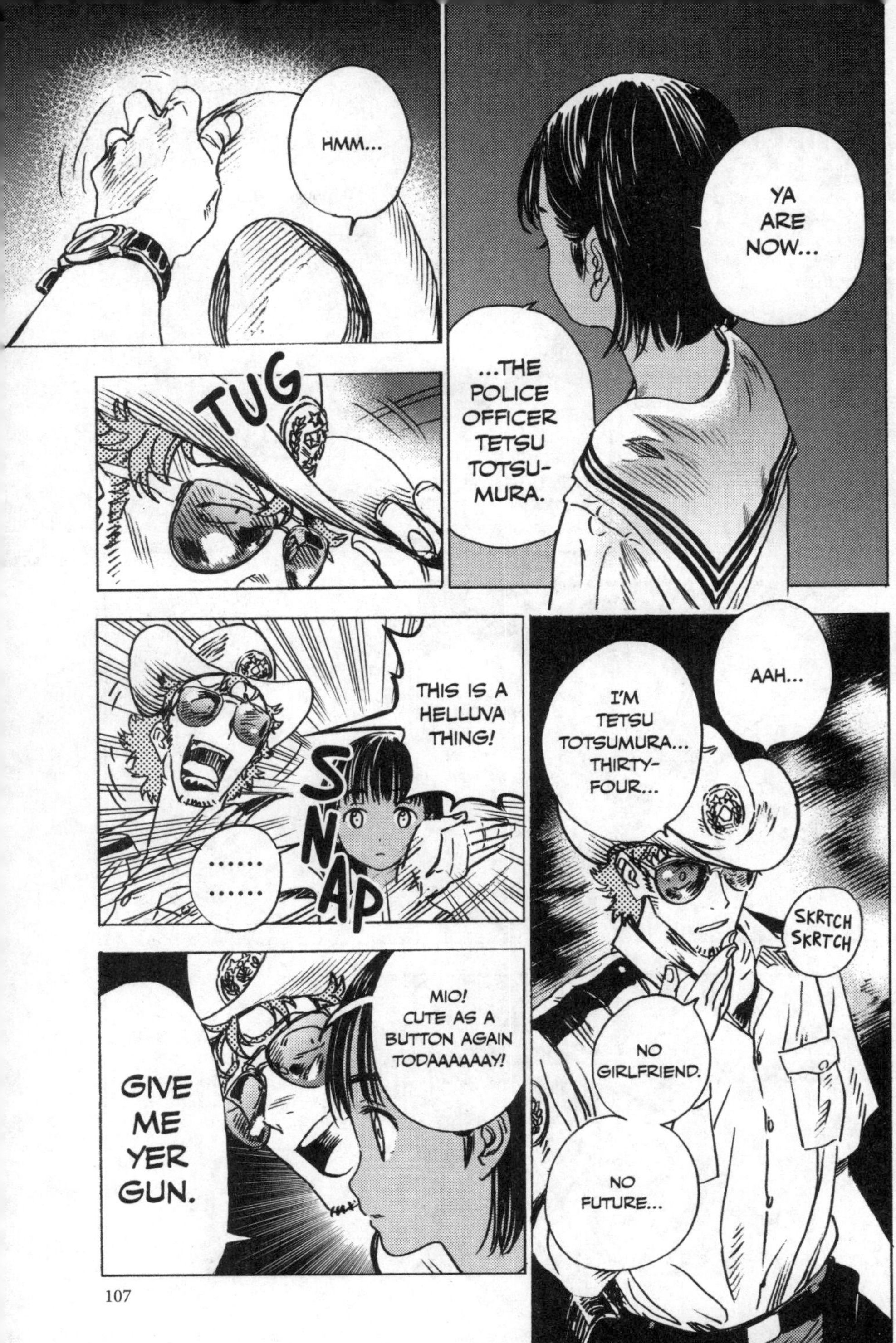
YA ARE NOW...
...THE POLICE OFFICER TETSU TOTSU-MURA.
HMM...
TUG
AAH...
I'M TETSU TOTSUMURA... THIRTY-FOUR...
SKRTCH SKRTCH
NO GIRLFRIEND.
NO FUTURE...
THIS IS A HELLUVA THING!
SNAP
......
......
MIO! CUTE AS A BUTTON AGAIN TODAAAAAAY!
GIVE ME YER GUN.

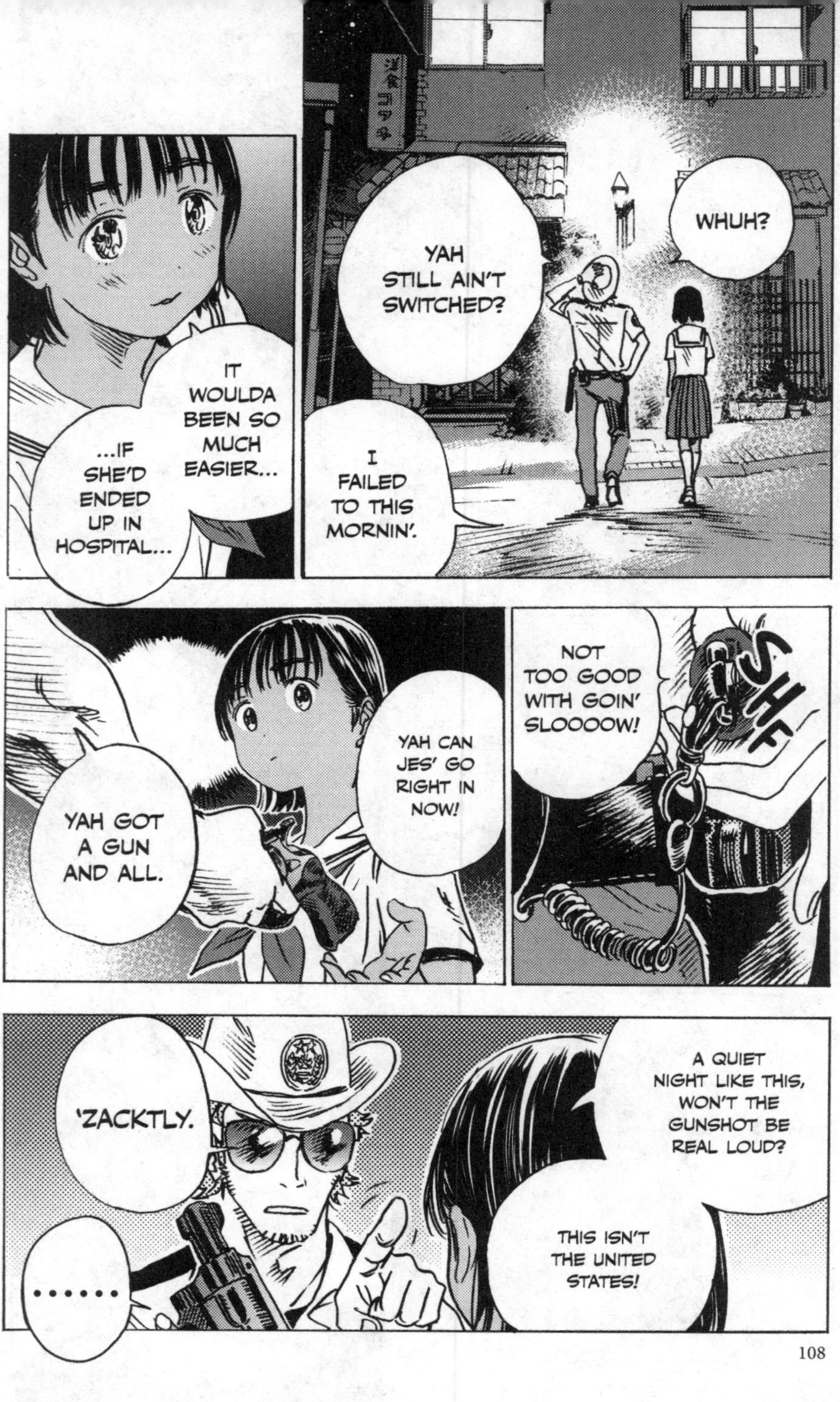
WHUH?
YAH STILL AIN'T SWITCHED?
I FAILED TO THIS MORNIN'.
IT WOULDA BEEN SO MUCH EASIER...
...IF SHE'D ENDED UP IN HOSPITAL...
NOT TOO GOOD WITH GOIN' SLOOOOW!
SHF
YAH CAN JES' GO RIGHT IN NOW!
YAH GOT A GUN AND ALL.
A QUIET NIGHT LIKE THIS, WON'T THE GUNSHOT BE REAL LOUD?
'ZACKTLY.
THIS ISN'T THE UNITED STATES!
......

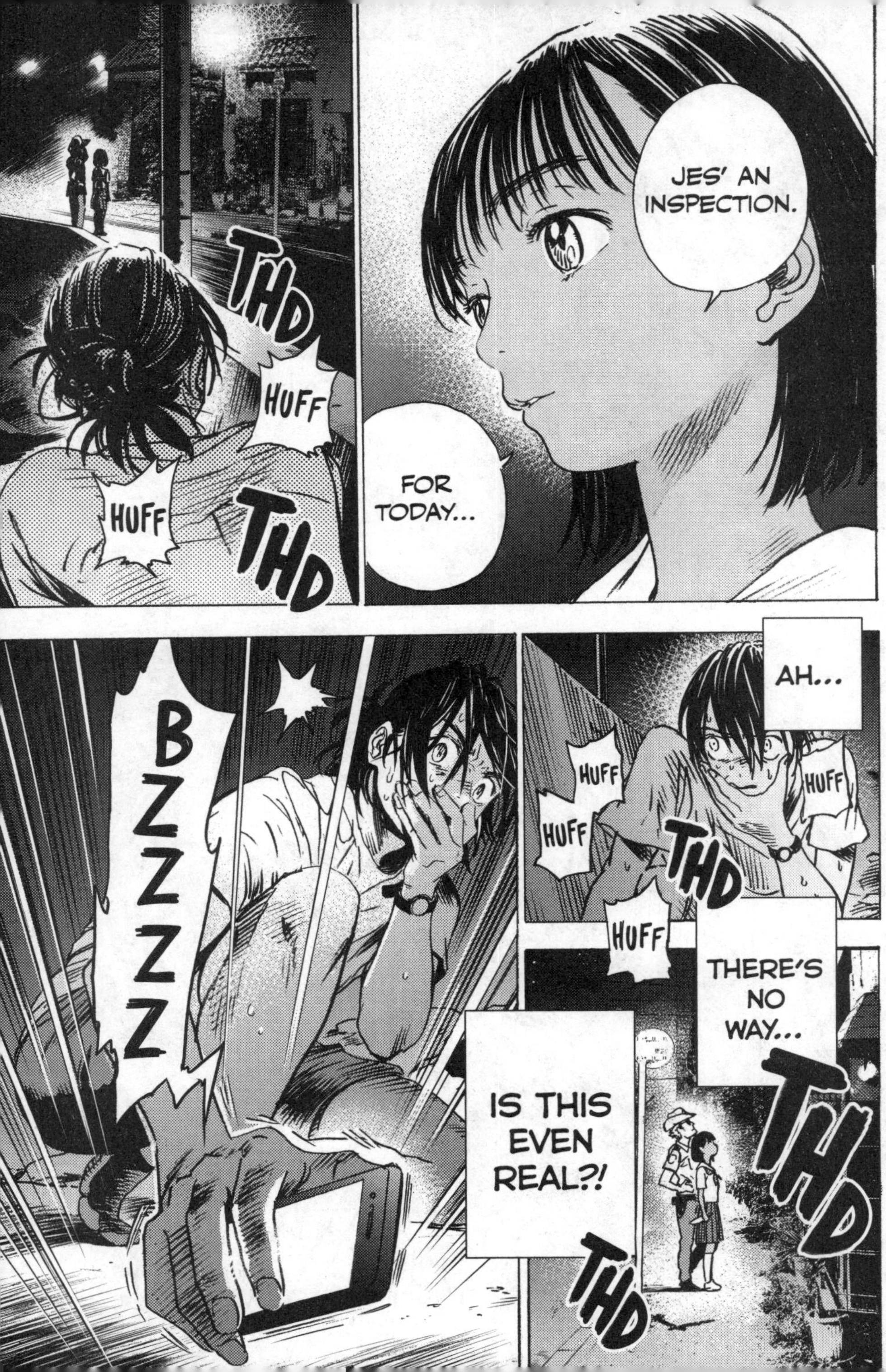
JES' AN INSPECTION.
FOR TODAY...
THD
HUFF
HUFF
THD
AH...
HUFF
HUFF
HUFF
THD
HUFF
THERE'S NO WAY...
IS THIS EVEN REAL?!
THD
THD
BZZZZ

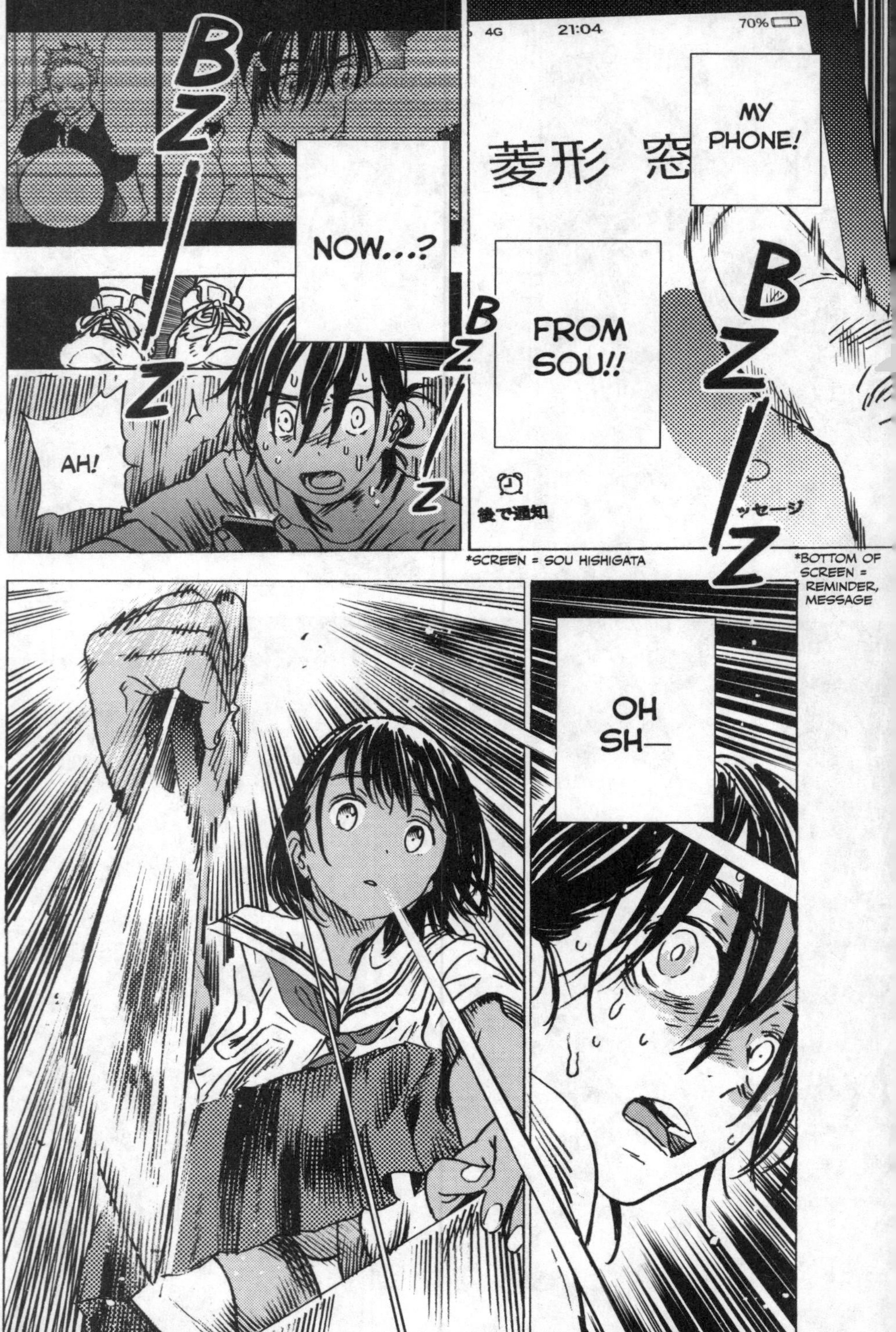

4G
21:04
70%
菱形 窓
MY PHONE!
BZZ
FROM SOU!!
後で通知
ッセージ
*SCREEN = SOU HISHIGATA
*BOTTOM OF SCREEN = REMINDER, MESSAGE
BZZ
NOW...?
BZZ
AH!
OH SH—

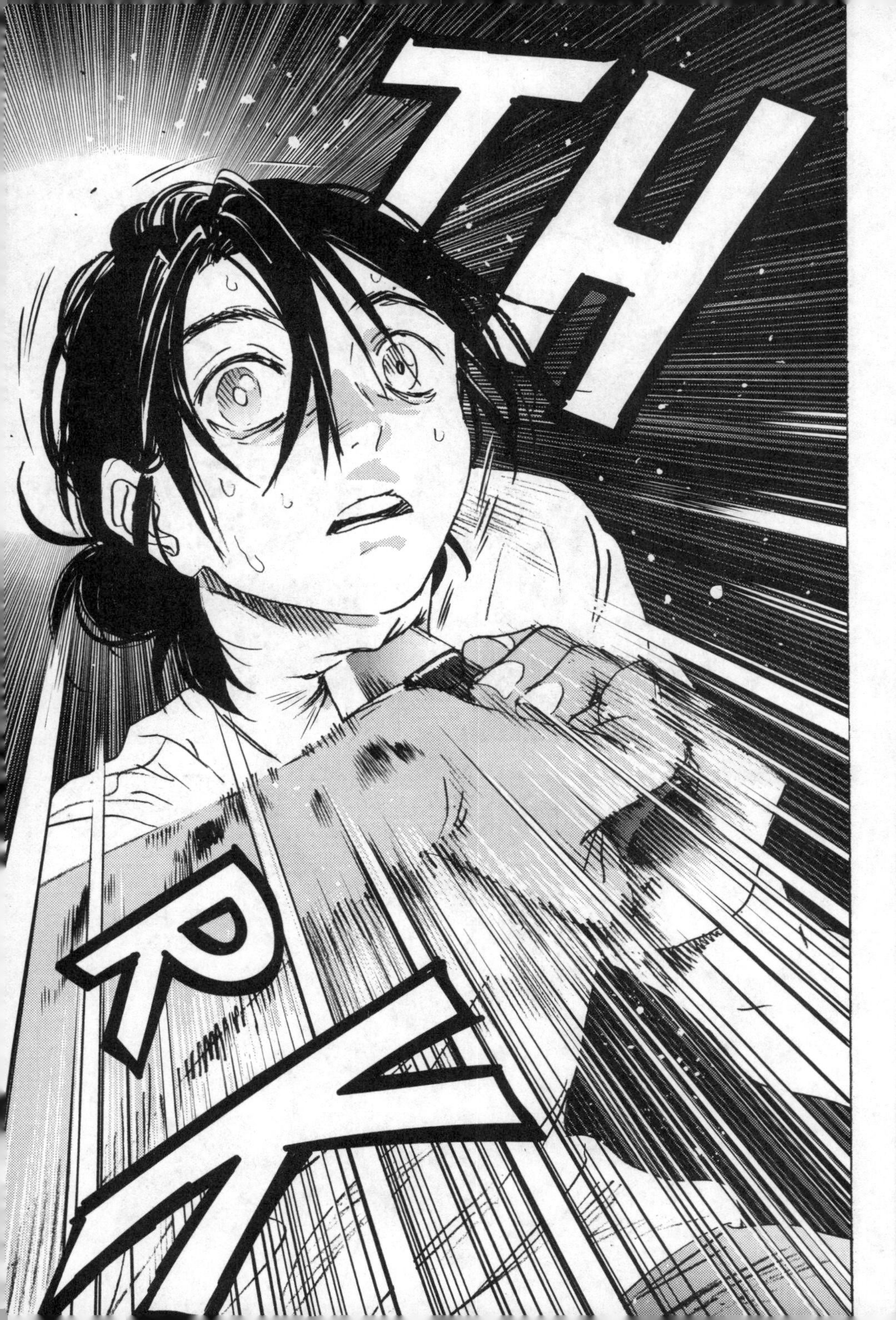
THRAK

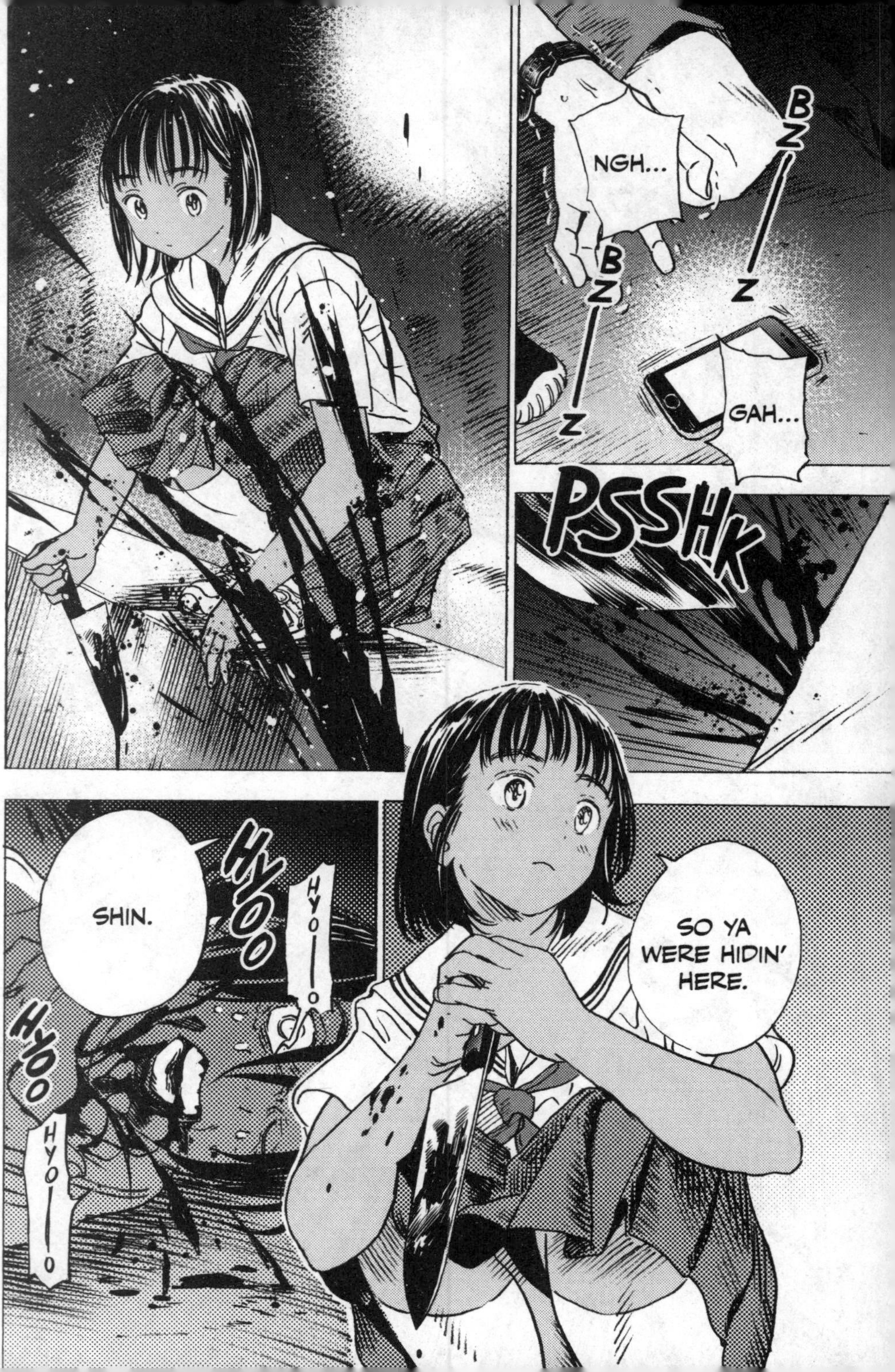
NGH...
BZ—Z
BZ—Z
GAH...
PSSHK
SO YA WERE HIDIN' HERE.
SHIN.
HYOO
HYO—O
HYOO
HYO—O

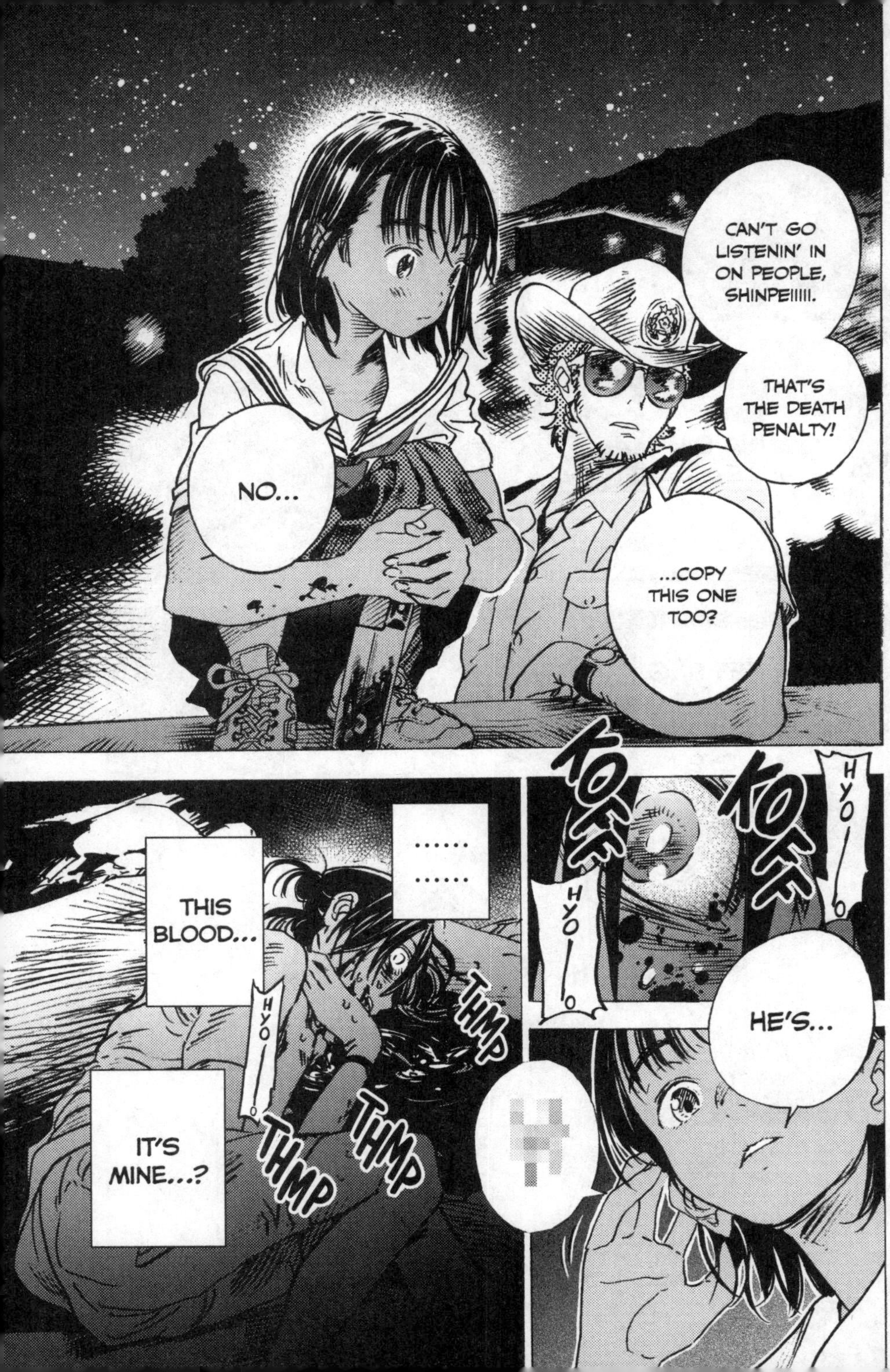
CAN'T GO LISTENIN' IN ON PEOPLE, SHINPEIIIII.
THAT'S THE DEATH PENALTY!
...COPY THIS ONE TOO?
NO...
HYO—O
KOFF
KOFF
HYO—O
HE'S...
......
......
THIS BLOOD...
HYO—O
THMP
THMP
THMP
IT'S MINE...?

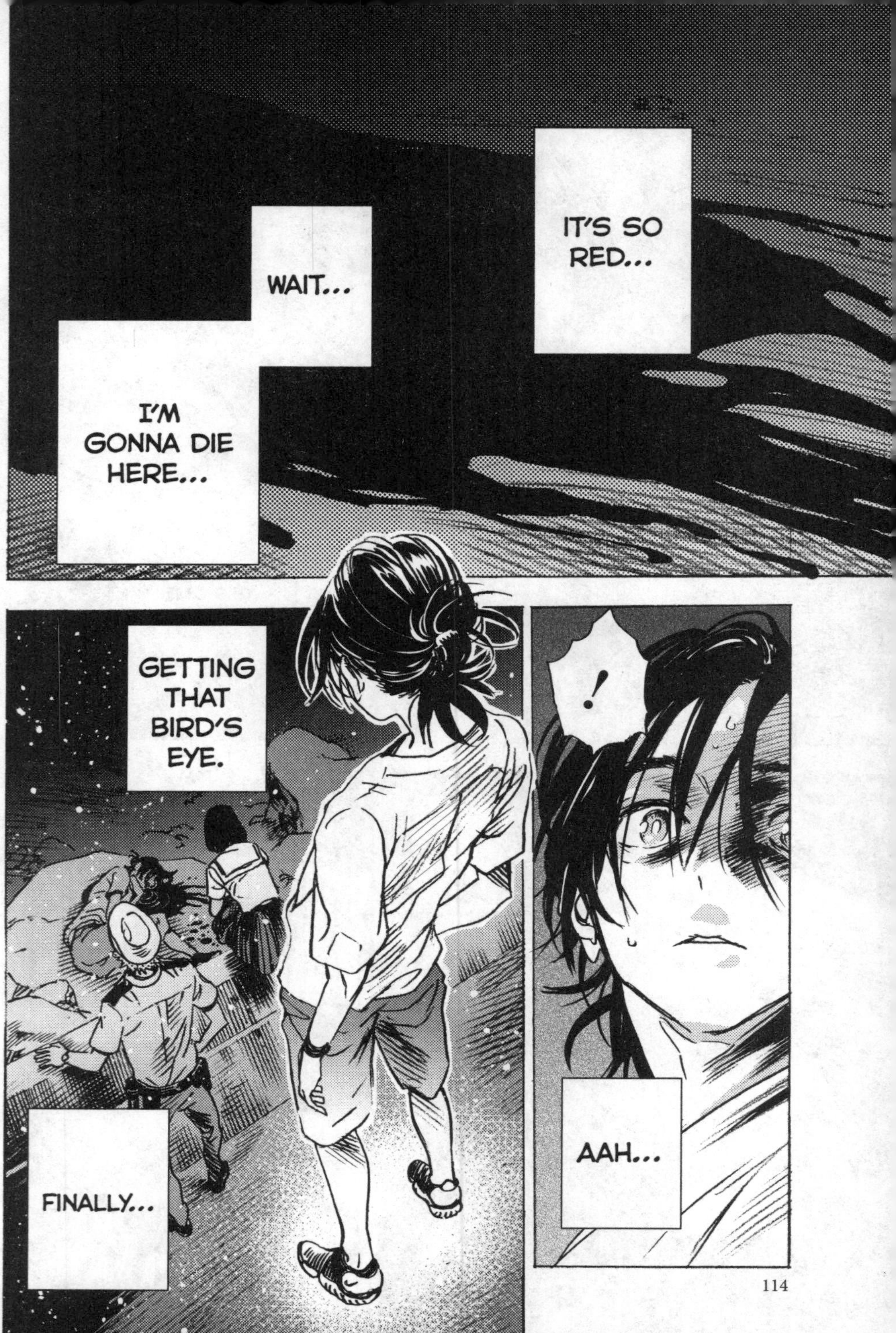
IT'S SO RED...
WAIT...
I'M GONNA DIE HERE...
!
AAH...
GETTING THAT BIRD'S EYE.
FINALLY...

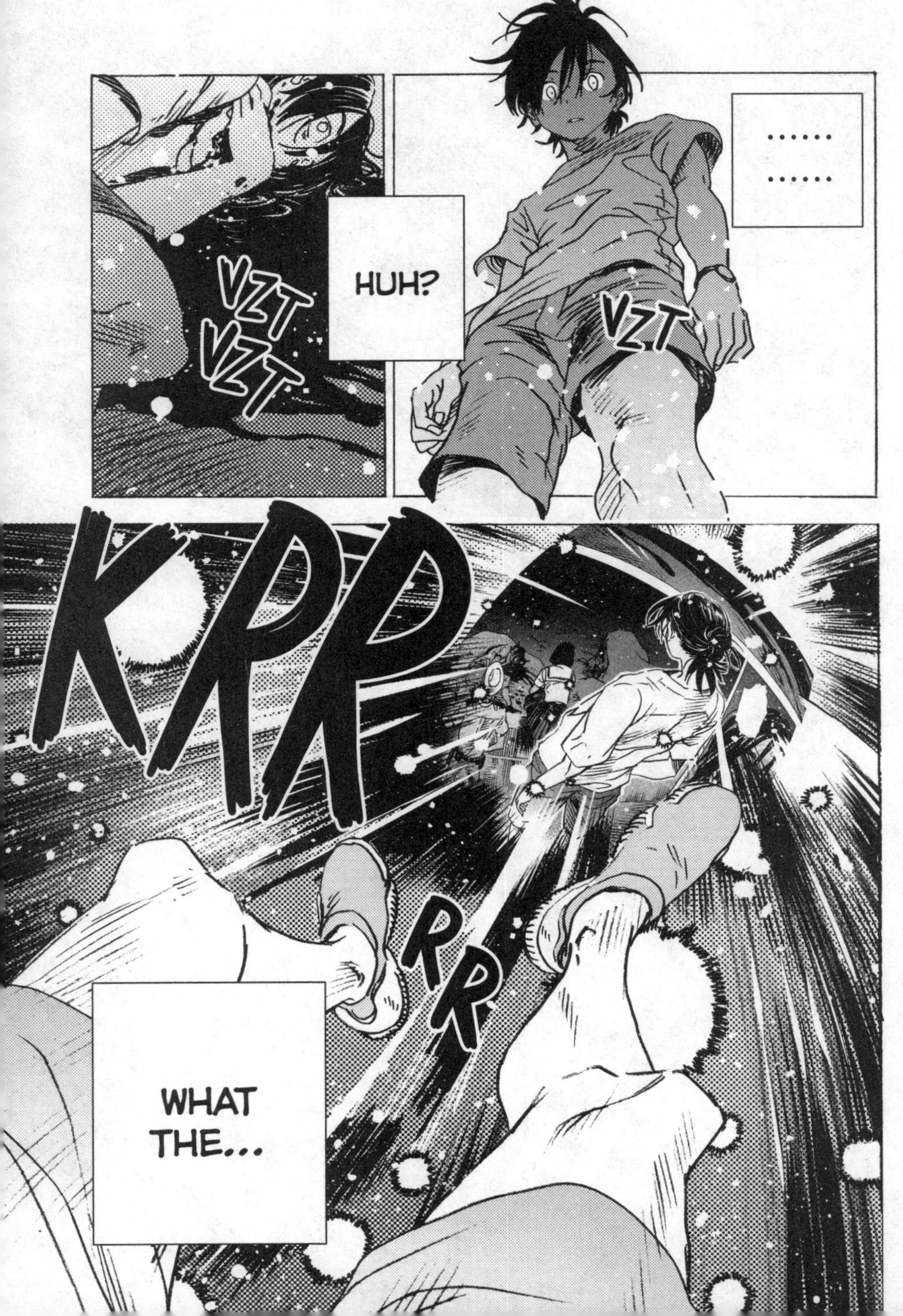
......
......
VZT
HUH?
VZT
VZT
KRR
RR
WHAT THE...

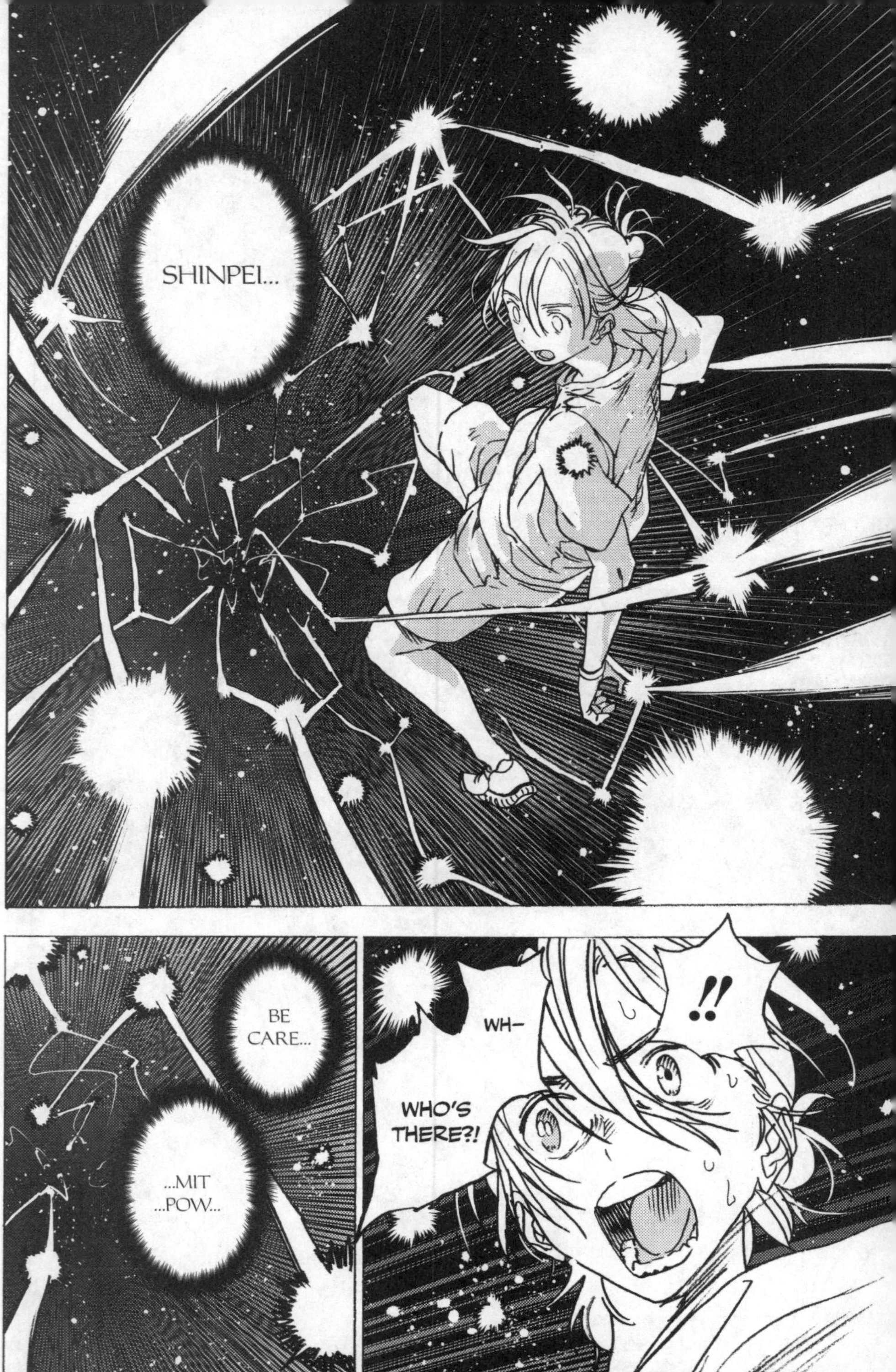
SHINPEI...
!!
WH-
WHO'S THERE?!
BE CARE...
...MIT ...POW...

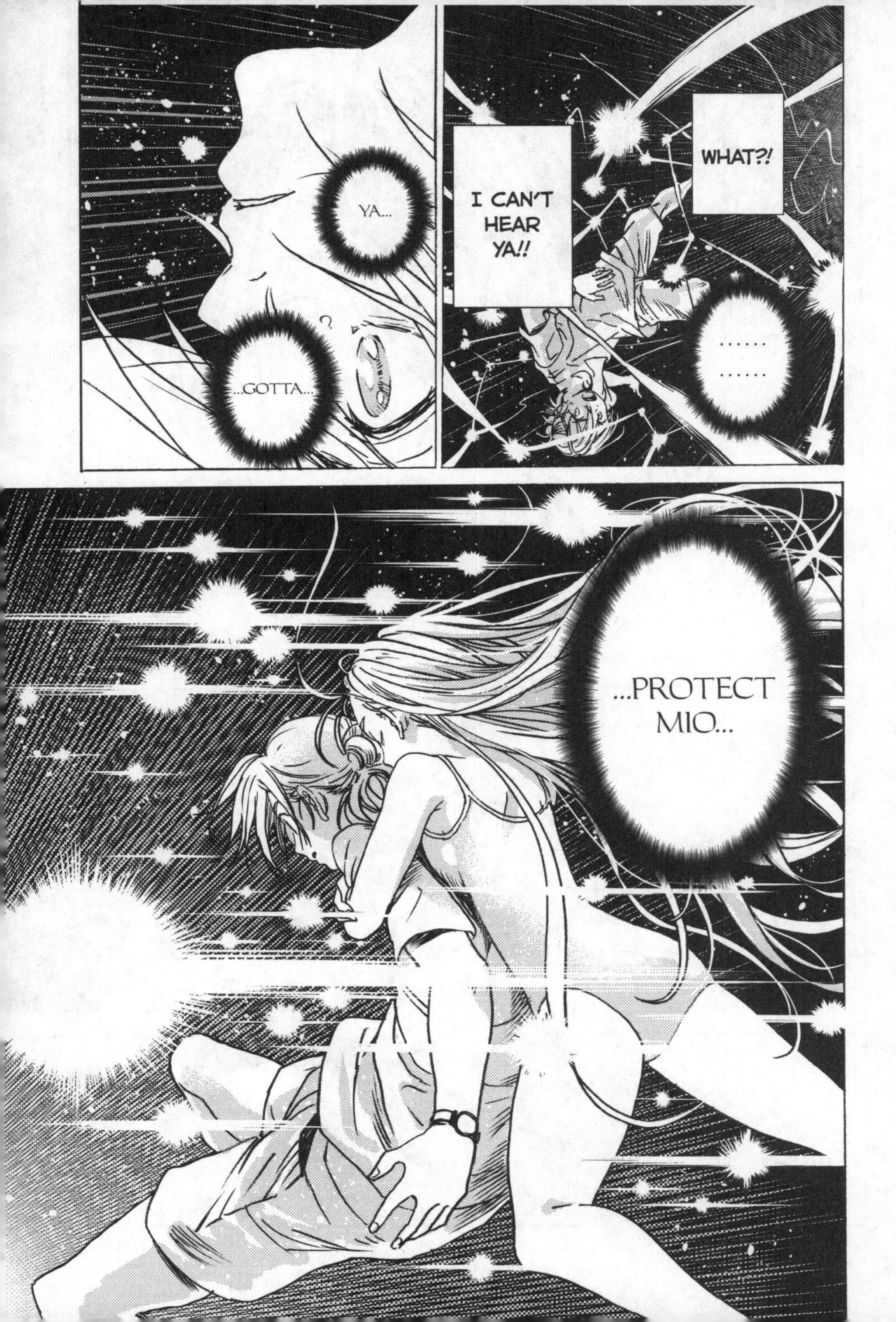
WHAT?!
I CAN'T HEAR YA!!
....
....
YA...
...GOTTA...
...PROTECT MIO...

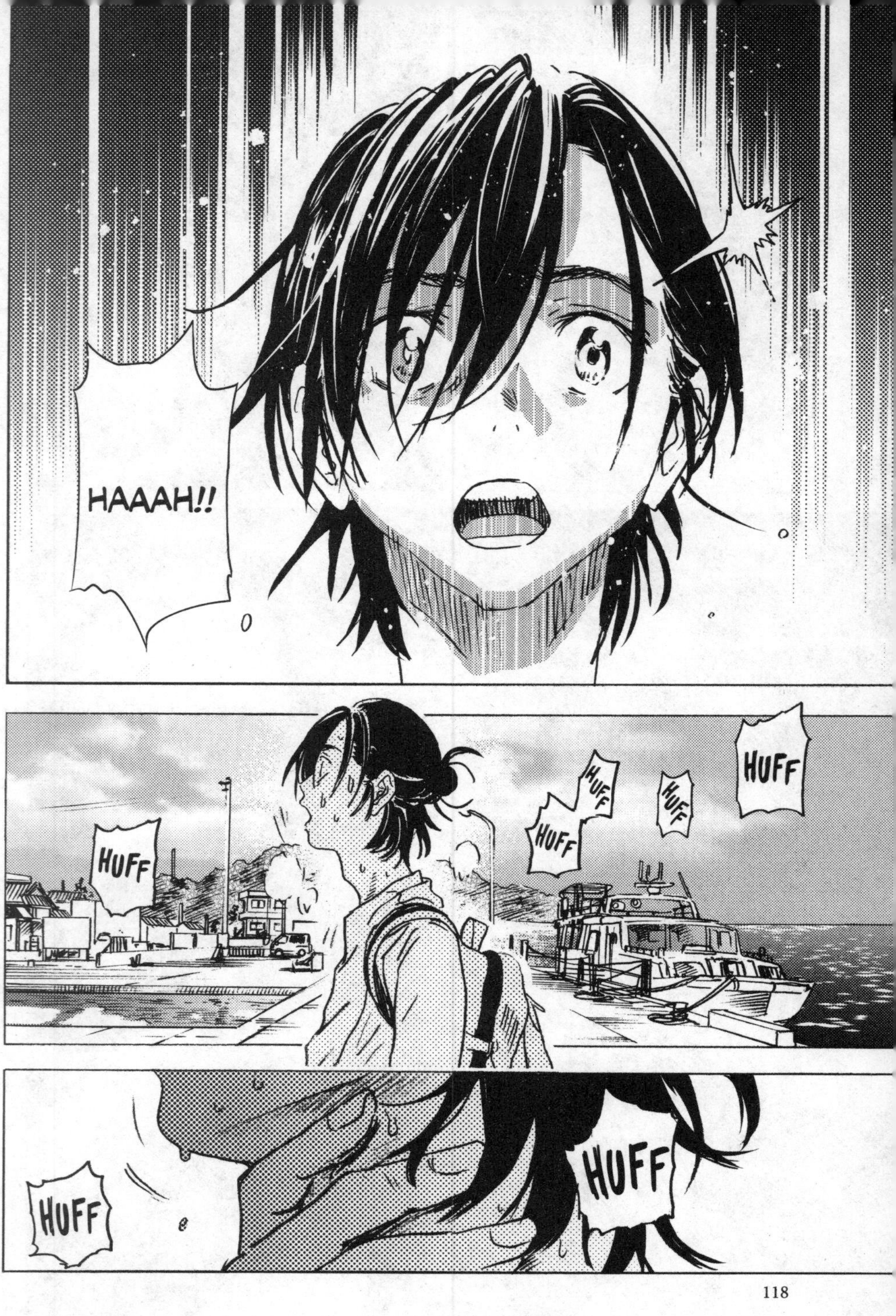
HAAAH!!
HUFF
HUFF
HUFF
HUFF
HUFF
HUFF
HUFF

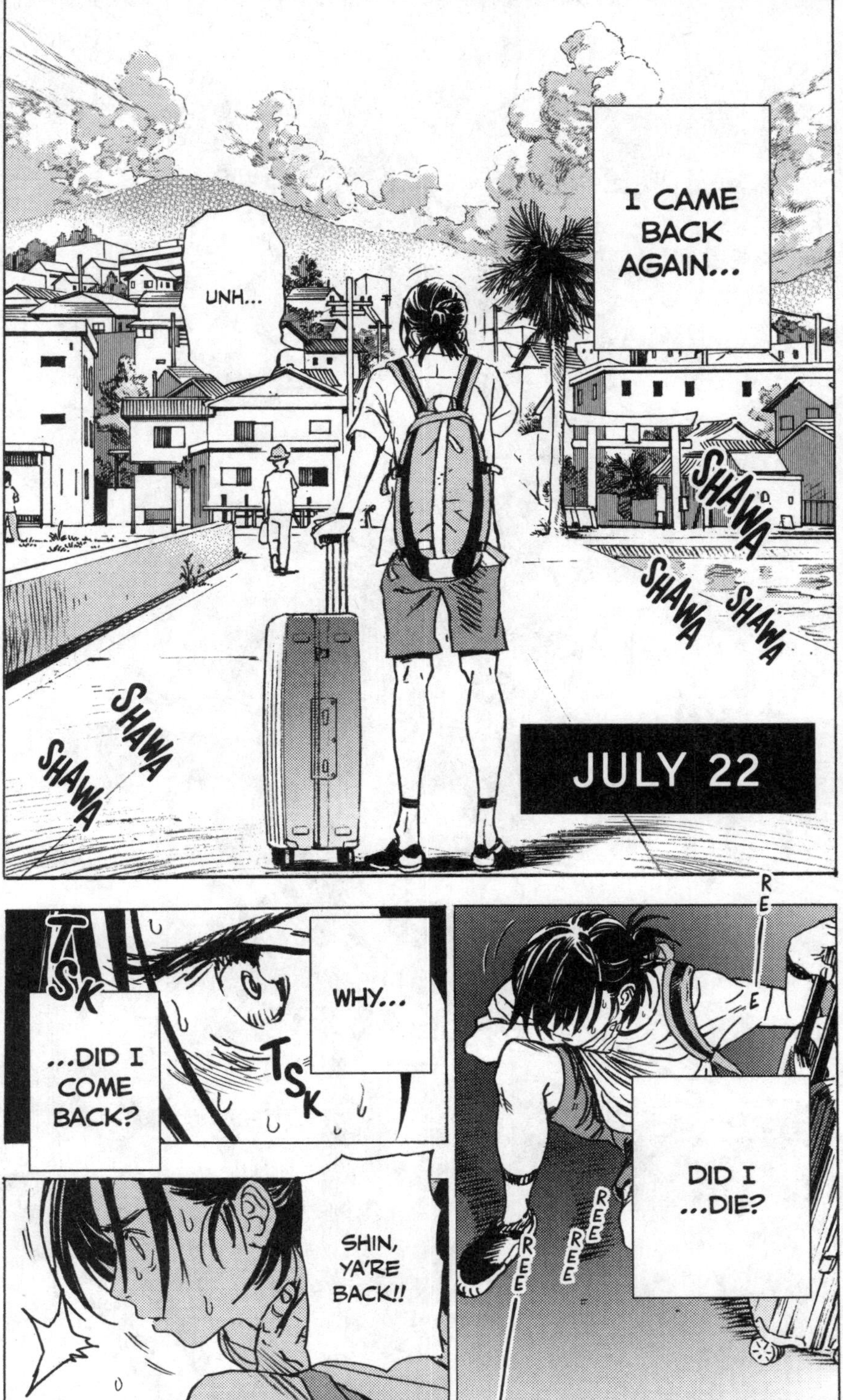
I CAME BACK AGAIN...
UNH...
SHAWA
SHAWA
SHAWA
JULY 22
SHAWA
SHAWA
REEE
DID I ...DIE?
REE
REE
REE
WHY...
TSK
...DID I COME BACK?
TSK
SHIN, YA'RE BACK!!

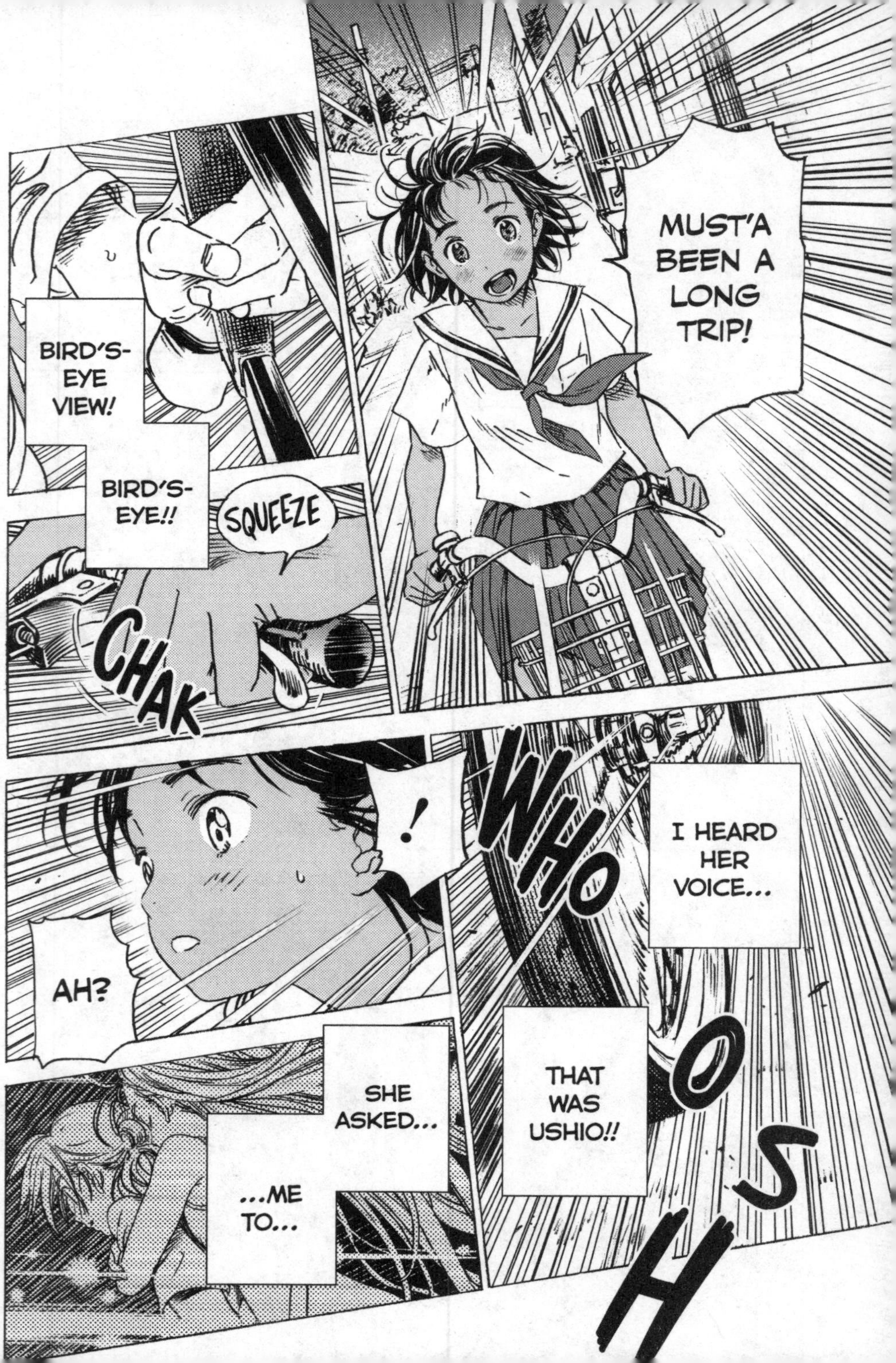
MUST'A BEEN A LONG TRIP!
BIRD'S-EYE VIEW!
BIRD'S-EYE!!
SQUEEZE
CHAK
WHOOSH
I HEARD HER VOICE...
THAT WAS USHIO!!
!
AH?
SHE ASKED...
...ME TO...

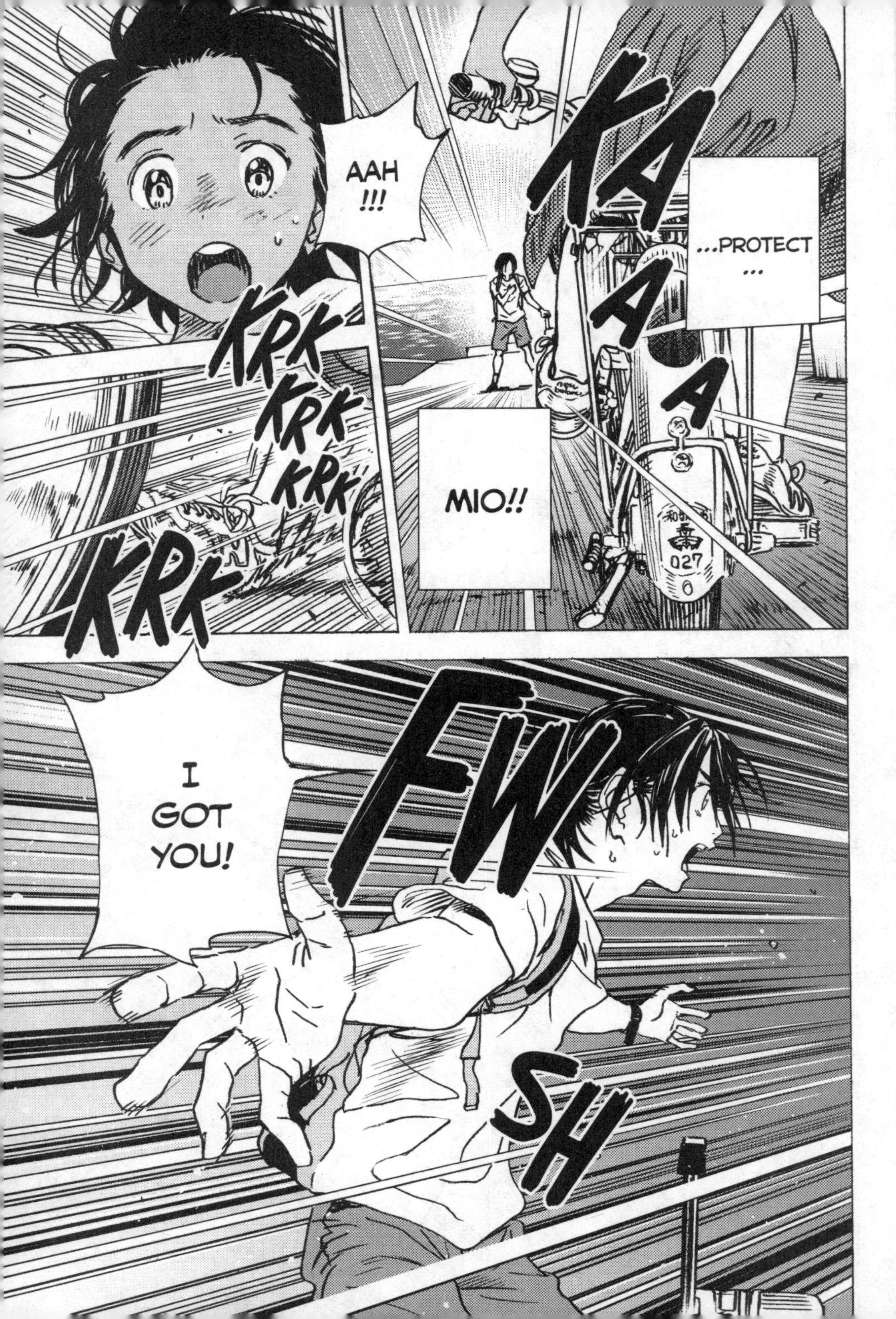
KAAAA
...PROTECT ...
MIO!!
AAH !!!
KRK KRK KRK KRK
KRK
FW
I GOT YOU!
SH

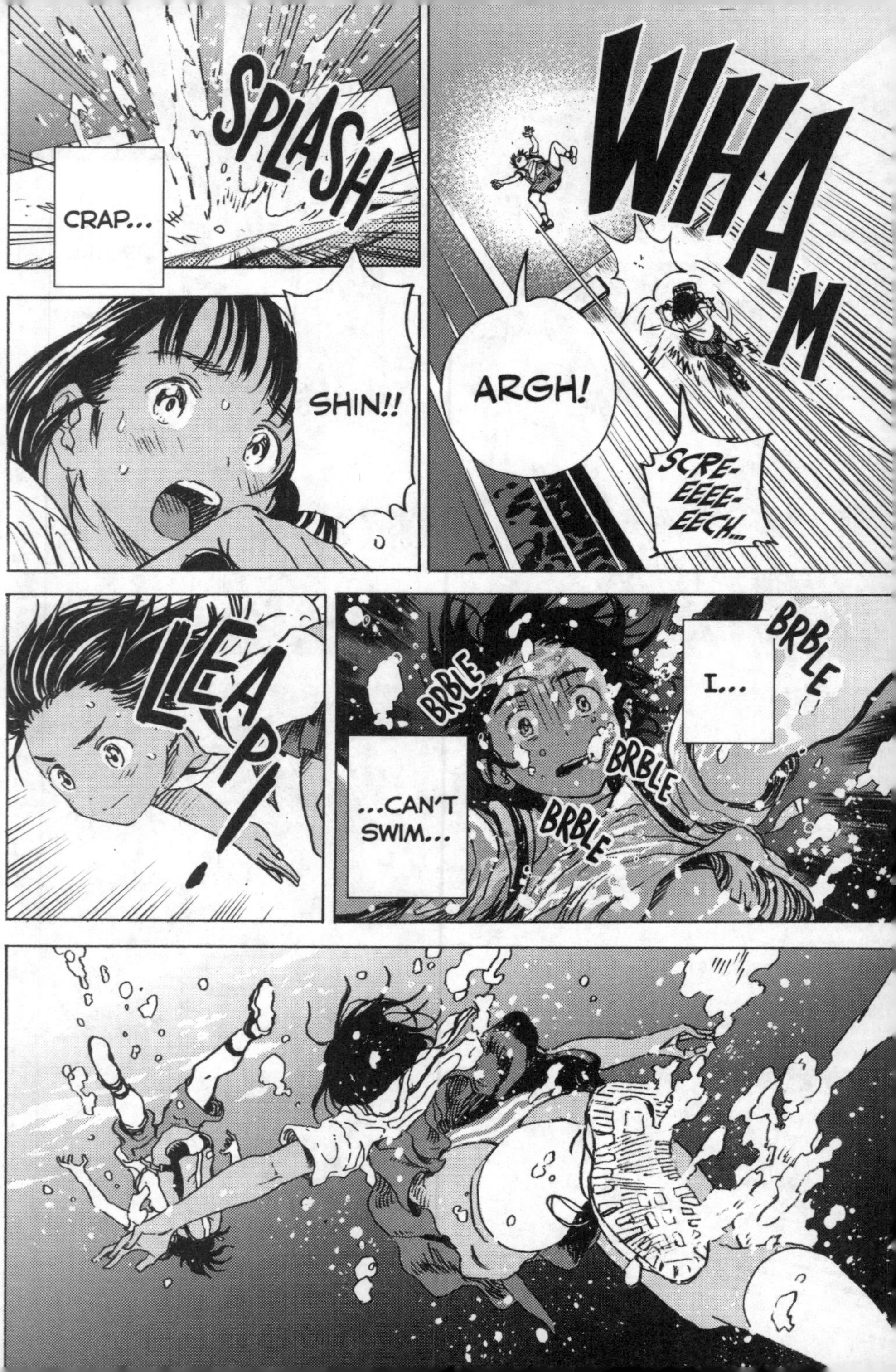
WHAM
ARGH!
SCRE-EEEE-EECH...
SPLASH
CRAP...
SHIN!!
BRBLE
I...
BRBLE
BRBLE
BRBLE
...CAN'T SWIM...
LLEAP!

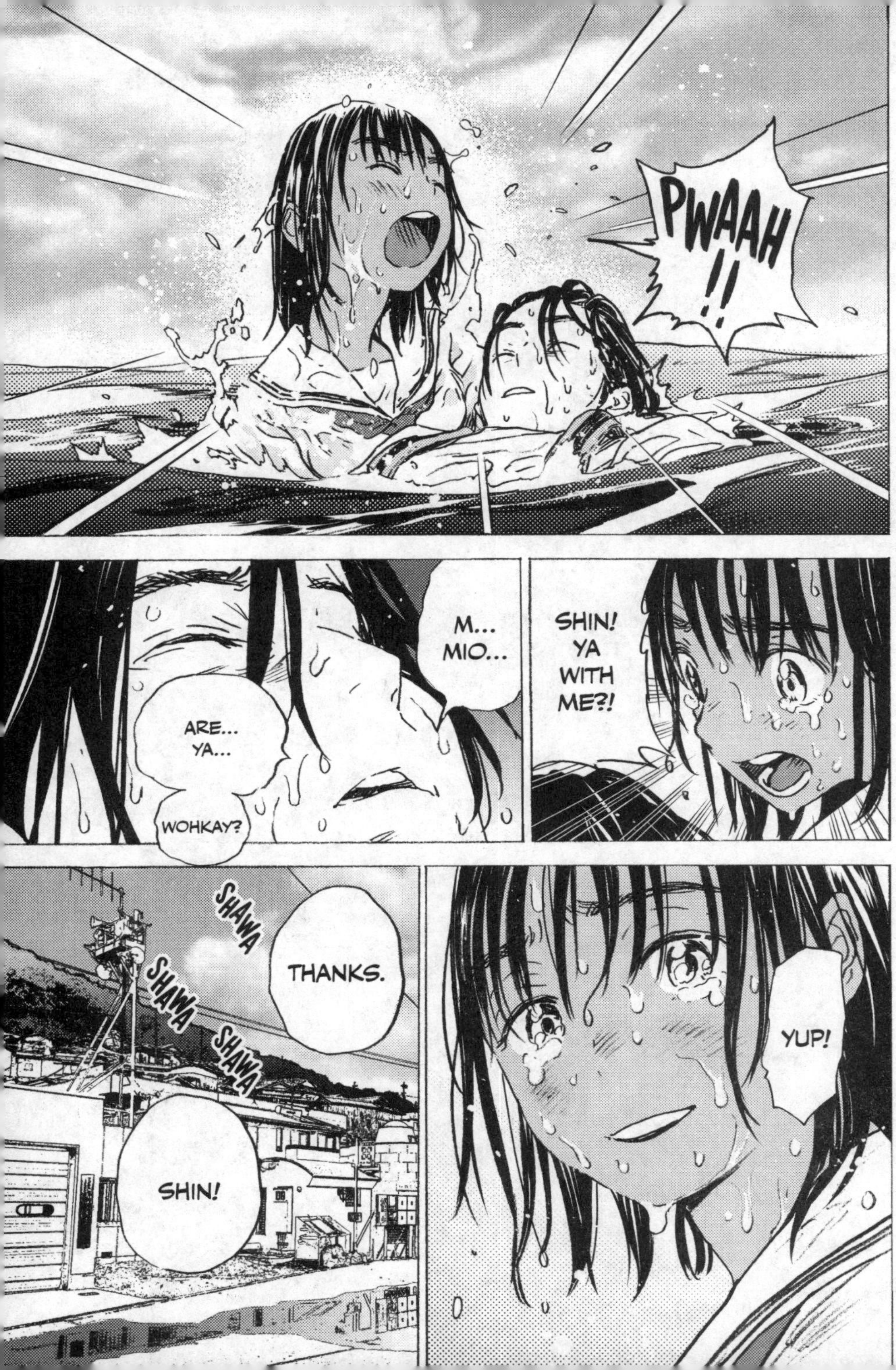
PWAAH!!
SHIN! YA WITH ME?!
M... MIO...
ARE... YA...
WOHKAY?
YUP!
THANKS.
SHAWA
SHAWA
SHAWA
SHIN!

Summertime rendering

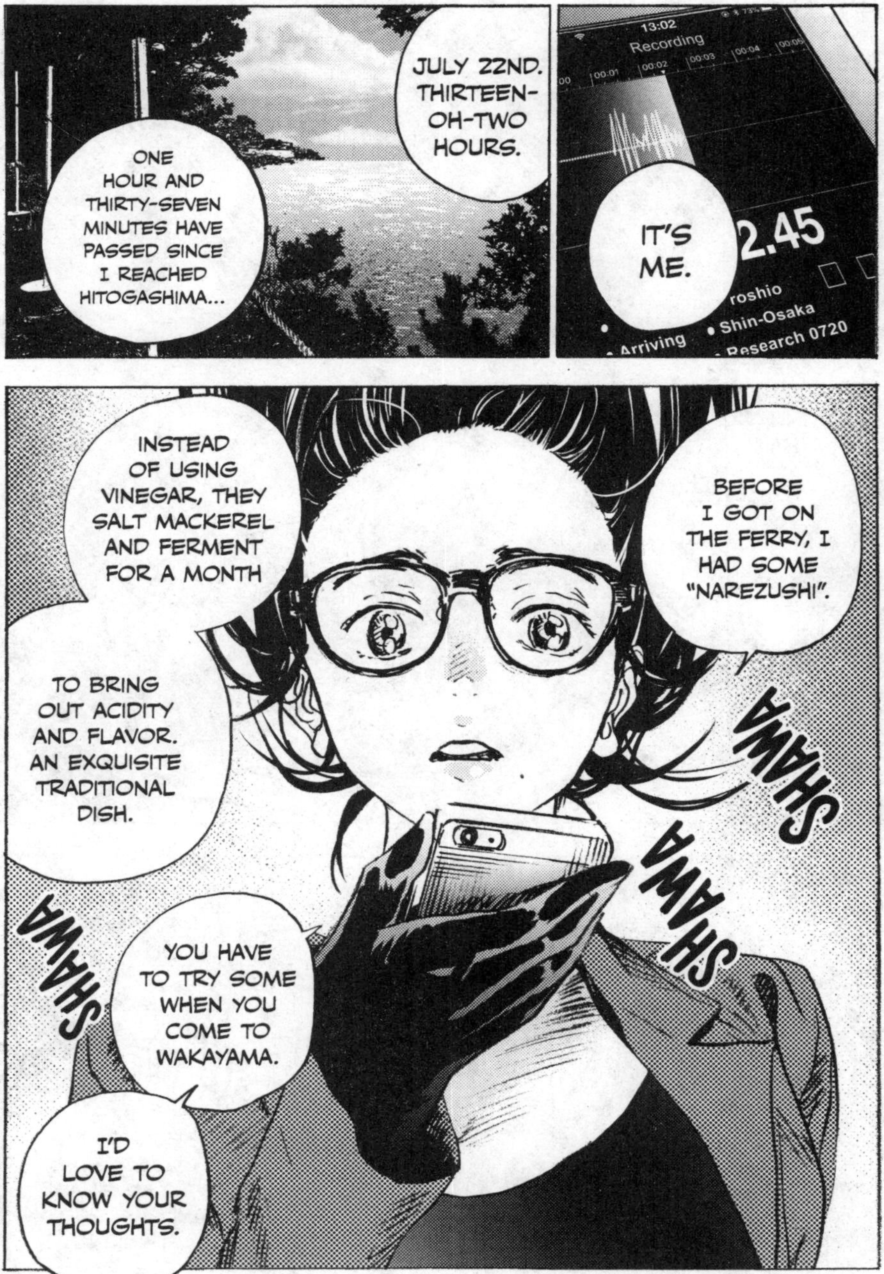
13:02
Recording
IT'S ME.
2.45
roshio
Arriving
Shin-Osaka
Research 0720
JULY 22ND. THIRTEEN-OH-TWO HOURS.
ONE HOUR AND THIRTY-SEVEN MINUTES HAVE PASSED SINCE I REACHED HITOGASHIMA...
BEFORE I GOT ON THE FERRY, I HAD SOME "NAREZUSHI".
SHAWA
SHAWA
INSTEAD OF USING VINEGAR, THEY SALT MACKEREL AND FERMENT FOR A MONTH
TO BRING OUT ACIDITY AND FLAVOR. AN EXQUISITE TRADITIONAL DISH.
SHAWA
YOU HAVE TO TRY SOME WHEN YOU COME TO WAKAYAMA.
I'D LOVE TO KNOW YOUR THOUGHTS.

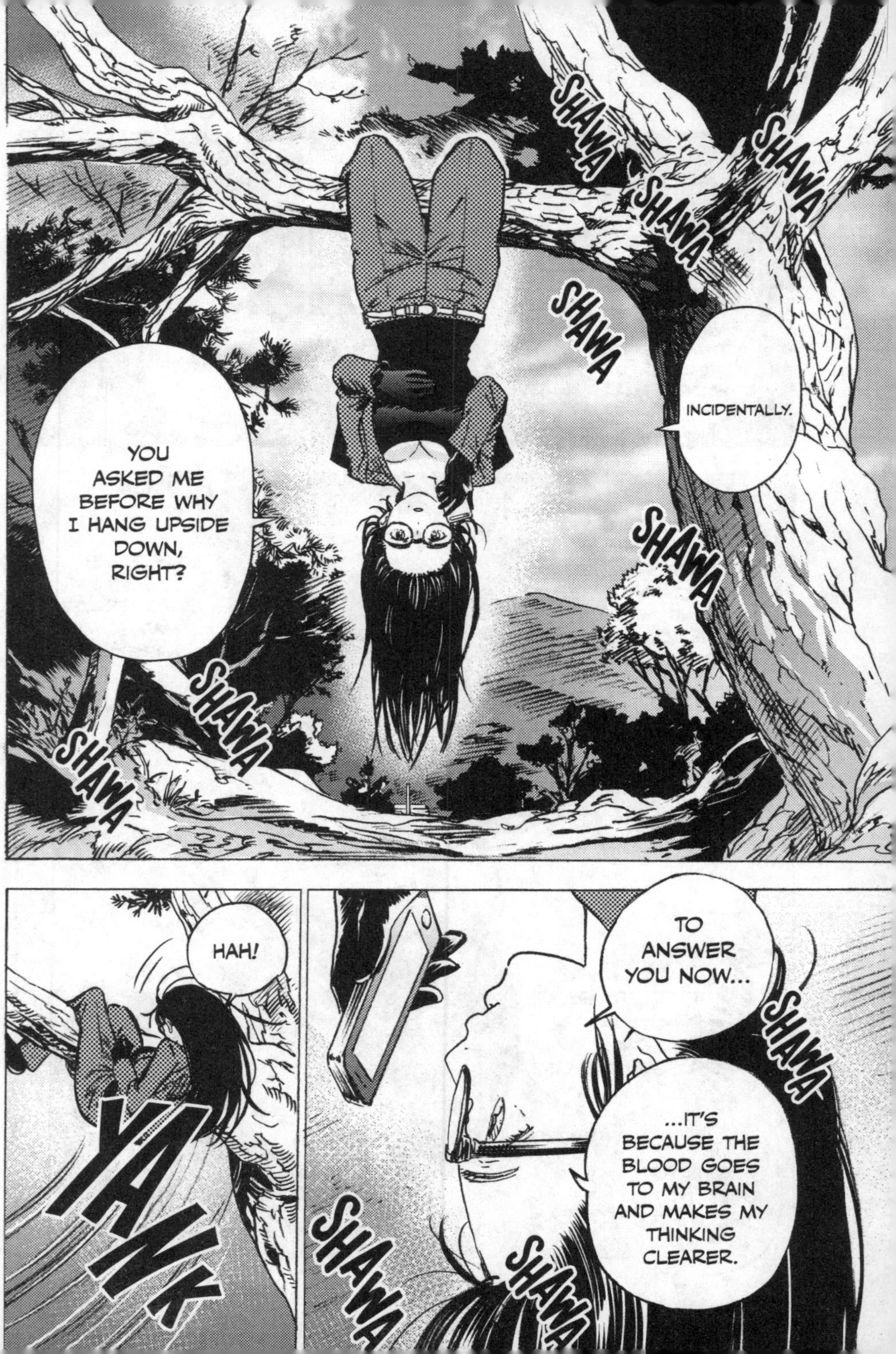
SHAWA
SHAWA
SHAWA
SHAWA
SHAWA
INCIDENTALLY.
SHAWA
YOU ASKED ME BEFORE WHY I HANG UPSIDE DOWN, RIGHT?
SHAWA
SHAWA
TO ANSWER YOU NOW...
SHAWA
...IT'S BECAUSE THE BLOOD GOES TO MY BRAIN AND MAKES MY THINKING CLEARER.
SHAWA
SHAWA
HAH!
YANK

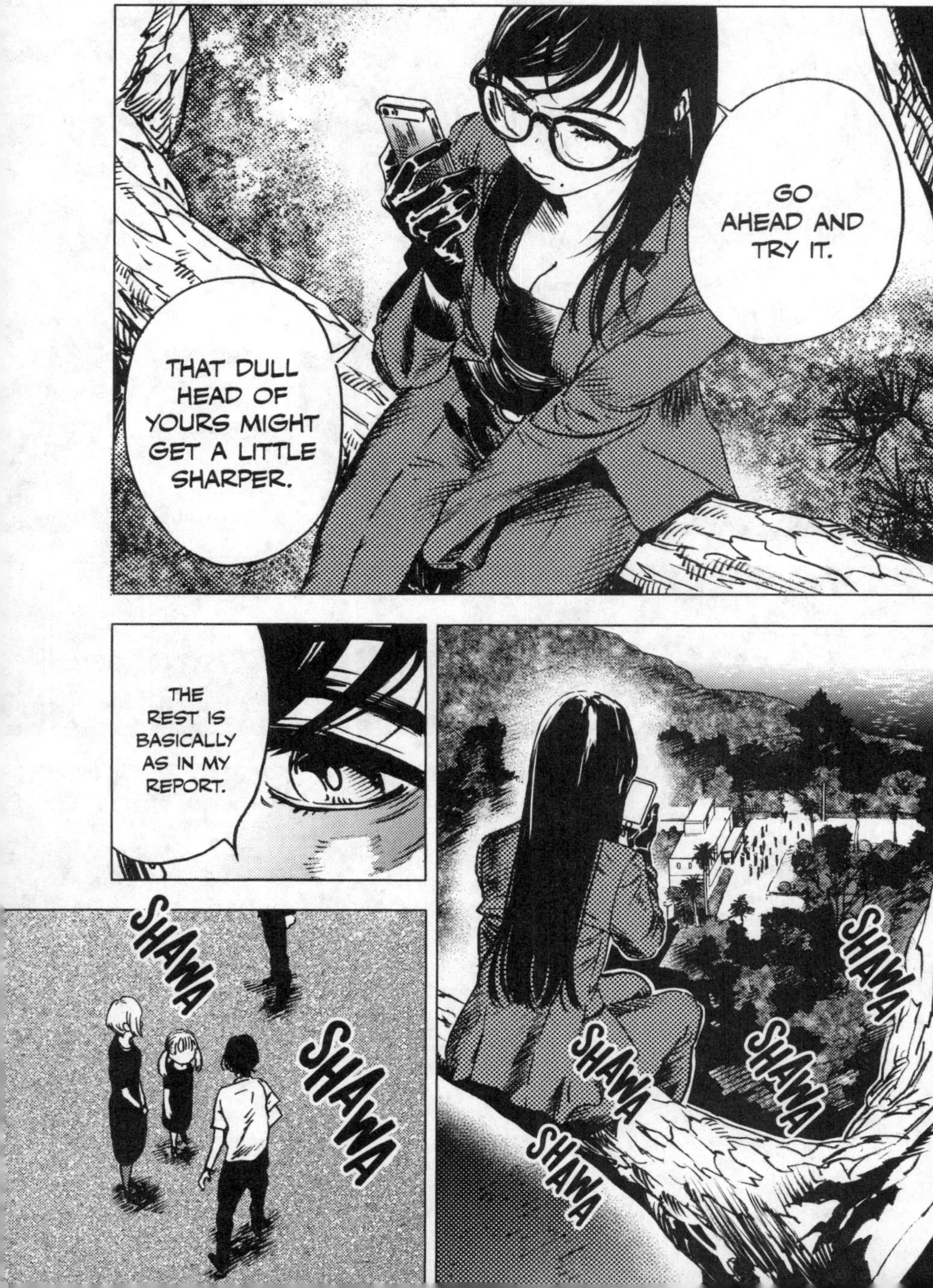
GO AHEAD AND TRY IT.
THAT DULL HEAD OF YOURS MIGHT GET A LITTLE SHARPER.
SHAWA
SHAWA
SHAWA
SHAWA
THE REST IS BASICALLY AS IN MY REPORT.
SHAWA
SHAWA

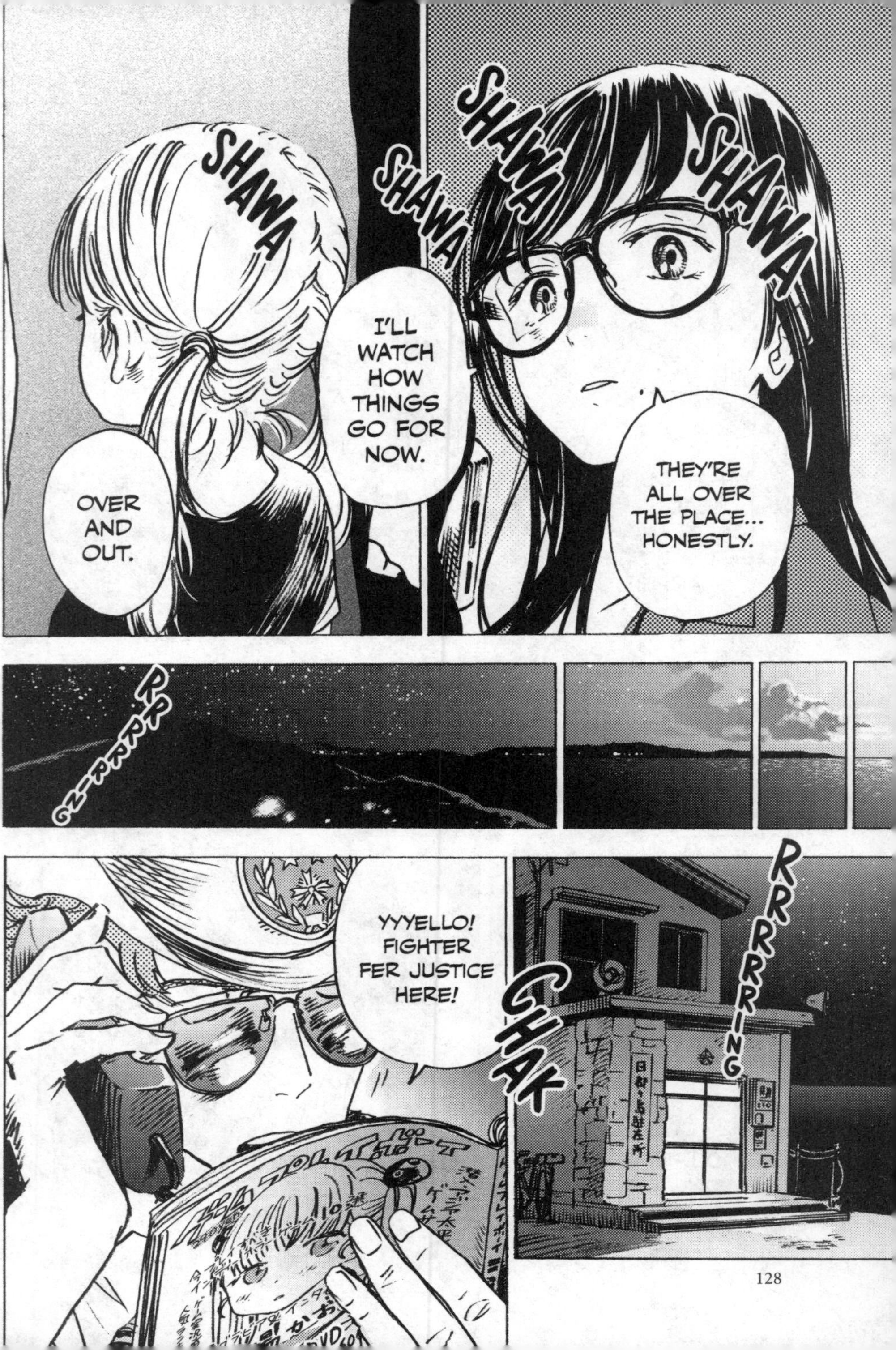
SHAWA
SHAWA
SHAWA
SHAWA
THEY'RE ALL OVER THE PLACE... HONESTLY.
SHAWA
I'LL WATCH HOW THINGS GO FOR NOW.
OVER AND OUT.
GZ-RRRRRRR
RRRRRRING
CHAK
YYYELLO! FIGHTER FER JUSTICE HERE!

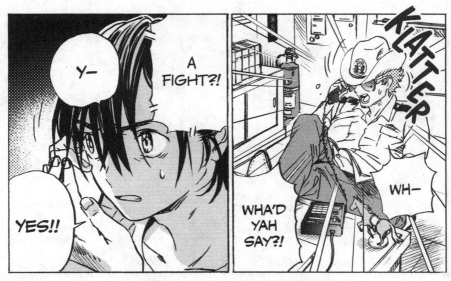

KLATTER
WH–
WHA'D YAH SAY?!
A FIGHT?!
Y–
YES!!
THAT VOICE! SHINPEI! YAH 'KAY?!
OH... UH-HUH.
PEOPLE FROM A BAR...
AT THE SHOPPING STREET... YES.
THANKS!
GET A BIRD'S-EYE VIEW...
WHAT I NEED TO DO...
...IS LIVE THROUGH TODAY.

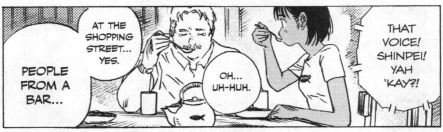

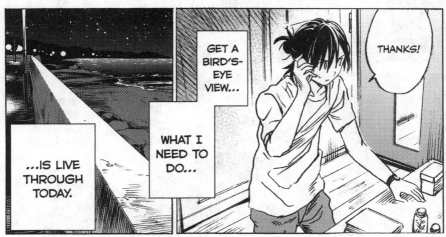

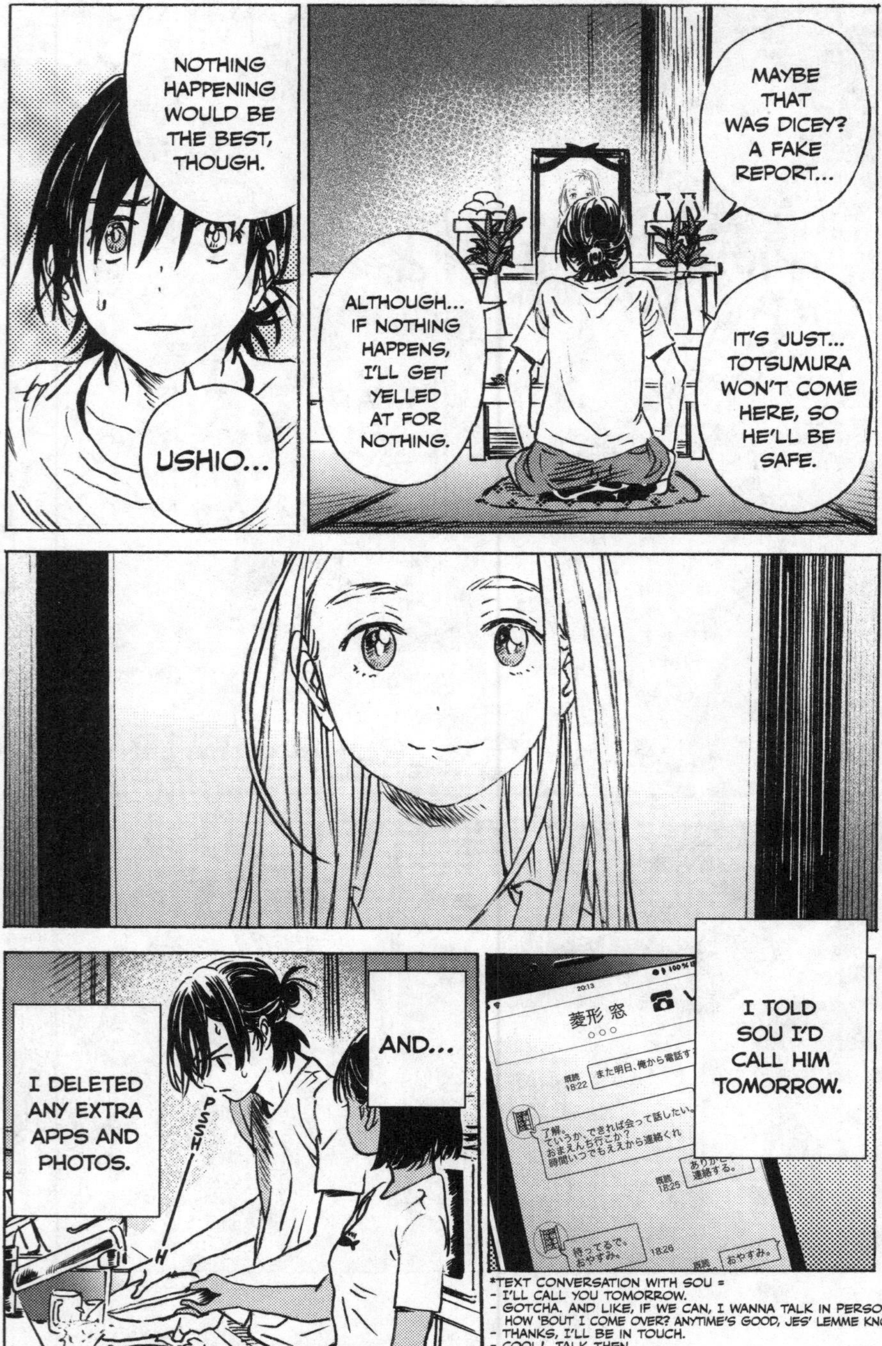
MAYBE THAT WAS DICEY? A FAKE REPORT...
IT'S JUST... TOTSUMURA WON'T COME HERE, SO HE'LL BE SAFE.
ALTHOUGH... IF NOTHING HAPPENS, I'LL GET YELLED AT FOR NOTHING.
NOTHING HAPPENING WOULD BE THE BEST, THOUGH.
USHIO...
I TOLD SOU I'D CALL HIM TOMORROW.
菱形 窓
了解。
ていうか、できれば会って話したい。
おまえんち行こか？
時間いつでもええから連絡くれ
待ってるで。おやすみ。
おやすみ。
AND...
I DELETED ANY EXTRA APPS AND PHOTOS.
PSSHH

*TEXT CONVERSATION WITH SOU =
- I'LL CALL YOU TOMORROW.
- GOTCHA. AND LIKE, IF WE CAN, I WANNA TALK IN PERSON. HOW 'BOUT I COME OVER? ANYTIME'S GOOD, JES' LEMME KNOW.
- THANKS, I'LL BE IN TOUCH.
- COOL! TALK THEN.

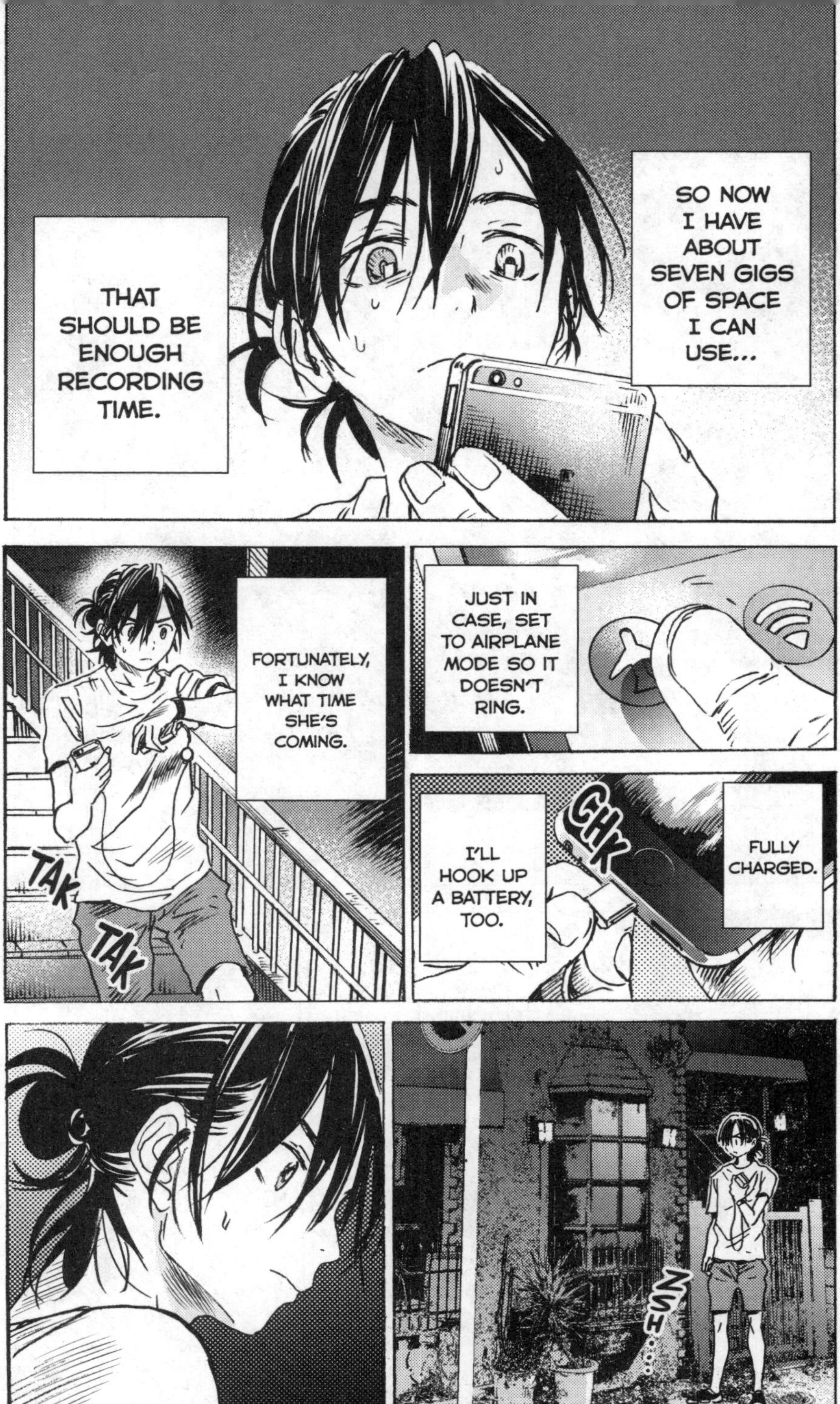
SO NOW I HAVE ABOUT SEVEN GIGS OF SPACE I CAN USE...
THAT SHOULD BE ENOUGH RECORDING TIME.
JUST IN CASE, SET TO AIRPLANE MODE SO IT DOESN'T RING.
FULLY CHARGED.
CHK
I'LL HOOK UP A BATTERY, TOO.
FORTUNATELY, I KNOW WHAT TIME SHE'S COMING.
TAK
TAK
ZSH...

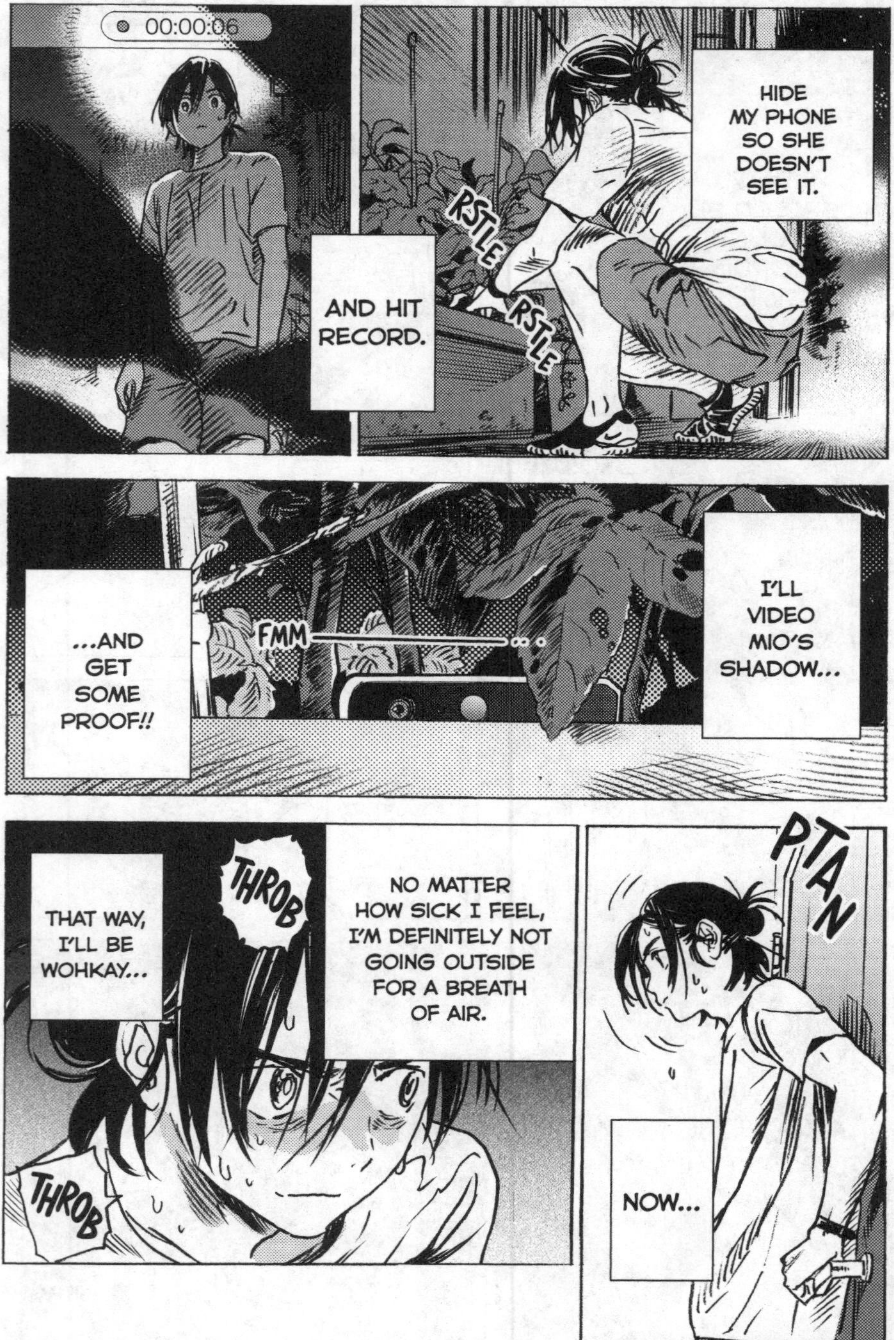
HIDE MY PHONE SO SHE DOESN'T SEE IT.
RSTLE
RSTLE
AND HIT RECORD.
00:00:06
I'LL VIDEO MIO'S SHADOW...
FMM
...AND GET SOME PROOF!!
PTAN
NOW...
NO MATTER HOW SICK I FEEL, I'M DEFINITELY NOT GOING OUTSIDE FOR A BREATH OF AIR.
THROB
THAT WAY, I'LL BE WOHKAY...
THROB

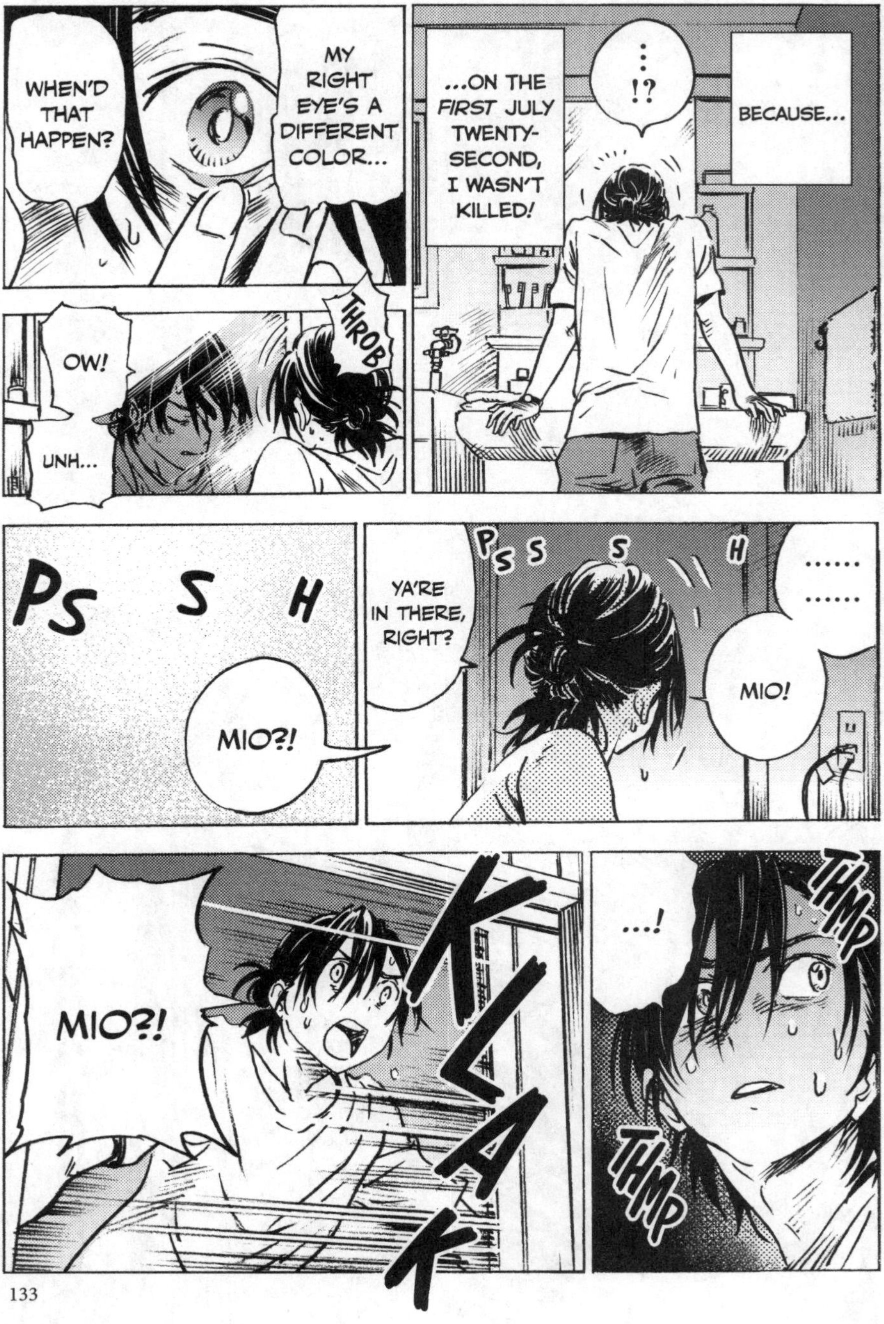
BECAUSE...
...
!?
...ON THE *FIRST* JULY TWENTY-SECOND, I WASN'T KILLED!
MY RIGHT EYE'S A DIFFERENT COLOR...
WHEN'D THAT HAPPEN?
THROB
OW!
UNH...
......
......
MIO!
PSSSH
YA'RE IN THERE, RIGHT?
PS S H
MIO?!
THMP
...!
THMP
KLAK
MIO?!

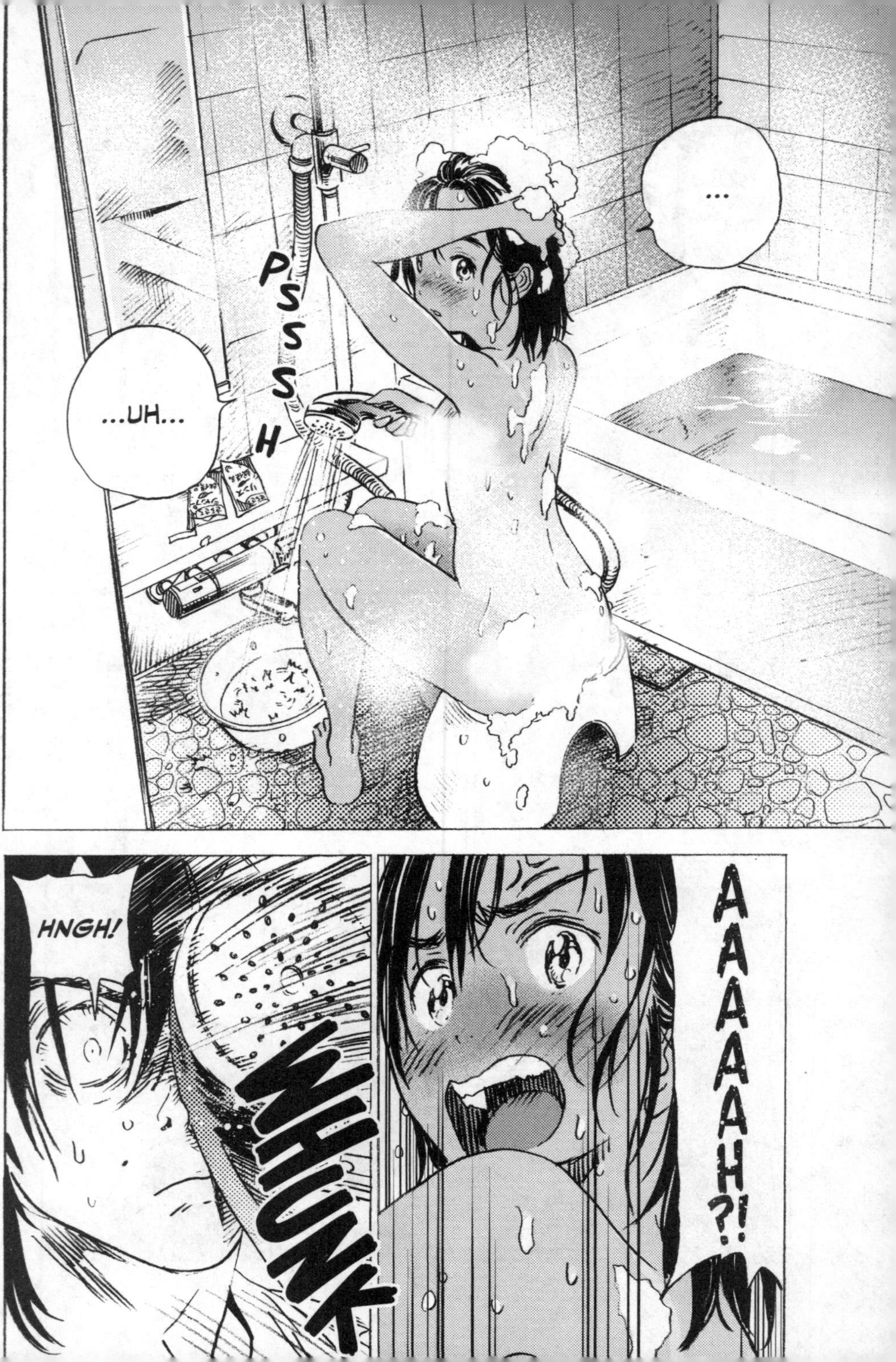
...
PSSSH
...UH...
AAAAAH?!
HNGH!
WHUNK

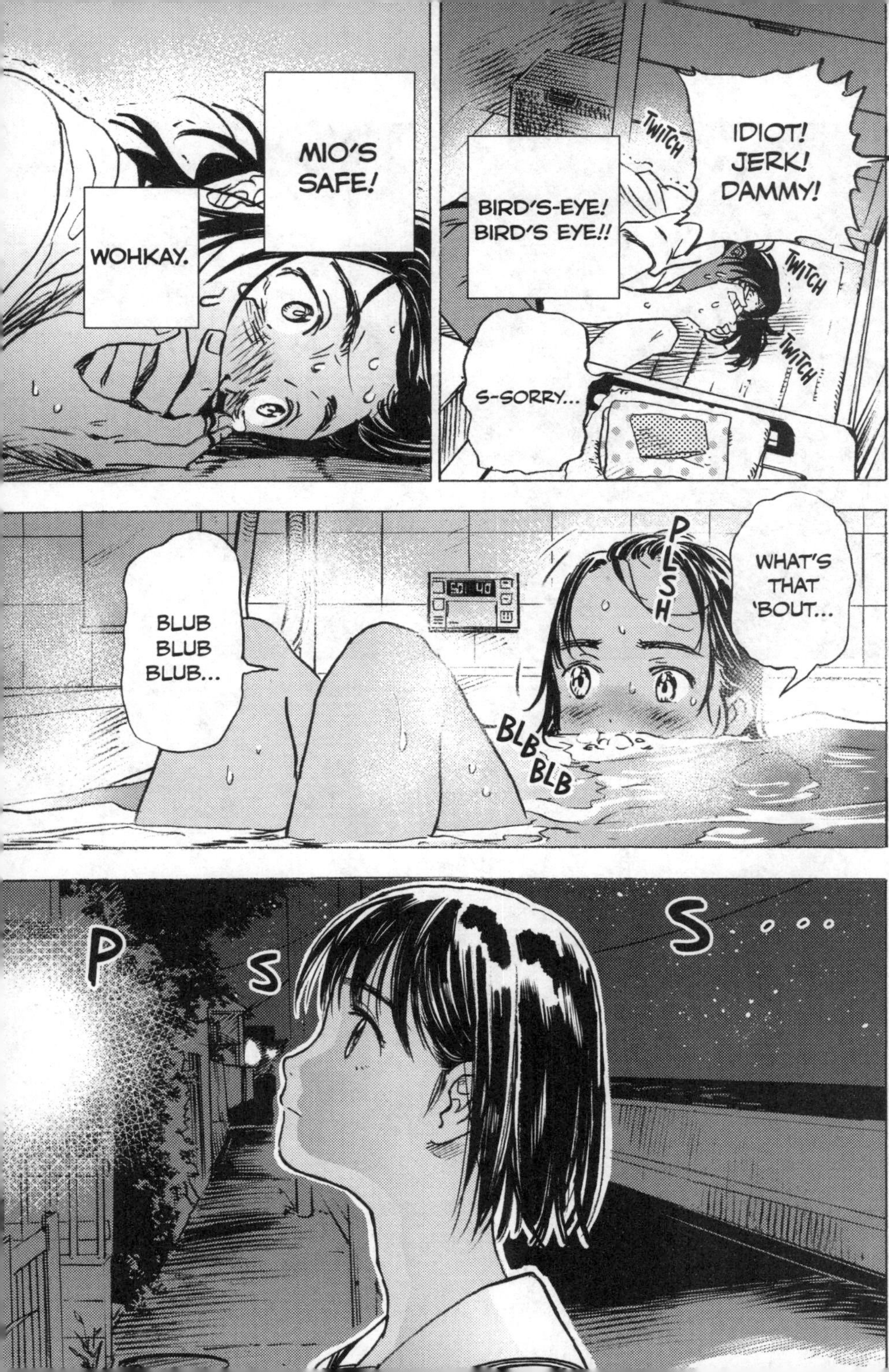

IDIOT! JERK! DAMMY!
TWITCH
TWITCH
TWITCH
BIRD'S-EYE! BIRD'S EYE!!
S-SORRY...
MIO'S SAFE!
WOHKAY.
WHAT'S THAT 'BOUT...
PLSH
BLB BLB
BLUB BLUB BLUB...
P S S...

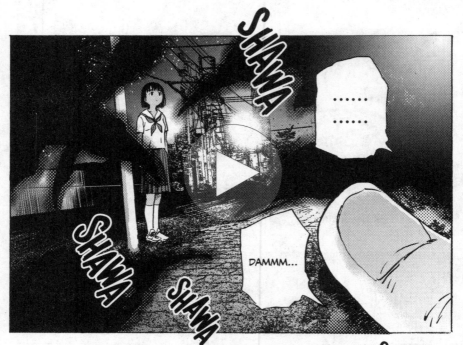

SHAWA

......
......

DAMMM...

SHAWA

SHAWA

KNOCK
KNOCK

GOT HER
PERFECTLY
RIIIIIGHT
THERE.

SHAWA

SHAWA

SHAWA

SHAWA

RE
REE
REE
RE
E.
RE

JULY 23

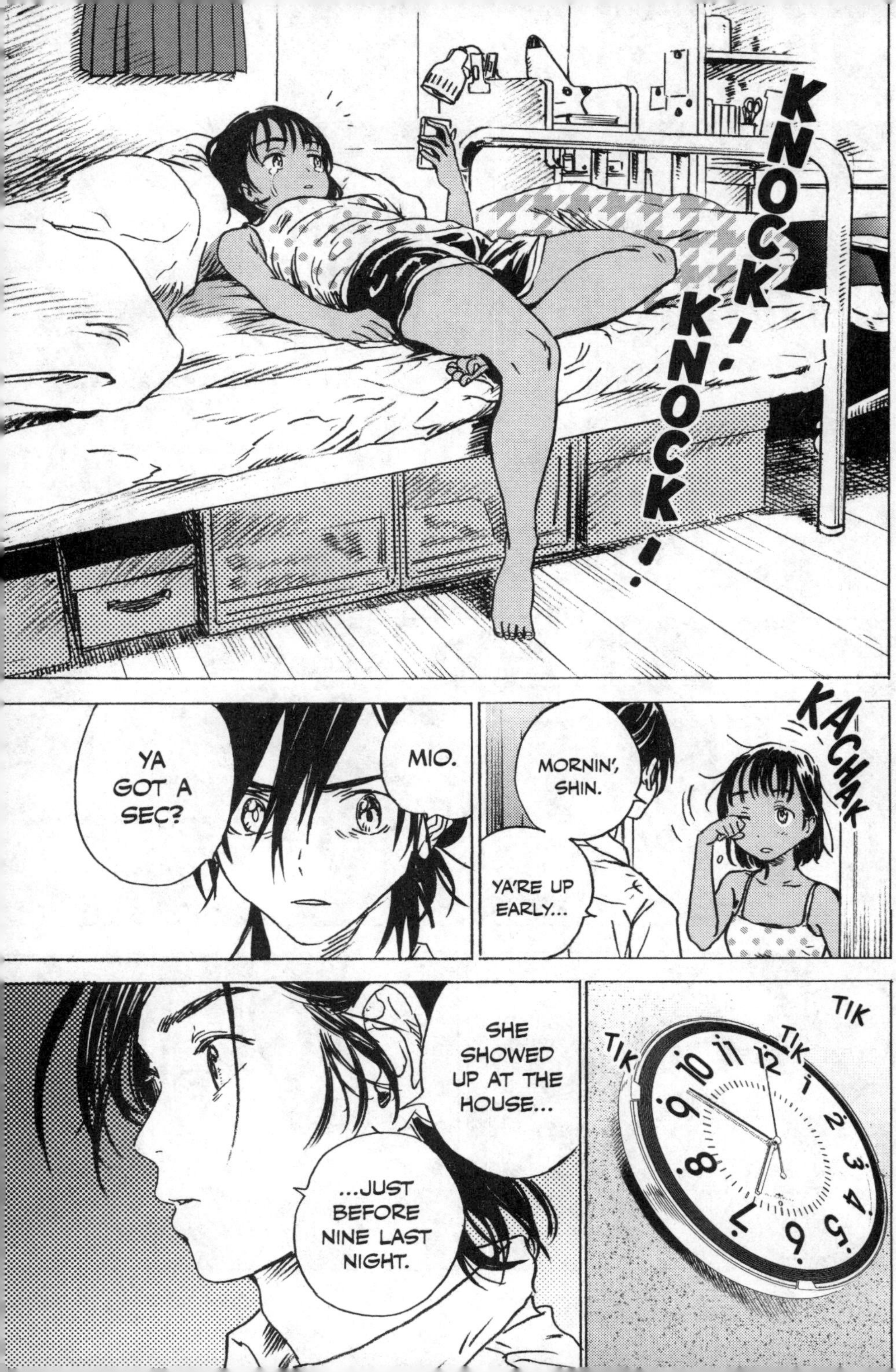
KNOCK!
KNOCK!
KACHAK
MORNIN', SHIN.
YA'RE UP EARLY...
MIO.
YA GOT A SEC?
TIK
TIK
TIK
SHE SHOWED UP AT THE HOUSE...
...JUST BEFORE NINE LAST NIGHT.

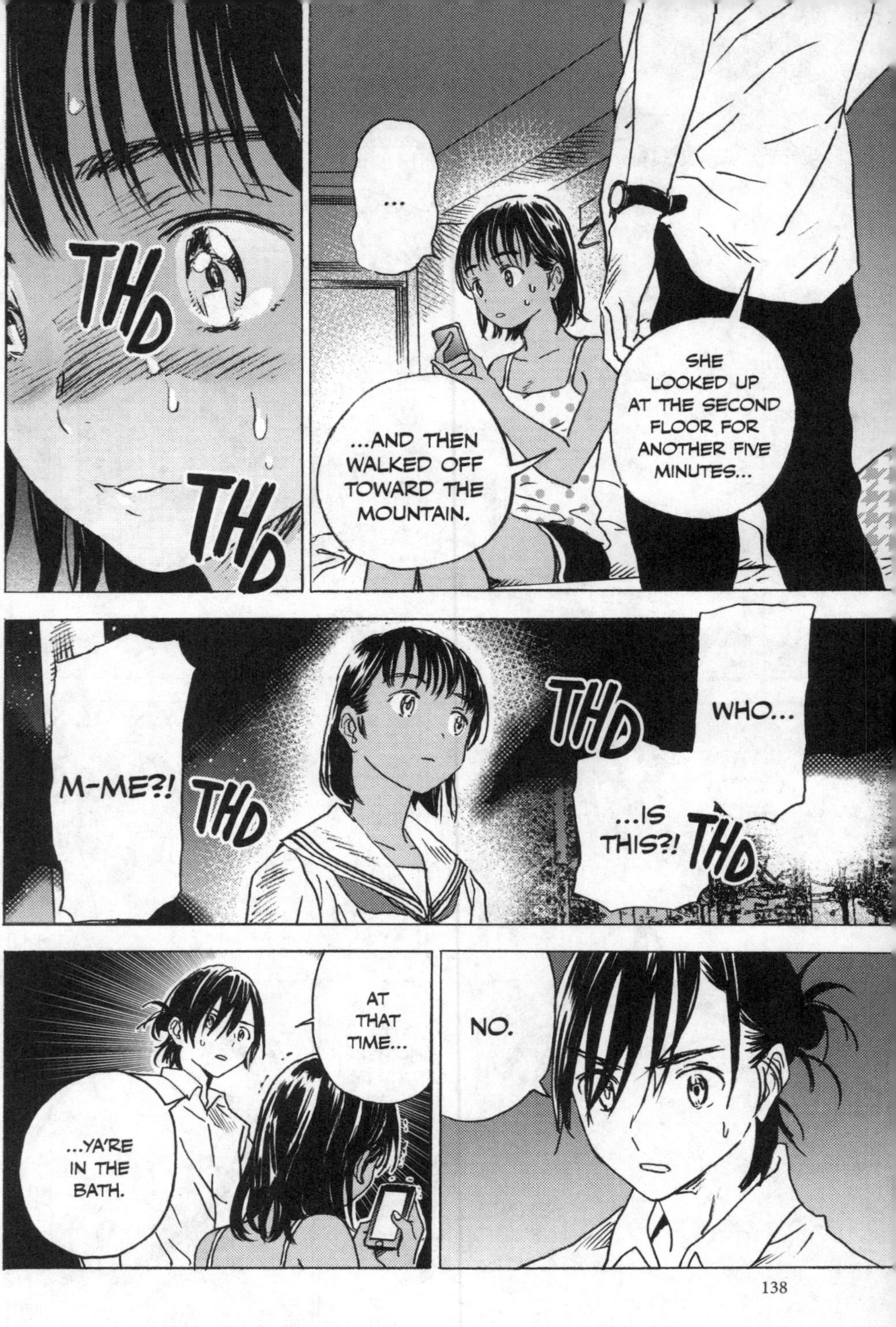
SHE LOOKED UP AT THE SECOND FLOOR FOR ANOTHER FIVE MINUTES...
...AND THEN WALKED OFF TOWARD THE MOUNTAIN.
...
THD
THD
WHO...
THD
...IS THIS?!
THD
THD
M-ME?!
NO.
AT THAT TIME...
...YA'RE IN THE BATH.

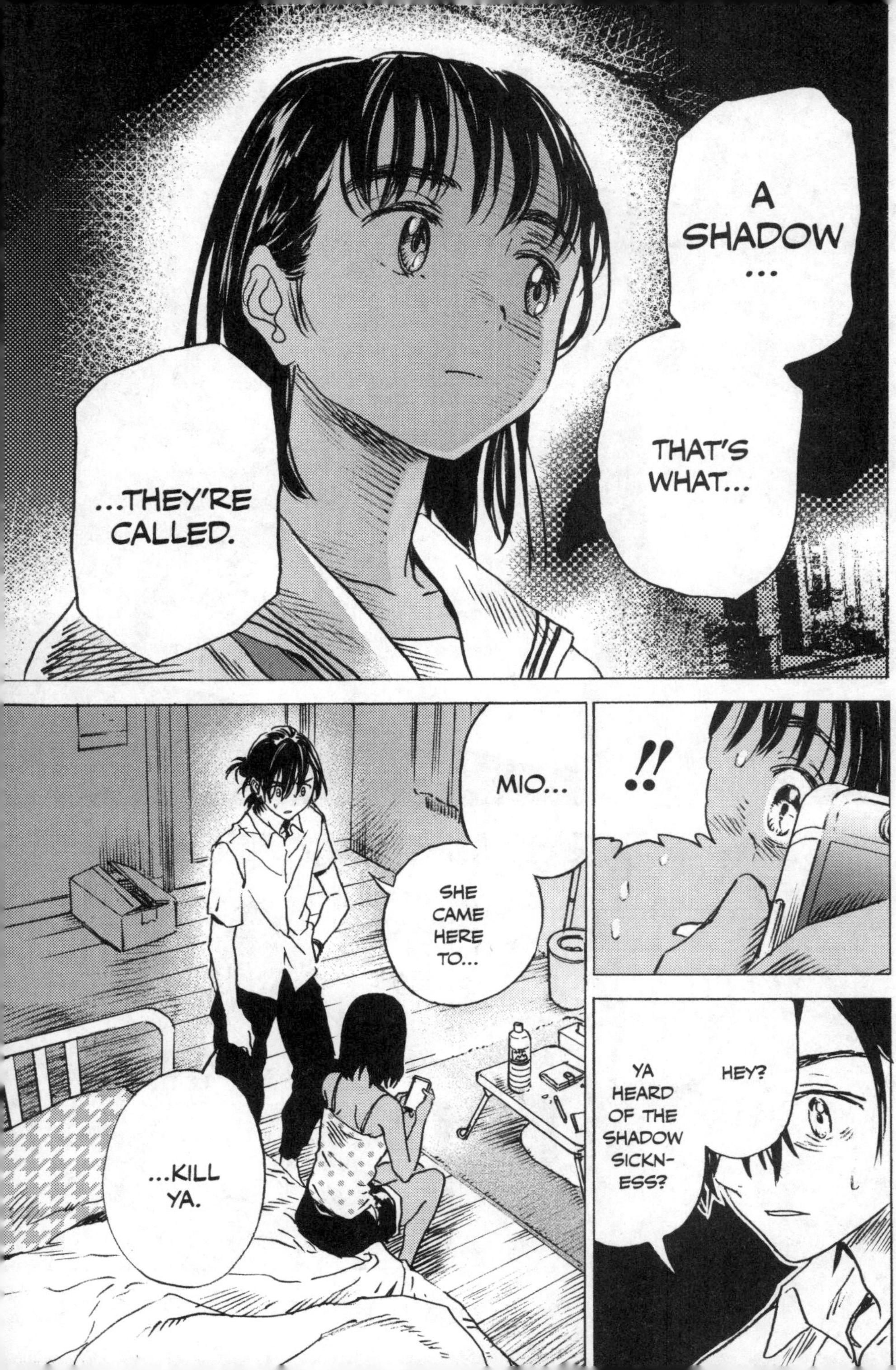
A SHADOW ...
THAT'S WHAT...
...THEY'RE CALLED.
!!
HEY?
YA HEARD OF THE SHADOW SICKN-ESS?
MIO...
SHE CAME HERE TO...
...KILL YA.

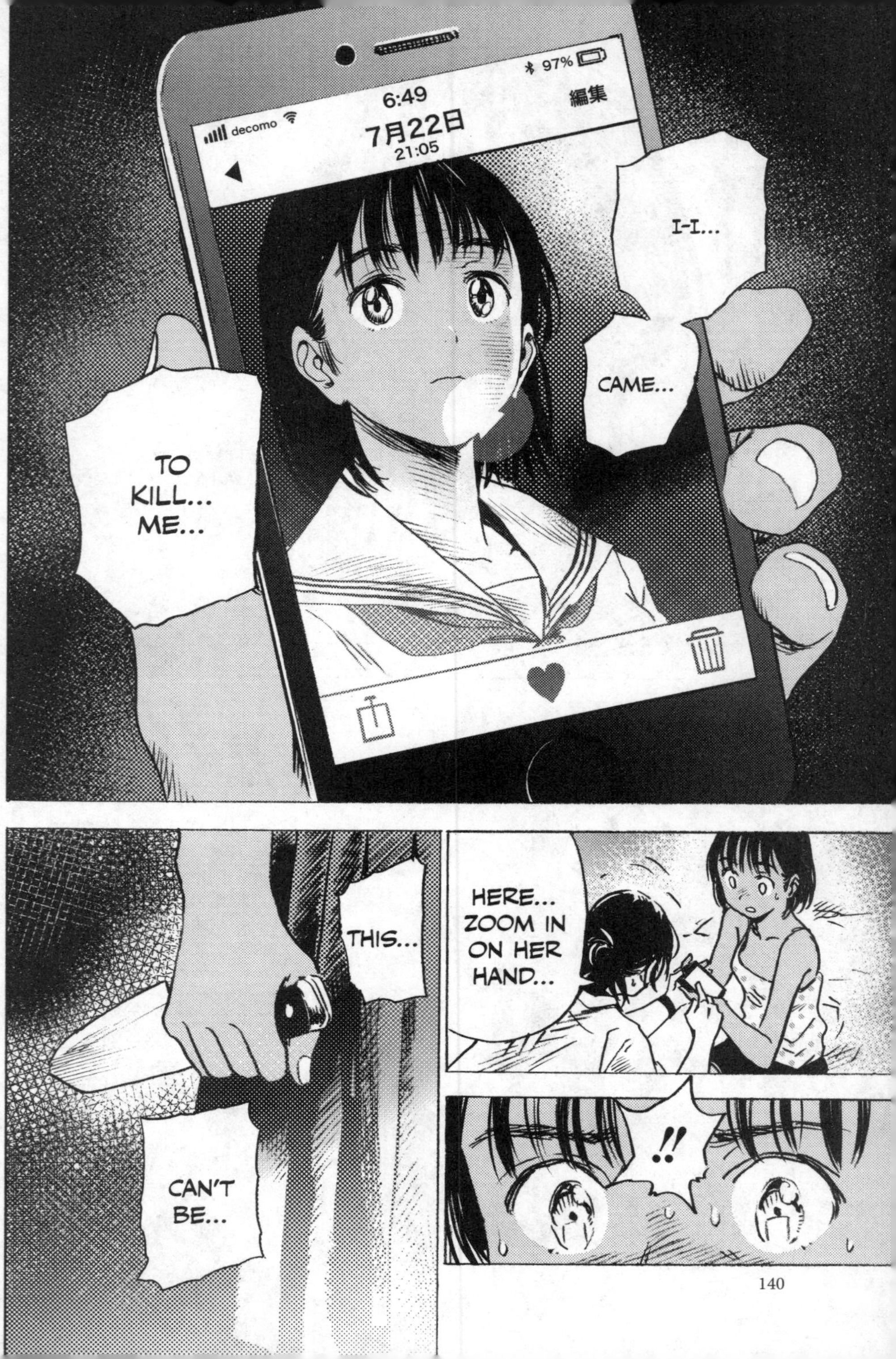
6:49
7月22日
21:05
編集
decomo
97%
I-I...
CAME...
TO KILL... ME...
HERE... ZOOM IN ON HER HAND...
!!
THIS...
CAN'T BE...

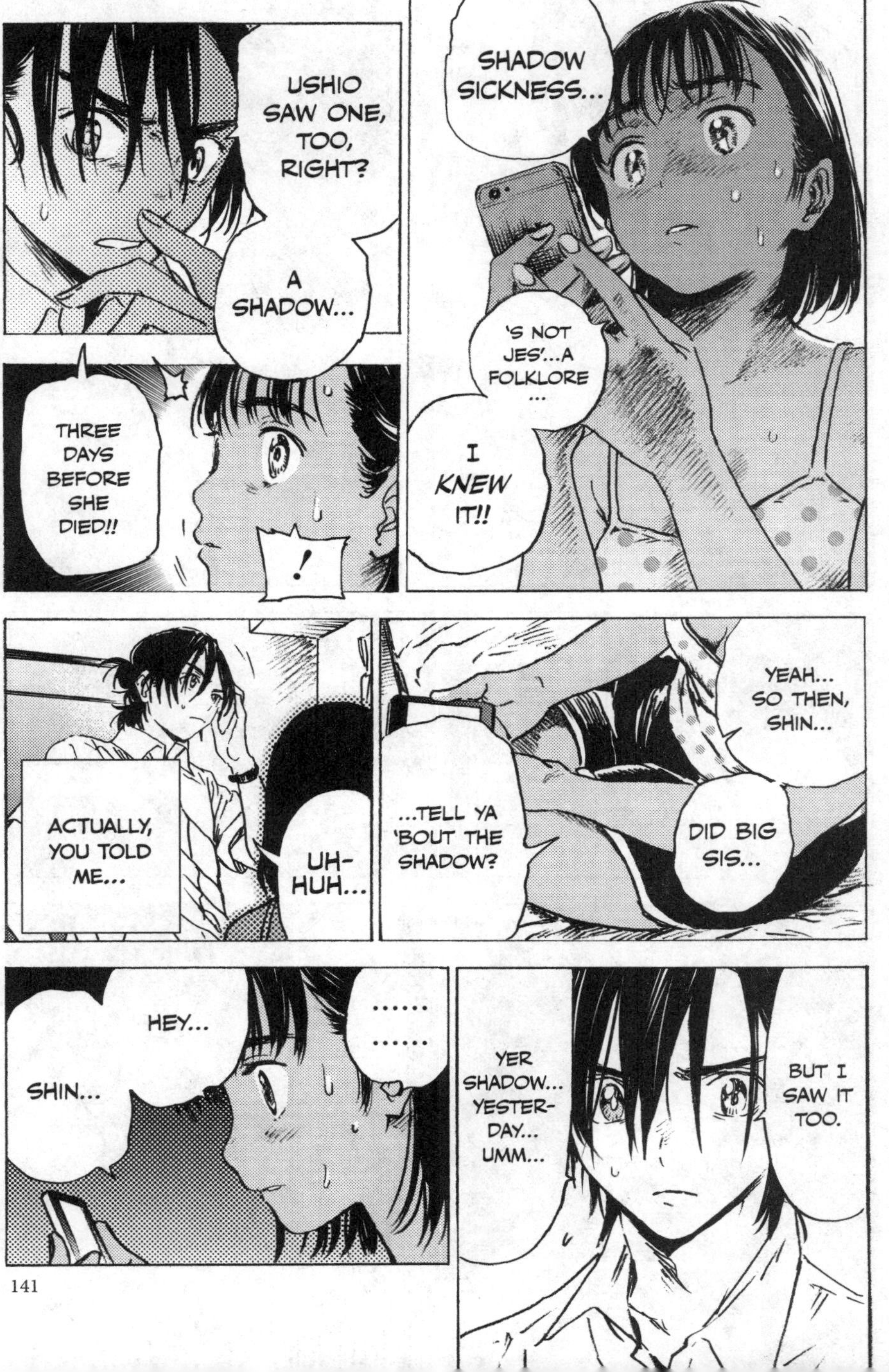
SHADOW SICKNESS...
'S NOT JES'...A FOLKLORE ...
I *KNEW* IT!!
USHIO SAW ONE, TOO, RIGHT?
A SHADOW...
THREE DAYS BEFORE SHE DIED!!
!
YEAH... SO THEN, SHIN...
DID BIG SIS...
...TELL YA 'BOUT THE SHADOW?
UH-HUH...
ACTUALLY, YOU TOLD ME...
BUT I SAW IT TOO.
YER SHADOW... YESTER-DAY... UMM...
......
......
HEY...
SHIN...

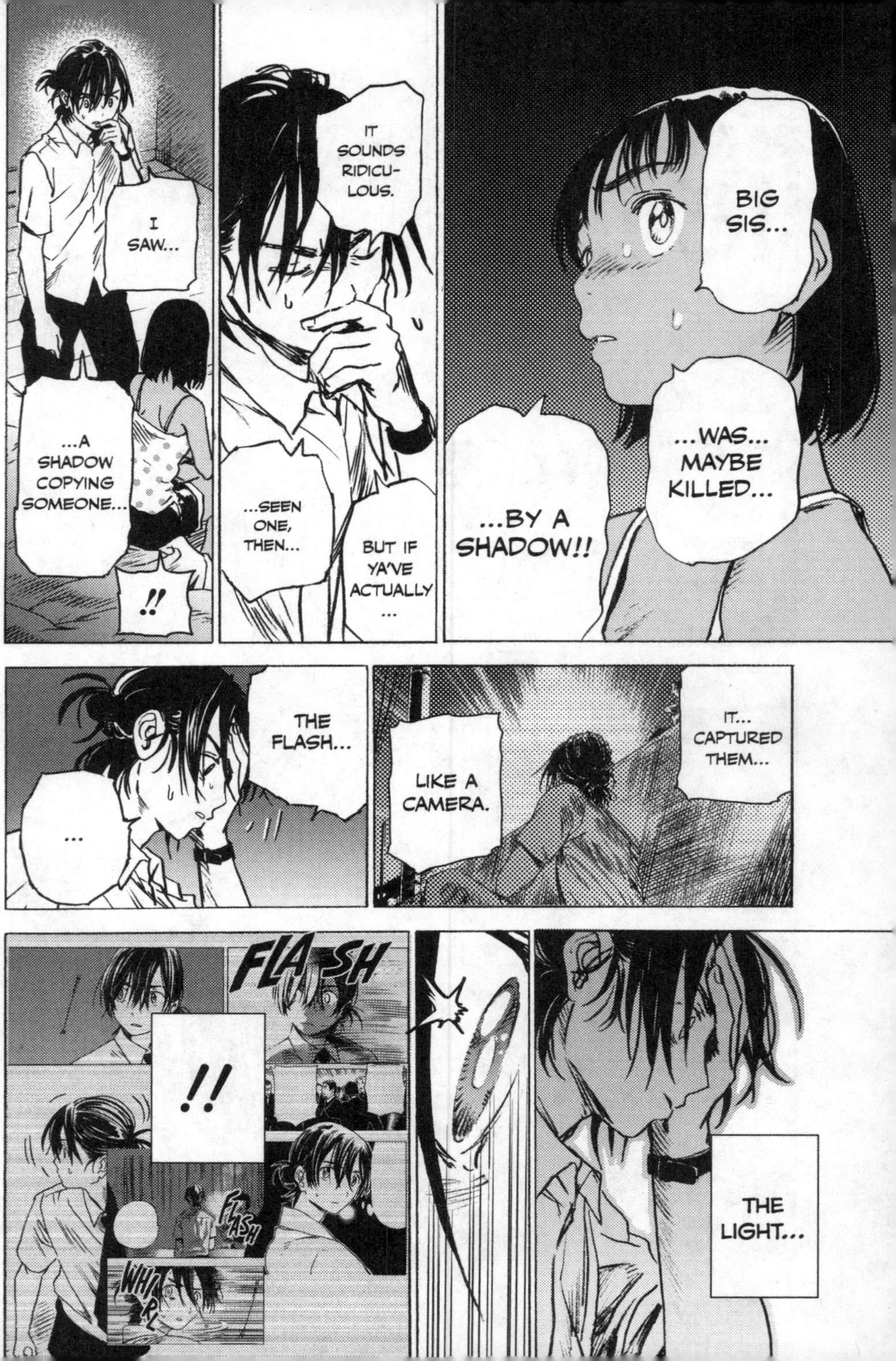
BIG SIS...
...WAS... MAYBE KILLED...
...BY A SHADOW!!
IT SOUNDS RIDICU-LOUS.
BUT IF YA'VE ACTUALLY ...
...SEEN ONE, THEN...
I SAW...
...A SHADOW COPYING SOMEONE...
!!
IT... CAPTURED THEM...
LIKE A CAMERA.
THE FLASH...
...
THE LIGHT...
FLASH
!!
FLASH
WHIRL

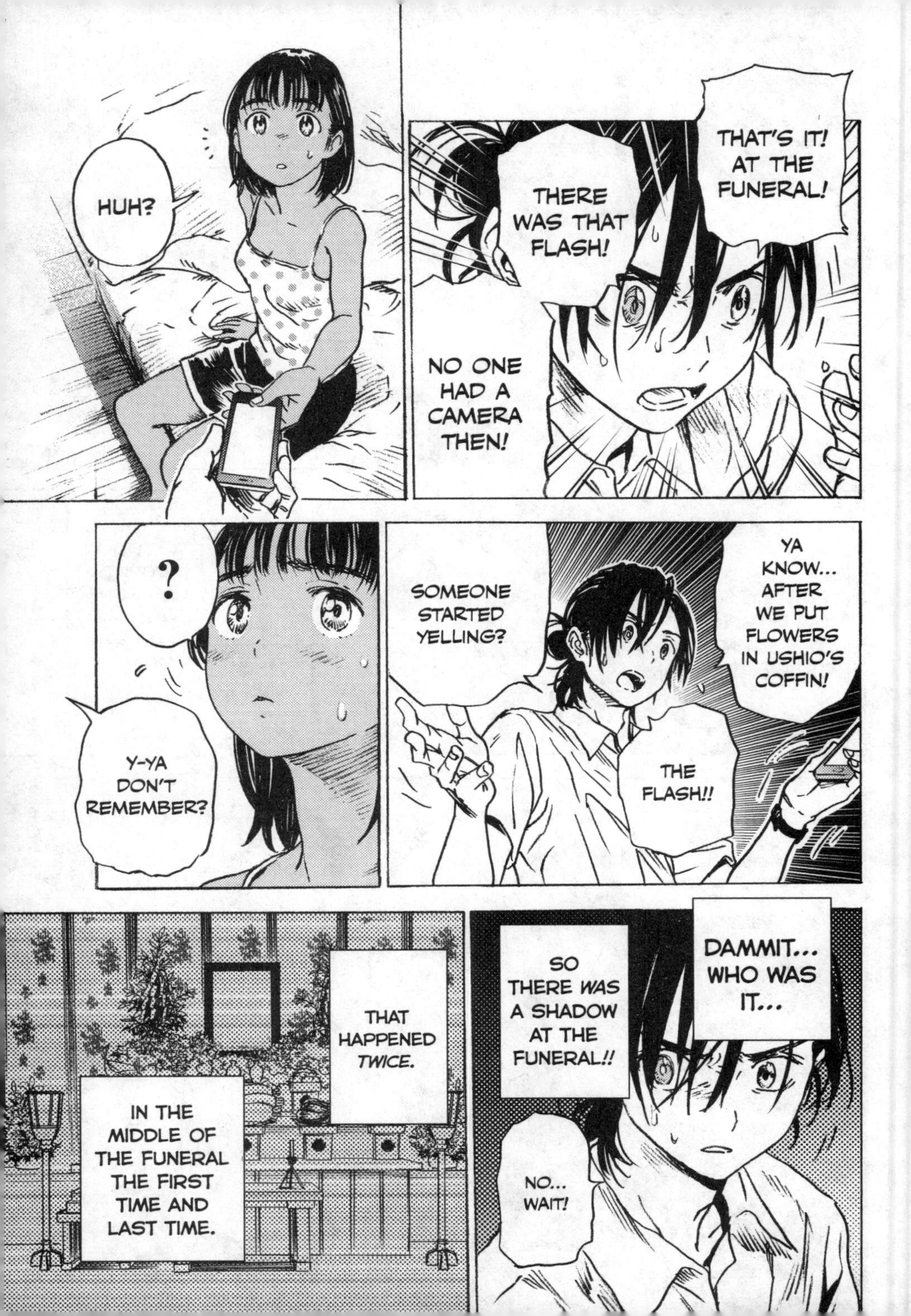
THAT'S IT! AT THE FUNERAL!
THERE WAS THAT FLASH!
NO ONE HAD A CAMERA THEN!
HUH?
YA KNOW... AFTER WE PUT FLOWERS IN USHIO'S COFFIN!
SOMEONE STARTED YELLING?
THE FLASH!!
?
Y-YA DON'T REMEMBER?
DAMMIT... WHO WAS IT...
SO THERE *WAS* A SHADOW AT THE FUNERAL!!
NO... WAIT!
THAT HAPPENED *TWICE*.
IN THE MIDDLE OF THE FUNERAL THE FIRST TIME AND LAST TIME.

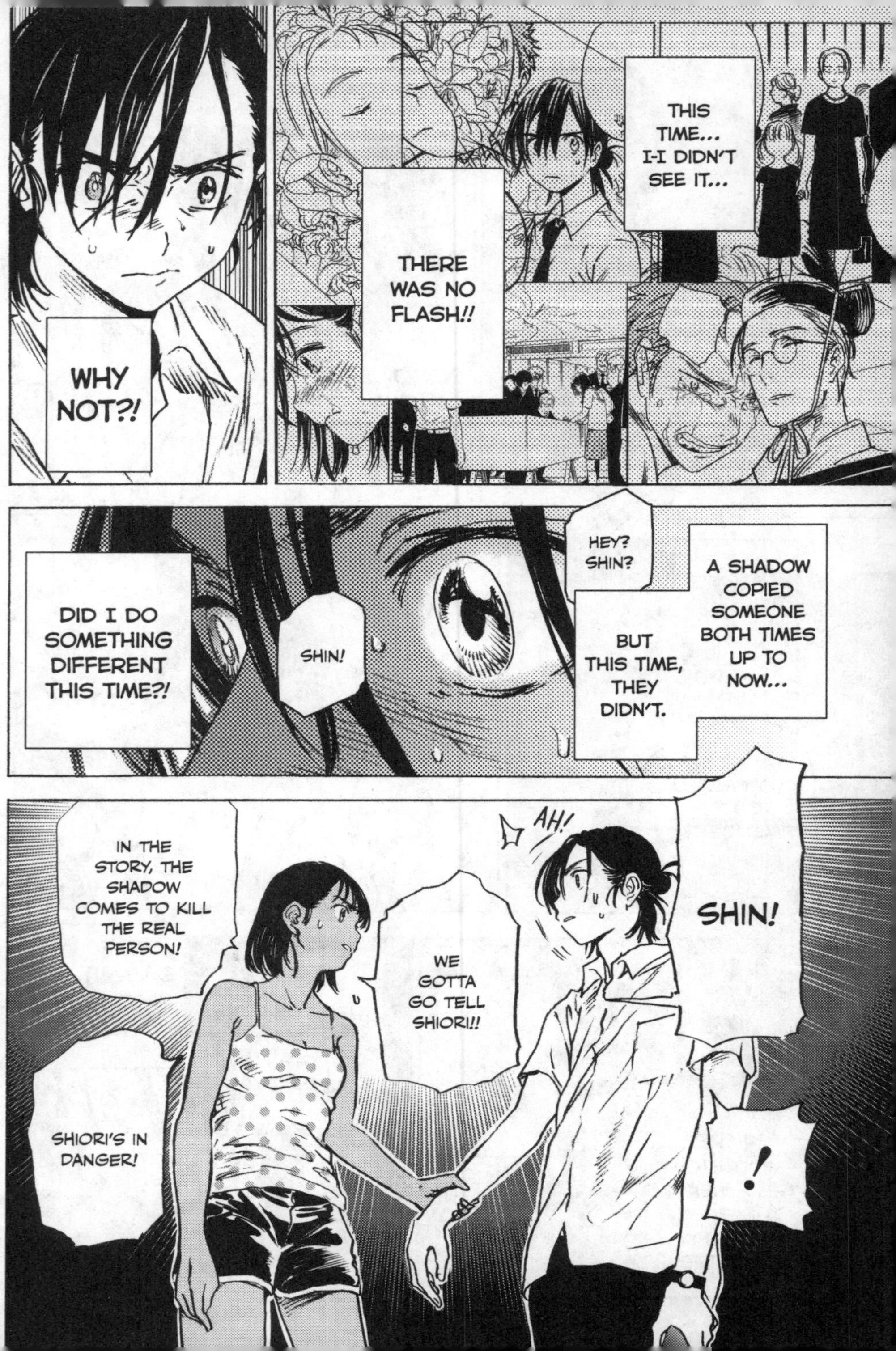

THIS TIME... I-I DIDN'T SEE IT...
THERE WAS NO FLASH!!
WHY NOT?!
A SHADOW COPIED SOMEONE BOTH TIMES UP TO NOW...
BUT THIS TIME, THEY DIDN'T.
HEY? SHIN?
SHIN!
DID I DO SOMETHING DIFFERENT THIS TIME?!
SHIN!
AH!
!
WE GOTTA GO TELL SHIORI!!
IN THE STORY, THE SHADOW COMES TO KILL THE REAL PERSON!
SHIORI'S IN DANGER!

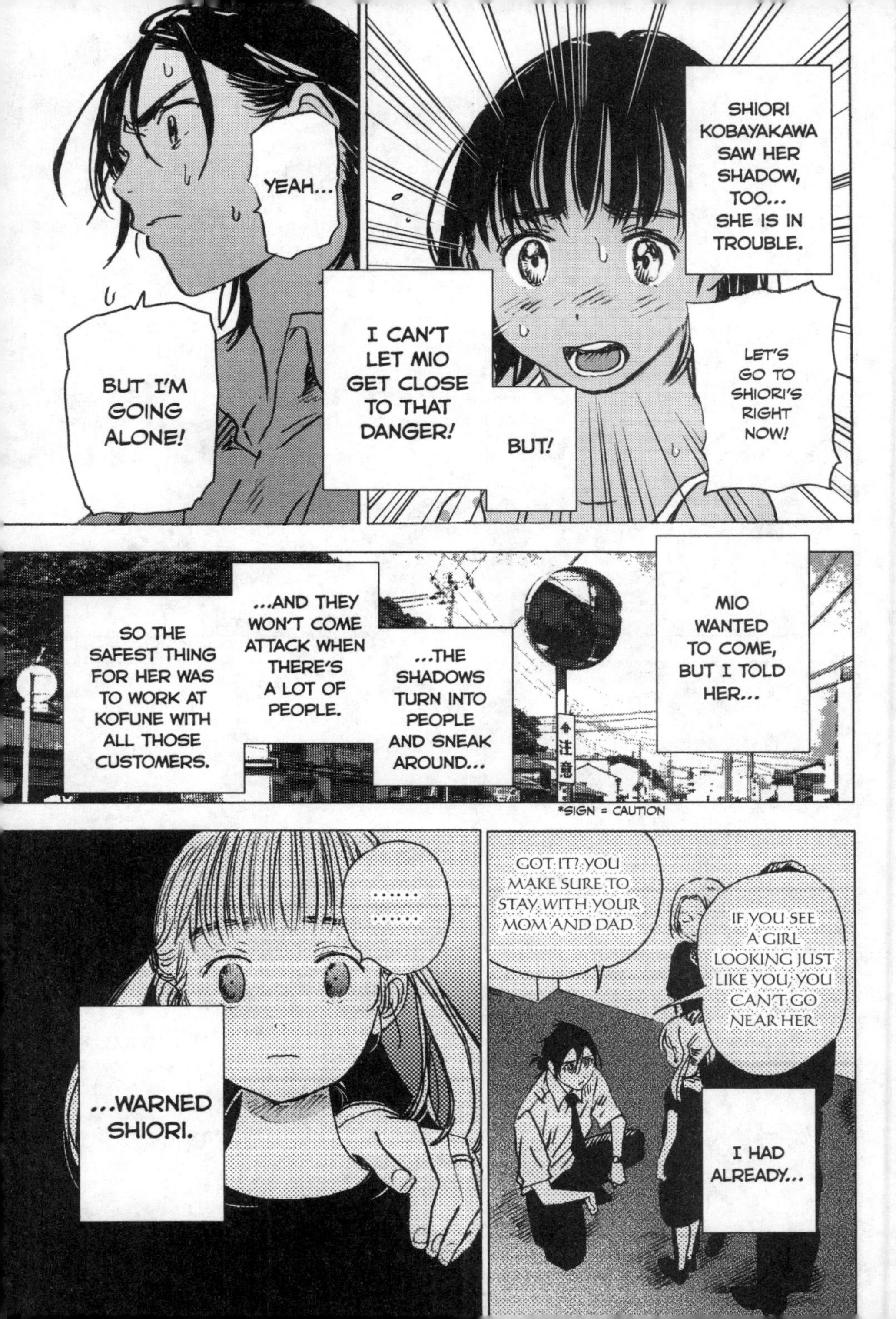
SHIORI KOBAYAKAWA SAW HER SHADOW, TOO... SHE IS IN TROUBLE.
LET'S GO TO SHIORI'S RIGHT NOW!
BUT!
I CAN'T LET MIO GET CLOSE TO THAT DANGER!
YEAH...
BUT I'M GOING ALONE!
MIO WANTED TO COME, BUT I TOLD HER...
...THE SHADOWS TURN INTO PEOPLE AND SNEAK AROUND...
...AND THEY WON'T COME ATTACK WHEN THERE'S A LOT OF PEOPLE.
SO THE SAFEST THING FOR HER WAS TO WORK AT KOFUNE WITH ALL THOSE CUSTOMERS.
注意
*SIGN = CAUTION
IF YOU SEE A GIRL LOOKING JUST LIKE YOU, YOU CAN'T GO NEAR HER.
GOT IT? YOU MAKE SURE TO STAY WITH YOUR MOM AND DAD.
I HAD ALREADY...
......
...WARNED SHIORI.

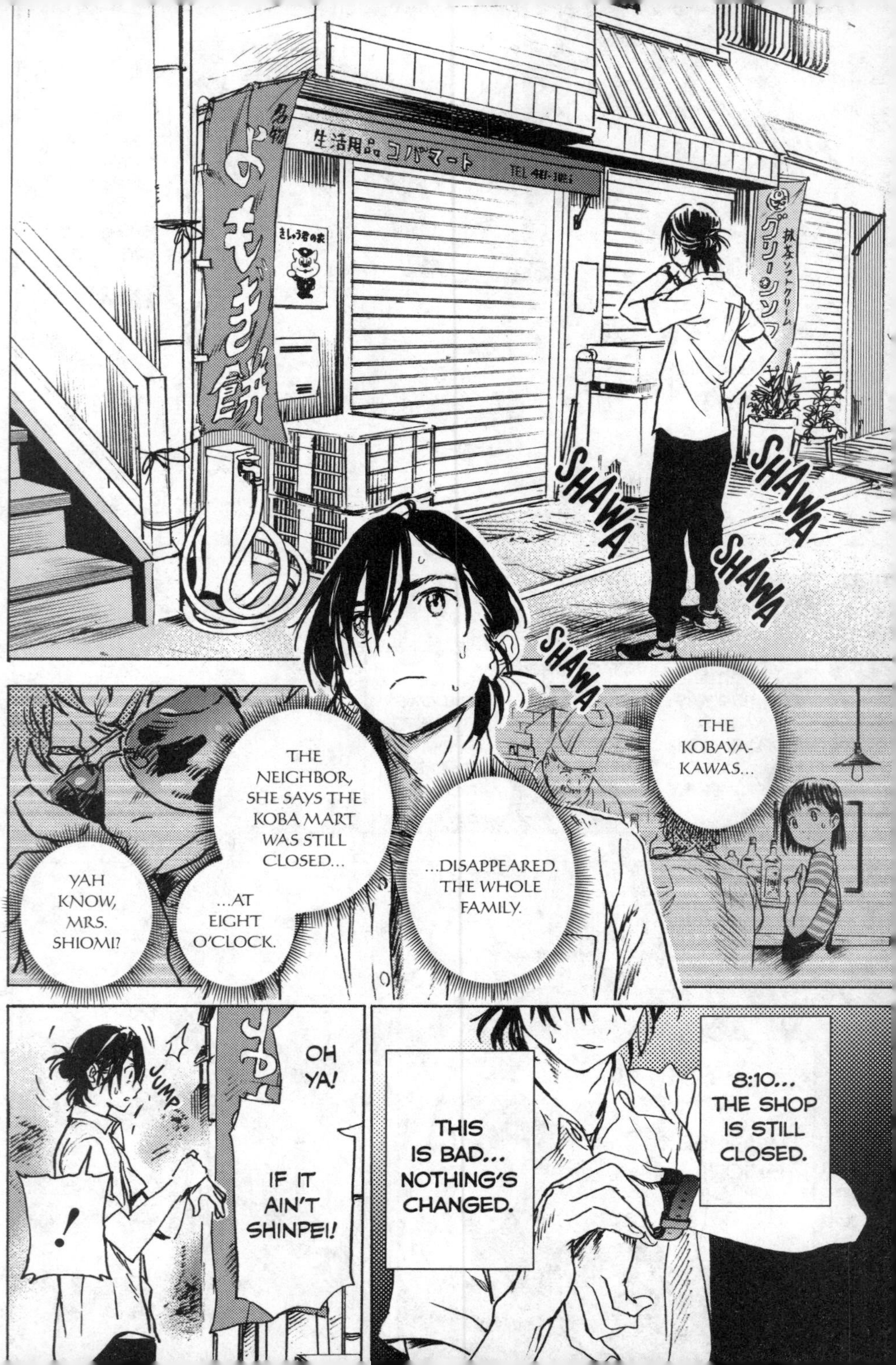

生活用品 コバマート
よもぎ餅
SHAWA SHAWA SHAWA SHAWA SHAWA
THE KOBAYA-KAWAS...
...DISAPPEARED. THE WHOLE FAMILY.
THE NEIGHBOR, SHE SAYS THE KOBA MART WAS STILL CLOSED...
...AT EIGHT O'CLOCK.
YAH KNOW, MRS. SHIOMI?
8:10... THE SHOP IS STILL CLOSED.
THIS IS BAD... NOTHING'S CHANGED.
OH YA!
IF IT AIN'T SHINPEI!
JUMP
!

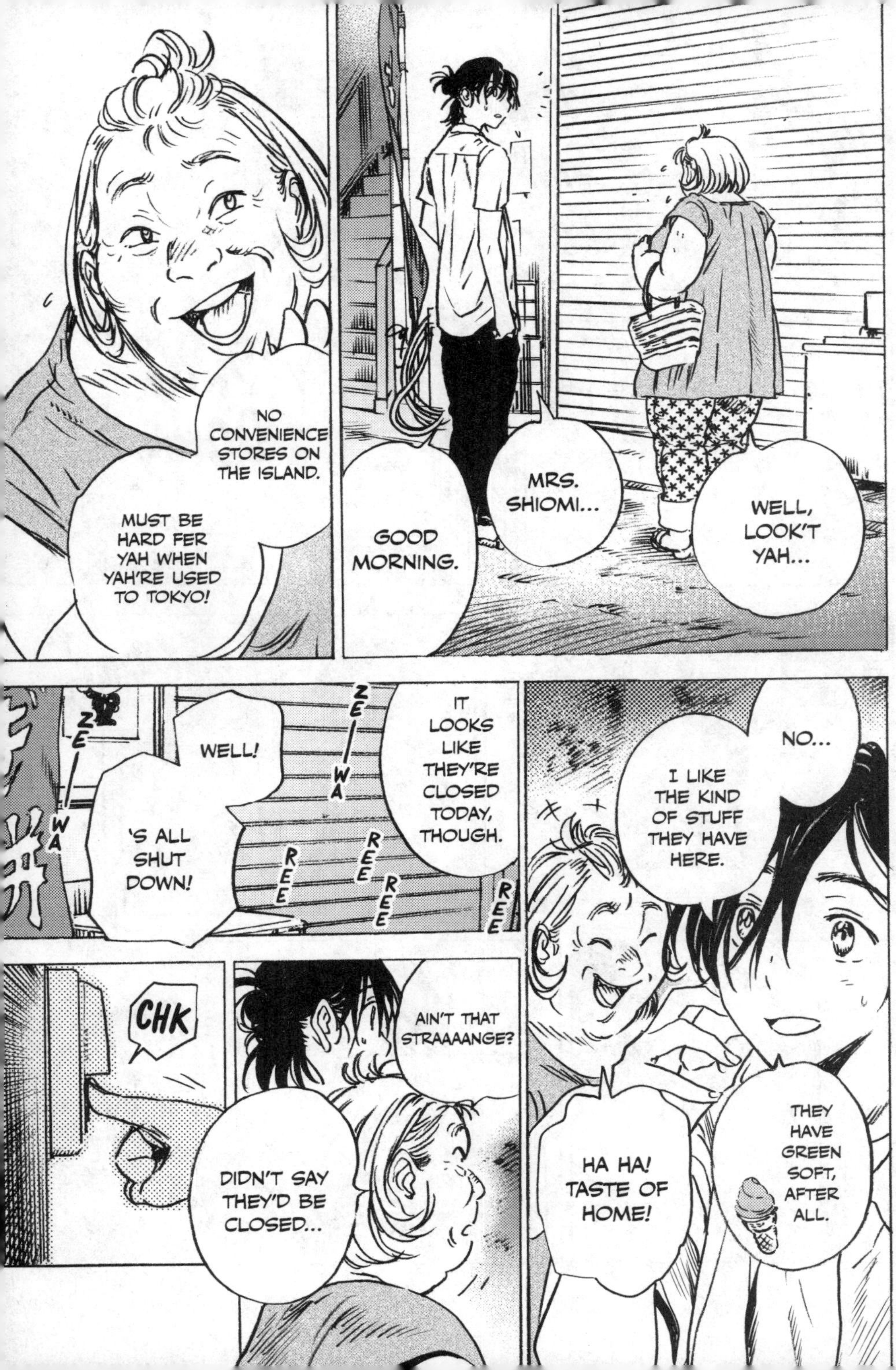
WELL, LOOK'T YAH...
MRS. SHIOMI...
GOOD MORNING.
NO CONVENIENCE STORES ON THE ISLAND.
MUST BE HARD FER YAH WHEN YAH'RE USED TO TOKYO!
NO...
I LIKE THE KIND OF STUFF THEY HAVE HERE.
THEY HAVE GREEN SOFT, AFTER ALL.
HA HA! TASTE OF HOME!
IT LOOKS LIKE THEY'RE CLOSED TODAY, THOUGH.
ZE-WA
REE
REE
REE
REE
WELL!
'S ALL SHUT DOWN!
ZE-WA
AIN'T THAT STRAAAANGE?
DIDN'T SAY THEY'D BE CLOSED...
CHK

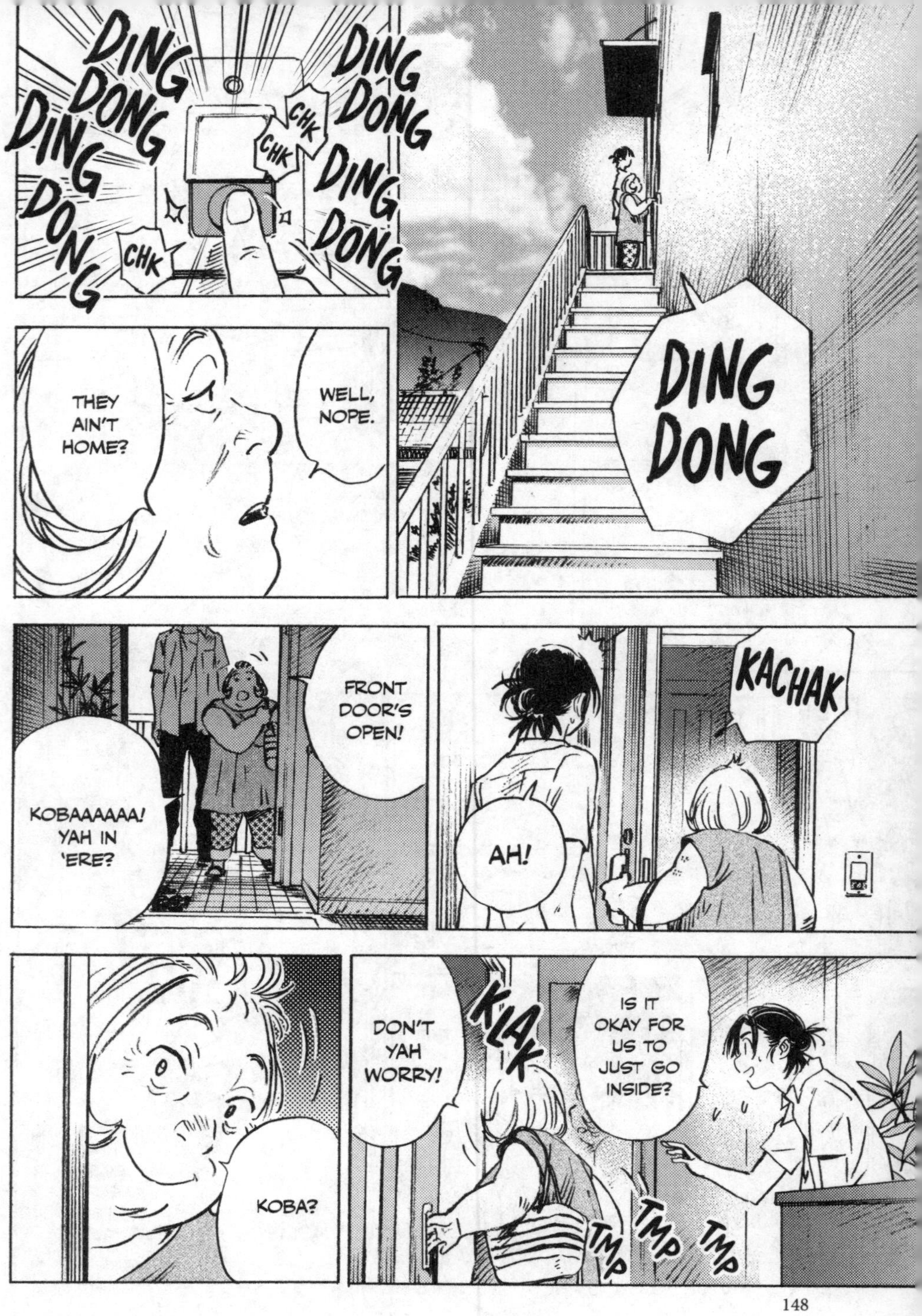
DING DONG
DING DONG DING DONG
CHK
CHK
CHK
DING DONG DING DONG
WELL, NOPE.
THEY AIN'T HOME?
KACHAK
AH!
FRONT DOOR'S OPEN!
KOBAAAAAA! YAH IN 'ERE?
IS IT OKAY FOR US TO JUST GO INSIDE?
K'LAK
DON'T YAH WORRY!
TMP TMP TMP
KOBA?

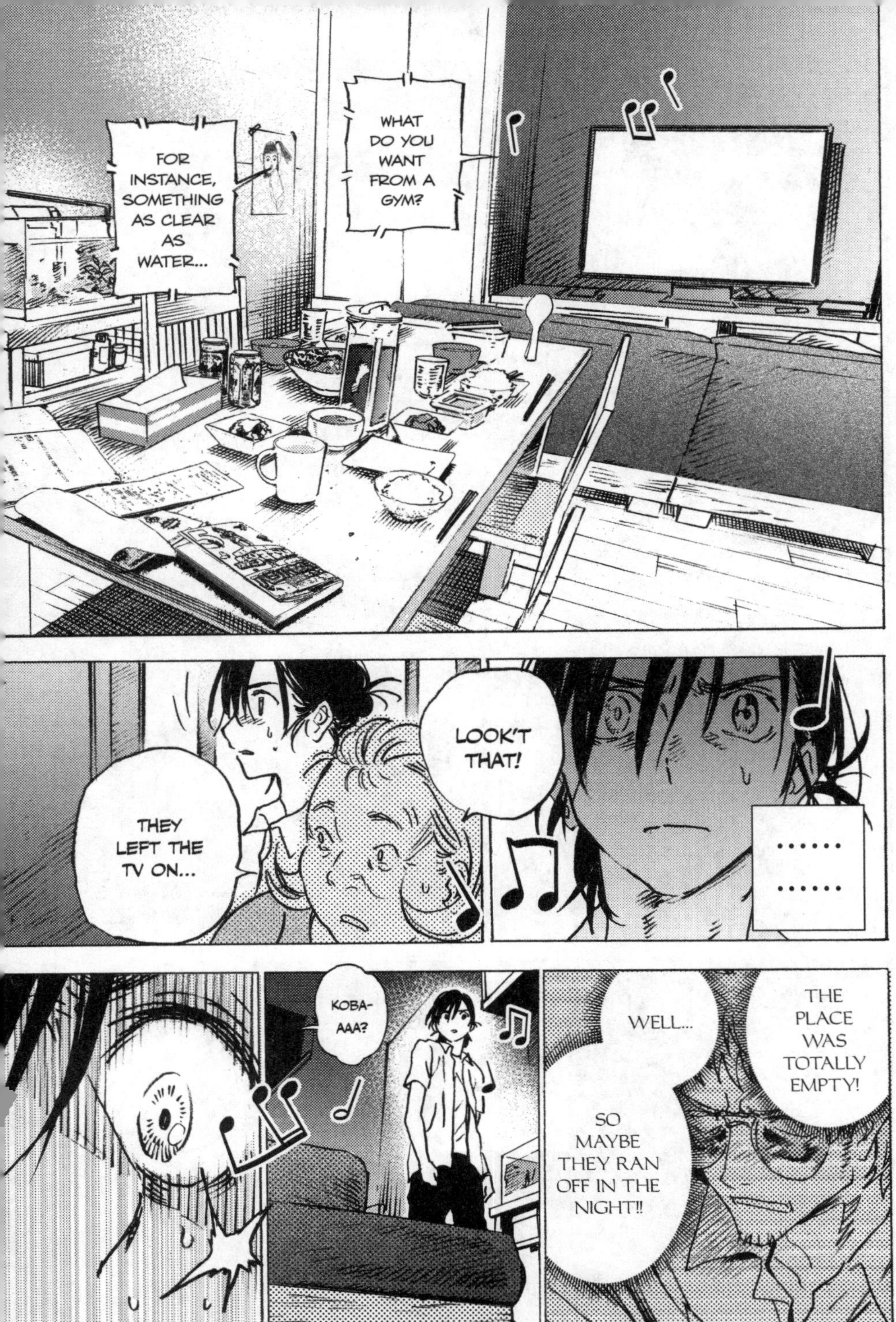
WHAT DO YOU WANT FROM A GYM?
FOR INSTANCE, SOMETHING AS CLEAR AS WATER...
......
......
LOOK'T THAT!
THEY LEFT THE TV ON...
THE PLACE WAS TOTALLY EMPTY!
WELL...
SO MAYBE THEY RAN OFF IN THE NIGHT!!
KOBA-AAA?

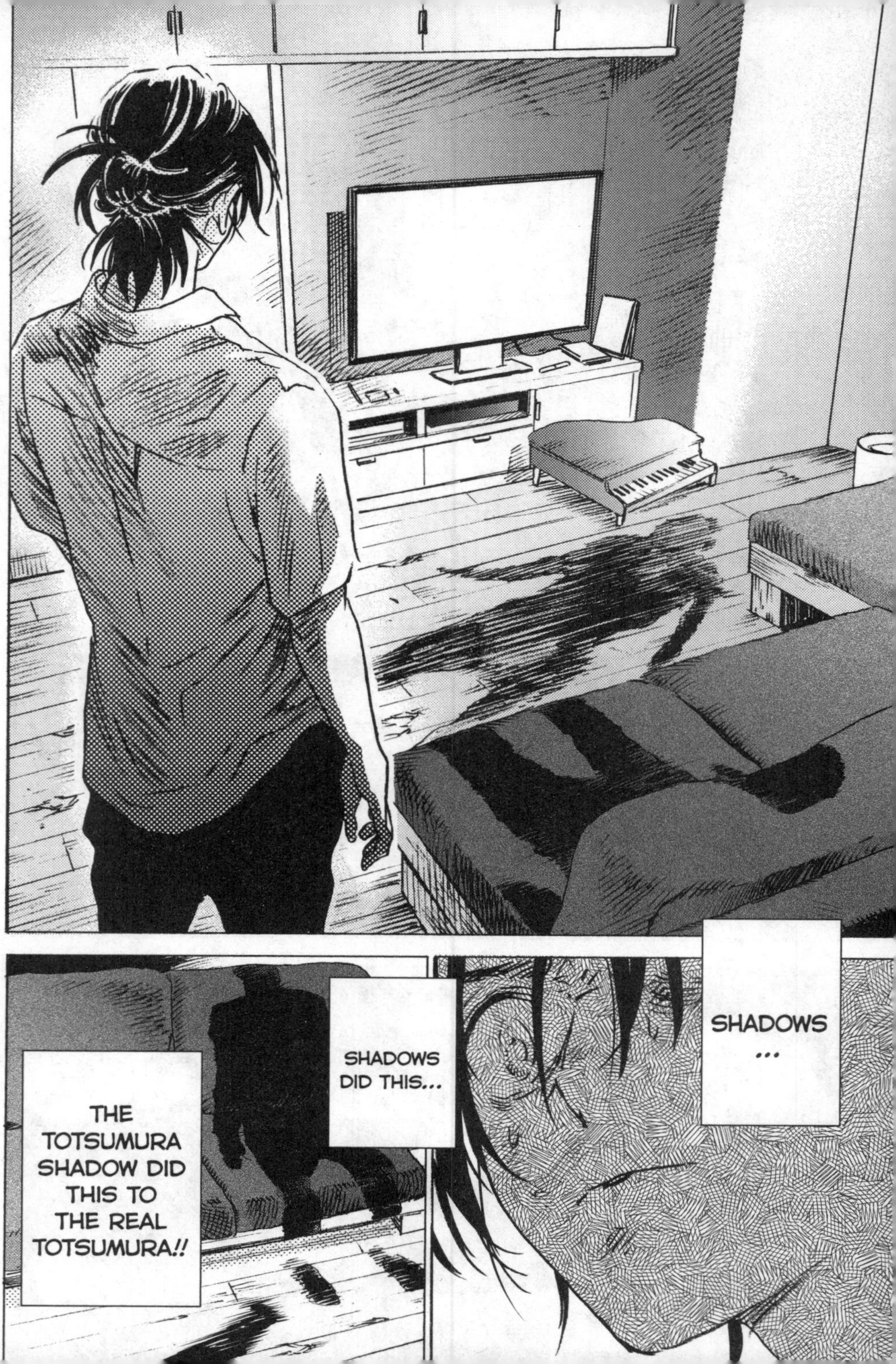
SHADOWS ...
SHADOWS DID THIS...
THE TOTSUMURA SHADOW DID THIS TO THE REAL TOTSUMURA!!

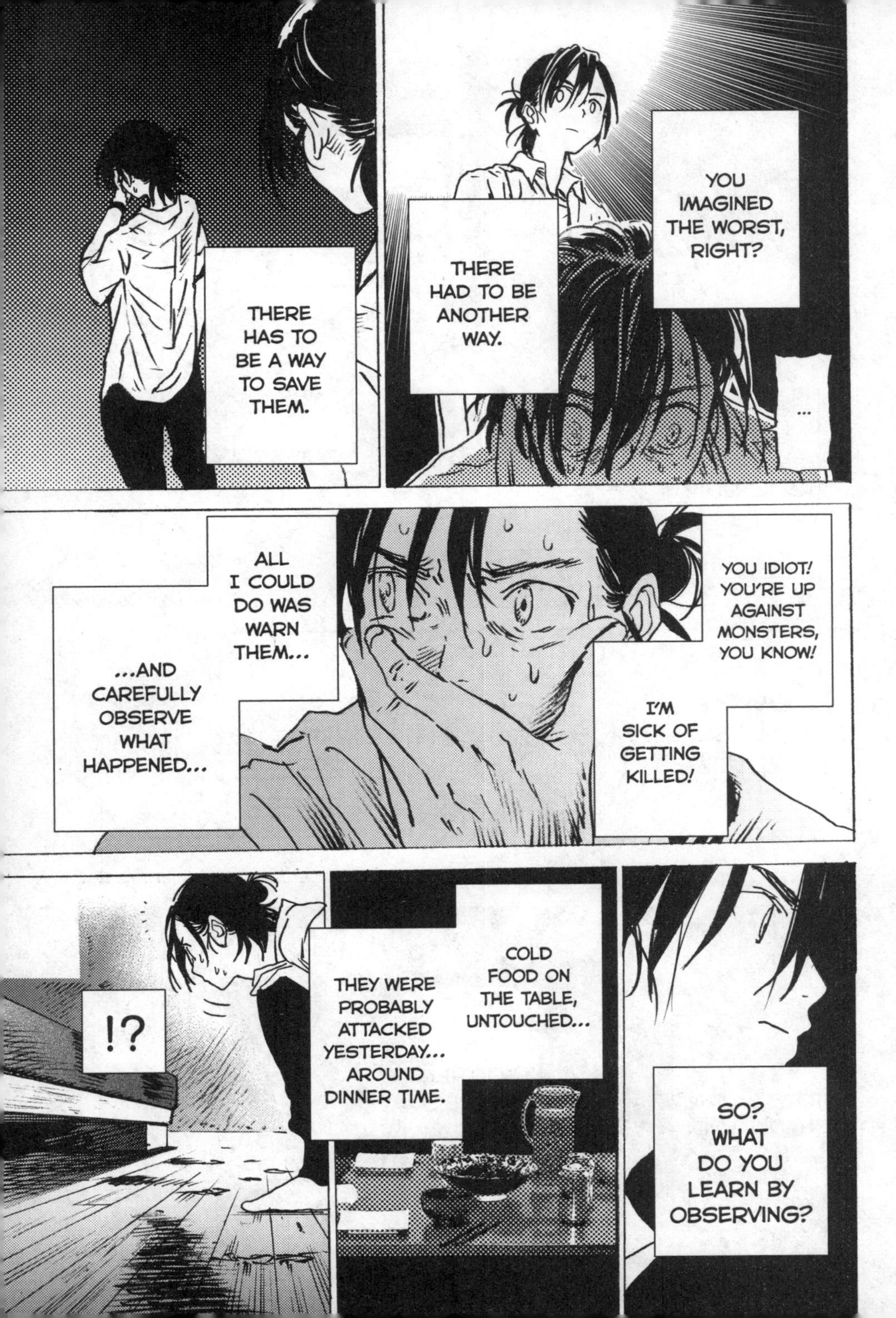
YOU IMAGINED THE WORST, RIGHT?
...
THERE HAD TO BE ANOTHER WAY.
THERE HAS TO BE A WAY TO SAVE THEM.
YOU IDIOT! YOU'RE UP AGAINST MONSTERS, YOU KNOW!
I'M SICK OF GETTING KILLED!
ALL I COULD DO WAS WARN THEM...
...AND CAREFULLY OBSERVE WHAT HAPPENED...
SO? WHAT DO YOU LEARN BY OBSERVING?
COLD FOOD ON THE TABLE, UNTOUCHED...
THEY WERE PROBABLY ATTACKED YESTERDAY... AROUND DINNER TIME.
!?

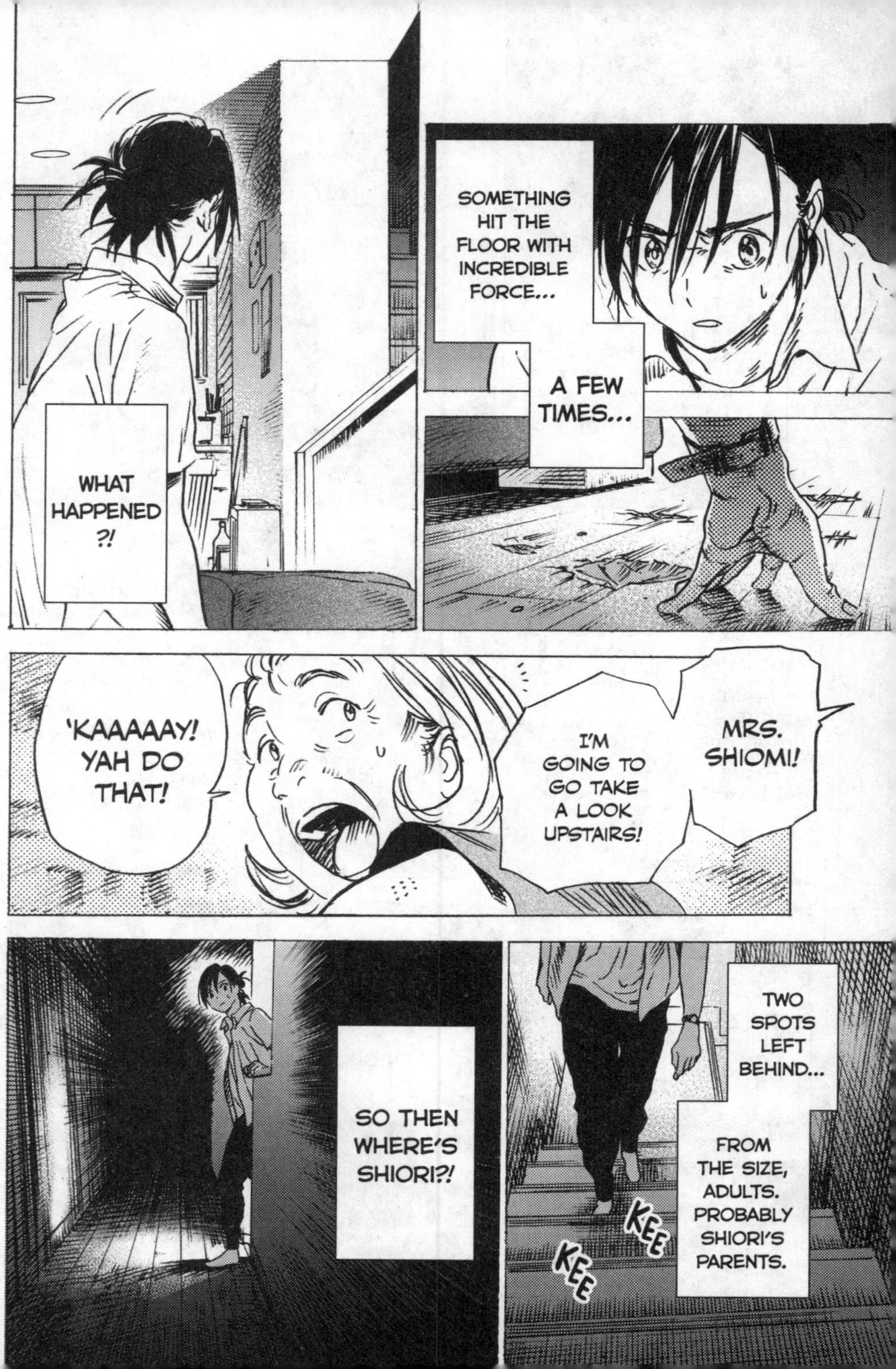
SOMETHING HIT THE FLOOR WITH INCREDIBLE FORCE...
A FEW TIMES...
WHAT HAPPENED ?!
MRS. SHIOMI!
I'M GOING TO GO TAKE A LOOK UPSTAIRS!
'KAAAAAY! YAH DO THAT!
TWO SPOTS LEFT BEHIND...
FROM THE SIZE, ADULTS. PROBABLY SHIORI'S PARENTS.
KEE
KEE
SO THEN WHERE'S SHIORI?!

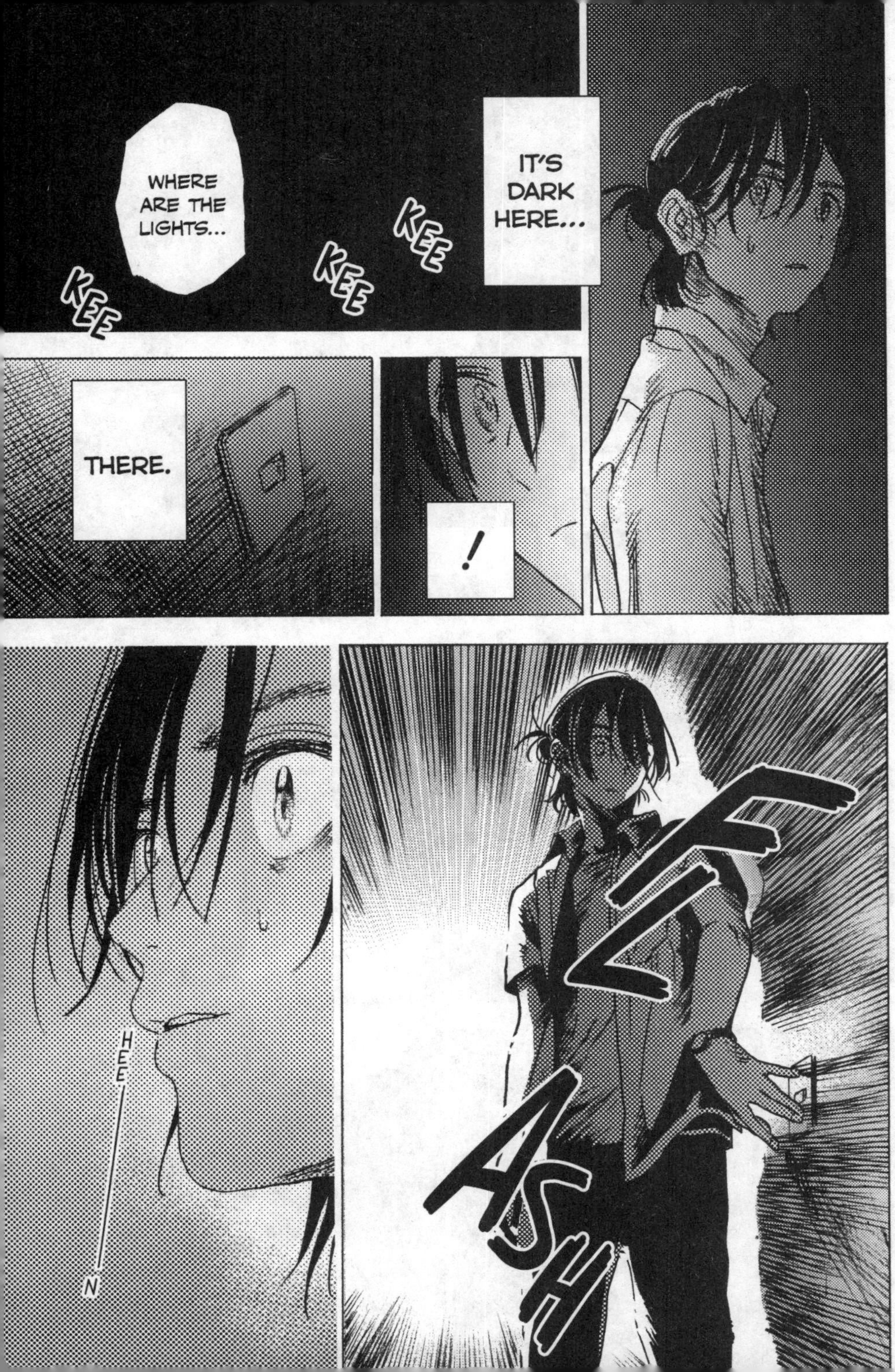

IT'S DARK HERE...
KEE
KEE
WHERE ARE THE LIGHTS...
KEE
!
THERE.
FLASH
HEE—N

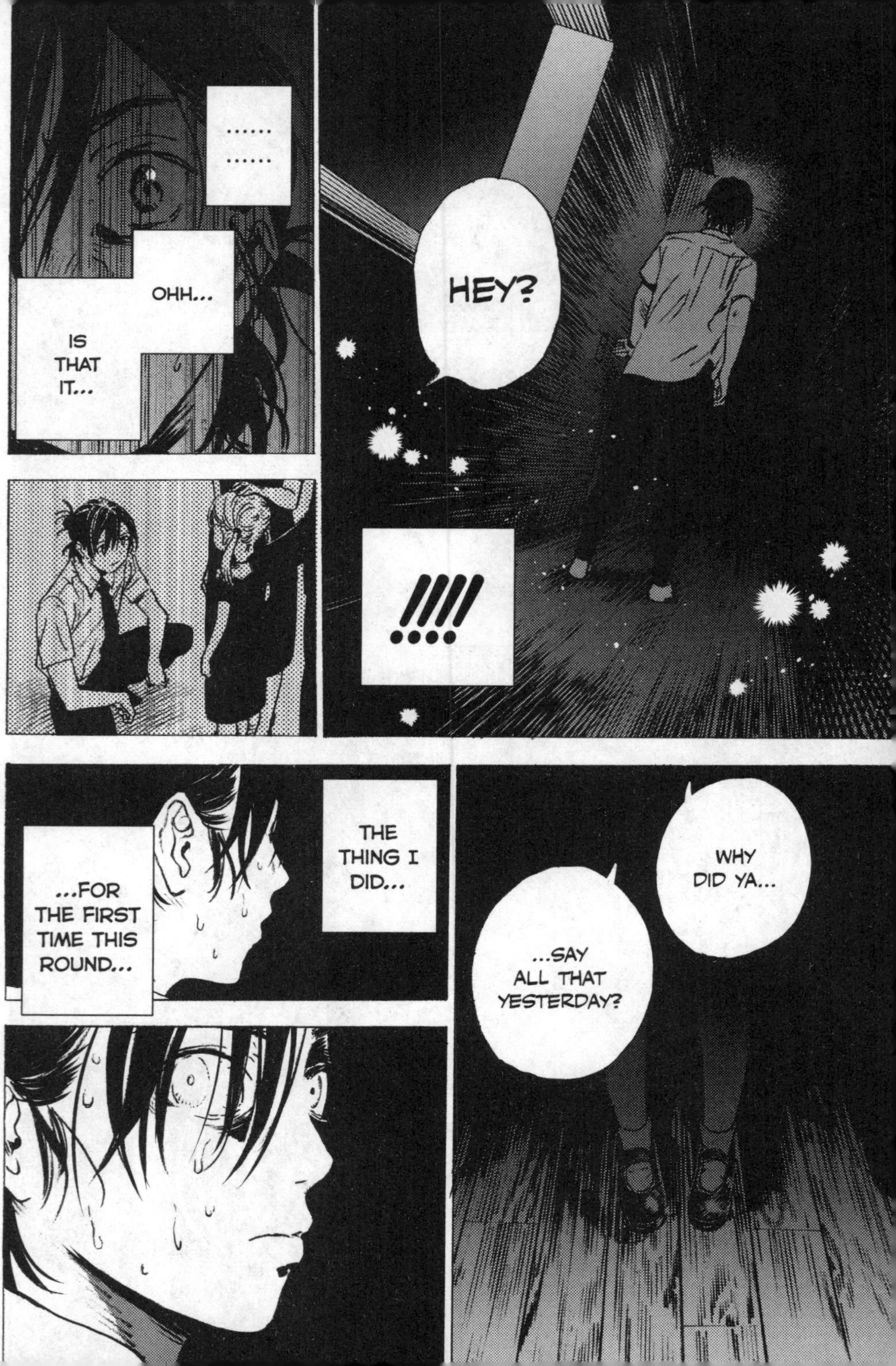
HEY?
!!!!
......
......
OHH...
IS THAT IT...
WHY DID YA...
...SAY ALL THAT YESTERDAY?
THE THING I DID...
...FOR THE FIRST TIME THIS ROUND...

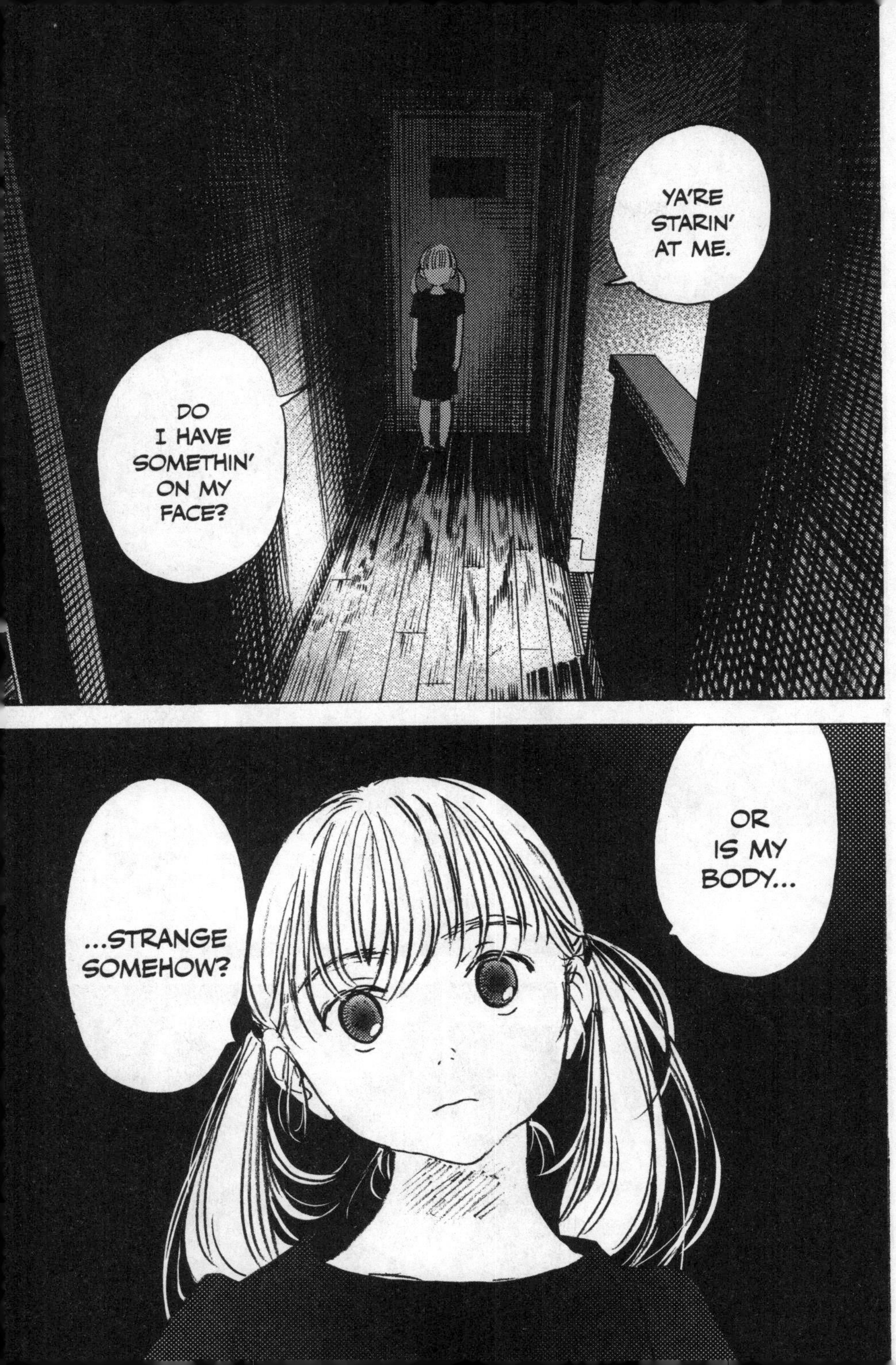
YA'RE STARIN' AT ME.
DO I HAVE SOMETHIN' ON MY FACE?
OR IS MY BODY...
...STRANGE SOMEHOW?

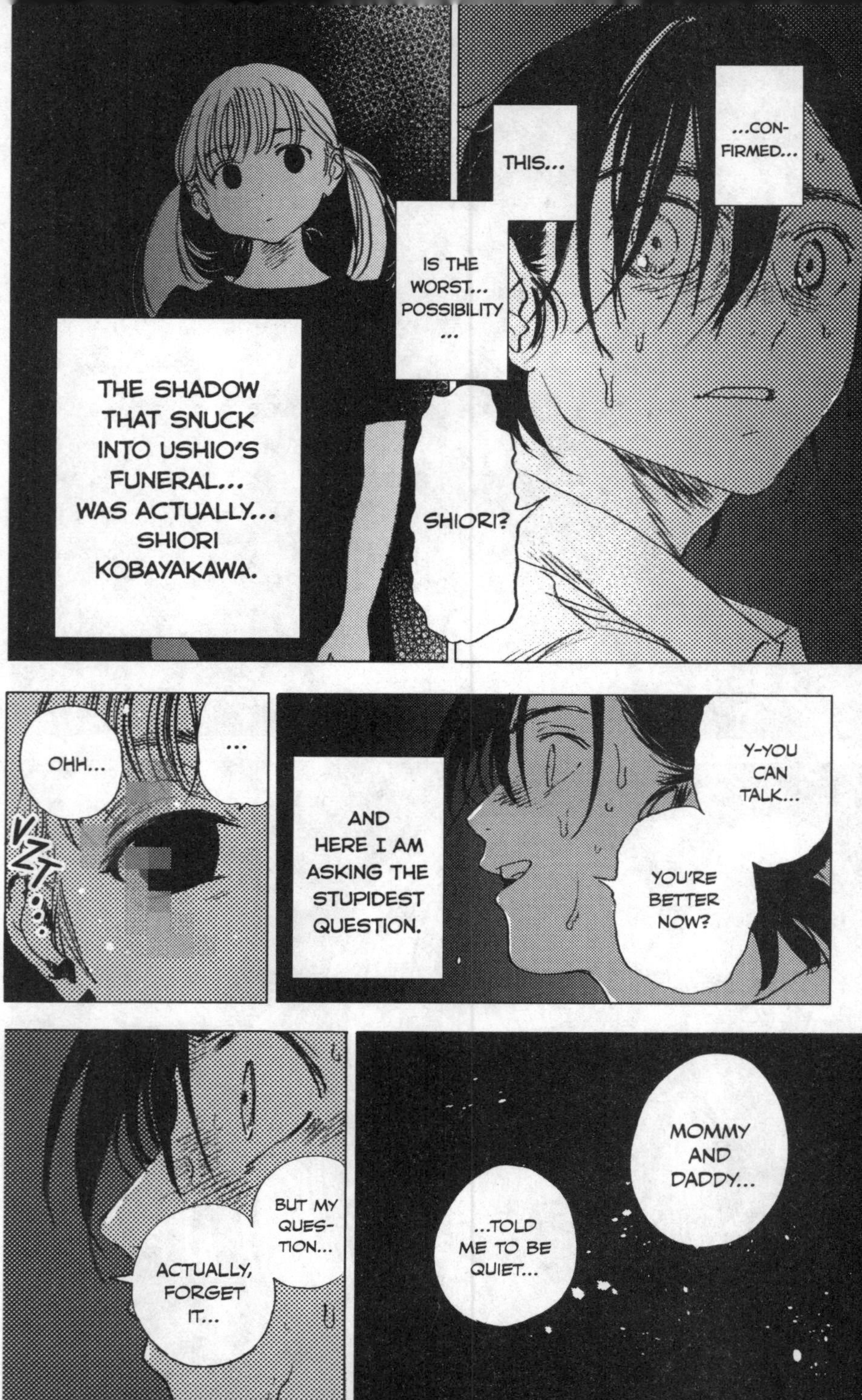
...CON-FIRMED...
THIS...
IS THE WORST... POSSIBILITY ...
SHIORI?
THE SHADOW THAT SNUCK INTO USHIO'S FUNERAL... WAS ACTUALLY... SHIORI KOBAYAKAWA.
Y-YOU CAN TALK...
YOU'RE BETTER NOW?
AND HERE I AM ASKING THE STUPIDEST QUESTION.
...
OHH...
VZT...
MOMMY AND DADDY...
...TOLD ME TO BE QUIET...
BUT MY QUES-TION...
ACTUALLY, FORGET IT...

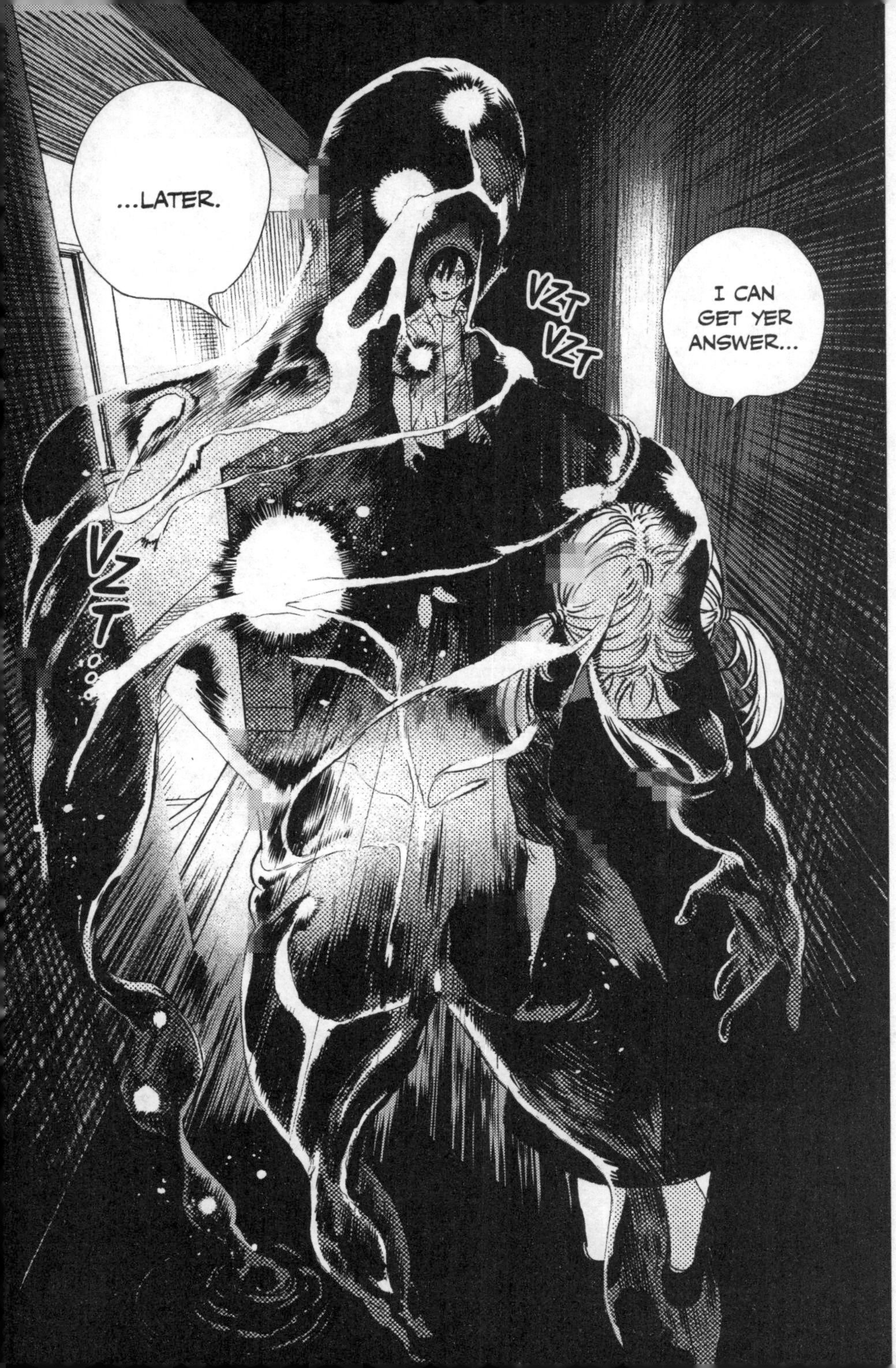
I CAN GET YER ANSWER...
VZT VZT
...LATER.
VZT...

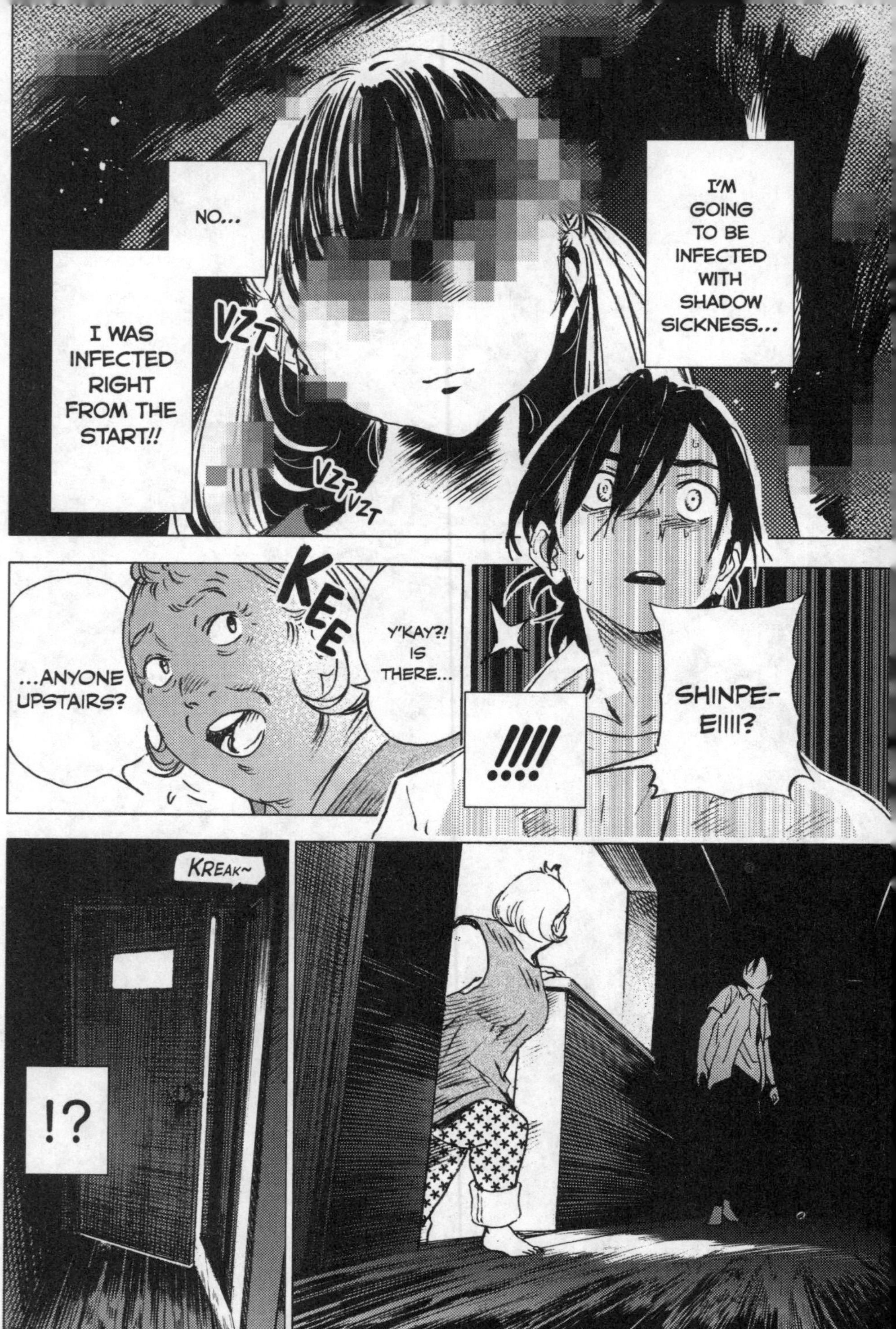
I'M GOING TO BE INFECTED WITH SHADOW SICKNESS...
NO...
VZT
I WAS INFECTED RIGHT FROM THE START!!
VZTVZT
SHINPE-EIIII?
!!!!
KEE
Y'KAY?! IS THERE...
...ANYONE UPSTAIRS?
KREAK~
!?

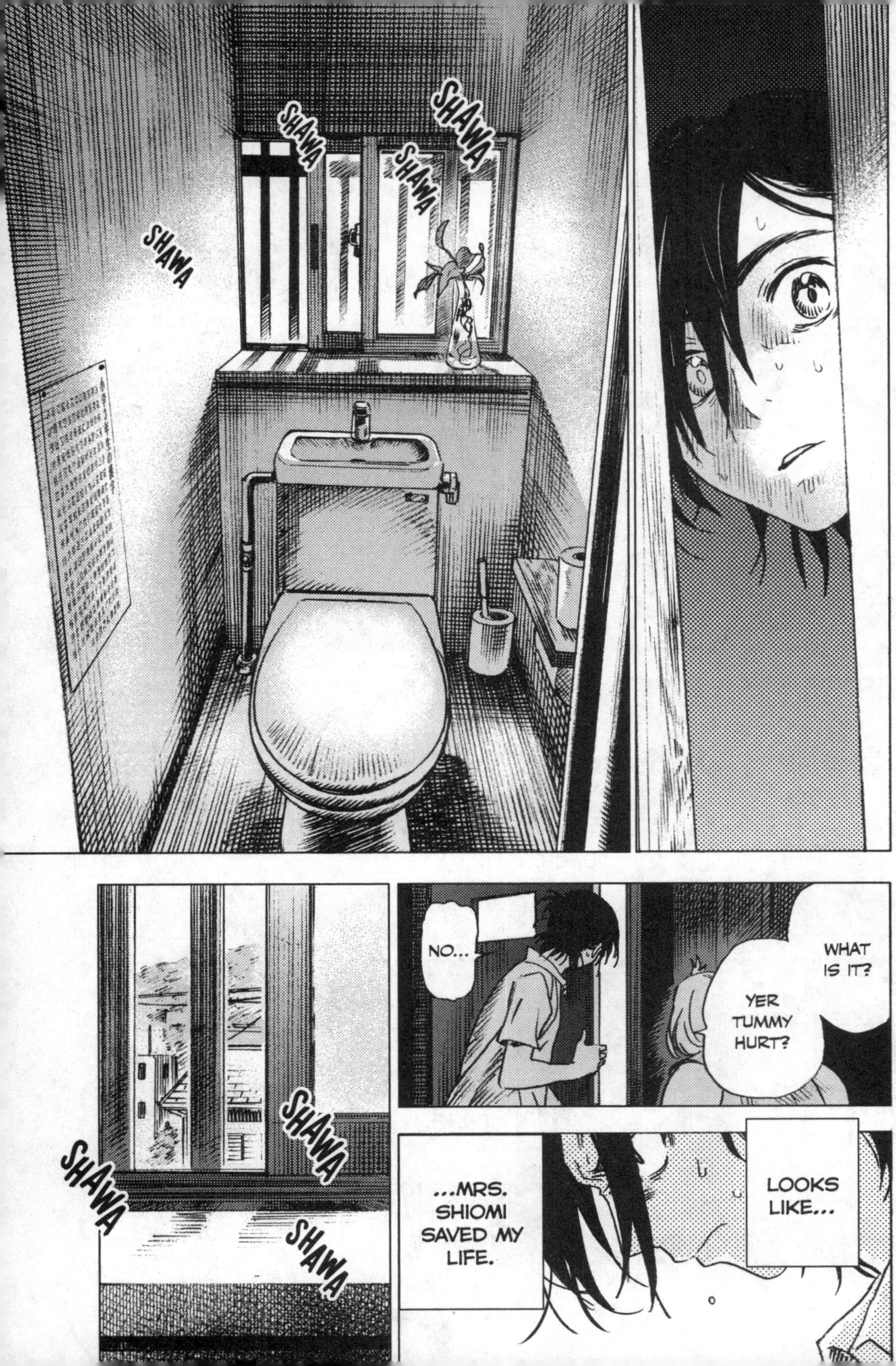
SHAWA
SHAWA
SHAWA
SHAWA
WHAT IS IT?
YER TUMMY HURT?
NO...
LOOKS LIKE...
...MRS. SHIOMI SAVED MY LIFE.
SHAWA
SHAWA
SHAWA

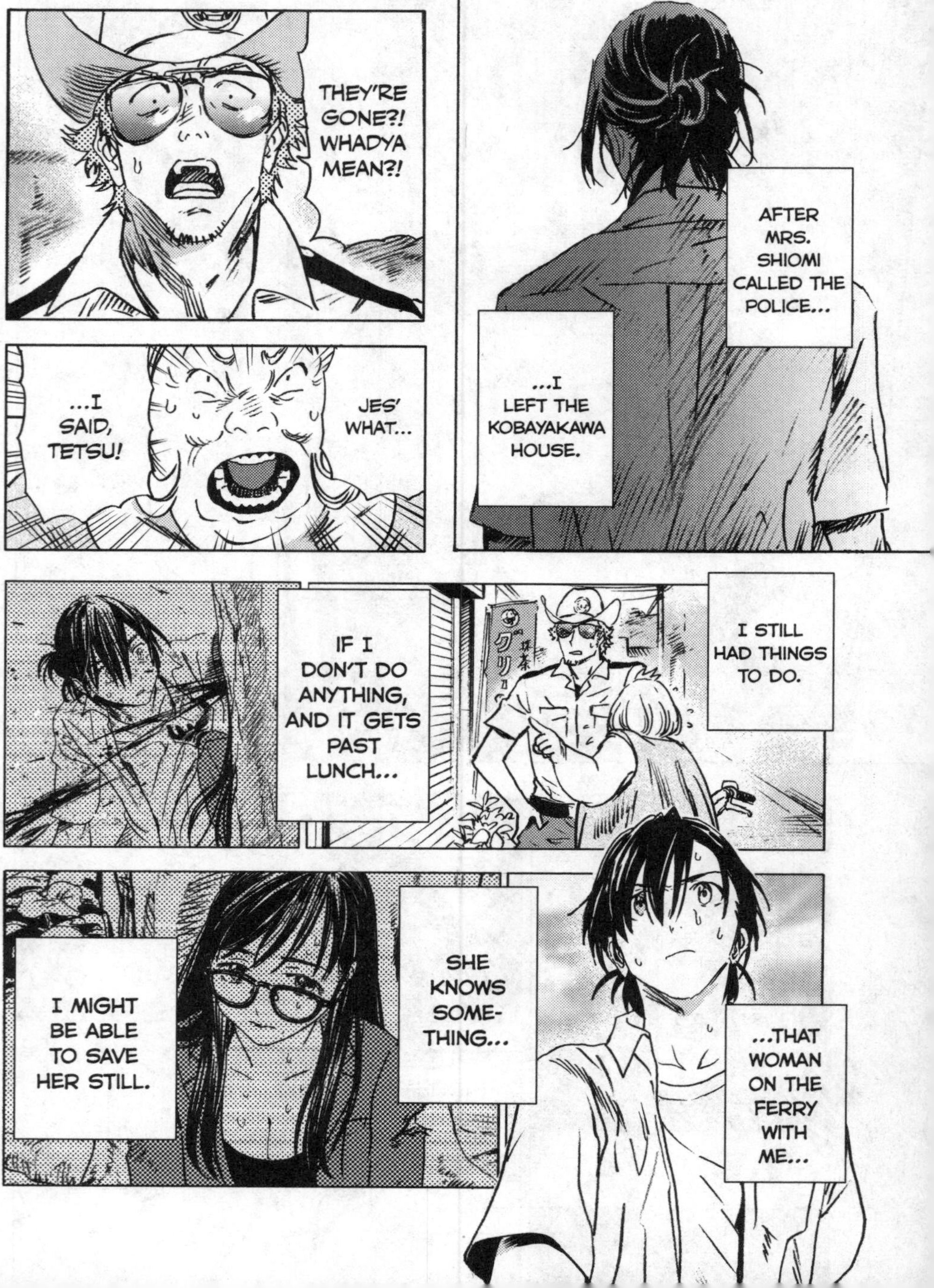
AFTER MRS. SHIOMI CALLED THE POLICE...
...I LEFT THE KOBAYAKAWA HOUSE.
THEY'RE GONE?! WHADYA MEAN?!
JES' WHAT...
...I SAID, TETSU!
I STILL HAD THINGS TO DO.
IF I DON'T DO ANYTHING, AND IT GETS PAST LUNCH...
SHE KNOWS SOME-THING...
...THAT WOMAN ON THE FERRY WITH ME...
I MIGHT BE ABLE TO SAVE HER STILL.

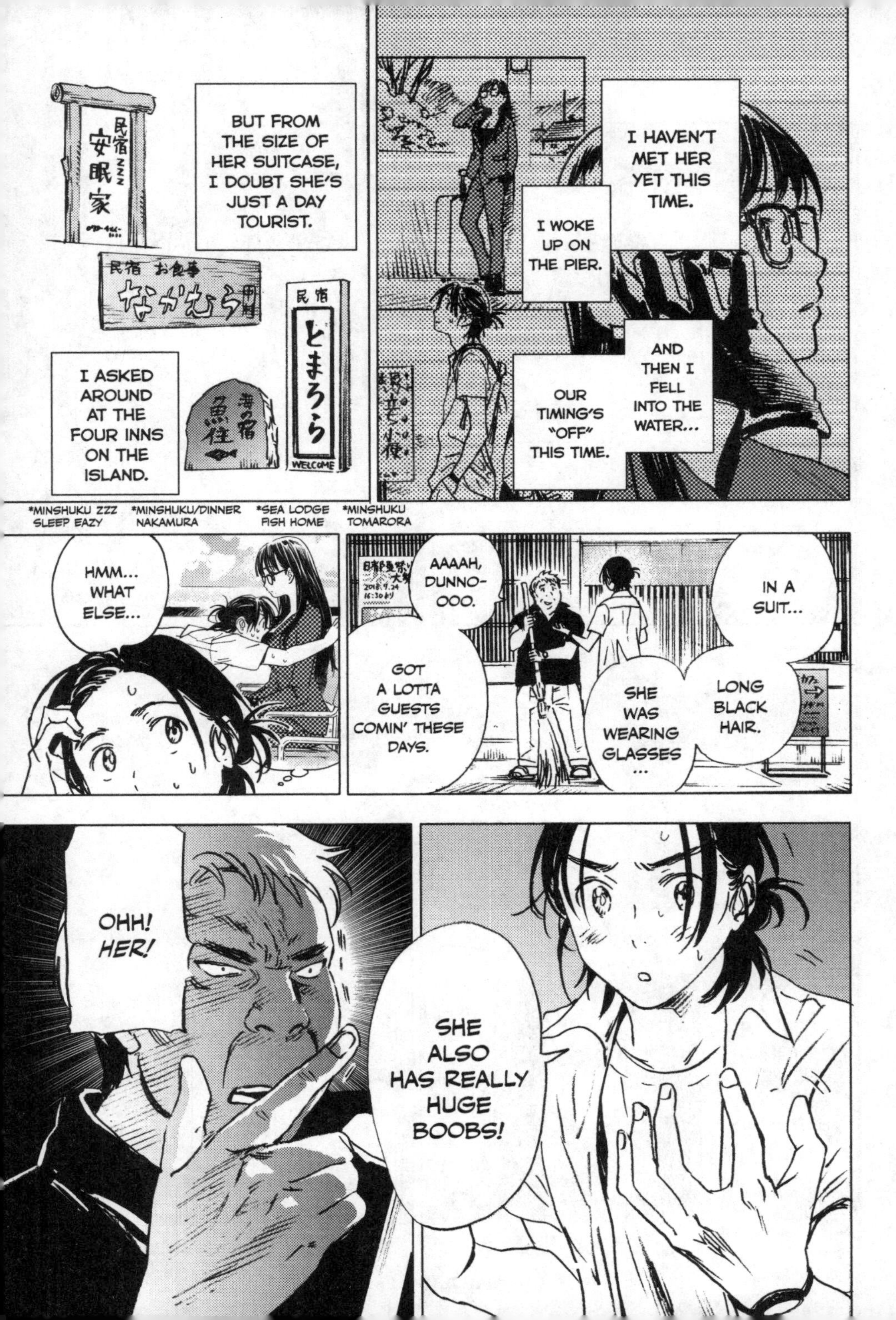
I HAVEN'T MET HER YET THIS TIME.
I WOKE UP ON THE PIER.
AND THEN I FELL INTO THE WATER...
OUR TIMING'S "OFF" THIS TIME.
BUT FROM THE SIZE OF HER SUITCASE, I DOUBT SHE'S JUST A DAY TOURIST.
民宿 安眠家 ZZZ
民宿 お食事 なかむら
民宿 とまろら WELCOME
海の宿 魚住
I ASKED AROUND AT THE FOUR INNS ON THE ISLAND.
*MINSHUKU ZZZ SLEEP EAZY
*MINSHUKU/DINNER NAKAMURA
*SEA LODGE FISH HOME
*MINSHUKU TOMARORA
IN A SUIT...
LONG BLACK HAIR.
SHE WAS WEARING GLASSES ...
AAAAH, DUNNO-OOO.
GOT A LOTTA GUESTS COMIN' THESE DAYS.
HMM... WHAT ELSE...
SHE ALSO HAS REALLY HUGE BOOBS!
OHH! HER!

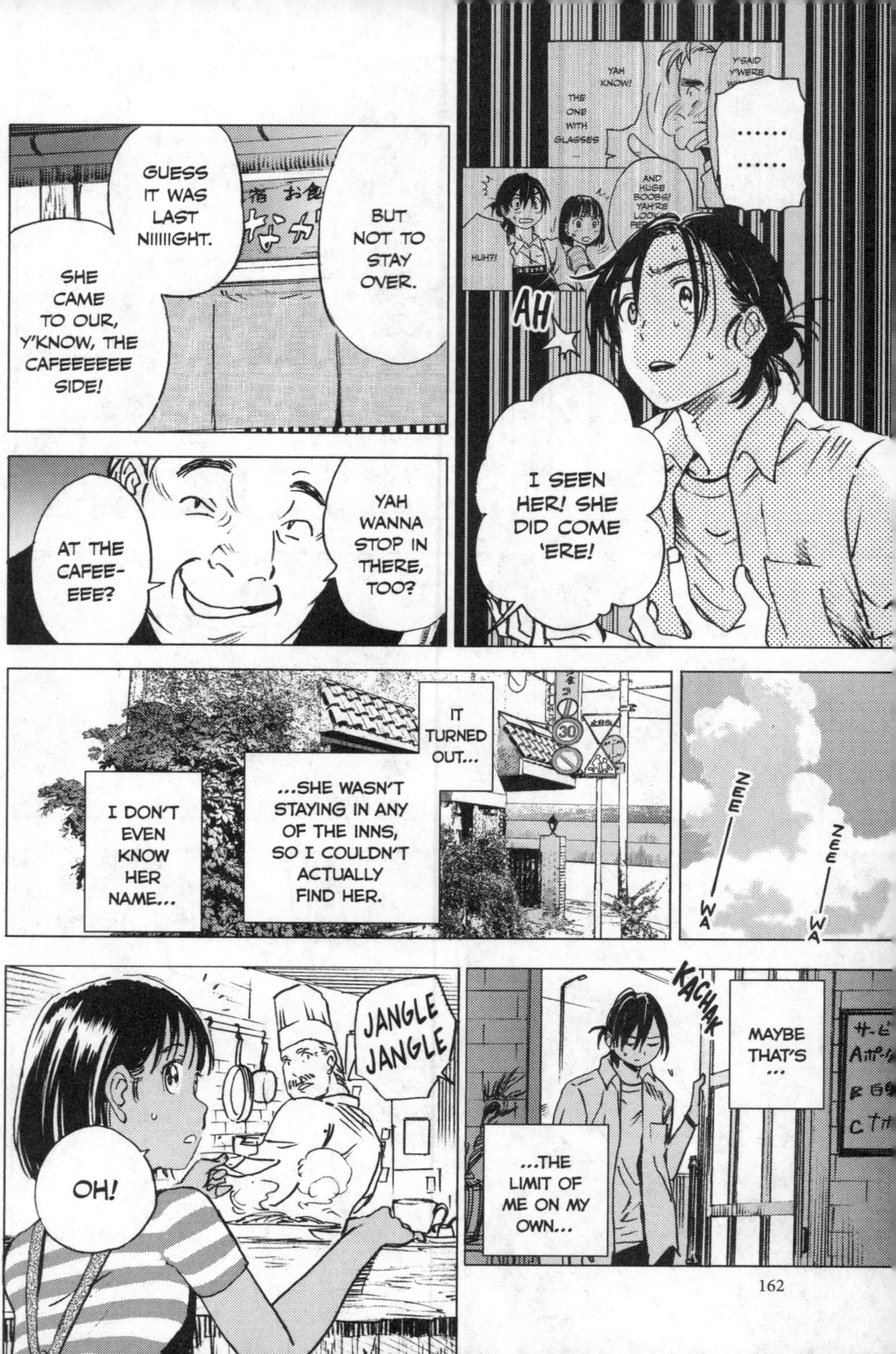

Y'SAID Y'WERE
YAH KNOW!
THE ONE WITH GLASSES
......
......
AND HUGE BOOBS! YAH'RE
HUH?!
AH
I SEEN HER! SHE DID COME 'ERE!
BUT NOT TO STAY OVER.
GUESS IT WAS LAST NIIIIIGHT.
SHE CAME TO OUR, Y'KNOW, THE CAFEEEEEE SIDE!
YAH WANNA STOP IN THERE, TOO?
AT THE CAFEE-EEE?
ZEE-WA
ZEE-WA
IT TURNED OUT...
...SHE WASN'T STAYING IN ANY OF THE INNS, SO I COULDN'T ACTUALLY FIND HER.
I DON'T EVEN KNOW HER NAME...
KACHAK
MAYBE THAT'S...
...THE LIMIT OF ME ON MY OWN...
JANGLE JANGLE
OH!

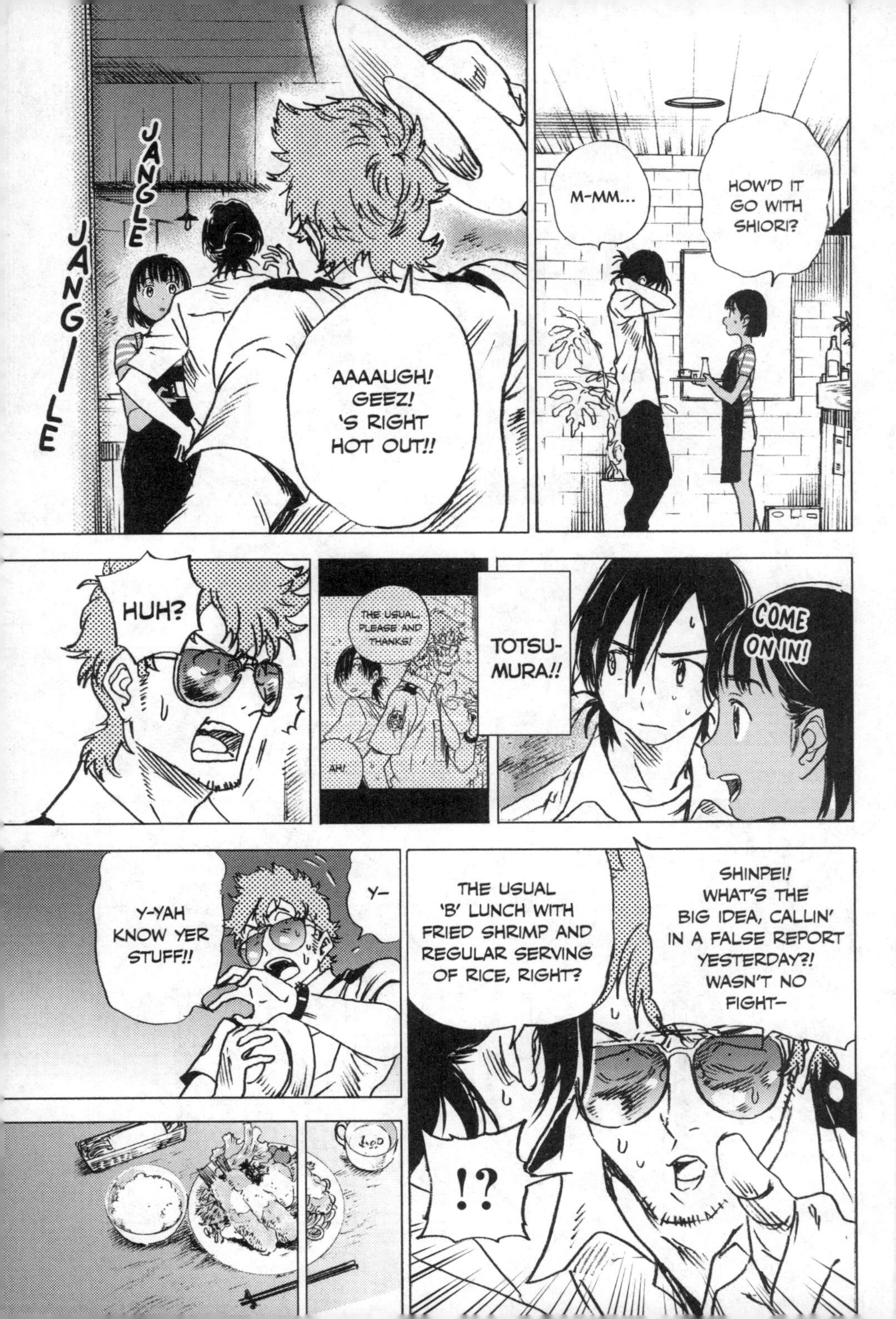
HOW'D IT GO WITH SHIORI?
M-MM...
AAAAUGH! GEEZ! 'S RIGHT HOT OUT!!
JANGLE
JANGLE
COME ON IN!
TOTSU-MURA!!
THE USUAL, PLEASE AND THANKS!
AH!
HUH?
SHINPEI! WHAT'S THE BIG IDEA, CALLIN' IN A FALSE REPORT YESTERDAY?! WASN'T NO FIGHT–
THE USUAL 'B' LUNCH WITH FRIED SHRIMP AND REGULAR SERVING OF RICE, RIGHT?
!?
Y–
Y-YAH KNOW YER STUFF!!

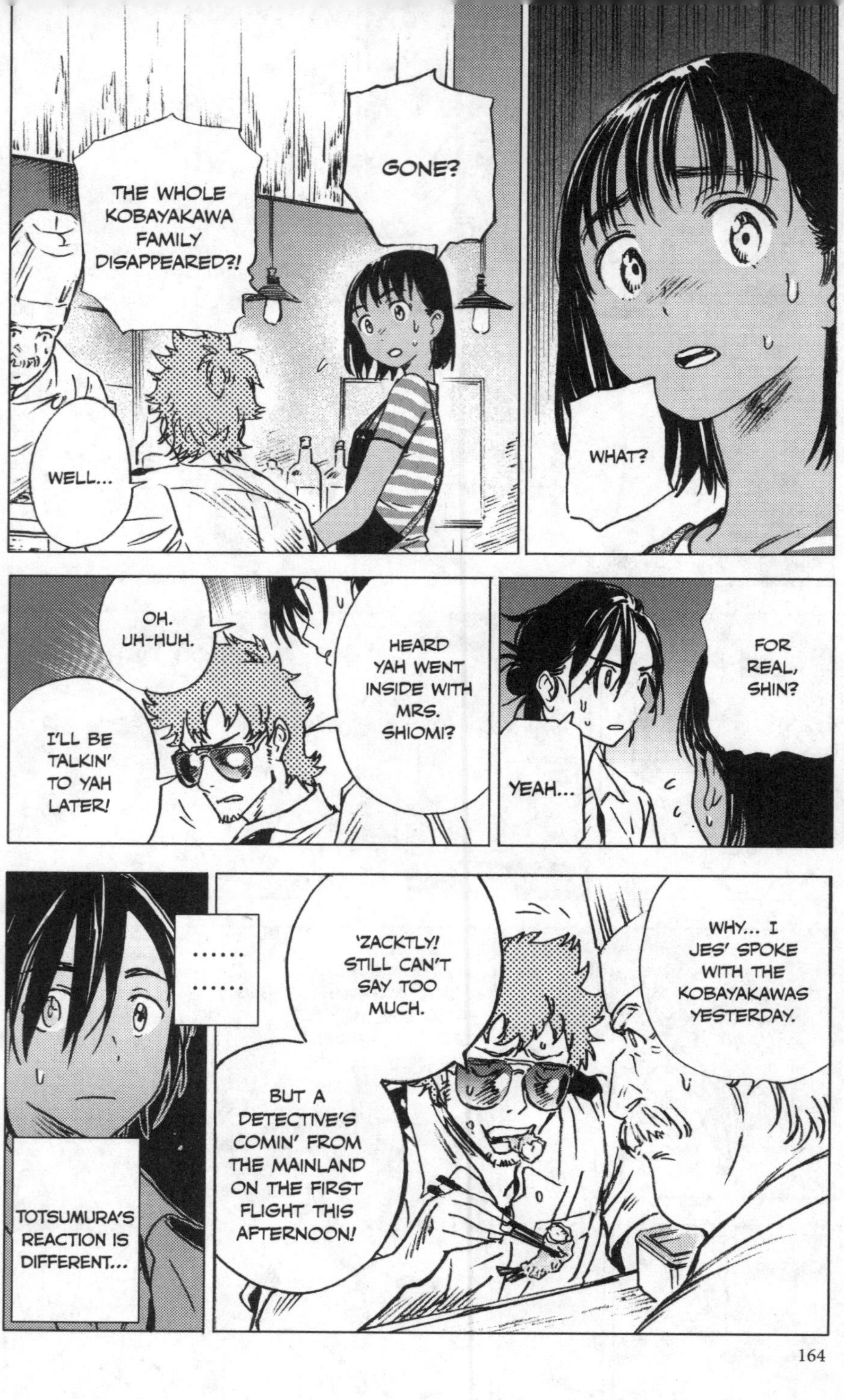
WHAT?
GONE?
THE WHOLE KOBAYAKAWA FAMILY DISAPPEARED?!
WELL...
FOR REAL, SHIN?
YEAH...
HEARD YAH WENT INSIDE WITH MRS. SHIOMI?
OH. UH-HUH.
I'LL BE TALKIN' TO YAH LATER!
WHY... I JES' SPOKE WITH THE KOBAYAKAWAS YESTERDAY.
'ZACKTLY! STILL CAN'T SAY TOO MUCH.
BUT A DETECTIVE'S COMIN' FROM THE MAINLAND ON THE FIRST FLIGHT THIS AFTERNOON!
......
......
TOTSUMURA'S REACTION IS DIFFERENT...

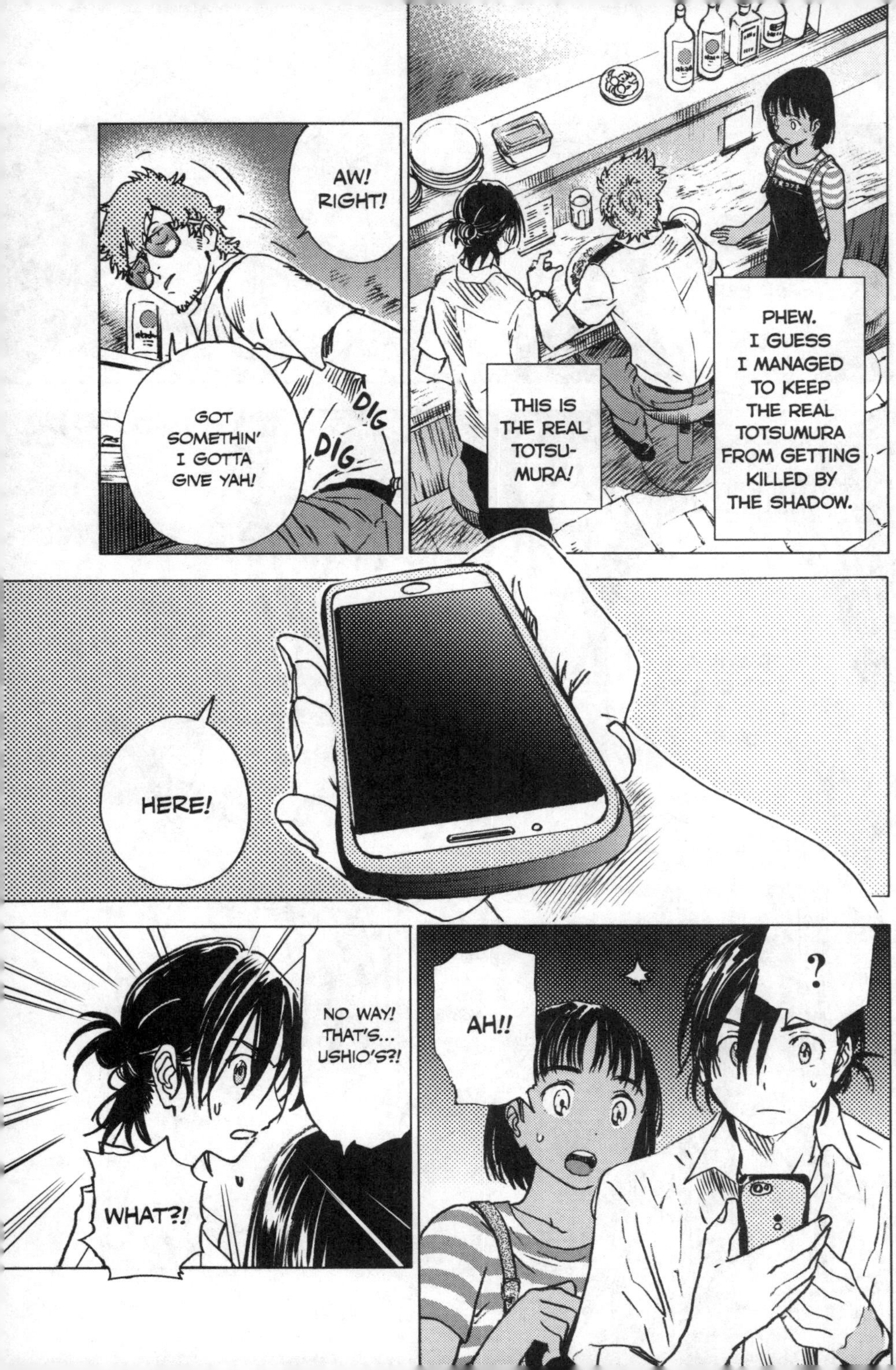
PHEW. I GUESS I MANAGED TO KEEP THE REAL TOTSUMURA FROM GETTING KILLED BY THE SHADOW.
THIS IS THE REAL TOTSU-MURA!
AW! RIGHT!
GOT SOMETHIN' I GOTTA GIVE YAH!
DIG
DIG
HERE!
?
AH!!
NO WAY! THAT'S... USHIO'S?!
WHAT?!

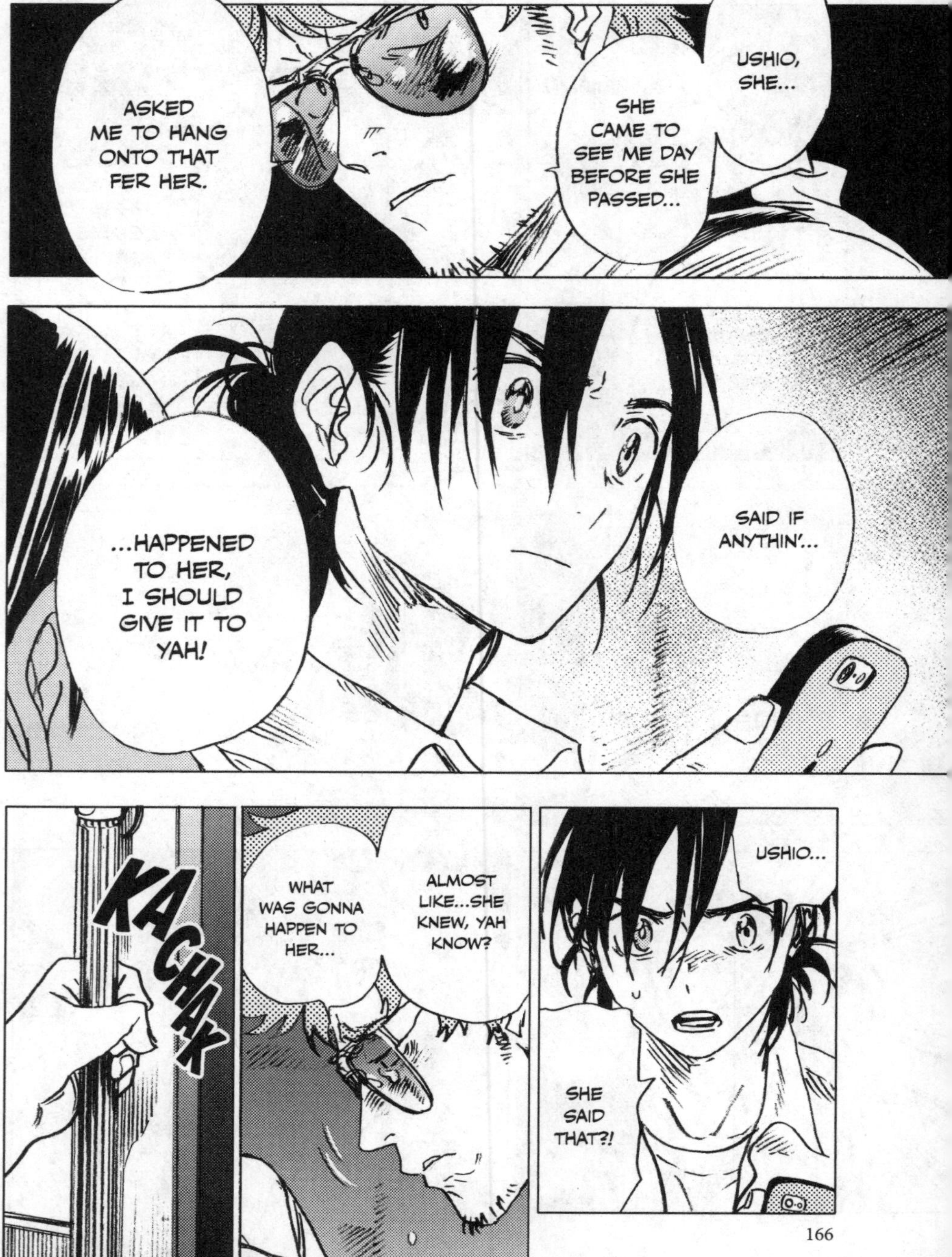
USHIO, SHE...
SHE CAME TO SEE ME DAY BEFORE SHE PASSED...
ASKED ME TO HANG ONTO THAT FER HER.
SAID IF ANYTHIN'...
...HAPPENED TO HER, I SHOULD GIVE IT TO YAH!
USHIO...
SHE SAID THAT?!
ALMOST LIKE...SHE KNEW, YAH KNOW?
WHAT WAS GONNA HAPPEN TO HER...
KACHAK

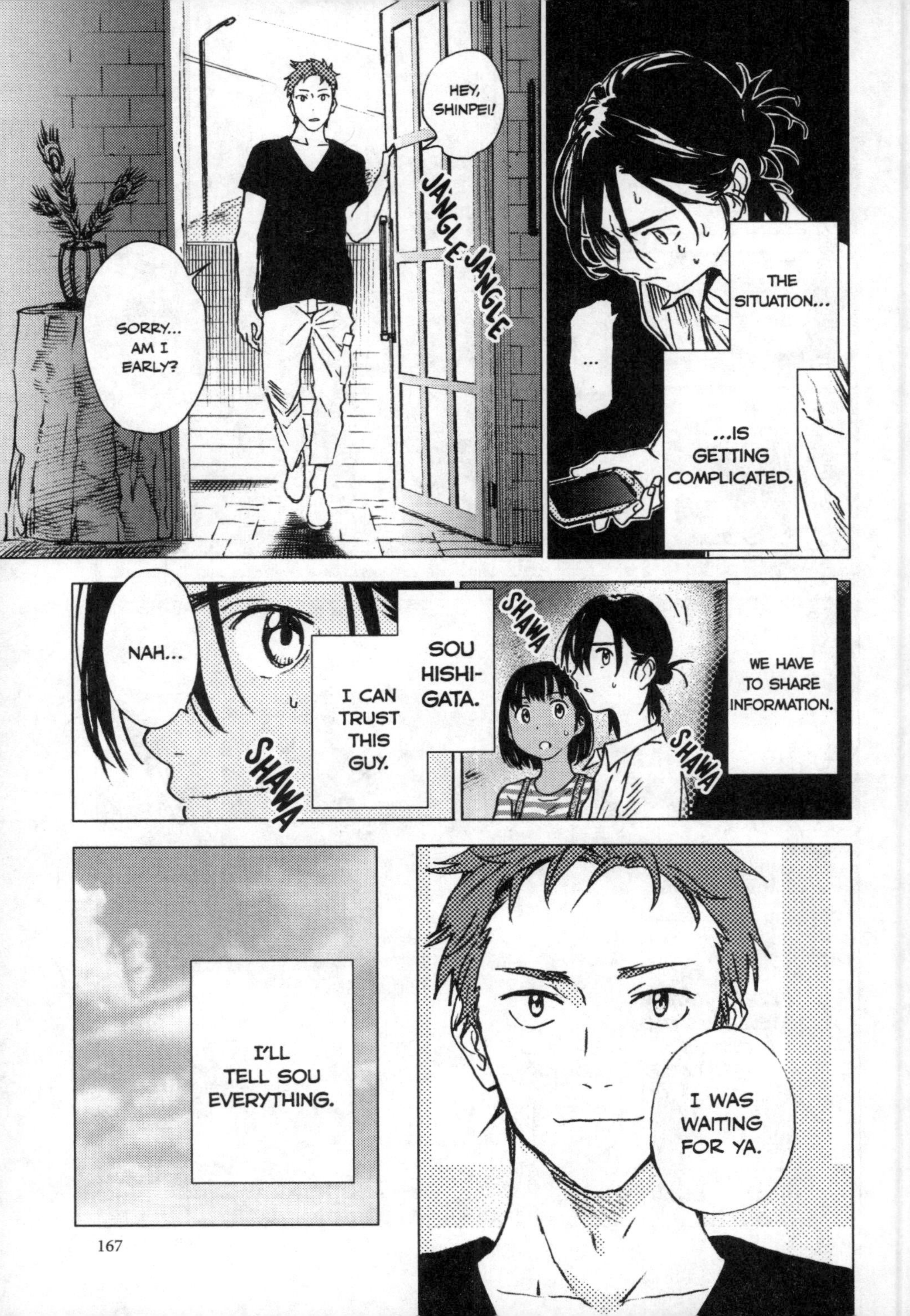
THE SITUATION...
...
...IS GETTING COMPLICATED.
HEY, SHINPEI!
JANGLE JANGLE
SORRY... AM I EARLY?
WE HAVE TO SHARE INFORMATION.
SHAWA
SHAWA
SOU HISHIGATA.
I CAN TRUST THIS GUY.
NAH...
SHAWA
I WAS WAITING FOR YA.
I'LL TELL SOU EVERYTHING.

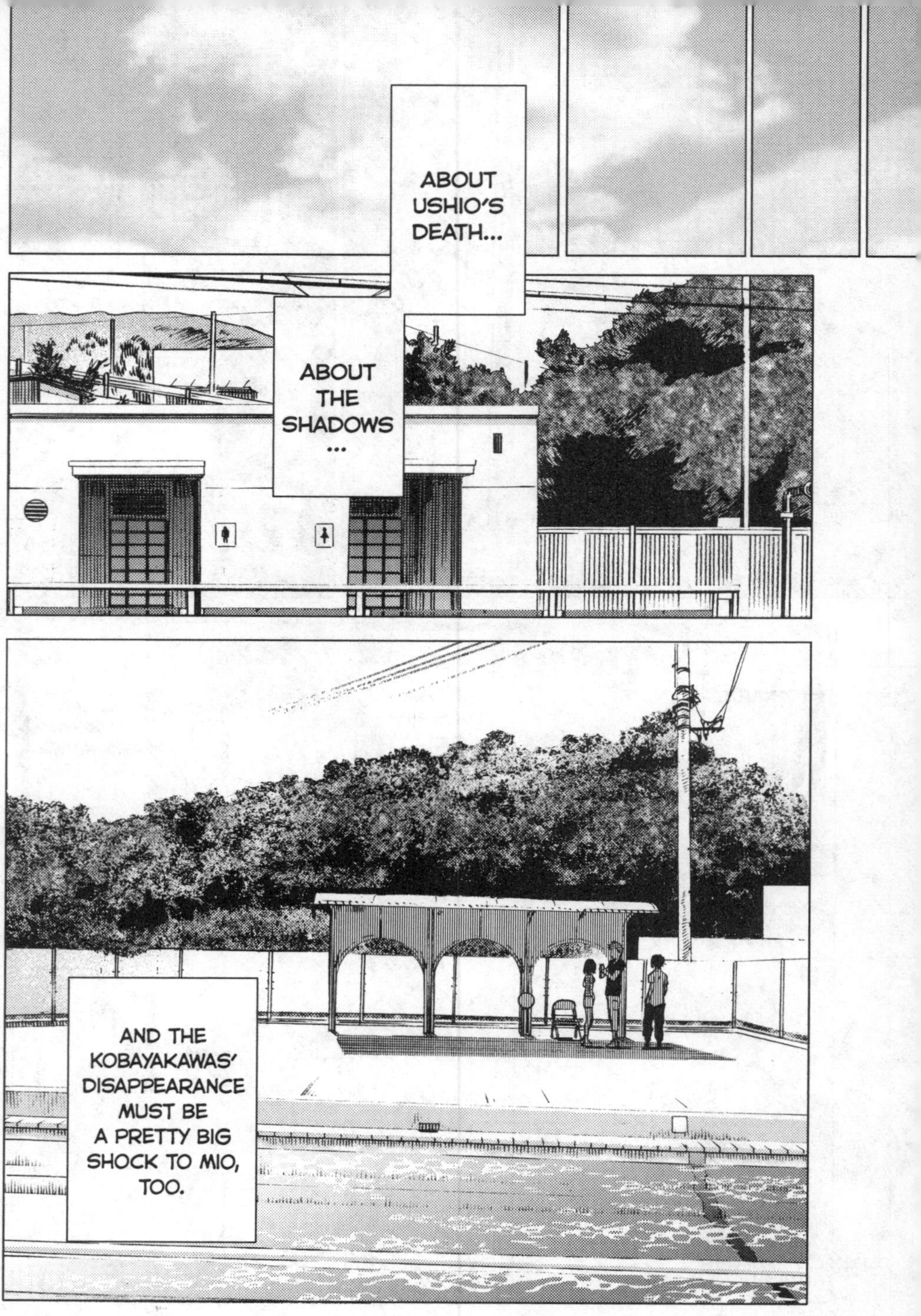
ABOUT USHIO'S DEATH...
ABOUT THE SHADOWS...
AND THE KOBAYAKAWAS' DISAPPEARANCE MUST BE A PRETTY BIG SHOCK TO MIO, TOO.

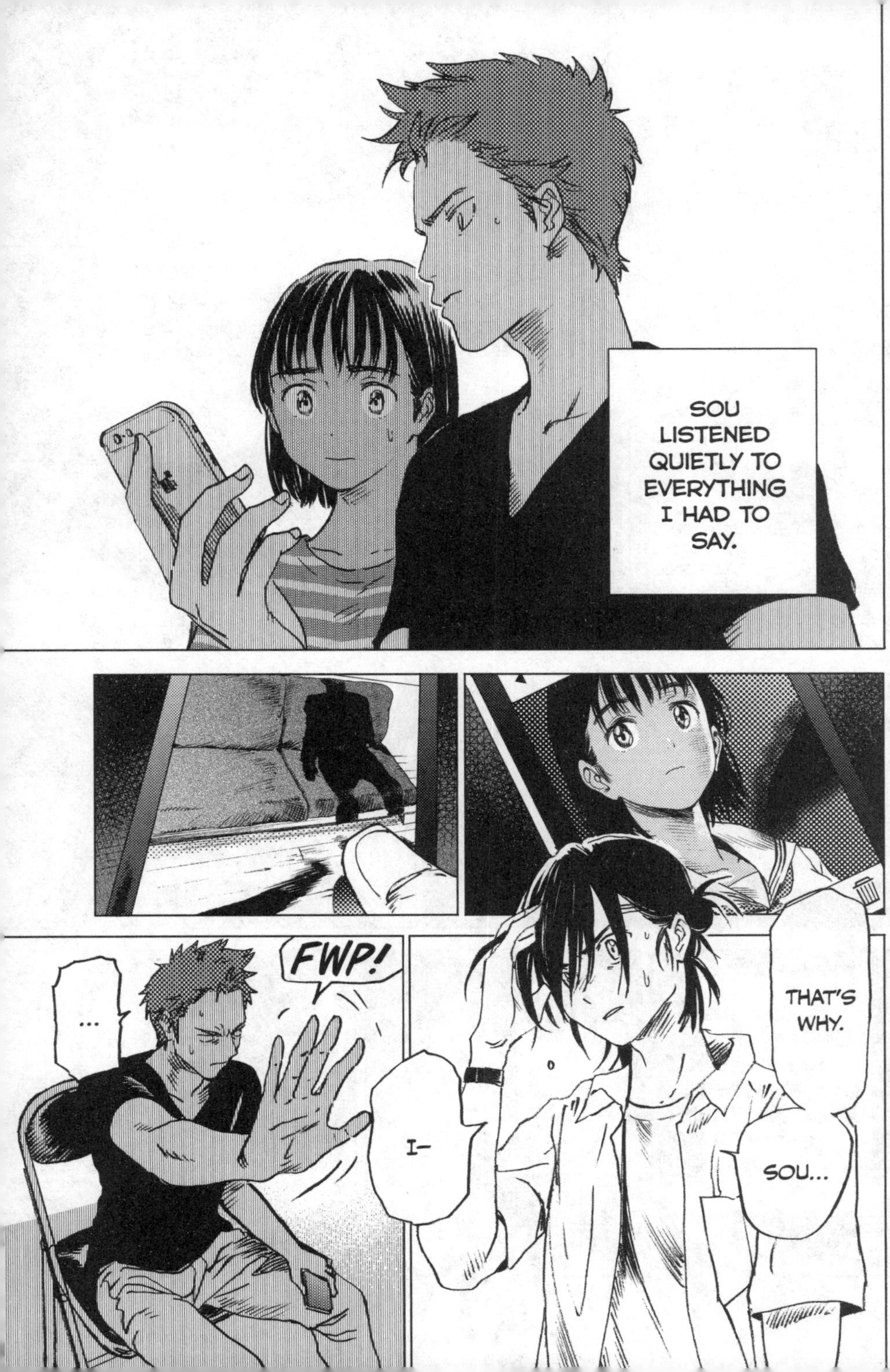
SOU LISTENED QUIETLY TO EVERYTHING I HAD TO SAY.
THAT'S WHY.
SOU...
I–
FWP!
...

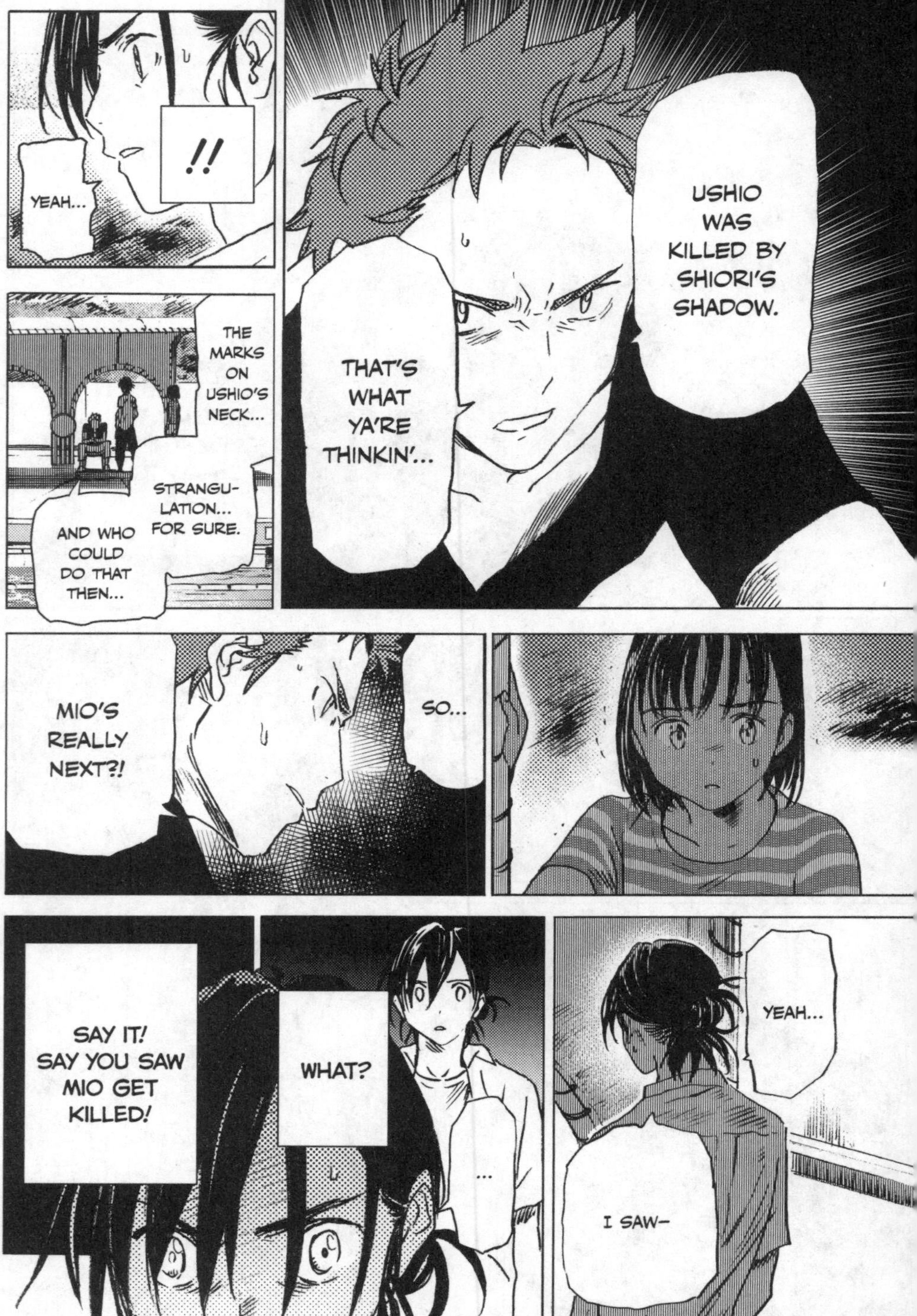
USHIO WAS KILLED BY SHIORI'S SHADOW.
THAT'S WHAT YA'RE THINKIN'...
!!
YEAH...
THE MARKS ON USHIO'S NECK...
STRANGULATION... FOR SURE.
AND WHO COULD DO THAT THEN...
SO...
MIO'S REALLY NEXT?!
YEAH...
I SAW—
WHAT?
...
SAY IT! SAY YOU SAW MIO GET KILLED!

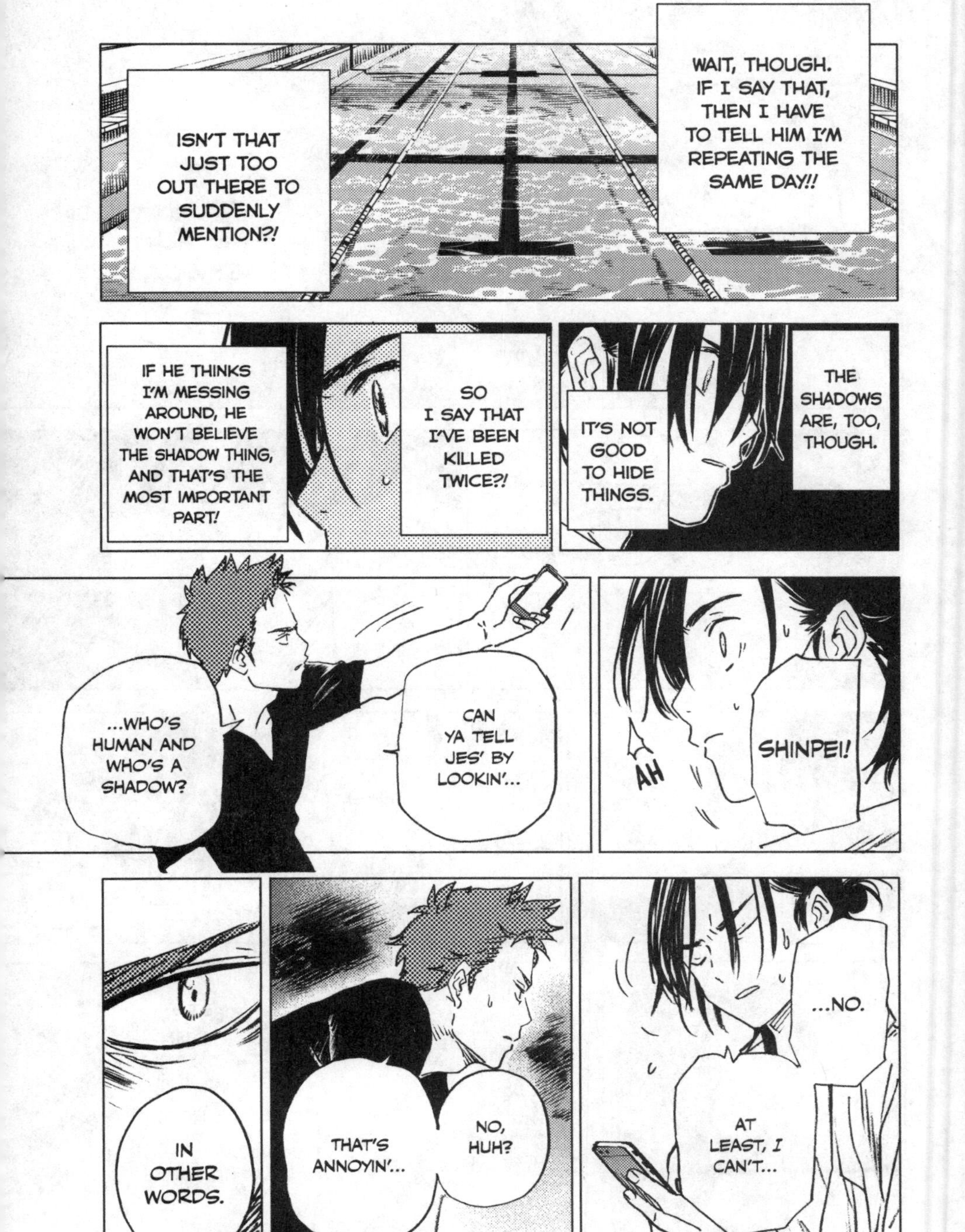
WAIT, THOUGH. IF I SAY THAT, THEN I HAVE TO TELL HIM I'M REPEATING THE SAME DAY!!
ISN'T THAT JUST TOO OUT THERE TO SUDDENLY MENTION?!
THE SHADOWS ARE, TOO, THOUGH.
IT'S NOT GOOD TO HIDE THINGS.
SO I SAY THAT I'VE BEEN KILLED TWICE?!
IF HE THINKS I'M MESSING AROUND, HE WON'T BELIEVE THE SHADOW THING, AND THAT'S THE MOST IMPORTANT PART!
SHINPEI!
AH
CAN YA TELL JES' BY LOOKIN'...
...WHO'S HUMAN AND WHO'S A SHADOW?
...NO.
AT LEAST, I CAN'T...
NO, HUH?
THAT'S ANNOYIN'...
IN OTHER WORDS.

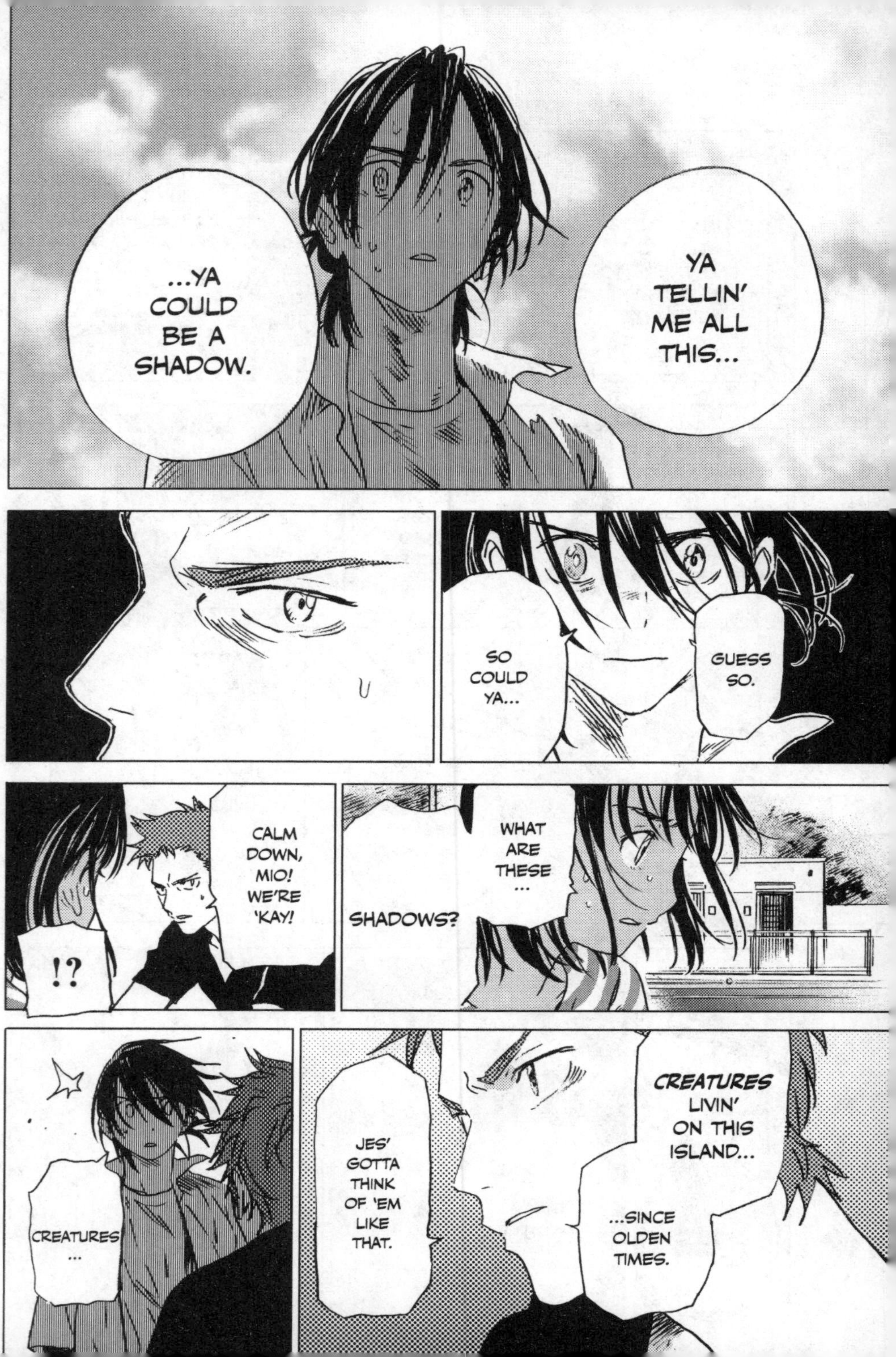
YA TELLIN' ME ALL THIS...
...YA COULD BE A SHADOW.
GUESS SO.
SO COULD YA...
WHAT ARE THESE ...
SHADOWS?
CALM DOWN, MIO! WE'RE 'KAY!
!?
CREATURES LIVIN' ON THIS ISLAND...
...SINCE OLDEN TIMES.
JES' GOTTA THINK OF 'EM LIKE THAT.
CREATURES ...

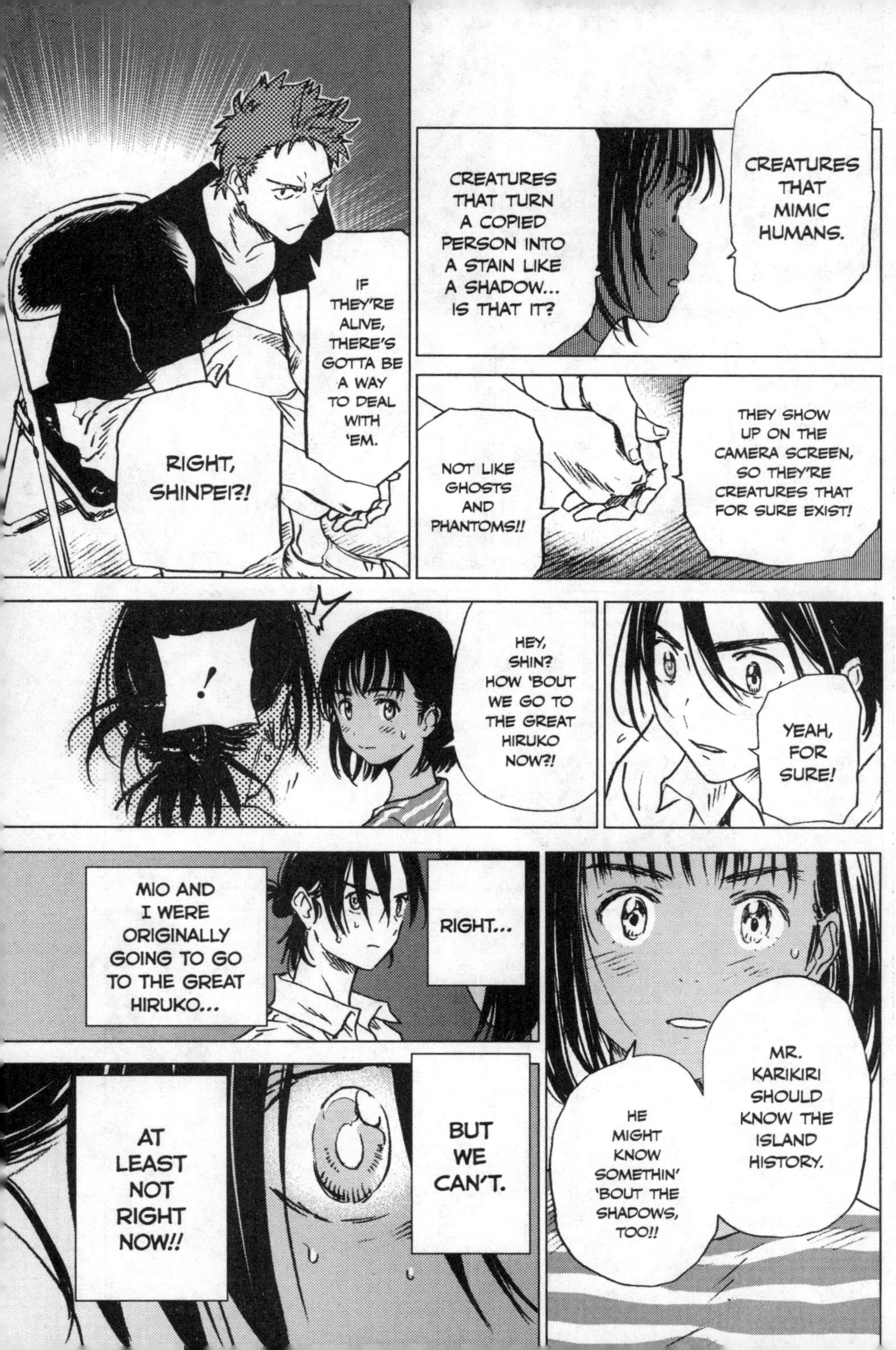
CREATURES THAT MIMIC HUMANS.
CREATURES THAT TURN A COPIED PERSON INTO A STAIN LIKE A SHADOW... IS THAT IT?
THEY SHOW UP ON THE CAMERA SCREEN, SO THEY'RE CREATURES THAT FOR SURE EXIST!
NOT LIKE GHOSTS AND PHANTOMS!!
IF THEY'RE ALIVE, THERE'S GOTTA BE A WAY TO DEAL WITH 'EM.
RIGHT, SHINPEI?!
YEAH, FOR SURE!
HEY, SHIN? HOW 'BOUT WE GO TO THE GREAT HIRUKO NOW?!
!
MR. KARIKIRI SHOULD KNOW THE ISLAND HISTORY.
HE MIGHT KNOW SOMETHIN' 'BOUT THE SHADOWS, TOO!!
RIGHT...
MIO AND I WERE ORIGINALLY GOING TO GO TO THE GREAT HIRUKO...
BUT WE CAN'T.
AT LEAST NOT RIGHT NOW!!

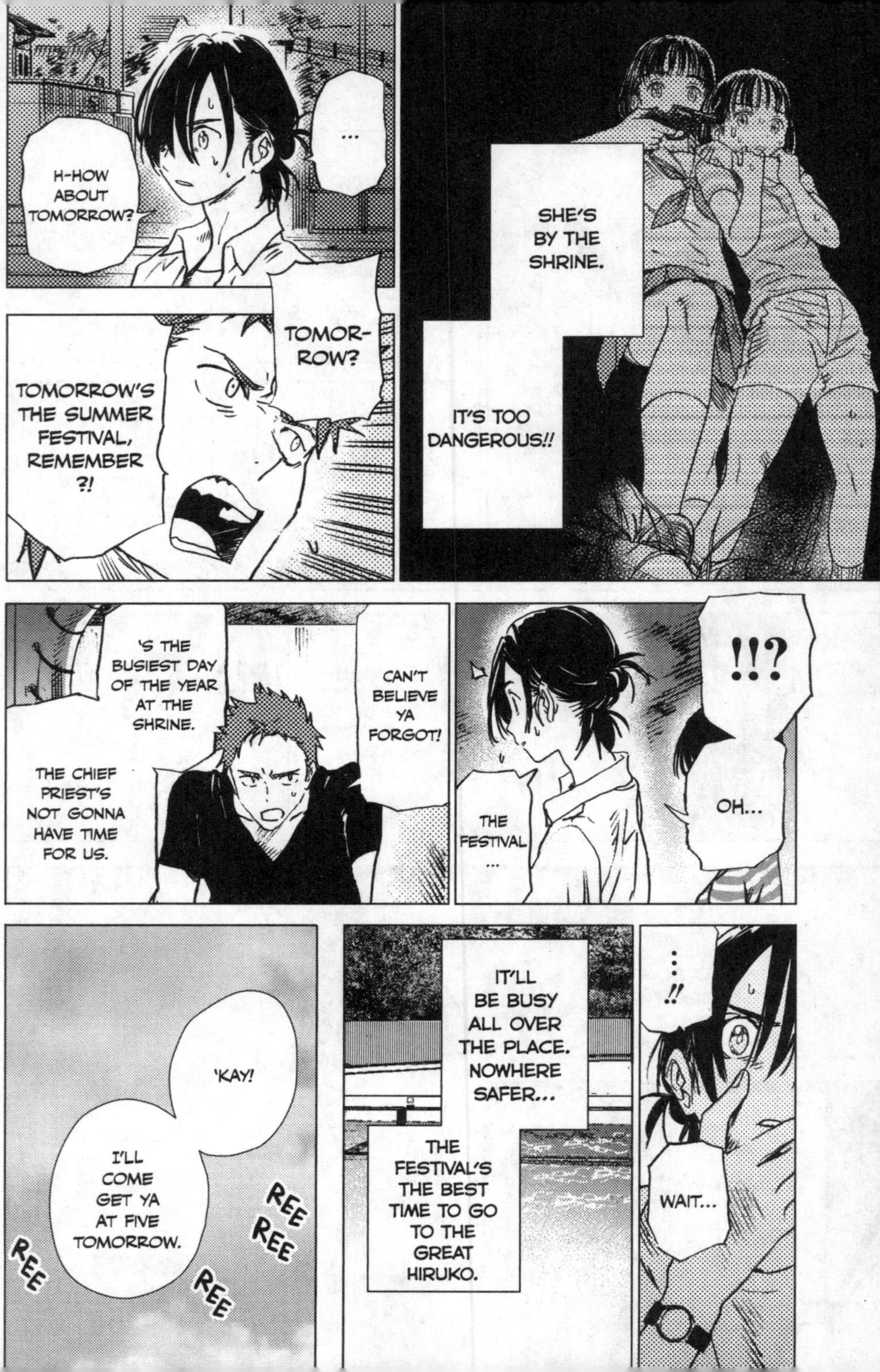
SHE'S BY THE SHRINE.
IT'S TOO DANGEROUS!!
...
H-HOW ABOUT TOMORROW?
TOMORROW?
TOMORROW'S THE SUMMER FESTIVAL, REMEMBER ?!
!!?
OH...
THE FESTIVAL ...
CAN'T BELIEVE YA FORGOT!
'S THE BUSIEST DAY OF THE YEAR AT THE SHRINE.
THE CHIEF PRIEST'S NOT GONNA HAVE TIME FOR US.
...!!
WAIT...
IT'LL BE BUSY ALL OVER THE PLACE. NOWHERE SAFER...
THE FESTIVAL'S THE BEST TIME TO GO TO THE GREAT HIRUKO.
'KAY!
I'LL COME GET YA AT FIVE TOMORROW.
REE
REE
REE
REE

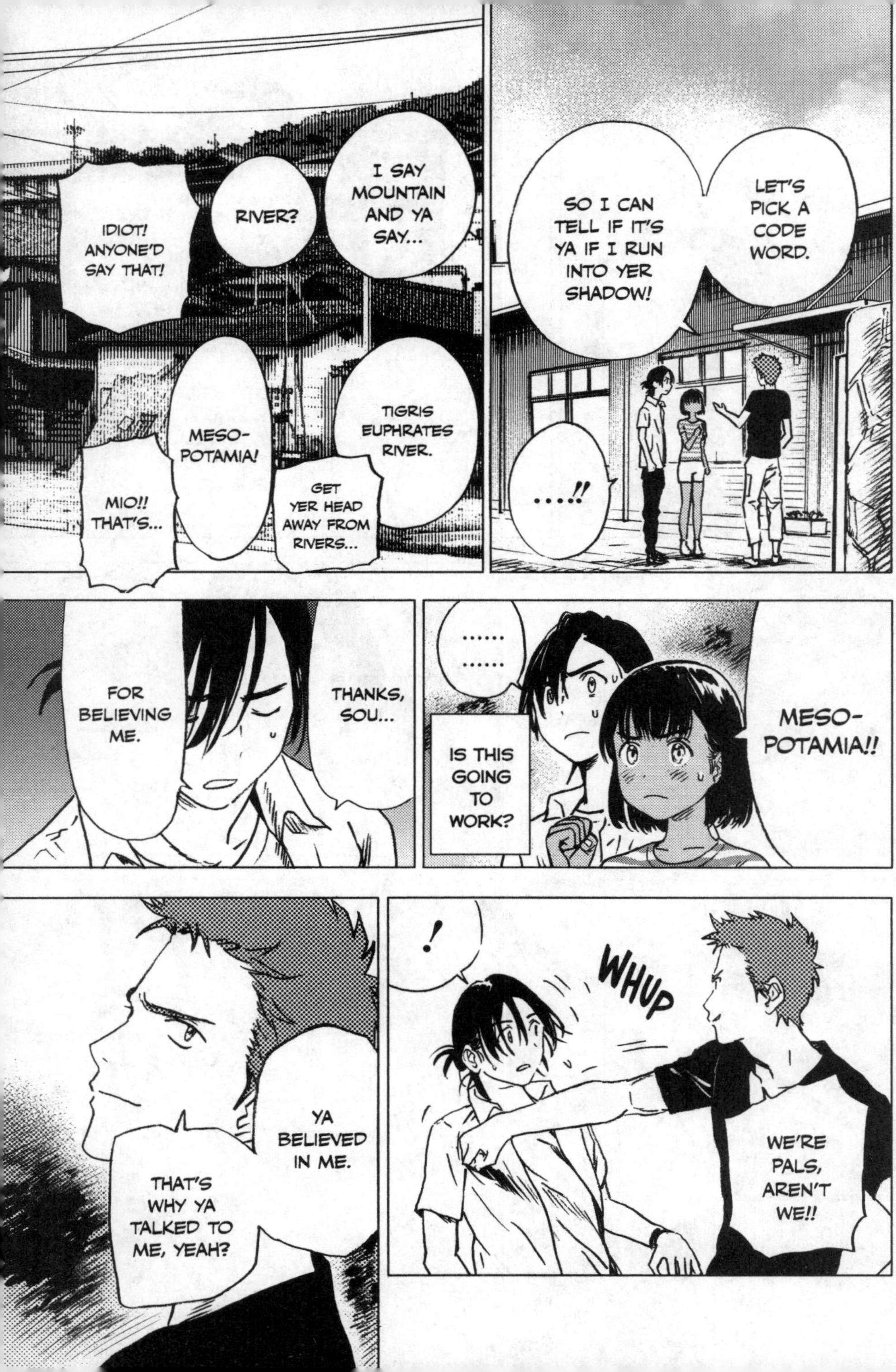
LET'S PICK A CODE WORD.
SO I CAN TELL IF IT'S YA IF I RUN INTO YER SHADOW!
....!!
I SAY MOUNTAIN AND YA SAY...
RIVER?
IDIOT! ANYONE'D SAY THAT!
TIGRIS EUPHRATES RIVER.
GET YER HEAD AWAY FROM RIVERS...
MESO-POTAMIA!
MIO!! THAT'S...
MESO-POTAMIA!!
......
......
IS THIS GOING TO WORK?
THANKS, SOU...
FOR BELIEVING ME.
!
WHUP
WE'RE PALS, AREN'T WE!!
YA BELIEVED IN ME.
THAT'S WHY YA TALKED TO ME, YEAH?

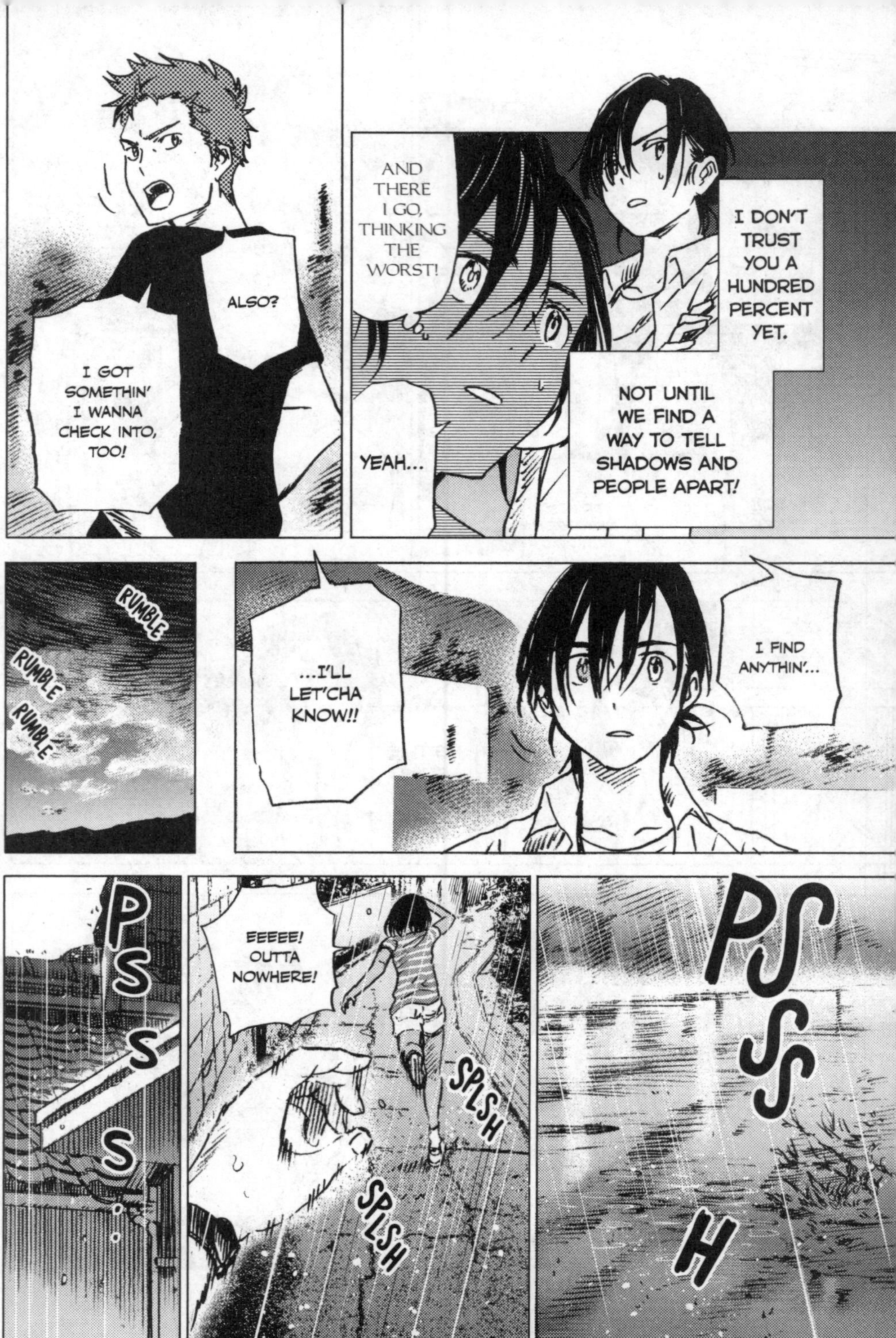
I DON'T TRUST YOU A HUNDRED PERCENT YET.
NOT UNTIL WE FIND A WAY TO TELL SHADOWS AND PEOPLE APART!
AND THERE I GO, THINKING THE WORST!
YEAH...
ALSO?
I GOT SOMETHIN' I WANNA CHECK INTO, TOO!
I FIND ANYTHIN'...
...I'LL LET'CHA KNOW!!
RUMBLE
RUMBLE
RUMBLE
PSSSH
EEEEE! OUTTA NOWHERE!
SPLSH
SPLSH
PSSS...

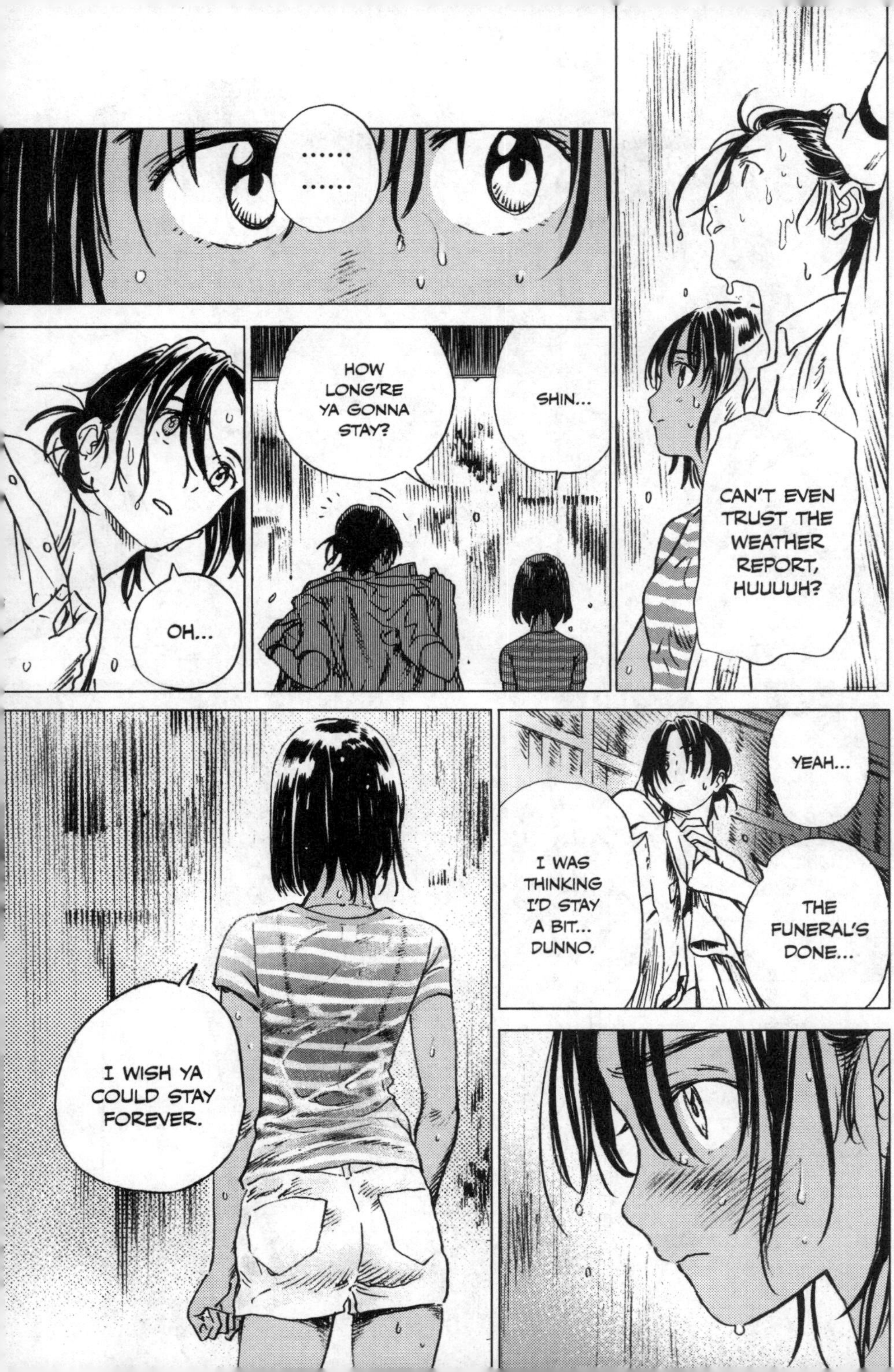
CAN'T EVEN TRUST THE WEATHER REPORT, HUUUUH?
......
......
SHIN...
HOW LONG'RE YA GONNA STAY?
OH...
YEAH...
THE FUNERAL'S DONE...
I WAS THINKING I'D STAY A BIT... DUNNO.
I WISH YA COULD STAY FOREVER.

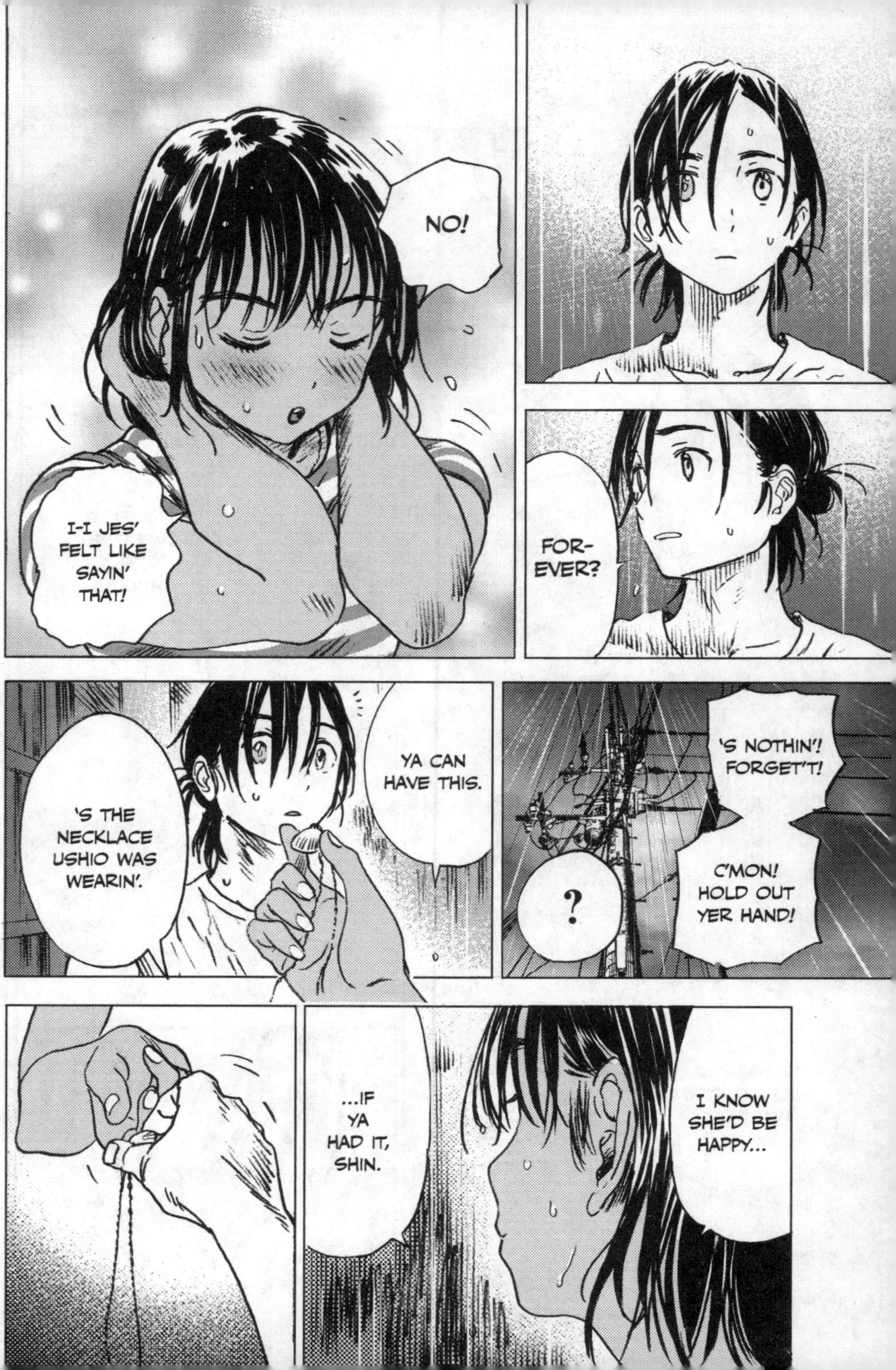
FOR-EVER?
NO!
I-I JES' FELT LIKE SAYIN' THAT!
'S NOTHIN'! FORGET'T!
C'MON! HOLD OUT YER HAND!
?
YA CAN HAVE THIS.
'S THE NECKLACE USHIO WAS WEARIN'.
I KNOW SHE'D BE HAPPY...
...IF YA HAD IT, SHIN.

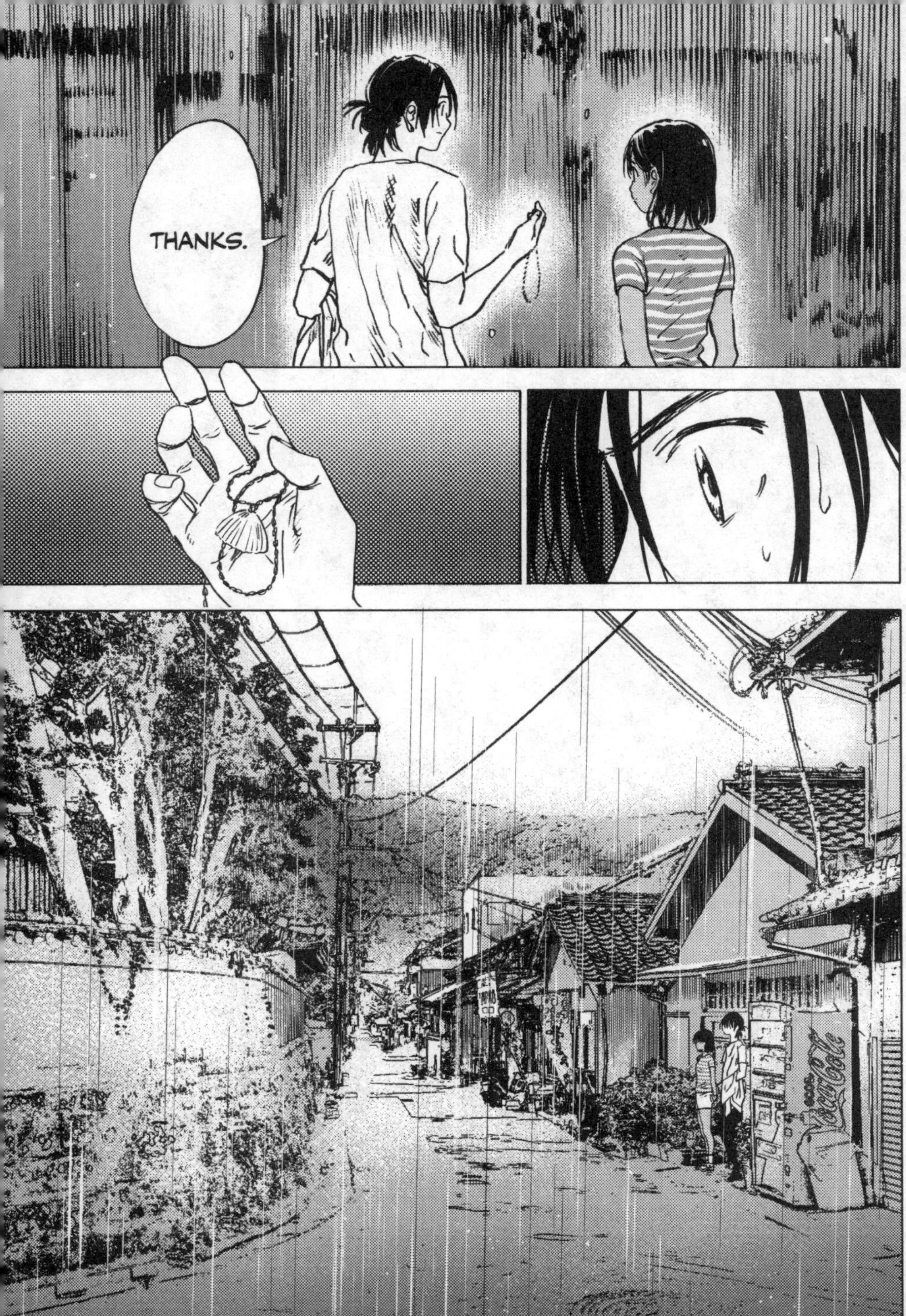
THANKS.

Summertime rendering

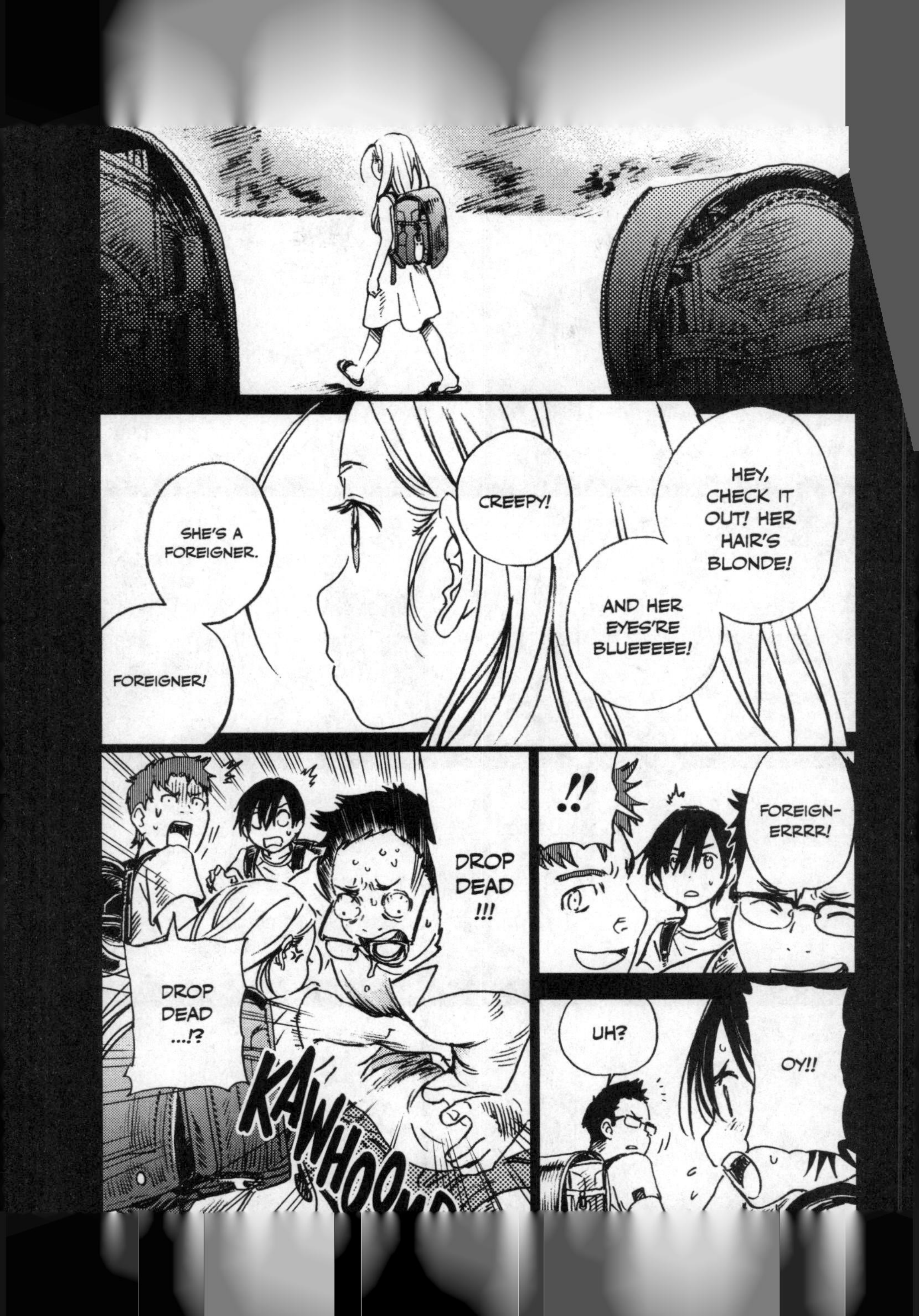
HEY, CHECK IT OUT! HER HAIR'S BLONDE!
CREEPY!
AND HER EYES'RE BLUEEEEE!
SHE'S A FOREIGNER.
FOREIGNER!
FOREIGN-ERRRR!
!!
OY!!
UH?
DROP DEAD!!!
DROP DEAD ...!?
KAWHOOM

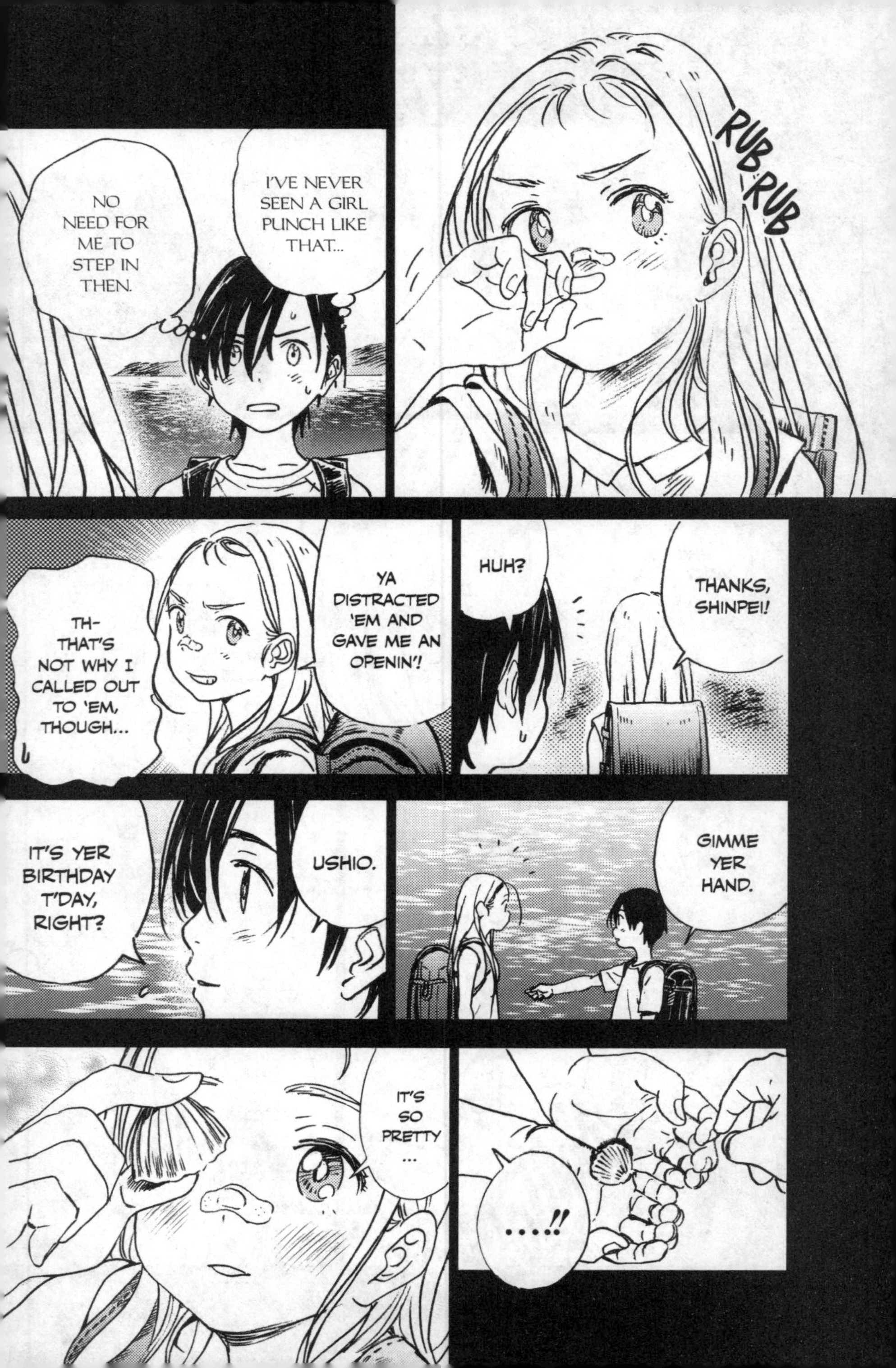
RUB RUB
I'VE NEVER SEEN A GIRL PUNCH LIKE THAT...
NO NEED FOR ME TO STEP IN THEN.
THANKS, SHINPEI!
HUH?
YA DISTRACTED 'EM AND GAVE ME AN OPENIN'!
TH- THAT'S NOT WHY I CALLED OUT TO 'EM, THOUGH...
GIMME YER HAND.
USHIO.
IT'S YER BIRTHDAY T'DAY, RIGHT?
....!!
IT'S SO PRETTY ...

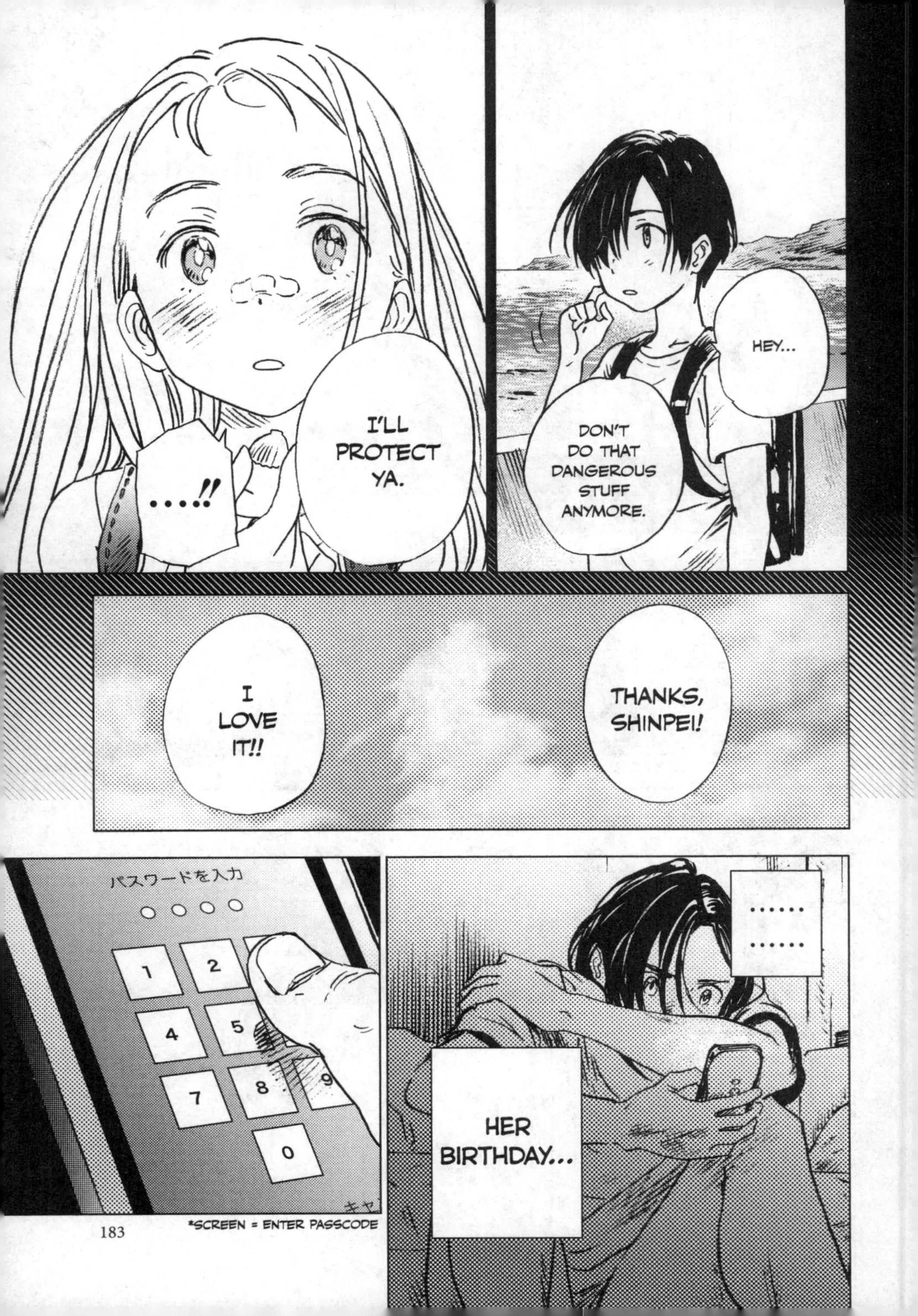
HEY...
DON'T DO THAT DANGEROUS STUFF ANYMORE.
I'LL PROTECT YA.
....!!
THANKS, SHINPEI!
I LOVE IT!!
......
......
HER BIRTHDAY...
パスワードを入力
1 2 4 5 7 8 9 0
キャ

*SCREEN = ENTER PASSCODE

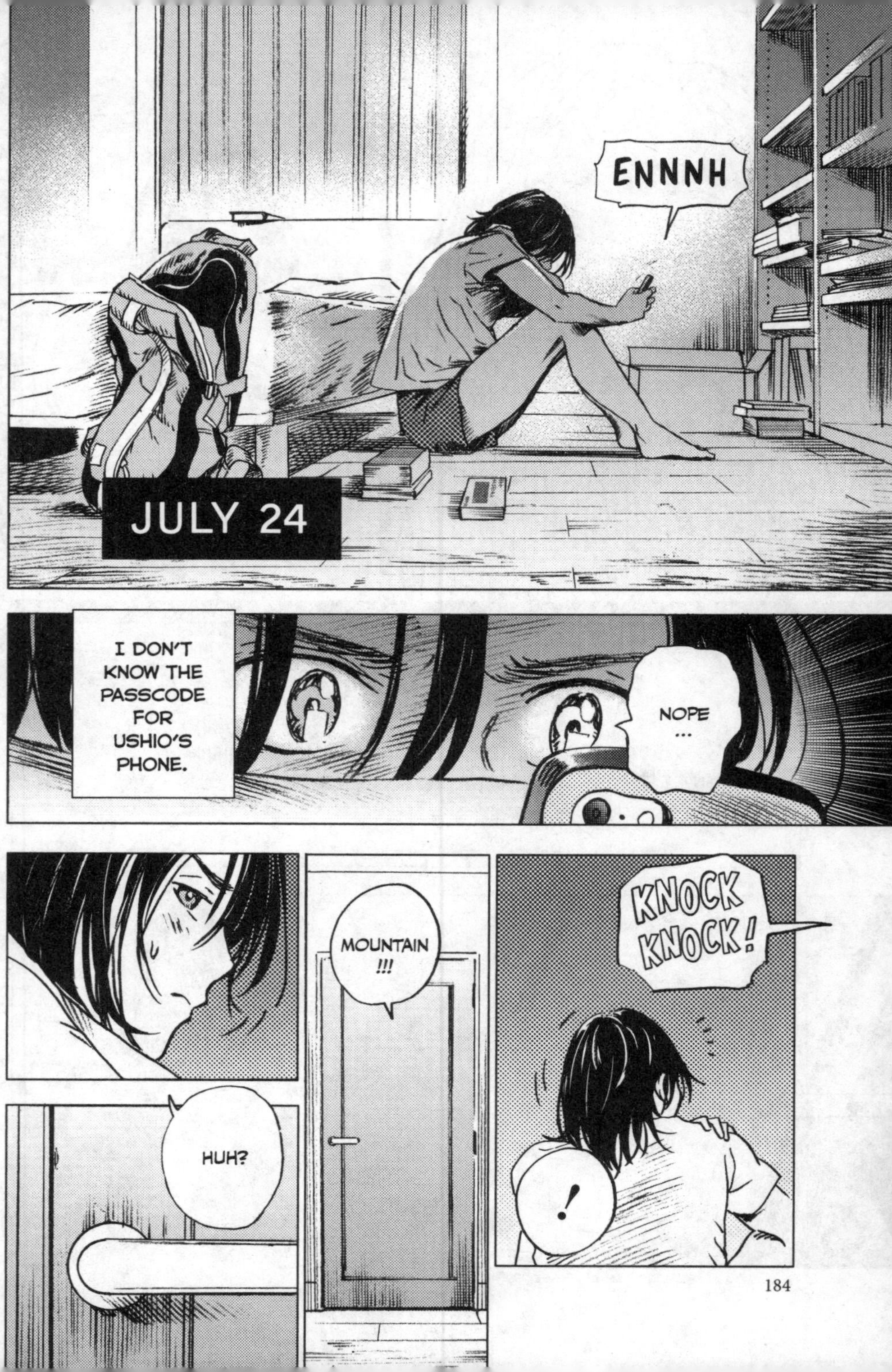
ENNNH
JULY 24
I DON'T KNOW THE PASSCODE FOR USHIO'S PHONE.
NOPE ...
KNOCK KNOCK!
!
MOUNTAIN !!!
HUH?

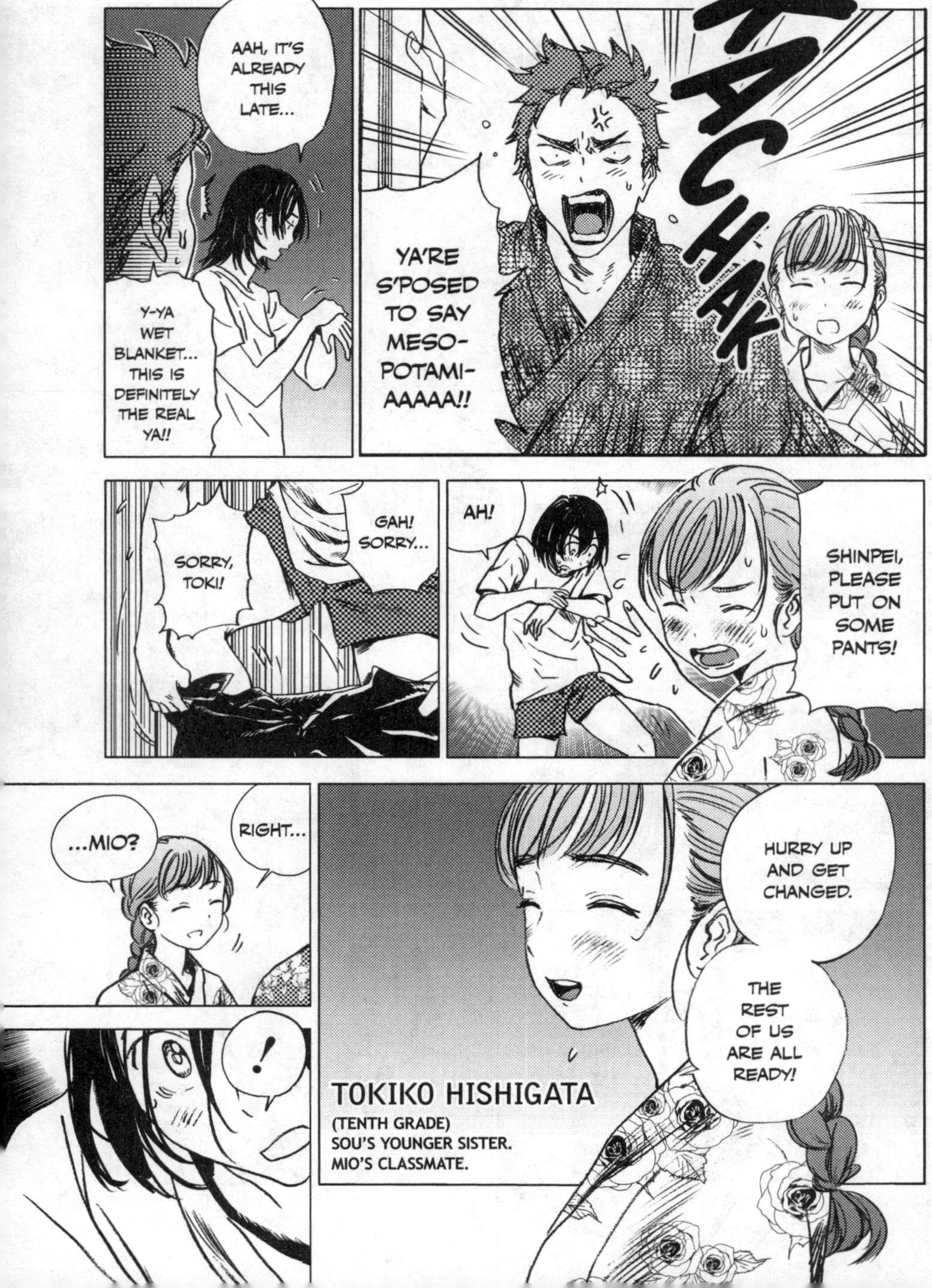
KACHAK
YA'RE S'POSED TO SAY MESO-POTAMI-AAAAA!!
AAH, IT'S ALREADY THIS LATE...
Y-YA WET BLANKET... THIS IS DEFINITELY THE REAL YA!!
SHINPEI, PLEASE PUT ON SOME PANTS!
AH!
GAH! SORRY...
SORRY, TOKI!
HURRY UP AND GET CHANGED.
THE REST OF US ARE ALL READY!
TOKIKO HISHIGATA
(TENTH GRADE)
SOU'S YOUNGER SISTER.
MIO'S CLASSMATE.
RIGHT...
...MIO?
!

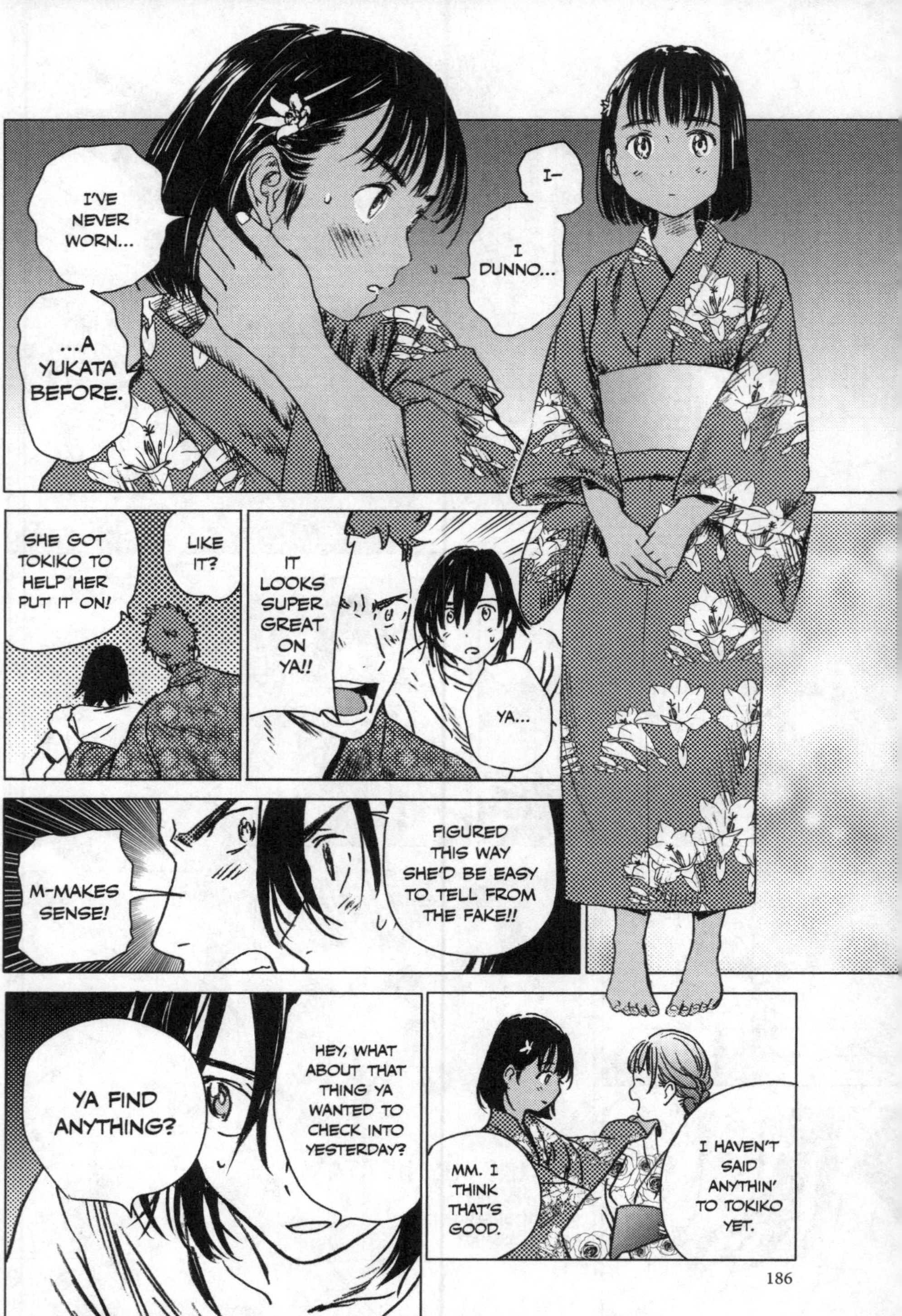
I—
I DUNNO...
I'VE NEVER WORN...
...A YUKATA BEFORE.
IT LOOKS SUPER GREAT ON YA!!
YA...
LIKE IT?
SHE GOT TOKIKO TO HELP HER PUT IT ON!
FIGURED THIS WAY SHE'D BE EASY TO TELL FROM THE FAKE!!
M-MAKES SENSE!
I HAVEN'T SAID ANYTHIN' TO TOKIKO YET.
MM. I THINK THAT'S GOOD.
HEY, WHAT ABOUT THAT THING YA WANTED TO CHECK INTO YESTERDAY?
YA FIND ANYTHING?

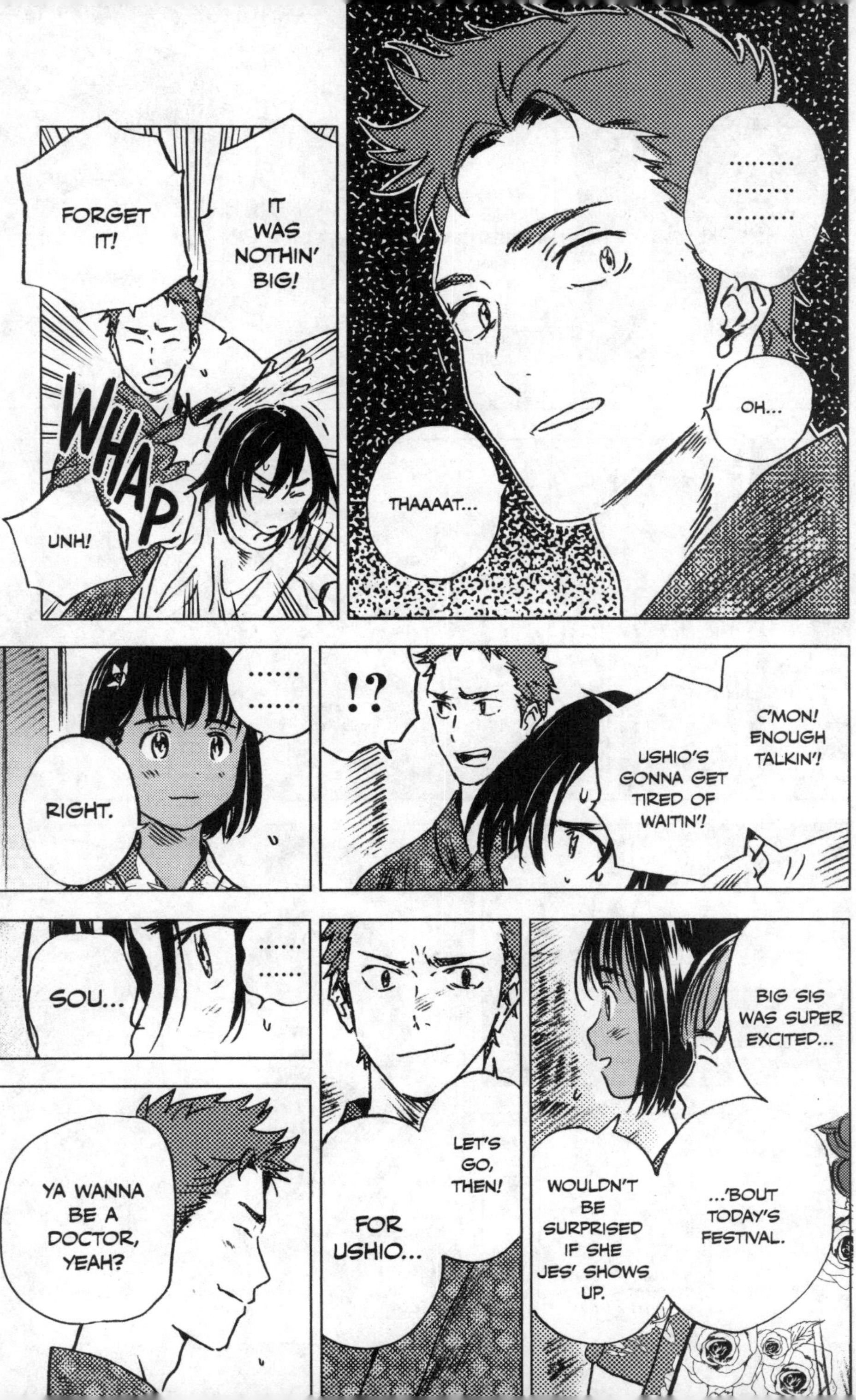
....
OH...
THAAAAT...
IT WAS NOTHIN' BIG!
FORGET IT!
WHAP
UNH!
C'MON! ENOUGH TALKIN'!
USHIO'S GONNA GET TIRED OF WAITIN'!
!?
....
RIGHT.
BIG SIS WAS SUPER EXCITED...
...'BOUT TODAY'S FESTIVAL.
WOULDN'T BE SURPRISED IF SHE JES' SHOWS UP.
LET'S GO, THEN!
FOR USHIO...
....
SOU...
YA WANNA BE A DOCTOR, YEAH?

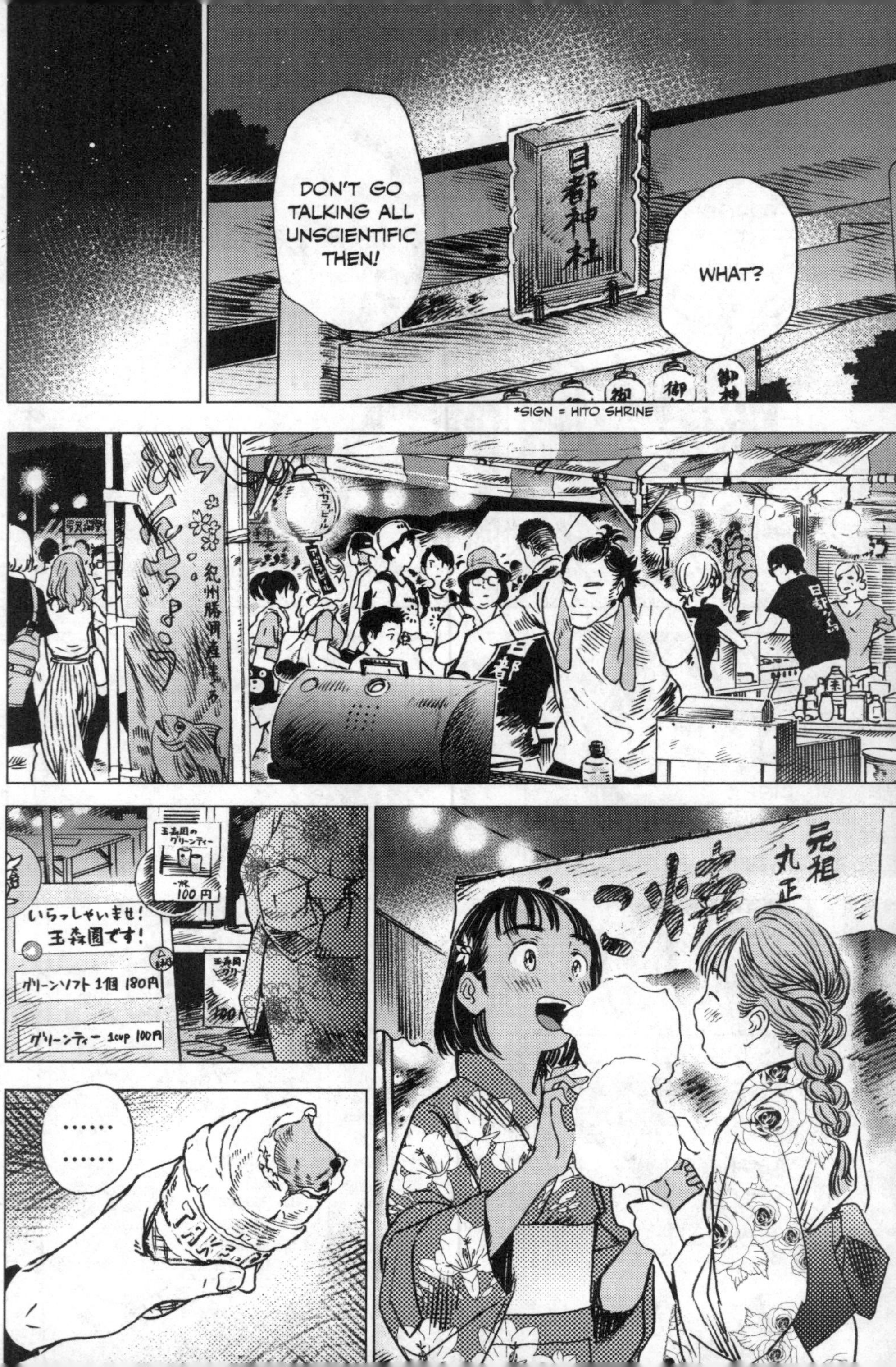
DON'T GO TALKING ALL UNSCIENTIFIC THEN!
WHAT?
日都神社
*SIGN = HITO SHRINE
元祖
丸正
いらっしゃいませ！
玉森園です！
グリーンソフト 1個 180円
グリーンティー 1cup 100円
……
……

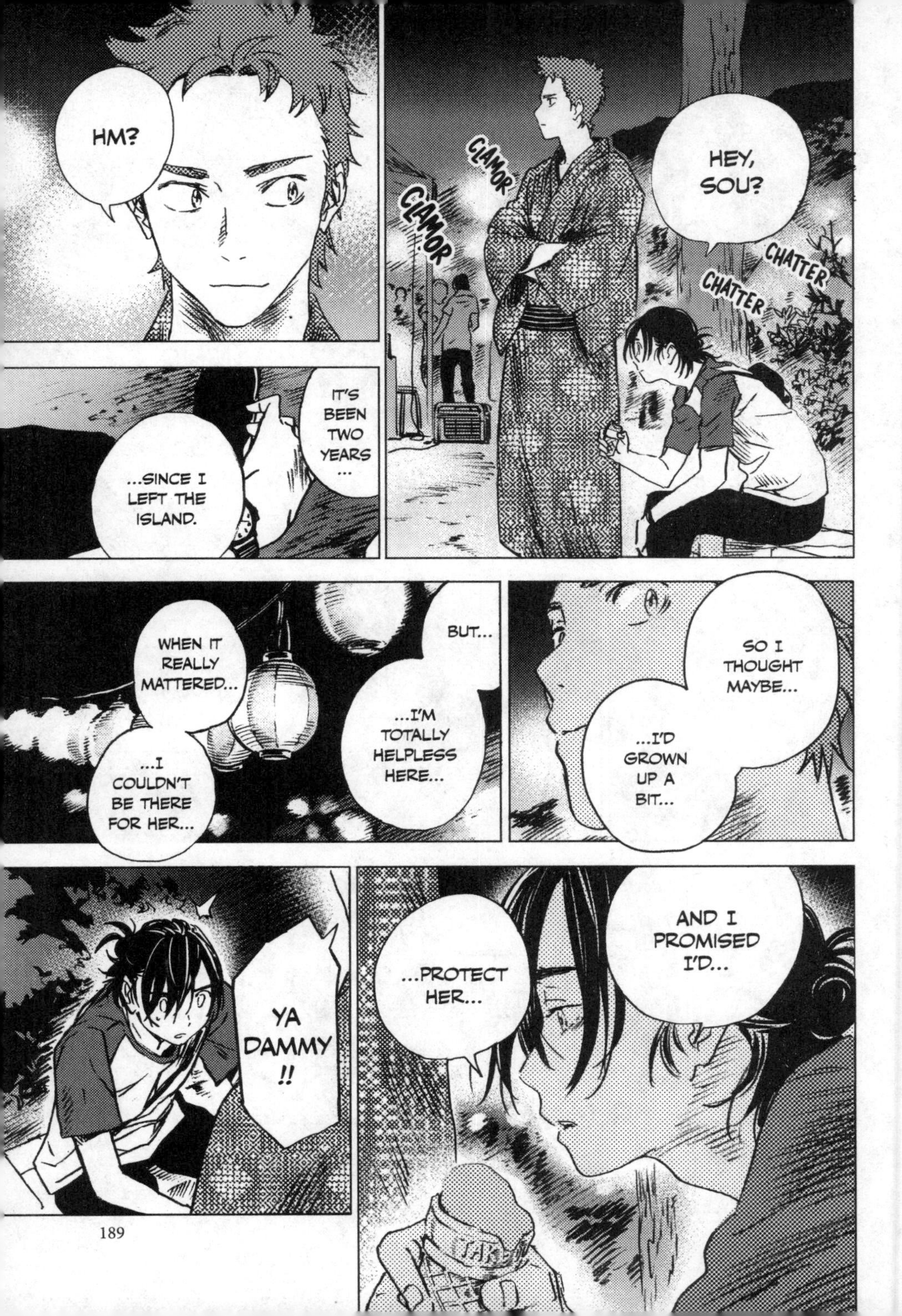
CLAMOR
CLAMOR
HEY, SOU?
CHATTER
CHATTER
HM?
IT'S BEEN TWO YEARS...
...SINCE I LEFT THE ISLAND.
SO I THOUGHT MAYBE...
...I'D GROWN UP A BIT...
BUT...
...I'M TOTALLY HELPLESS HERE...
WHEN IT REALLY MATTERED...
...I COULDN'T BE THERE FOR HER...
AND I PROMISED I'D...
...PROTECT HER...
YA DAMMY !!

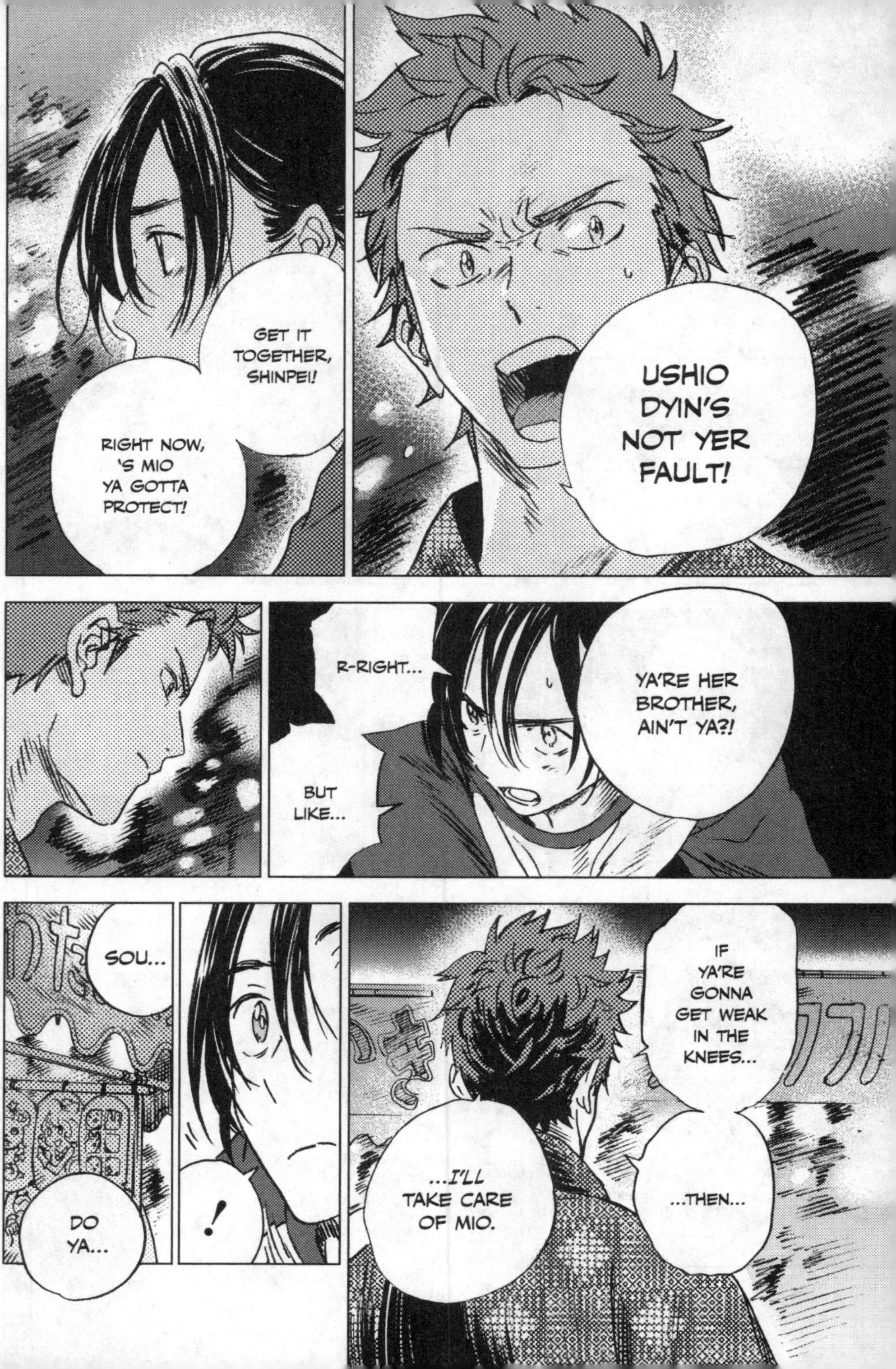
USHIO DYIN'S NOT YER FAULT!
GET IT TOGETHER, SHINPEI!
RIGHT NOW, 'S MIO YA GOTTA PROTECT!
YA'RE HER BROTHER, AIN'T YA?!
R-RIGHT...
BUT LIKE...
IF YA'RE GONNA GET WEAK IN THE KNEES...
...THEN...
...I'LL TAKE CARE OF MIO.
!
SOU...
DO YA...

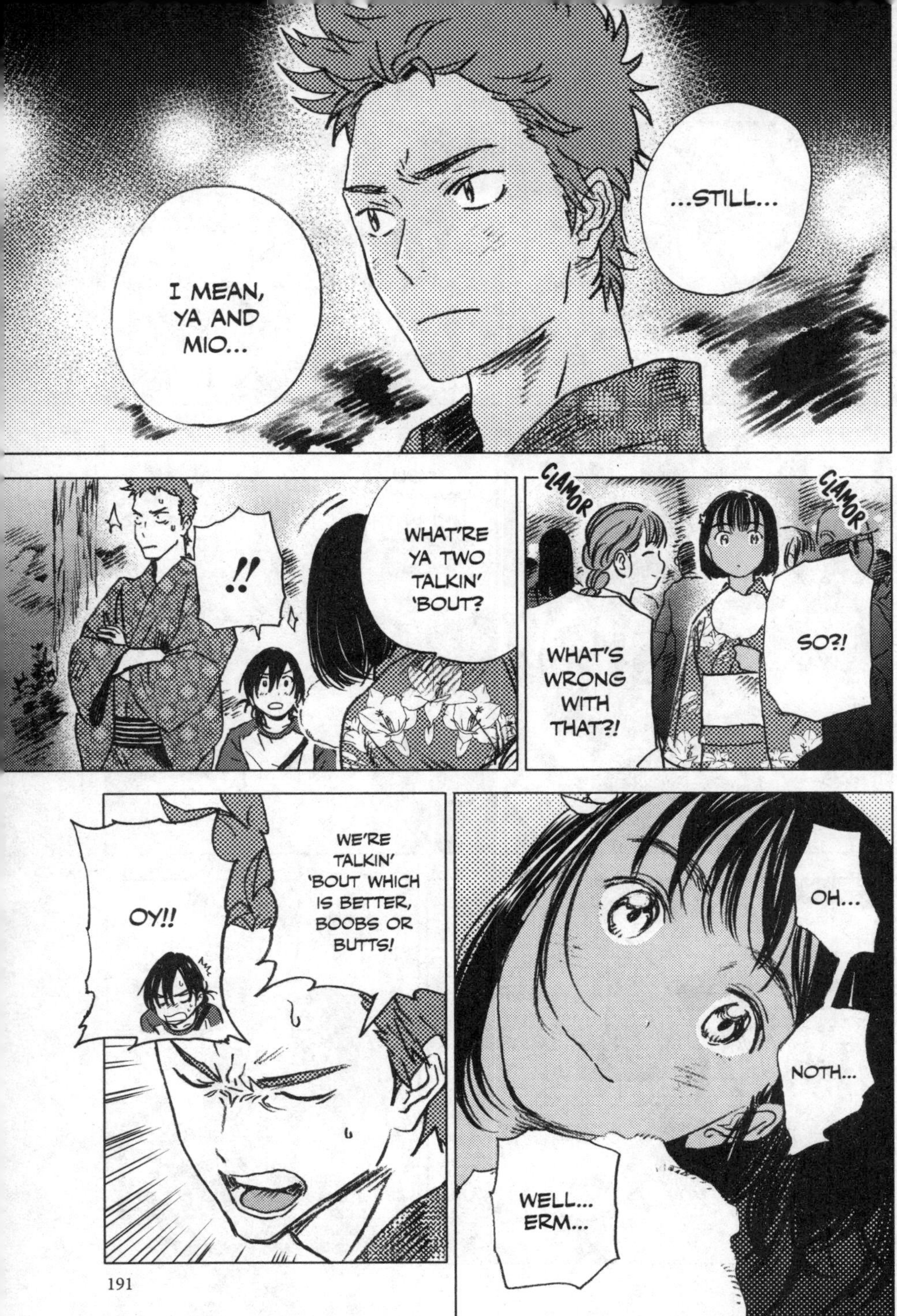
...STILL...
I MEAN, YA AND MIO...
CLAMOR
CLAMOR
SO?!
WHAT'S WRONG WITH THAT?!
WHAT'RE YA TWO TALKIN' 'BOUT?
!!
OH...
NOTH...
WELL... ERM...
WE'RE TALKIN' 'BOUT WHICH IS BETTER, BOOBS OR BUTTS!
OY!!

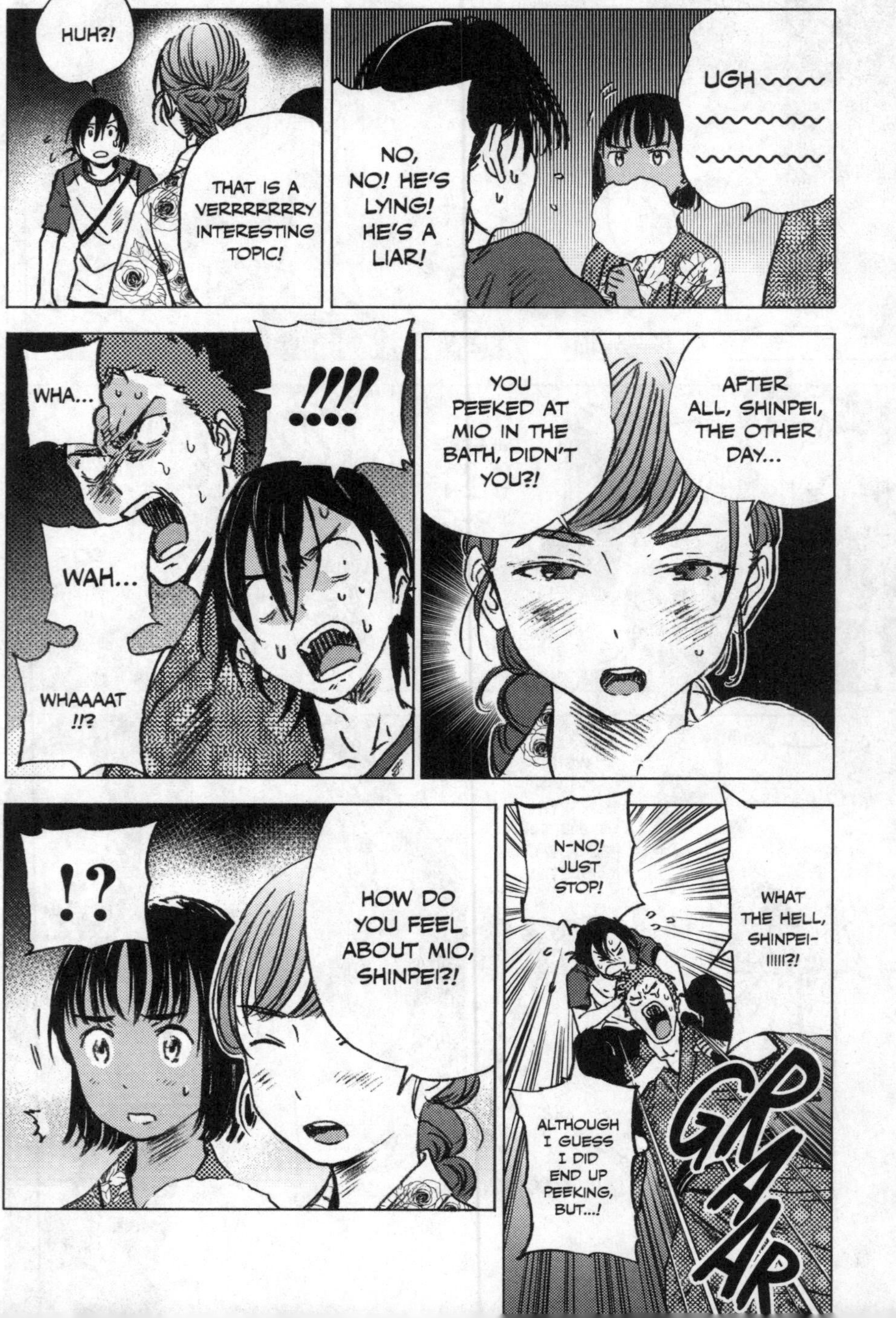
UGH ~~~~~~~~~
NO, NO! HE'S LYING! HE'S A LIAR!
THAT IS A VERRRRRRRY INTERESTING TOPIC!
HUH?!
AFTER ALL, SHINPEI, THE OTHER DAY...
YOU PEEKED AT MIO IN THE BATH, DIDN'T YOU?!
!!!!
WHA...
WAH...
WHAAAAT!!?
WHAT THE HELL, SHINPEI-!!!!!?!
N-NO! JUST STOP!
ALTHOUGH I GUESS I DID END UP PEEKING, BUT...!
GRAHAR
HOW DO YOU FEEL ABOUT MIO, SHINPEI?!
!?

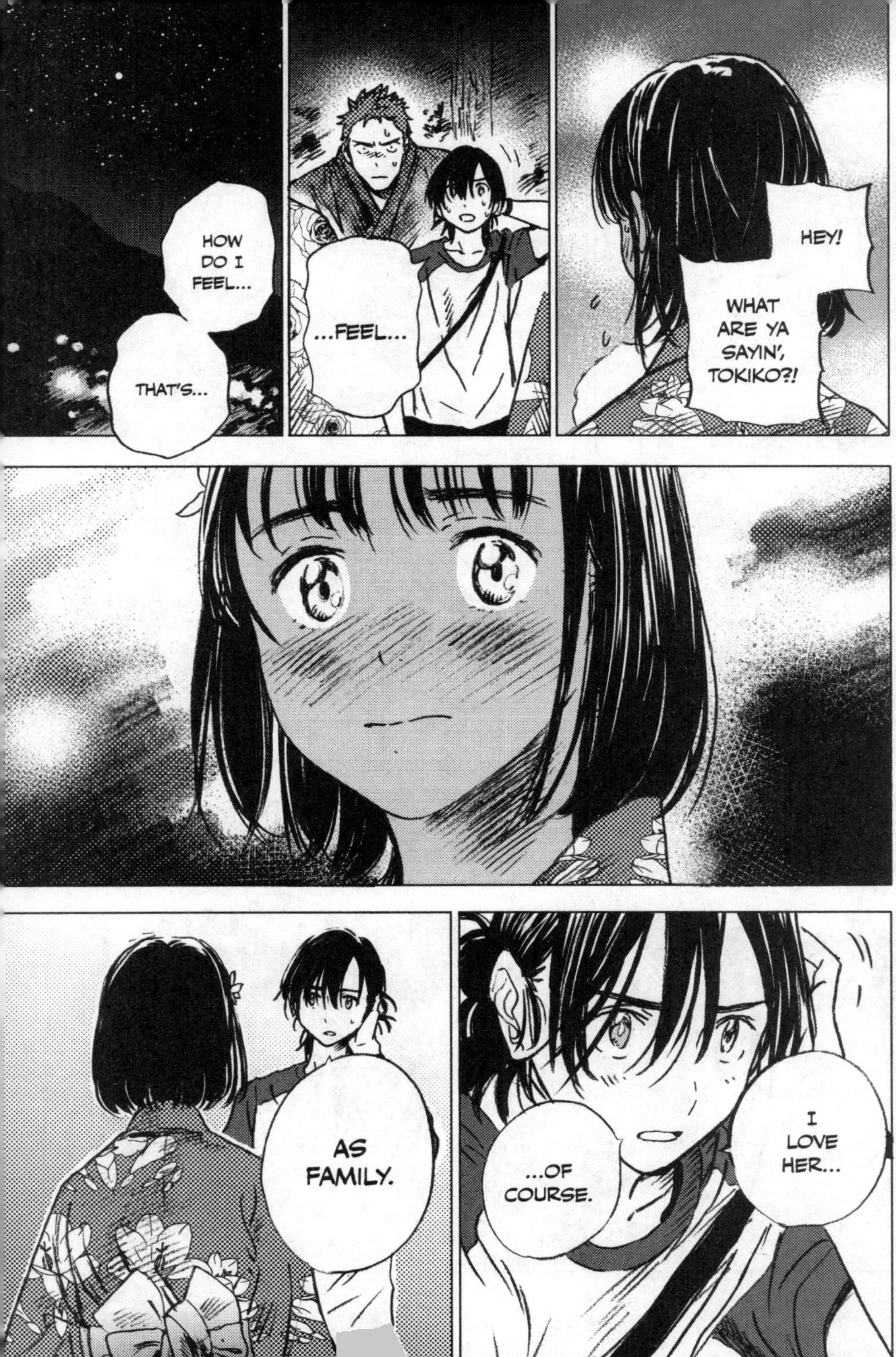
HEY!
WHAT ARE YA SAYIN', TOKIKO?!
...FEEL...
HOW DO I FEEL...
THAT'S...
I LOVE HER...
...OF COURSE.
AS FAMILY.

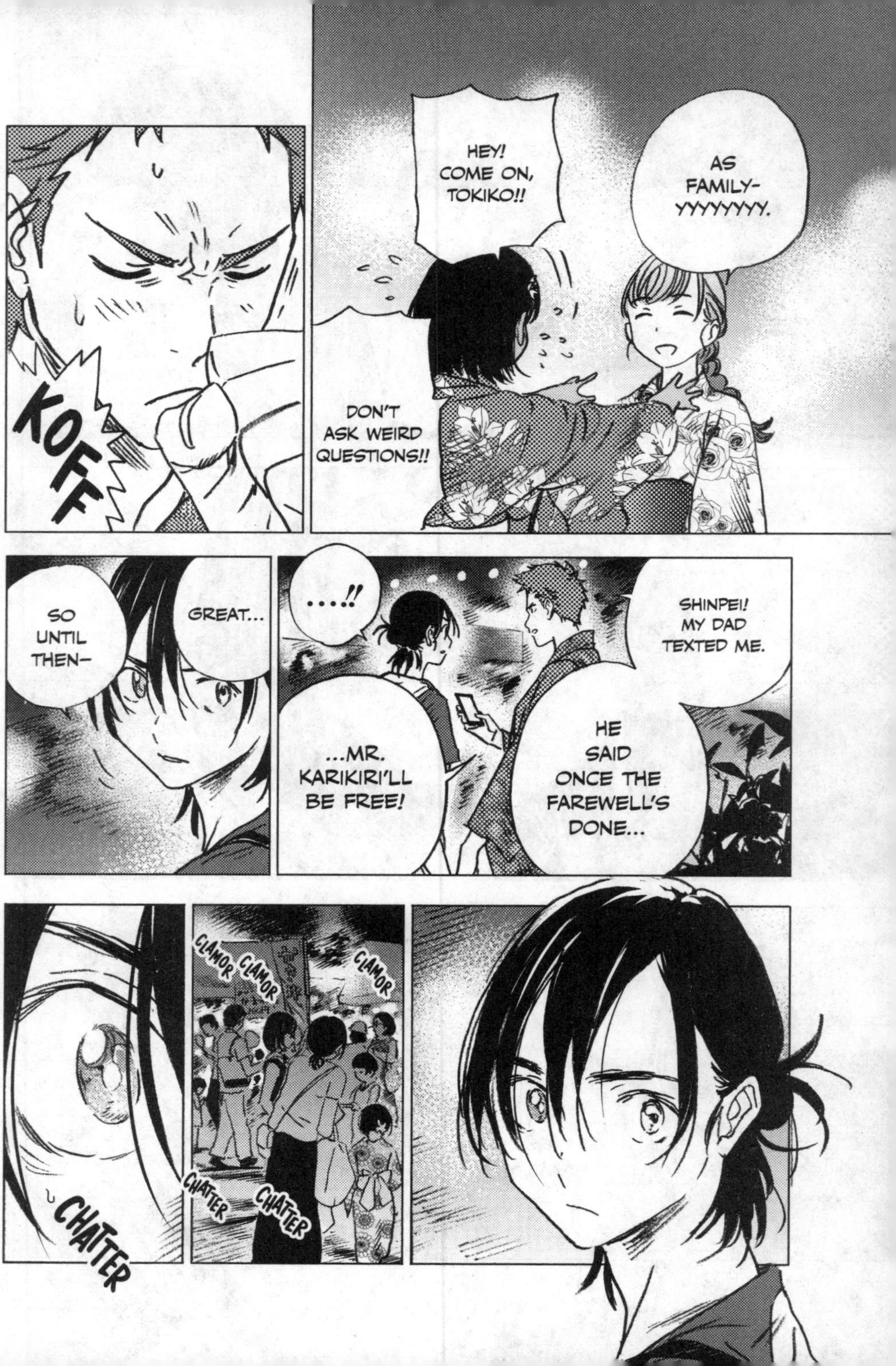
AS FAMILY-YYYYYYYY.
HEY! COME ON, TOKIKO!!
DON'T ASK WEIRD QUESTIONS!!
KOFF
SHINPEI! MY DAD TEXTED ME.
....!!
HE SAID ONCE THE FAREWELL'S DONE...
...MR. KARIKIRI'LL BE FREE!
GREAT...
SO UNTIL THEN-
CLAMOR
CLAMOR
CLAMOR
CHATTER
CHATTER
CHATTER

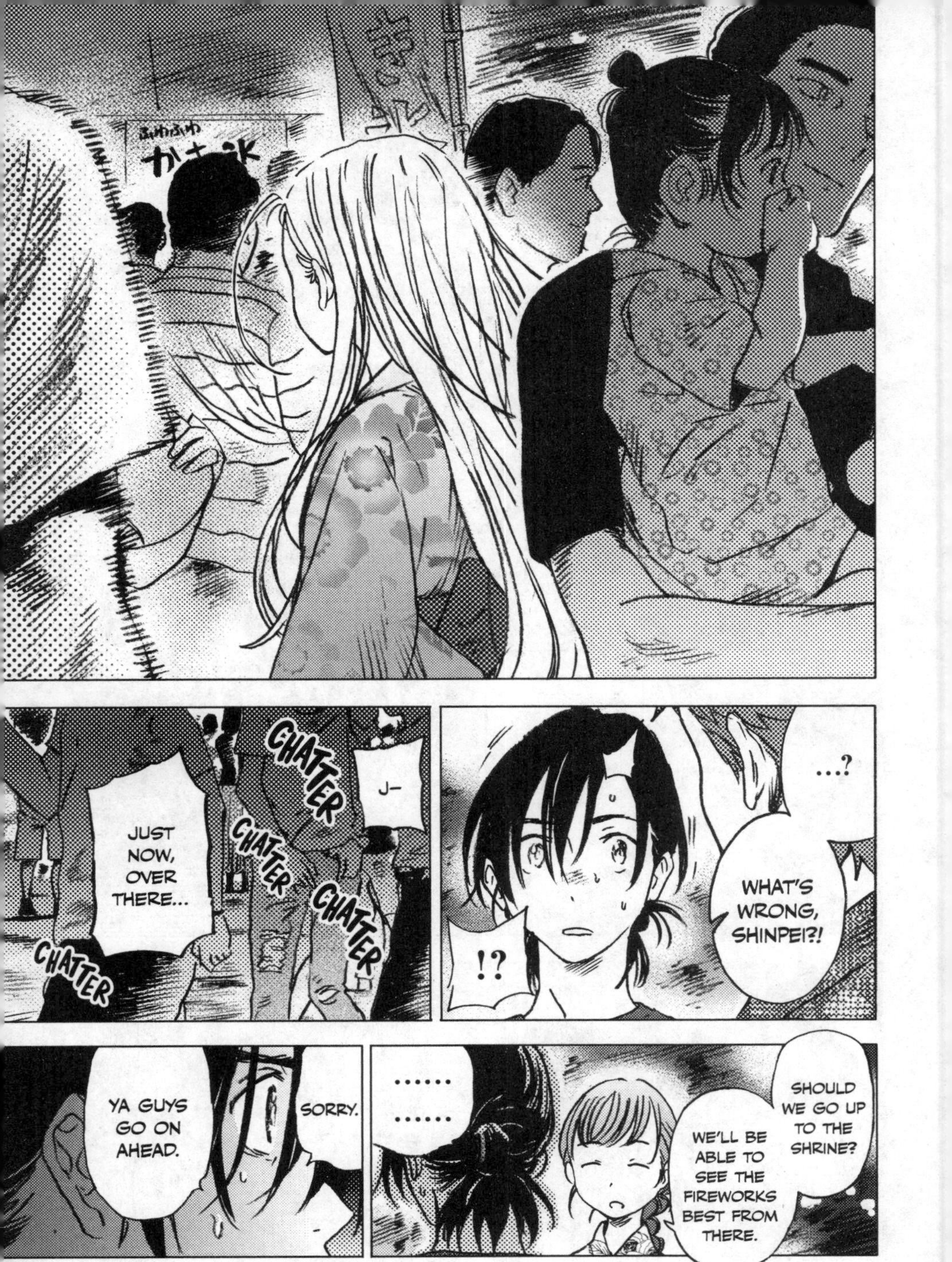
…?
WHAT'S WRONG, SHINPEI?!
!?
J–
CHATTER
JUST NOW, OVER THERE…
CHATTER
CHATTER
CHATTER
CHATTER
SHOULD WE GO UP TO THE SHRINE?
WE'LL BE ABLE TO SEE THE FIREWORKS BEST FROM THERE.
……
……
SORRY.
YA GUYS GO ON AHEAD.

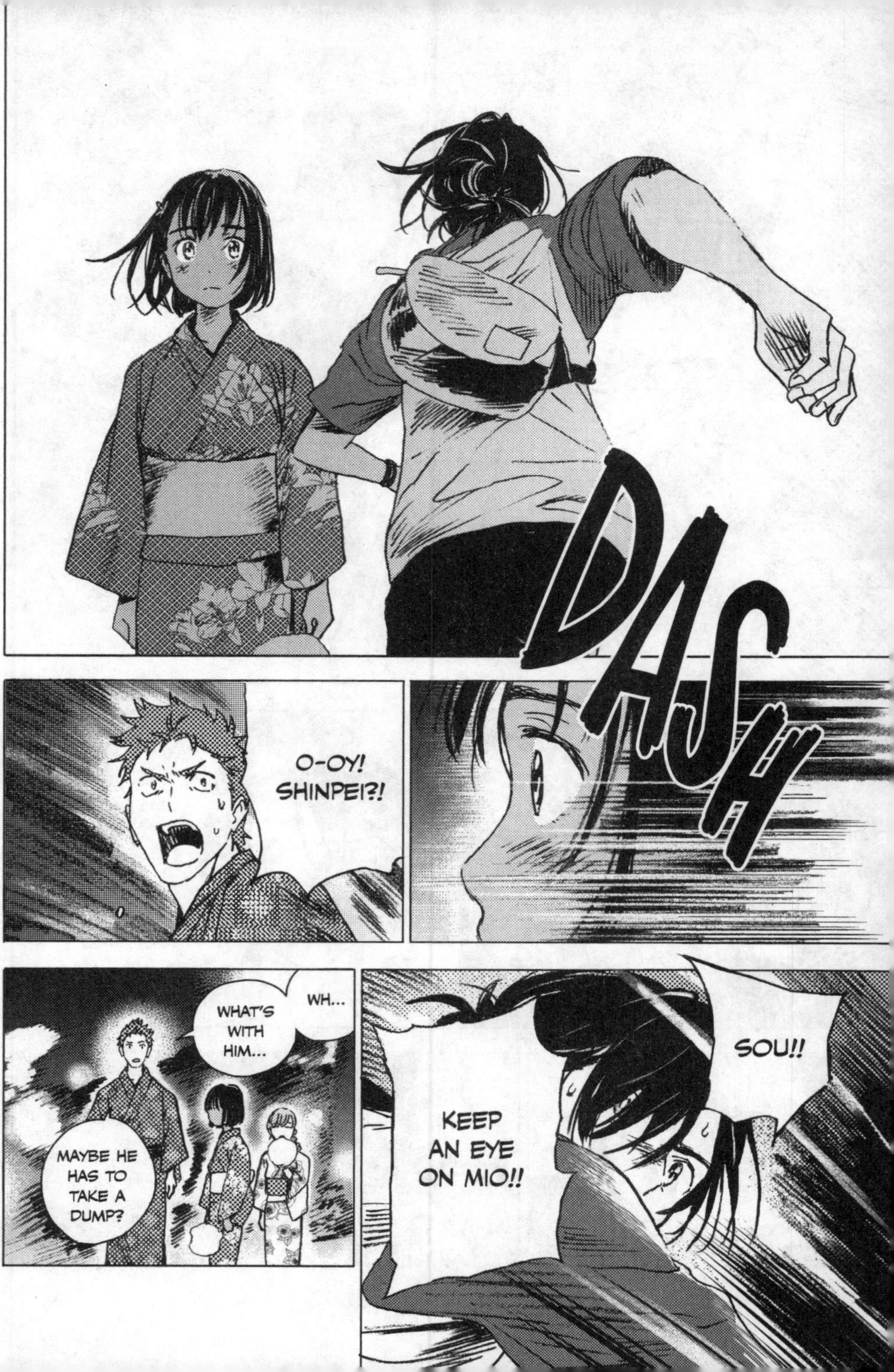
DASH
O-OY! SHINPEI?!
SOU!!
KEEP AN EYE ON MIO!!
WH...
WHAT'S WITH HIM...
MAYBE HE HAS TO TAKE A DUMP?

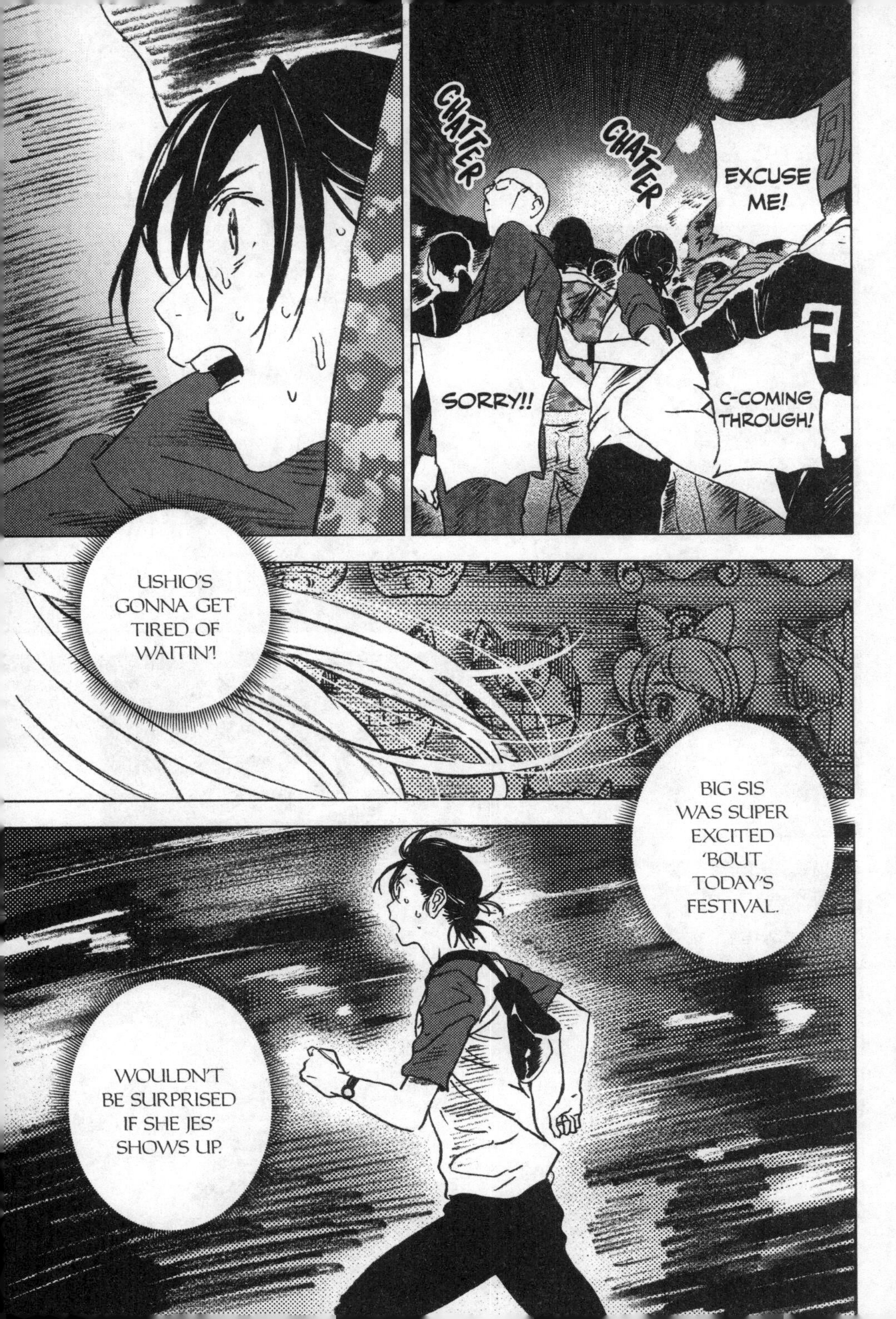
EXCUSE ME!
CHATTER
CHATTER
C-COMING THROUGH!
SORRY!!
USHIO'S GONNA GET TIRED OF WAITIN'!
BIG SIS WAS SUPER EXCITED 'BOUT TODAY'S FESTIVAL.
WOULDN'T BE SURPRISED IF SHE JES' SHOWS UP.

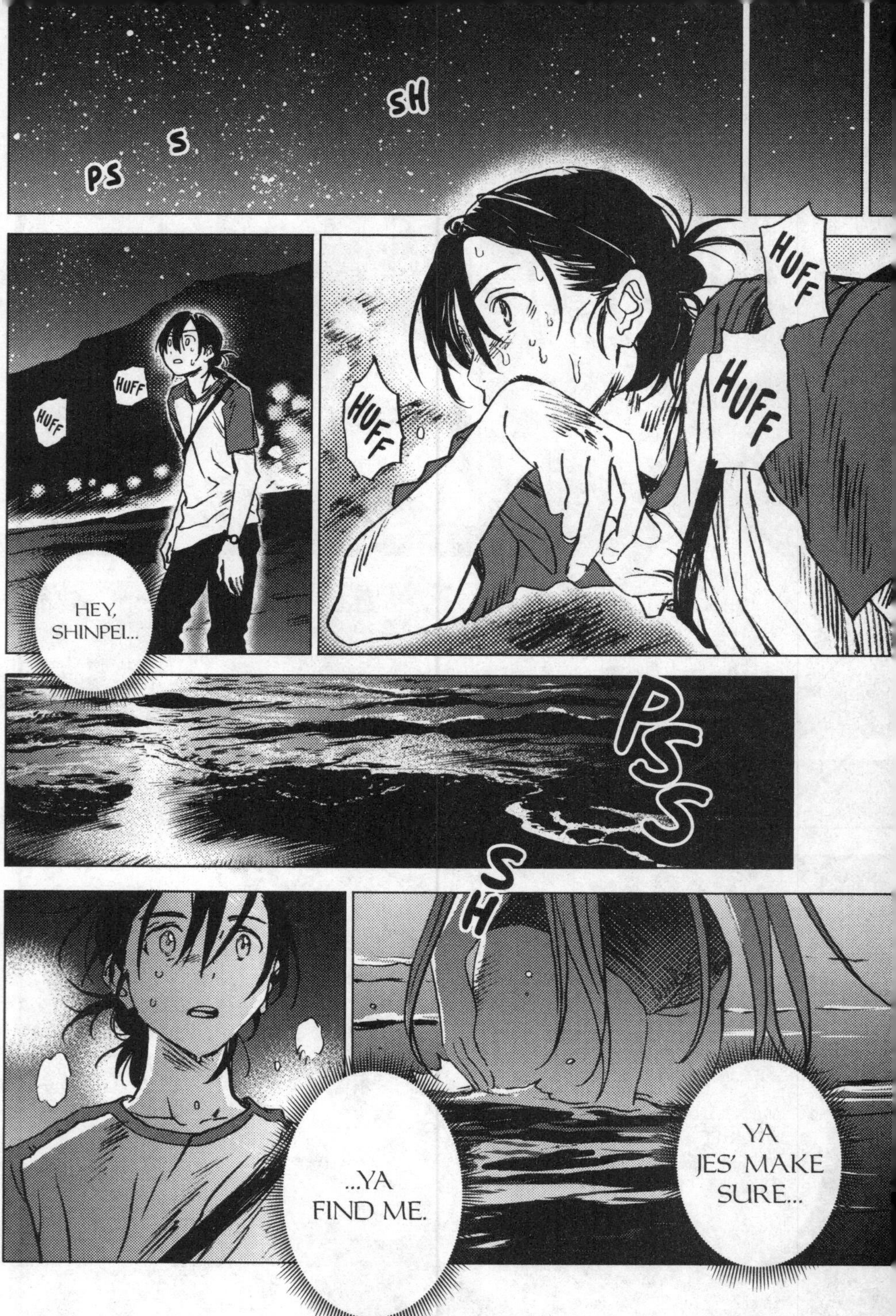
PS
S
SH
HUFF
HUFF
HUFF
HUFF
HUFF
HEY, SHINPEI...
PSS
SH
YA JES' MAKE SURE...
...YA FIND ME.

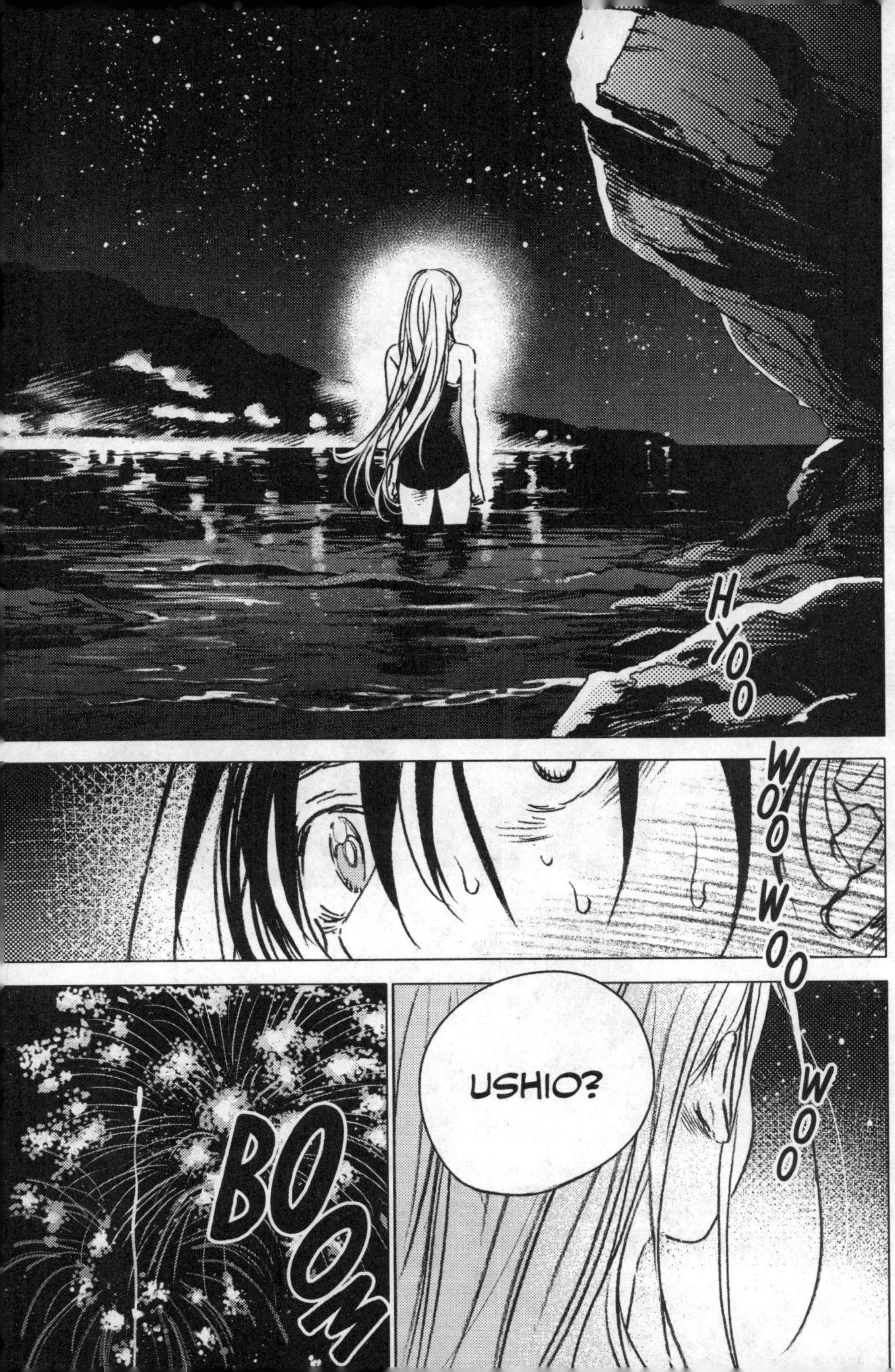
HYOO
WOOWOOWOO
WOO
USHIO?
BOOM

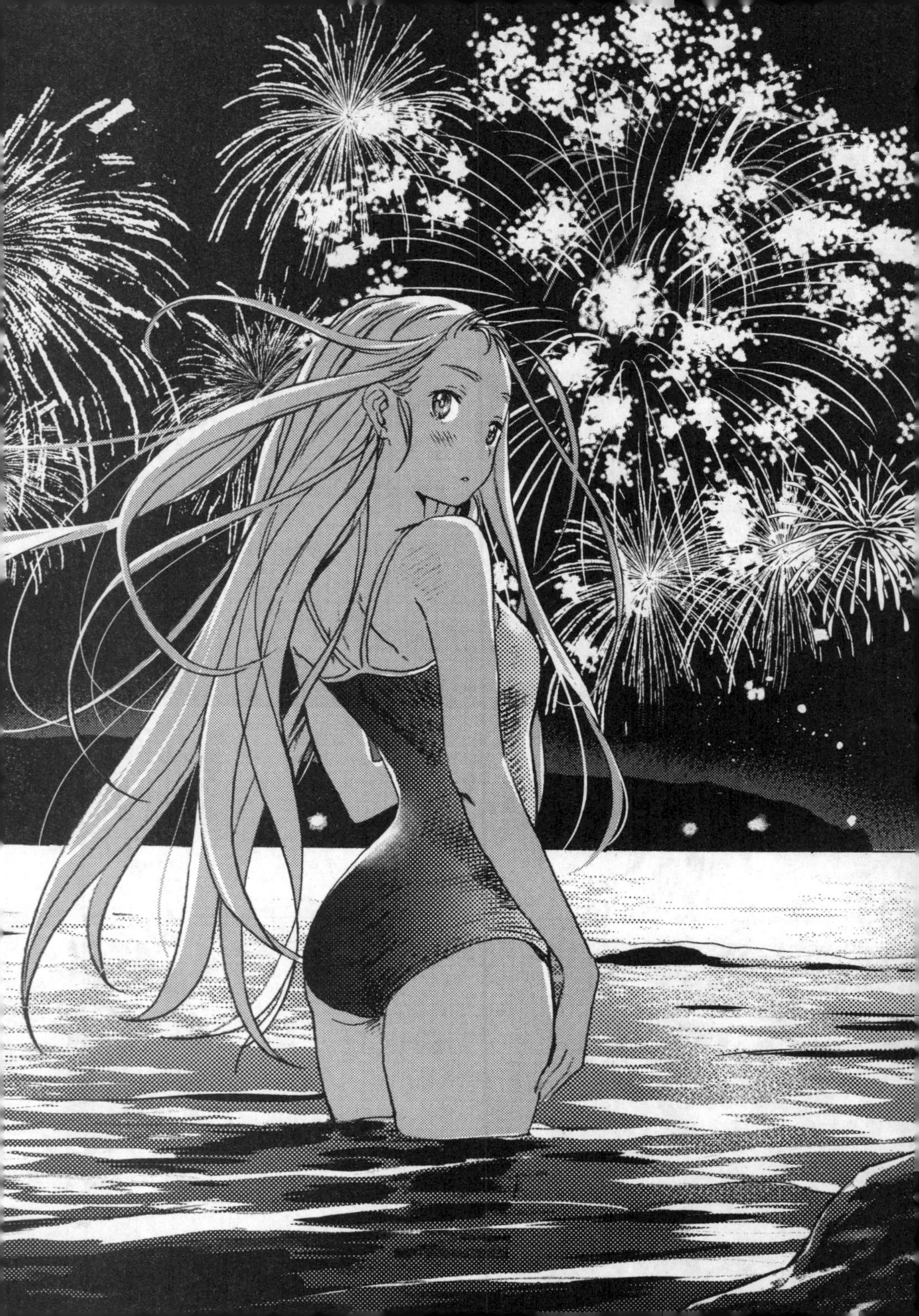

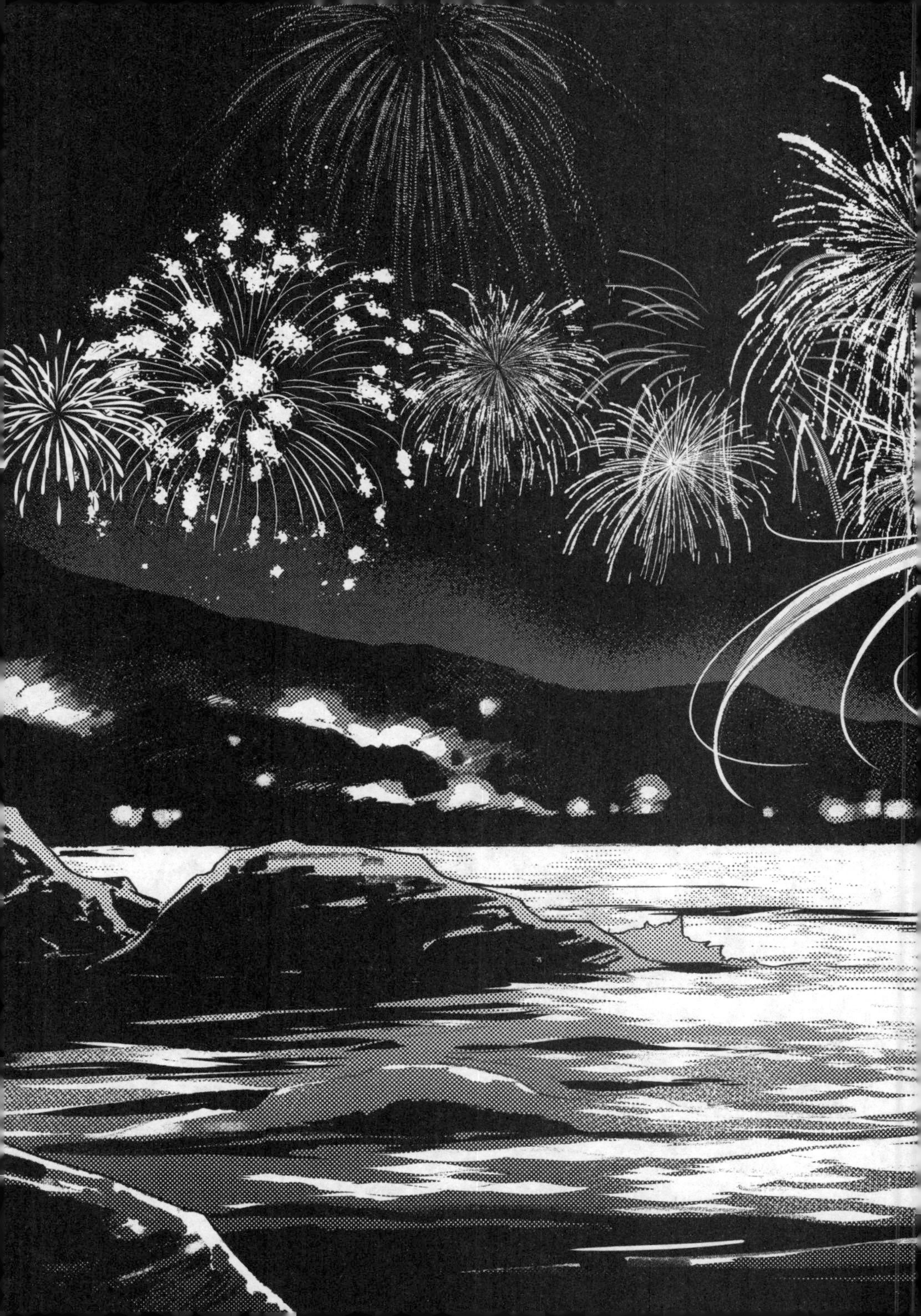

Summertime rendering

サマータイムレンダ

Summer time rendering

[Vortex]

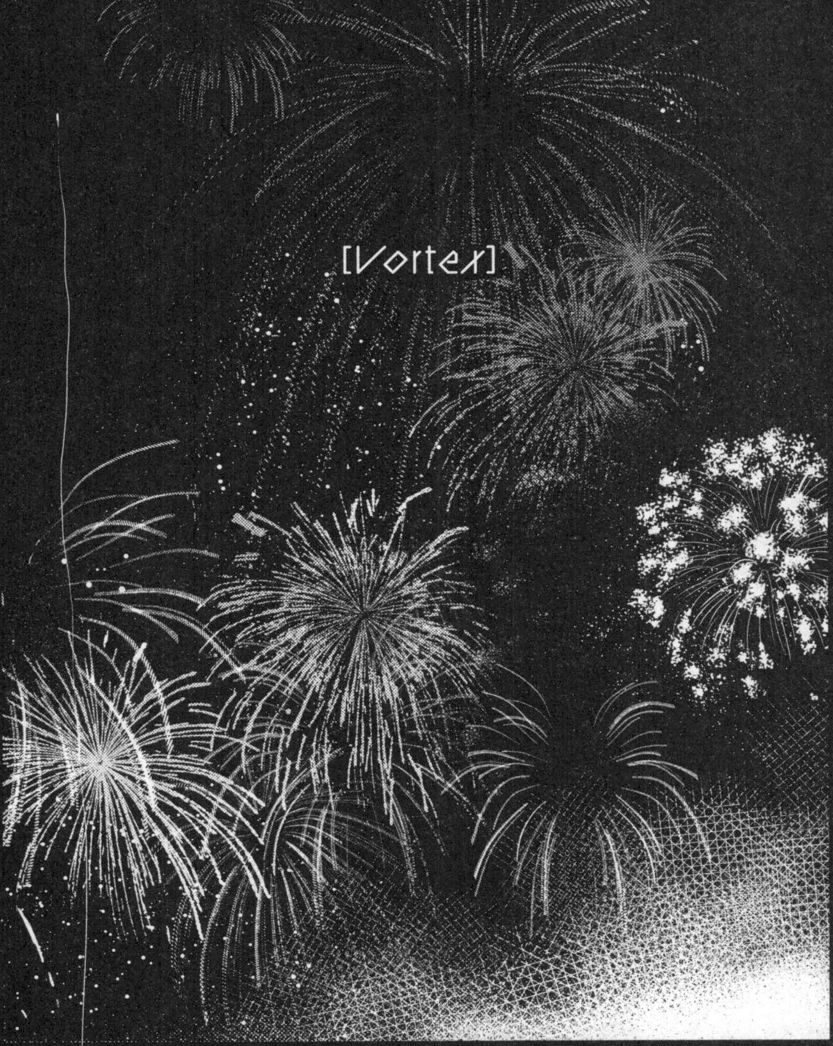

田中靖規

TANAKA YASUKI

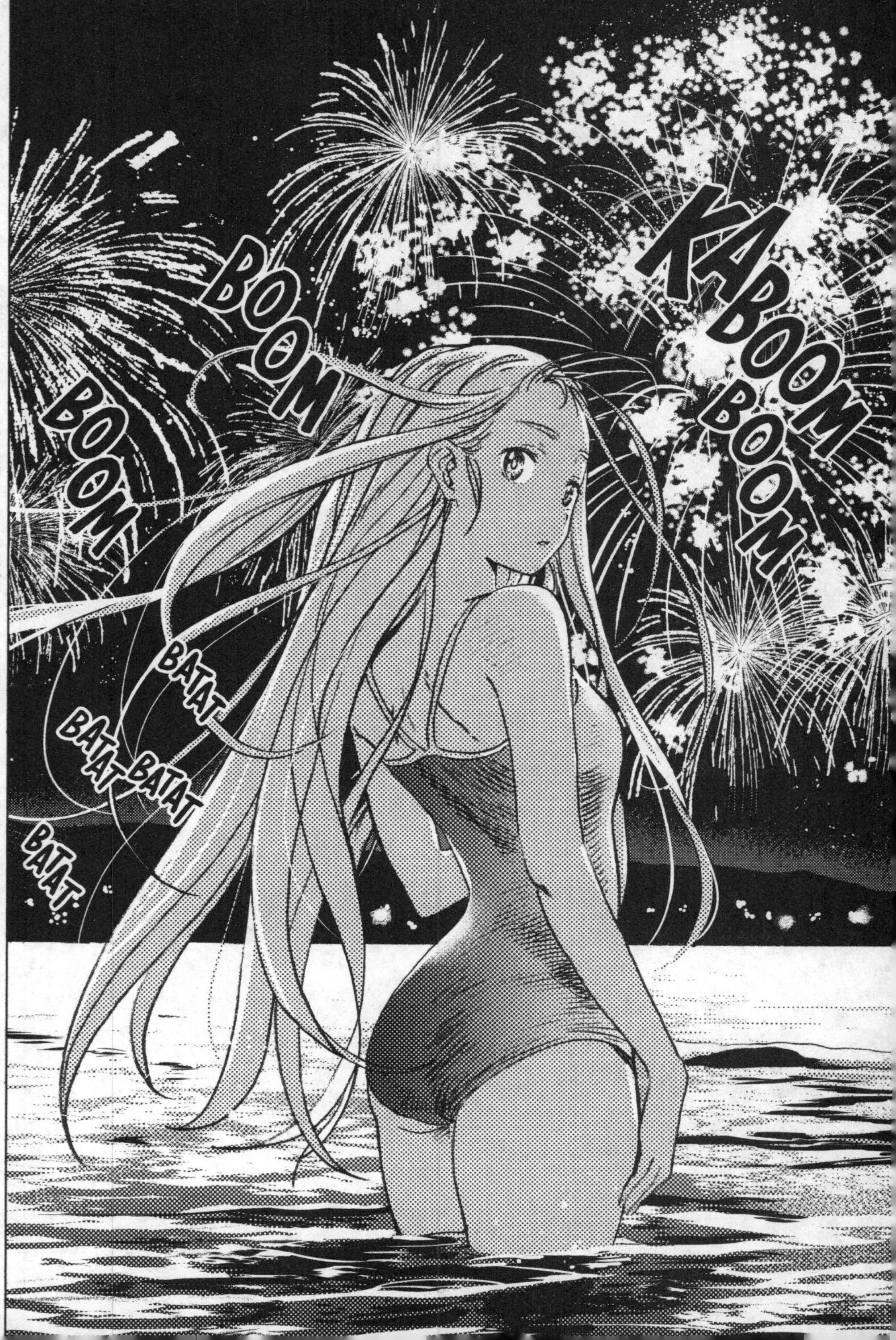
KABOOM
BOOM
BOOM
BOOM
BOOM
BATAT
BATAT
BATAT
BATAT

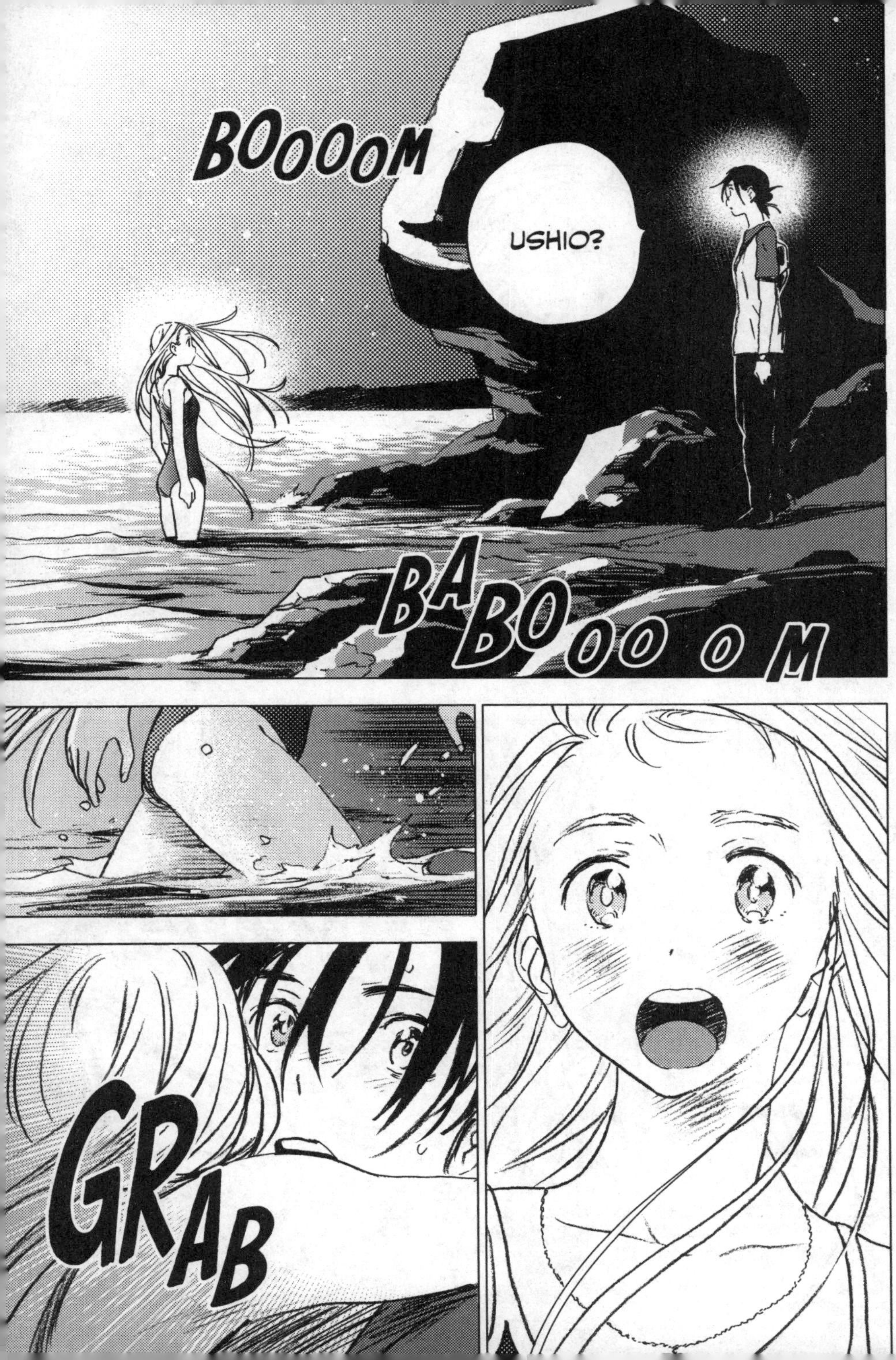
BOOOOM
USHIO?
BABOOO OM
GRAB

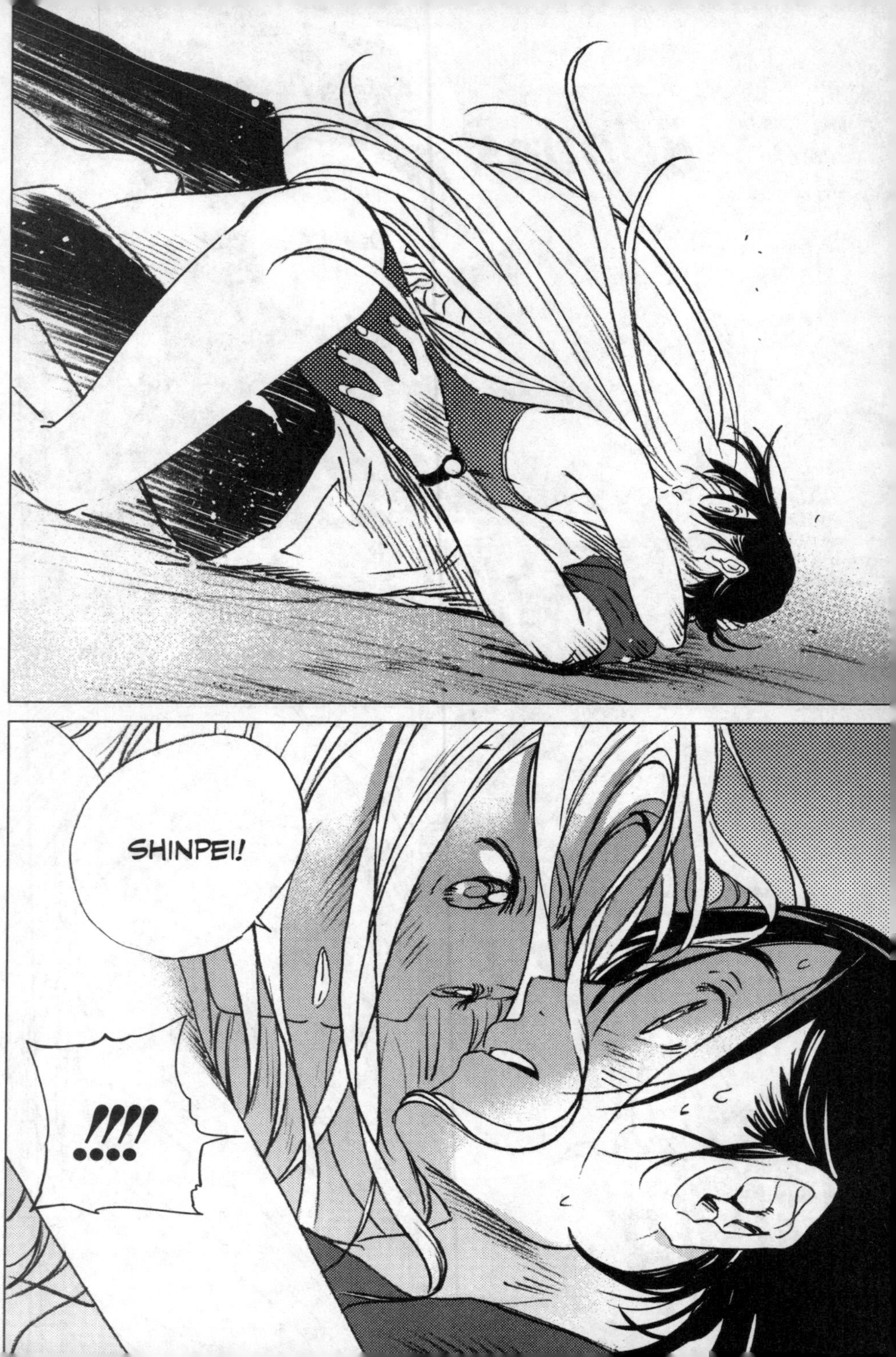
SHINPEI!
!!!!

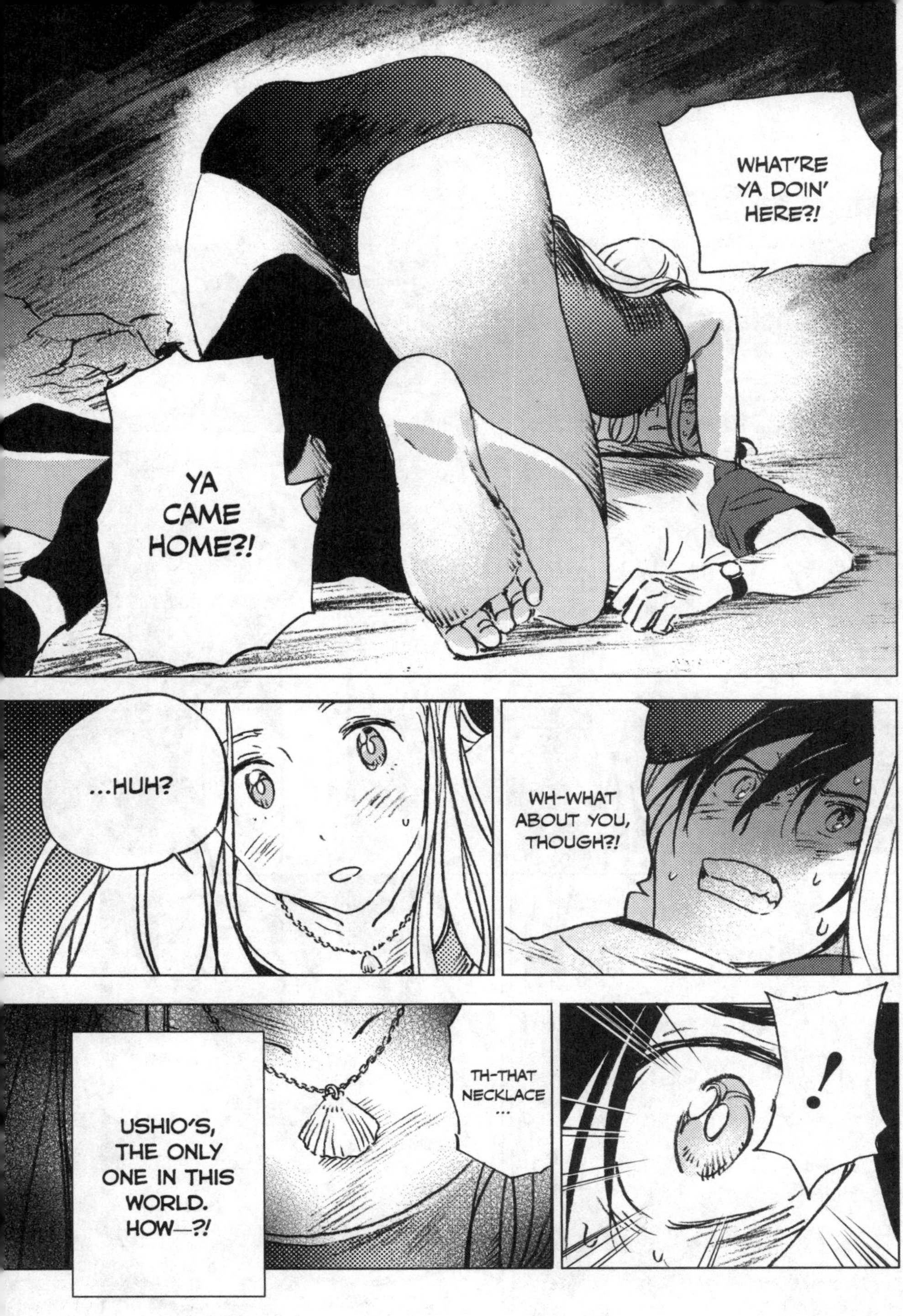
WHAT'RE YA DOIN' HERE?!
YA CAME HOME?!
WH-WHAT ABOUT YOU, THOUGH?!
...HUH?
!
TH-THAT NECKLACE ...
USHIO'S, THE ONLY ONE IN THIS WORLD. HOW—?!

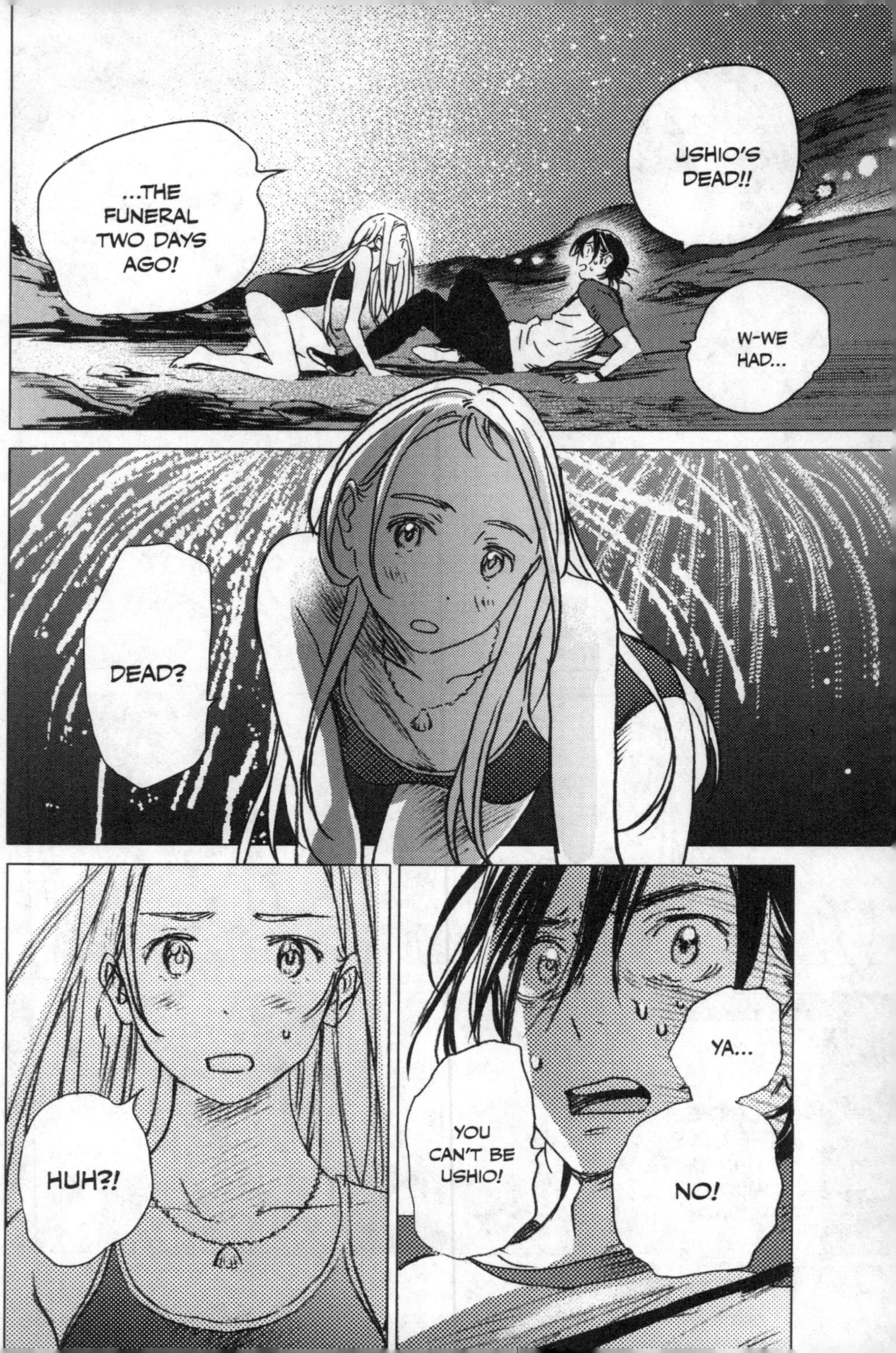
USHIO'S DEAD!!
W-WE HAD...
...THE FUNERAL TWO DAYS AGO!
DEAD?
YA...
NO!
YOU CAN'T BE USHIO!
HUH?!

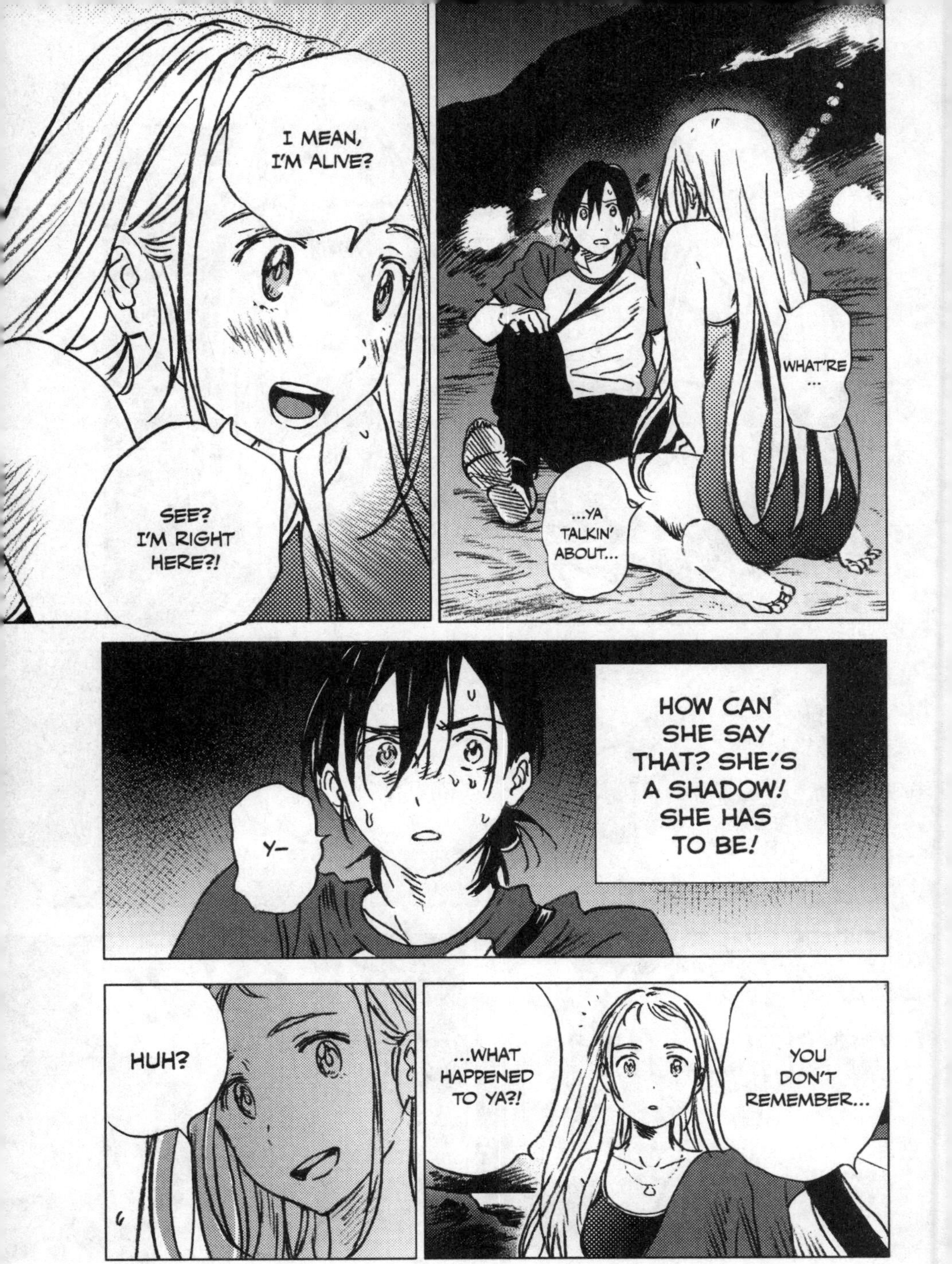
WHAT'RE ...
...YA TALKIN' ABOUT...
I MEAN, I'M ALIVE?
SEE? I'M RIGHT HERE?!
HOW CAN SHE SAY THAT? SHE'S A SHADOW! SHE HAS TO BE!
Y-
YOU DON'T REMEMBER...
...WHAT HAPPENED TO YA?!
HUH?

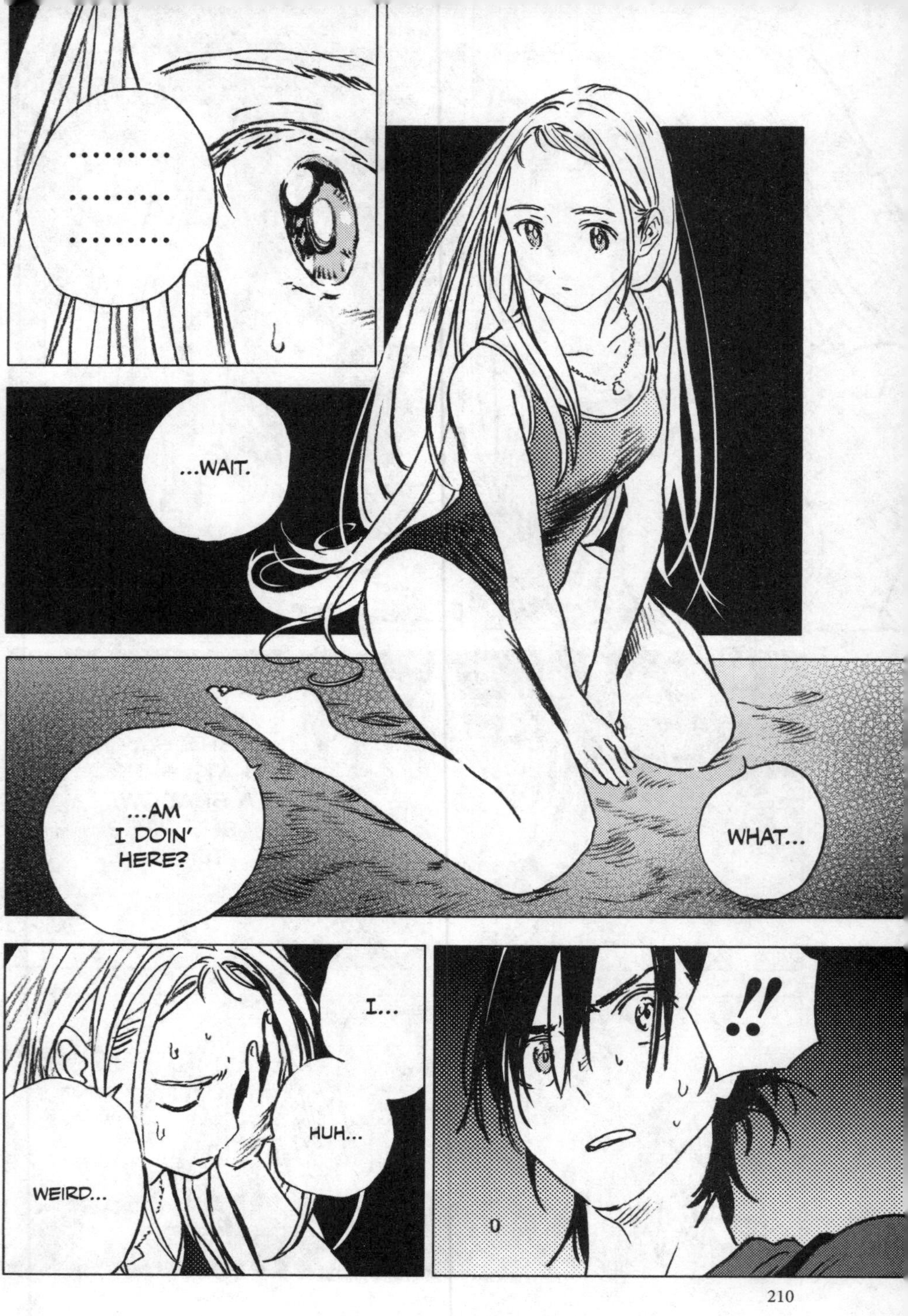

....
....
....
...WAIT.
WHAT...
...AM I DOIN' HERE?
!!
I...
HUH...
WEIRD...

I MEAN, I'M ALIVE?

SEE? I'M RIGHT HERE?!

WHAT'RE...

...YA TALKIN' ABOUT...

Y-

HOW CAN SHE SAY THAT? SHE'S A SHADOW! SHE HAS TO BE!

HUH?

...WHAT HAPPENED TO YA?!

YOU DON'T REMEMBER...

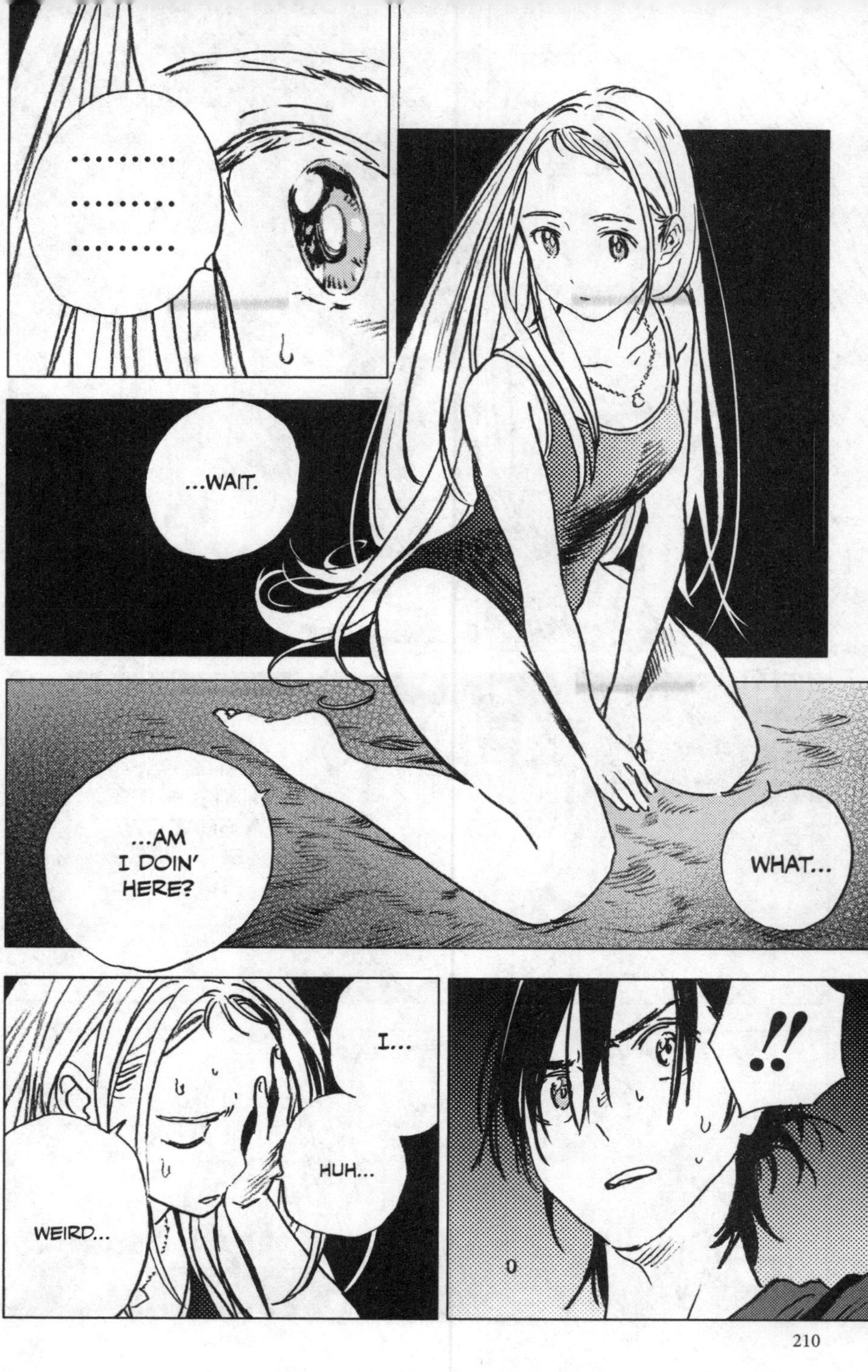
....
....
....
...WAIT.
WHAT...
...AM I DOIN' HERE?
!!
I...
HUH...
WEIRD...

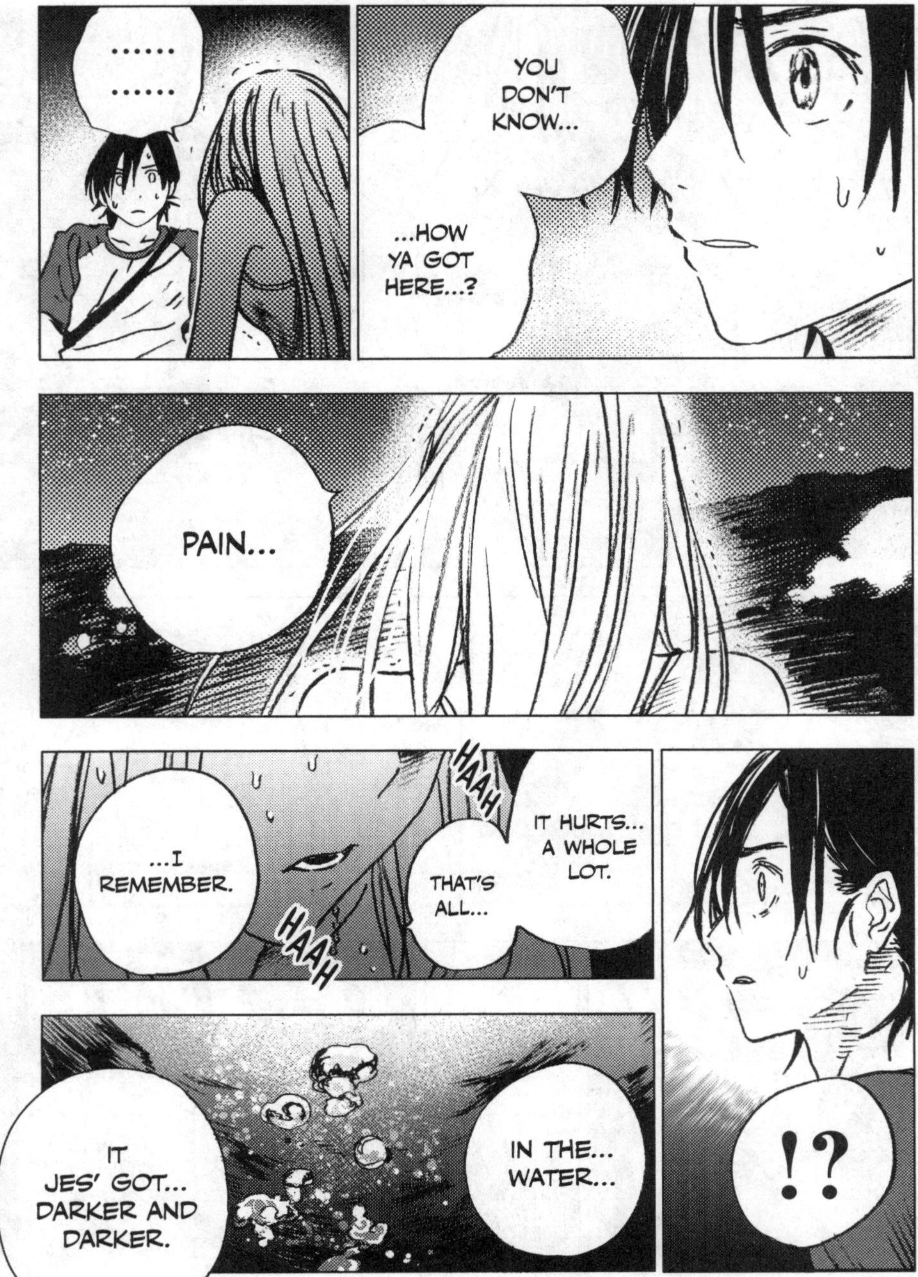
YOU DON'T KNOW...
...HOW YA GOT HERE...?
......
......
PAIN...
!?
IT HURTS... A WHOLE LOT.
HAAAH
THAT'S ALL...
...I REMEMBER.
HAAAH
IN THE... WATER...
IT JES' GOT... DARKER AND DARKER.

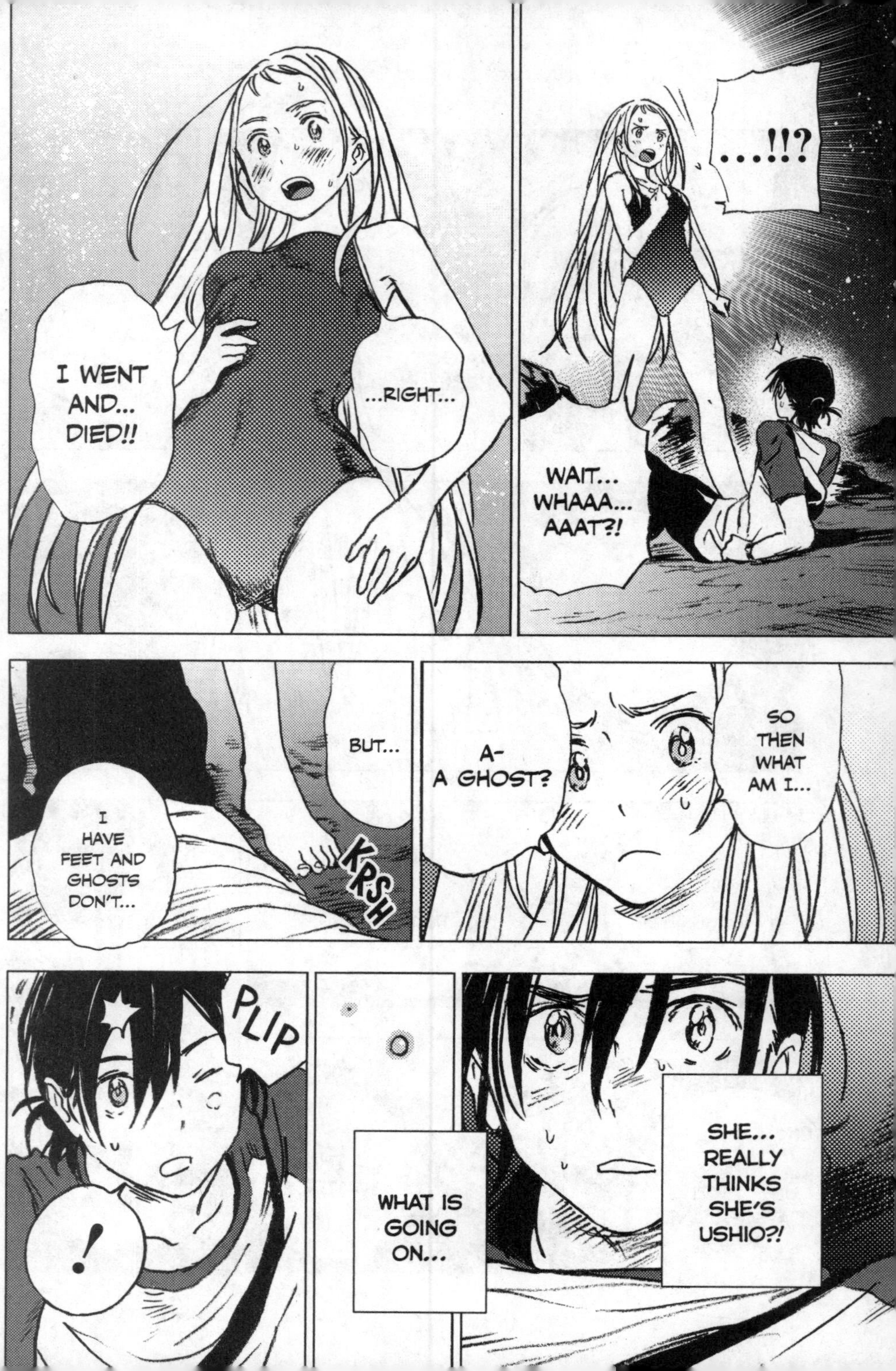
...!!?
WAIT... WHAAA... AAAT?!
...RIGHT...
I WENT AND... DIED!!
SO THEN WHAT AM I...
A- A GHOST?
BUT...
I HAVE FEET AND GHOSTS DON'T...
KRSH
SHE... REALLY THINKS SHE'S USHIO?!
WHAT IS GOING ON...
PLIP
!

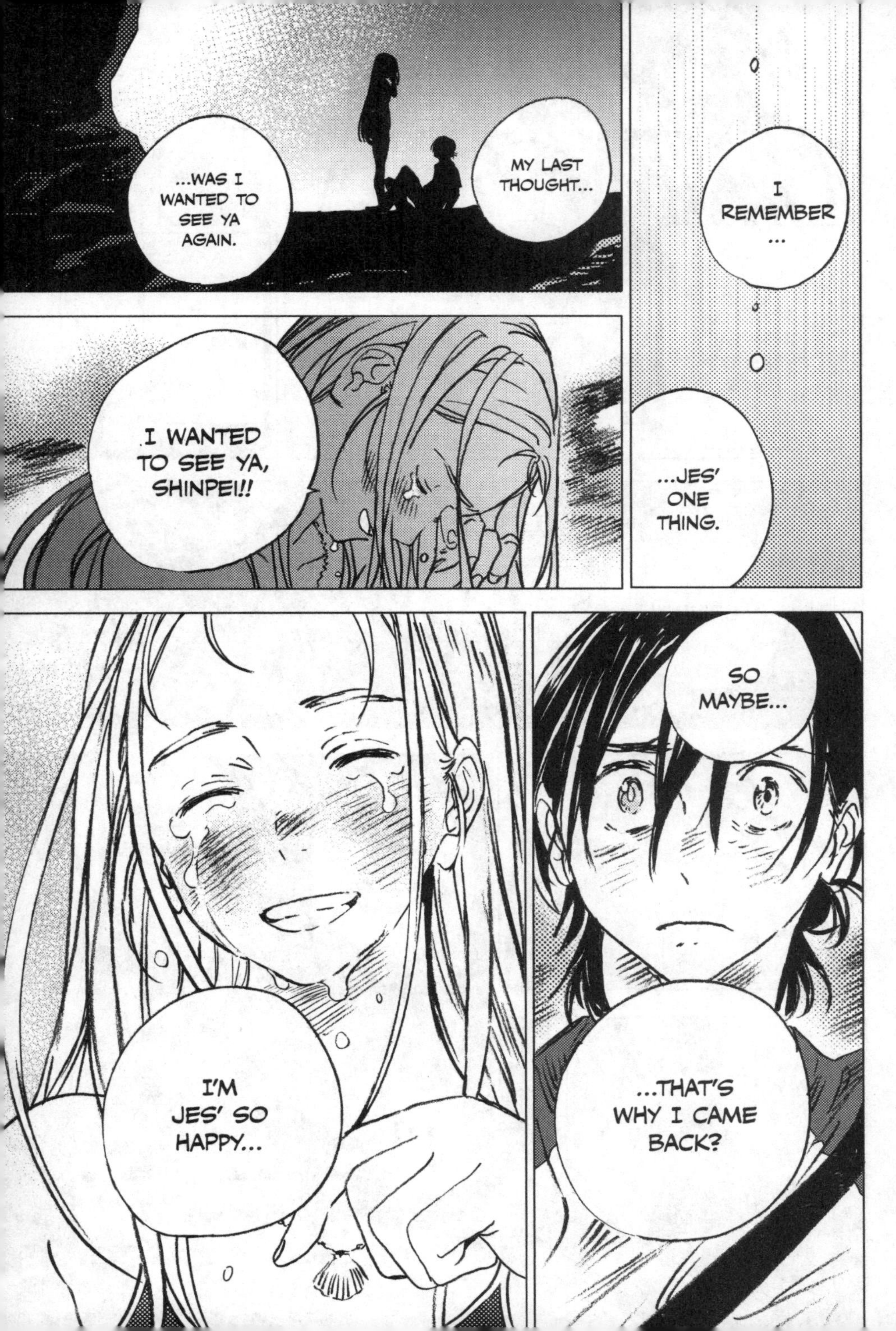
I REMEMBER ...
...JES' ONE THING.
MY LAST THOUGHT...
...WAS I WANTED TO SEE YA AGAIN.
I WANTED TO SEE YA, SHINPEI!!
SO MAYBE...
...THAT'S WHY I CAME BACK?
I'M JES' SO HAPPY...

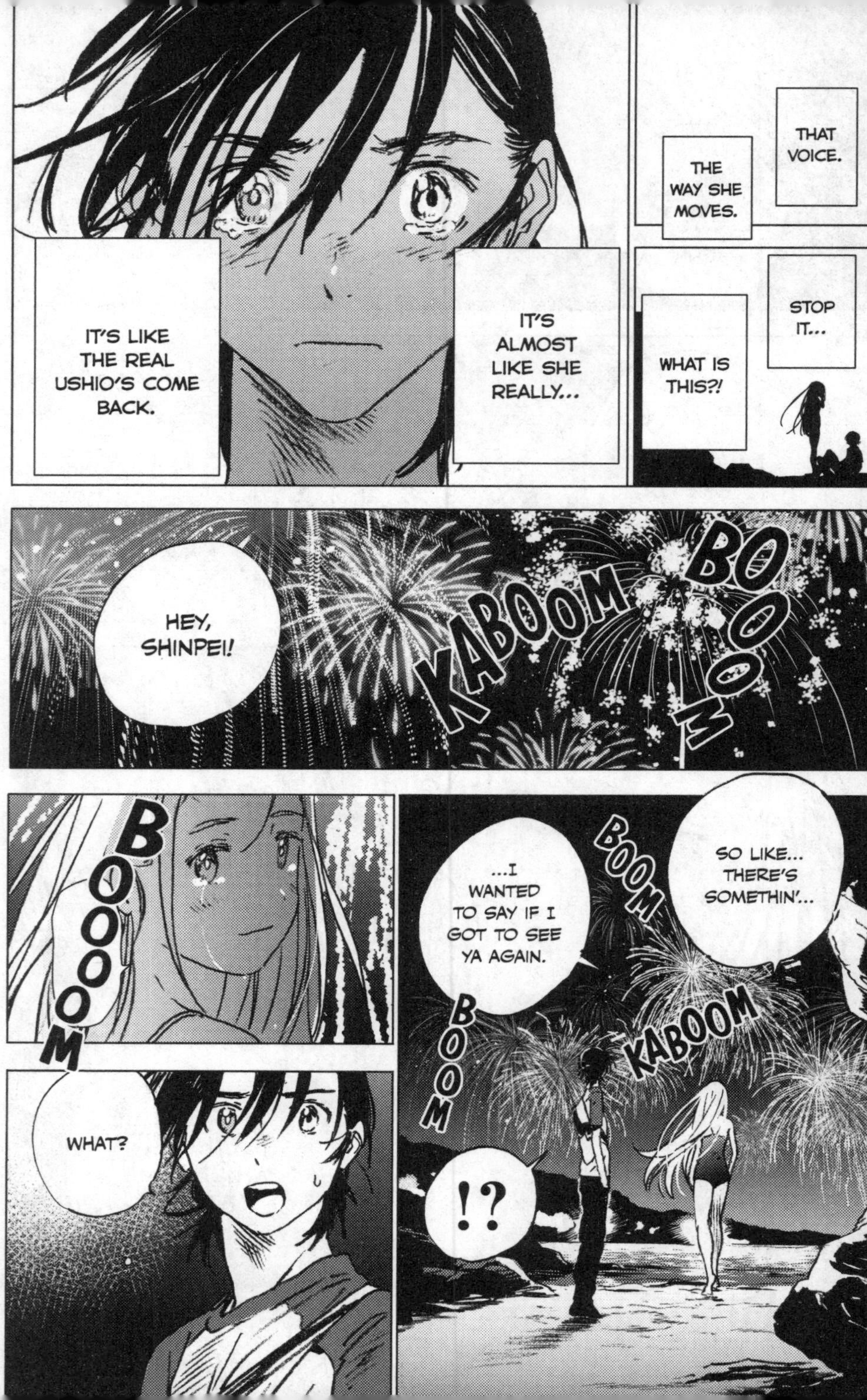
THAT VOICE.
THE WAY SHE MOVES.
STOP IT...
WHAT IS THIS?!
IT'S ALMOST LIKE SHE REALLY...
IT'S LIKE THE REAL USHIO'S COME BACK.
BOOOOM
KABOOM
HEY, SHINPEI!
SO LIKE... THERE'S SOMETHIN'...
BOOM
...I WANTED TO SAY IF I GOT TO SEE YA AGAIN.
KABOOM
BOOM
!?
BOOOOOM
WHAT?

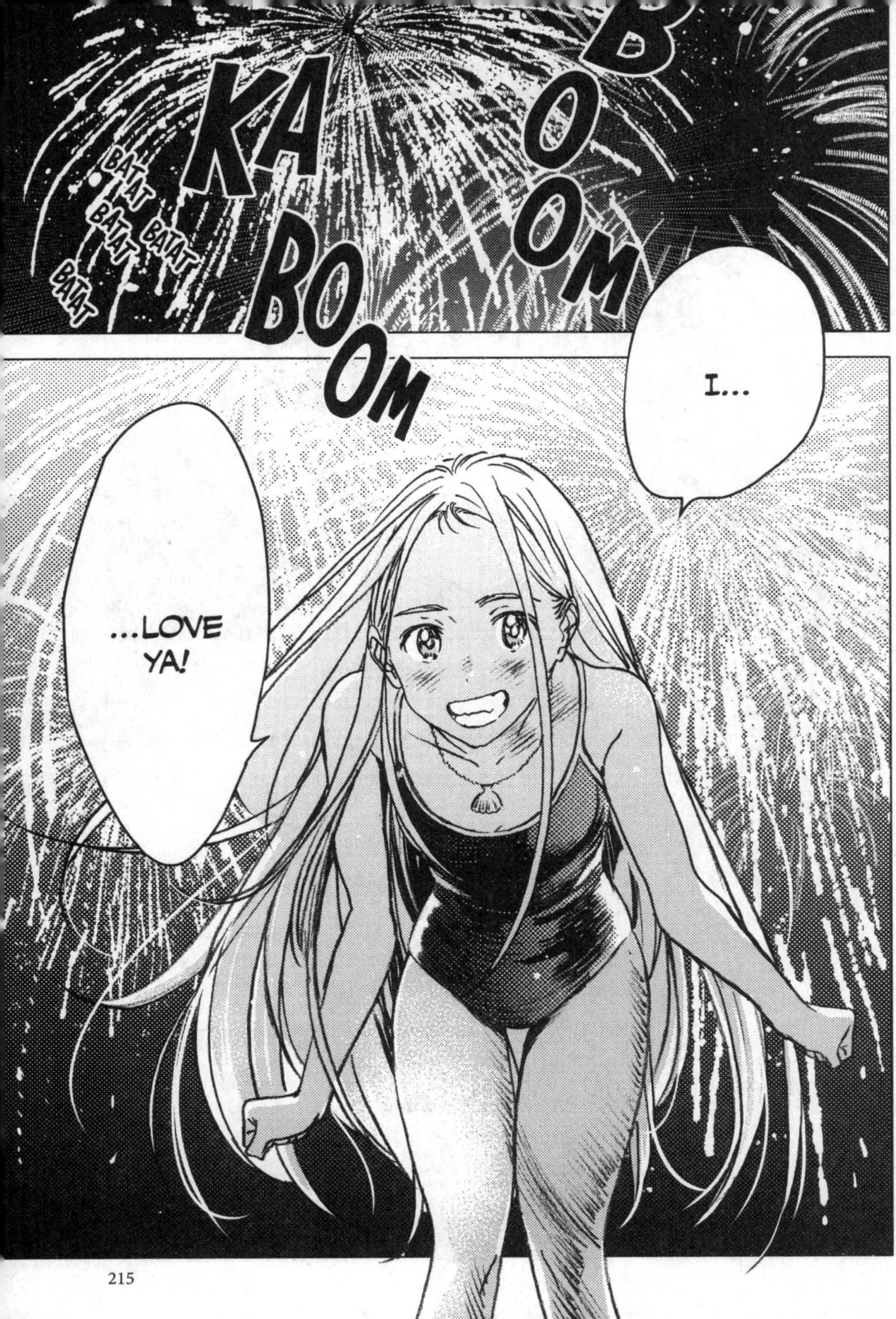
BOOM
KABOOM
BATAT BATAT
BATAT BATAT
BATAT
I...
...LOVE YA!

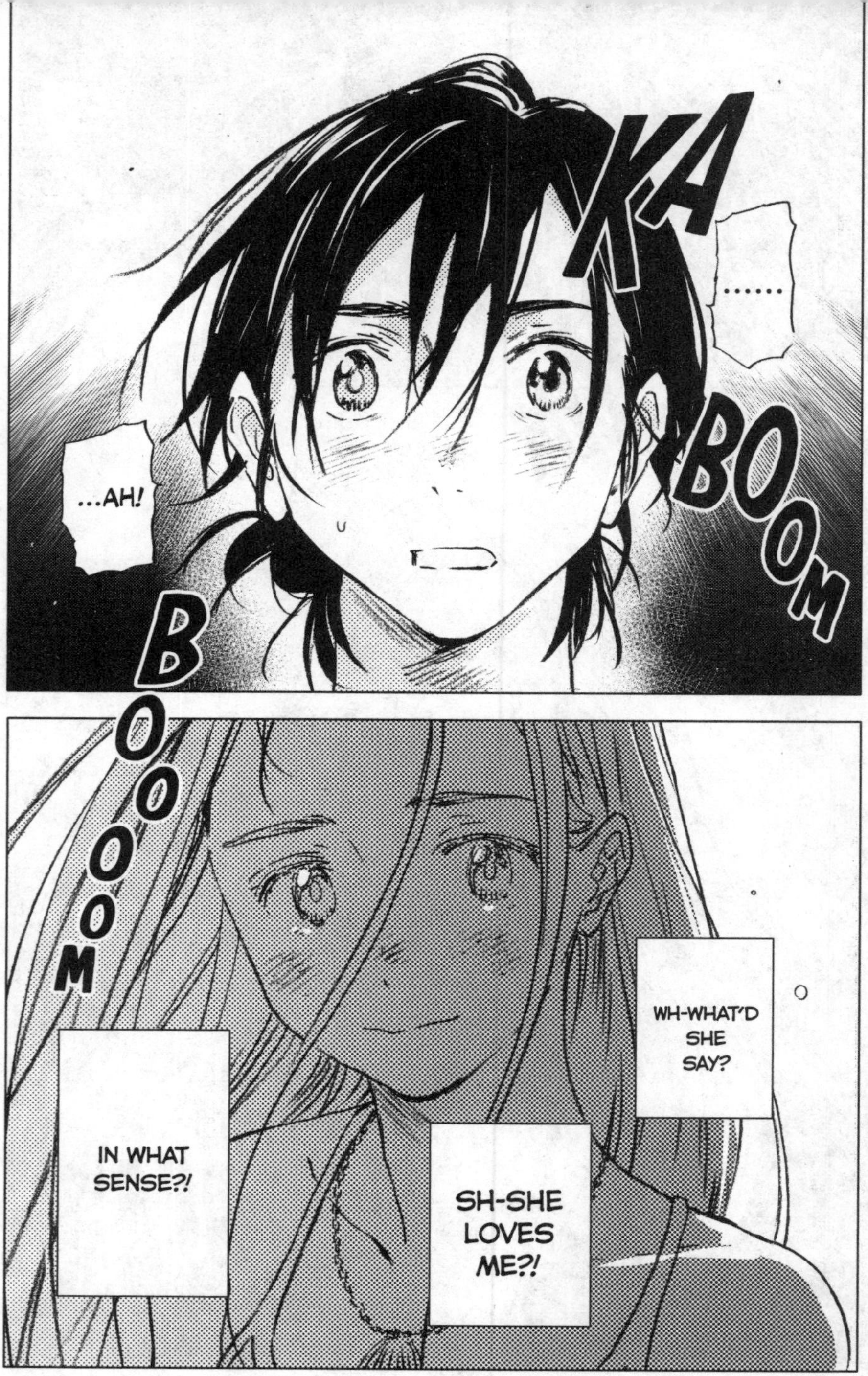
......
KABOOM
...AH!
BOOOOOOOM
WH-WHAT'D SHE SAY?
SH-SHE LOVES ME?!
IN WHAT SENSE?!

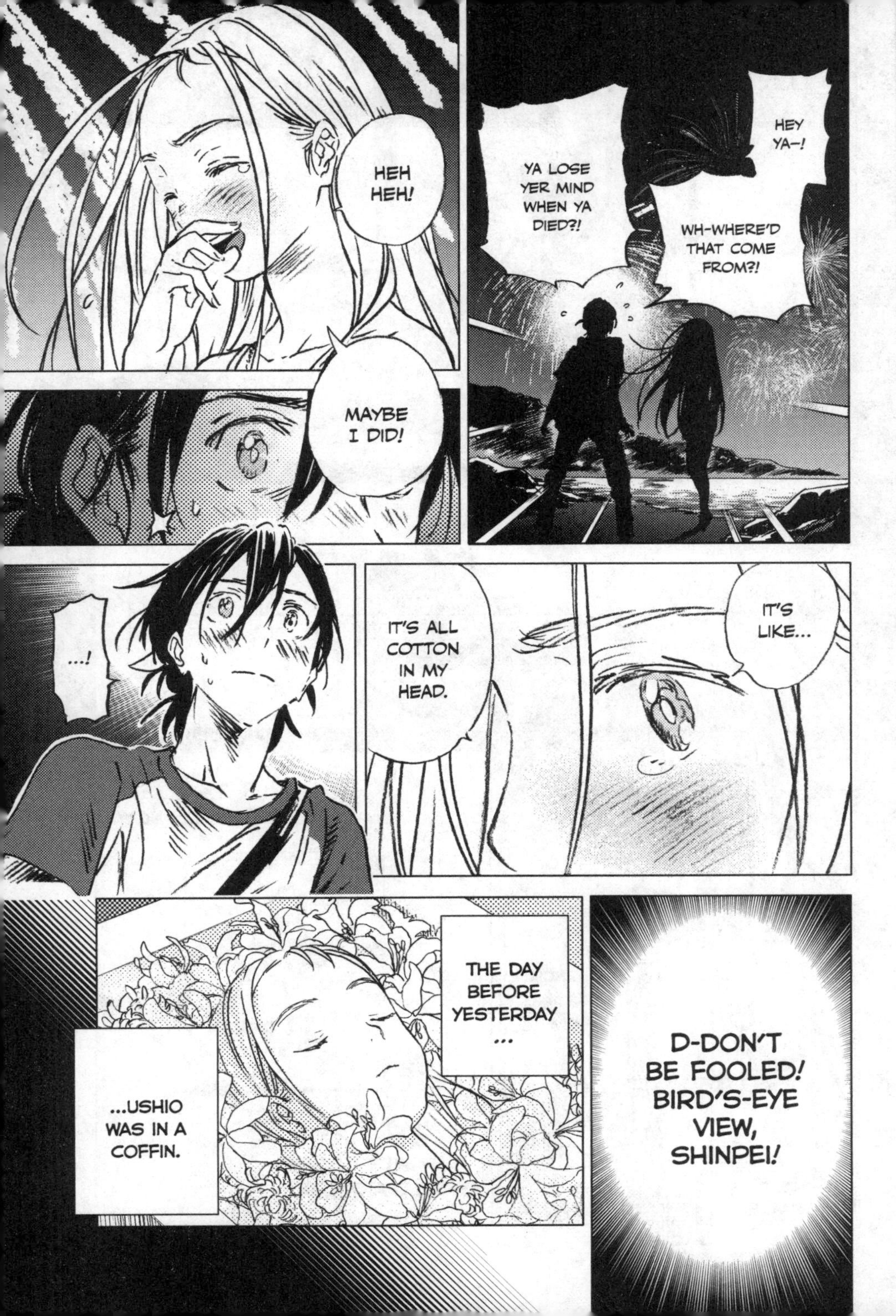
HEY YA—!
YA LOSE YER MIND WHEN YA DIED?!
WH-WHERE'D THAT COME FROM?!
HEH HEH!
MAYBE I DID!
IT'S LIKE...
IT'S ALL COTTON IN MY HEAD.
...!
D-DON'T BE FOOLED! BIRD'S-EYE VIEW, SHINPEI!
THE DAY BEFORE YESTERDAY...
...USHIO WAS IN A COFFIN.

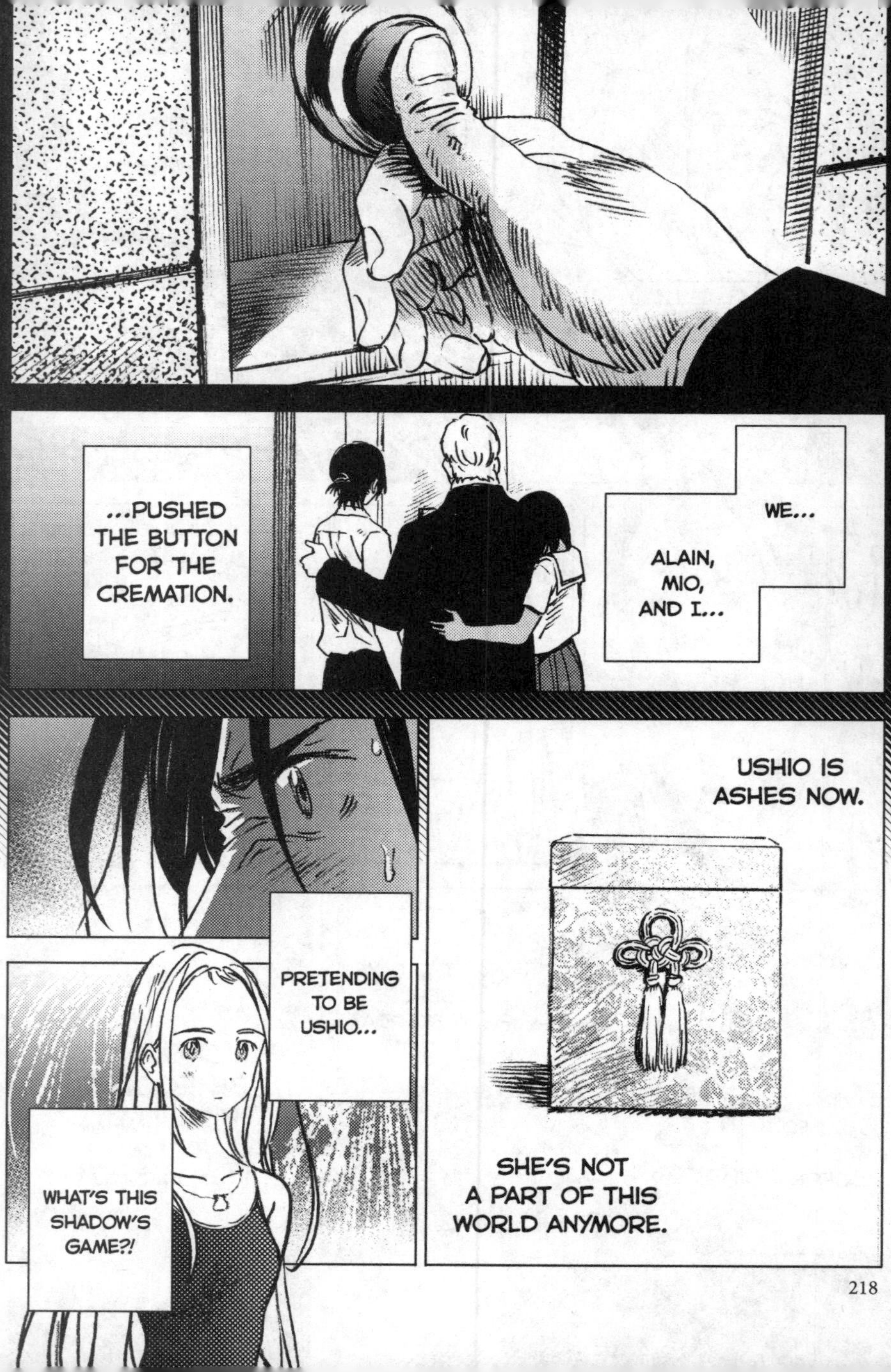
WE...
ALAIN, MIO, AND I...
...PUSHED THE BUTTON FOR THE CREMATION.
USHIO IS ASHES NOW.
SHE'S NOT A PART OF THIS WORLD ANYMORE.
PRETENDING TO BE USHIO...
WHAT'S THIS SHADOW'S GAME?!

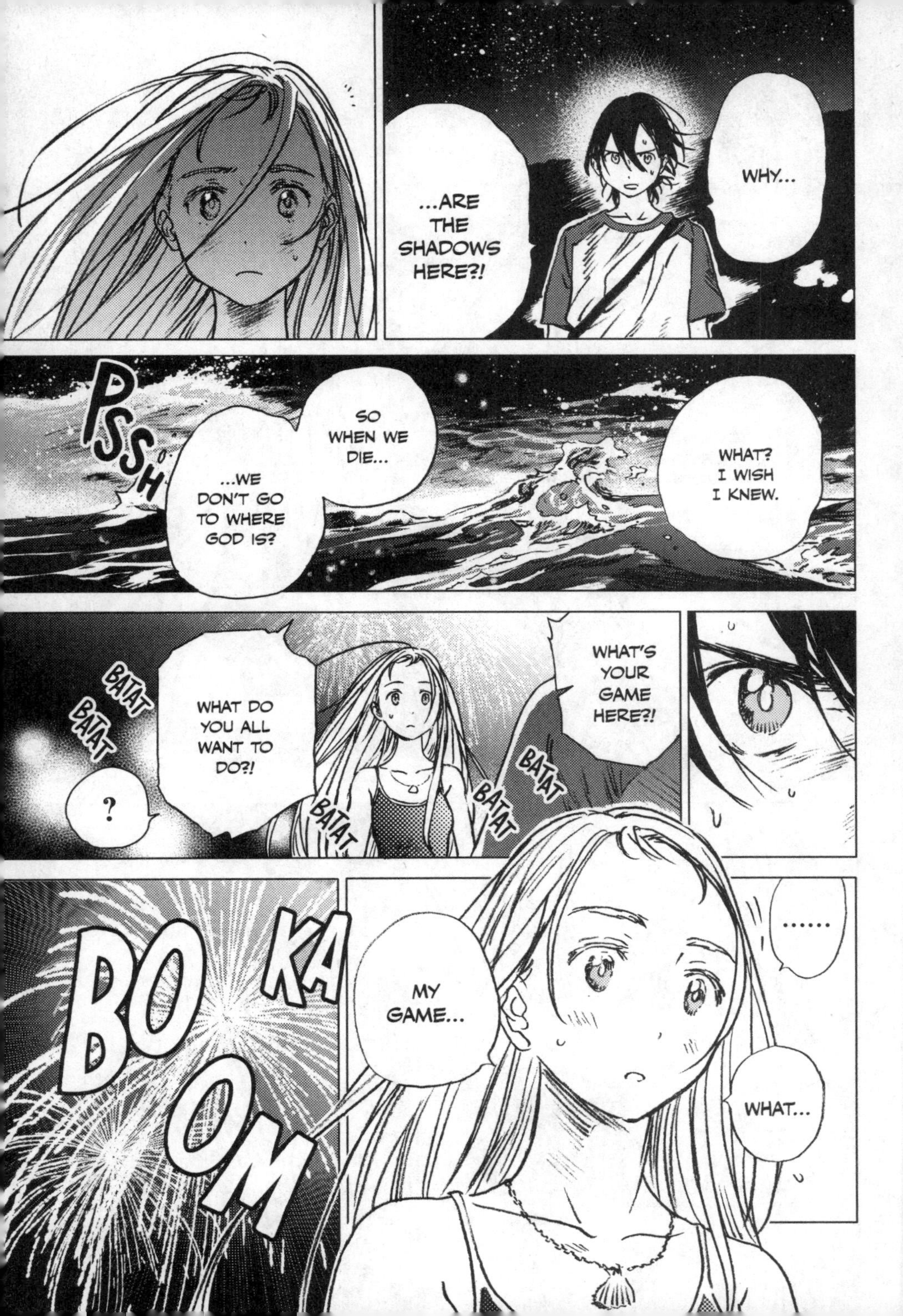
WHY...
...ARE THE SHADOWS HERE?!
WHAT? I WISH I KNEW.
SO WHEN WE DIE...
...WE DON'T GO TO WHERE GOD IS?
PSSH
WHAT'S YOUR GAME HERE?!
BATAT
BATAT
WHAT DO YOU ALL WANT TO DO?!
BATAT
BATAT
?
......
WHAT...
MY GAME...
KA
BOOM

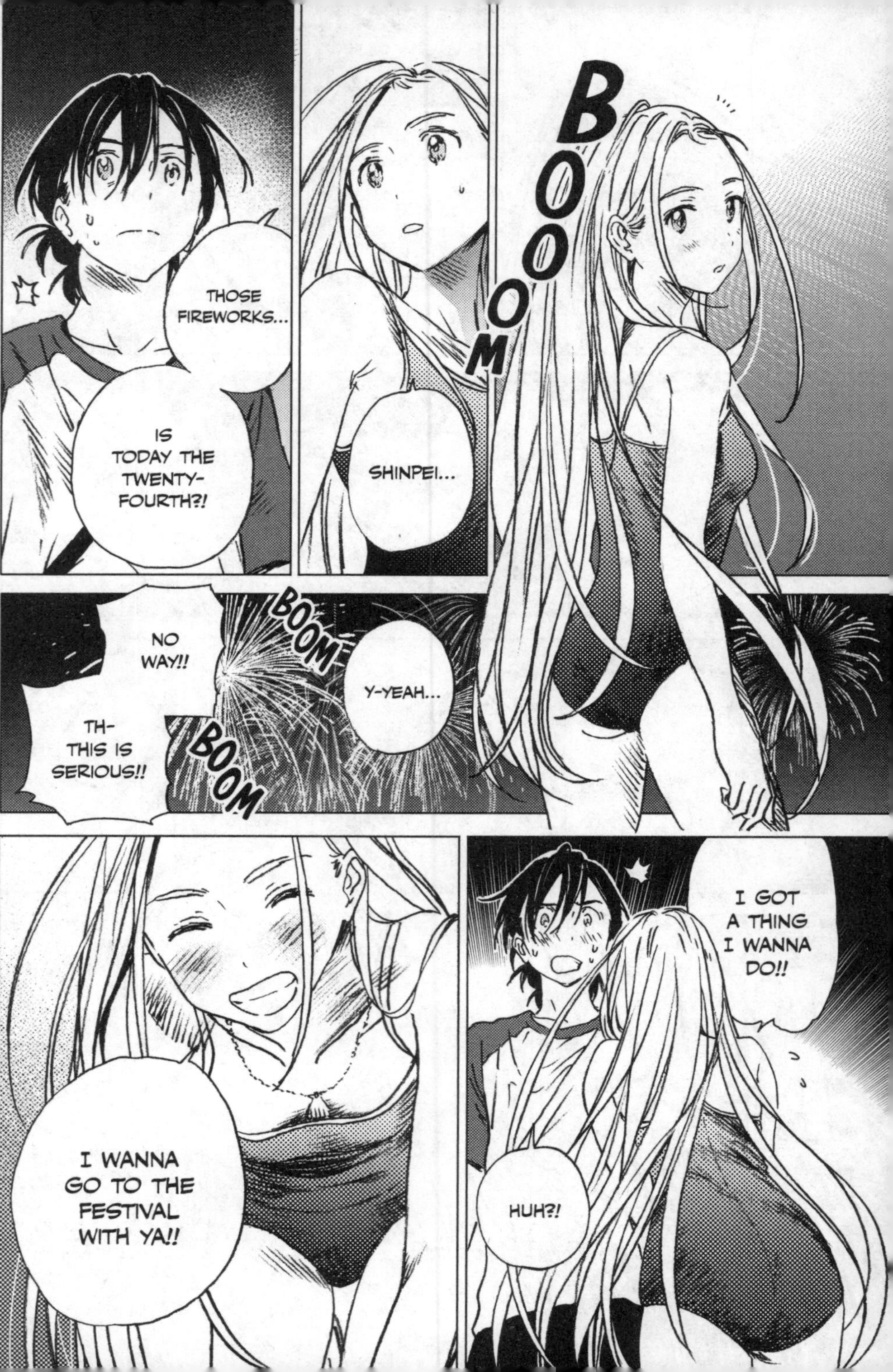
BOOOOM
SHINPEI...
THOSE FIREWORKS...
IS TODAY THE TWENTY-FOURTH?!
Y-YEAH...
BOOM
BOOM
NO WAY!!
TH- THIS IS SERIOUS!!
I GOT A THING I WANNA DO!!
HUH?!
I WANNA GO TO THE FESTIVAL WITH YA!!

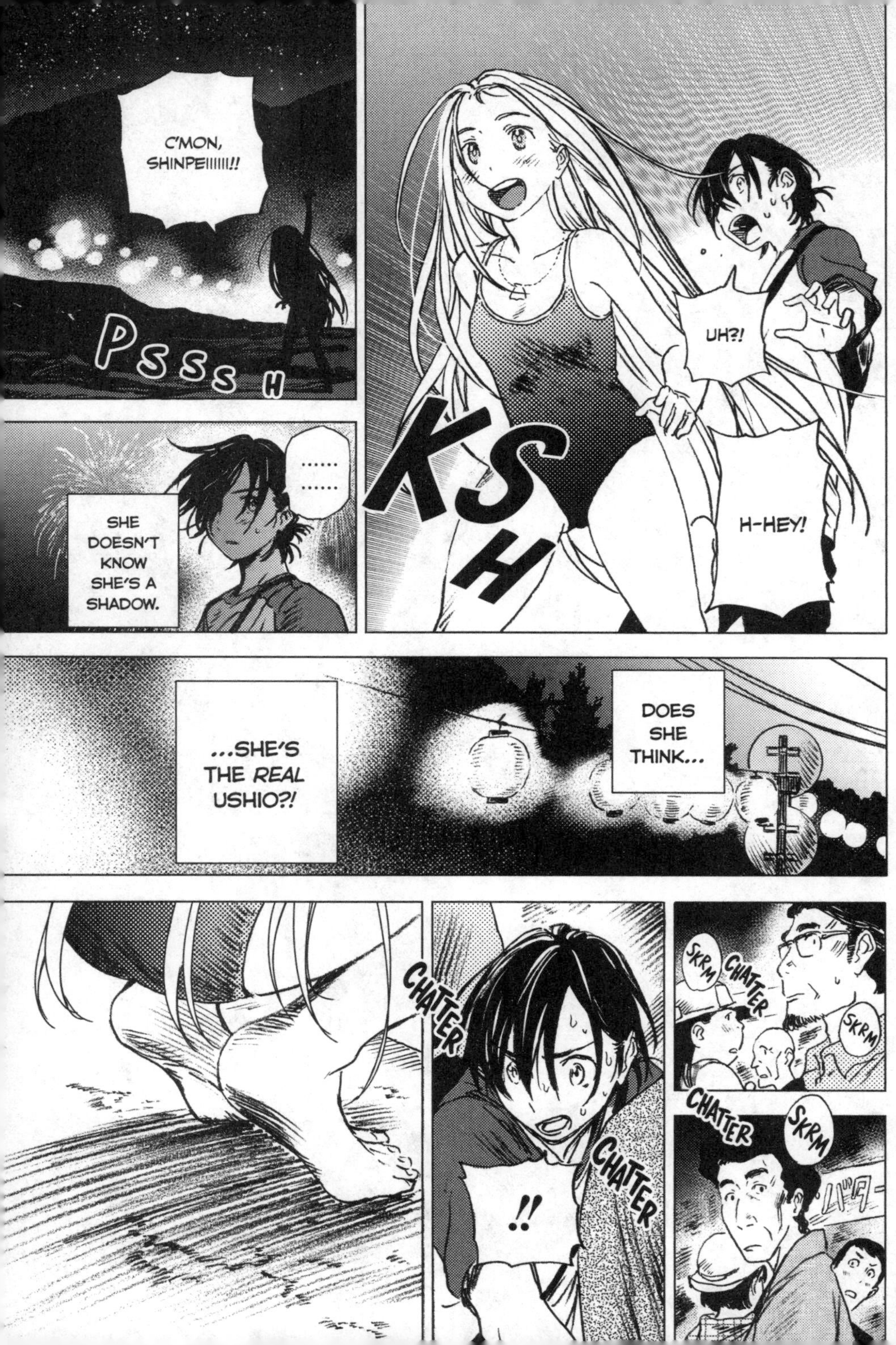
UH?!
H-HEY!
KSH
C'MON, SHINPEIIIIIII!!
PSSSH
....
SHE DOESN'T KNOW SHE'S A SHADOW.
DOES SHE THINK...
...SHE'S THE REAL USHIO?!
SKRM
CHATTER
SKRM
CHATTER
SKRM
CHATTER
CHATTER
!!

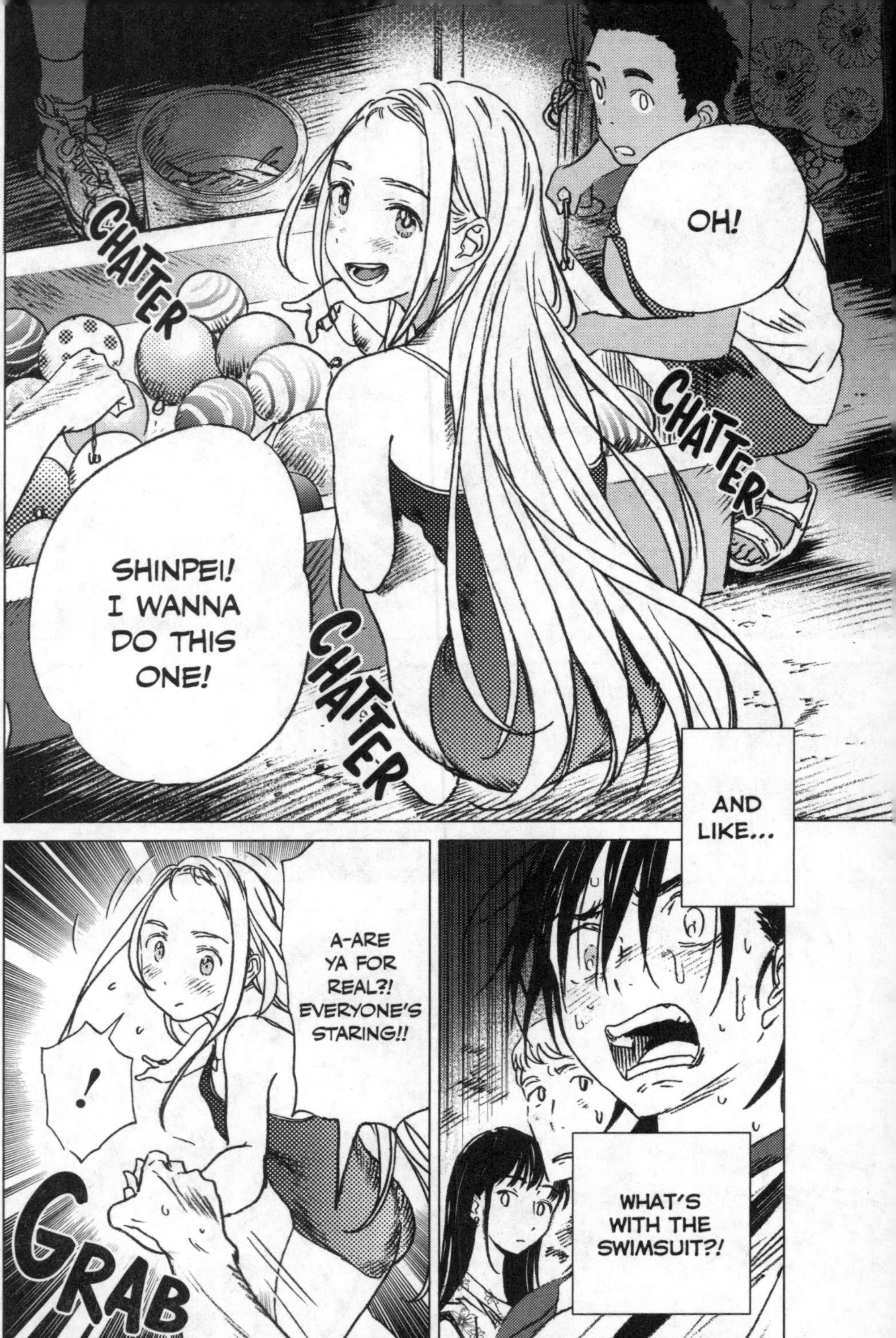
OH!
CHATTER
CHATTER
SHINPEI! I WANNA DO THIS ONE!
CHATTER
AND LIKE...
WHAT'S WITH THE SWIMSUIT?!
A-ARE YA FOR REAL?! EVERYONE'S STARING!!
!
GRAB

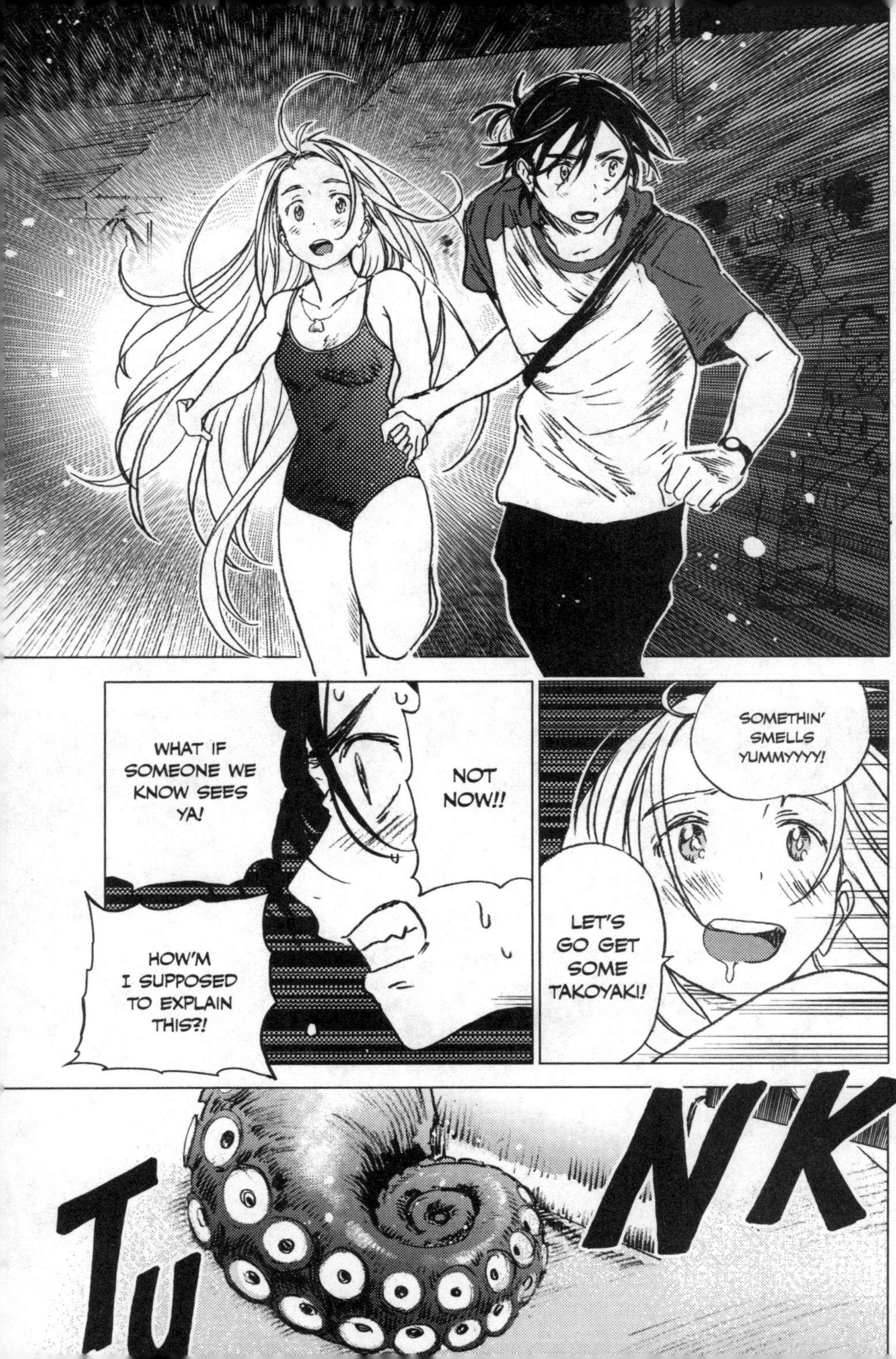
SOMETHIN' SMELLS YUMMYYYY!
LET'S GO GET SOME TAKOYAKI!
NOT NOW!!
WHAT IF SOMEONE WE KNOW SEES YA!
HOW'M I SUPPOSED TO EXPLAIN THIS?!
TuNK

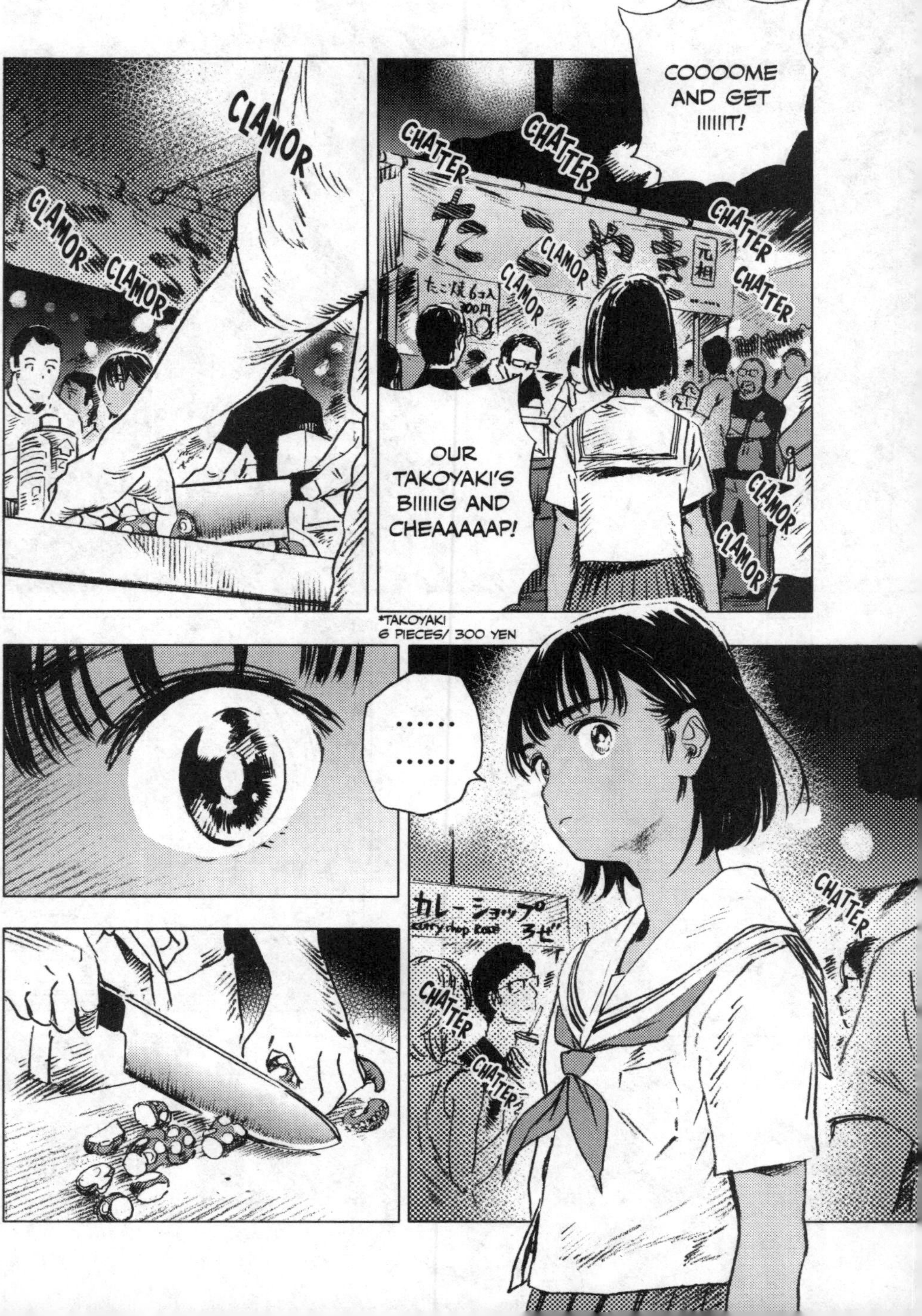
COOOOME AND GET IIIIIIT!
CHATTER
CHATTER
たこやき
CHATTER
CHATTER
CLAMOR
CLAMOR
OUR TAKOYAKI'S BIIIIIG AND CHEAAAAAP!
CLAMOR
CLAMOR
*TAKOYAKI
6 PIECES/ 300 YEN
CLAMOR
CLAMOR
CLAMOR
CLAMOR
CHATTER
カレーショップ ろぜ
CHATTER
CHATTER
......
......

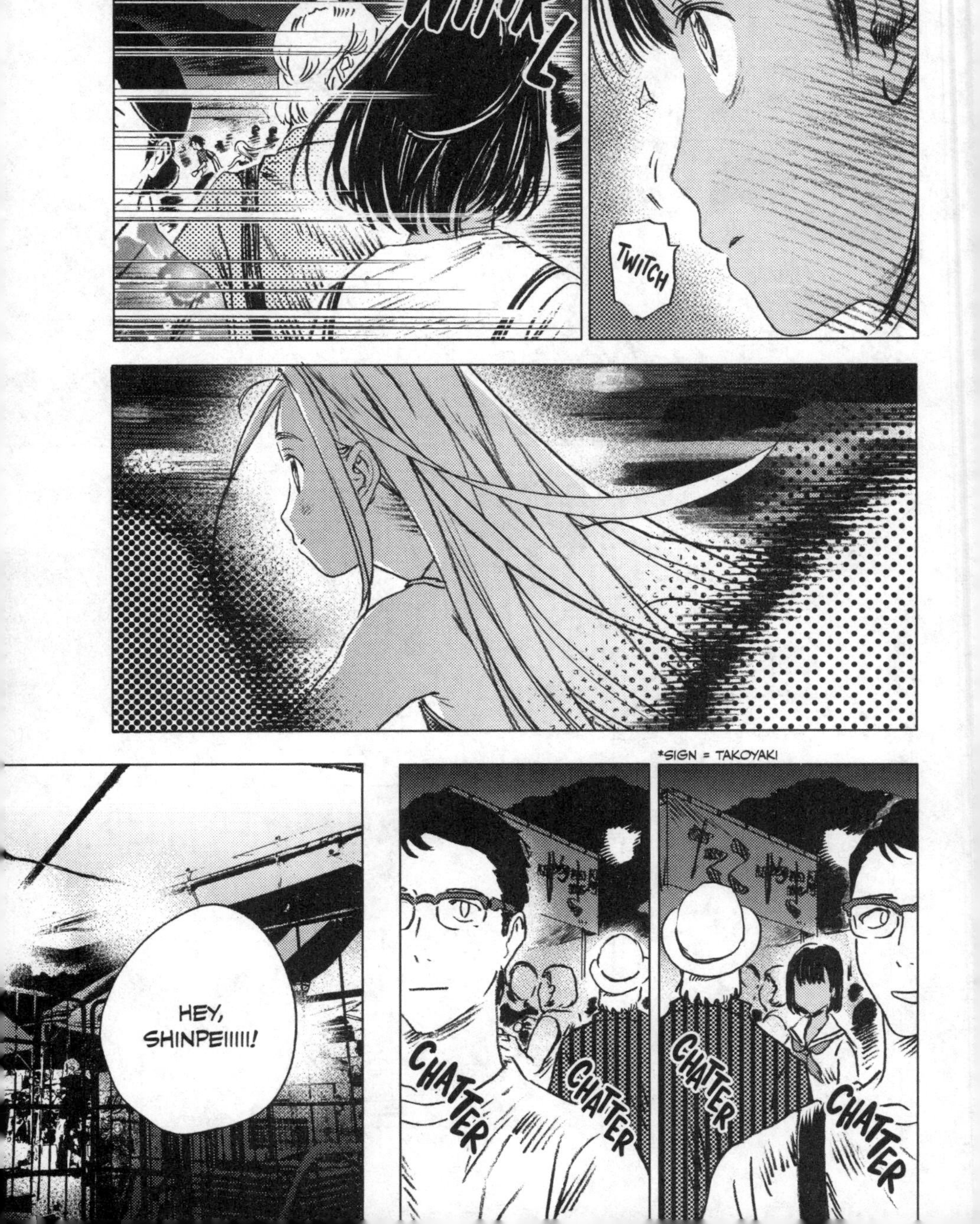
TWITCH
WHIRL
*SIGN = TAKOYAKI
CHATTER
CHATTER
CHATTER
CHATTER
HEY, SHINPEIIIIII!

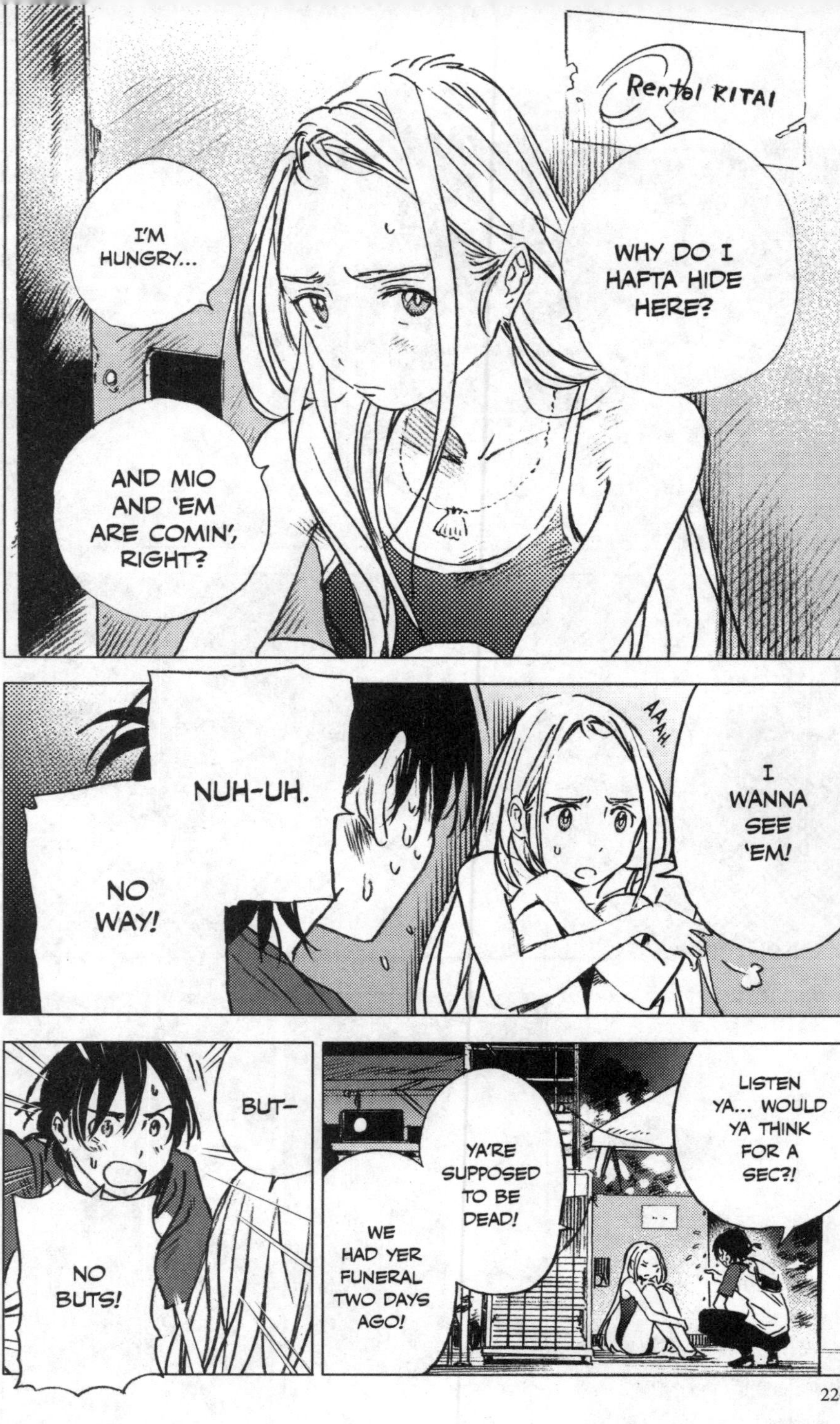
Rental KITAI
WHY DO I HAFTA HIDE HERE?
I'M HUNGRY...
AND MIO AND 'EM ARE COMIN', RIGHT?
AAAH.
I WANNA SEE 'EM!
NUH-UH.
NO WAY!
LISTEN YA... WOULD YA THINK FOR A SEC?!
YA'RE SUPPOSED TO BE DEAD!
WE HAD YER FUNERAL TWO DAYS AGO!
BUT-
NO BUTS!

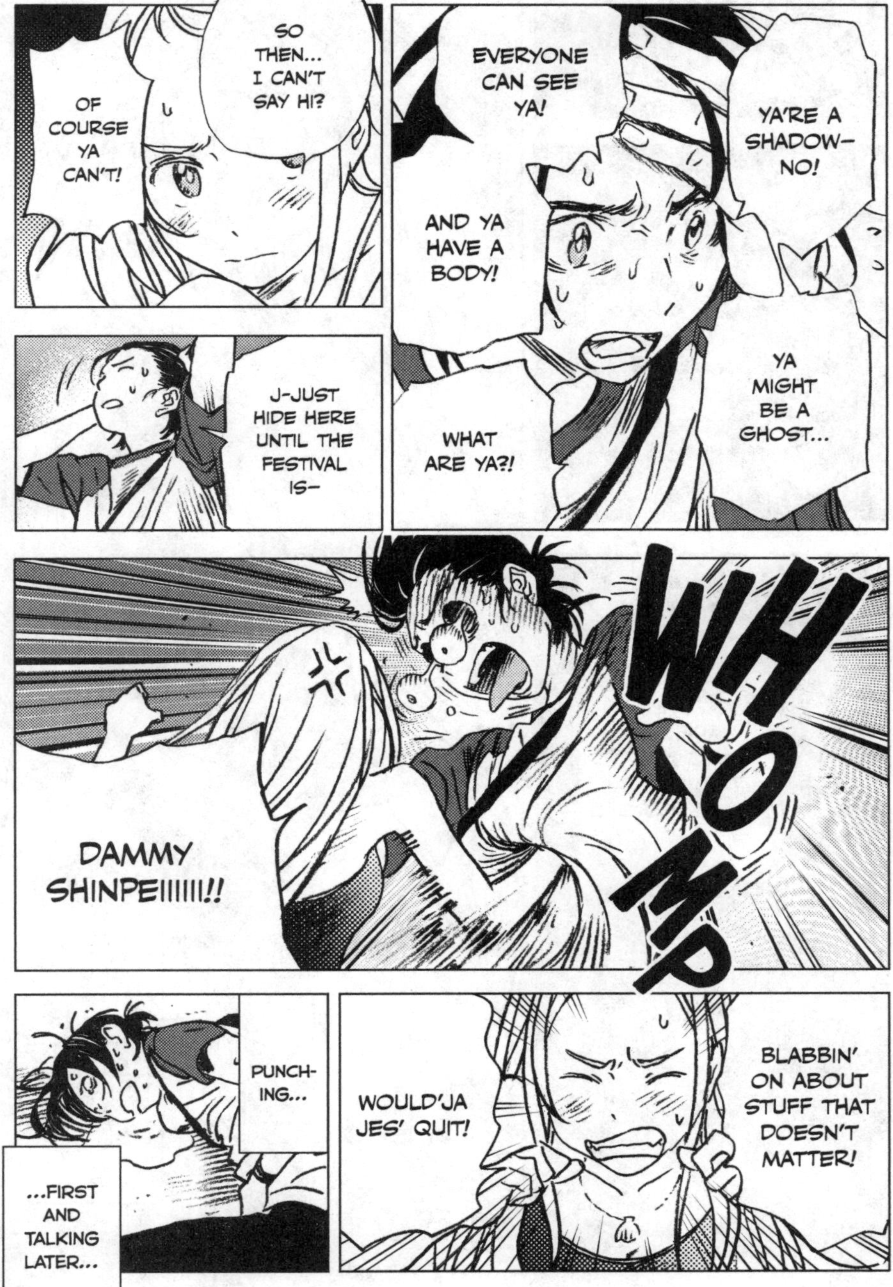
YA'RE A SHADOW—NO!
EVERYONE CAN SEE YA!
AND YA HAVE A BODY!
YA MIGHT BE A GHOST...
WHAT ARE YA?!
SO THEN... I CAN'T SAY HI?
OF COURSE YA CAN'T!
J-JUST HIDE HERE UNTIL THE FESTIVAL IS—
WHOMP
DAMMY SHINPEIIIIIII!!
BLABBIN' ON ABOUT STUFF THAT DOESN'T MATTER!
WOULD'JA JES' QUIT!
PUNCHING...
...FIRST AND TALKING LATER...

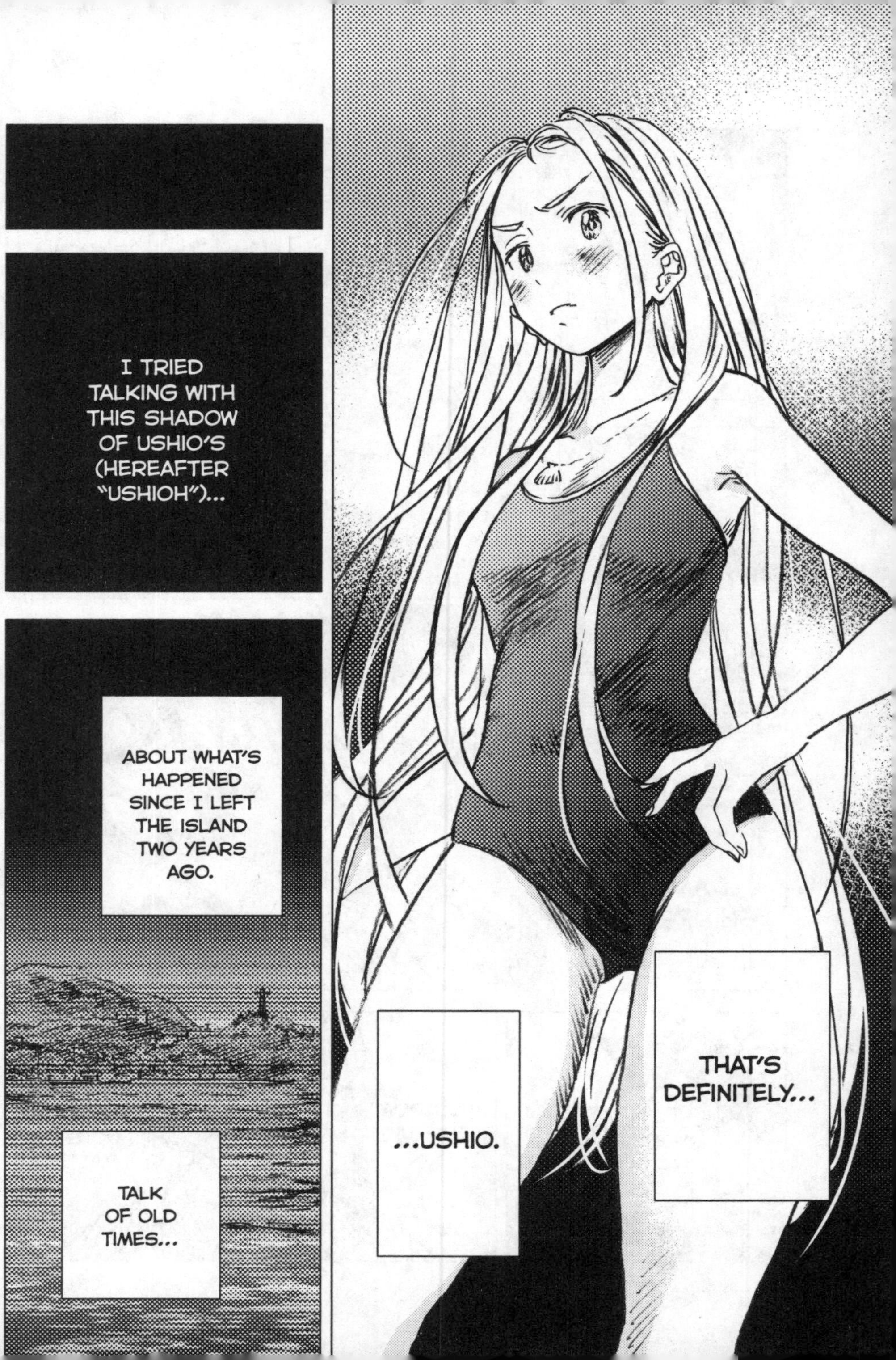

THAT'S DEFINITELY...
...USHIO.
I TRIED TALKING WITH THIS SHADOW OF USHIO'S (HEREAFTER "USHIOH")...
ABOUT WHAT'S HAPPENED SINCE I LEFT THE ISLAND TWO YEARS AGO.
TALK OF OLD TIMES...

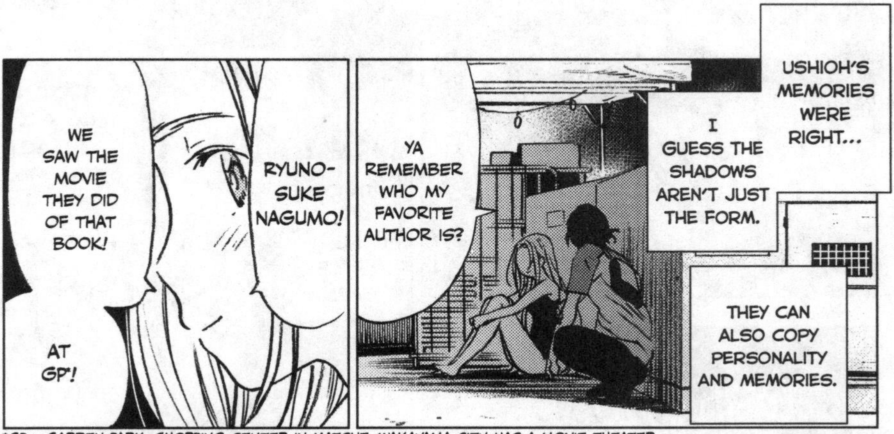
USHIOH'S MEMORIES WERE RIGHT...
I GUESS THE SHADOWS AREN'T JUST THE FORM.
THEY CAN ALSO COPY PERSONALITY AND MEMORIES.
YA REMEMBER WHO MY FAVORITE AUTHOR IS?
RYUNO-SUKE NAGUMO!
WE SAW THE MOVIE THEY DID OF THAT BOOK!
AT GP*!

*GP = GARDEN PARK. SHOPPING CENTER IN MATSUE, WAKAYAMA CITY. HAS A MOVIE THEATER.

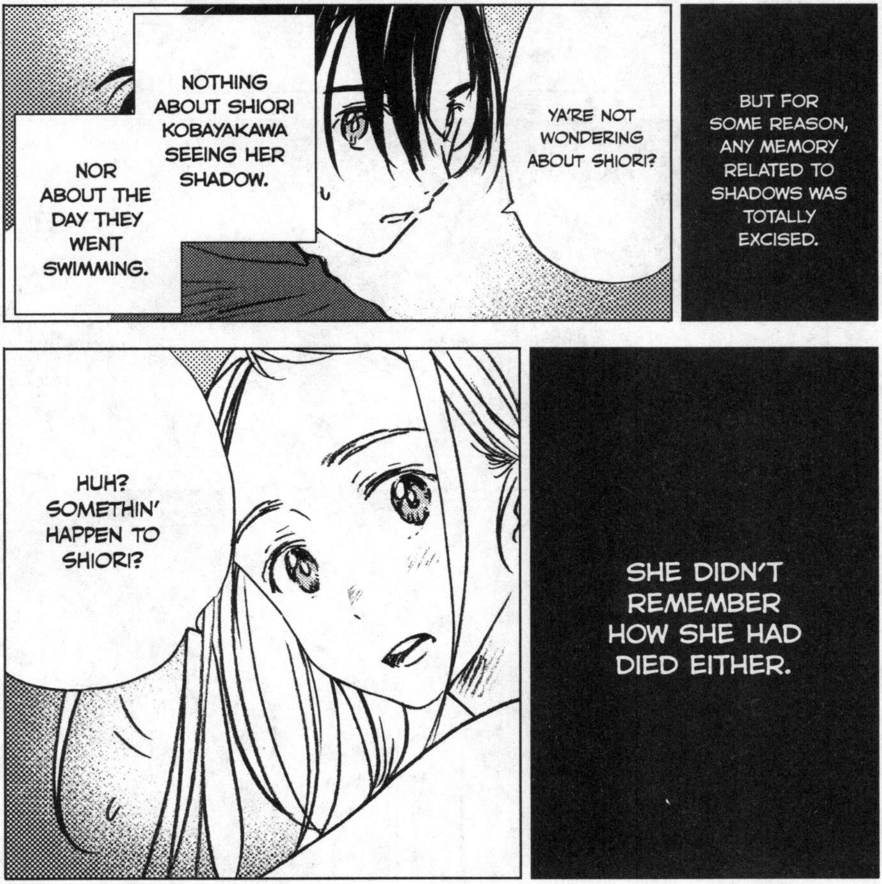
BUT FOR SOME REASON, ANY MEMORY RELATED TO SHADOWS WAS TOTALLY EXCISED.
YA'RE NOT WONDERING ABOUT SHIORI?
NOTHING ABOUT SHIORI KOBAYAKAWA SEEING HER SHADOW.
NOR ABOUT THE DAY THEY WENT SWIMMING.
SHE DIDN'T REMEMBER HOW SHE HAD DIED EITHER.
HUH? SOMETHIN' HAPPEN TO SHIORI?

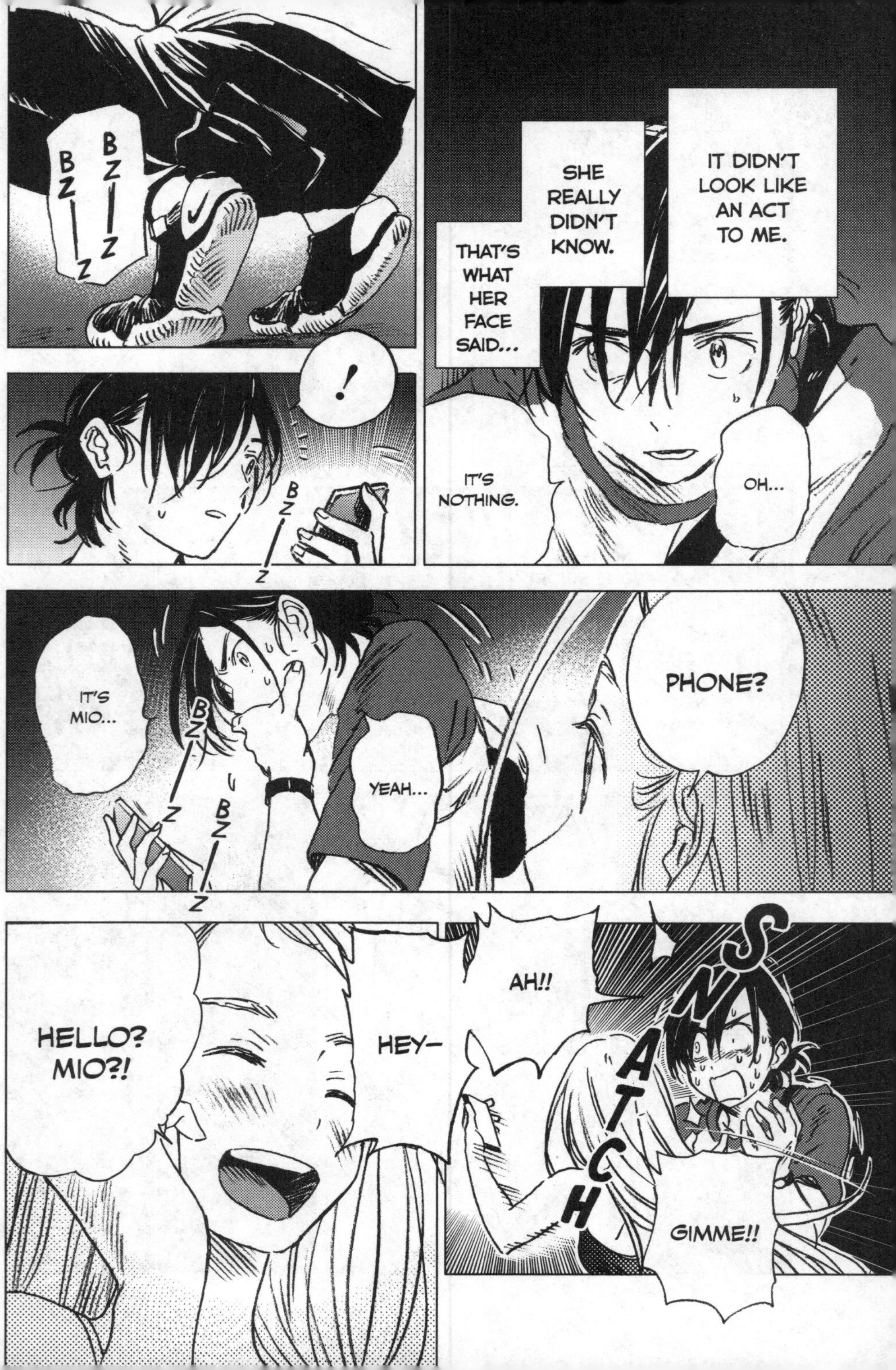
IT DIDN'T LOOK LIKE AN ACT TO ME.
SHE REALLY DIDN'T KNOW.
THAT'S WHAT HER FACE SAID...
OH...
IT'S NOTHING.
BZZZ
BZZZ
!
BZZ
PHONE?
YEAH...
IT'S MIO...
BZZ
BZZ
SNATCH
AH!!
GIMME!!
HEY–
HELLO? MIO?!

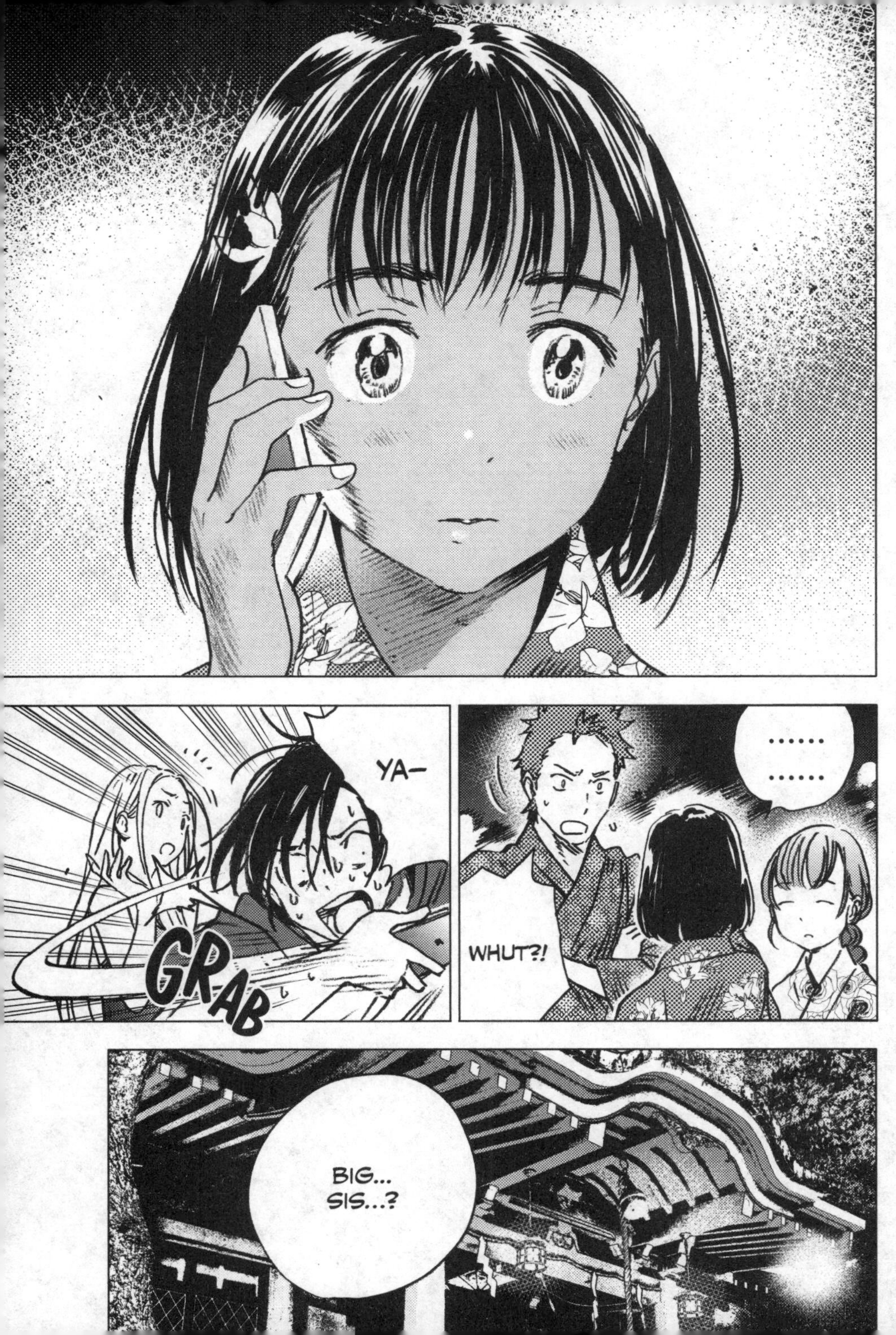
......
......
WHUT?!
YA-
GRAB
BIG...
SIS...?

Summertime rendering

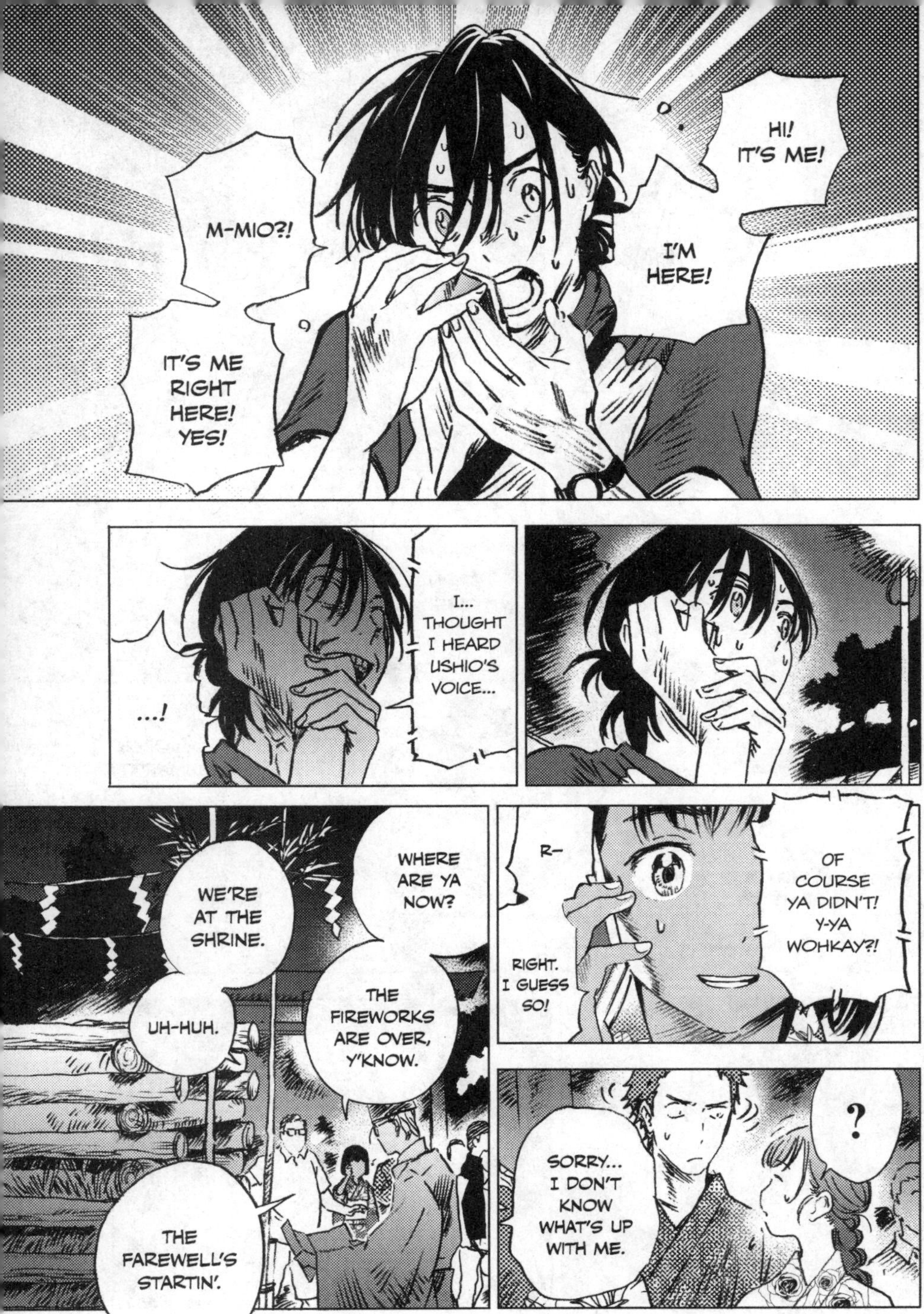
HI! IT'S ME!
I'M HERE!
M-MIO?!
IT'S ME RIGHT HERE! YES!
I... THOUGHT I HEARD USHIO'S VOICE...
...!
OF COURSE YA DIDN'T! Y-YA WOHKAY?!
R–
RIGHT. I GUESS SO!
?
SORRY... I DON'T KNOW WHAT'S UP WITH ME.
WHERE ARE YA NOW?
WE'RE AT THE SHRINE.
THE FIREWORKS ARE OVER, Y'KNOW.
UH-HUH.
THE FAREWELL'S STARTIN'.

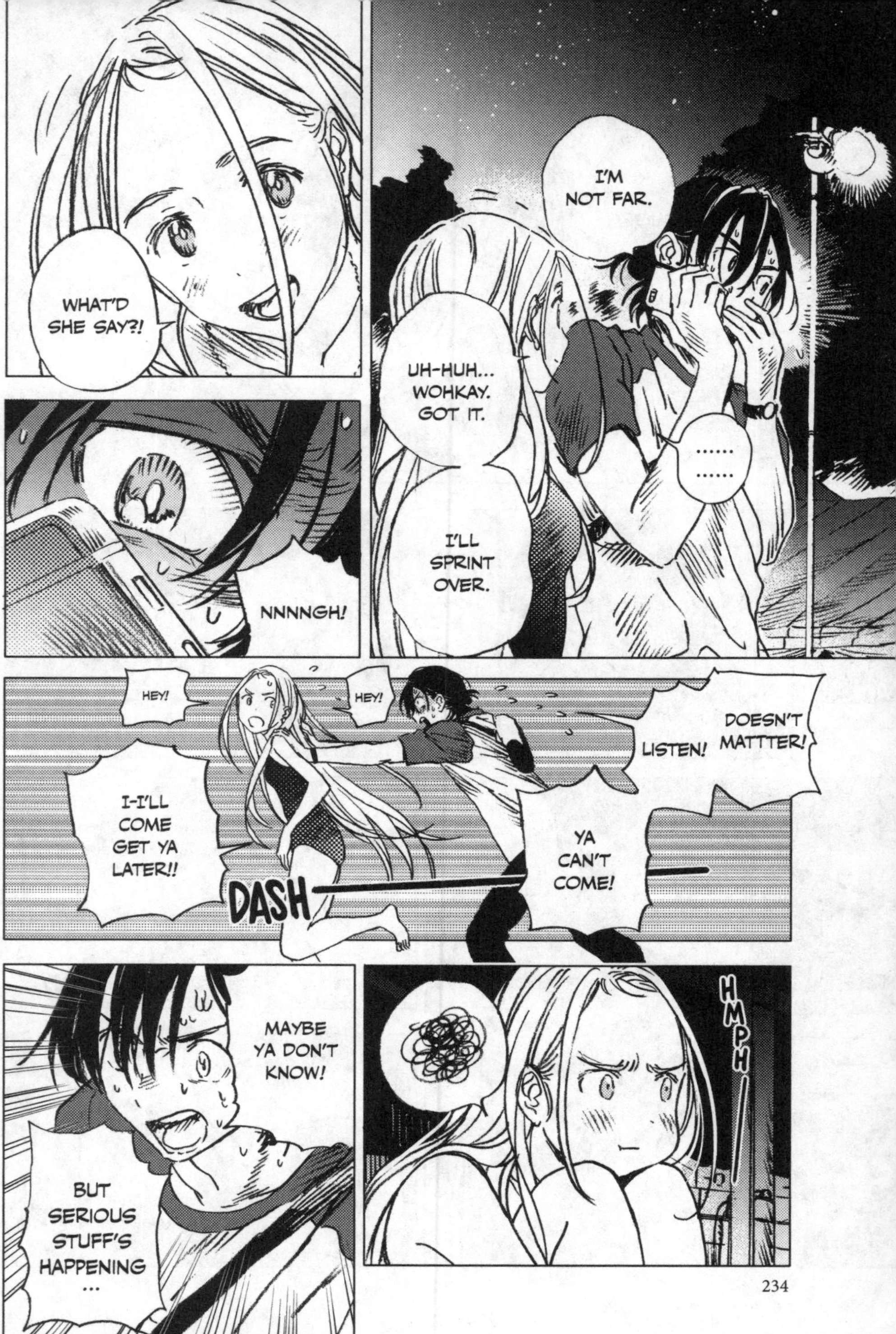
I'M NOT FAR.
UH-HUH... WOHKAY. GOT IT.
....
I'LL SPRINT OVER.
WHAT'D SHE SAY?!
NNNNGH!
DOESN'T MATTTER!
LISTEN!
HEY!
HEY!
YA CAN'T COME!
I-I'LL COME GET YA LATER!!
DASH
HMPH
MAYBE YA DON'T KNOW!
BUT SERIOUS STUFF'S HAPPENING ...

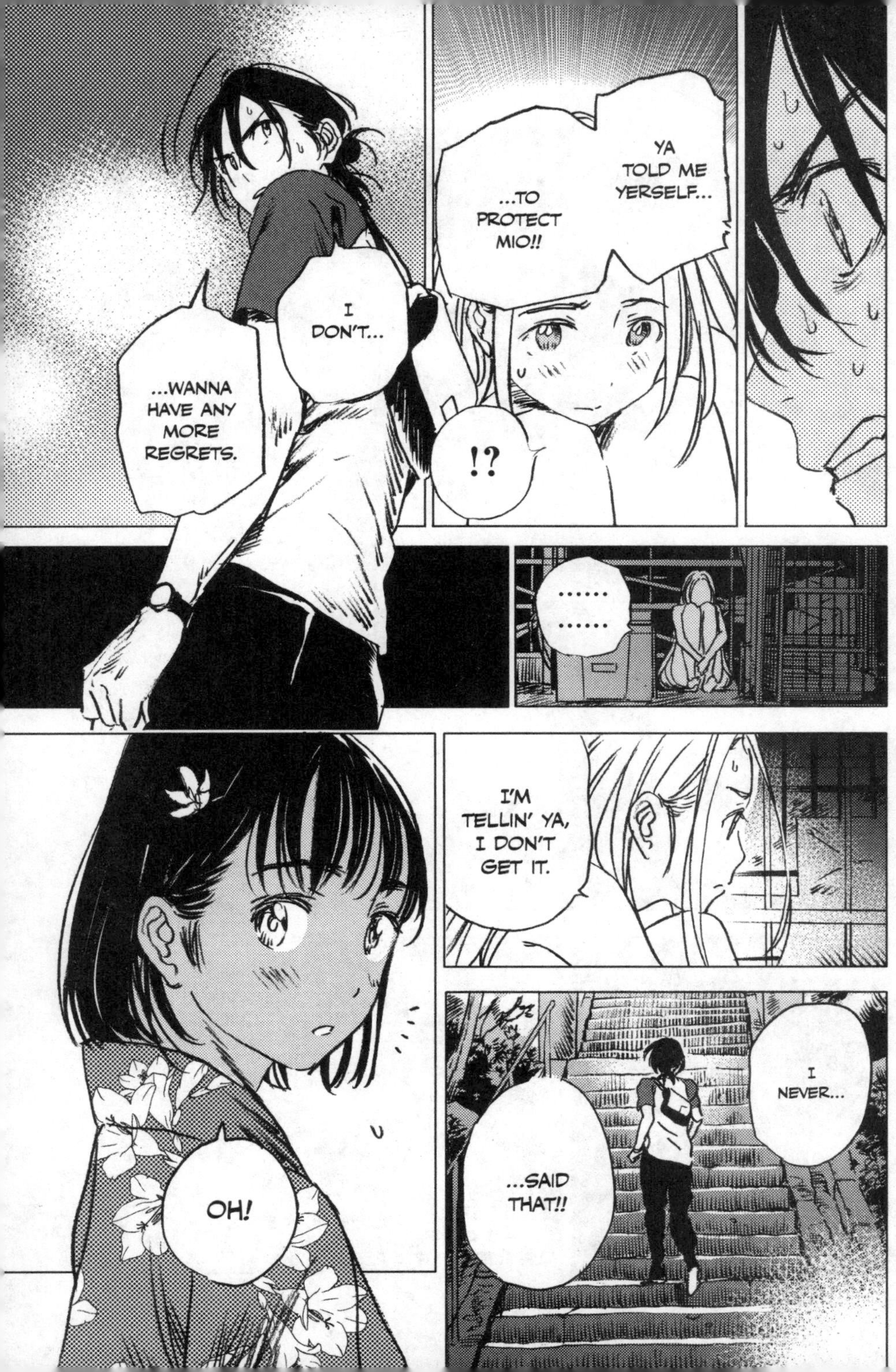
YA TOLD ME YERSELF...
...TO PROTECT MIO!!
!?
I DON'T...
...WANNA HAVE ANY MORE REGRETS.
......
......
I'M TELLIN' YA, I DON'T GET IT.
I NEVER...
...SAID THAT!!
OH!

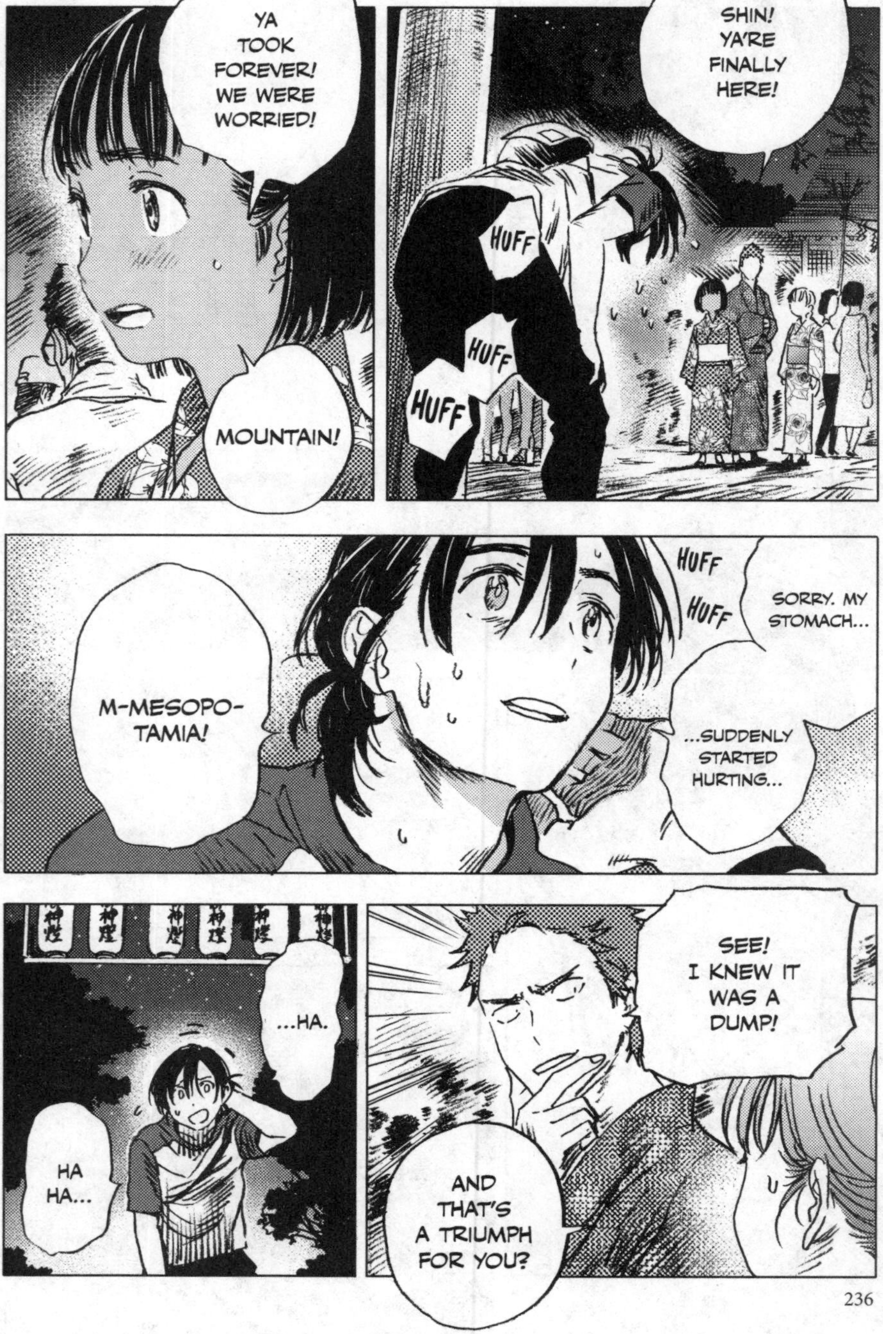
SHIN! YA'RE FINALLY HERE!
HUFF
HUFF
HUFF
YA TOOK FOREVER! WE WERE WORRIED!
MOUNTAIN!
HUFF
HUFF
SORRY. MY STOMACH...
...SUDDENLY STARTED HURTING...
M-MESOPOTAMIA!
SEE! I KNEW IT WAS A DUMP!
AND THAT'S A TRIUMPH FOR YOU?
...HA.
HA HA...

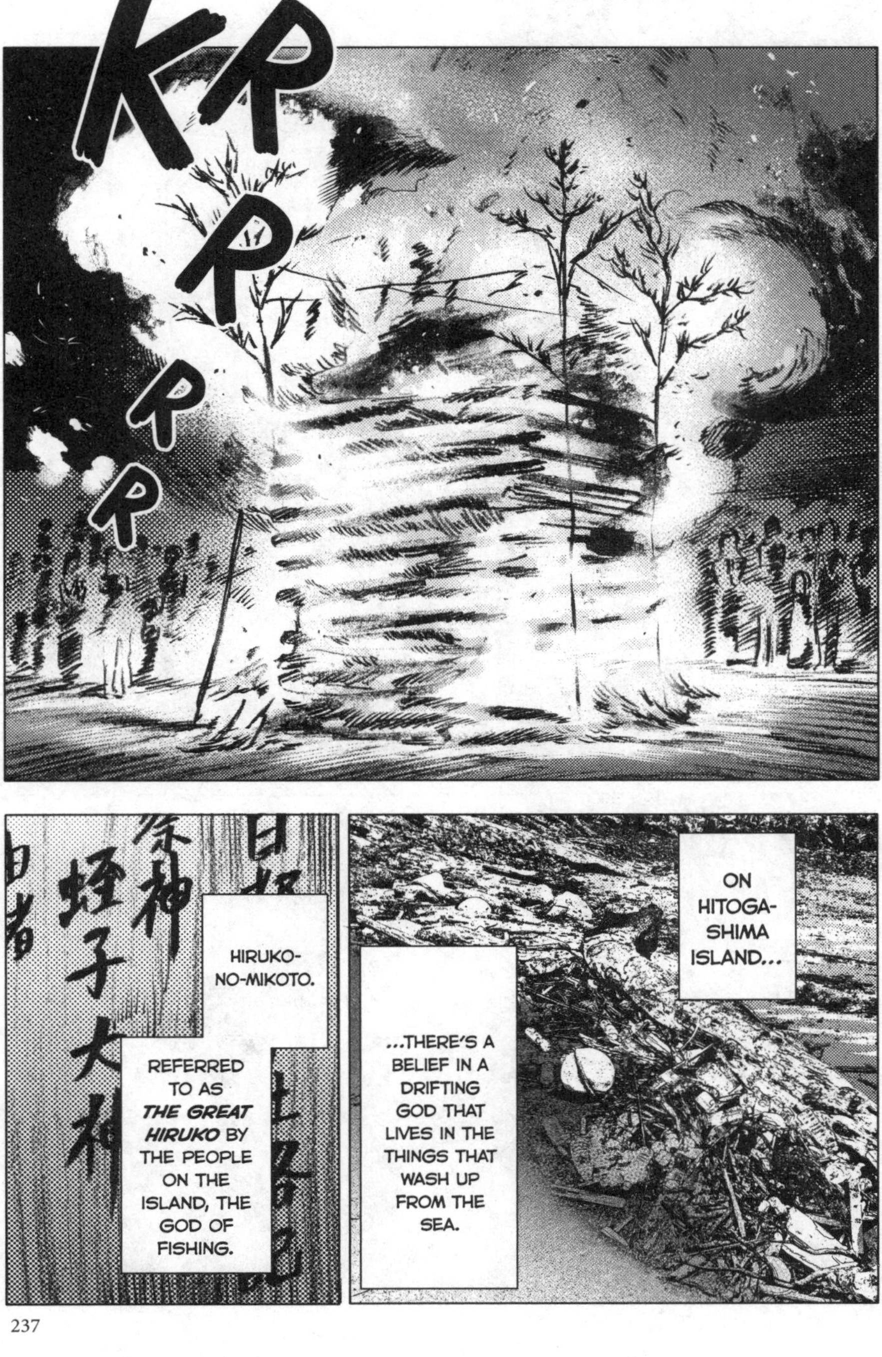
KRRRRR
ON HITOGA-SHIMA ISLAND...
...THERE'S A BELIEF IN A DRIFTING GOD THAT LIVES IN THE THINGS THAT WASH UP FROM THE SEA.
HIRUKO-NO-MIKOTO.
REFERRED TO AS *THE GREAT HIRUKO* BY THE PEOPLE ON THE ISLAND, THE GOD OF FISHING.

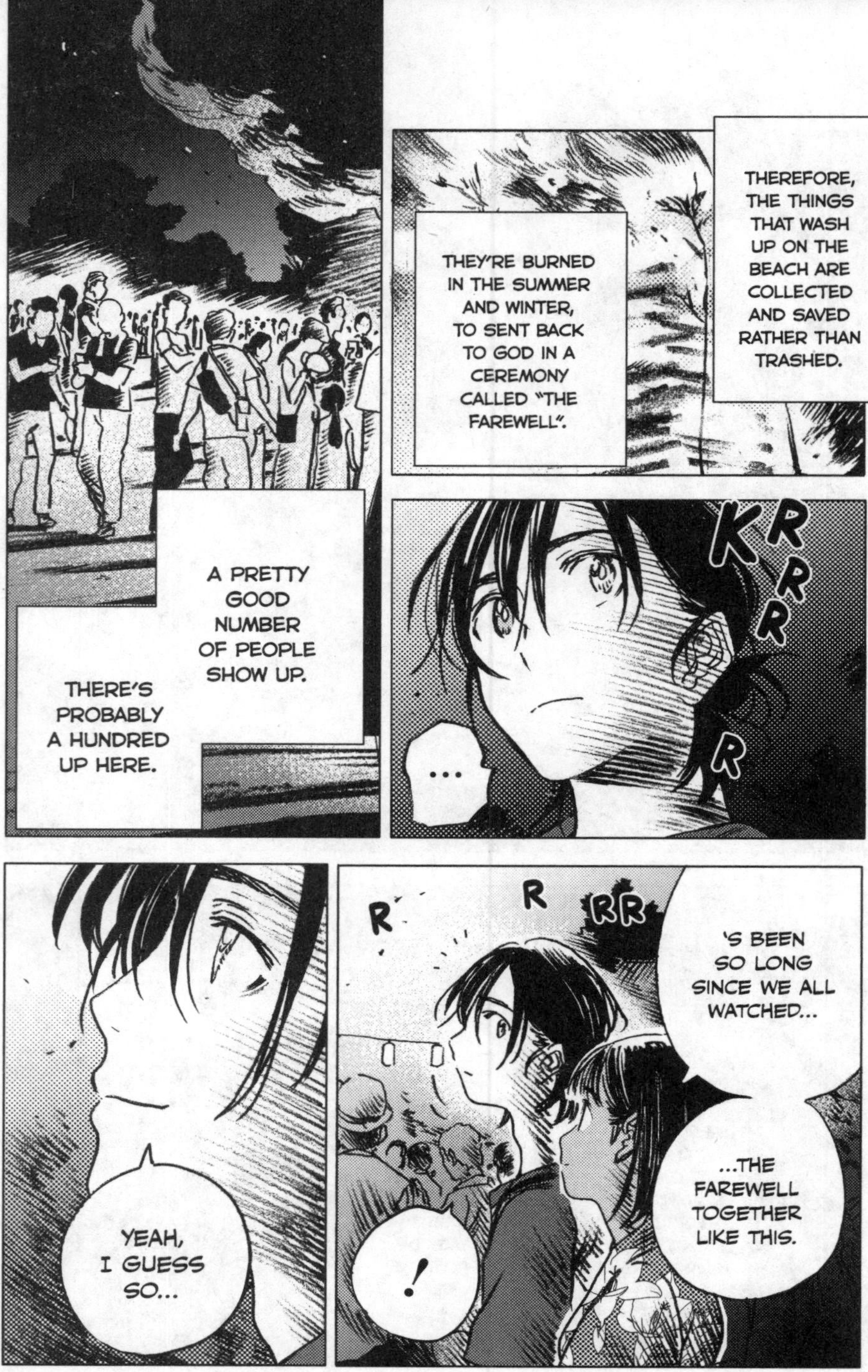
THEREFORE, THE THINGS THAT WASH UP ON THE BEACH ARE COLLECTED AND SAVED RATHER THAN TRASHED.
THEY'RE BURNED IN THE SUMMER AND WINTER, TO SENT BACK TO GOD IN A CEREMONY CALLED "THE FAREWELL".
KRRRR
R
...
A PRETTY GOOD NUMBER OF PEOPLE SHOW UP.
THERE'S PROBABLY A HUNDRED UP HERE.
RR
R
R
'S BEEN SO LONG SINCE WE ALL WATCHED...
...THE FAREWELL TOGETHER LIKE THIS.
!
YEAH, I GUESS SO...

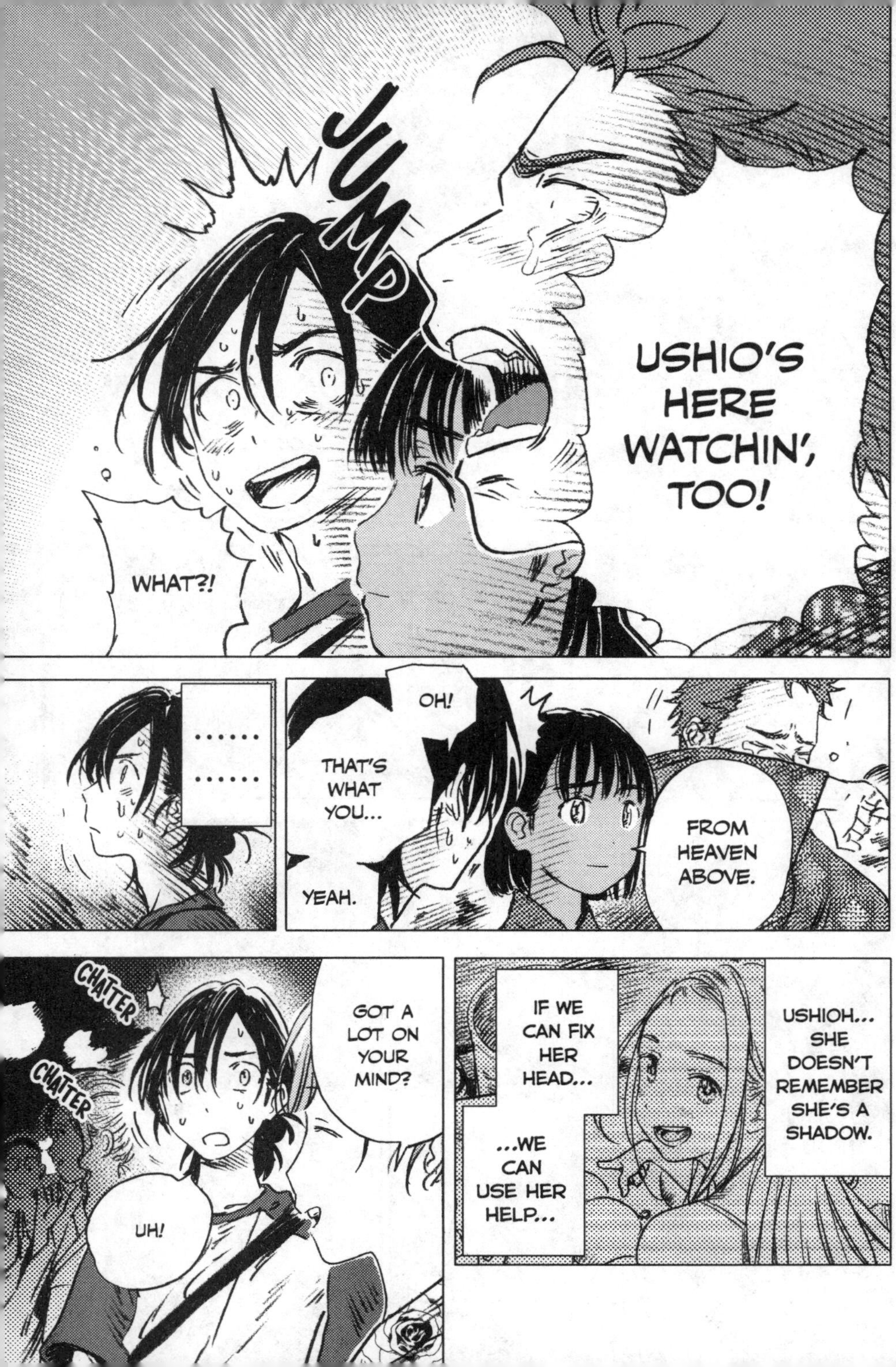

JUMP
USHIO'S HERE WATCHIN', TOO!
WHAT?!
FROM HEAVEN ABOVE.
OH!
THAT'S WHAT YOU...
YEAH.
......
......
USHIOH... SHE DOESN'T REMEMBER SHE'S A SHADOW.
IF WE CAN FIX HER HEAD...
...WE CAN USE HER HELP...
CHATTER
CHATTER
GOT A LOT ON YOUR MIND?
UH!

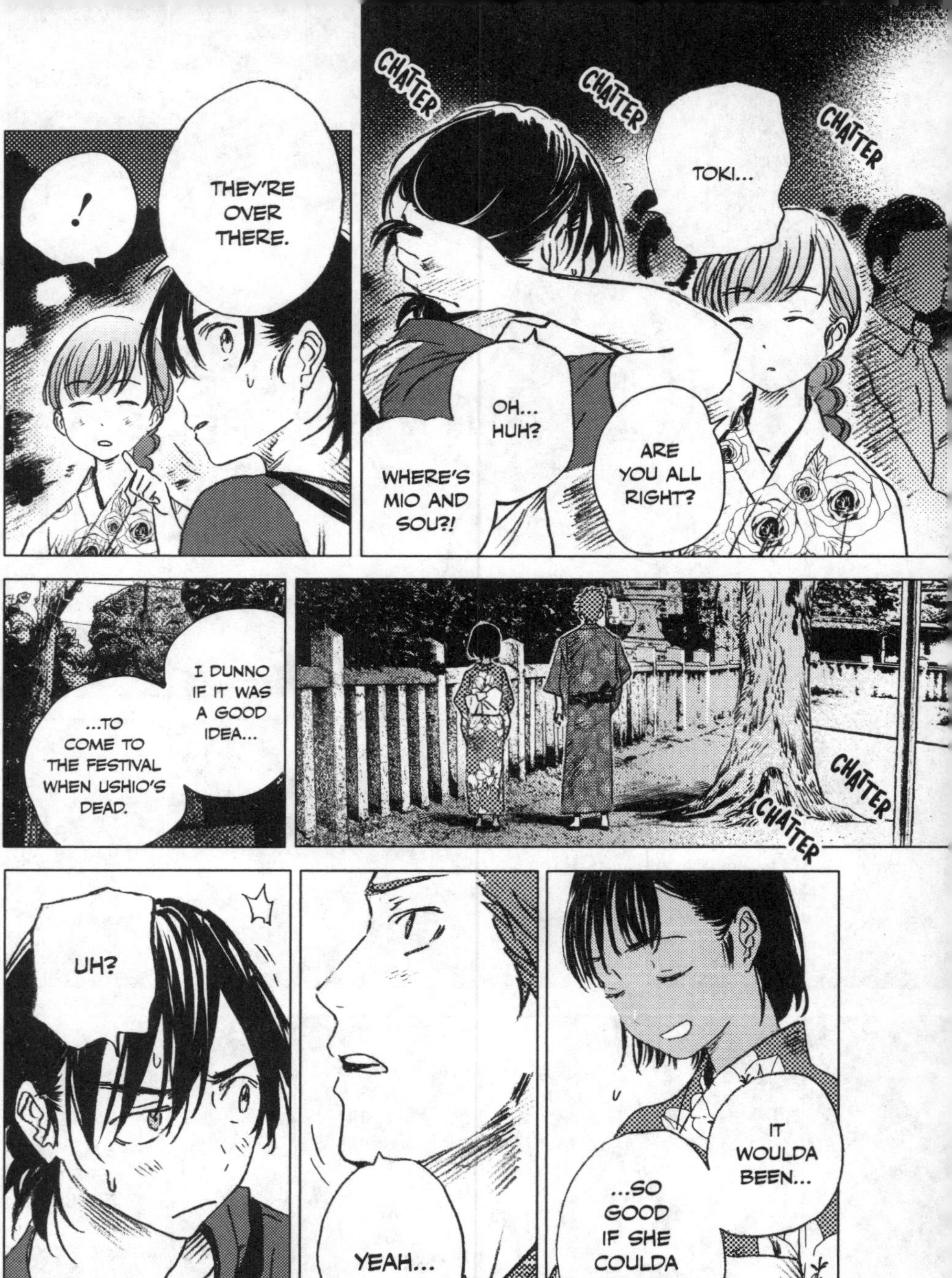
CHATTER
CHATTER
CHATTER
TOKI...
ARE YOU ALL RIGHT?
OH... HUH?
WHERE'S MIO AND SOU?!
THEY'RE OVER THERE.
!
CHATTER
CHATTER
I DUNNO IF IT WAS A GOOD IDEA...
...TO COME TO THE FESTIVAL WHEN USHIO'S DEAD.
IT WOULDA BEEN...
...SO GOOD IF SHE COULDA COME, TOO.
YEAH...
UH?

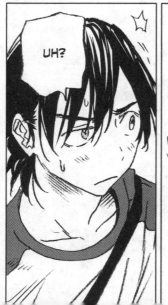

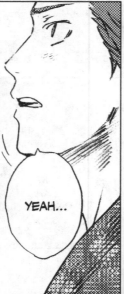

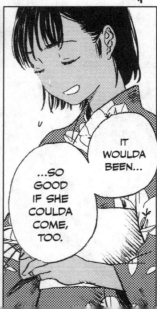

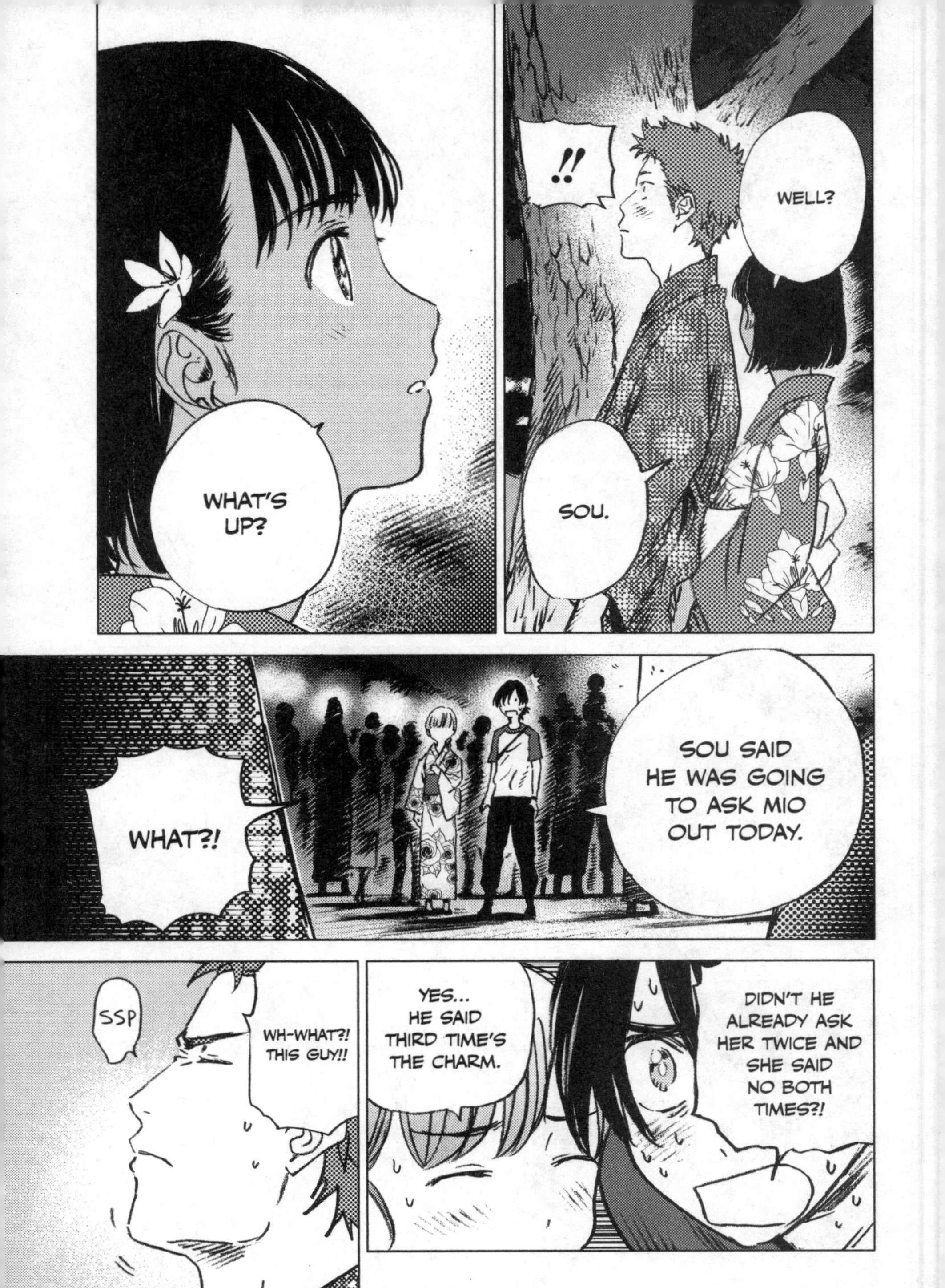

WELL?
!!
SOU.
WHAT'S UP?
SOU SAID HE WAS GOING TO ASK MIO OUT TODAY.
WHAT?!
DIDN'T HE ALREADY ASK HER TWICE AND SHE SAID NO BOTH TIMES?!
YES... HE SAID THIRD TIME'S THE CHARM.
WH-WHAT?! THIS GUY!!
SSP

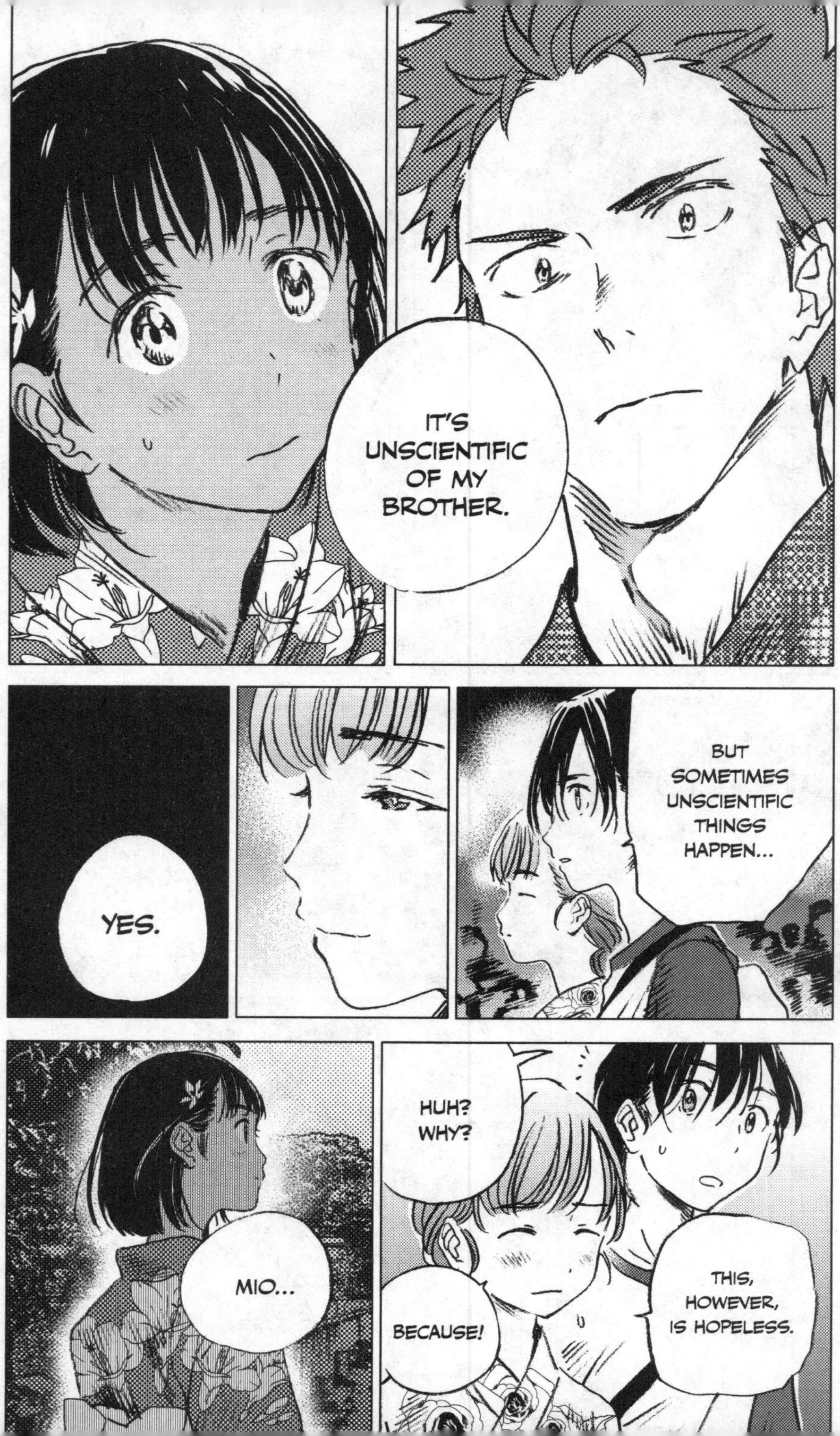
IT'S UNSCIENTIFIC OF MY BROTHER.
BUT SOMETIMES UNSCIENTIFIC THINGS HAPPEN...
YES.
THIS, HOWEVER, IS HOPELESS.
HUH? WHY?
BECAUSE!
MIO...

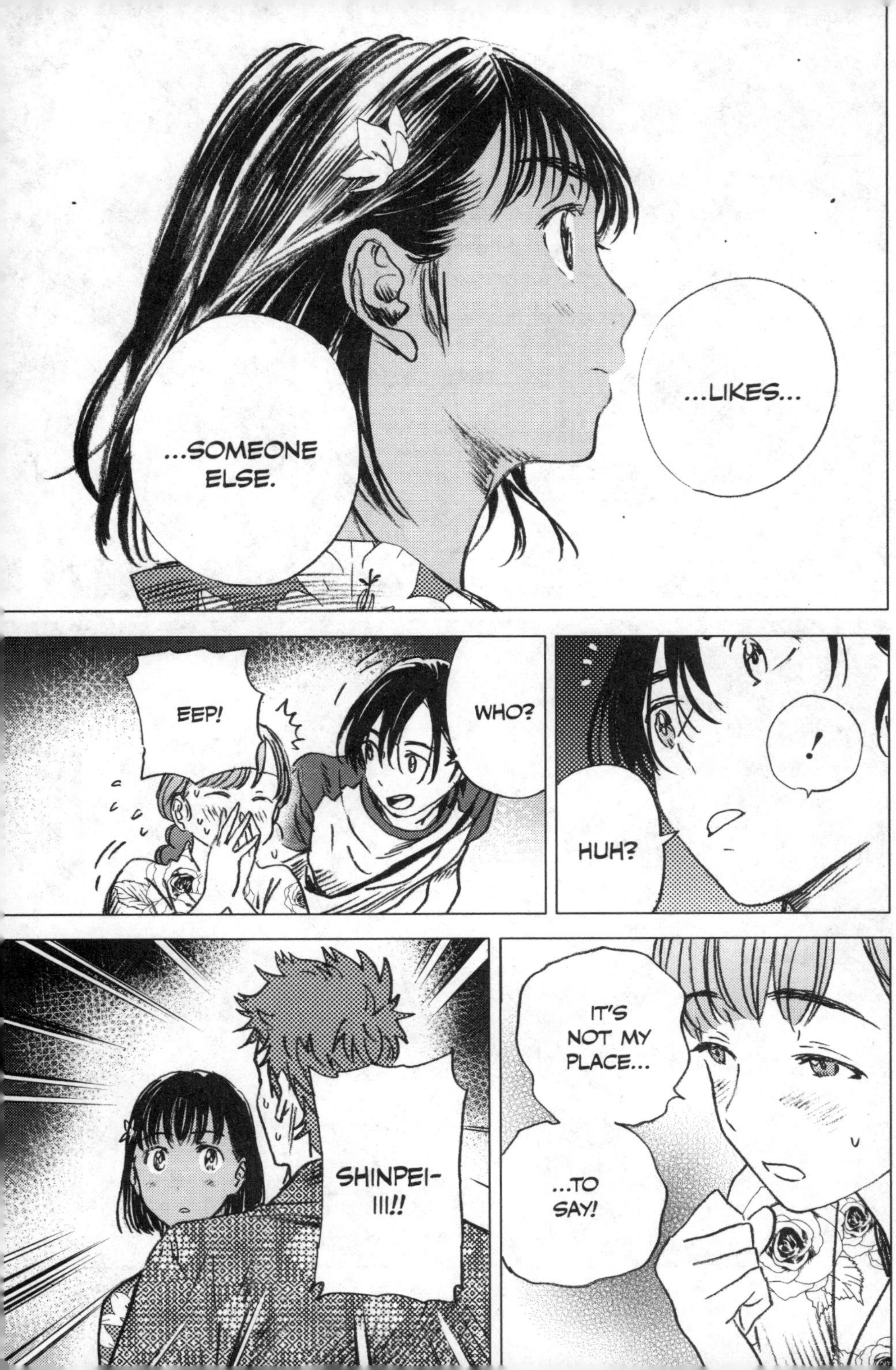
...LIKES...
...SOMEONE ELSE.
!
HUH?
WHO?
EEP!
IT'S NOT MY PLACE...
...TO SAY!
SHINPEI-IIII!!

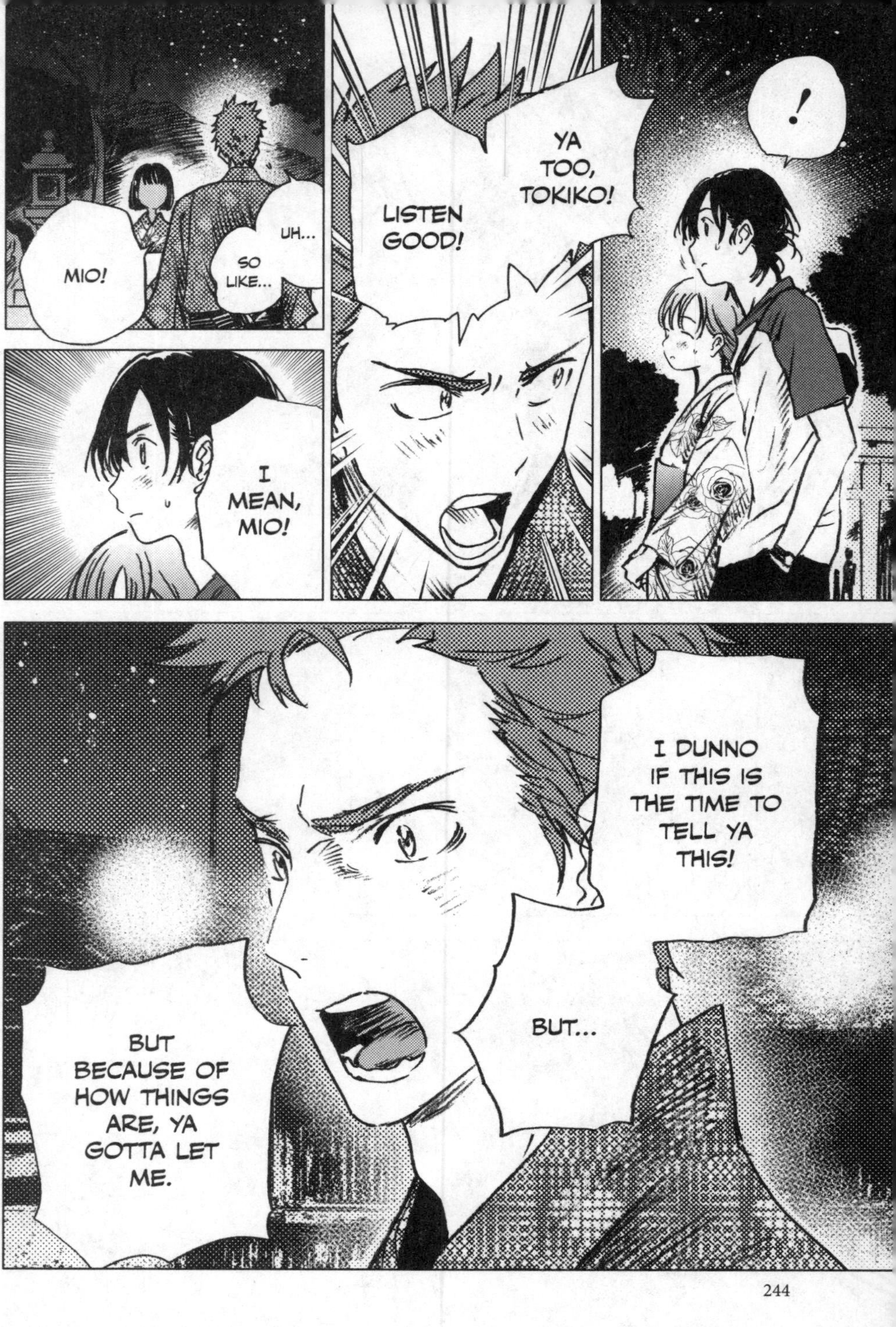
!
YA TOO, TOKIKO!
LISTEN GOOD!
UH...
SO LIKE...
MIO!
I MEAN, MIO!
I DUNNO IF THIS IS THE TIME TO TELL YA THIS!
BUT...
BUT BECAUSE OF HOW THINGS ARE, YA GOTTA LET ME.

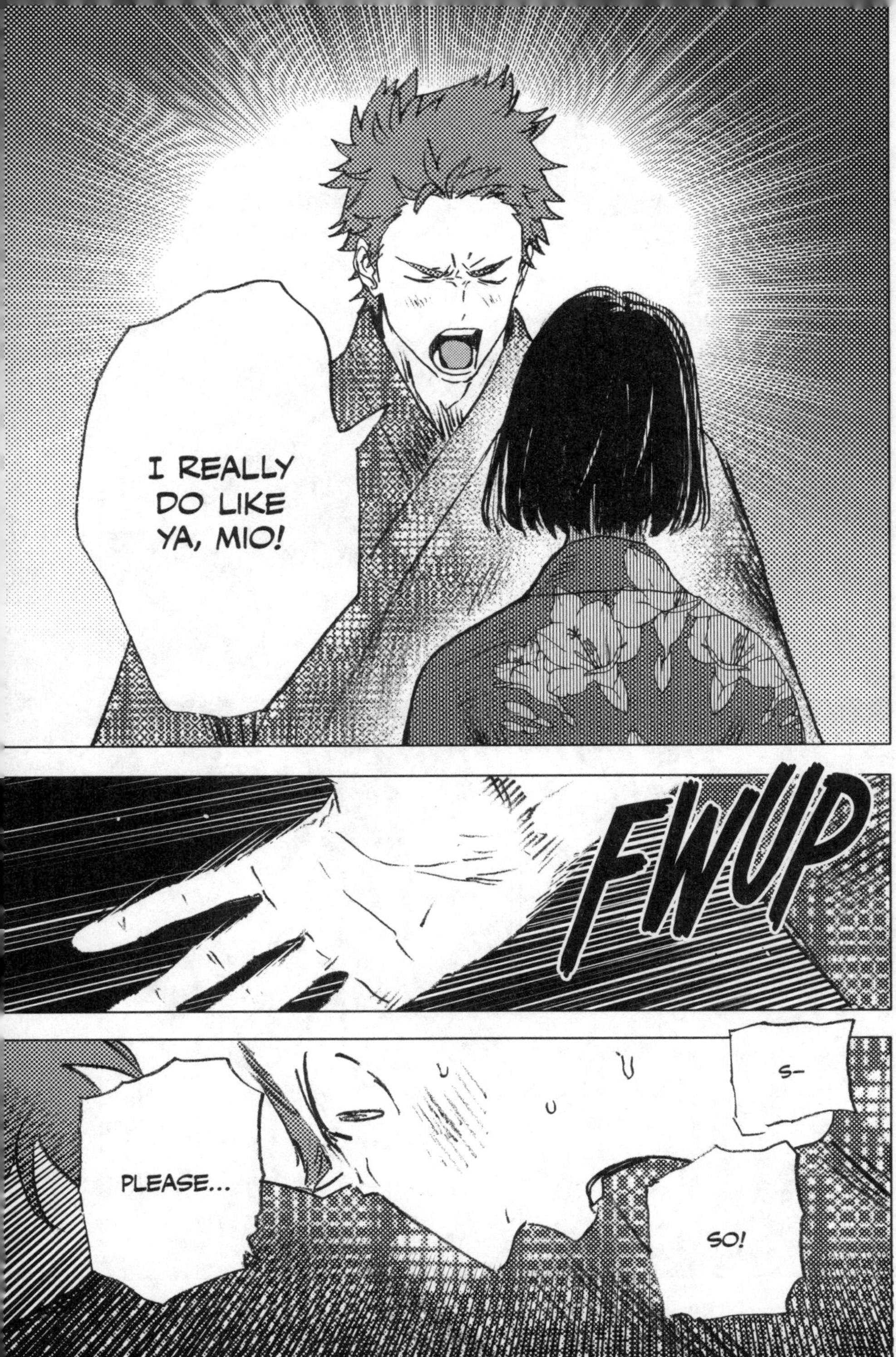
I REALLY DO LIKE YA, MIO!
FWUP
S-
SO!
PLEASE...

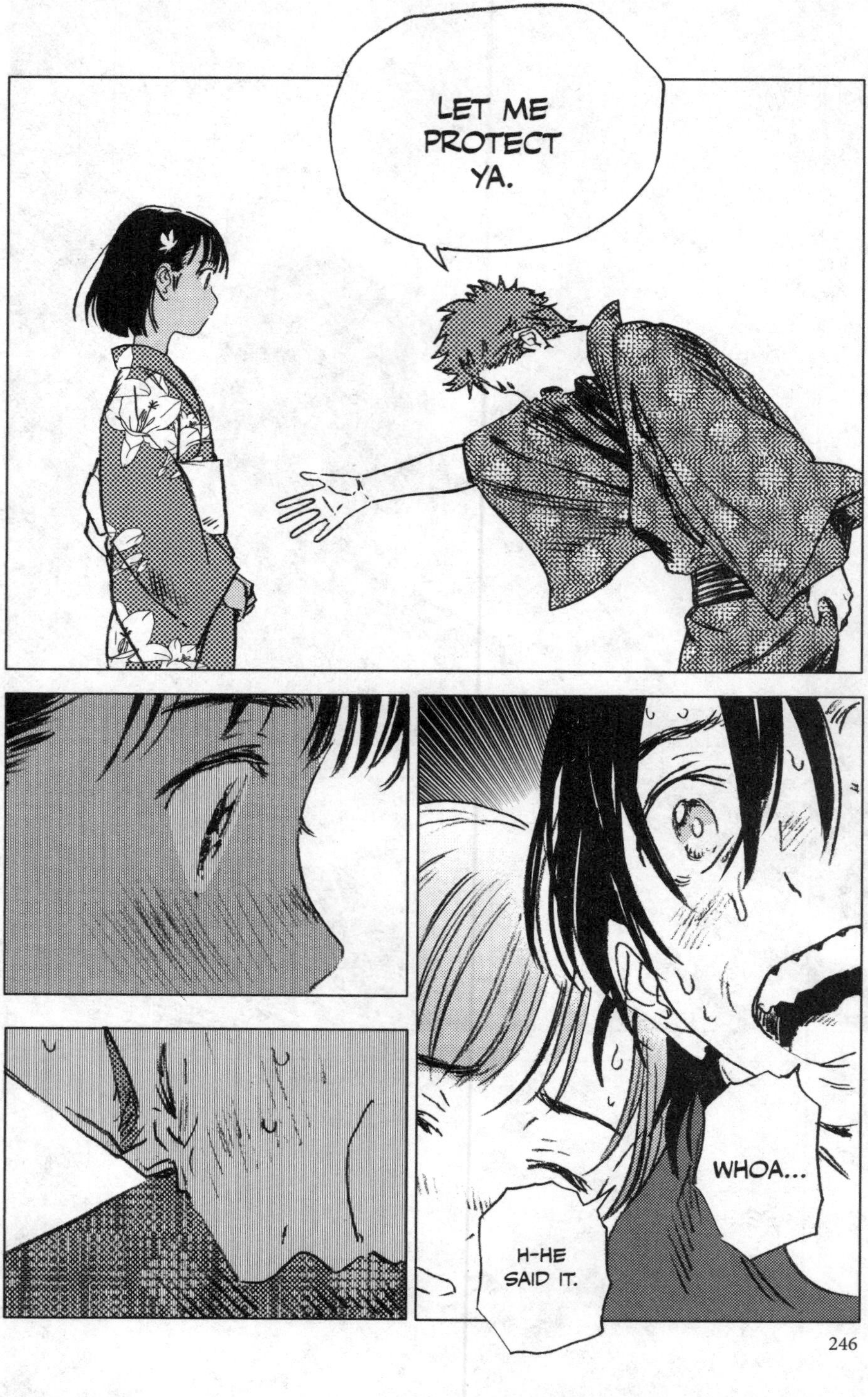
LET ME PROTECT YA.
WHOA...
H-HE SAID IT.

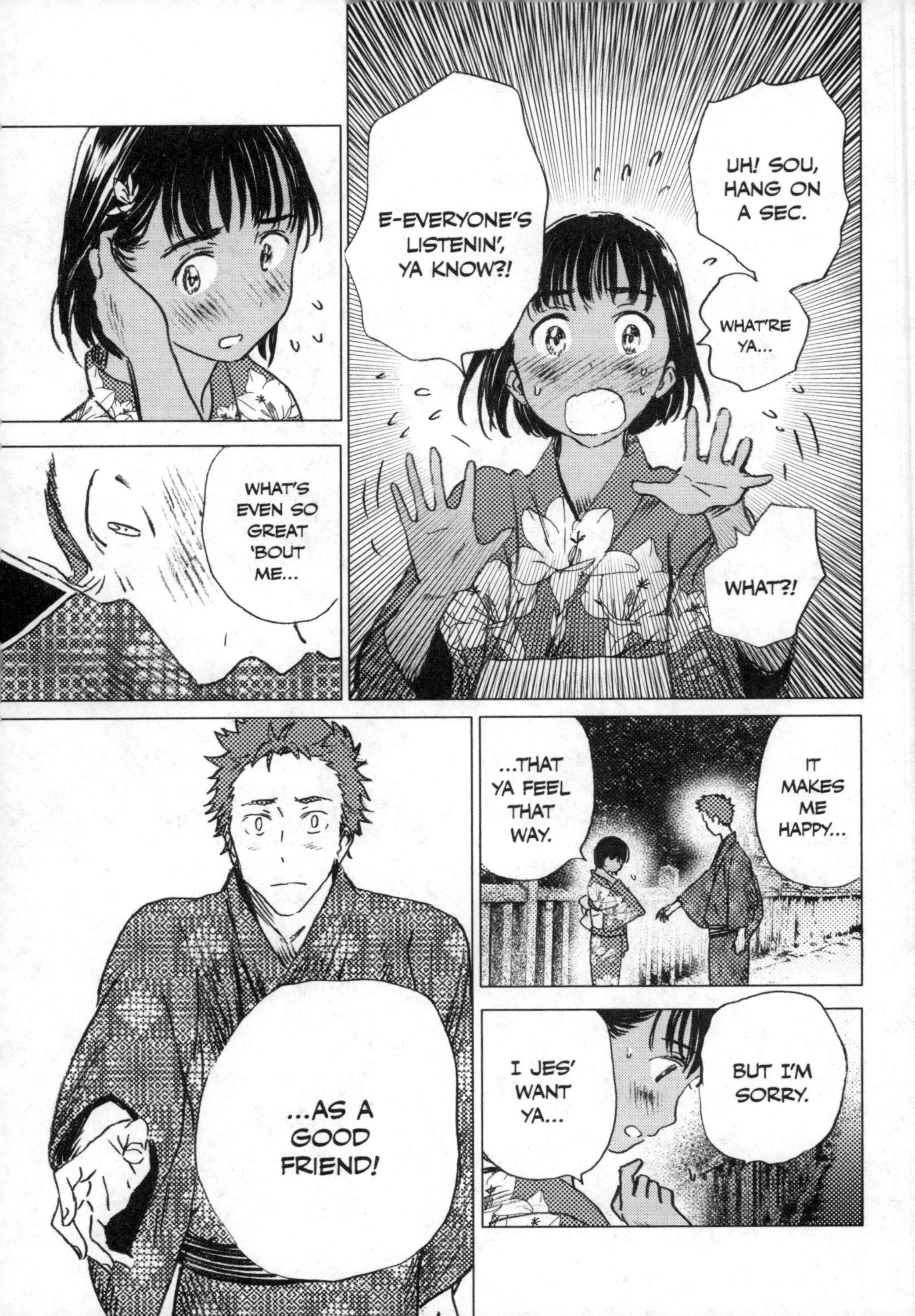
UH! SOU, HANG ON A SEC.
WHAT'RE YA...
WHAT?!
E-EVERYONE'S LISTENIN', YA KNOW?!
WHAT'S EVEN SO GREAT 'BOUT ME...
IT MAKES ME HAPPY...
...THAT YA FEEL THAT WAY.
BUT I'M SORRY.
I JES' WANT YA...
...AS A GOOD FRIEND!

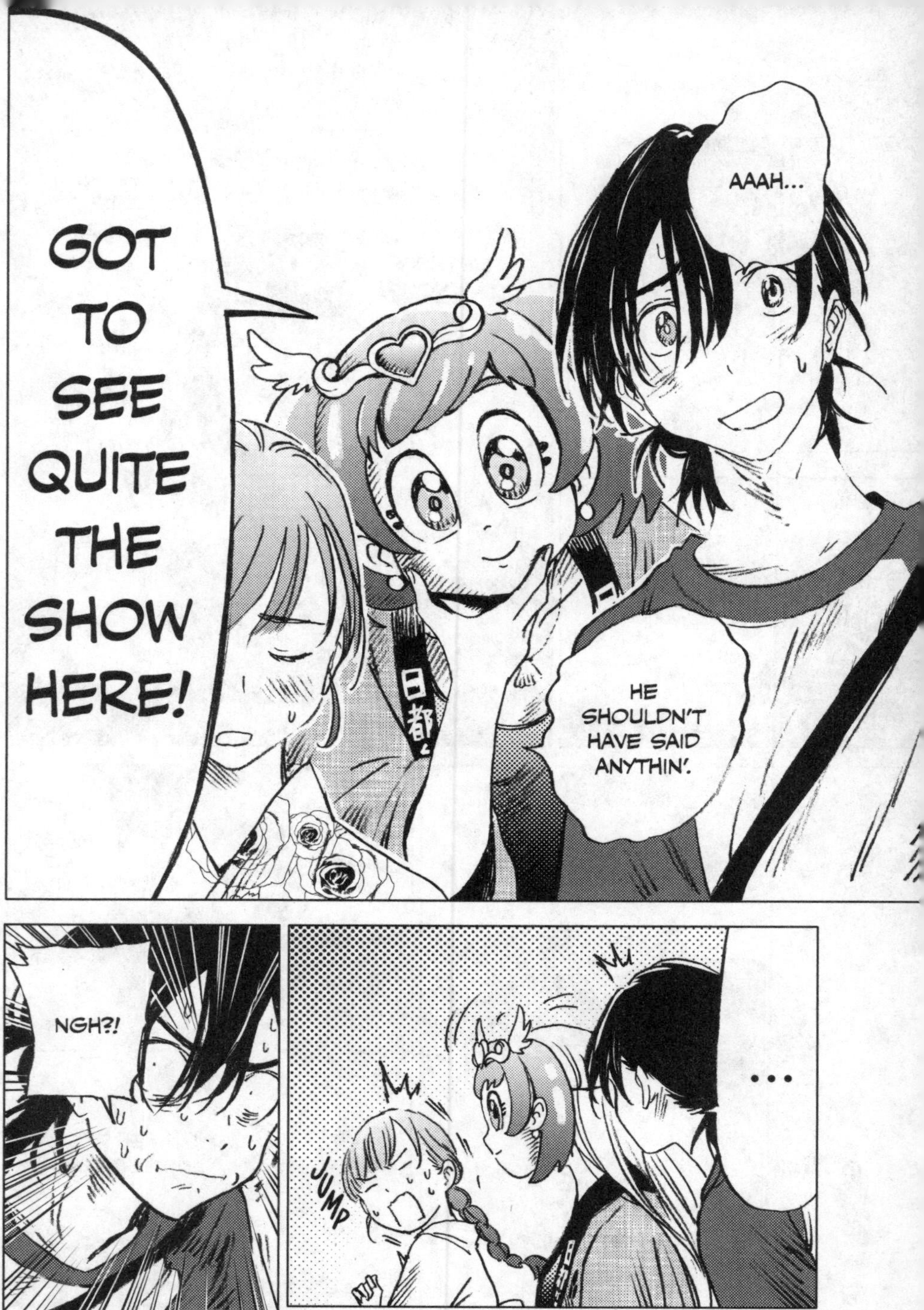
AAAH...
GOT TO SEE QUITE THE SHOW HERE!
HE SHOULDN'T HAVE SAID ANYTHIN'.
日都
...
JUMP
NGH?!

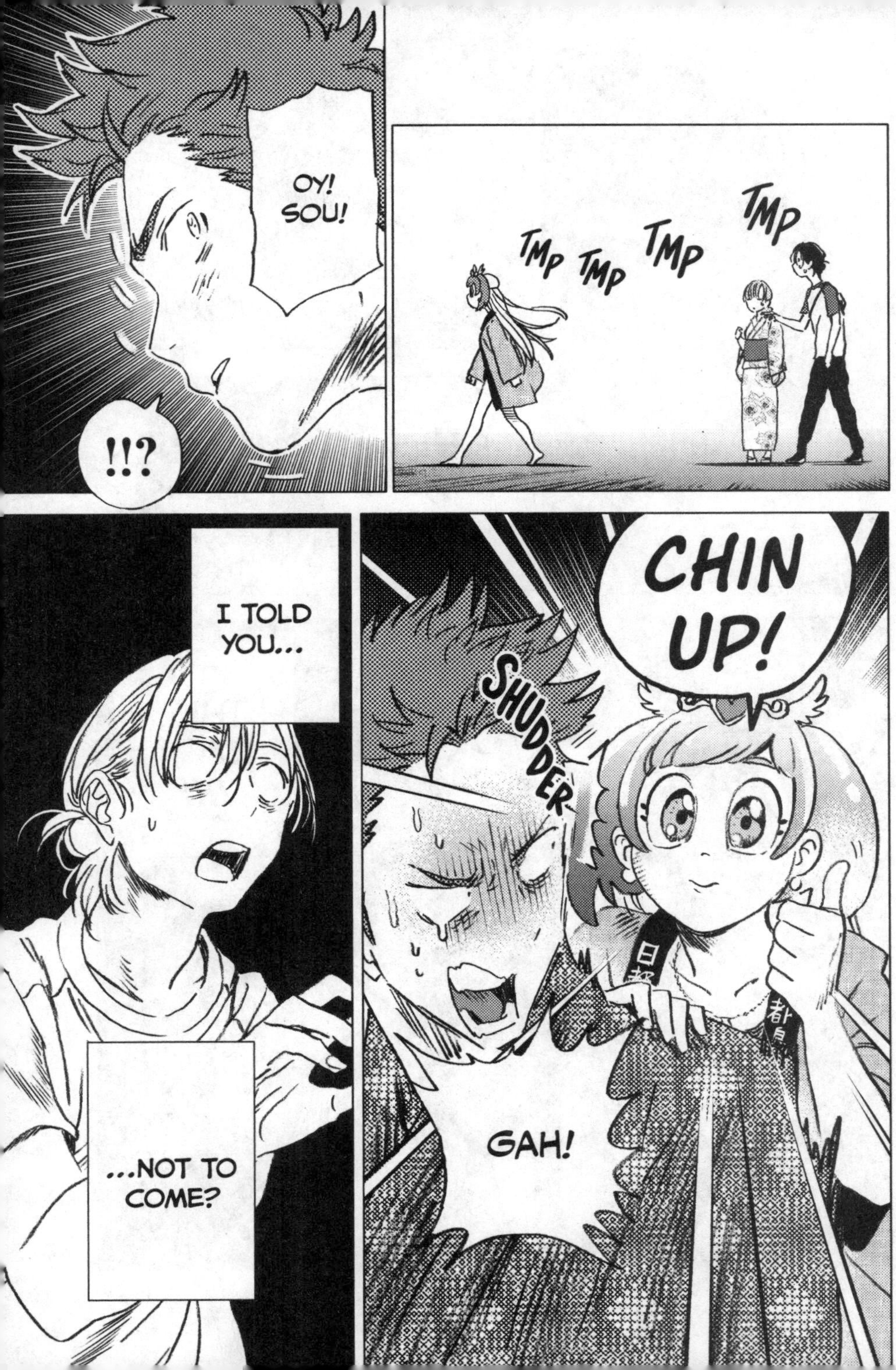
TMP
TMP
TMP
TMP
OY! SOU!
!!?
CHIN UP!
SHUDDER
GAH!
I TOLD YOU...
...NOT TO COME?

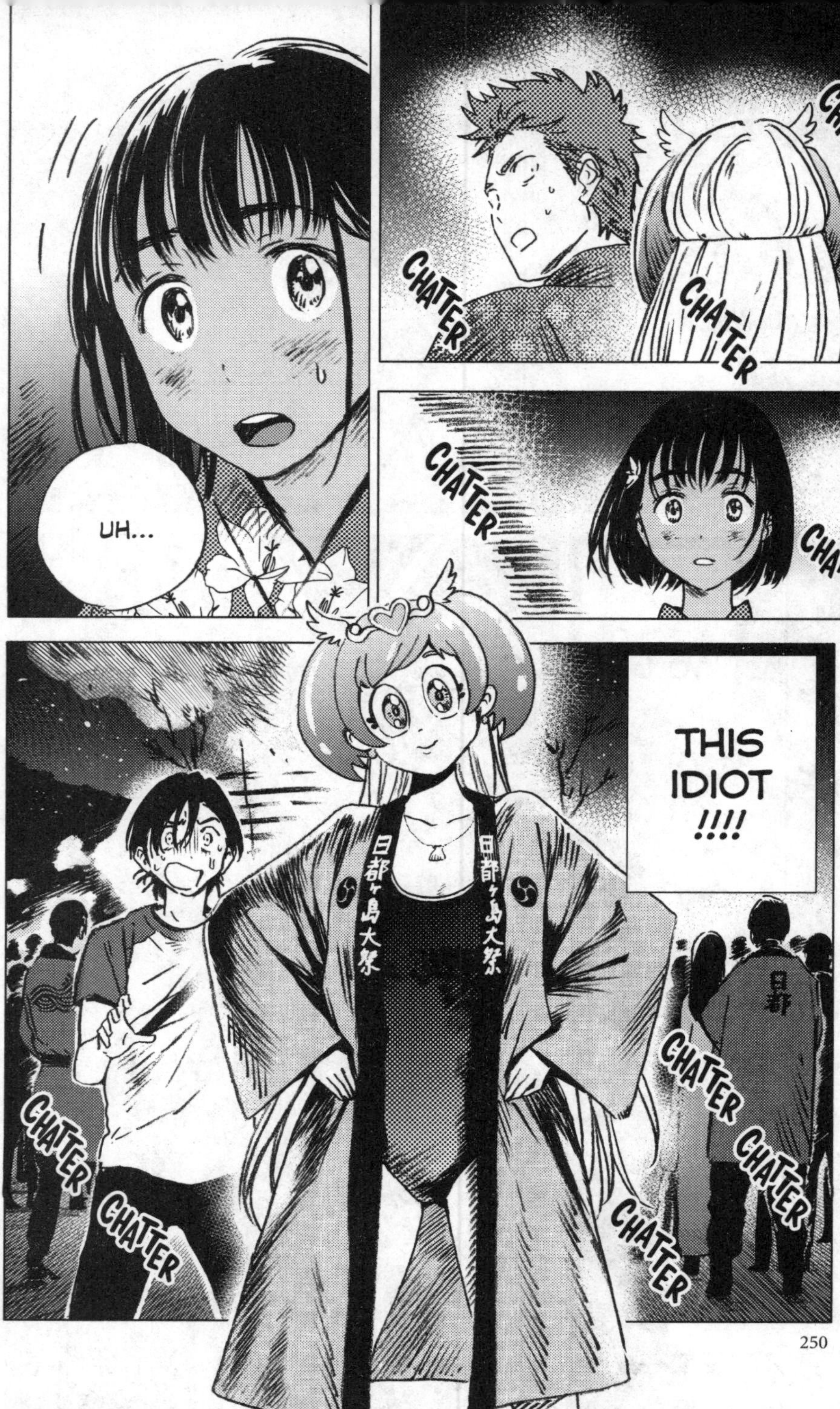
CHATTER
CHATTER
CHATTER
CHATTER
CHATTER
UH...
THIS IDIOT !!!!
日都ヶ島大祭
日都ヶ島大祭
CHATTER
CHATTER
CHATTER
CHATTER
CHATTER

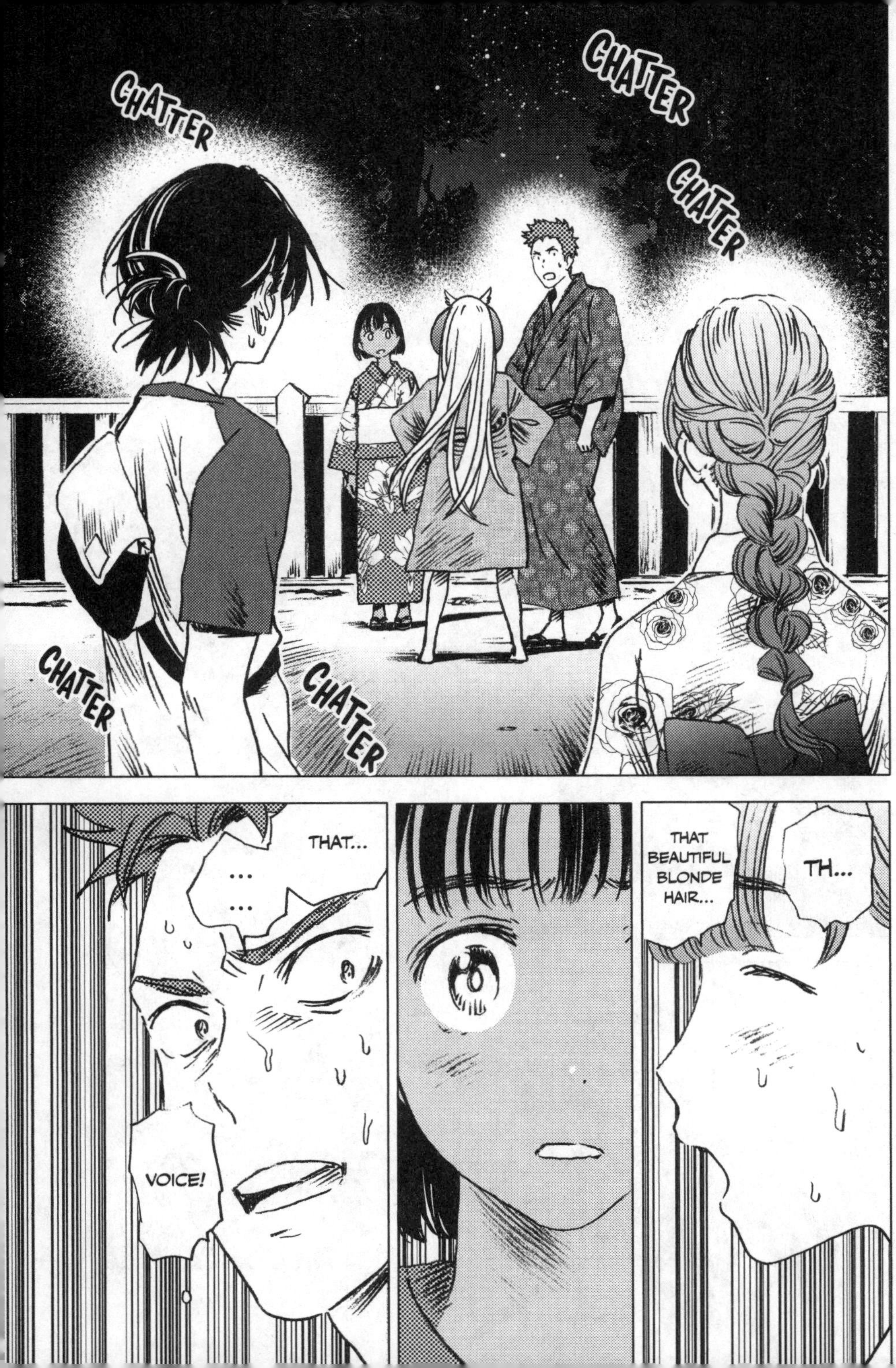
CHATTER
CHATTER
CHATTER
CHATTER
CHATTER
TH...
THAT BEAUTIFUL BLONDE HAIR...
THAT...
...
...
VOICE!

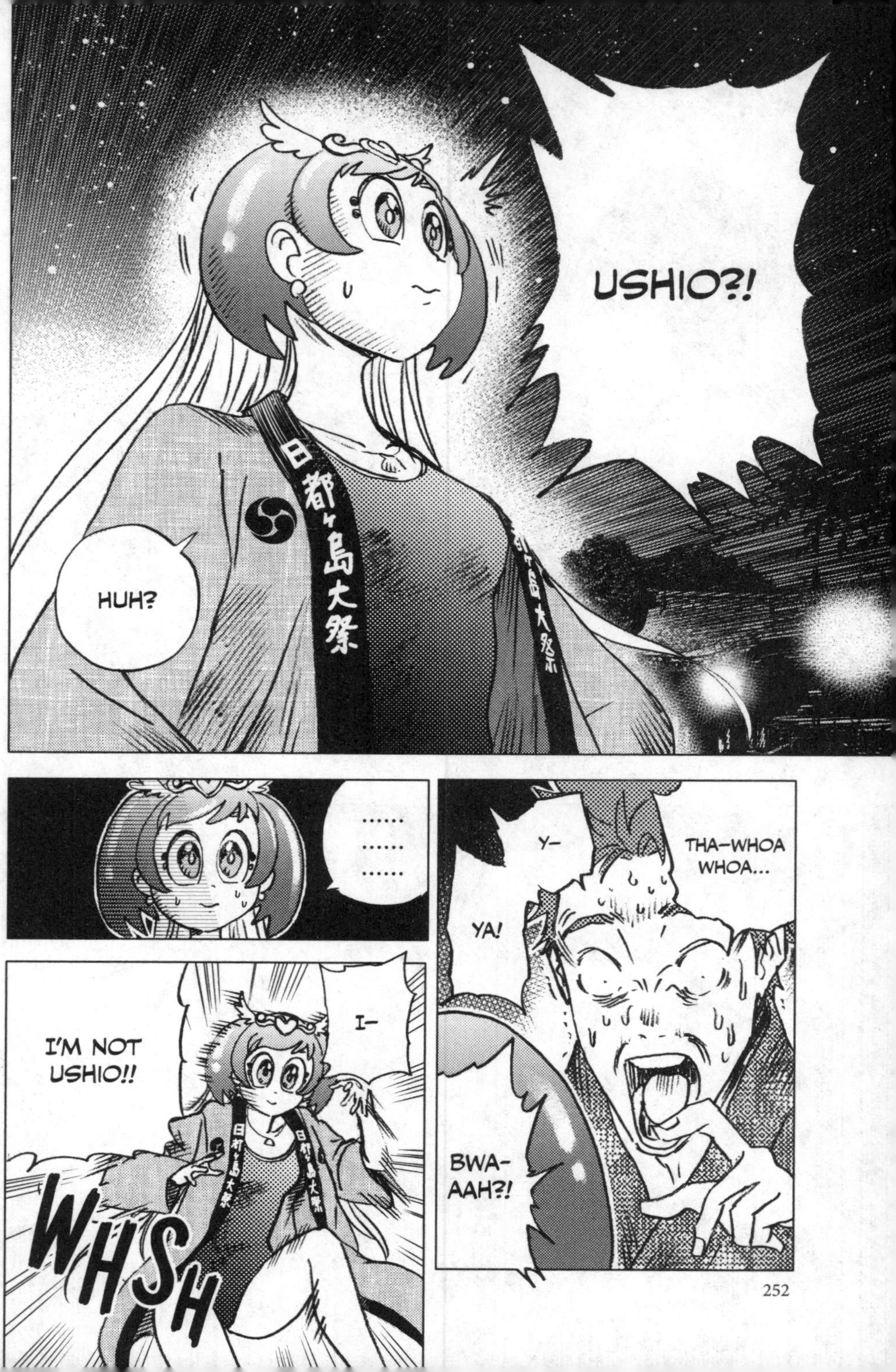
USHIO?!
HUH?
THA-WHOA WHOA...
Y-
YA!
BWA-AAH?!
......
......
......
I-
I'M NOT USHIO!!
WHSH

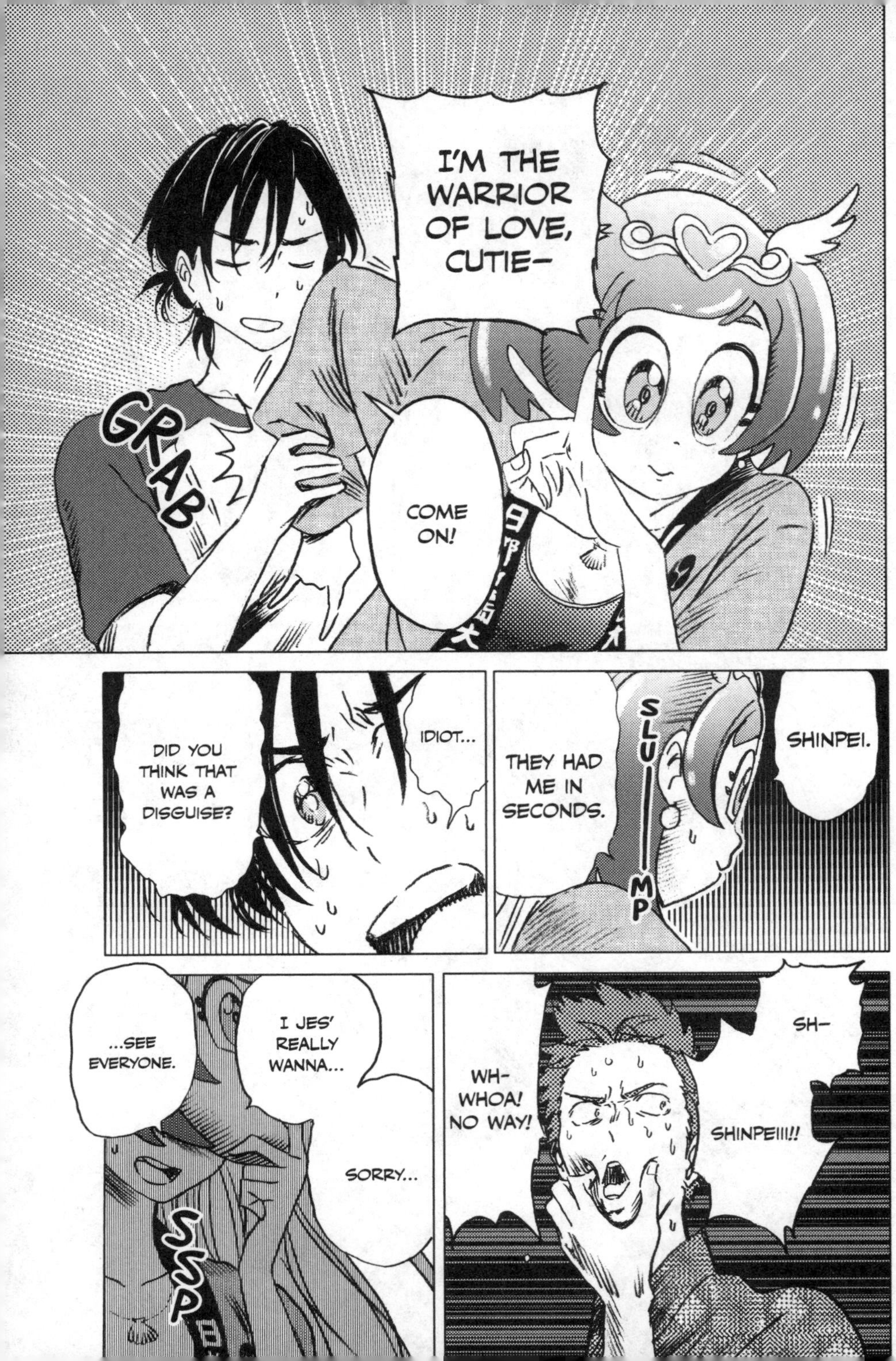
I'M THE WARRIOR OF LOVE, CUTIE–
GRAB
COME ON!
SHINPEI.
THEY HAD ME IN SECONDS.
SLU–MP
IDIOT...
DID YOU THINK THAT WAS A DISGUISE?
SH–
SHINPEIII!!
WH– WHOA! NO WAY!
I JES' REALLY WANNA...
...SEE EVERYONE.
SORRY...
SSP

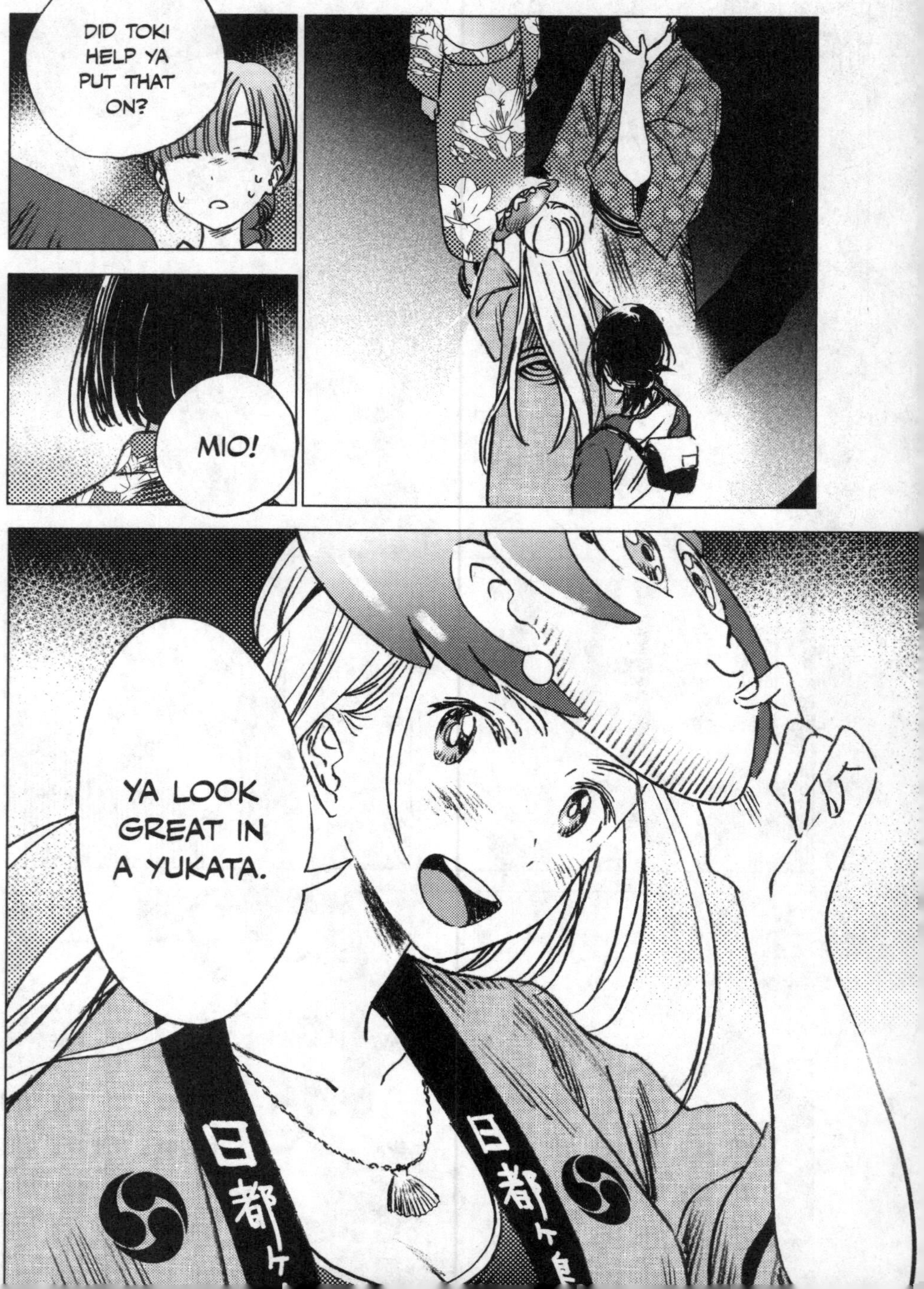
DID TOKI HELP YA PUT THAT ON?
MIO!
YA LOOK GREAT IN A YUKATA.

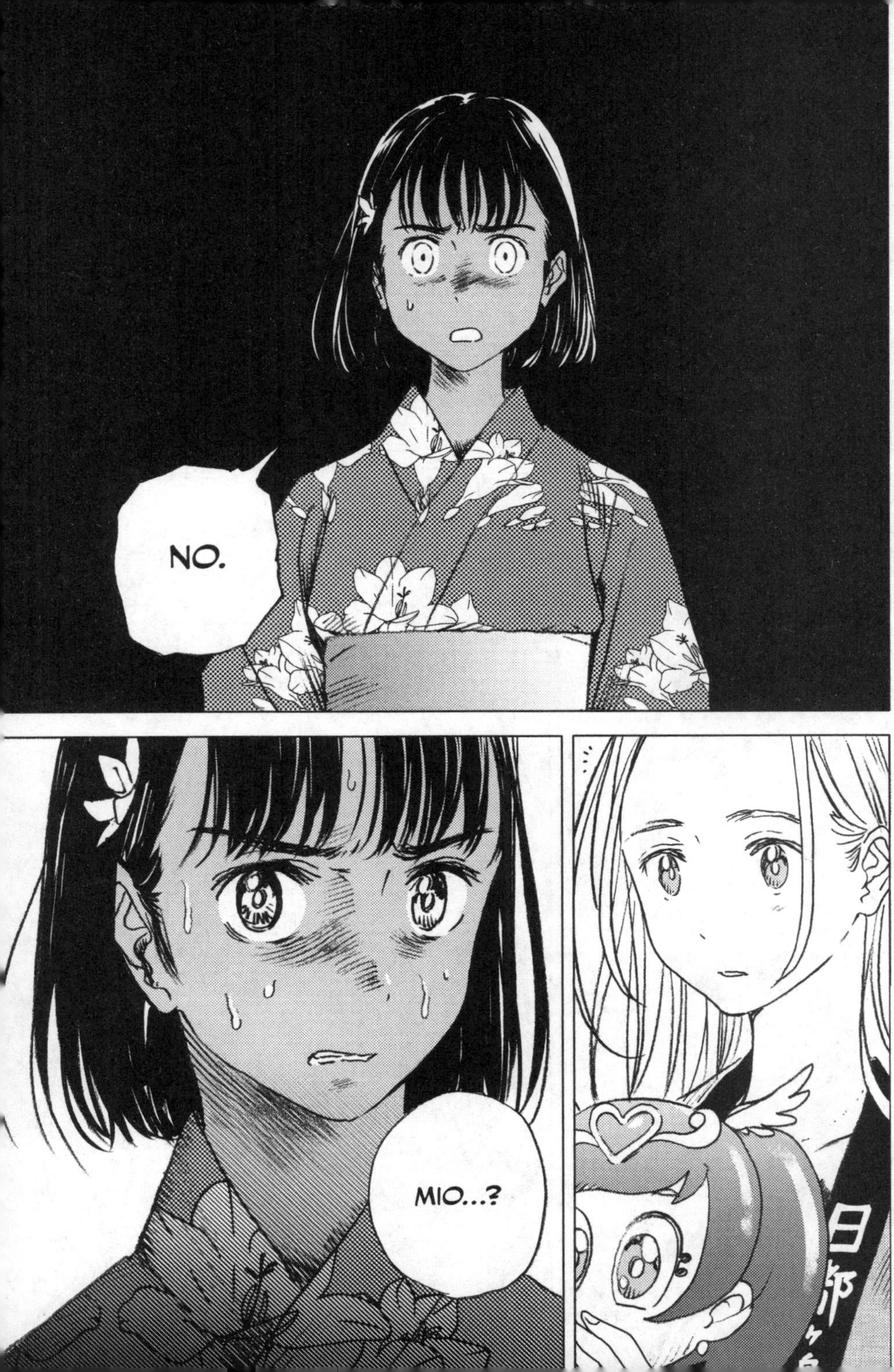
NO.
MIO...?

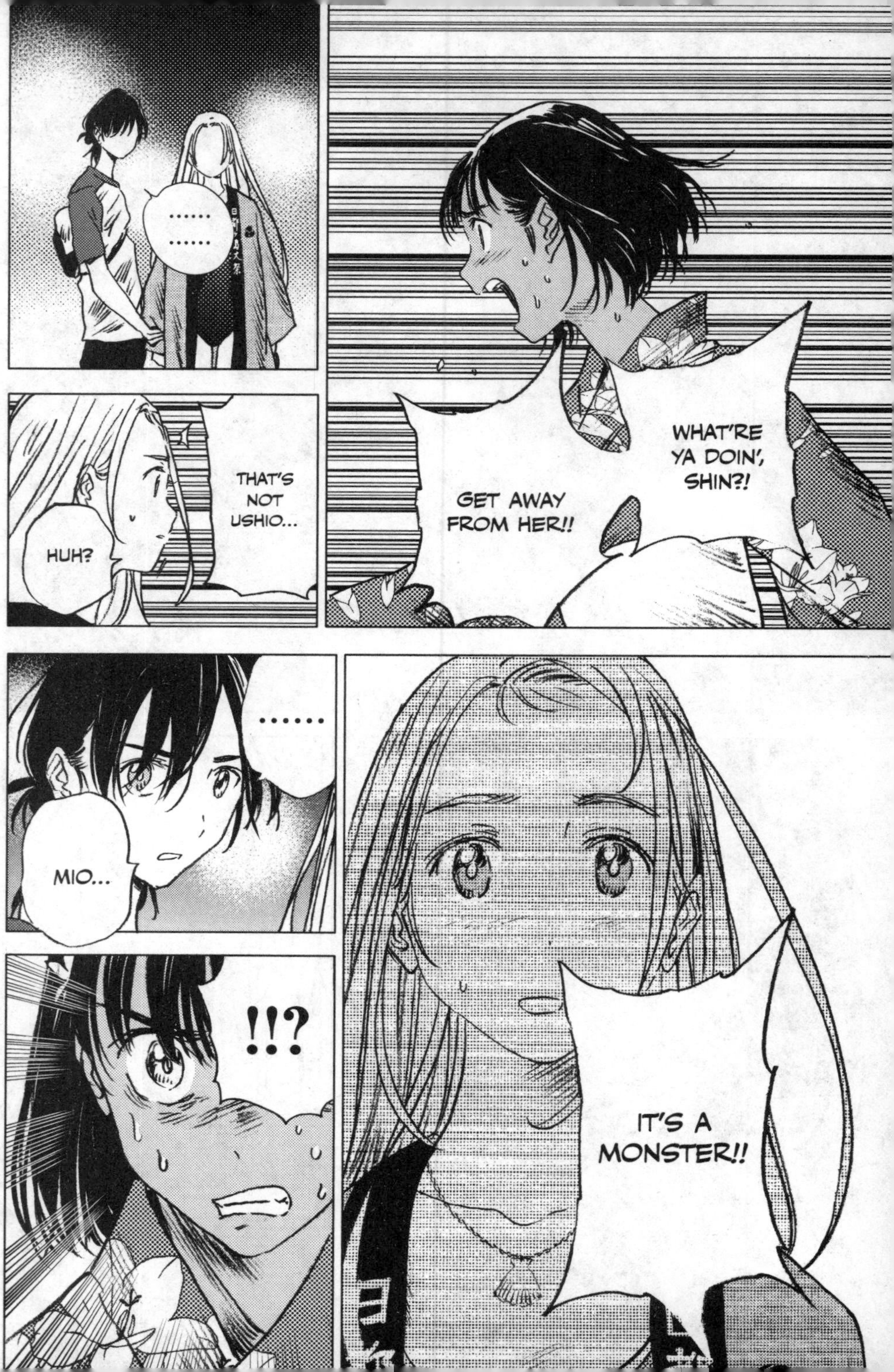
WHAT'RE YA DOIN', SHIN?!
GET AWAY FROM HER!!
......
......
THAT'S NOT USHIO...
HUH?
IT'S A MONSTER!!
......
MIO...
!!?

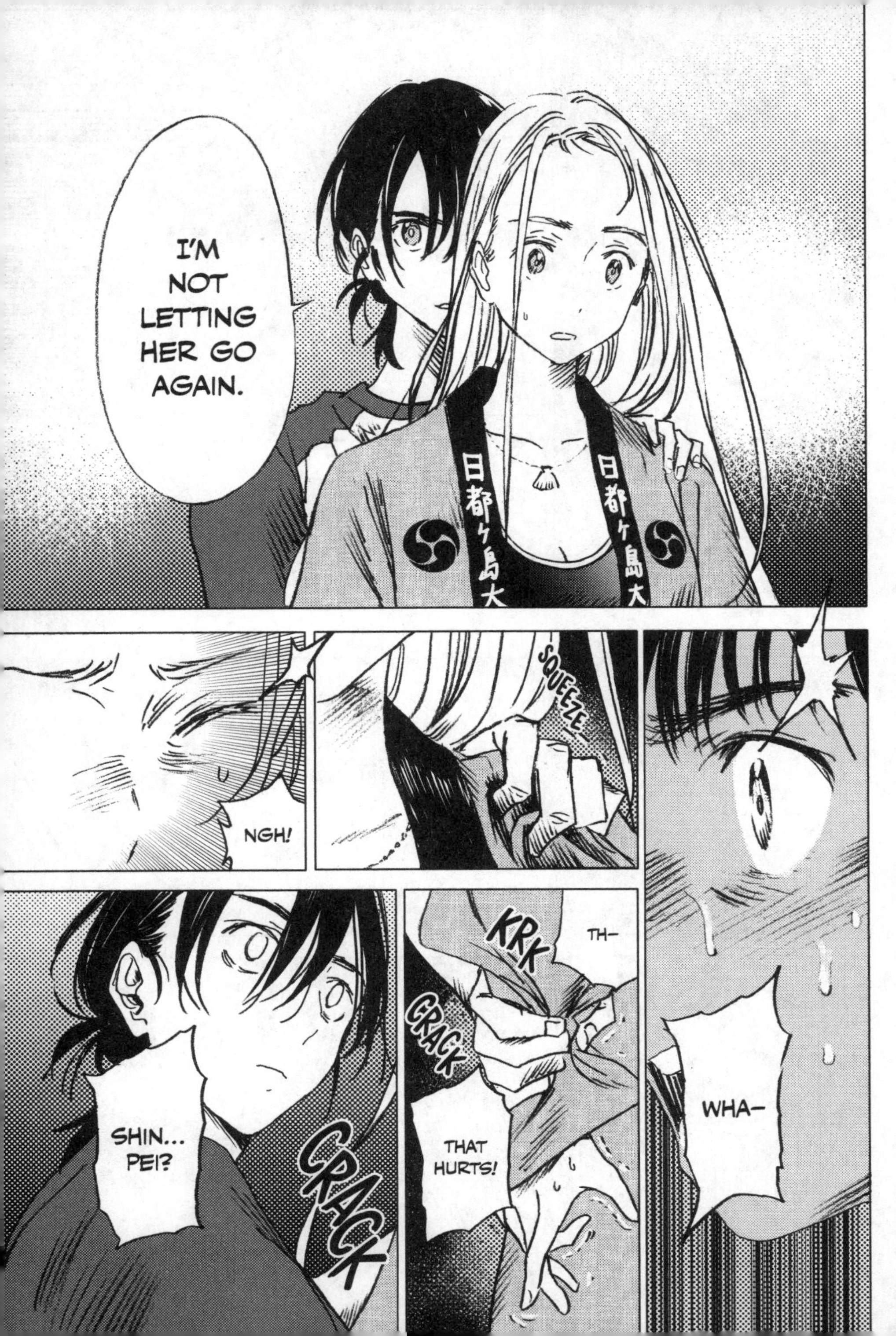
I'M NOT LETTING HER GO AGAIN.
日都ケ島大
日都ケ島大
WHA-
SQUEEZE
NGH!
KRK
TH-
CRACK
THAT HURTS!
CRACK
SHIN... PEI?

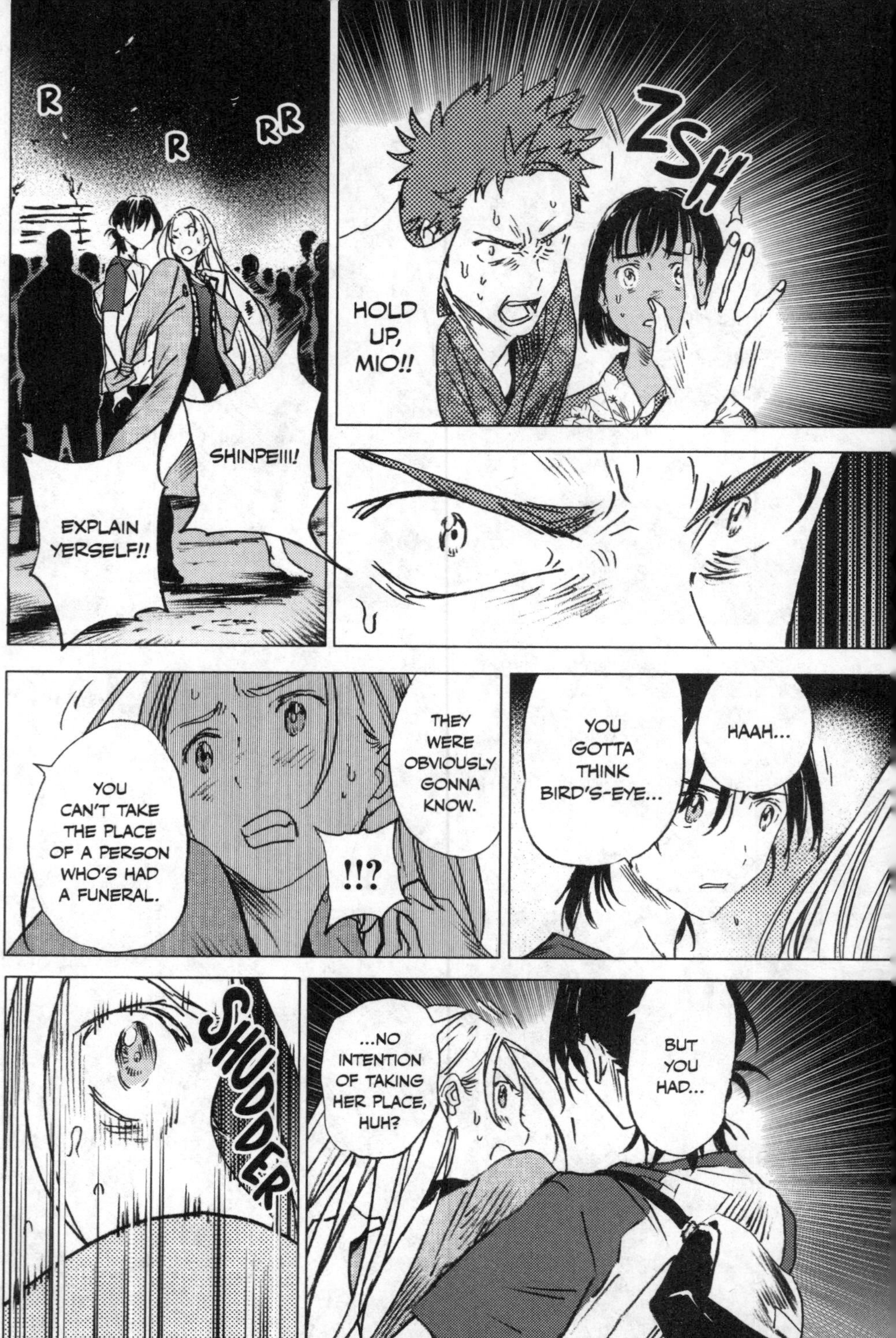
ZSH
HOLD UP, MIO!!
R
R
RR
SHINPEIII!
EXPLAIN YERSELF!!
HAAH...
YOU GOTTA THINK BIRD'S-EYE...
THEY WERE OBVIOUSLY GONNA KNOW.
!!?
YOU CAN'T TAKE THE PLACE OF A PERSON WHO'S HAD A FUNERAL.
BUT YOU HAD...
...NO INTENTION OF TAKING HER PLACE, HUH?
SHUDDER

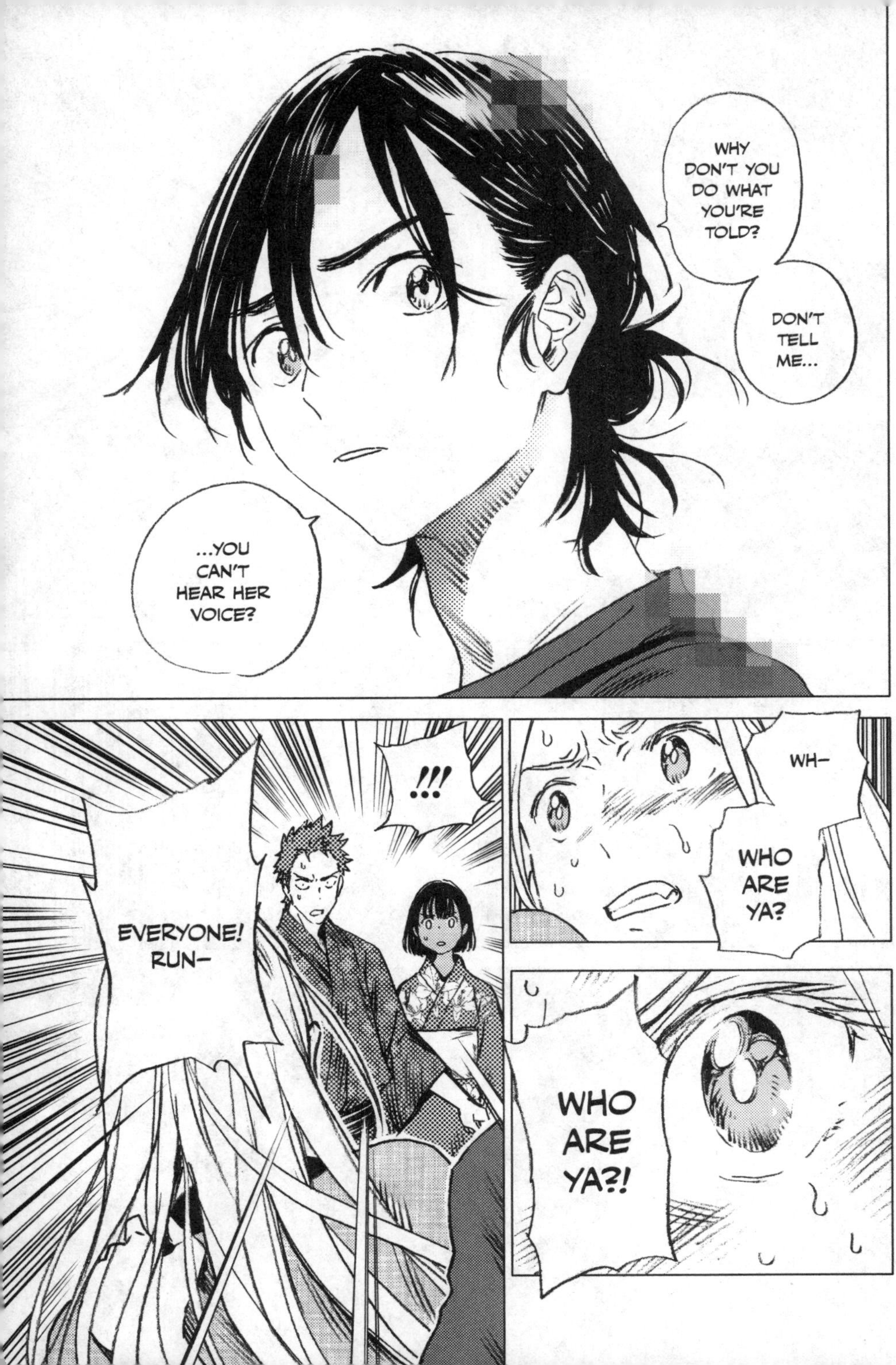
WHY DON'T YOU DO WHAT YOU'RE TOLD?
DON'T TELL ME...
...YOU CAN'T HEAR HER VOICE?
WH-
WHO ARE YA?
WHO ARE YA?!
!!!
EVERYONE! RUN-

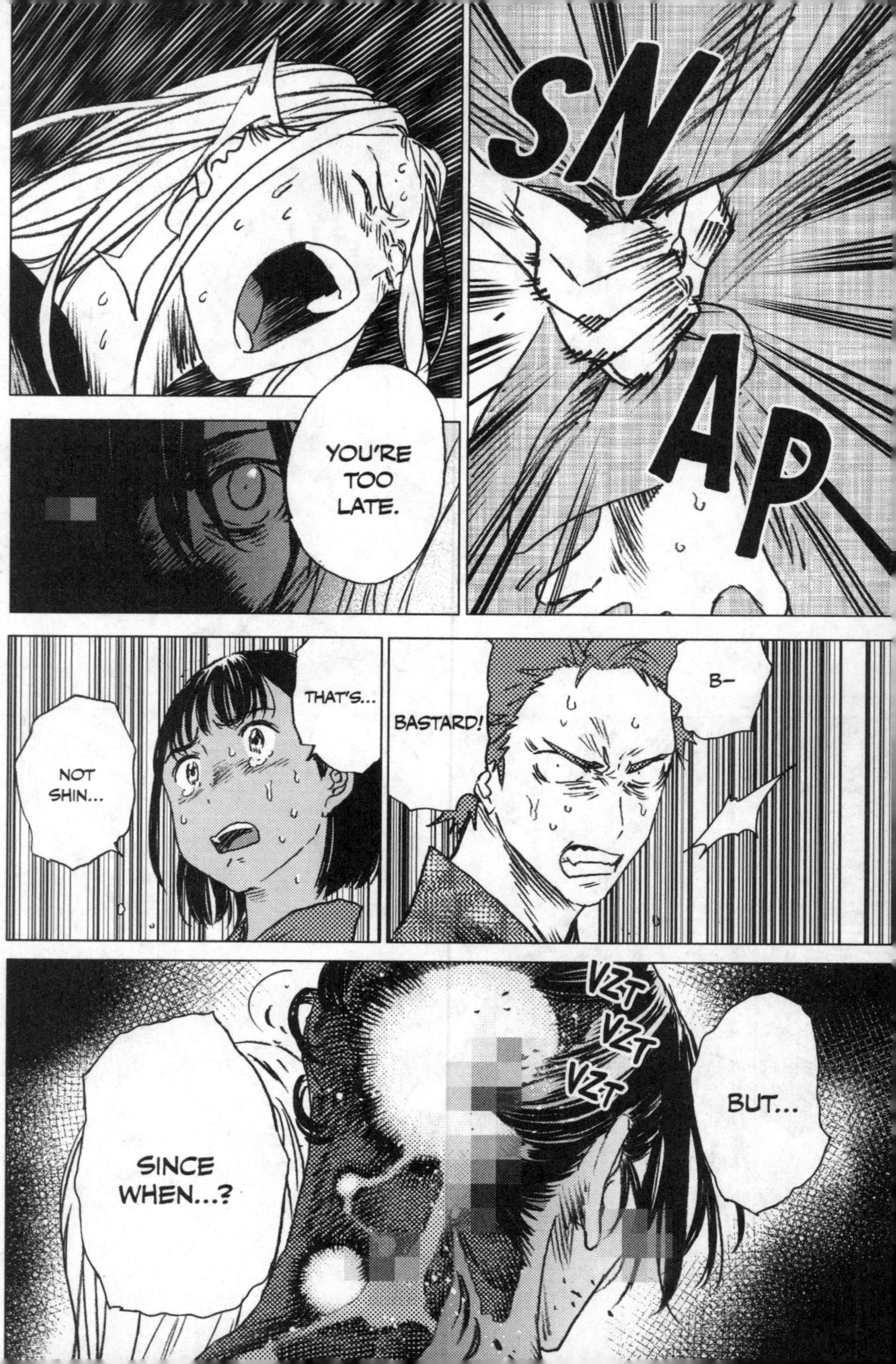
SN
AP
YOU'RE TOO LATE.
B-
BASTARD!
THAT'S...
NOT SHIN...
VZT
VZT
VZT
BUT...
SINCE WHEN...?

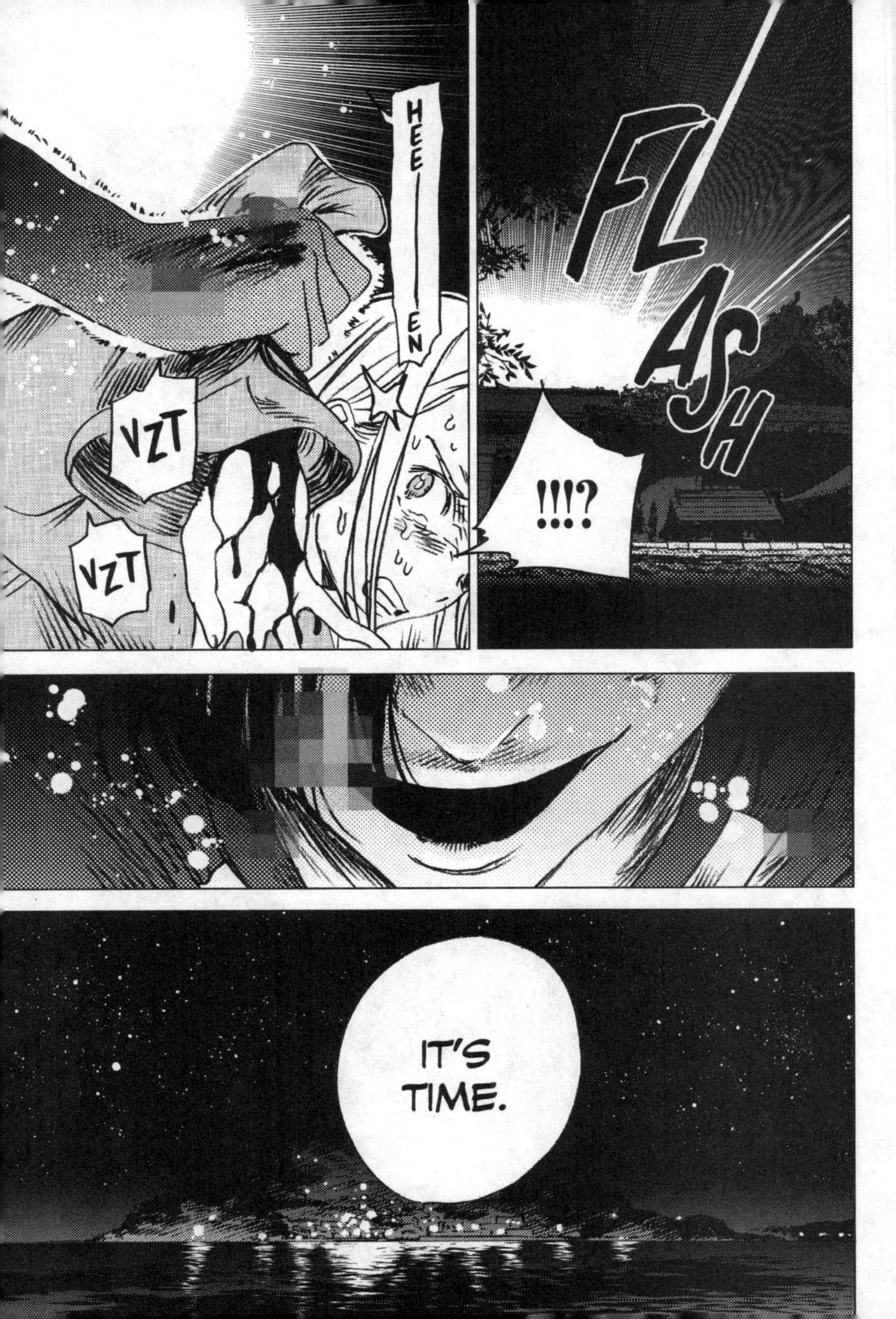
FLASH
!!!?
HEE—EN
VZT
VZT
IT'S TIME.

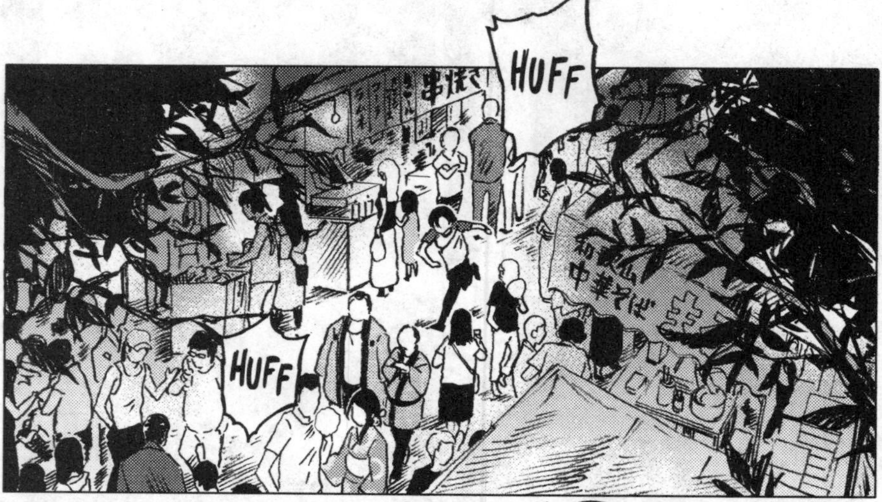
HUFF
中華そば
HUFF

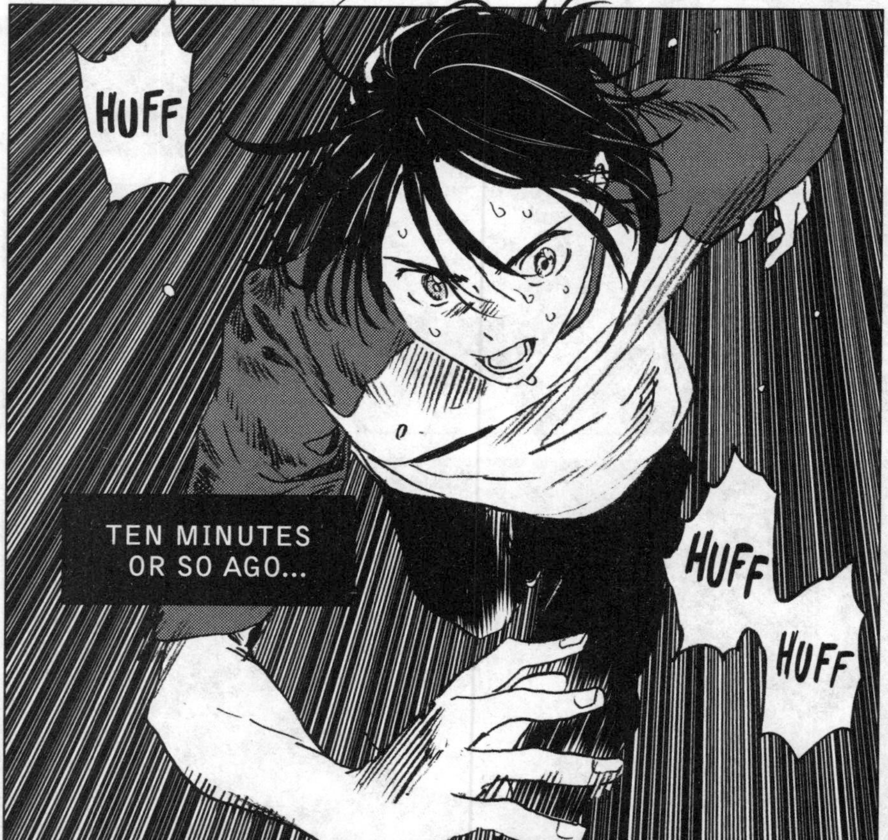
HUFF
TEN MINUTES OR SO AGO...
HUFF
HUFF

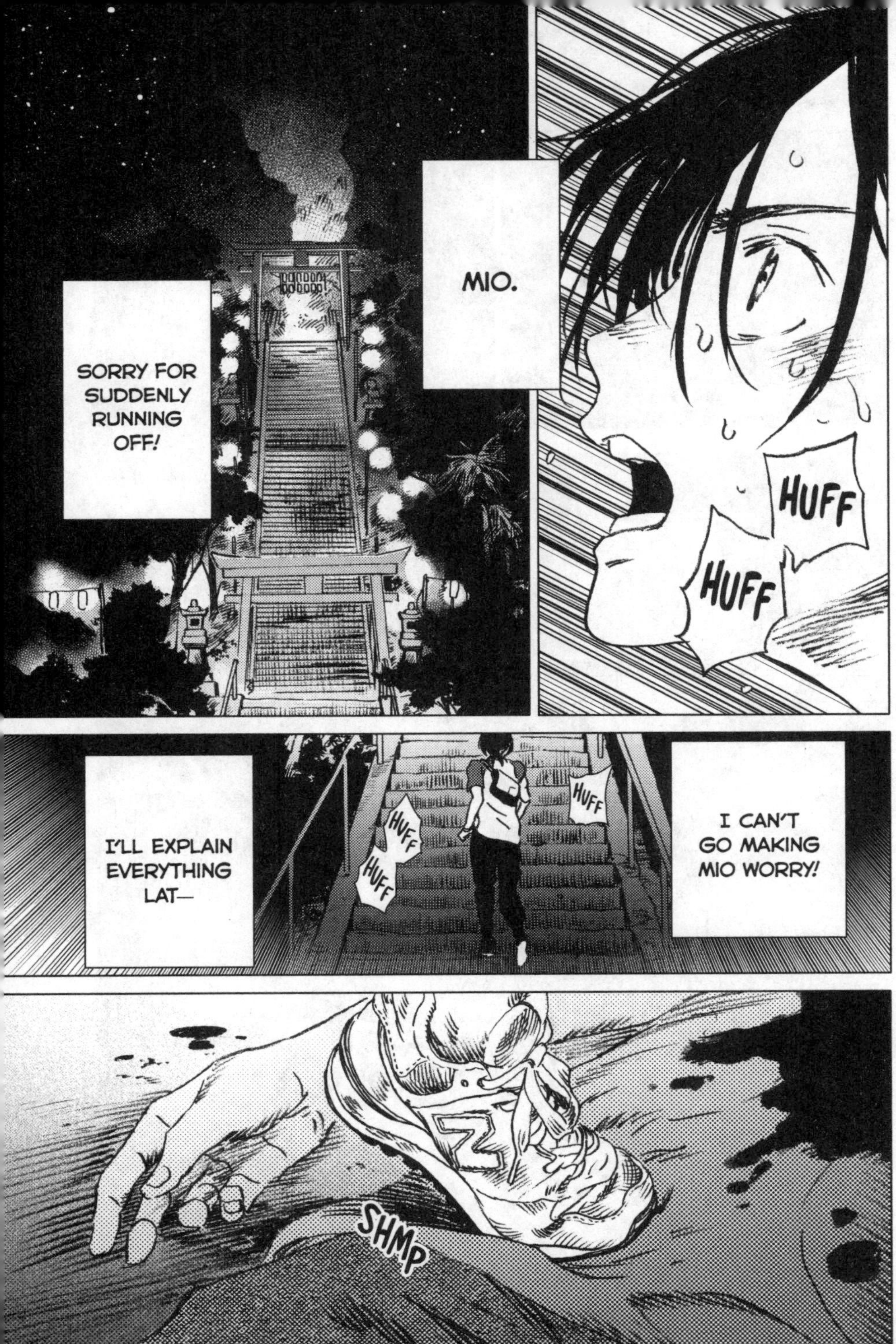
MIO.
HUFF
HUFF
SORRY FOR SUDDENLY RUNNING OFF!
I CAN'T GO MAKING MIO WORRY!
HUFF
HUFF
HUFF
I'LL EXPLAIN EVERYTHING LAT—
SHMP

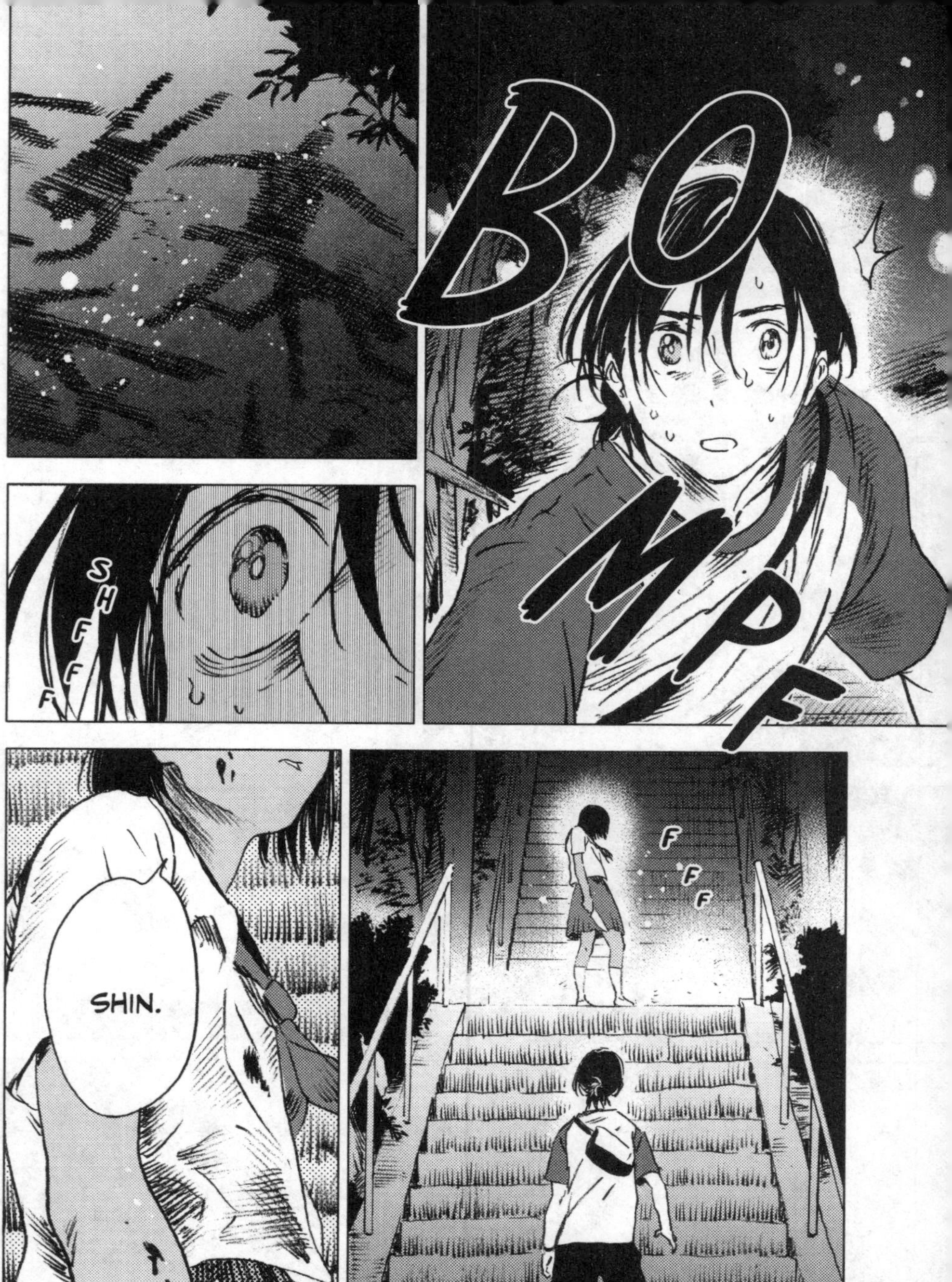
BOMPF
SHFFFF
FFF
SHIN.

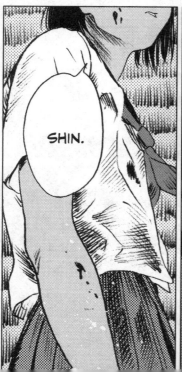

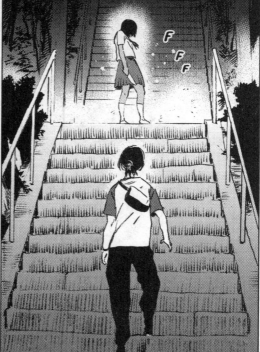

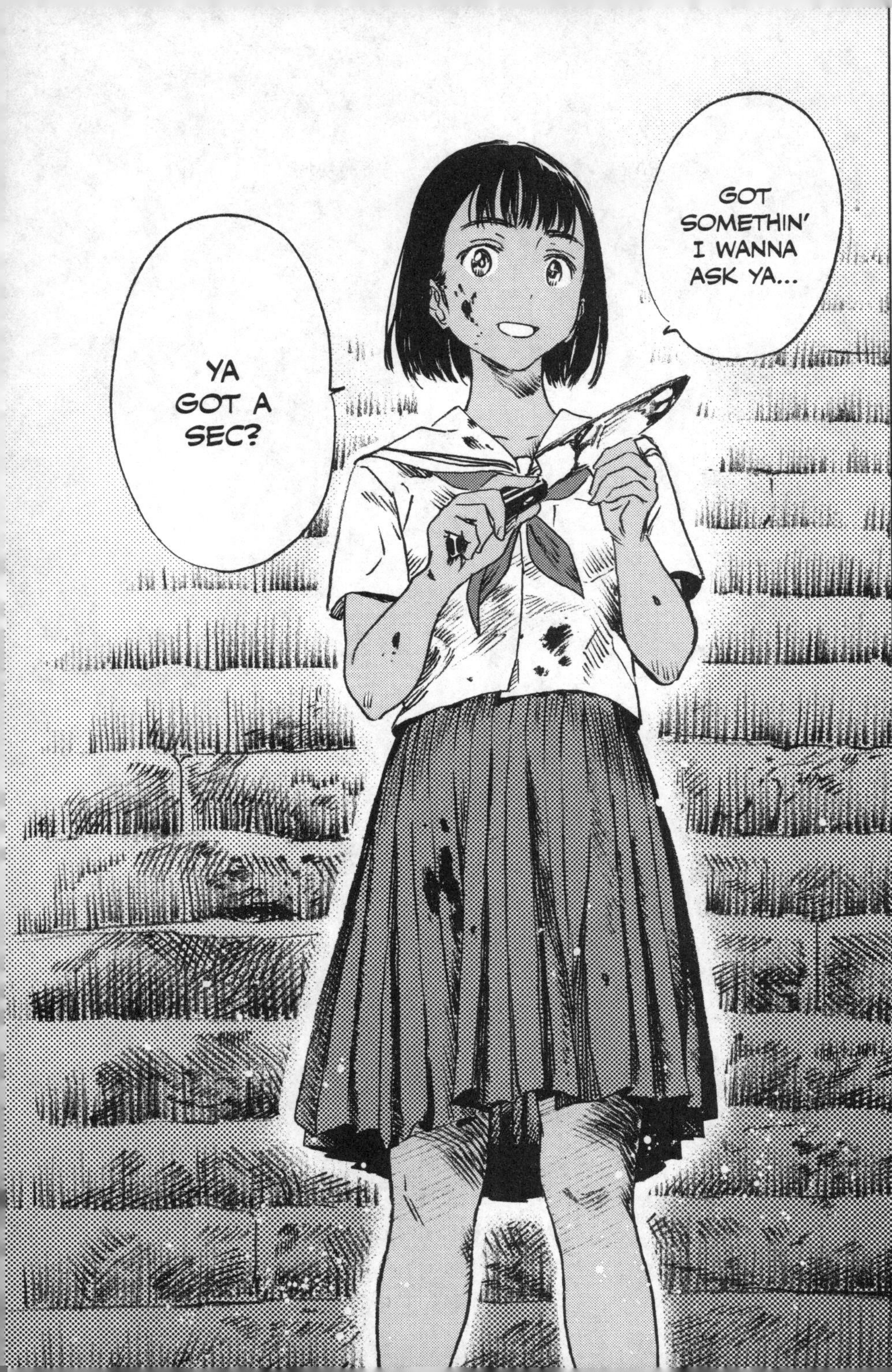
GOT SOMETHIN' I WANNA ASK YA...
YA GOT A SEC?

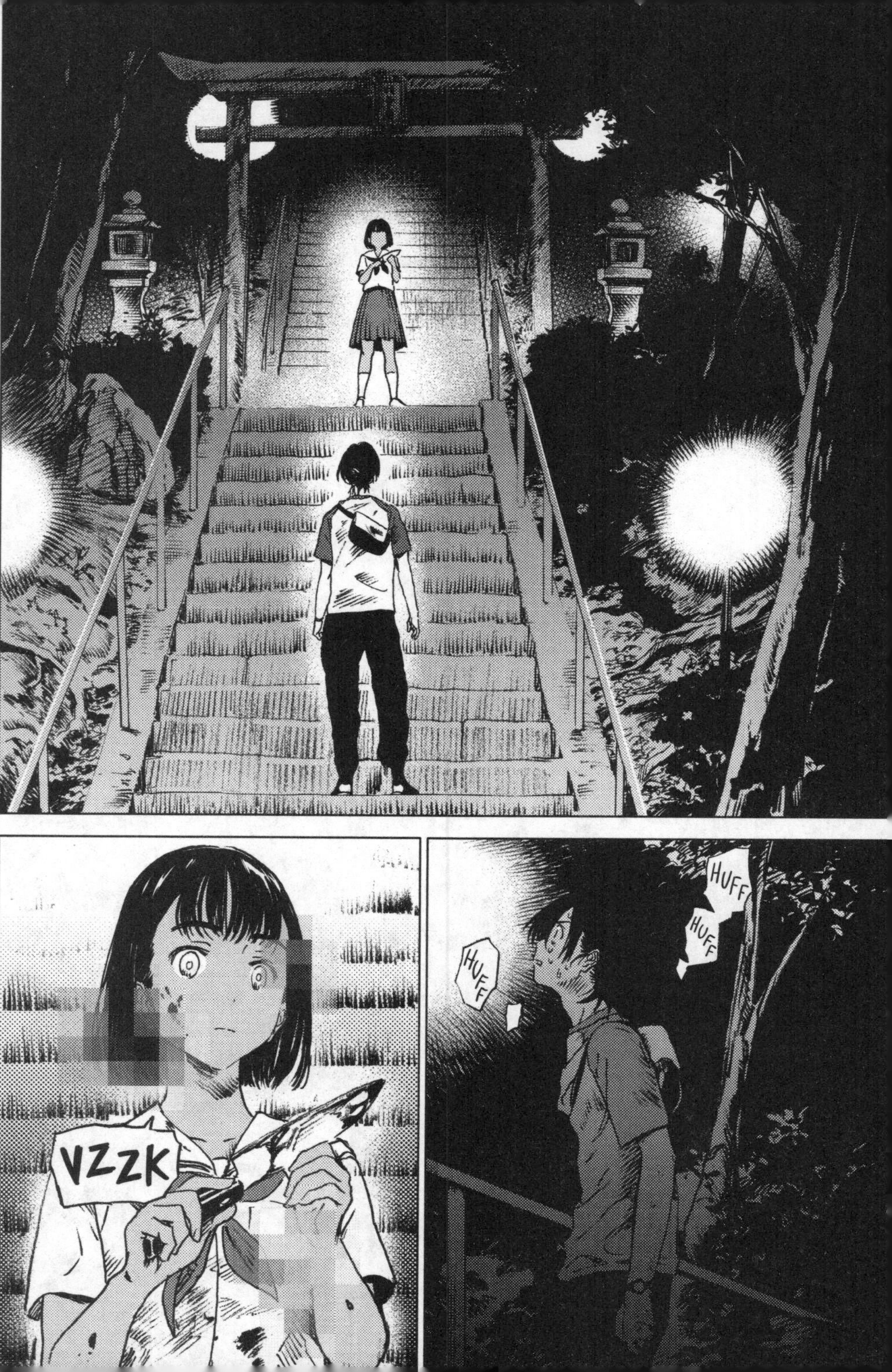
HUFF
HUFF
HUFF
VZZK

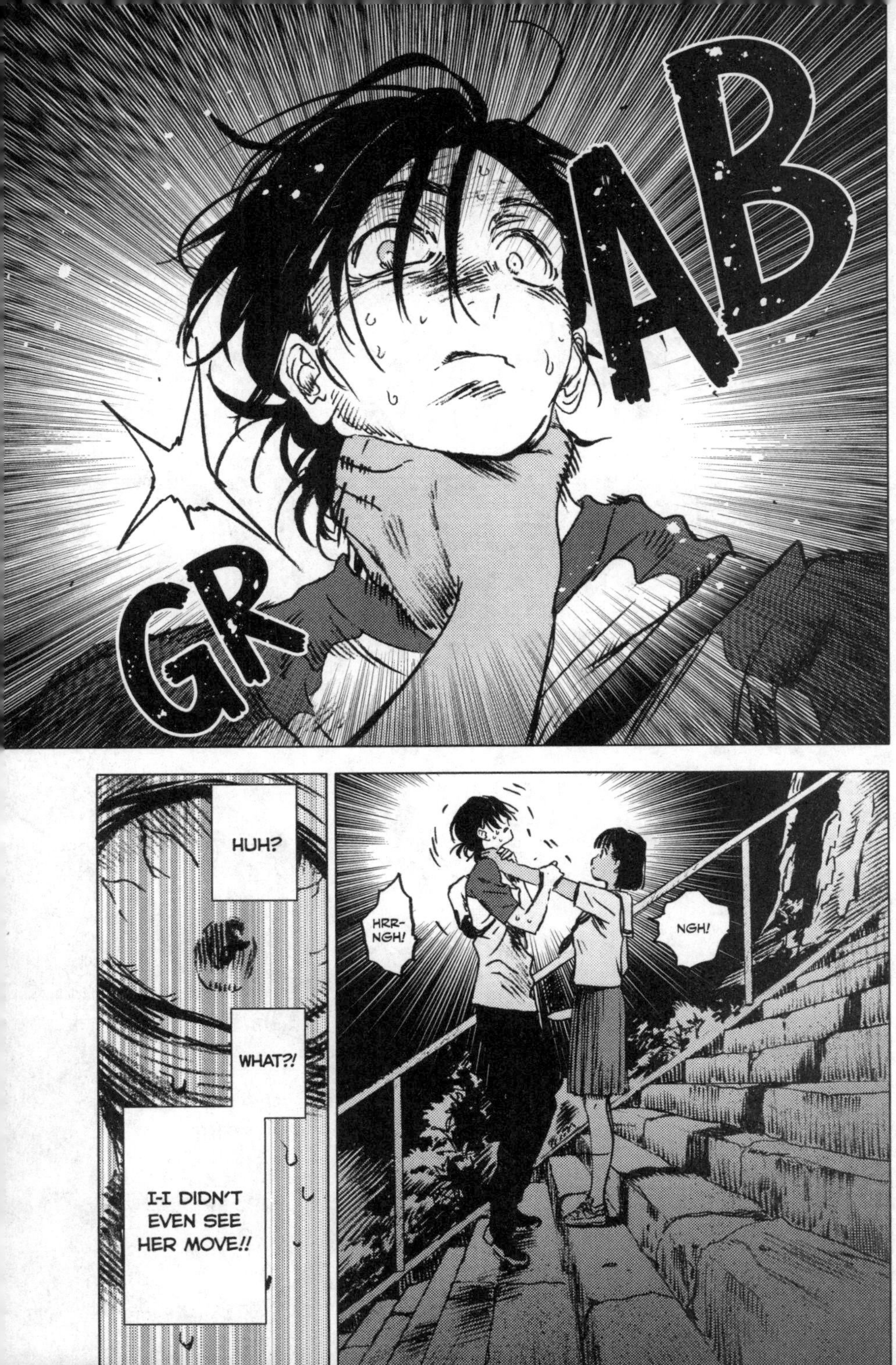
GRAB
NGH!
HRR-NGH!
HUH?
WHAT?!
I-I DIDN'T EVEN SEE HER MOVE!!

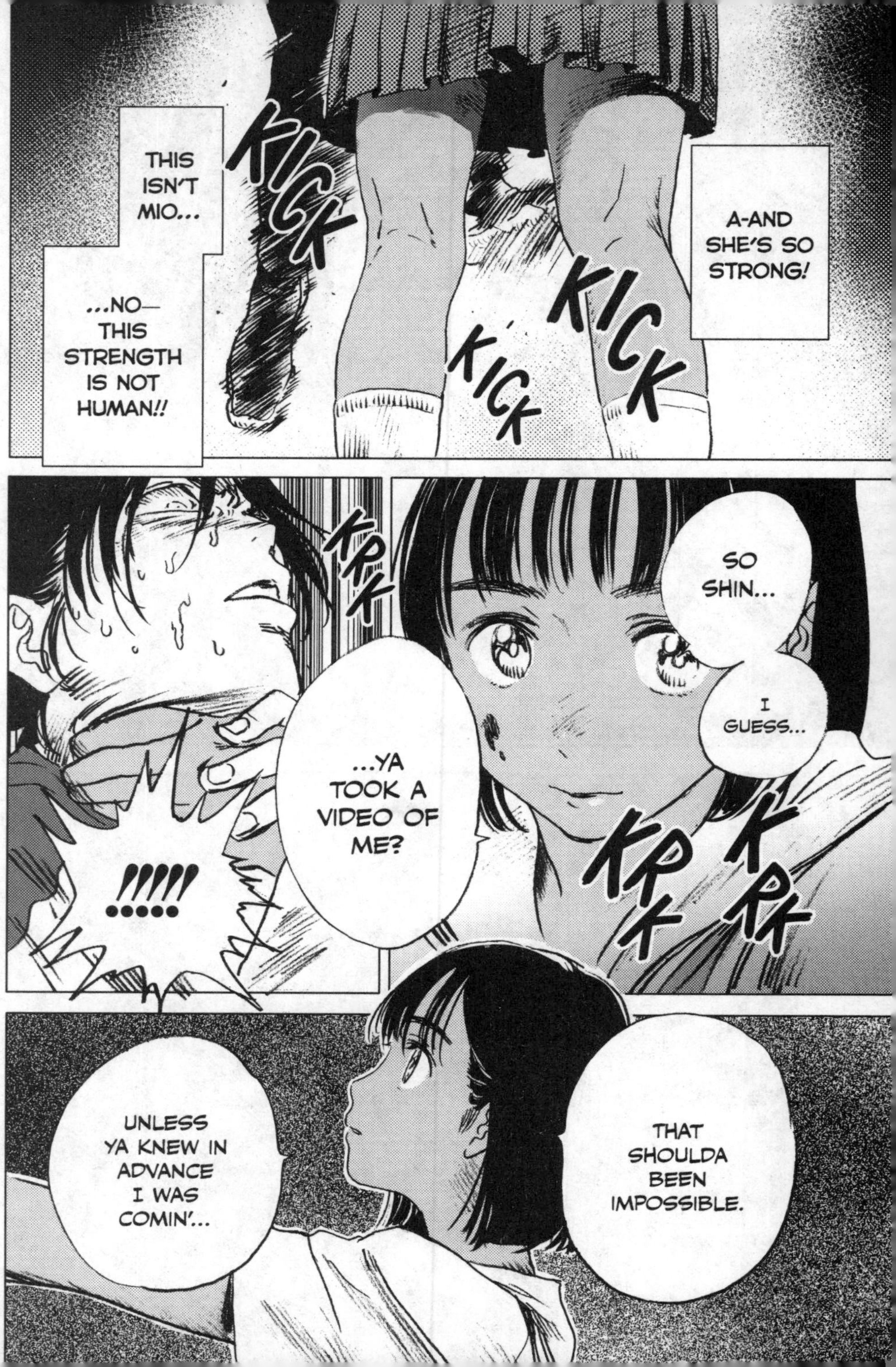
A-AND SHE'S SO STRONG!
KICK
KICK
KICK
THIS ISN'T MIO...
...NO— THIS STRENGTH IS NOT HUMAN!!
SO SHIN...
I GUESS...
KRK
KRK
KRK
...YA TOOK A VIDEO OF ME?
!!!!!
THAT SHOULDA BEEN IMPOSSIBLE.
UNLESS YA KNEW IN ADVANCE I WAS COMIN'...

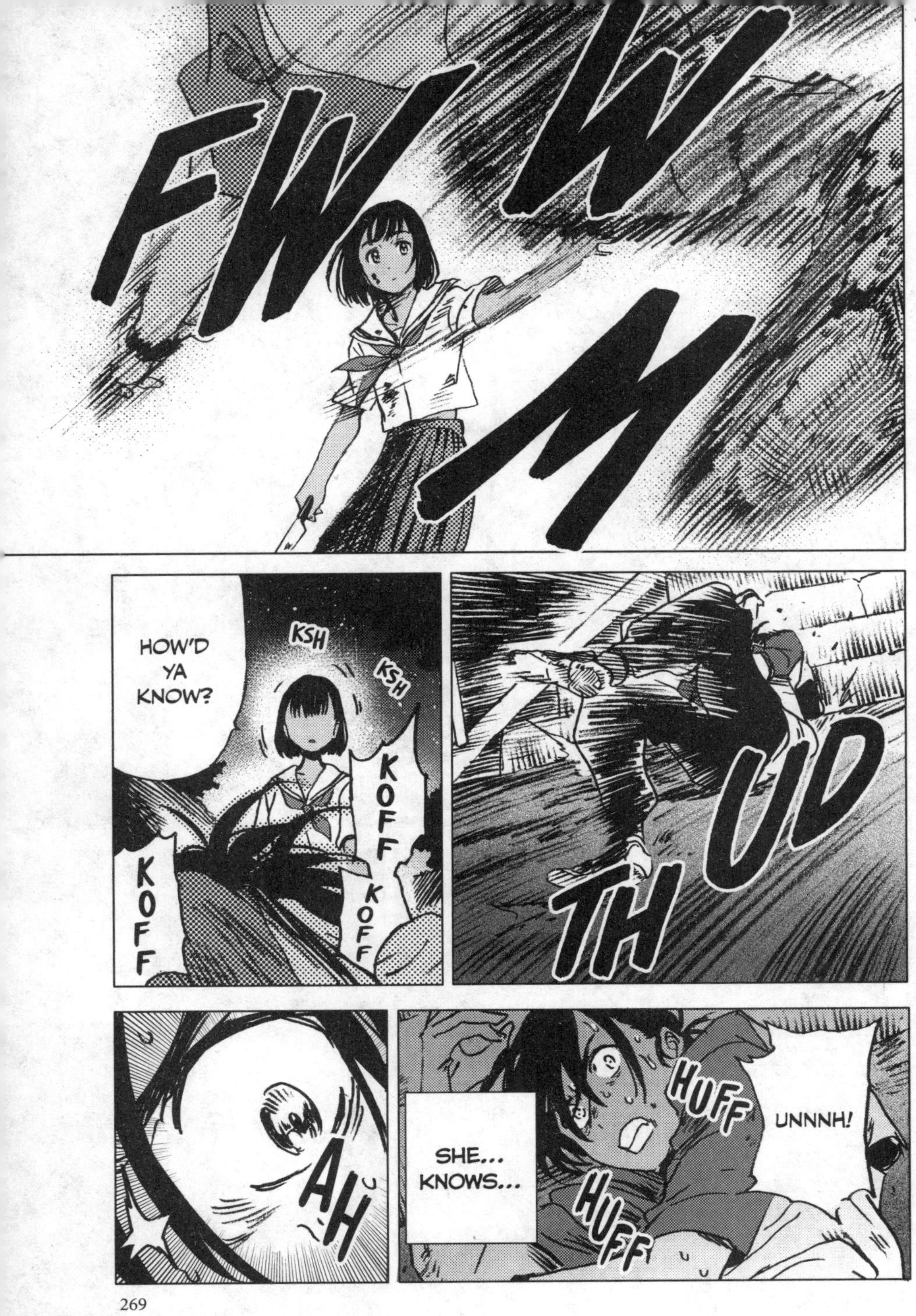
FWWM
THUD
KSH
KSH
HOW'D YA KNOW?
KOFF
KOFF
KOFF
KOFF
UNNNH!
HUFF
HUFF
SHE... KNOWS...
AH

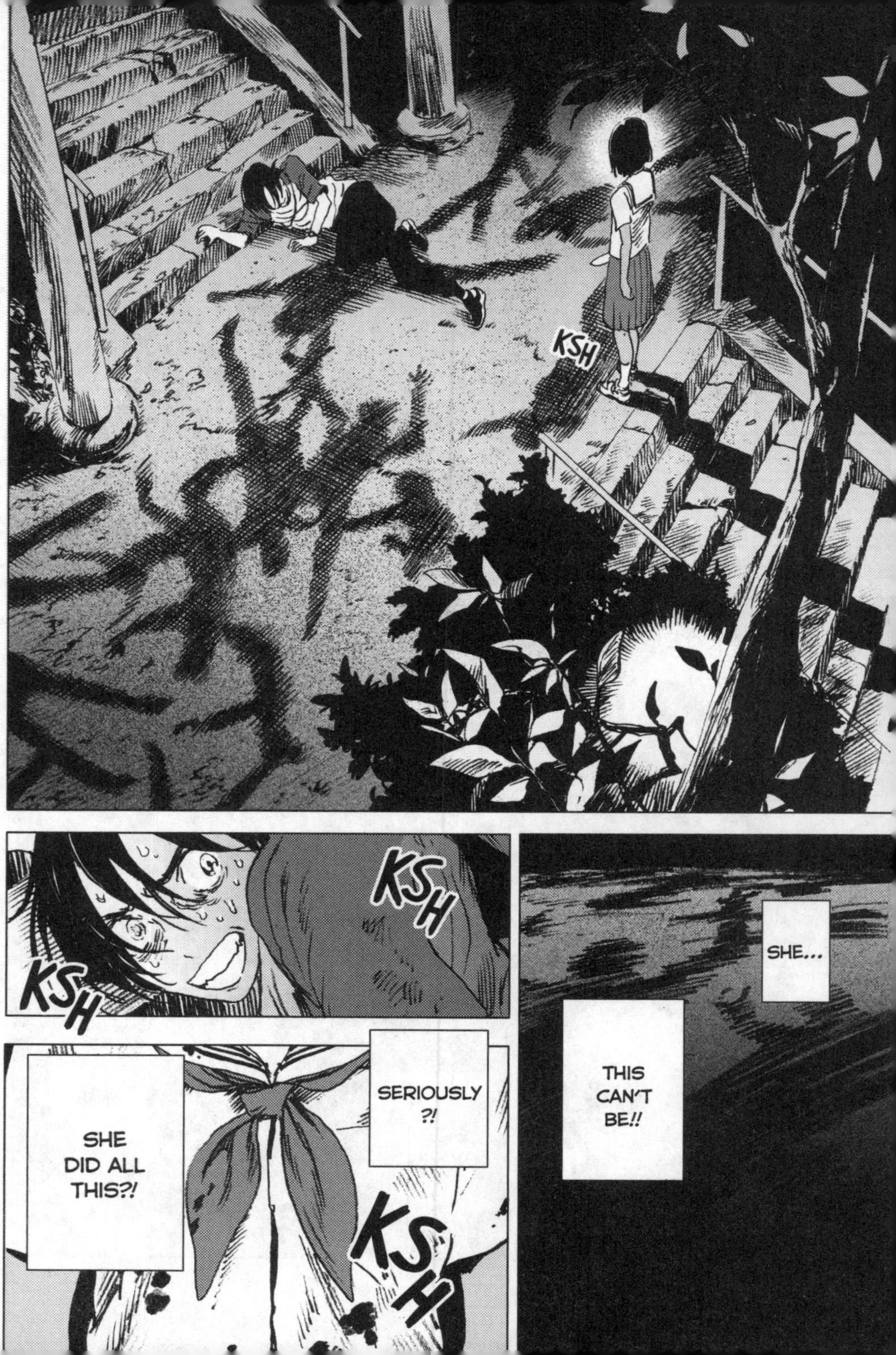
KSH
SHE...
THIS CAN'T BE!!
KSH
KSH
SERIOUSLY ?!
SHE DID ALL THIS?!
KSH

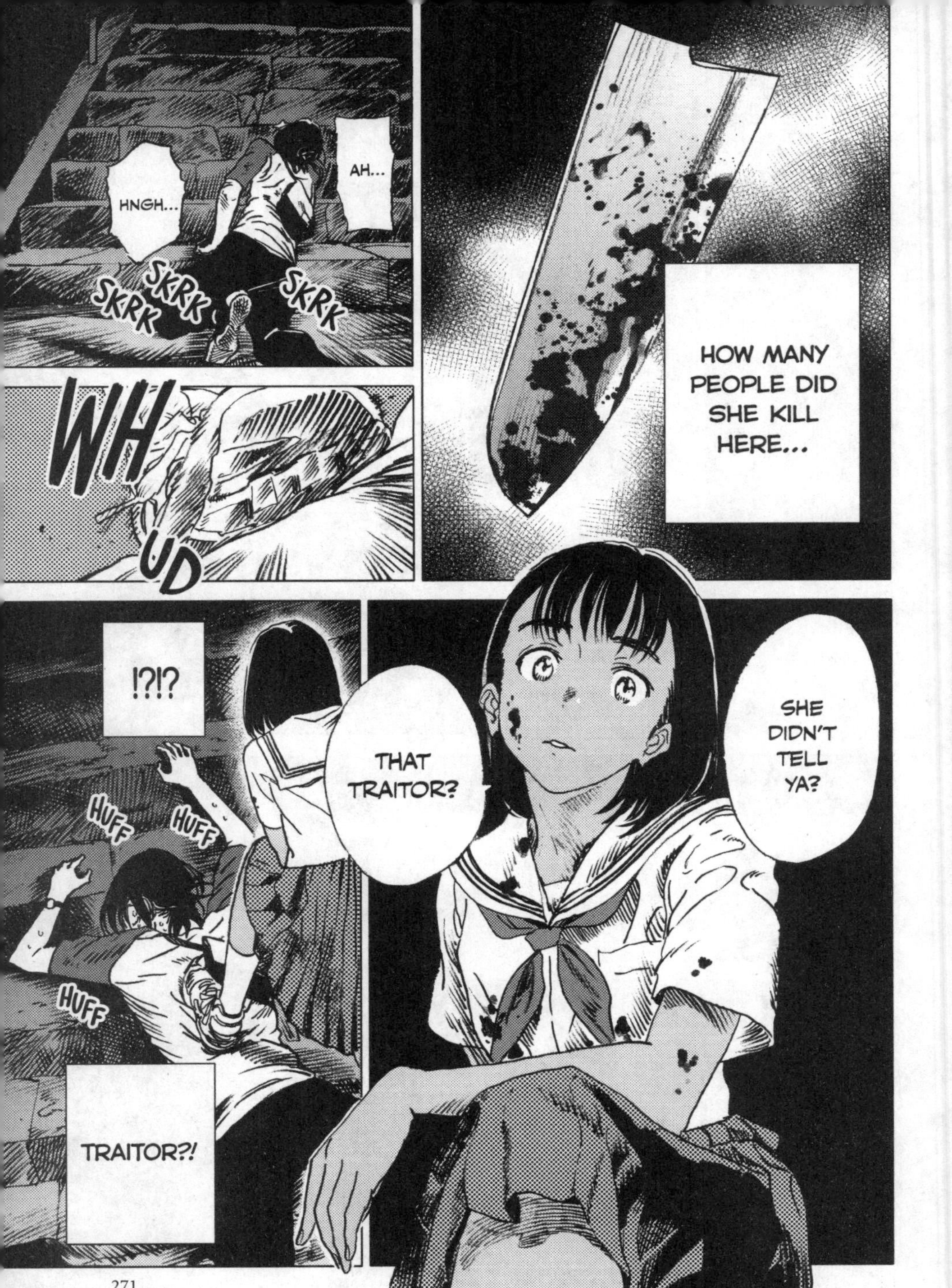
HOW MANY PEOPLE DID SHE KILL HERE...
AH...
HNGH...
SKRK
SKRK
SKRK
WHUD
SHE DIDN'T TELL YA?
THAT TRAITOR?
!?!?
HUFF
HUFF
HUFF
TRAITOR?!

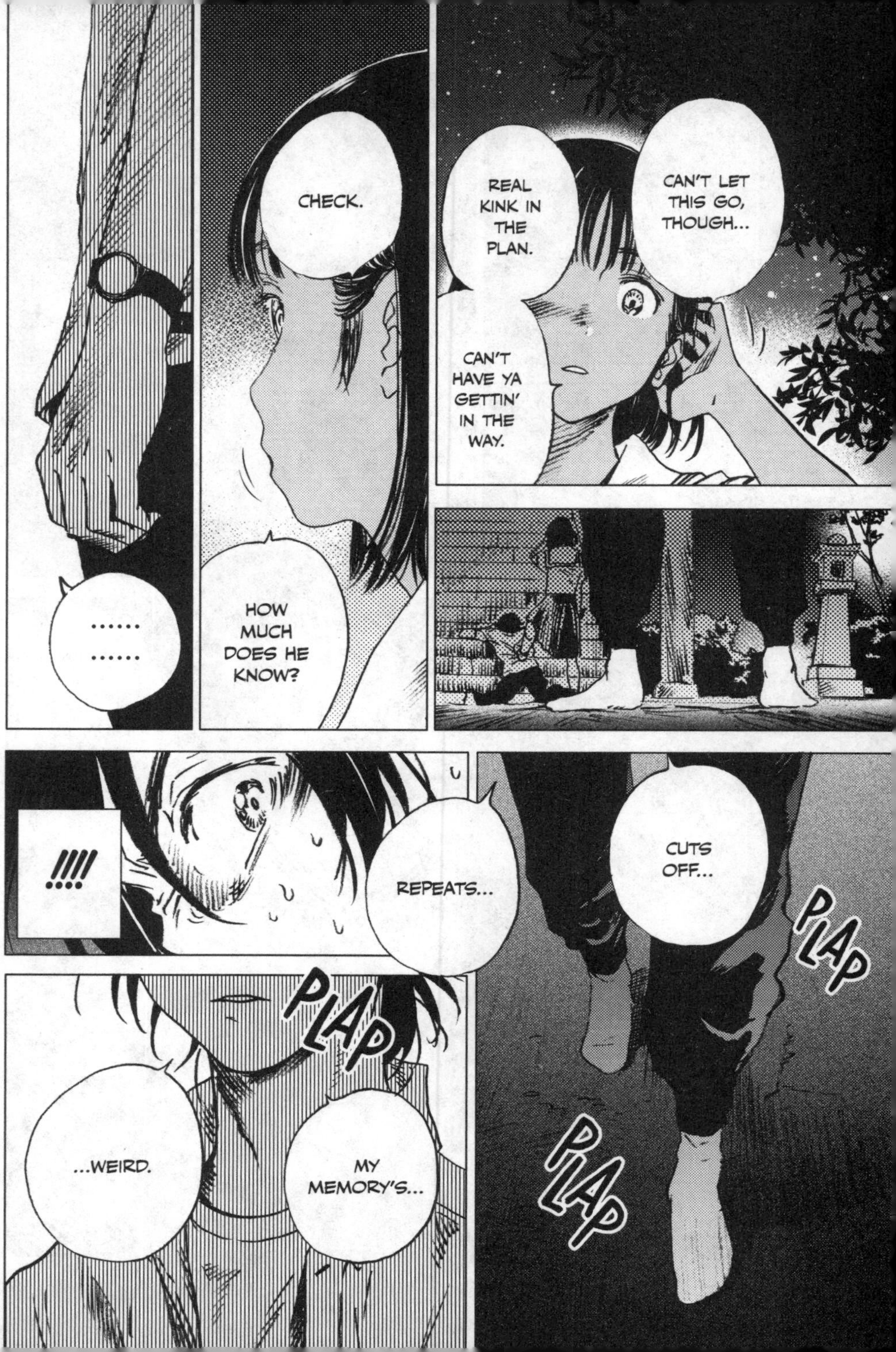

CAN'T LET THIS GO, THOUGH...
REAL KINK IN THE PLAN.
CAN'T HAVE YA GETTIN' IN THE WAY.
CHECK.
HOW MUCH DOES HE KNOW?
......
......
CUTS OFF...
PLAP
PLAP
REPEATS...
!!!!
PLAP
MY MEMORY'S...
...WEIRD.

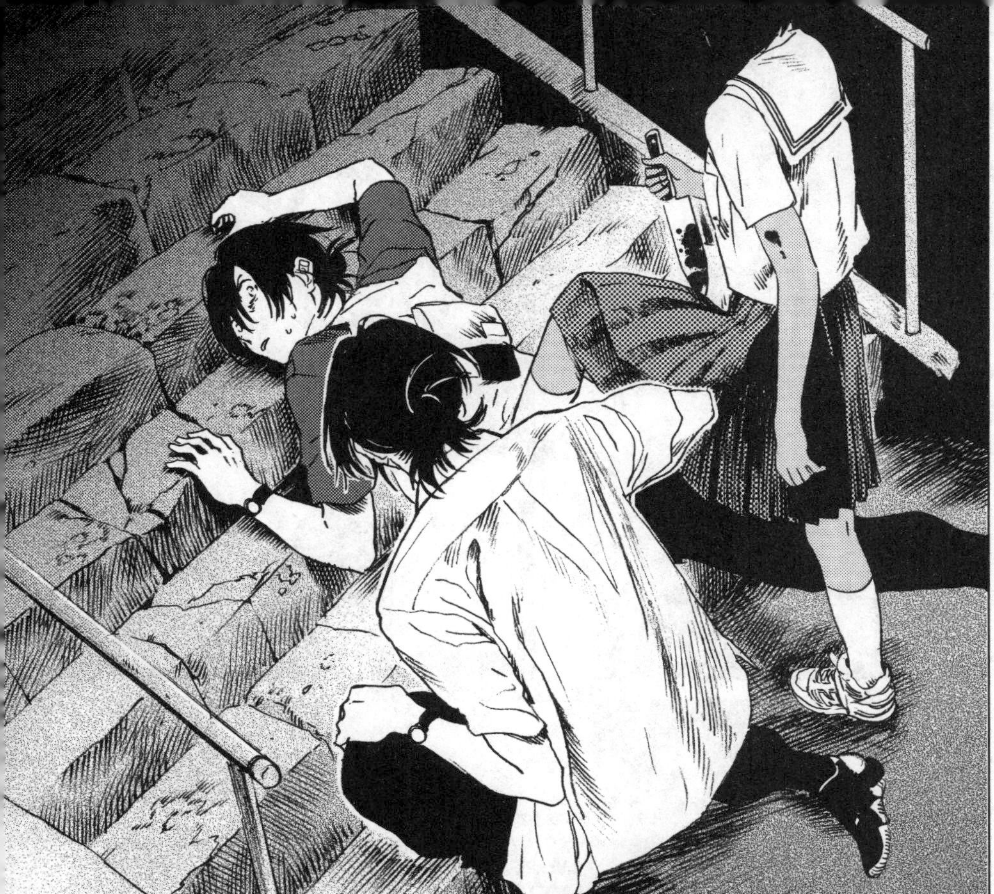

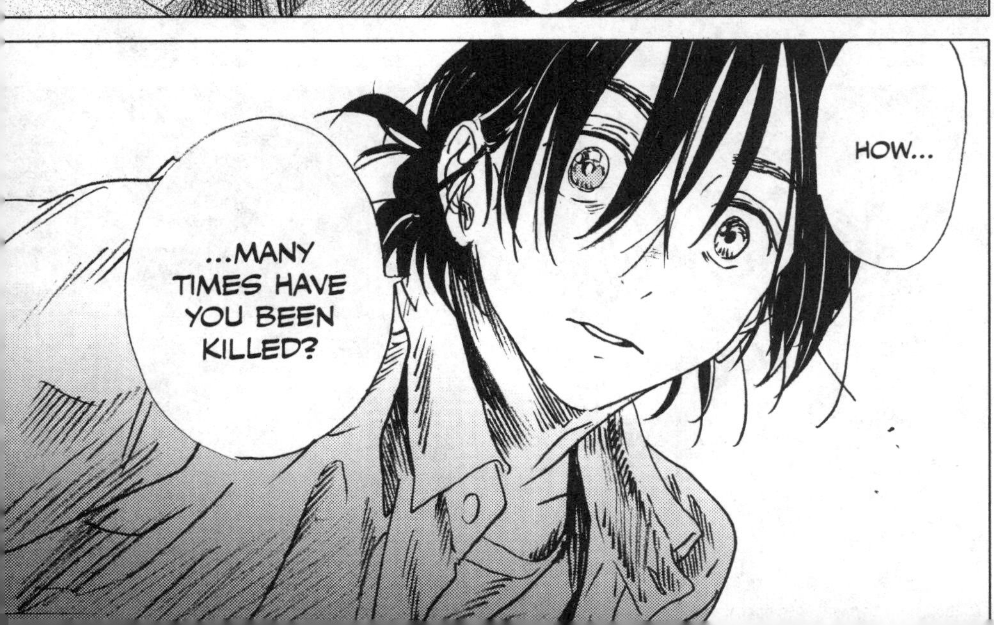
HOW...
...MANY TIMES HAVE YOU BEEN KILLED?

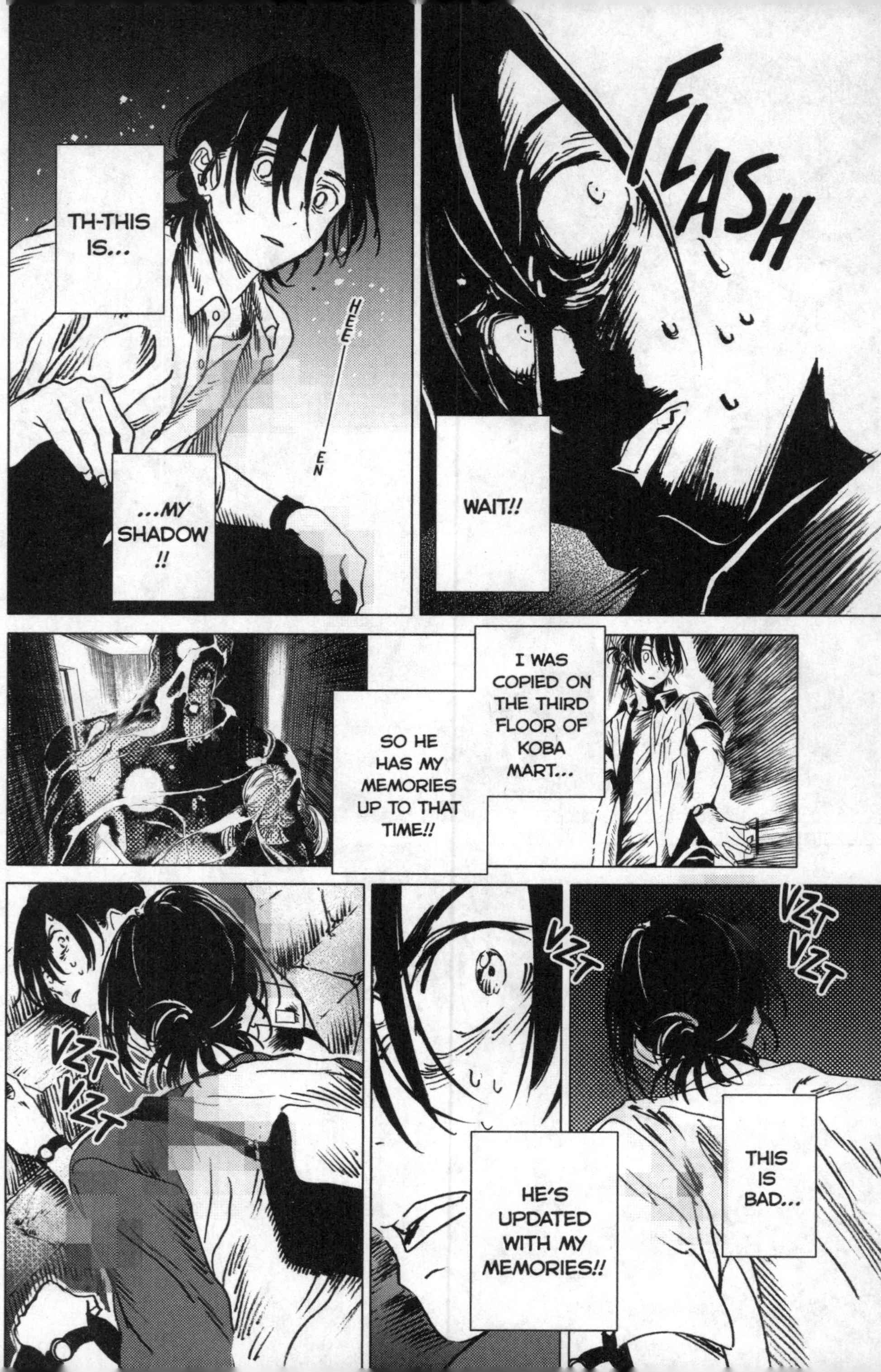
FLASH
WAIT!!
TH-THIS IS...
...MY SHADOW!!
HEEEN
I WAS COPIED ON THE THIRD FLOOR OF KOBA MART...
SO HE HAS MY MEMORIES UP TO THAT TIME!!
VZT VZT
THIS IS BAD...
VZT
HE'S UPDATED WITH MY MEMORIES!!
VZT VZT

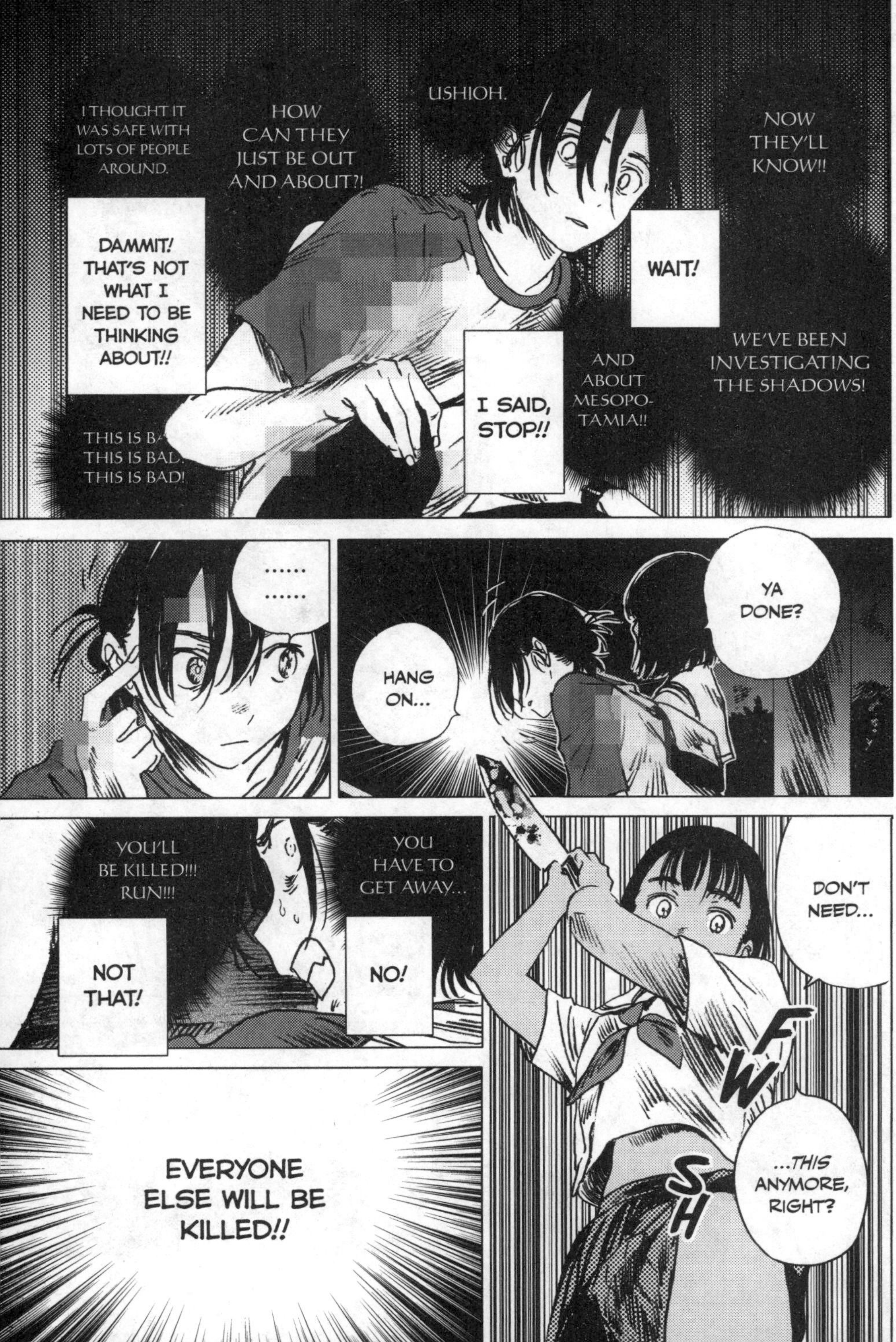
NOW THEY'LL KNOW!!
WE'VE BEEN INVESTIGATING THE SHADOWS!
WAIT!
USHIOH.
AND ABOUT MESOPOTAMIA!!
I SAID, STOP!!
HOW CAN THEY JUST BE OUT AND ABOUT?!
I THOUGHT IT WAS SAFE WITH LOTS OF PEOPLE AROUND.
DAMMIT! THAT'S NOT WHAT I NEED TO BE THINKING ABOUT!!
THIS IS BA
THIS IS BAD.
THIS IS BAD!
YA DONE?
HANG ON...
......
......
DON'T NEED...
FW
SH
...THIS ANYMORE, RIGHT?
YOU HAVE TO GET AWAY...
NO!
YOU'LL BE KILLED!!! RUN!!!
NOT THAT!
EVERYONE ELSE WILL BE KILLED!!

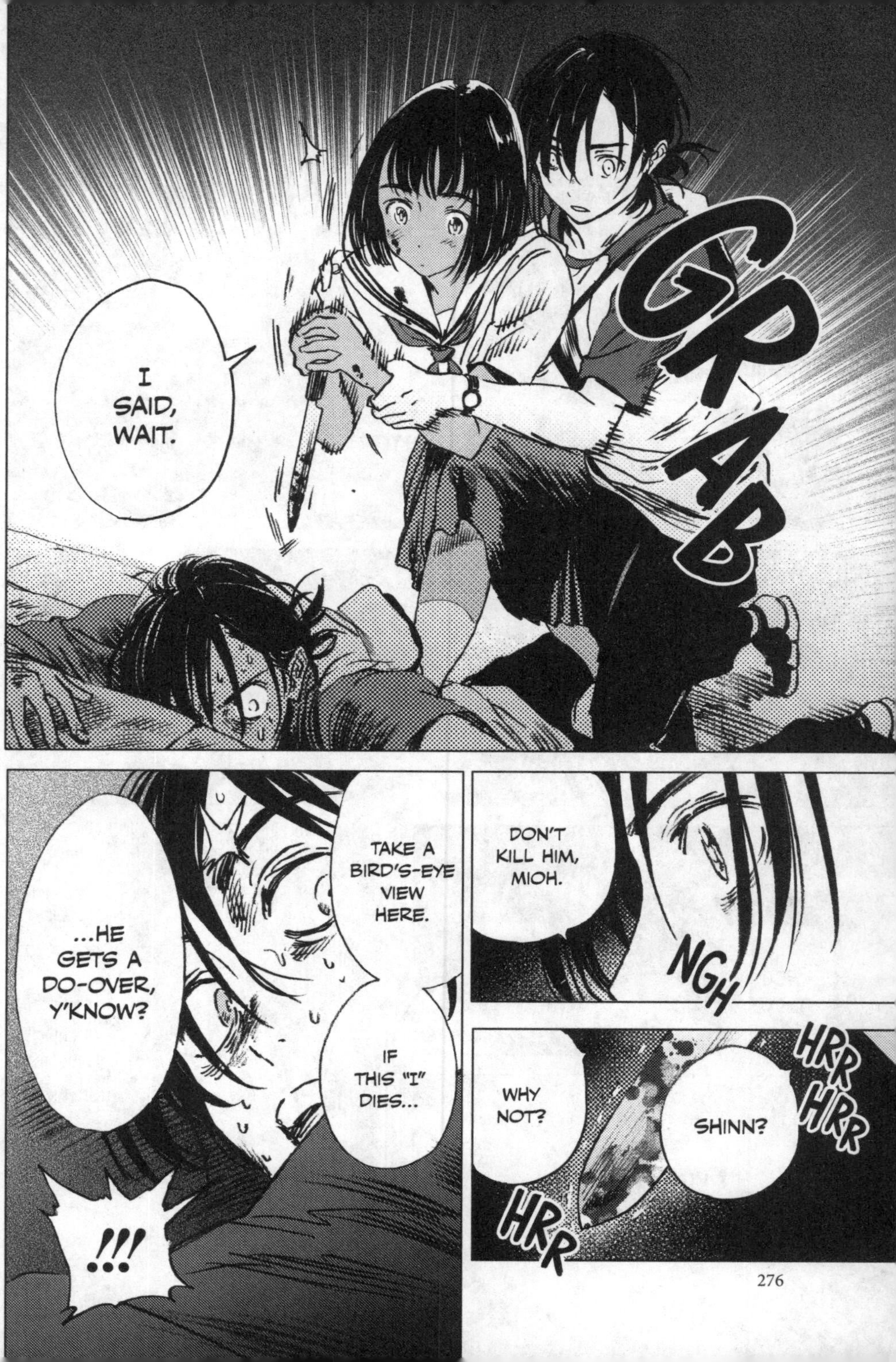
GRAB
I SAID, WAIT.
DON'T KILL HIM, MIOH.
NGH
HRR HRR
SHINN?
WHY NOT?
HRR
TAKE A BIRD'S-EYE VIEW HERE.
IF THIS "I" DIES...
...HE GETS A DO-OVER, Y'KNOW?
!!!

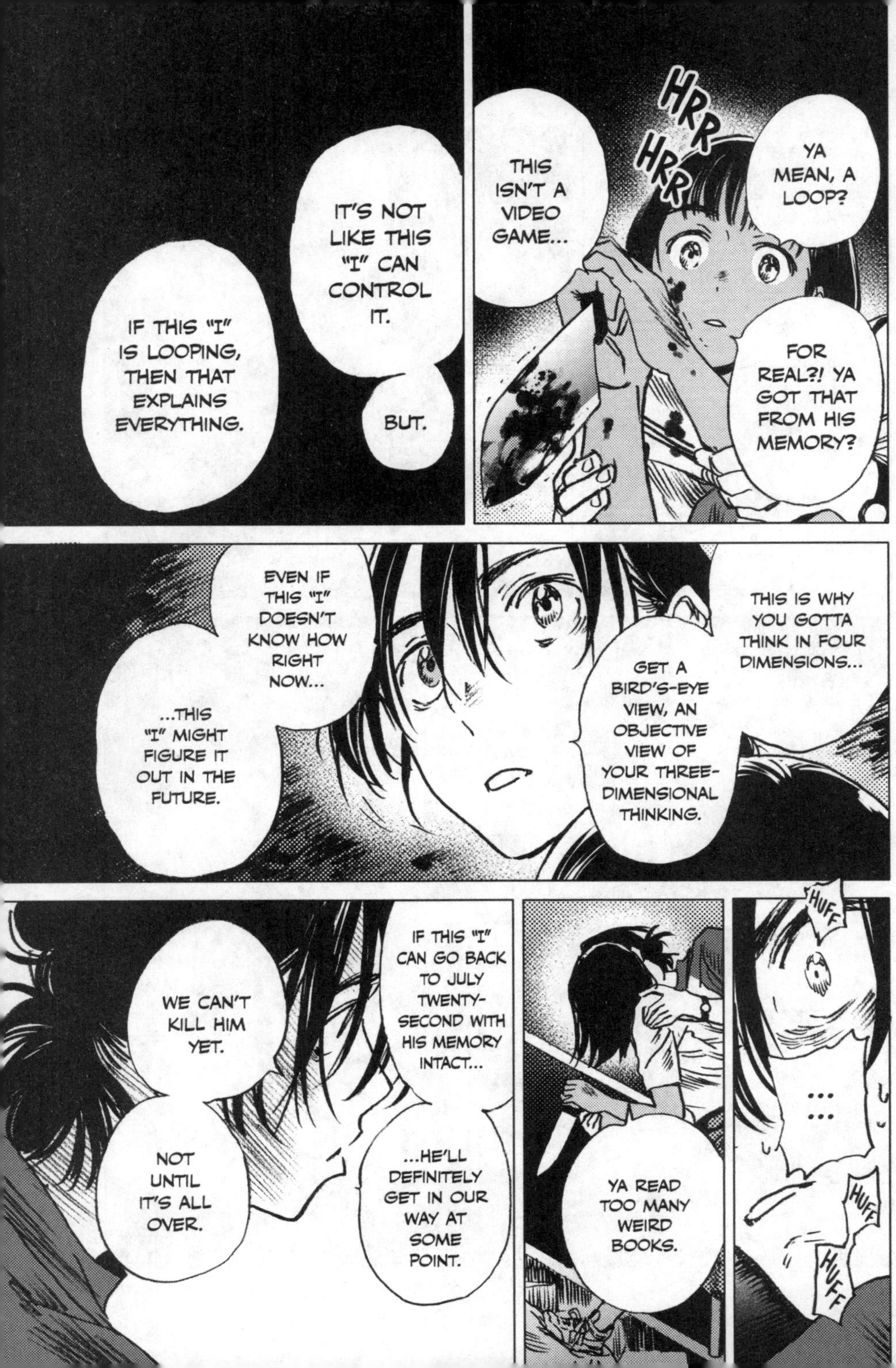
YA MEAN, A LOOP?
HRR HRR
FOR REAL?! YA GOT THAT FROM HIS MEMORY?
THIS ISN'T A VIDEO GAME...
IT'S NOT LIKE THIS "I" CAN CONTROL IT.
IF THIS "I" IS LOOPING, THEN THAT EXPLAINS EVERYTHING.
BUT.
THIS IS WHY YOU GOTTA THINK IN FOUR DIMENSIONS...
GET A BIRD'S-EYE VIEW, AN OBJECTIVE VIEW OF YOUR THREE-DIMENSIONAL THINKING.
EVEN IF THIS "I" DOESN'T KNOW HOW RIGHT NOW...
...THIS "I" MIGHT FIGURE IT OUT IN THE FUTURE.
HUFF
...
...
HUFF
HUFF
YA READ TOO MANY WEIRD BOOKS.
IF THIS "I" CAN GO BACK TO JULY TWENTY-SECOND WITH HIS MEMORY INTACT...
...HE'LL DEFINITELY GET IN OUR WAY AT SOME POINT.
WE CAN'T KILL HIM YET.
NOT UNTIL IT'S ALL OVER.

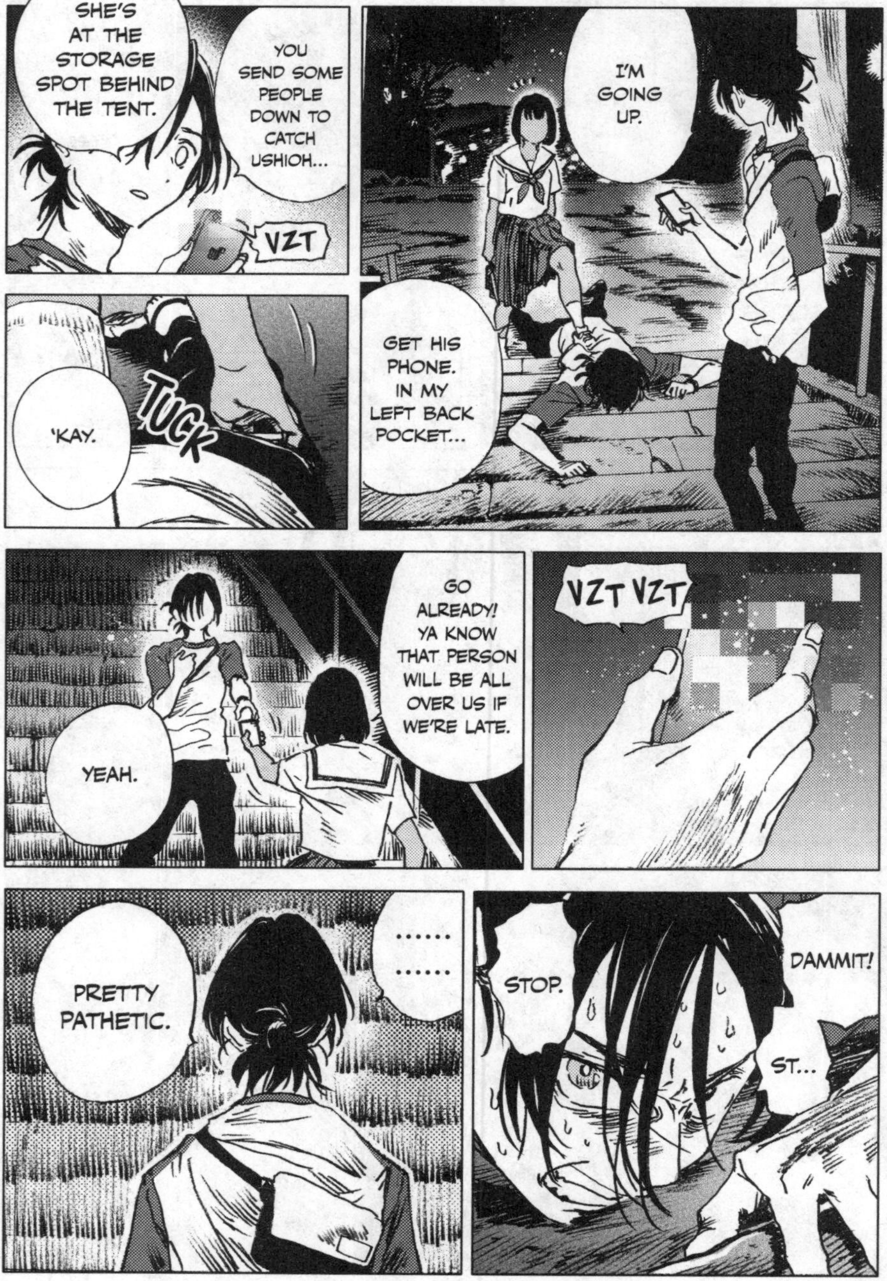
I'M GOING UP.
GET HIS PHONE. IN MY LEFT BACK POCKET...
YOU SEND SOME PEOPLE DOWN TO CATCH USHIOH...
SHE'S AT THE STORAGE SPOT BEHIND THE TENT.
VZT
TUCK
'KAY.
VZT VZT
GO ALREADY! YA KNOW THAT PERSON WILL BE ALL OVER US IF WE'RE LATE.
YEAH.
DAMMIT!
STOP.
ST...
......
......
PRETTY PATHETIC.

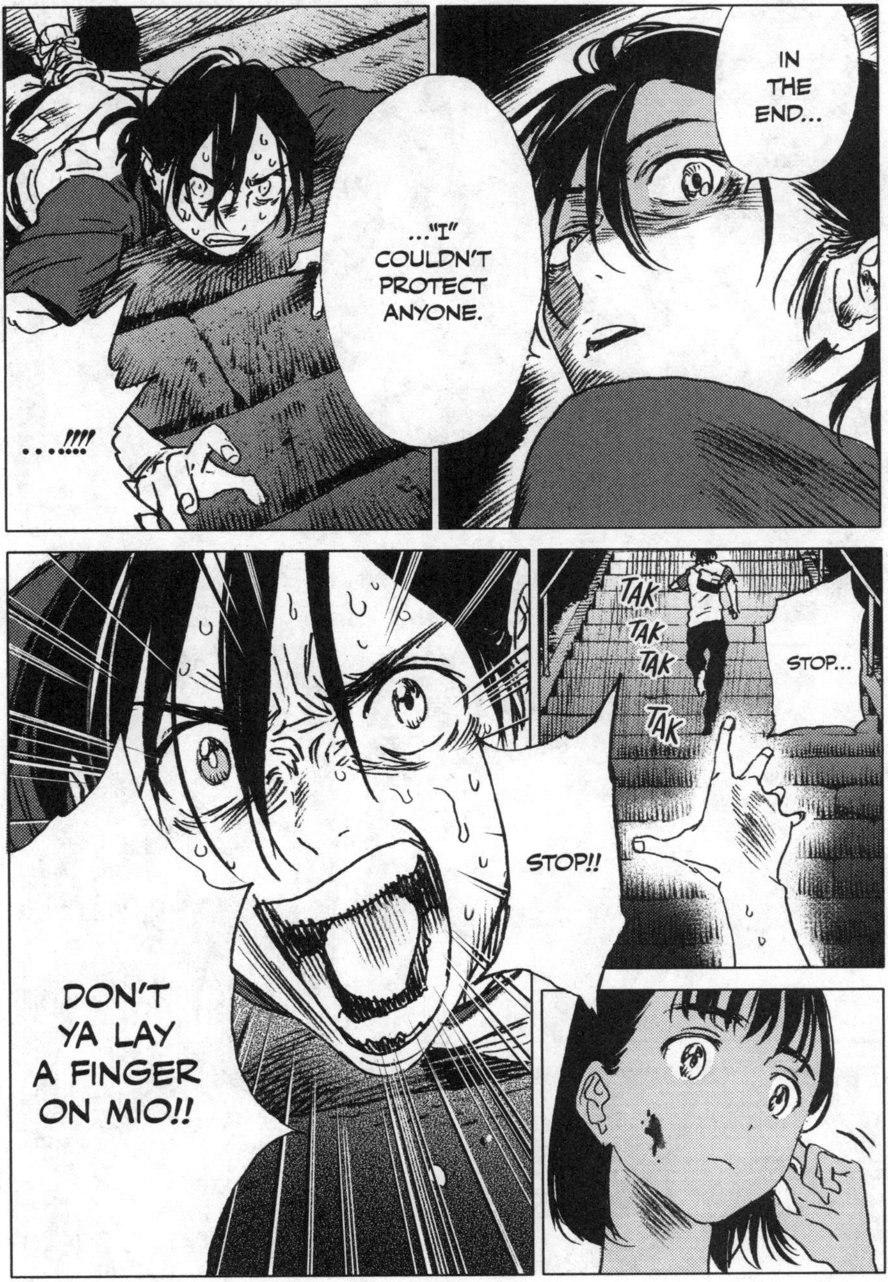
IN THE END...
..."I" COULDN'T PROTECT ANYONE.
......!!!!
TAK
TAK
TAK
TAK
STOP...
STOP!!
DON'T YA LAY A FINGER ON MIO!!

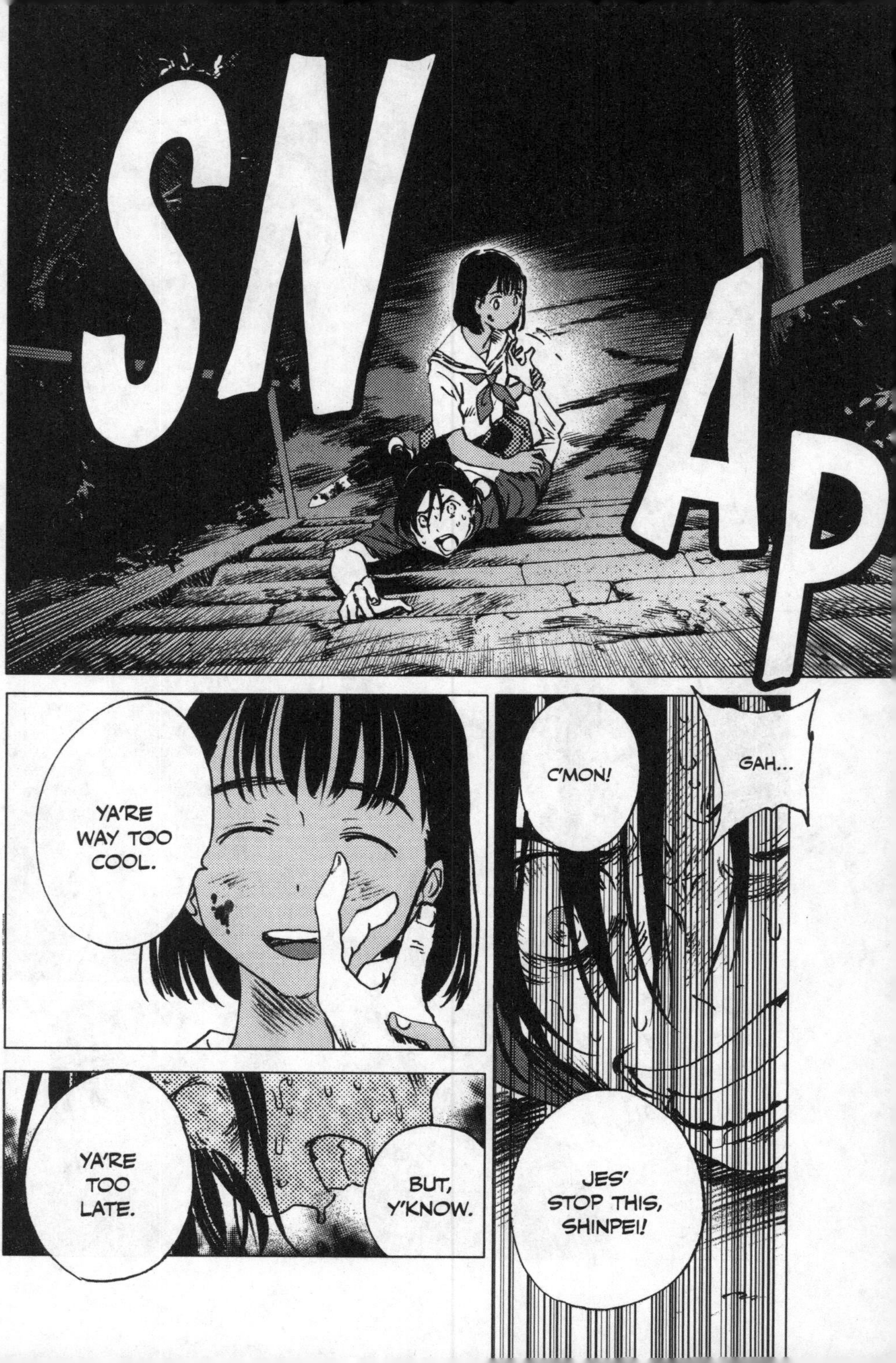
SNAP
GAH...
C'MON!
JES' STOP THIS, SHINPEI!
YA'RE WAY TOO COOL.
BUT, Y'KNOW.
YA'RE TOO LATE.

CRAWL

HNGH

NGAA-AAAH!!

...UN-NNH!

CRAWL

SOON...

MOTHER'S GOIN' TO WAKE UP.

JES' BE QUIET!

HRR

C'MON!

NOT KNOWIN' WHEN TO GIVE UP'S PATHETIC, SHIN!

HRR HRR

M-MIOOO-OOOO!!

GRAB

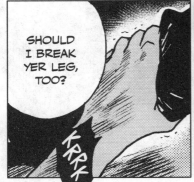

SHOULD I BREAK YER LEG, TOO?

KRRK

HRR HRR

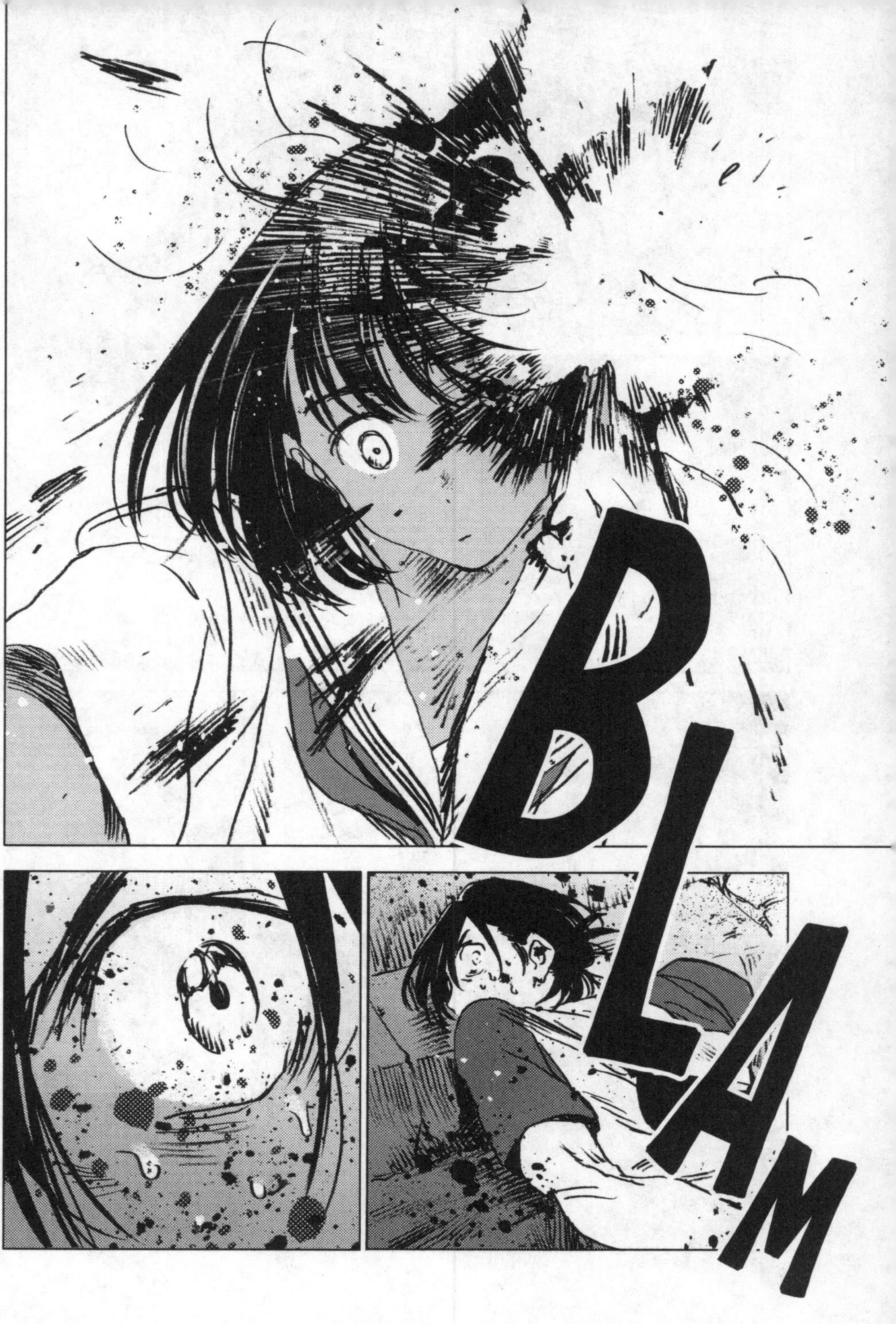
BLAM

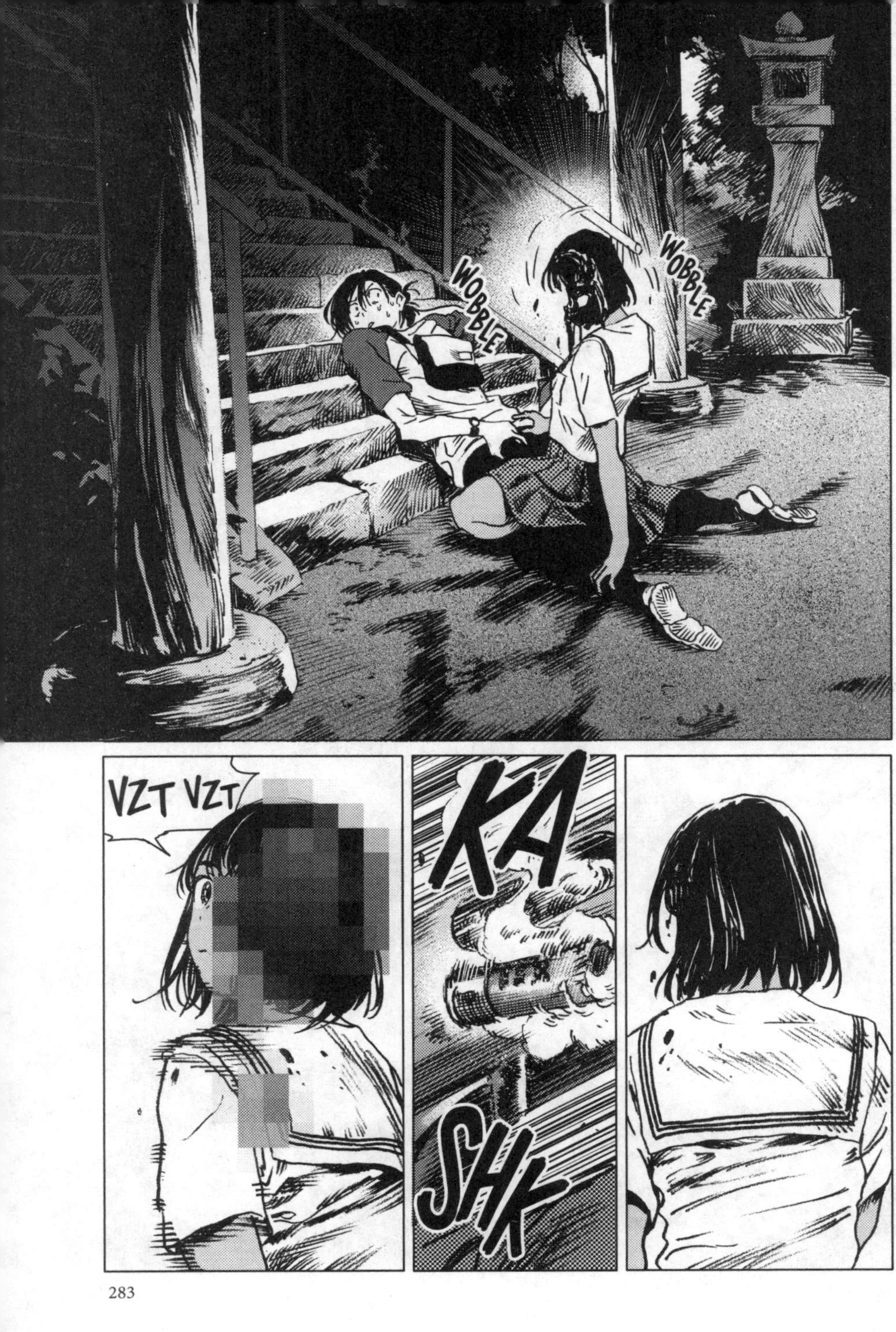
WOBBLE
WOBBLE
KA
SHK
VZT VZT

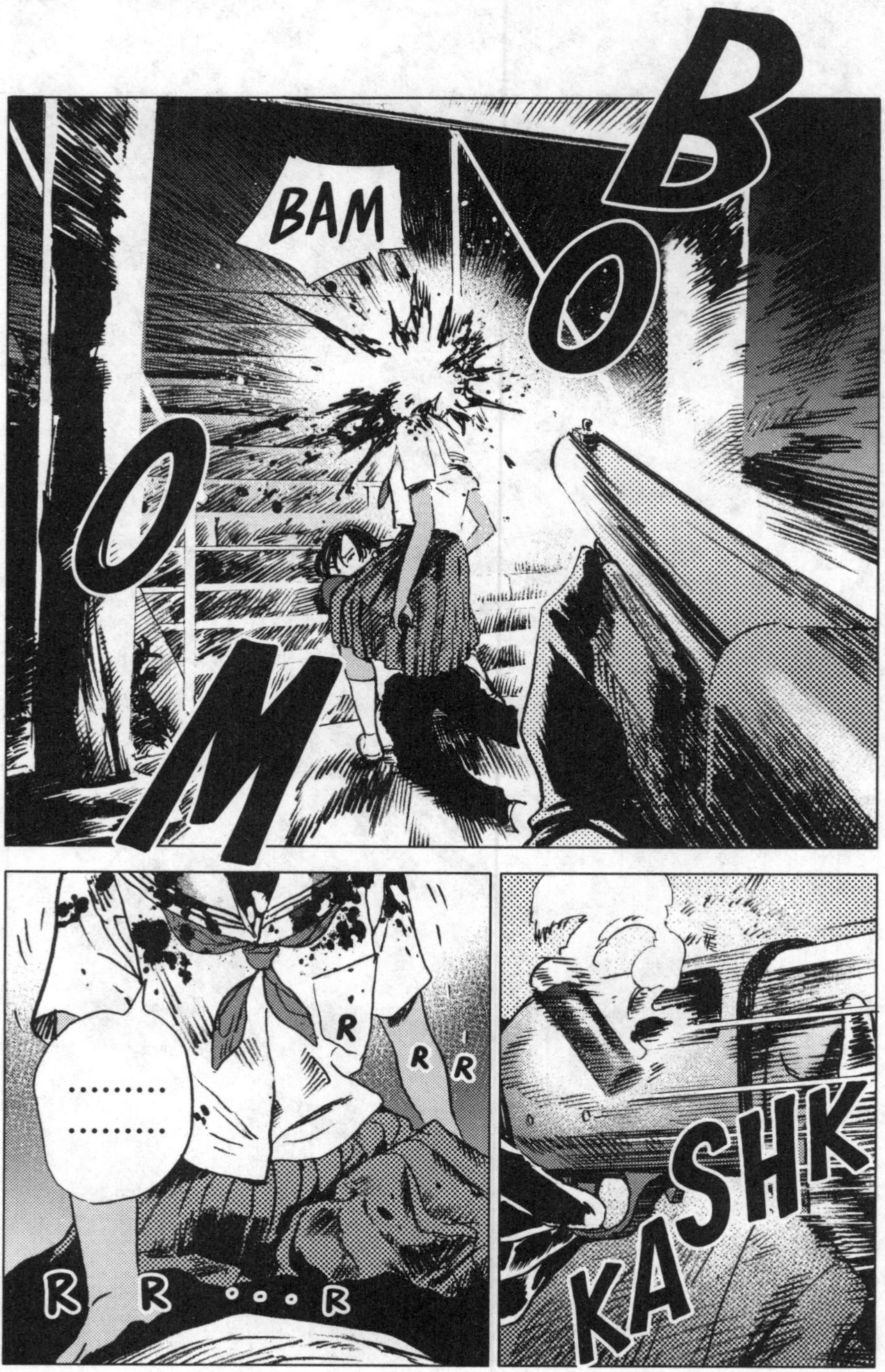
BAM
BOOM
KASHK
R
R R
....
....
R R ...R

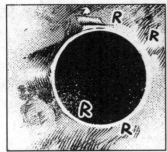

TH
U
D

AH...

HUFF

AH...
AH.

HUFF

YA
DON'T...

...HEAR
'BOUT
NAREZUSHI
ON HITOGA-
SHIMA,
HM?

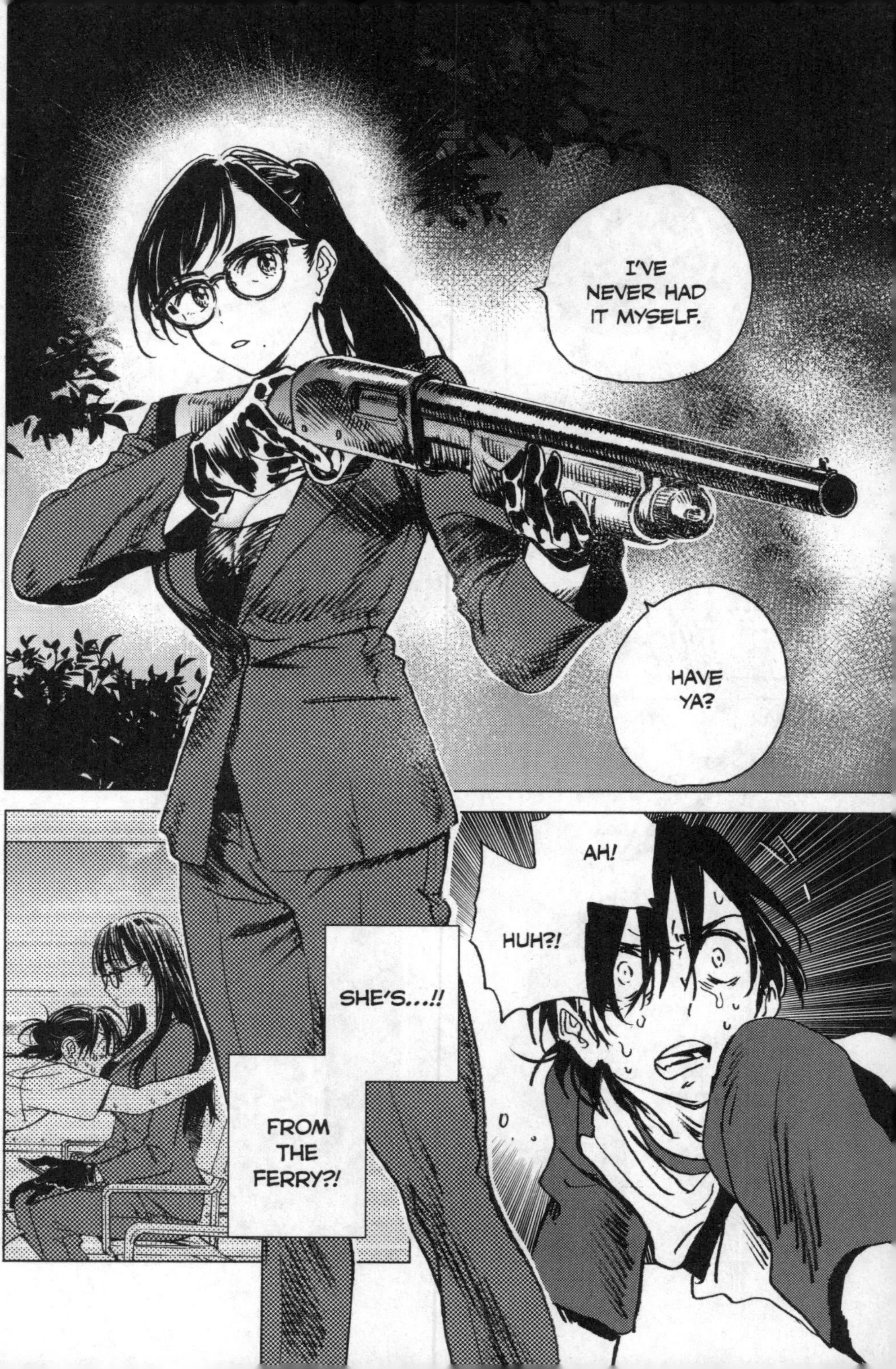

I'VE NEVER HAD IT MYSELF.
HAVE YA?
AH!
HUH?!
SHE'S...!!
FROM THE FERRY?!

!?!?

FSH

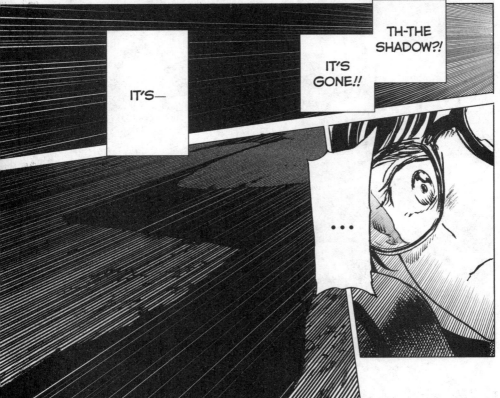

TH-THE SHADOW?!

IT'S GONE!!

IT'S—

...

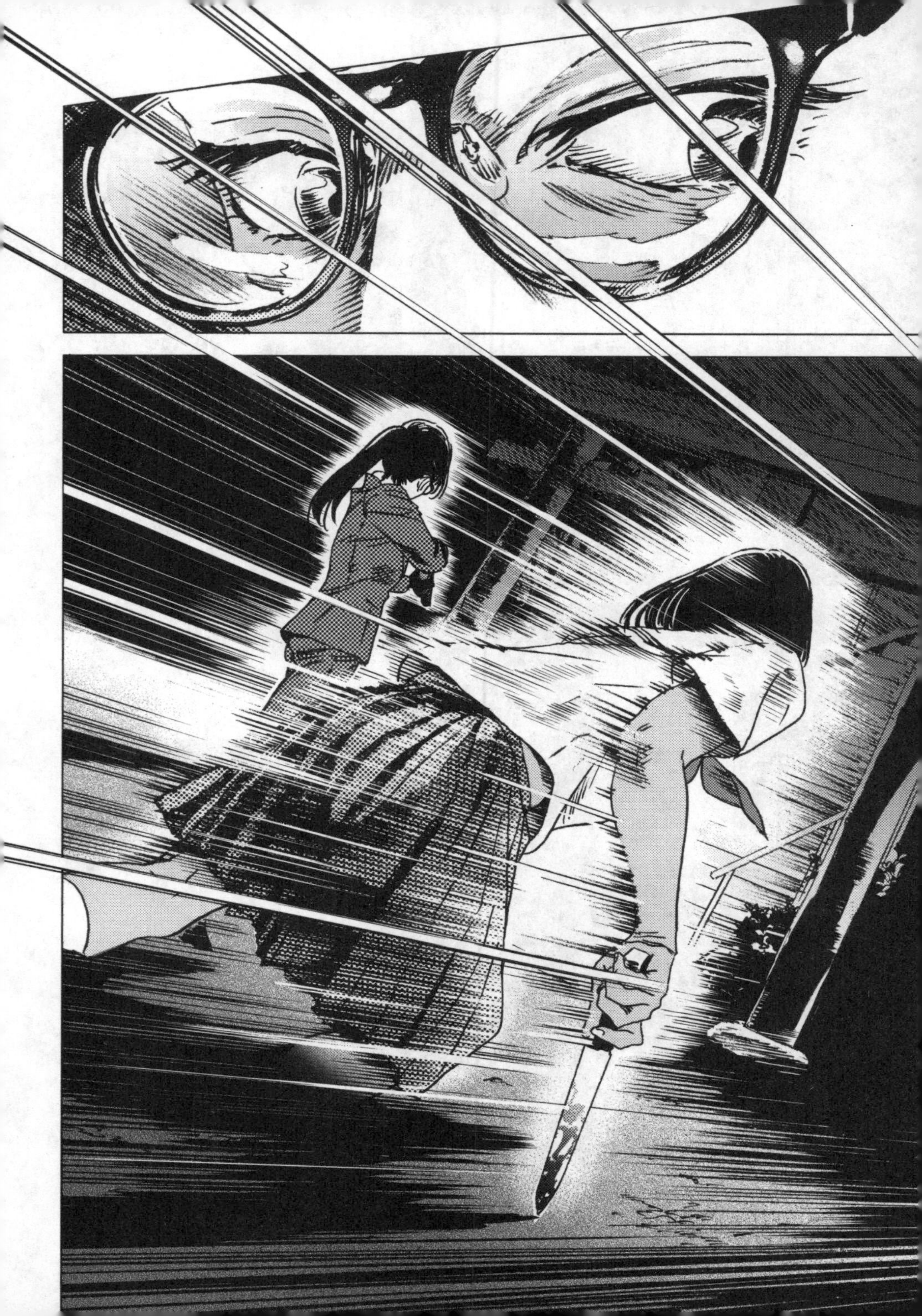

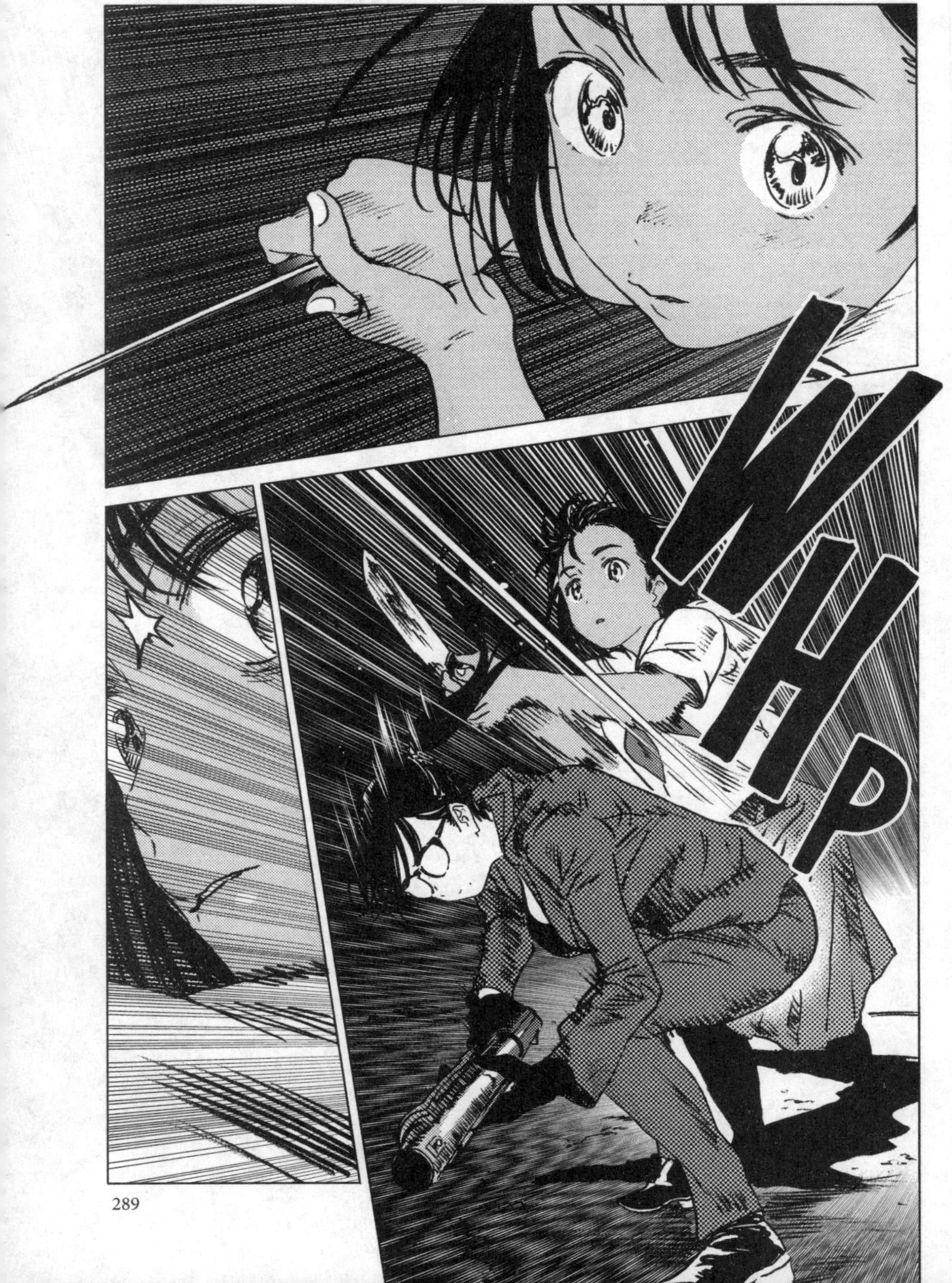
WHIP

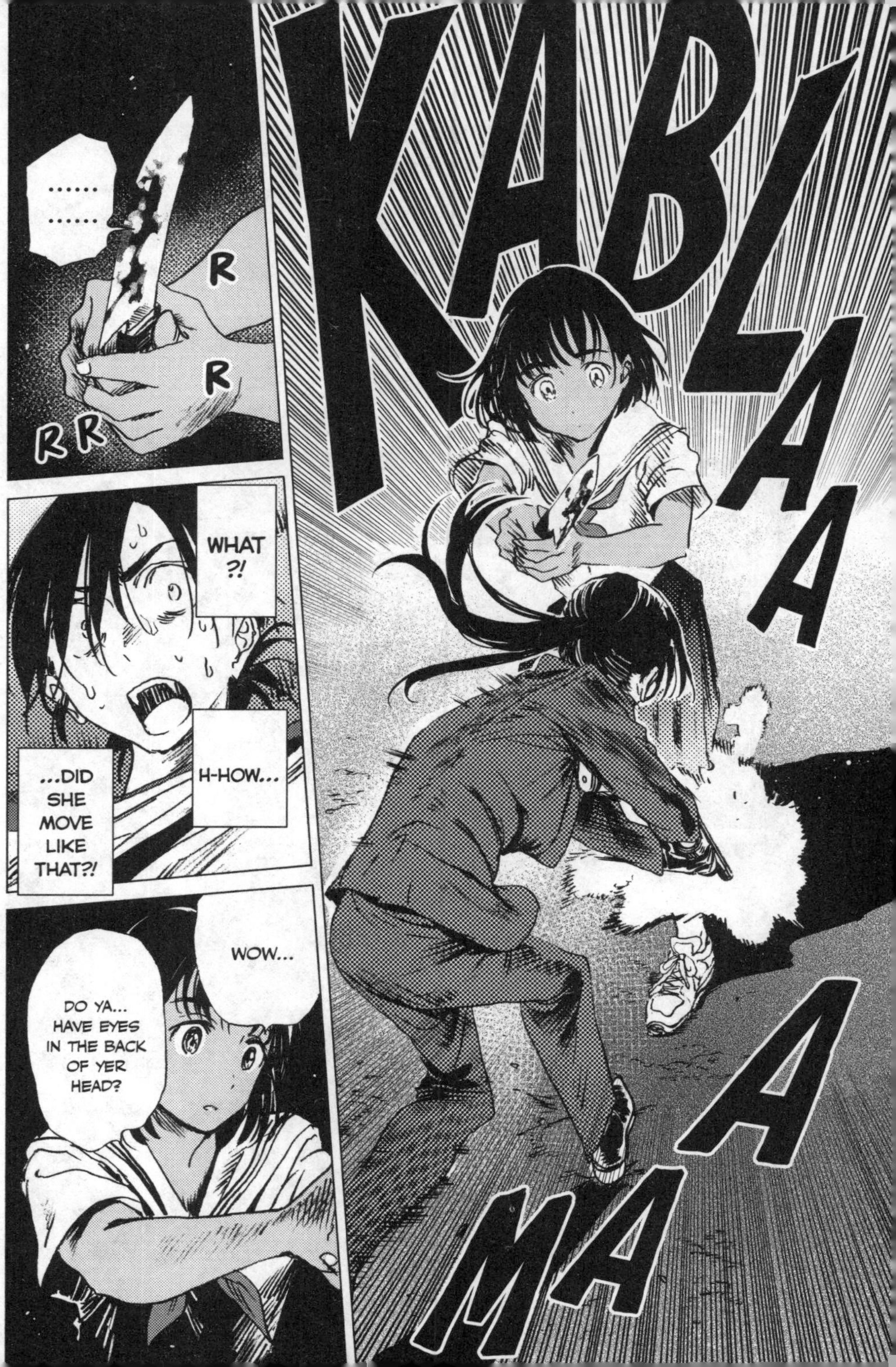
KABLAAA
AA
MA
……
……
R R R R
WHAT?!
H-HOW...
...DID SHE MOVE LIKE THAT?!
WOW...
DO YA... HAVE EYES IN THE BACK OF YER HEAD?

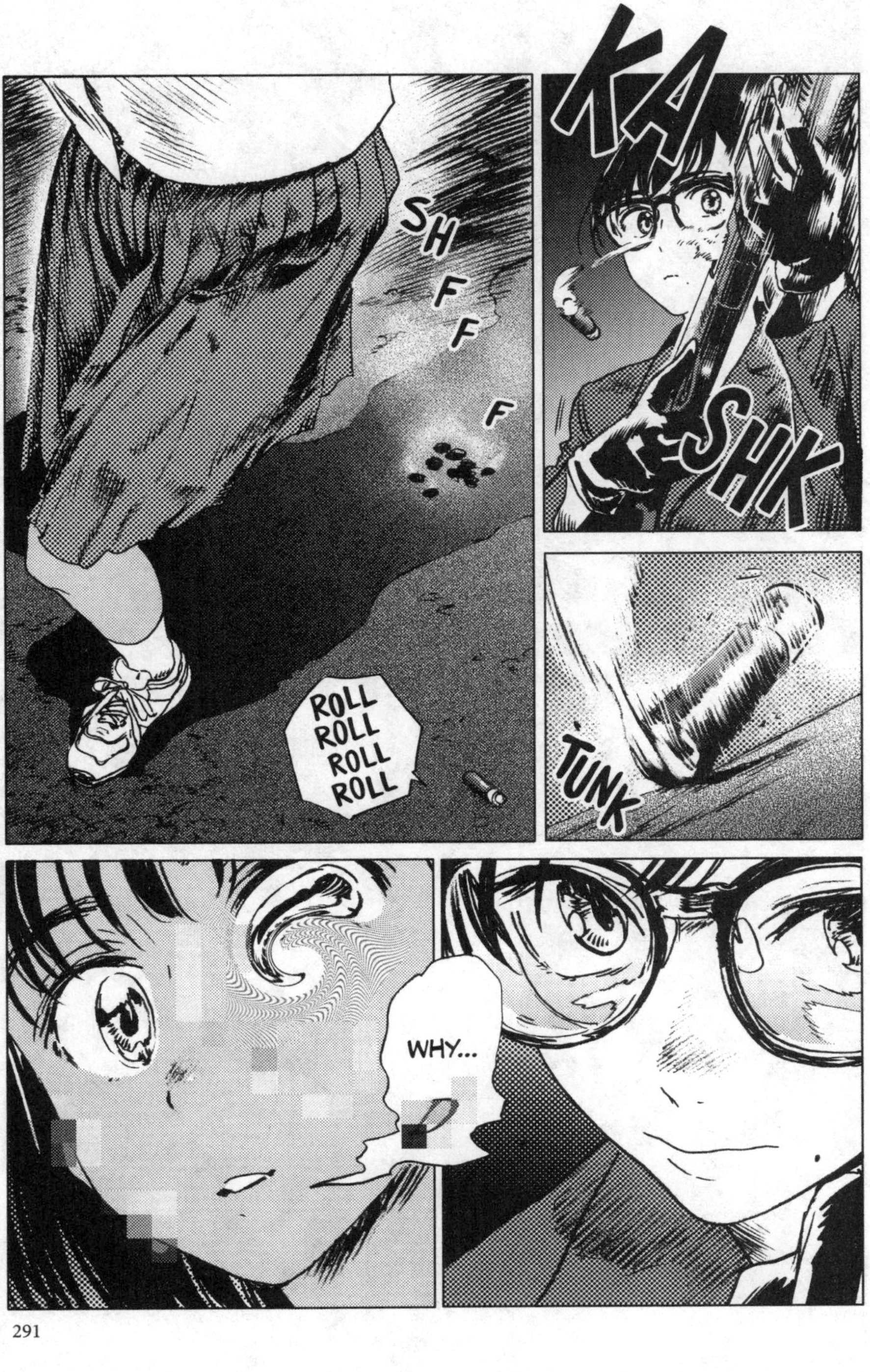
KA
SHK
TUNK
SH
F
F
F
ROLL
ROLL
ROLL
ROLL
WHY...

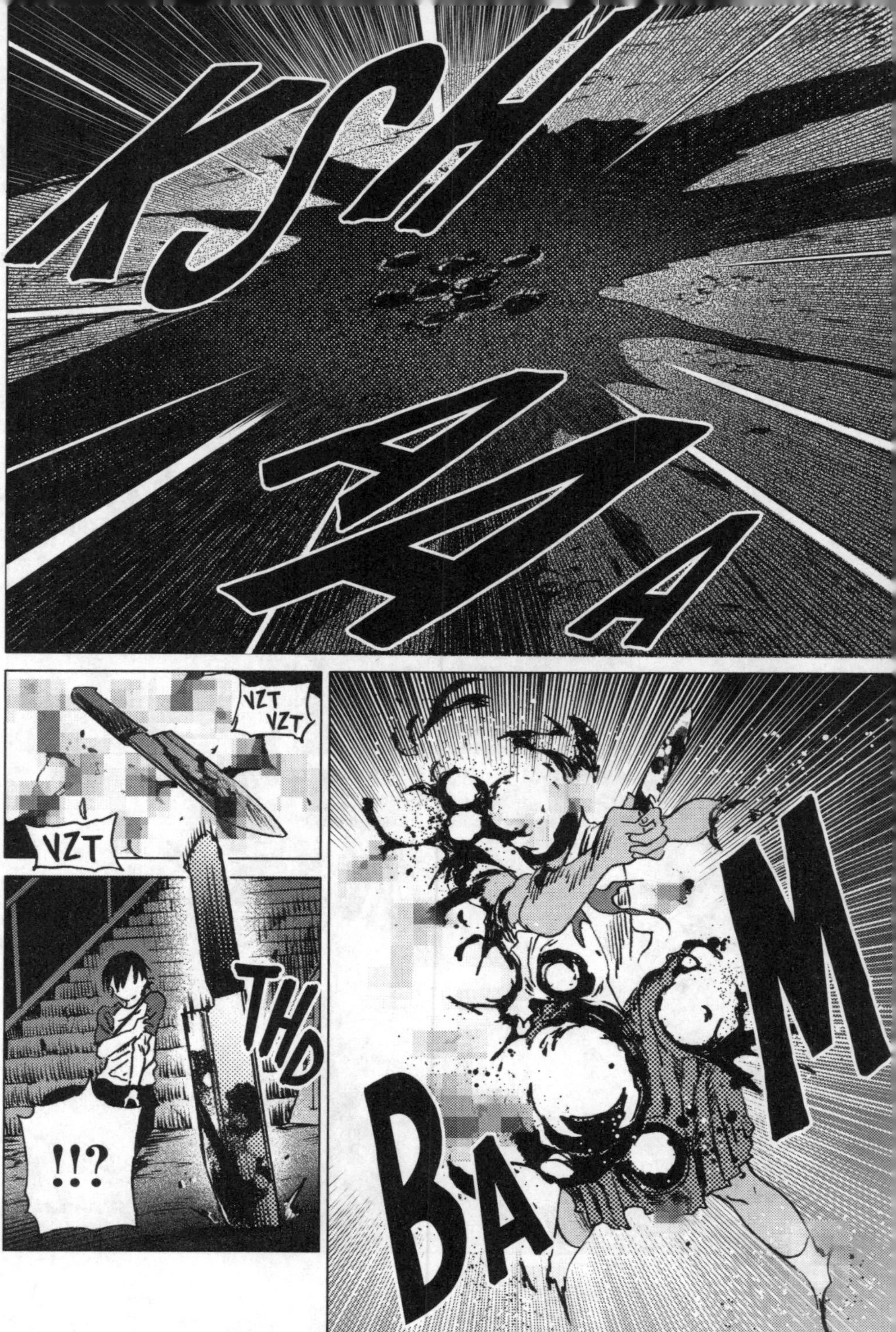

KSHAAA
BAM
VZT VZT
VZT
THD
!!?

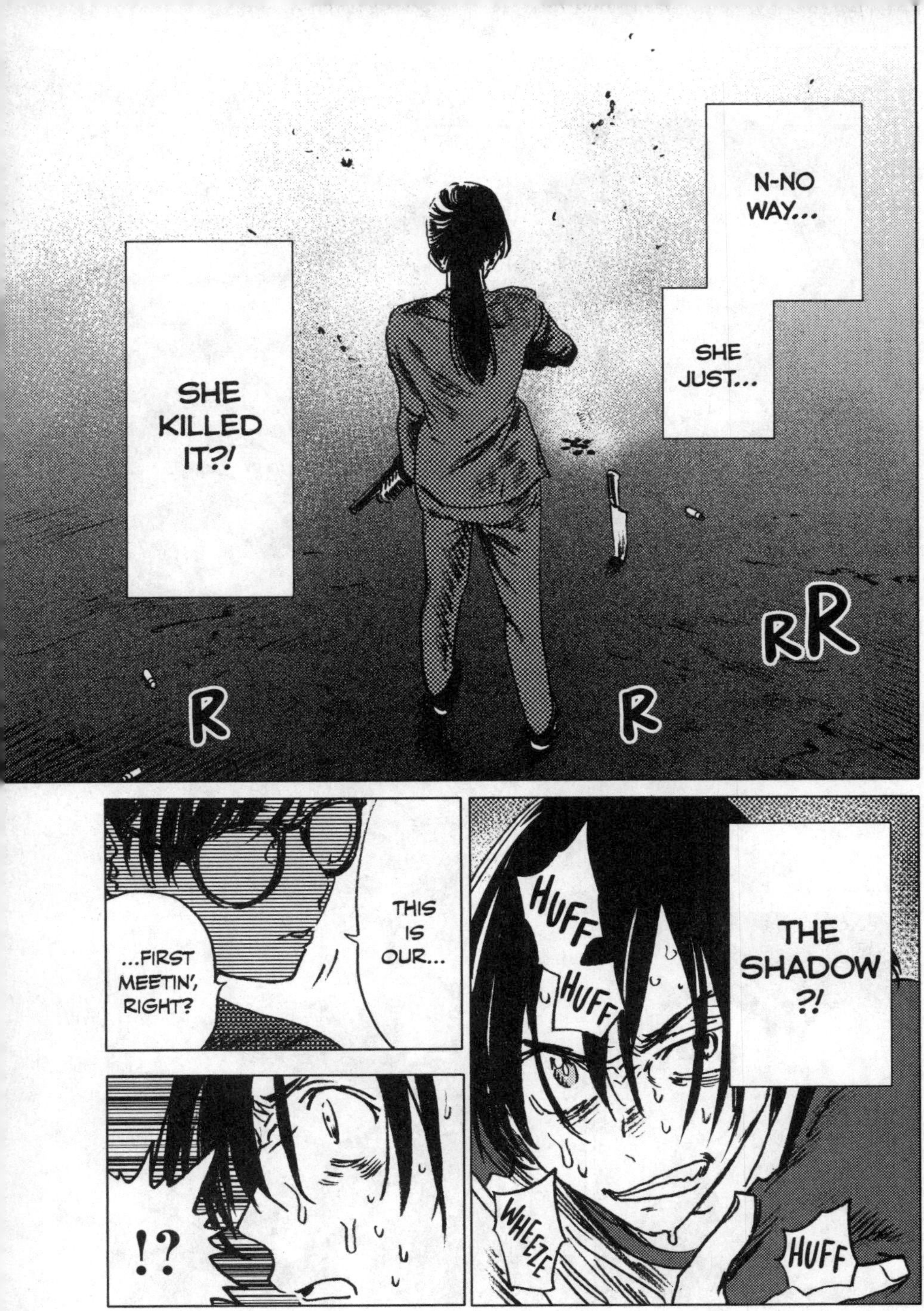
N-NO WAY...
SHE JUST...
SHE KILLED IT?!
RR
R
R
THE SHADOW ?!
HUFF
HUFF
WHEEZE
HUFF
THIS IS OUR...
...FIRST MEETIN', RIGHT?
!?

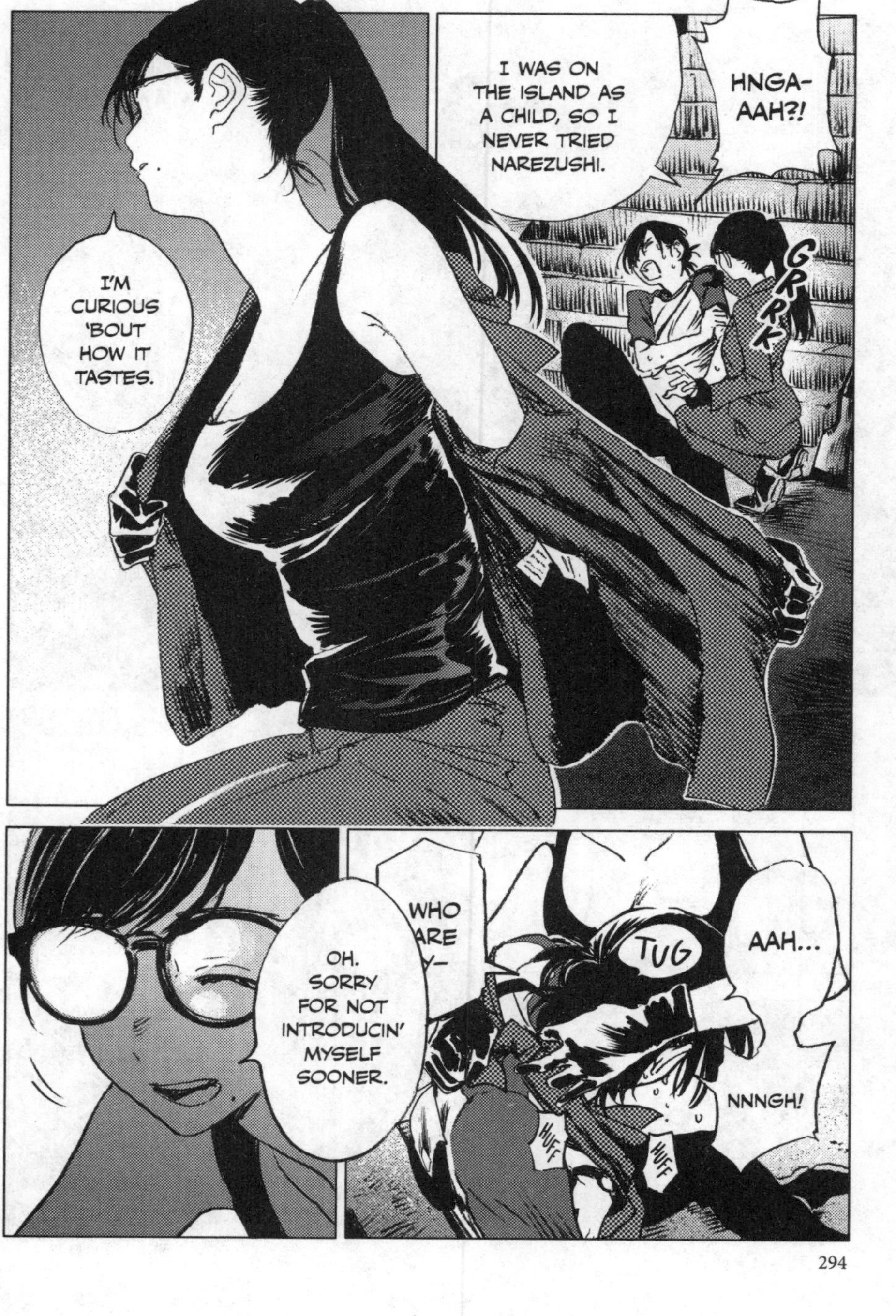

HNGA-AAH?!
I WAS ON THE ISLAND AS A CHILD, SO I NEVER TRIED NAREZUSHI.
GRRK
I'M CURIOUS 'BOUT HOW IT TASTES.
AAH...
TUG
WHO ARE Y—
NNNGH!
HUFF
HUFF
OH. SORRY FOR NOT INTRODUCIN' MYSELF SOONER.

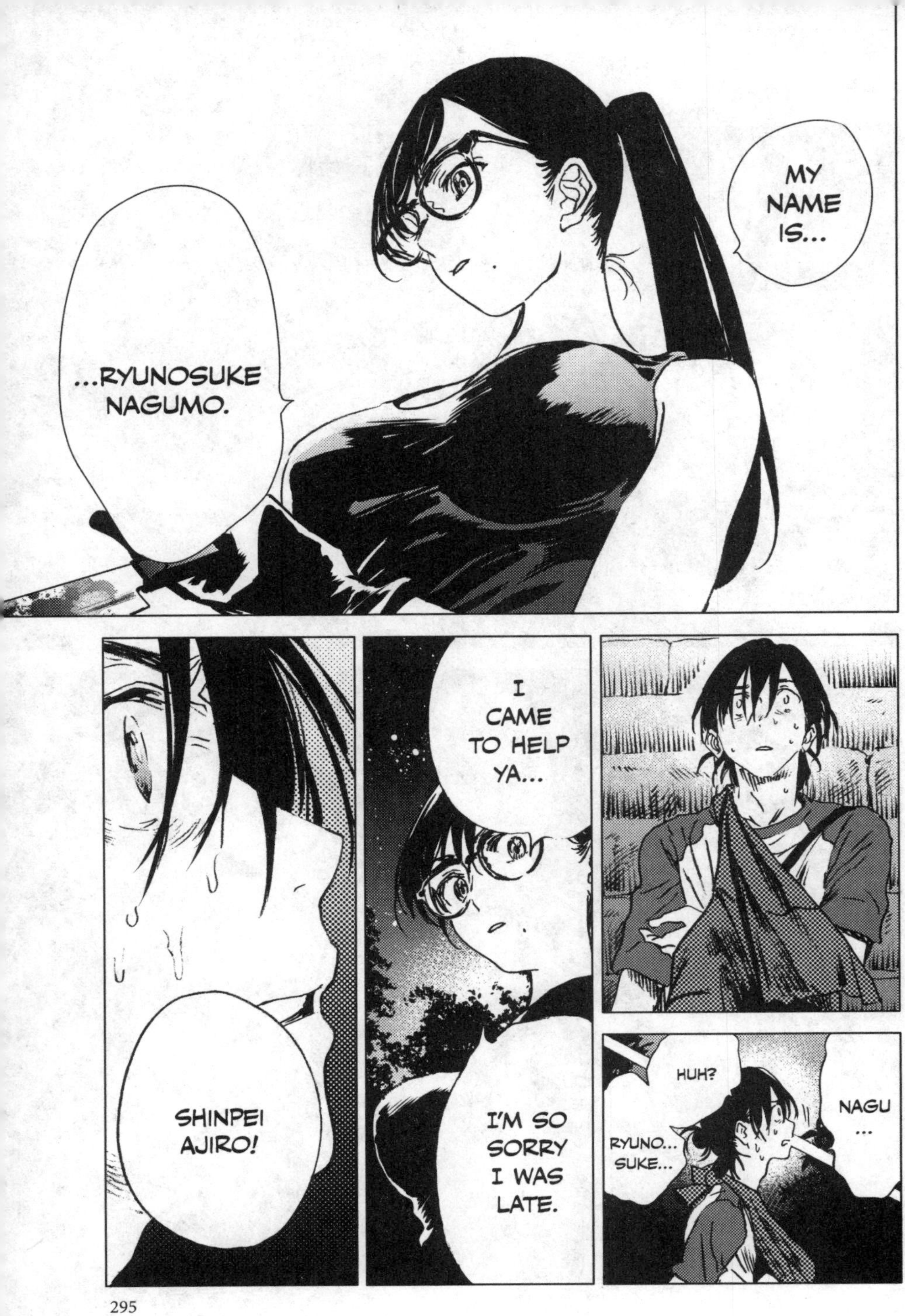
MY NAME IS...
...RYUNOSUKE NAGUMO.
HUH?
NAGU ...
RYUNO... SUKE...
I CAME TO HELP YA...
I'M SO SORRY I WAS LATE.
SHINPEI AJIRO!

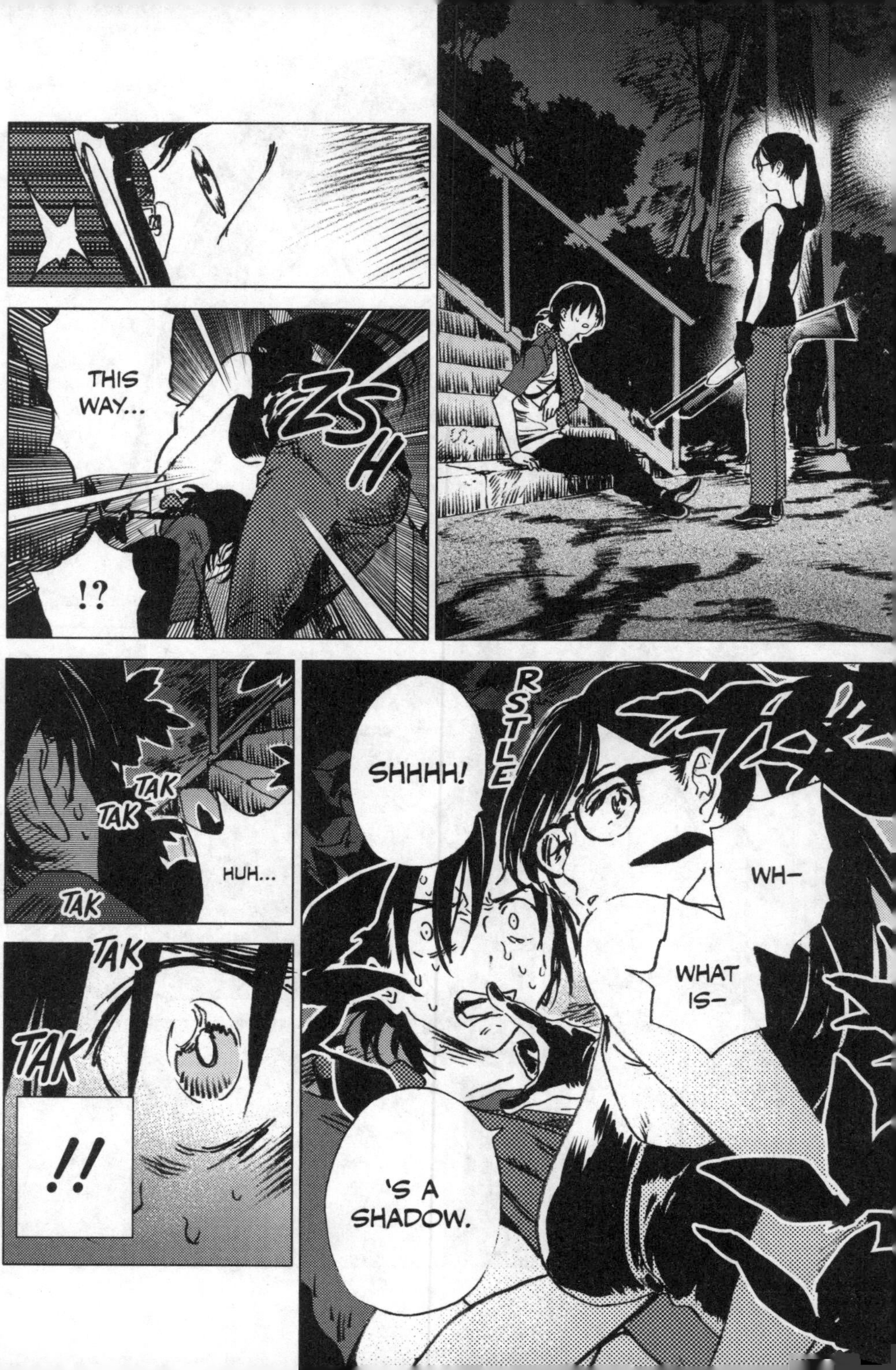
THIS WAY...
ZSH
!?
RSTLE
SHHHH!
WH-
WHAT IS-
'S A SHADOW.
TAK
TAK
HUH...
TAK
TAK
TAK
!!

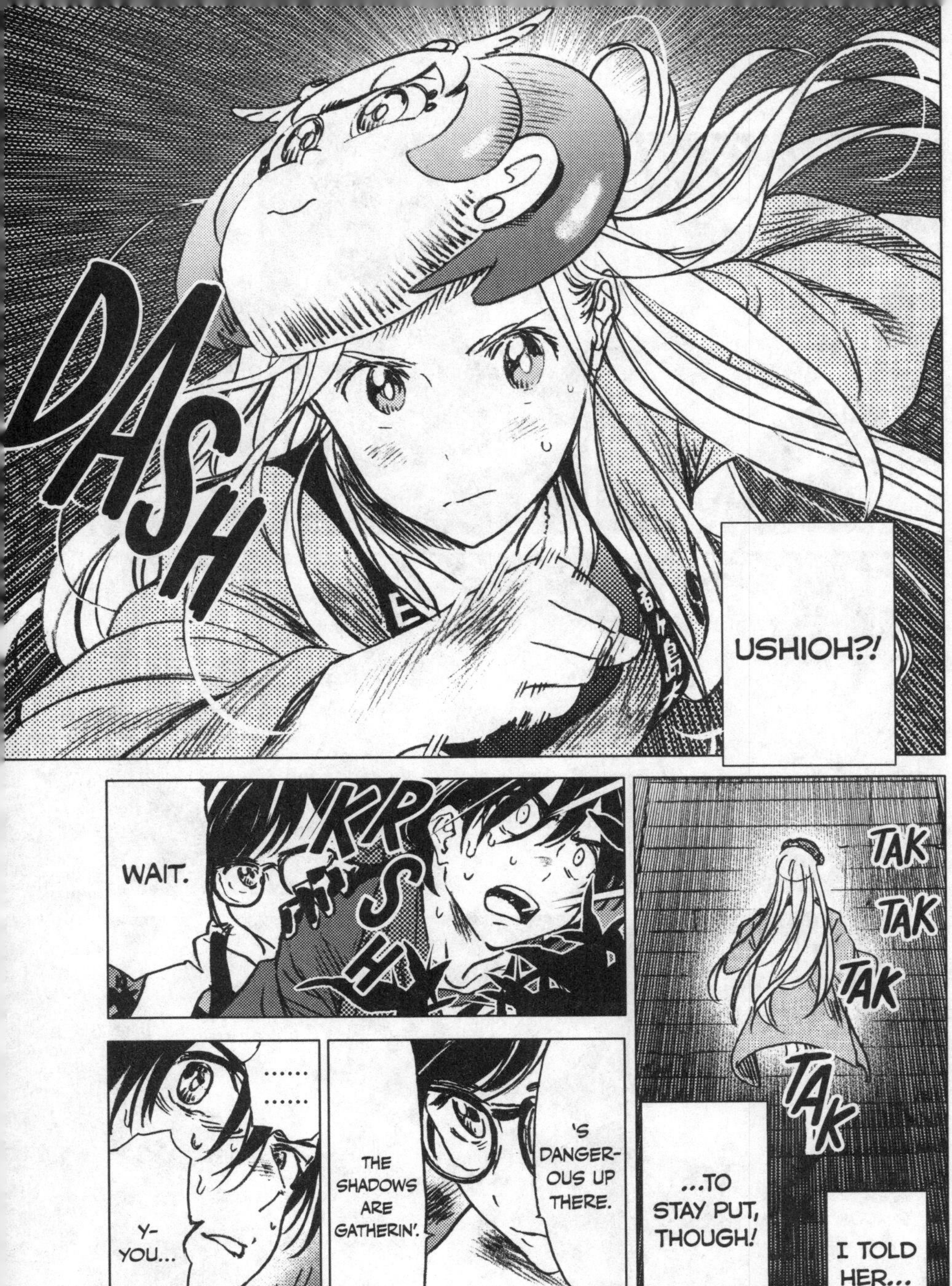
USHIOH?!
DASH
TAK
TAK
TAK
TAK
I TOLD HER...
...TO STAY PUT, THOUGH!
KRSH
WAIT.
'S DANGER-OUS UP THERE.
THE SHADOWS ARE GATHERIN'.
......
......
Y-YOU...

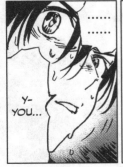

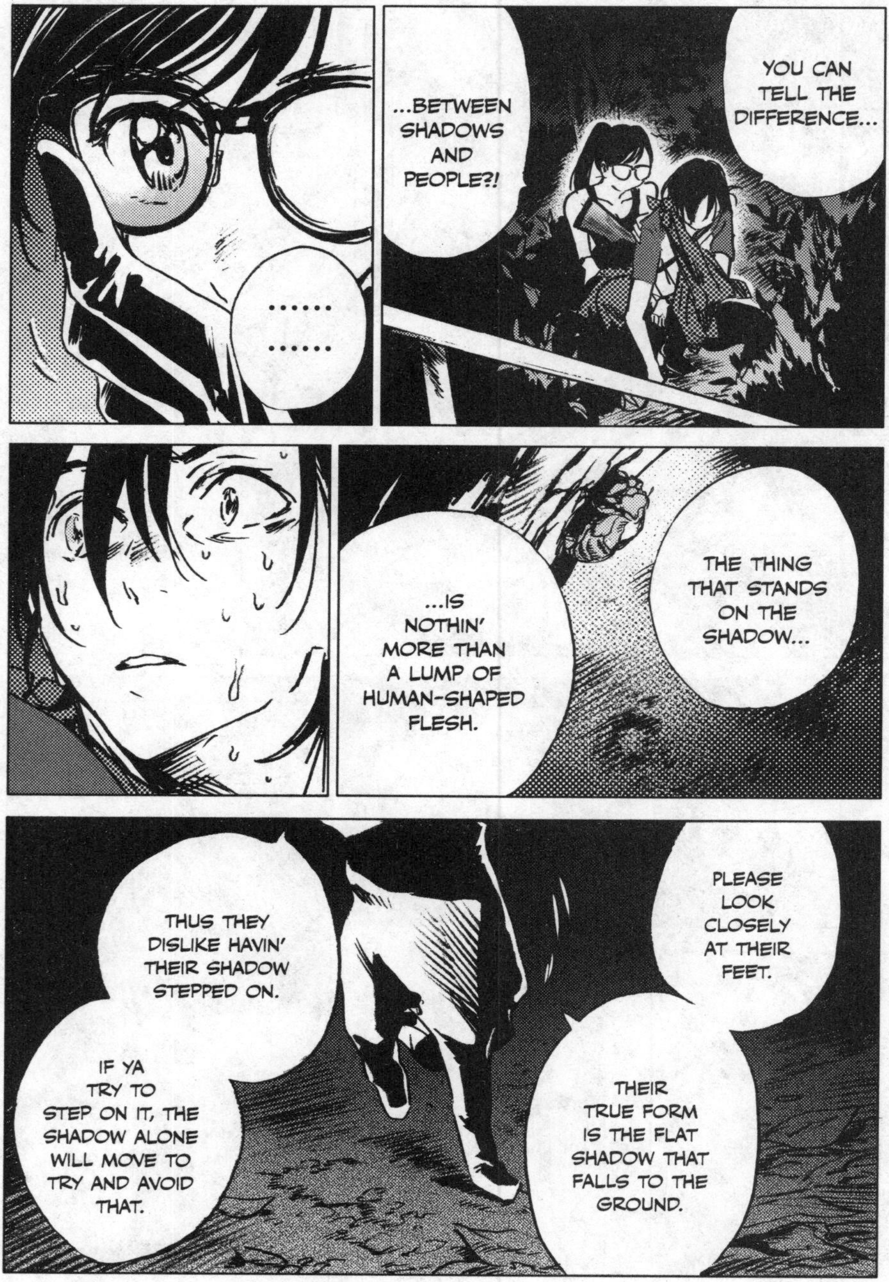
YOU CAN TELL THE DIFFERENCE...
...BETWEEN SHADOWS AND PEOPLE?!
......
......
THE THING THAT STANDS ON THE SHADOW...
...IS NOTHIN' MORE THAN A LUMP OF HUMAN-SHAPED FLESH.
PLEASE LOOK CLOSELY AT THEIR FEET.
THEIR TRUE FORM IS THE FLAT SHADOW THAT FALLS TO THE GROUND.
THUS THEY DISLIKE HAVIN' THEIR SHADOW STEPPED ON.
IF YA TRY TO STEP ON IT, THE SHADOW ALONE WILL MOVE TO TRY AND AVOID THAT.

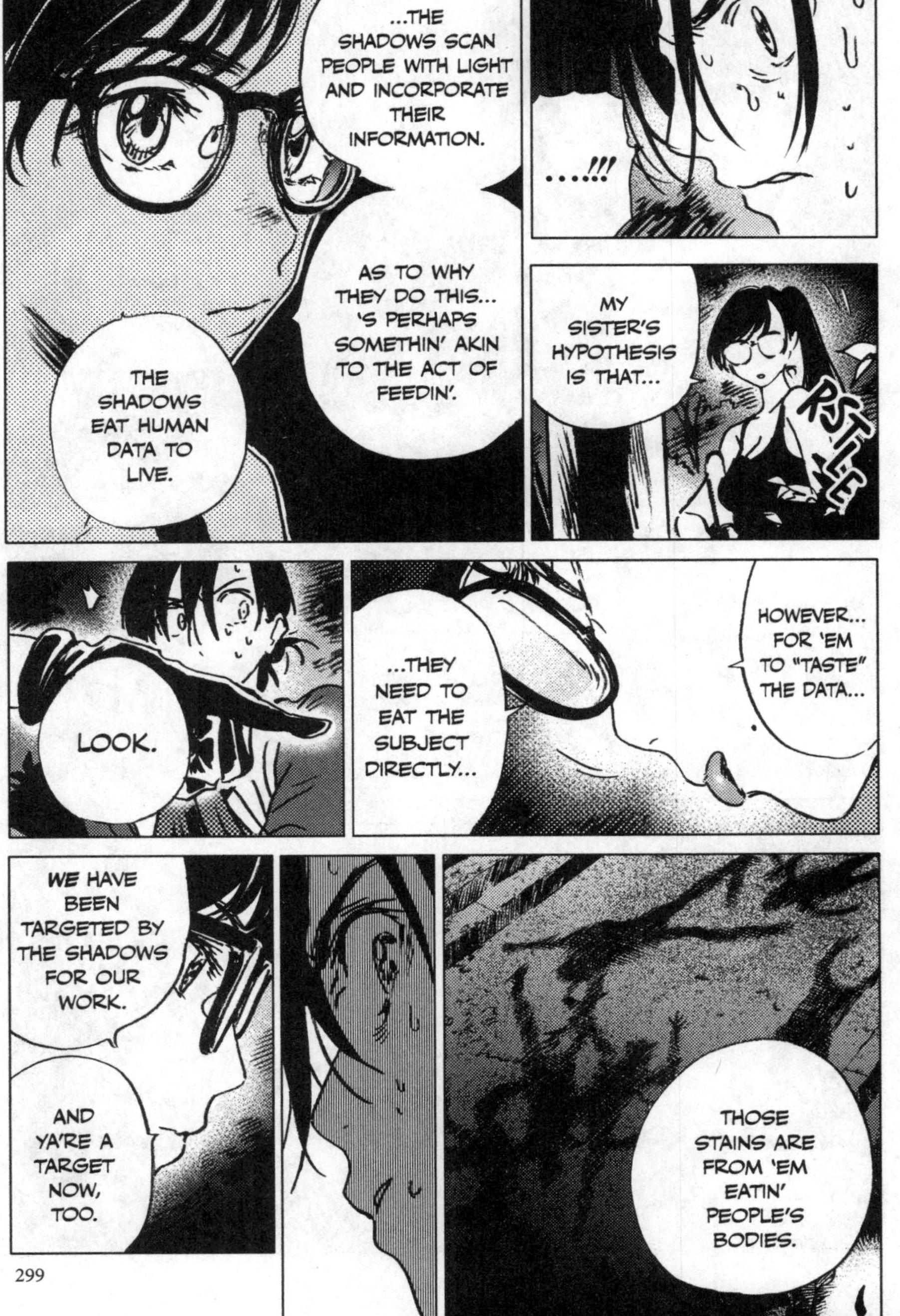
....!!!
MY SISTER'S HYPOTHESIS IS THAT...
RSTLE
...THE SHADOWS SCAN PEOPLE WITH LIGHT AND INCORPORATE THEIR INFORMATION.
AS TO WHY THEY DO THIS... 'S PERHAPS SOMETHIN' AKIN TO THE ACT OF FEEDIN'.
THE SHADOWS EAT HUMAN DATA TO LIVE.
HOWEVER... FOR 'EM TO "TASTE" THE DATA...
...THEY NEED TO EAT THE SUBJECT DIRECTLY...
LOOK.
THOSE STAINS ARE FROM 'EM EATIN' PEOPLE'S BODIES.
WE HAVE BEEN TARGETED BY THE SHADOWS FOR OUR WORK.
AND YA'RE A TARGET NOW, TOO.

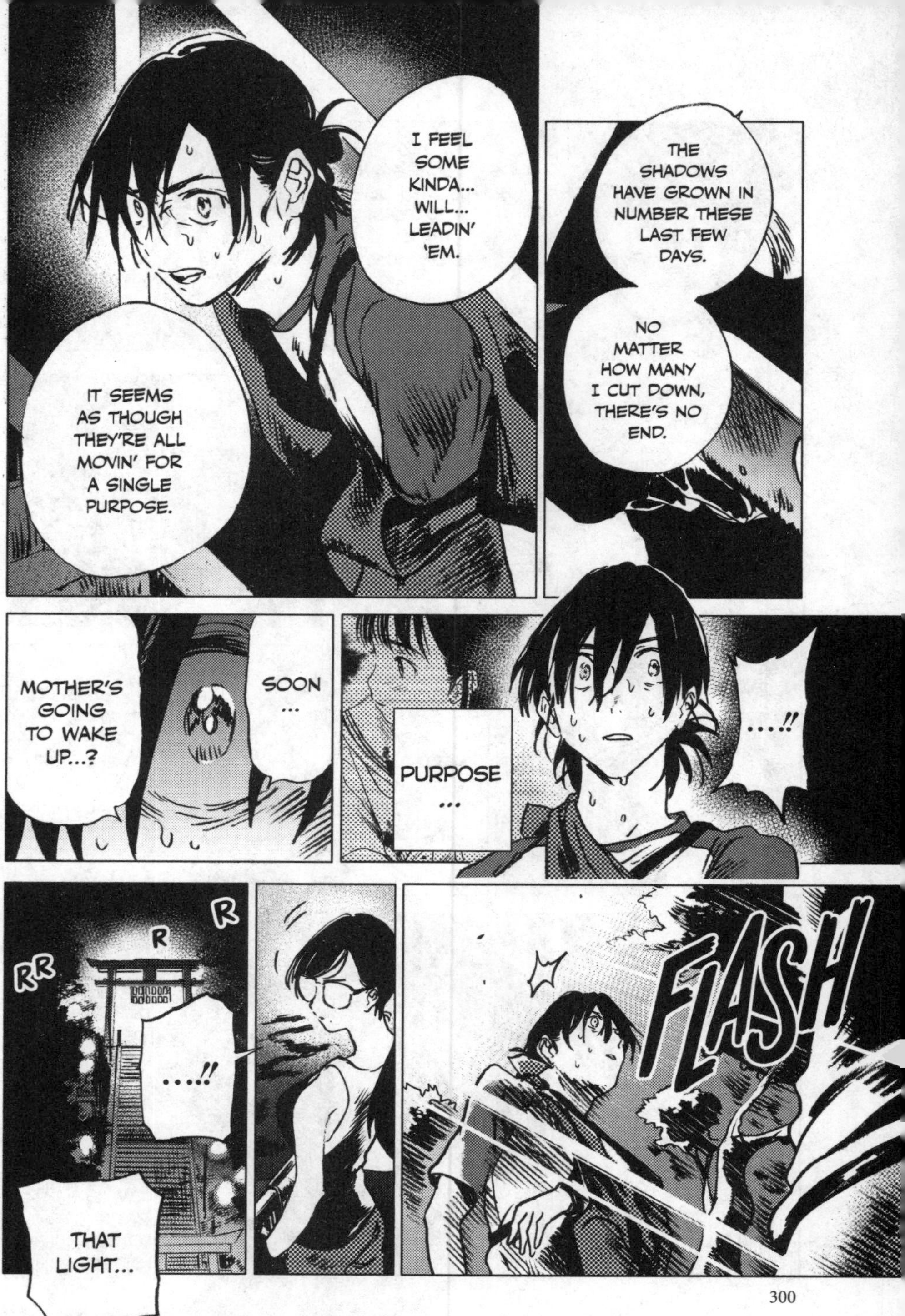
THE SHADOWS HAVE GROWN IN NUMBER THESE LAST FEW DAYS.
NO MATTER HOW MANY I CUT DOWN, THERE'S NO END.
I FEEL SOME KINDA... WILL... LEADIN' 'EM.
IT SEEMS AS THOUGH THEY'RE ALL MOVIN' FOR A SINGLE PURPOSE.
....!!
PURPOSE ...
SOON ...
MOTHER'S GOING TO WAKE UP...?
FLASH
....!!
R
R
RR
THAT LIGHT...

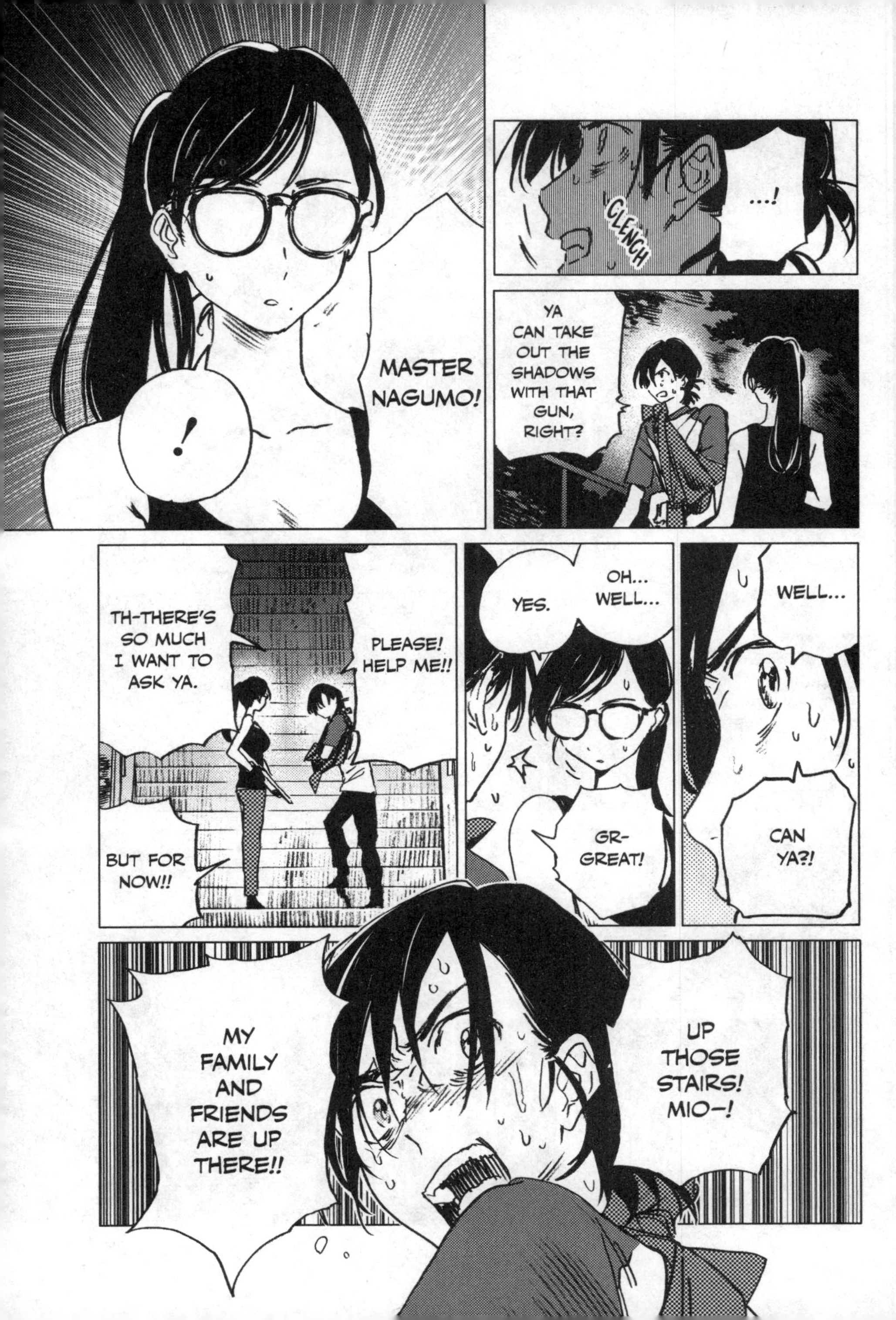
...!
CLENCH
YA CAN TAKE OUT THE SHADOWS WITH THAT GUN, RIGHT?
MASTER NAGUMO!
!
WELL...
CAN YA?!
OH... WELL...
YES.
GR-GREAT!
PLEASE! HELP ME!!
TH-THERE'S SO MUCH I WANT TO ASK YA.
BUT FOR NOW!!
UP THOSE STAIRS! MIO-!
MY FAMILY AND FRIENDS ARE UP THERE!!

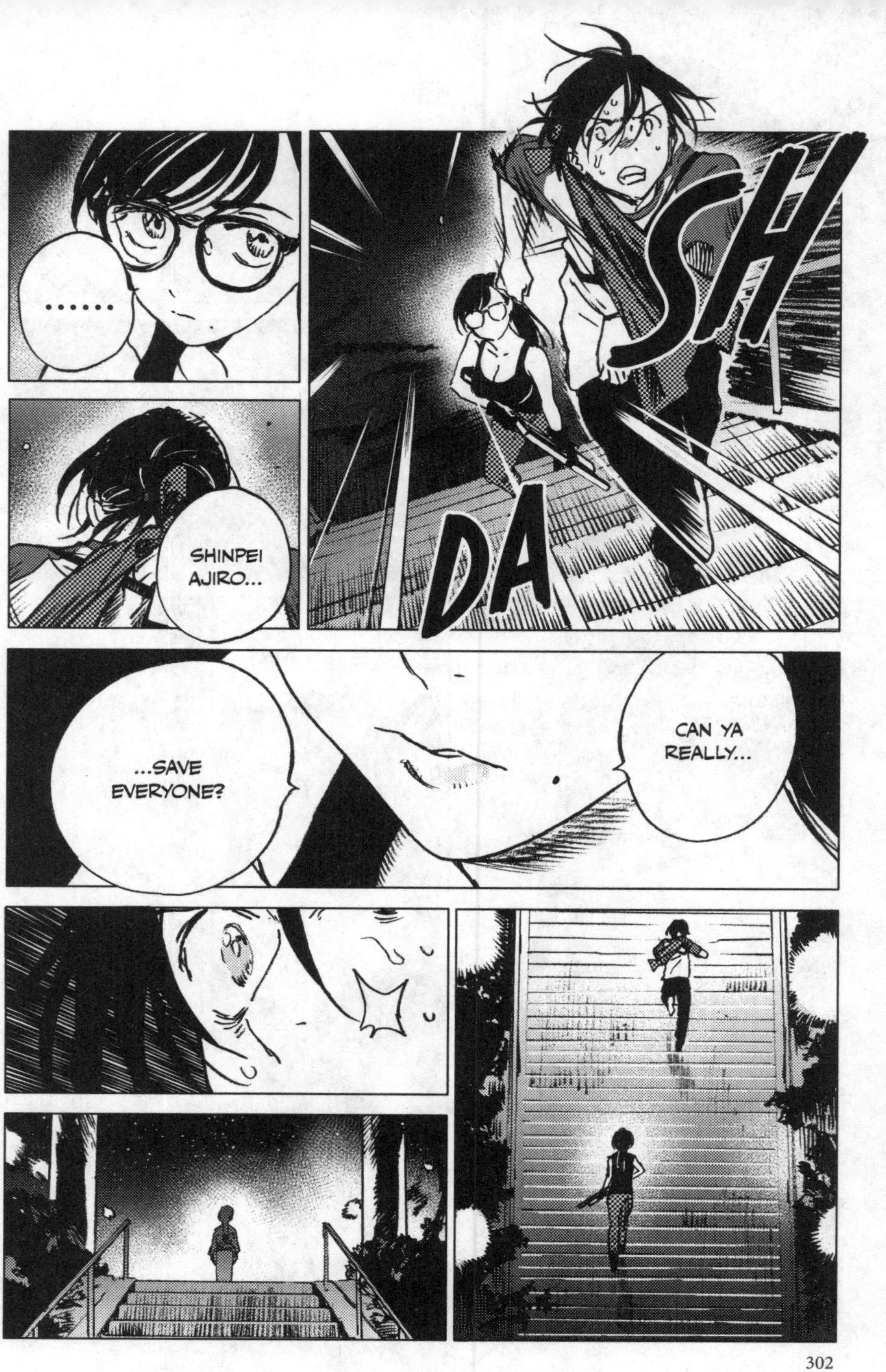
SH
DA
......
SHINPEI AJIRO...
CAN YA REALLY...
...SAVE EVERYONE?

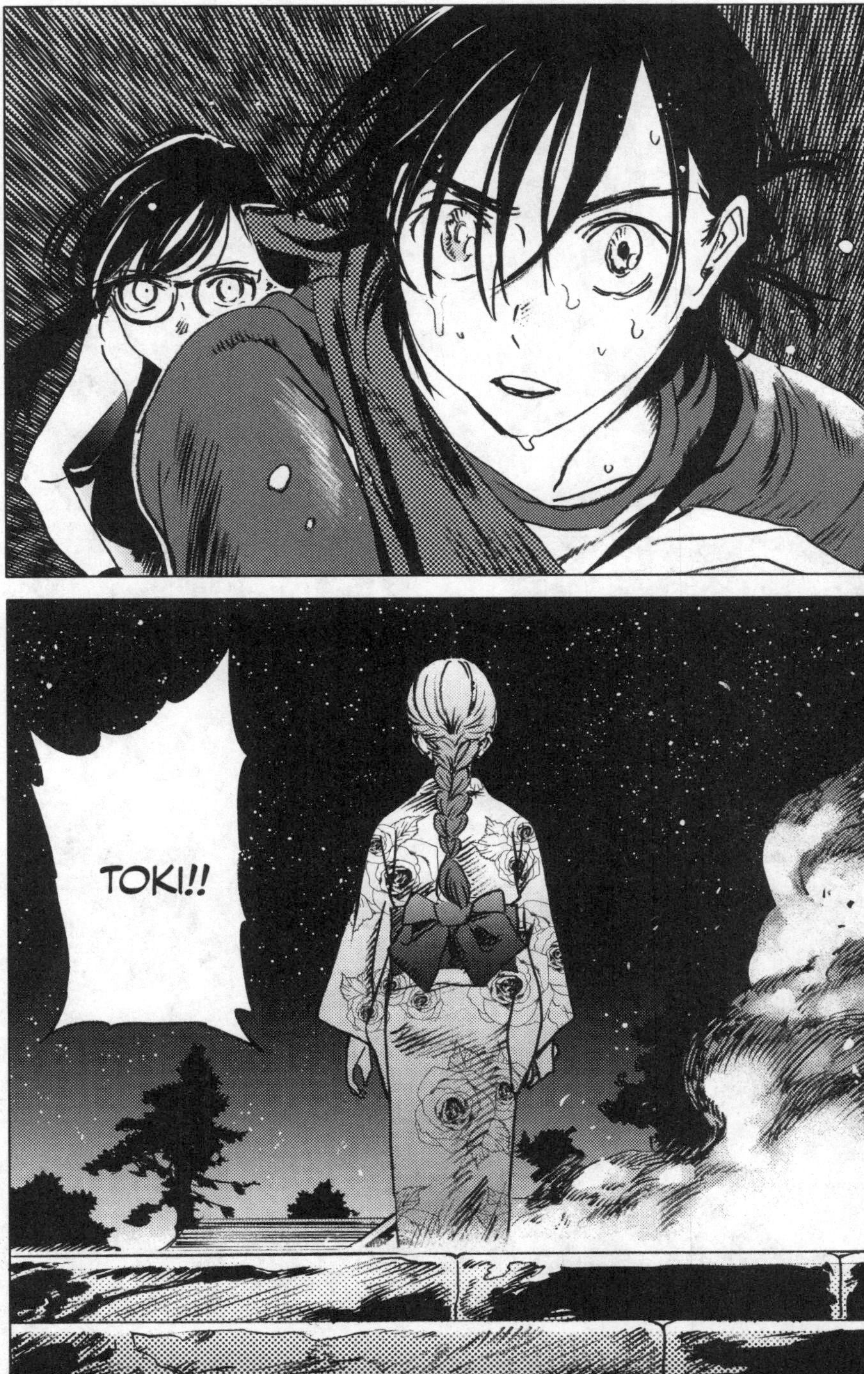
TOKI!!

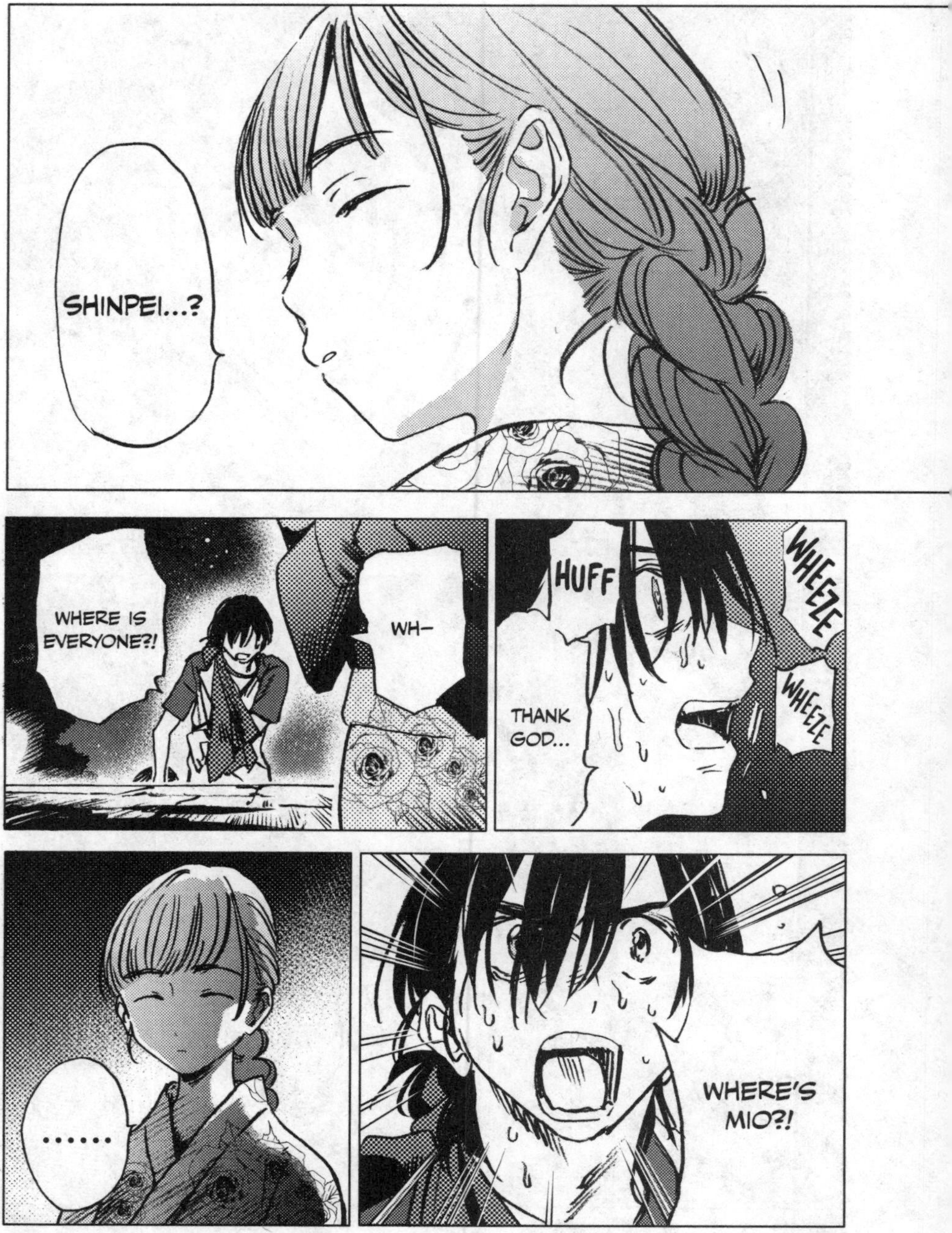
SHINPEI...?
WHEEZE
HUFF
WHEEZE
THANK GOD...
WH-
WHERE IS EVERYONE?!
WHERE'S MIO?!
......

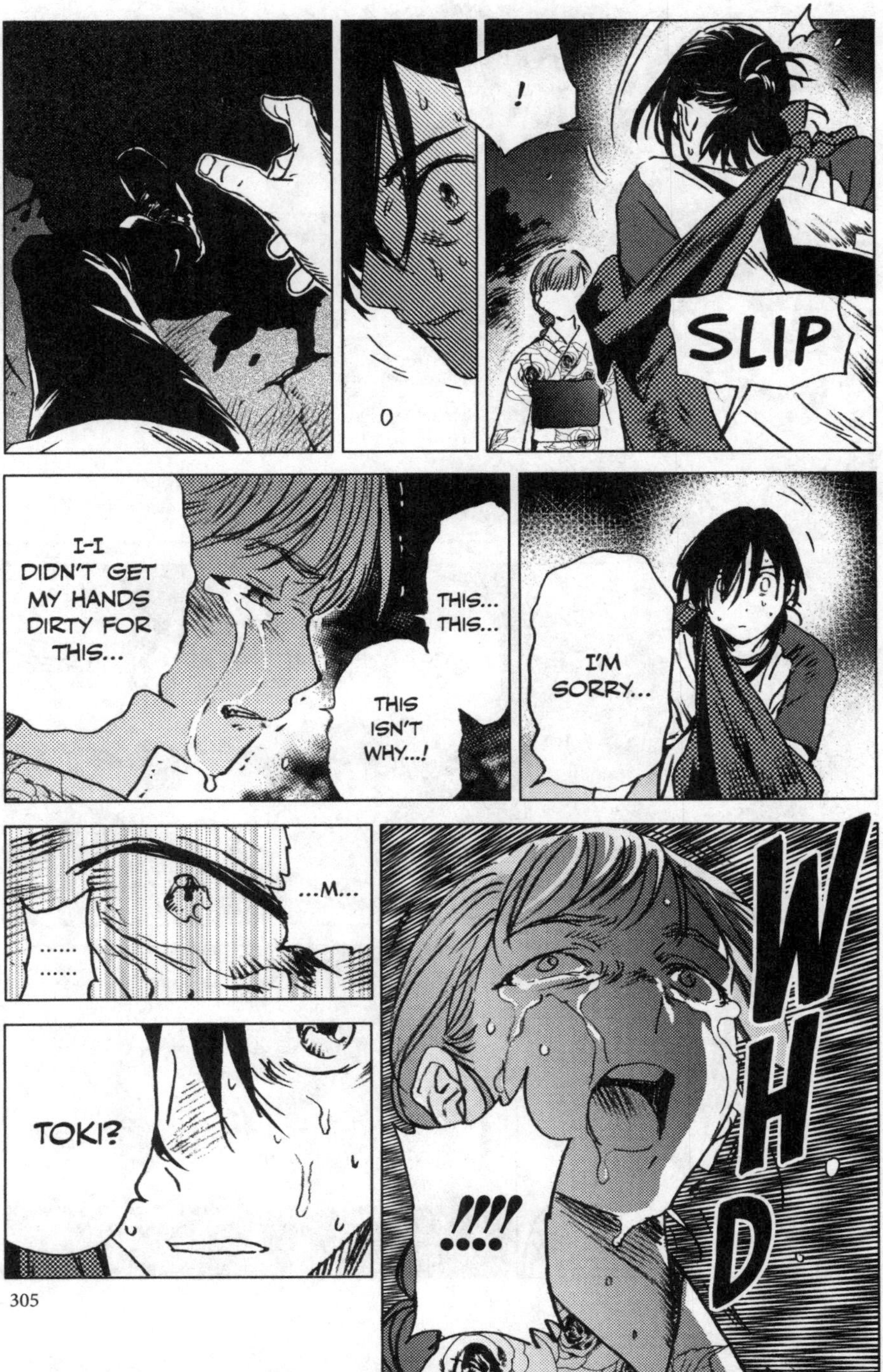
!
SLIP
0
I'M SORRY...
THIS... THIS...
THIS ISN'T WHY...!
I-I DIDN'T GET MY HANDS DIRTY FOR THIS...
...M...
......
......
TOKI?
WH.D
!!!!

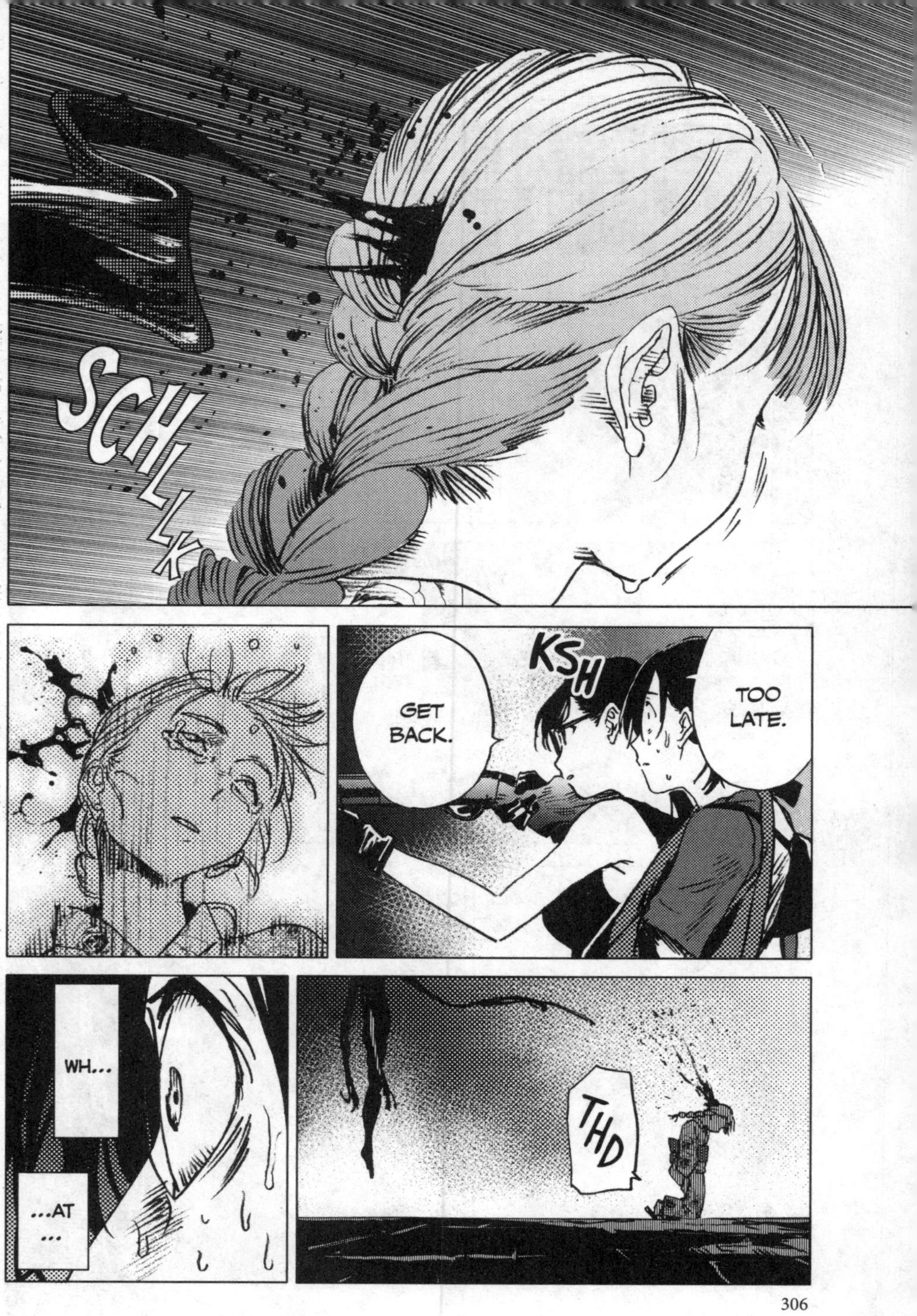
SCHLLK
TOO LATE.
KSH
GET BACK.
THD
WH...
...AT
...

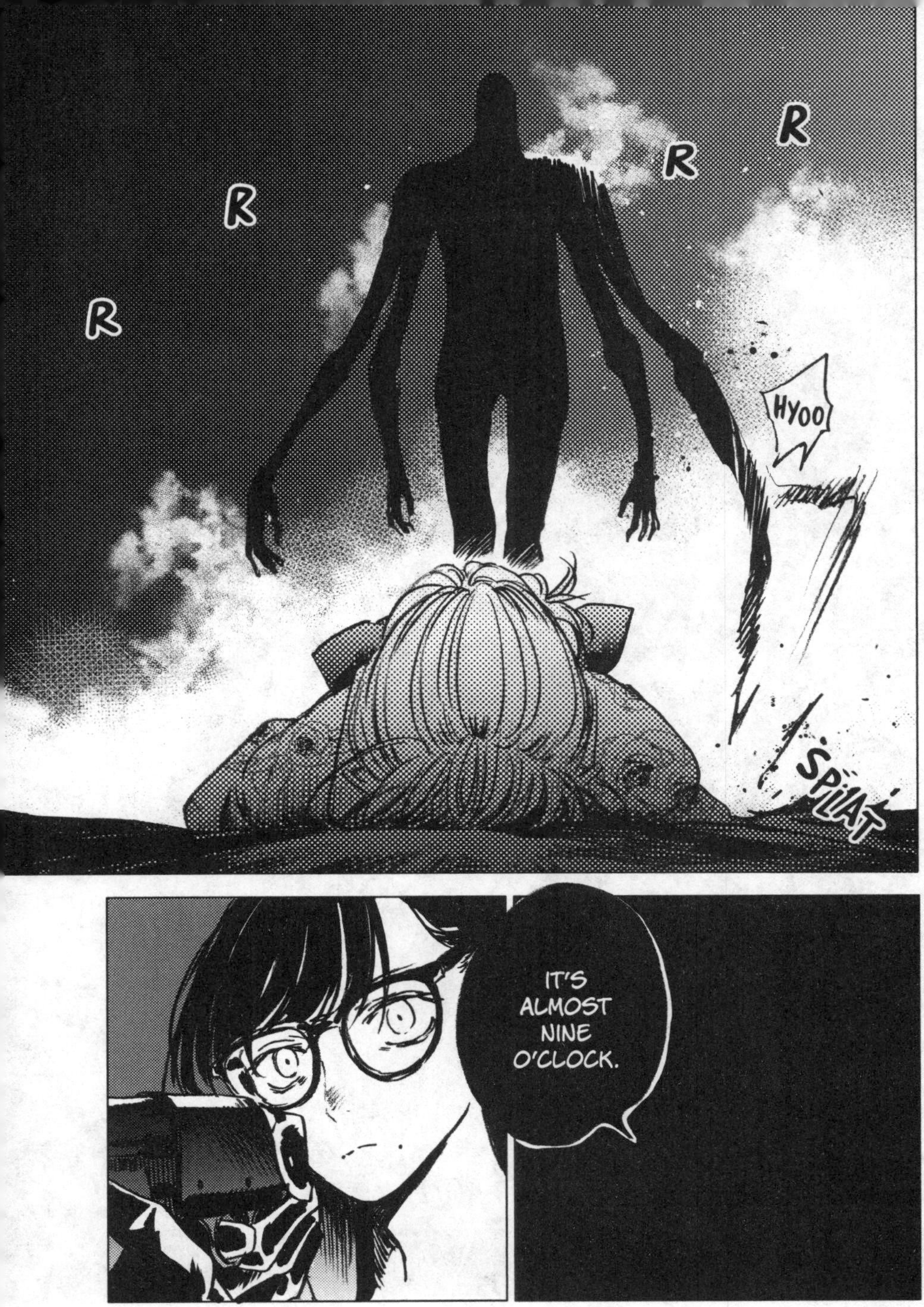
R
R
R
R
HYOO
SPLAT
IT'S ALMOST NINE O'CLOCK.

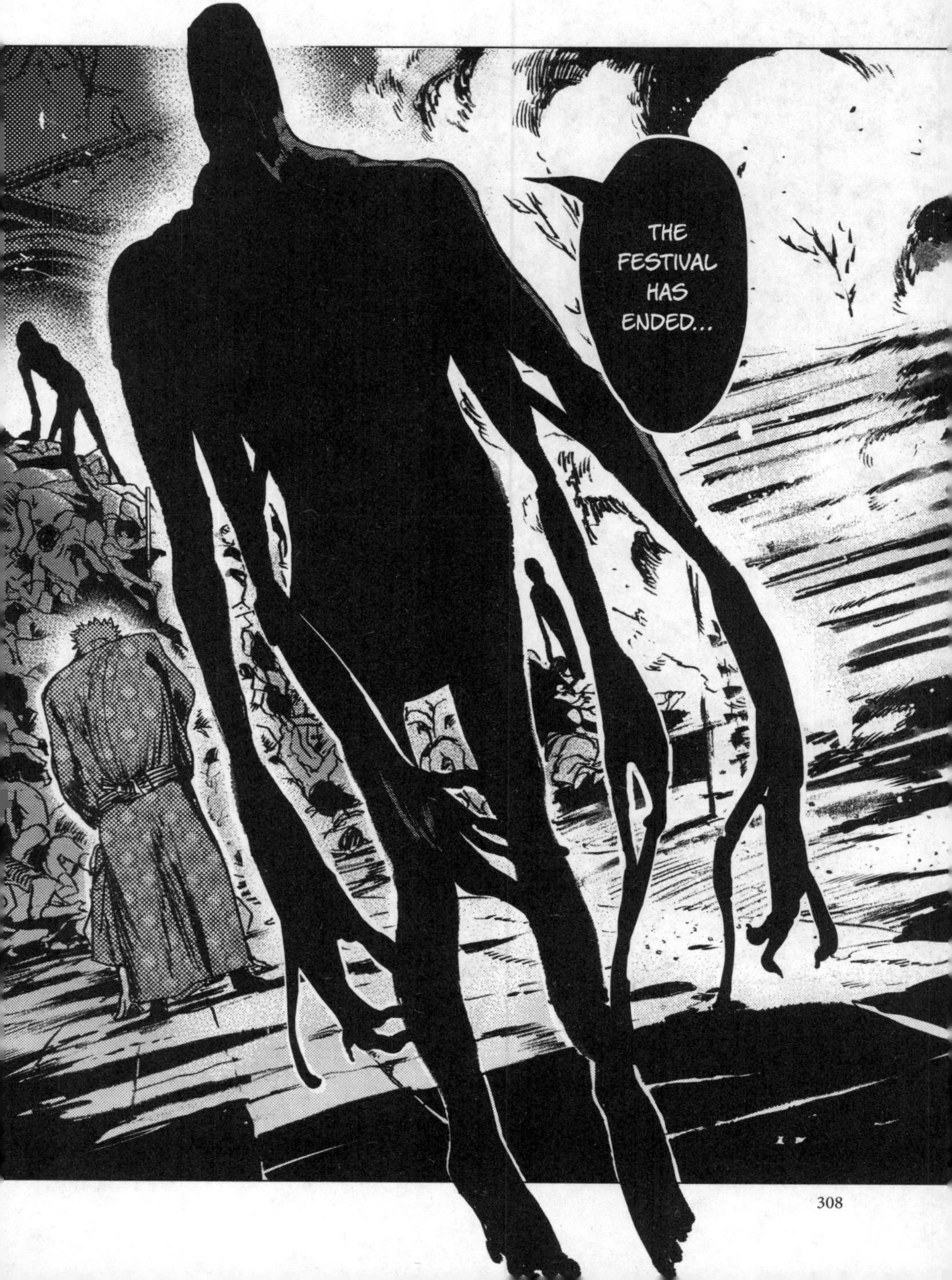
THE FESTIVAL HAS ENDED...

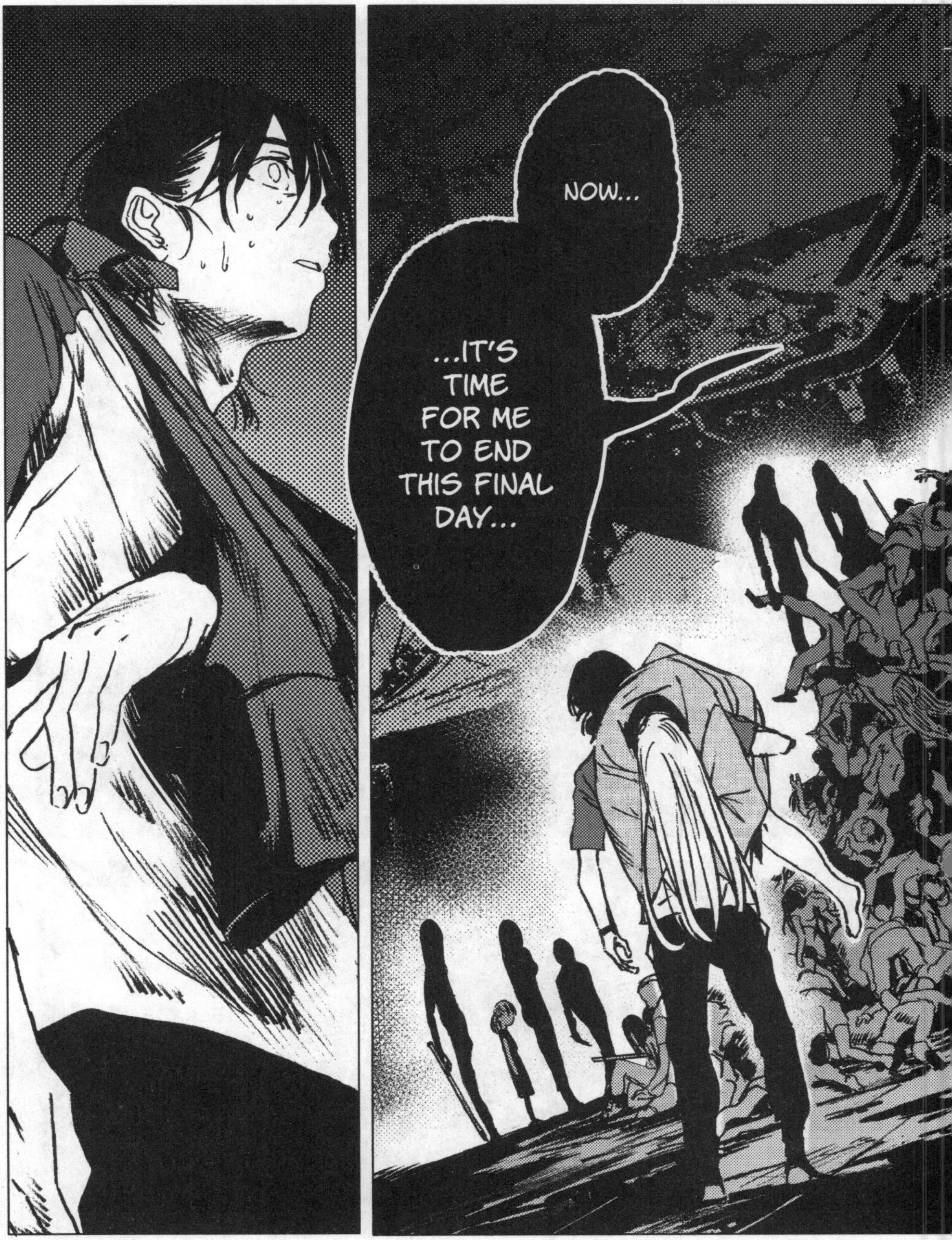
NOW...
...IT'S TIME FOR ME TO END THIS FINAL DAY...

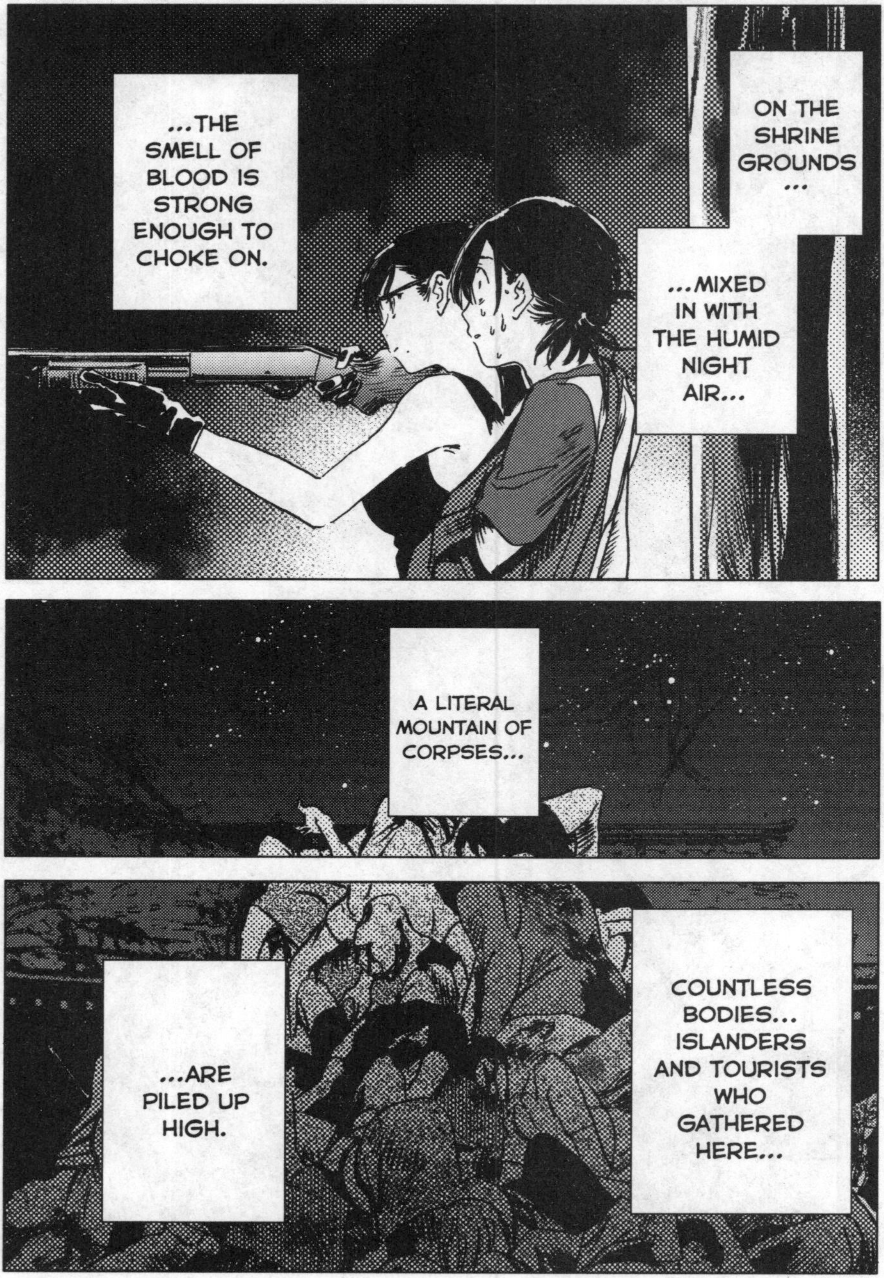
ON THE SHRINE GROUNDS...
...MIXED IN WITH THE HUMID NIGHT AIR...
...THE SMELL OF BLOOD IS STRONG ENOUGH TO CHOKE ON.
A LITERAL MOUNTAIN OF CORPSES...
COUNTLESS BODIES... ISLANDERS AND TOURISTS WHO GATHERED HERE...
...ARE PILED UP HIGH.

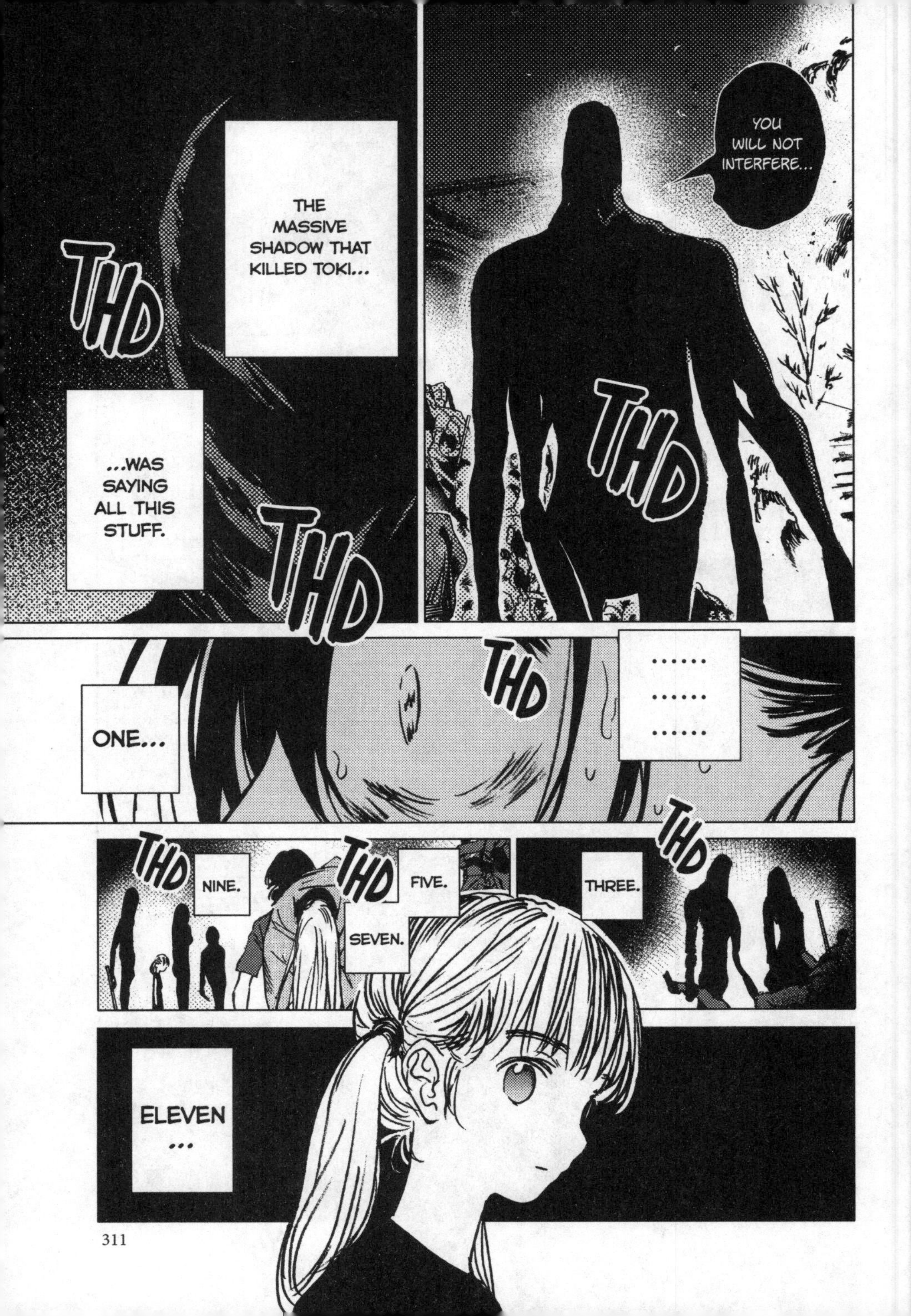
YOU WILL NOT INTERFERE...
THD
THE MASSIVE SHADOW THAT KILLED TOKI...
THD
...WAS SAYING ALL THIS STUFF.
THD
......
......
......
THD
ONE...
THD
THREE.
FIVE.
THD
SEVEN.
NINE.
THD
ELEVEN
...

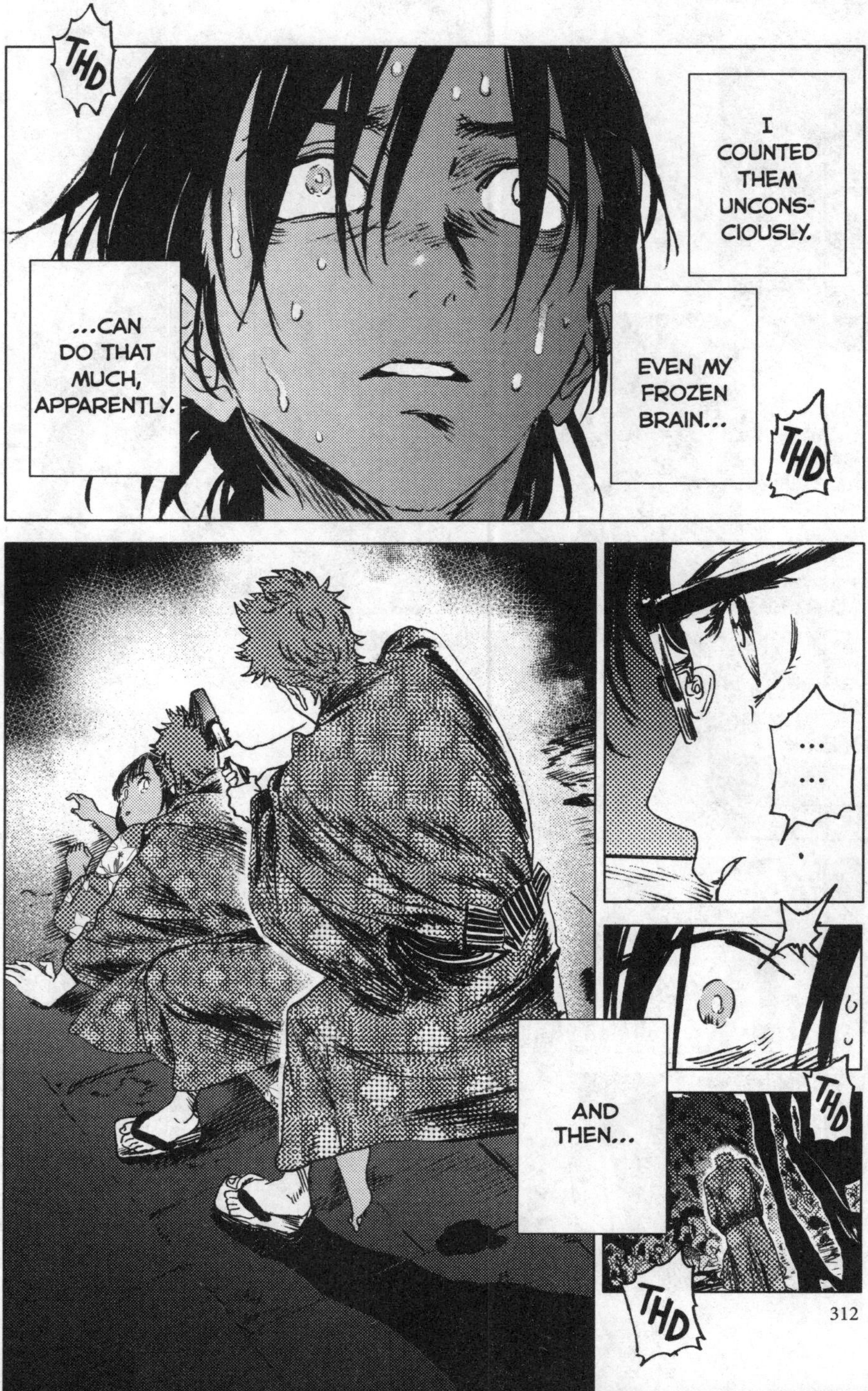
THD
I COUNTED THEM UNCONSCIOUSLY.
EVEN MY FROZEN BRAIN...
...CAN DO THAT MUCH, APPARENTLY.
THD
......
AND THEN...
THD
THD

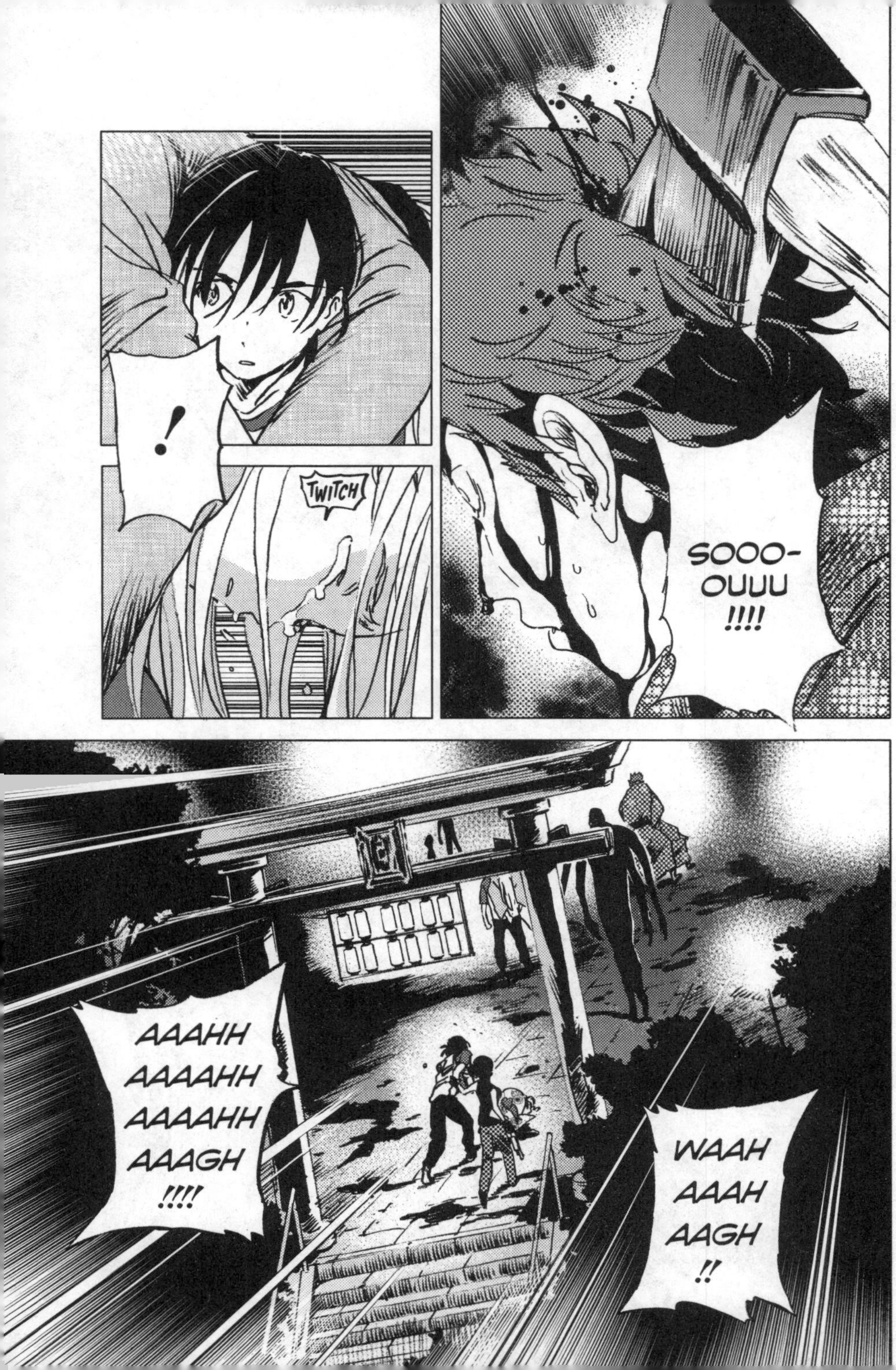
SOOO-OUUU!!!!
!
TWITCH
WAAH AAAH AAGH!!
AAAHH AAAAHH AAAAHH AAAGH!!!!

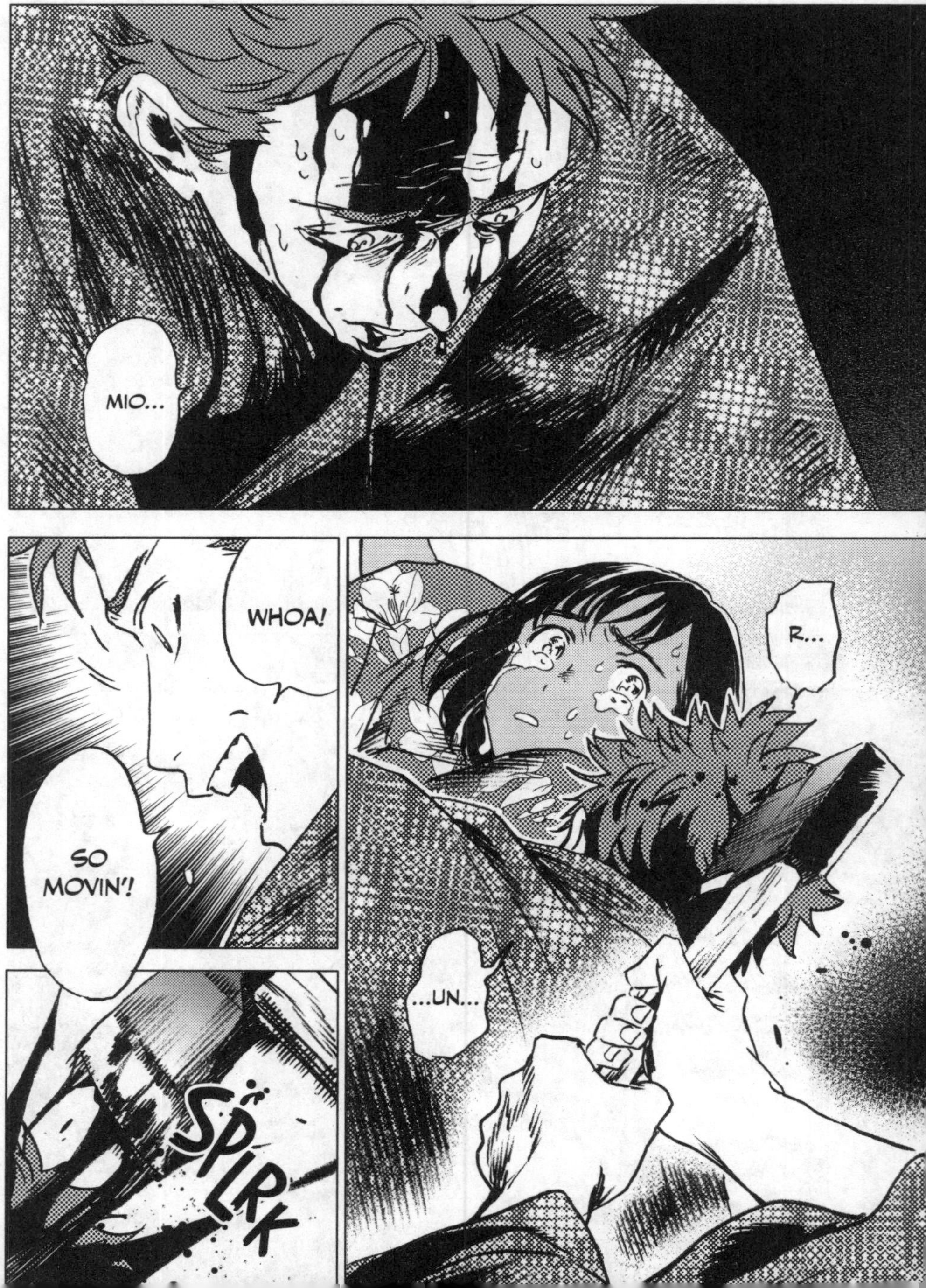
MIO...
R...
...UN...
WHOA!
SO MOVIN'!
SPLRK

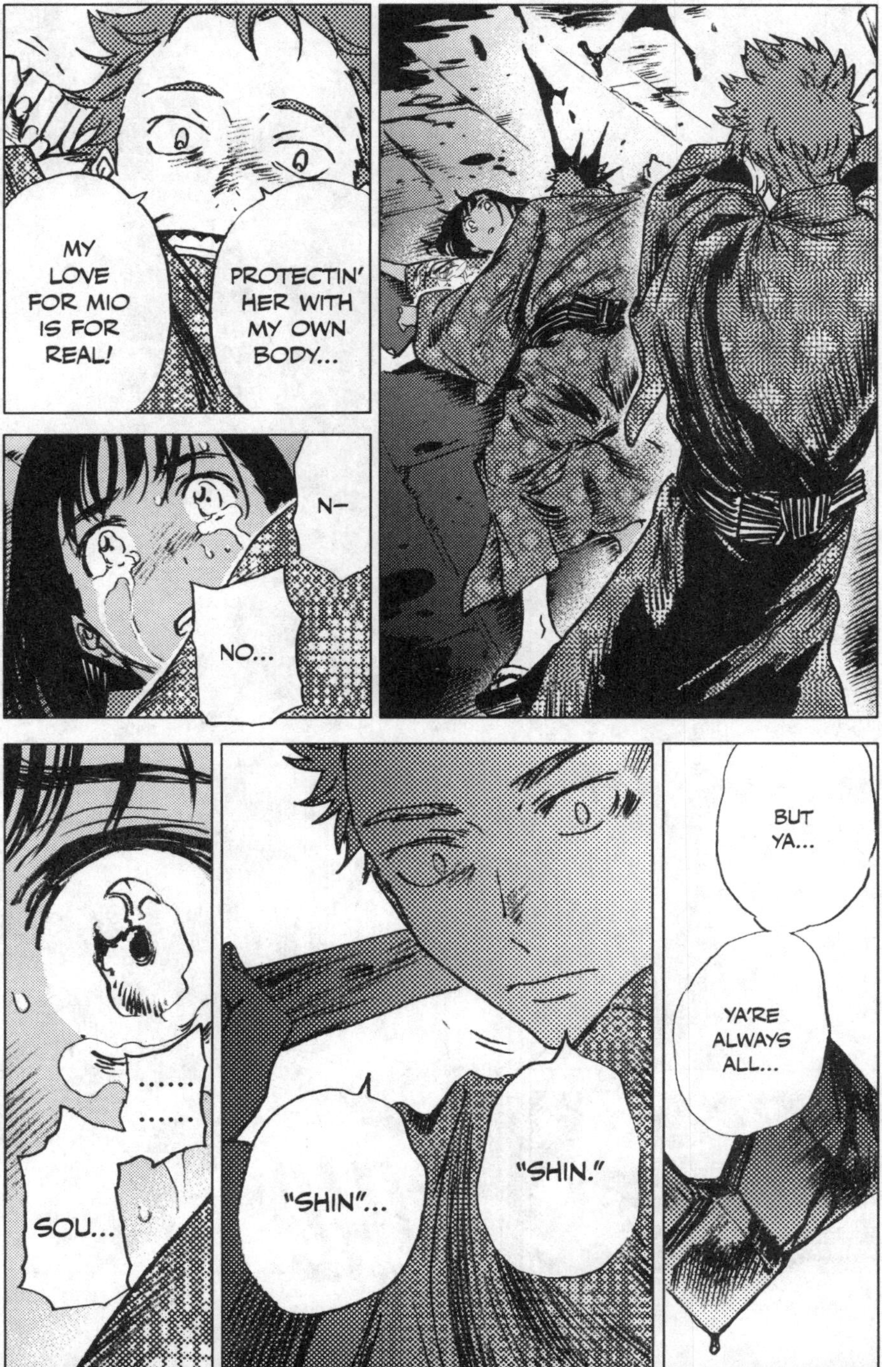
PROTECTIN' HER WITH MY OWN BODY...
MY LOVE FOR MIO IS FOR REAL!
N—
NO...
BUT YA...
YA'RE ALWAYS ALL...
"SHIN."
"SHIN"...
......
......
SOU...

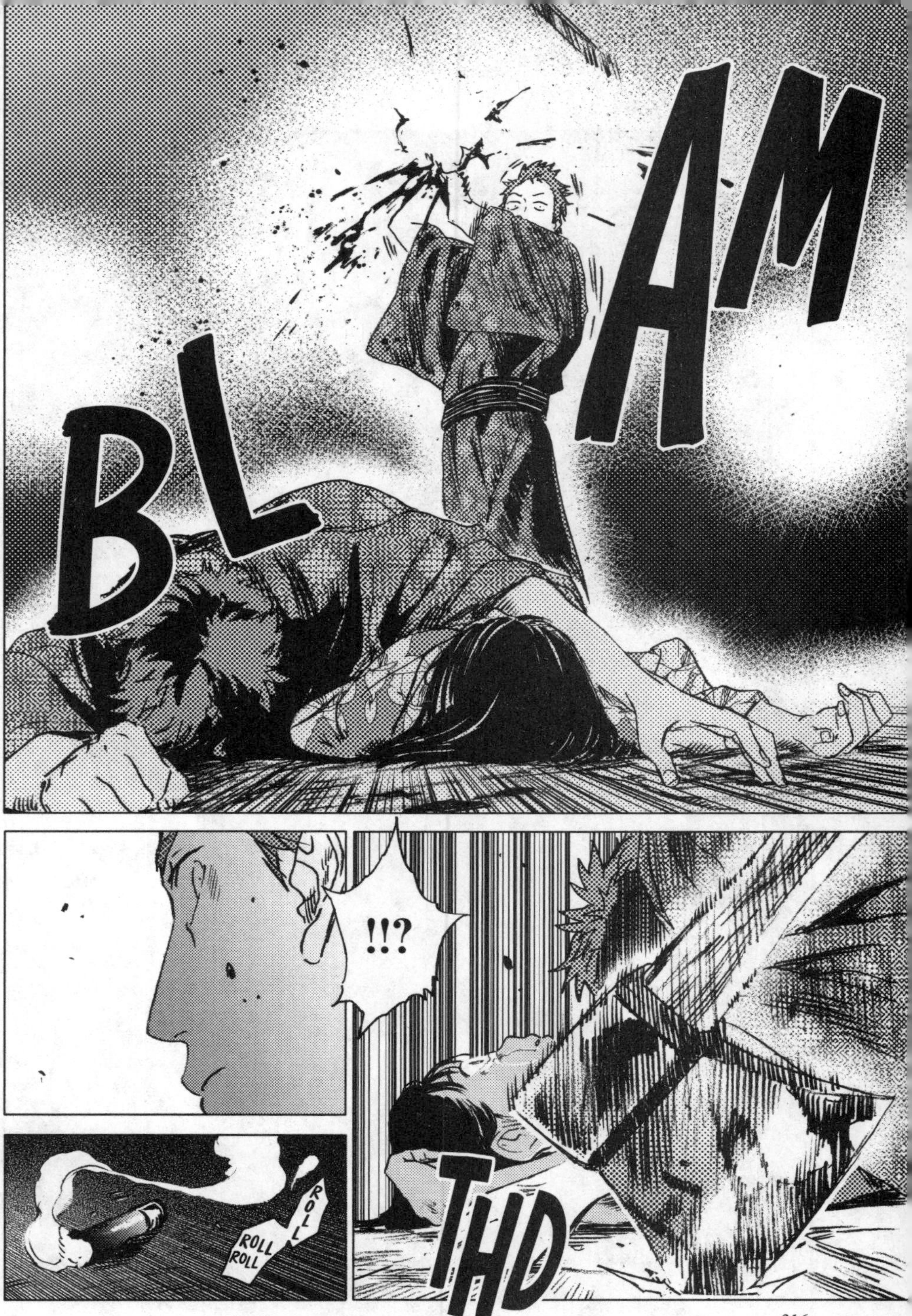
BLAM
!!?
THD
ROLL
ROLL
ROLL

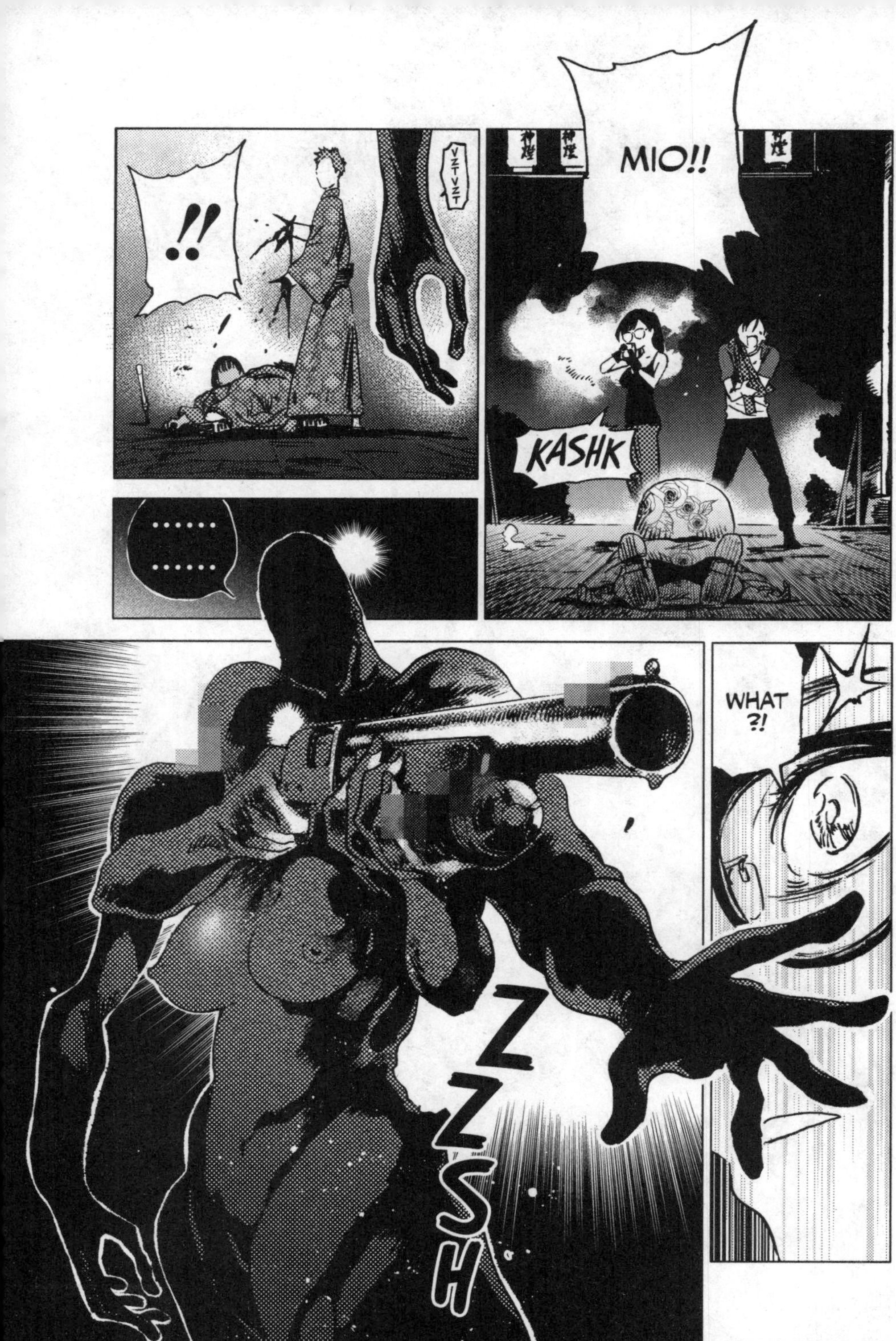
MIO!!
KASHK
!!
VZT VZT
!
......
......
WHAT ?!
ZZZSH

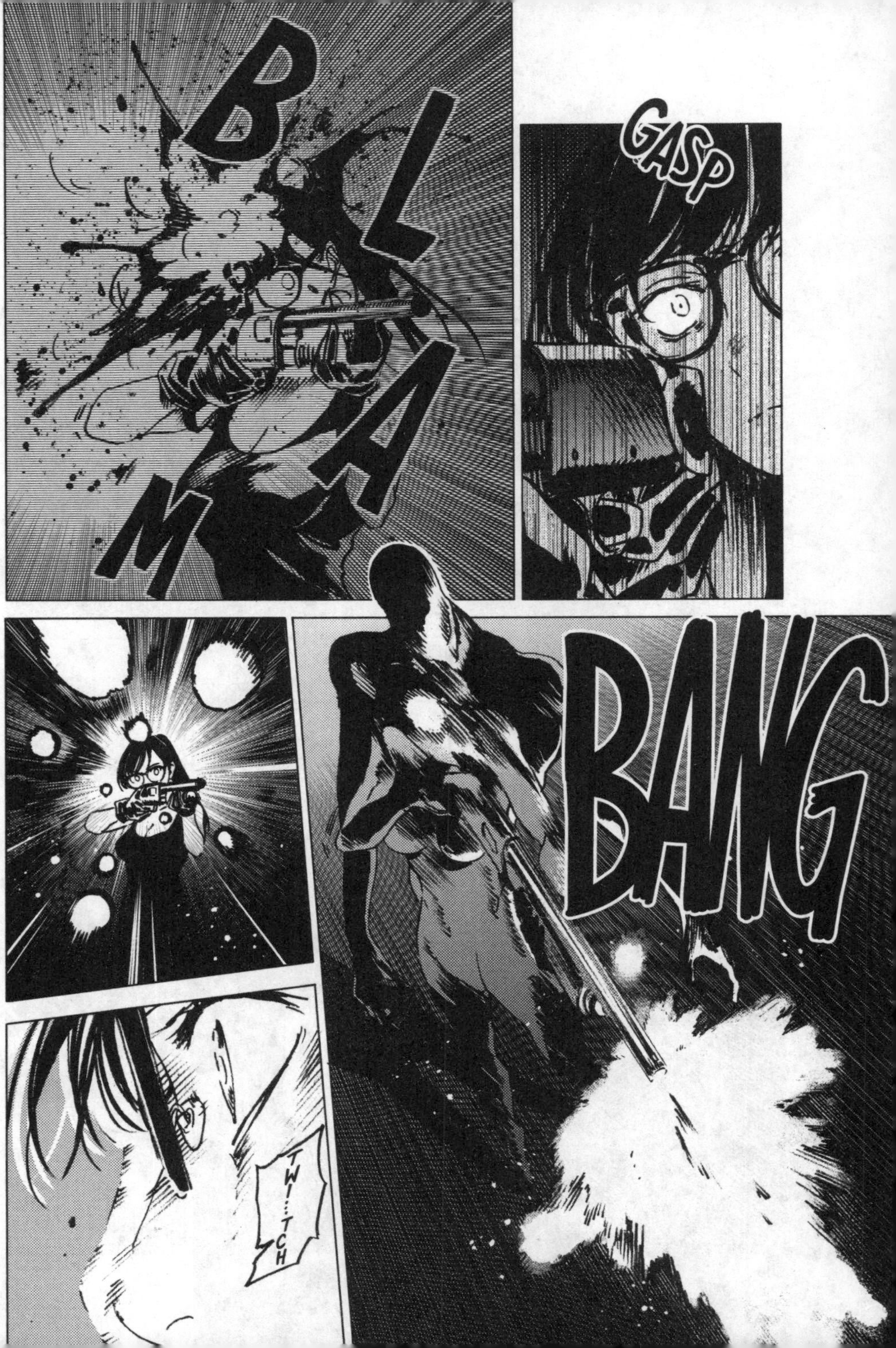
GASP
BLAM
BANG
TWI...TCH

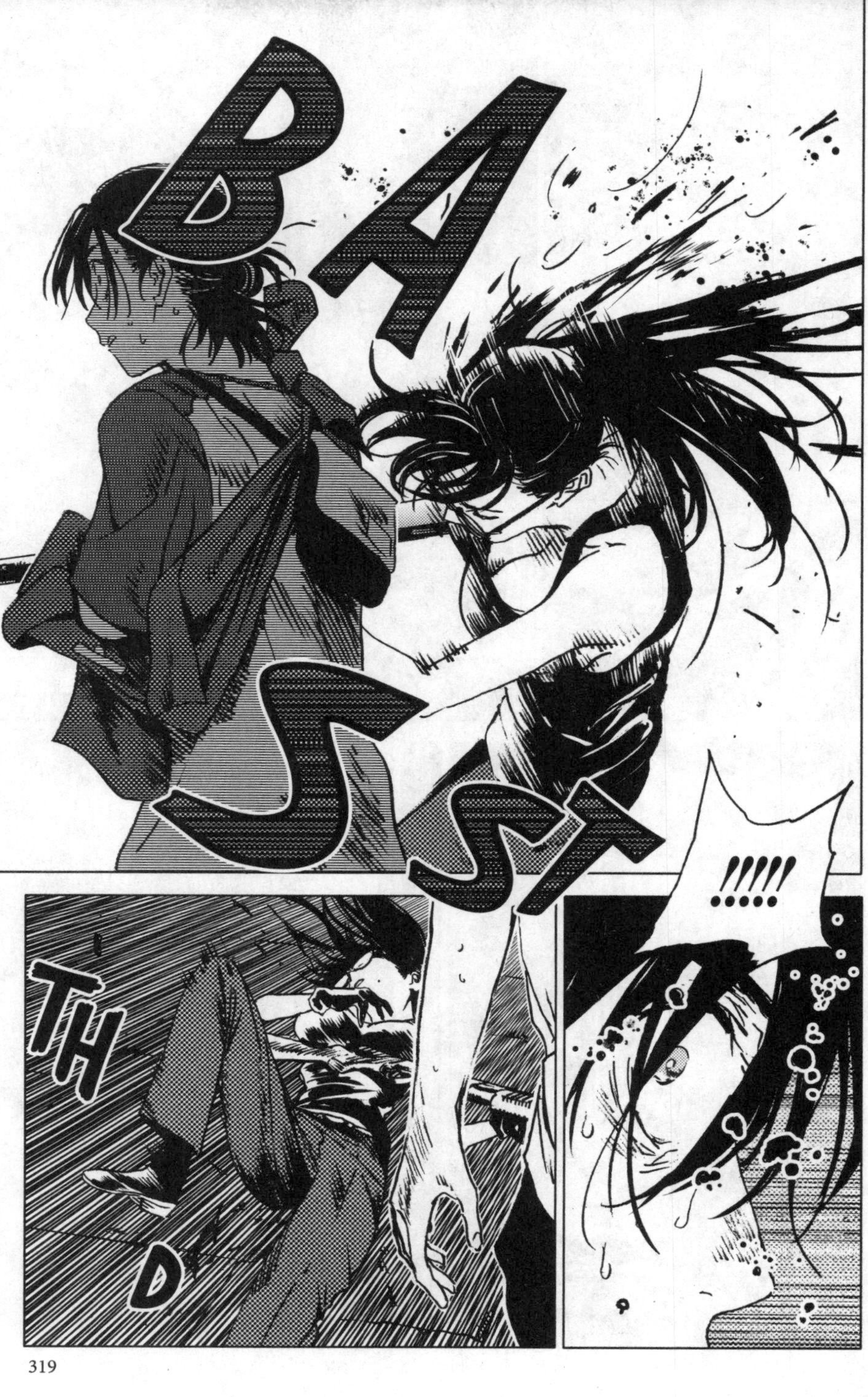
BASSST
!!!!!
TH
D

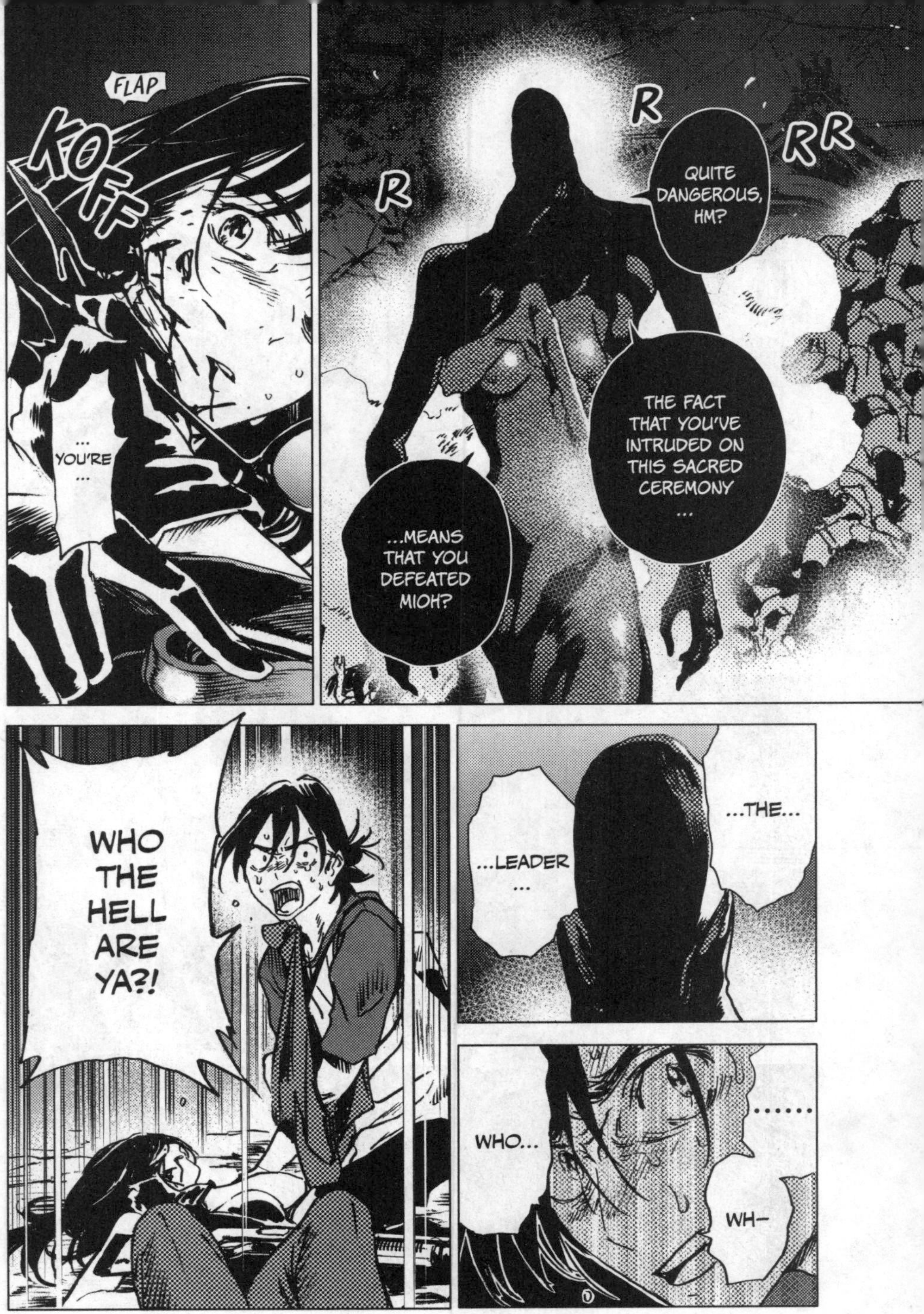
R
RR
QUITE DANGEROUS, HM?
R
THE FACT THAT YOU'VE INTRUDED ON THIS SACRED CEREMONY ...
...MEANS THAT YOU DEFEATED MIOH?
FLAP
KOFF
... YOU'RE ...
...THE...
...LEADER ...
......
WHO...
WH–
WHO THE HELL ARE YA?!

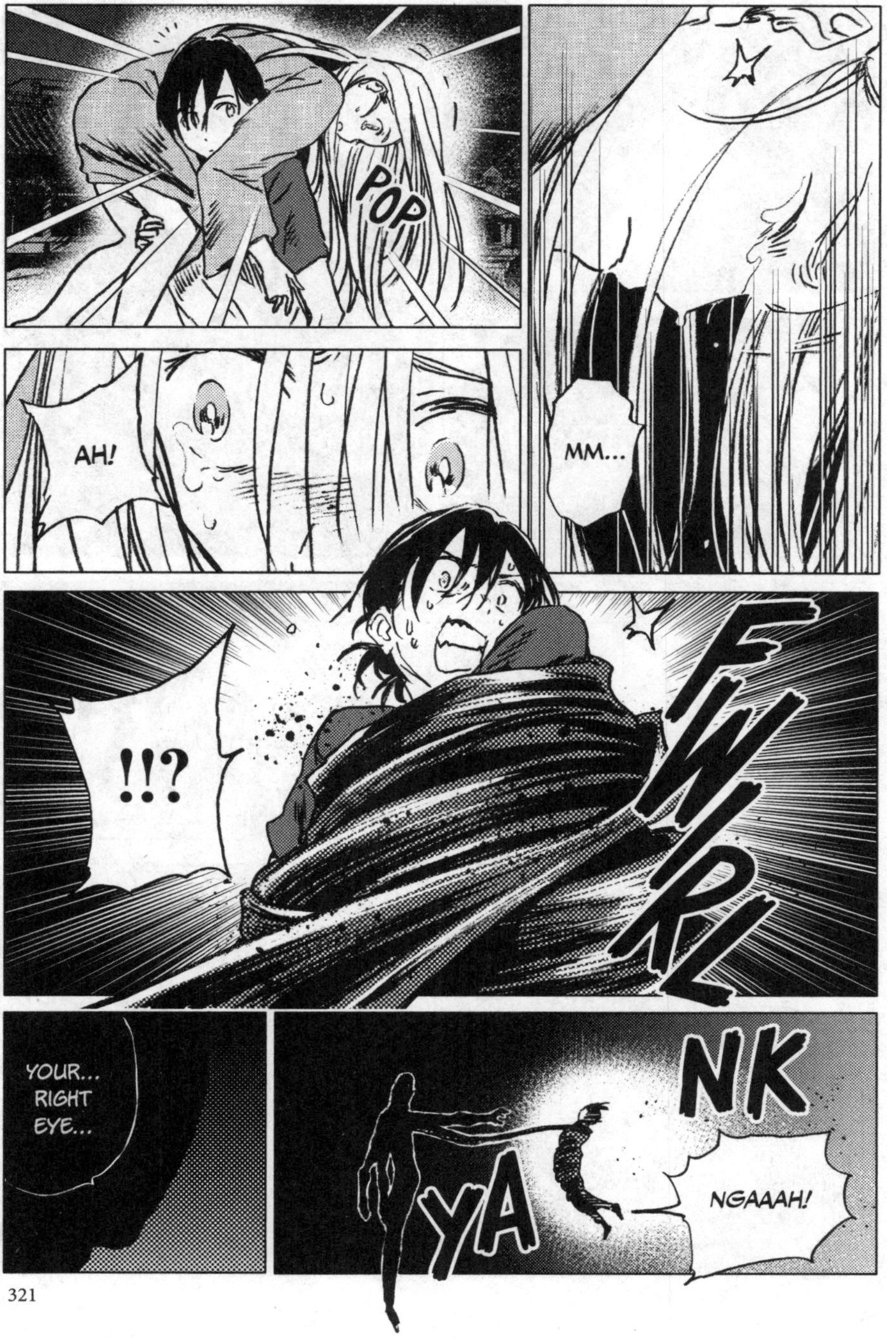
MM...
POP
AH!
!!?
FWIRL
YA
NK
NGAAAH!
YOUR... RIGHT EYE...

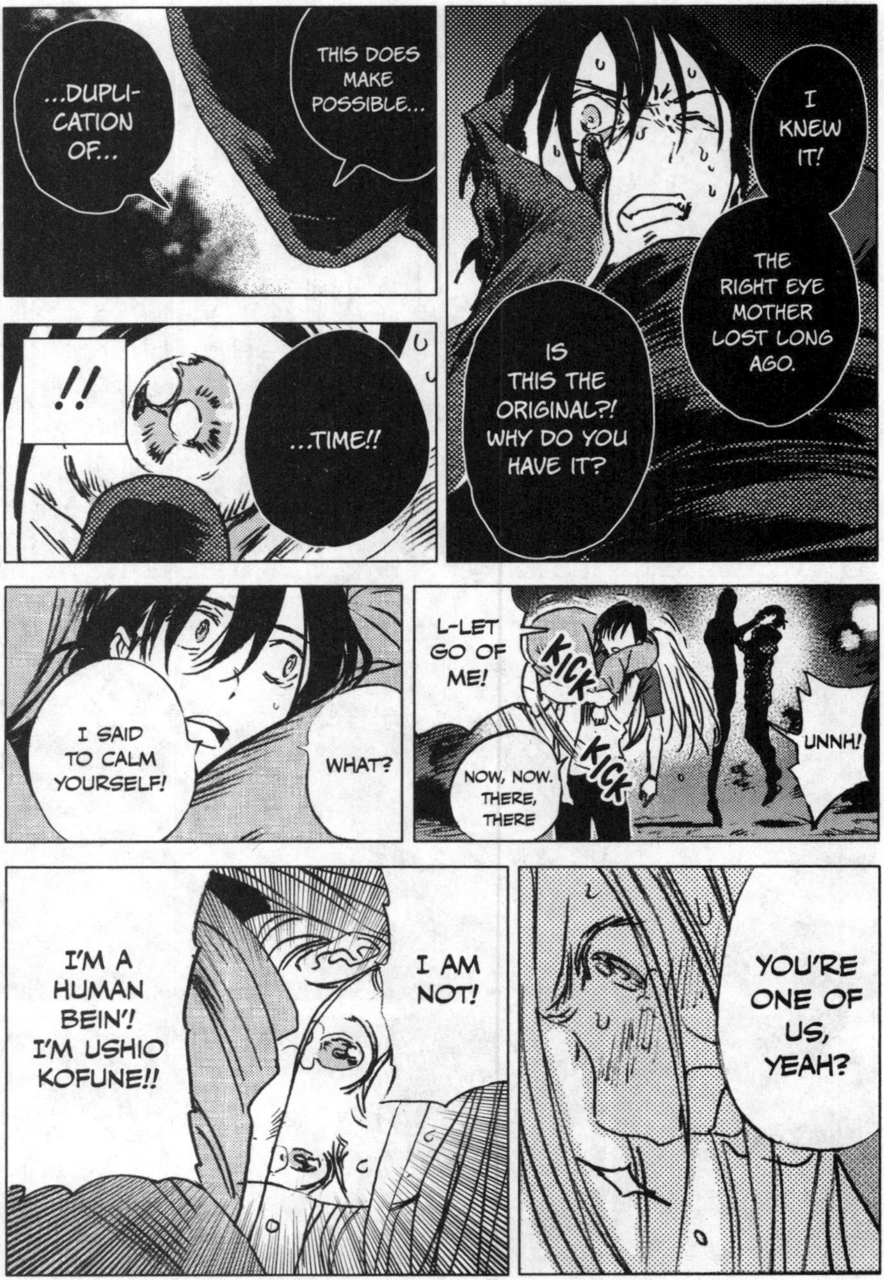
I KNEW IT!
THE RIGHT EYE MOTHER LOST LONG AGO.
IS THIS THE ORIGINAL?! WHY DO YOU HAVE IT?
THIS DOES MAKE POSSIBLE...
...DUPLICATION OF...
...TIME!!
!!
L-LET GO OF ME!
KICK
KICK
UNNH!
NOW, NOW. THERE, THERE
WHAT?
I SAID TO CALM YOURSELF!
YOU'RE ONE OF US, YEAH?
I AM NOT!
I'M A HUMAN BEIN'! I'M USHIO KOFUNE!!

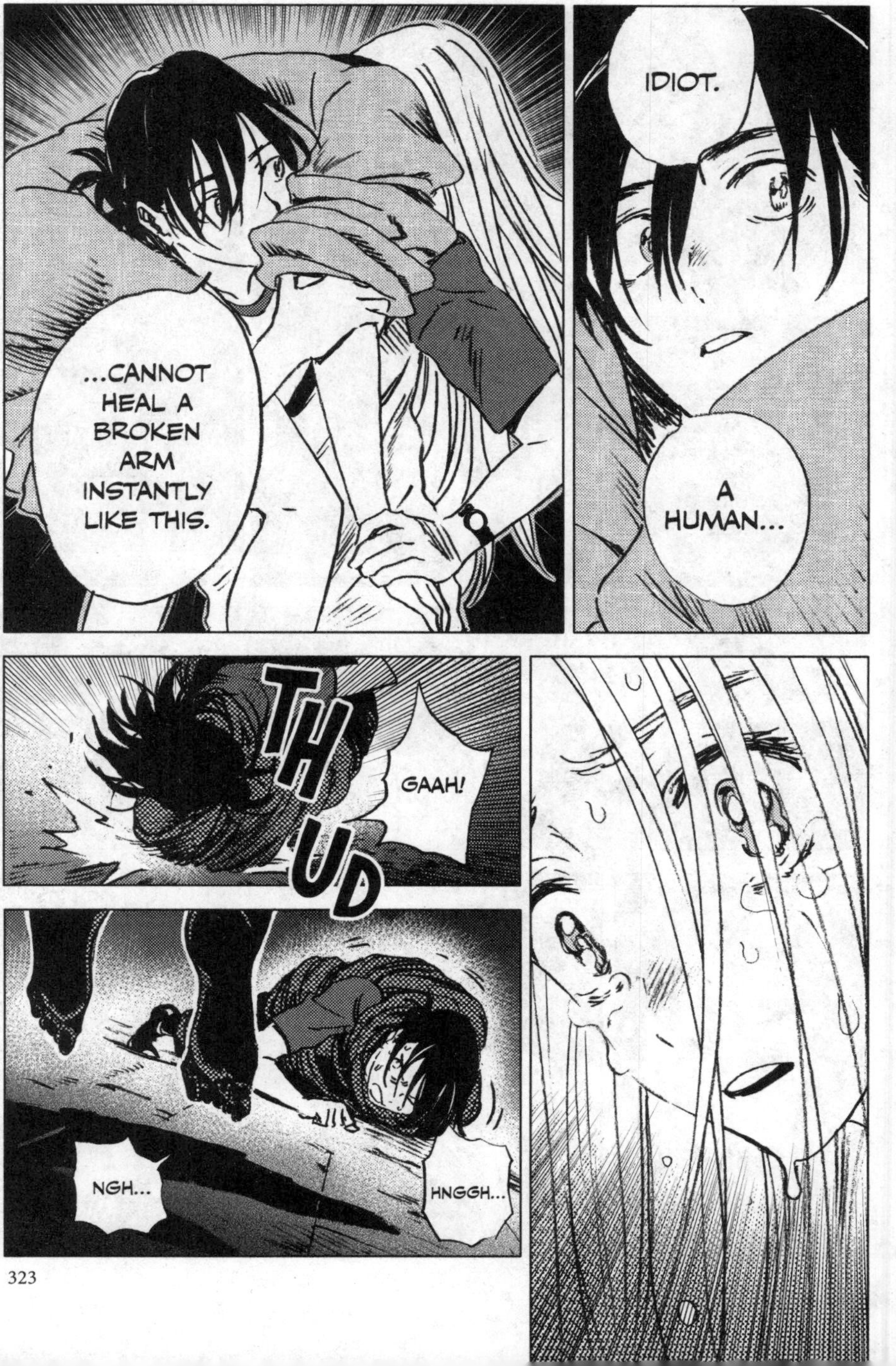
IDIOT.
A HUMAN...
...CANNOT HEAL A BROKEN ARM INSTANTLY LIKE THIS.
THUD
GAAH!
HNGGH...
NGH...

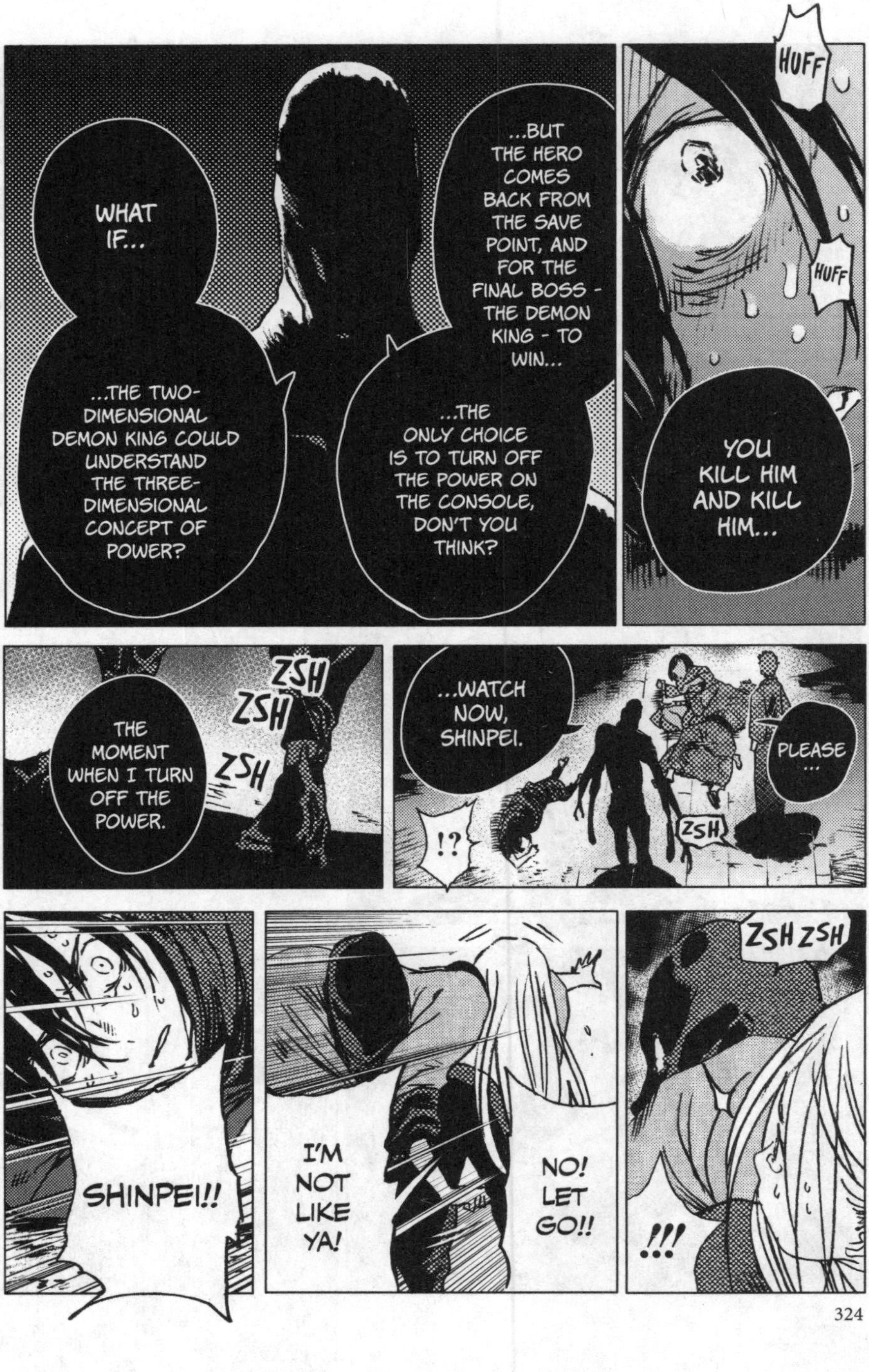
HUFF
HUFF
YOU KILL HIM AND KILL HIM...
WHAT IF...
...THE TWO-DIMENSIONAL DEMON KING COULD UNDERSTAND THE THREE-DIMENSIONAL CONCEPT OF POWER?
...BUT THE HERO COMES BACK FROM THE SAVE POINT, AND FOR THE FINAL BOSS - THE DEMON KING - TO WIN...
...THE ONLY CHOICE IS TO TURN OFF THE POWER ON THE CONSOLE, DON'T YOU THINK?
PLEASE ...
...WATCH NOW, SHINPEI.
ZSH
!?
ZSH
ZSH
ZSH
THE MOMENT WHEN I TURN OFF THE POWER.
ZSH ZSH
!!!
NO! LET GO!!
I'M NOT LIKE YA!
SHINPEI!!

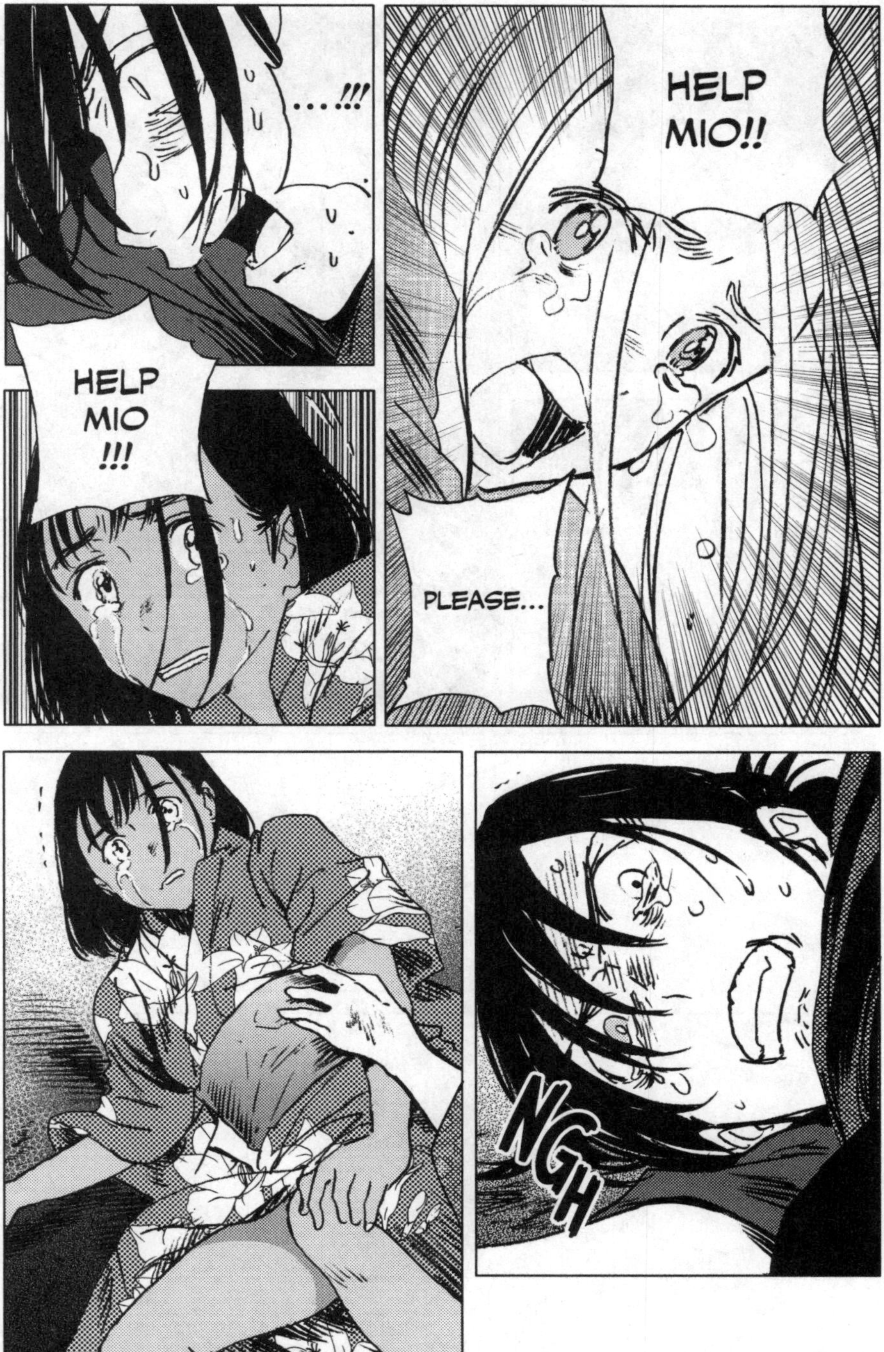

HELP MIO!!
PLEASE...
...!!!
HELP MIO !!!
NGH

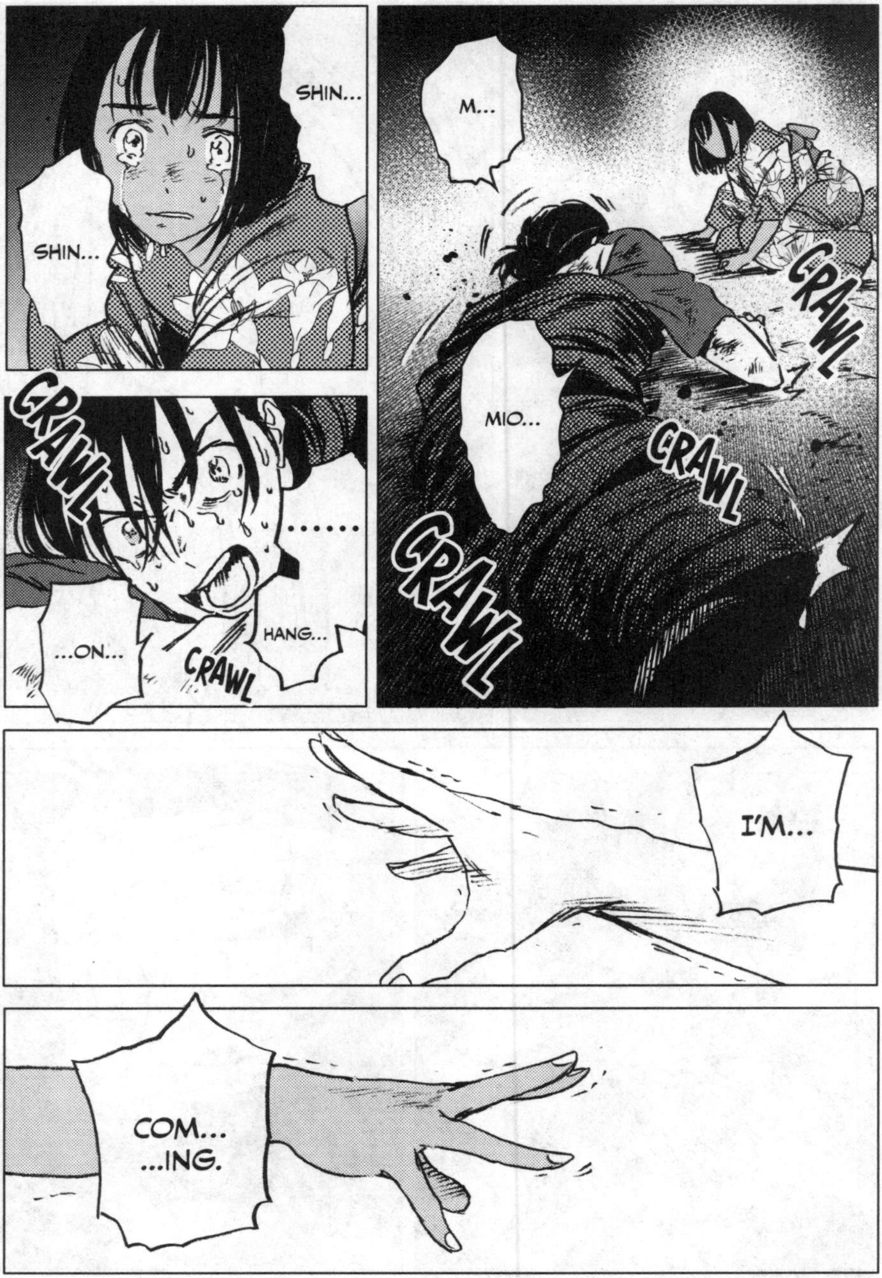
M...
CRAWL
MIO...
CRAWL
CRAWL
SHIN...
SHIN...
CRAWL
......
HANG...
CRAWL
...ON...
I'M...
COM...
...ING.

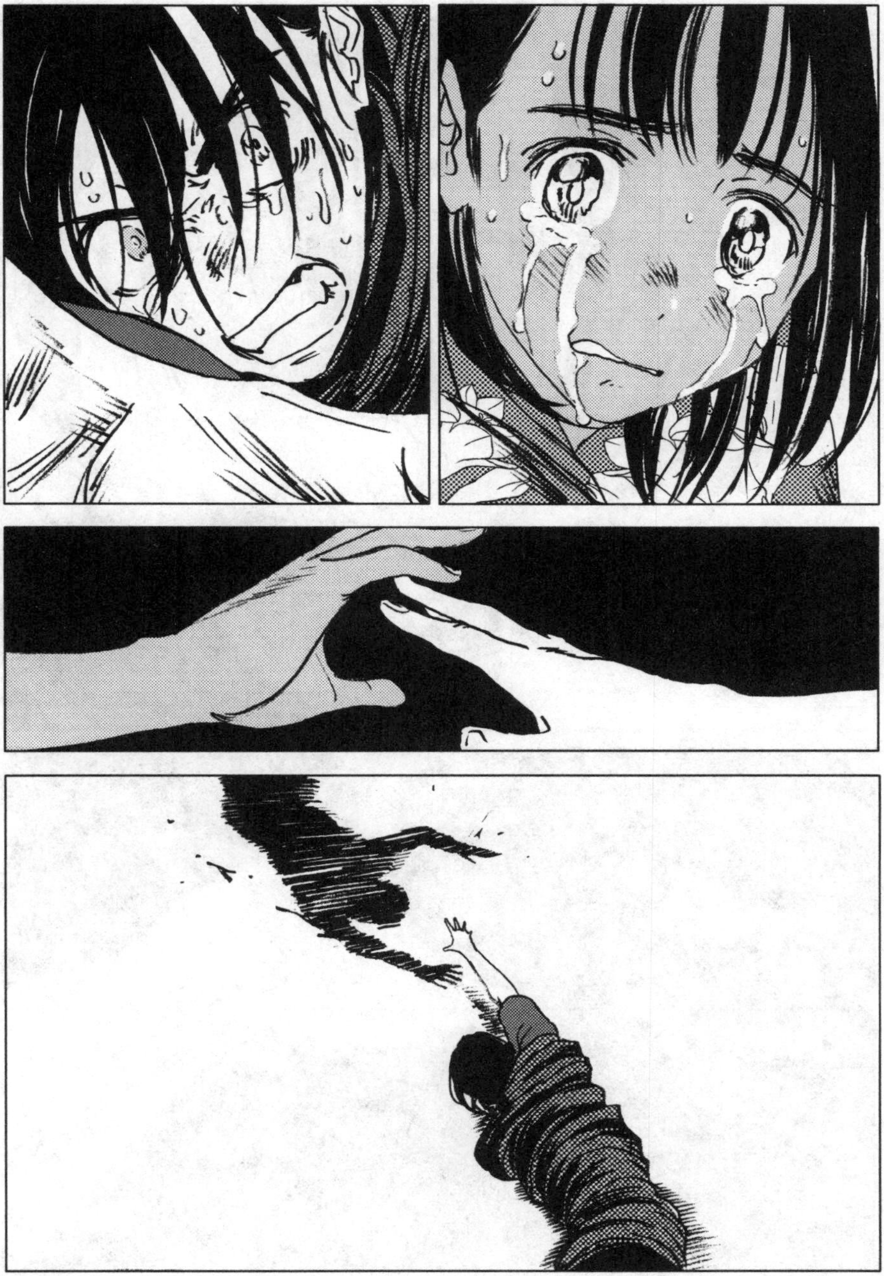

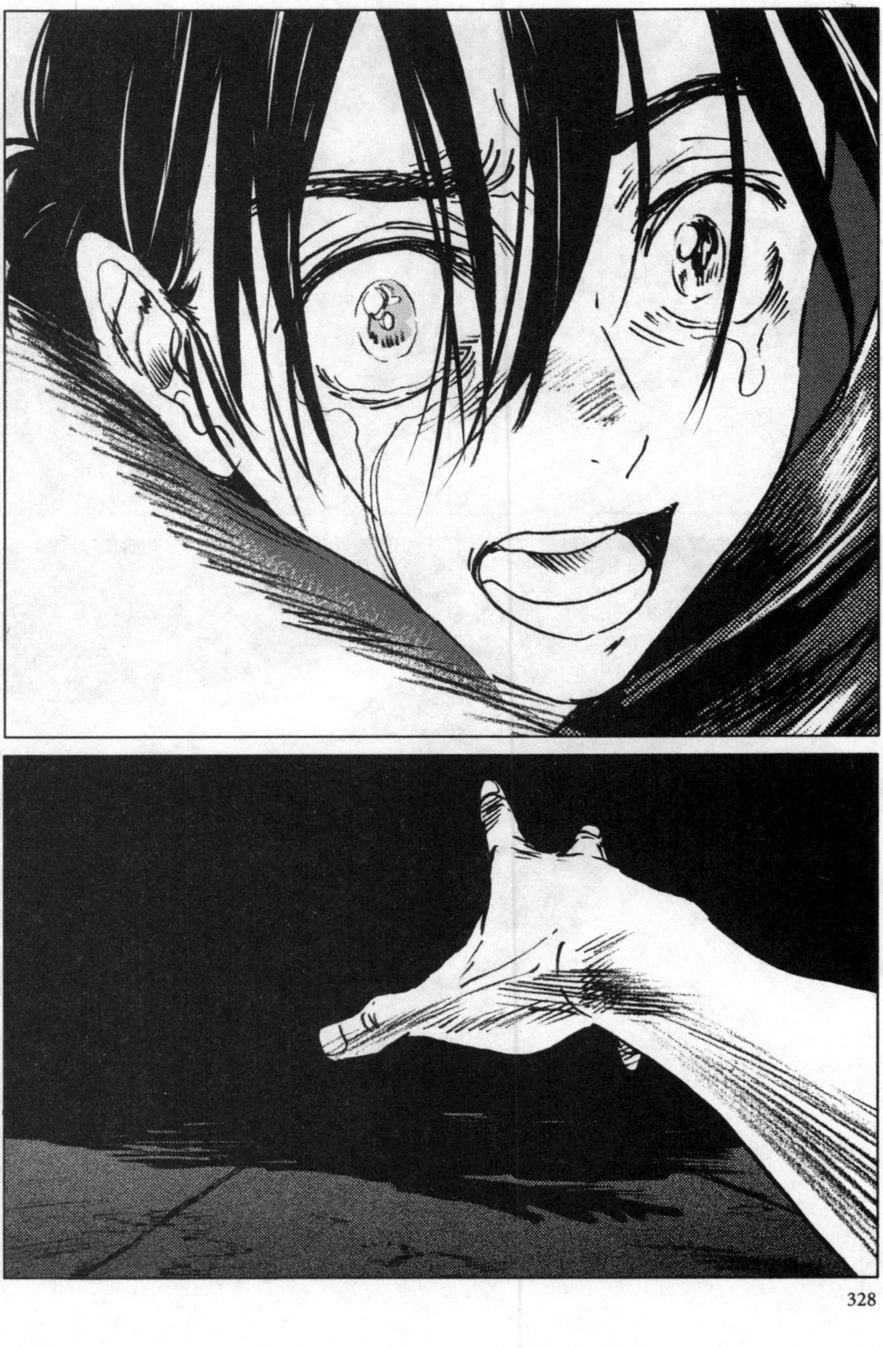

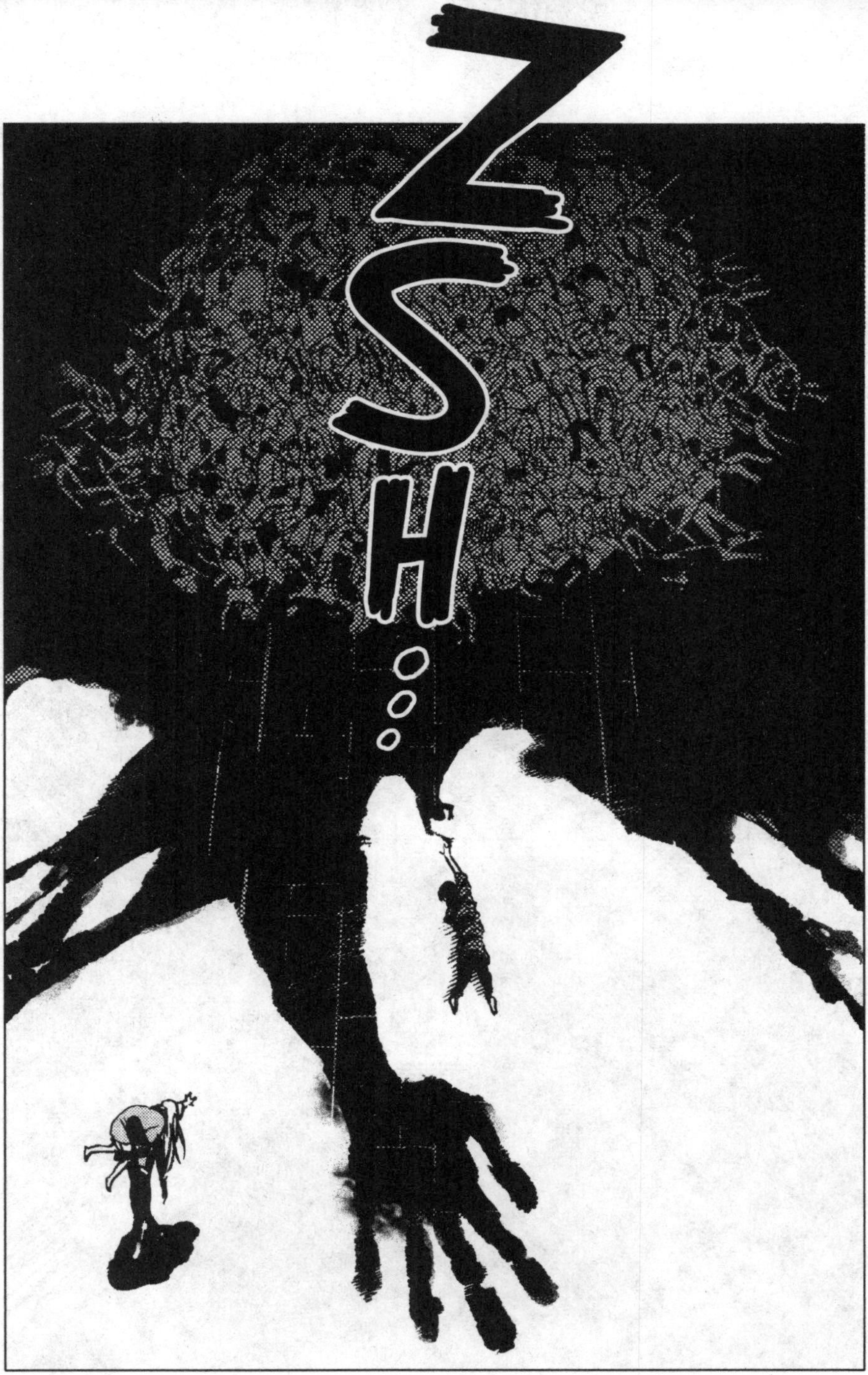
ZSH...

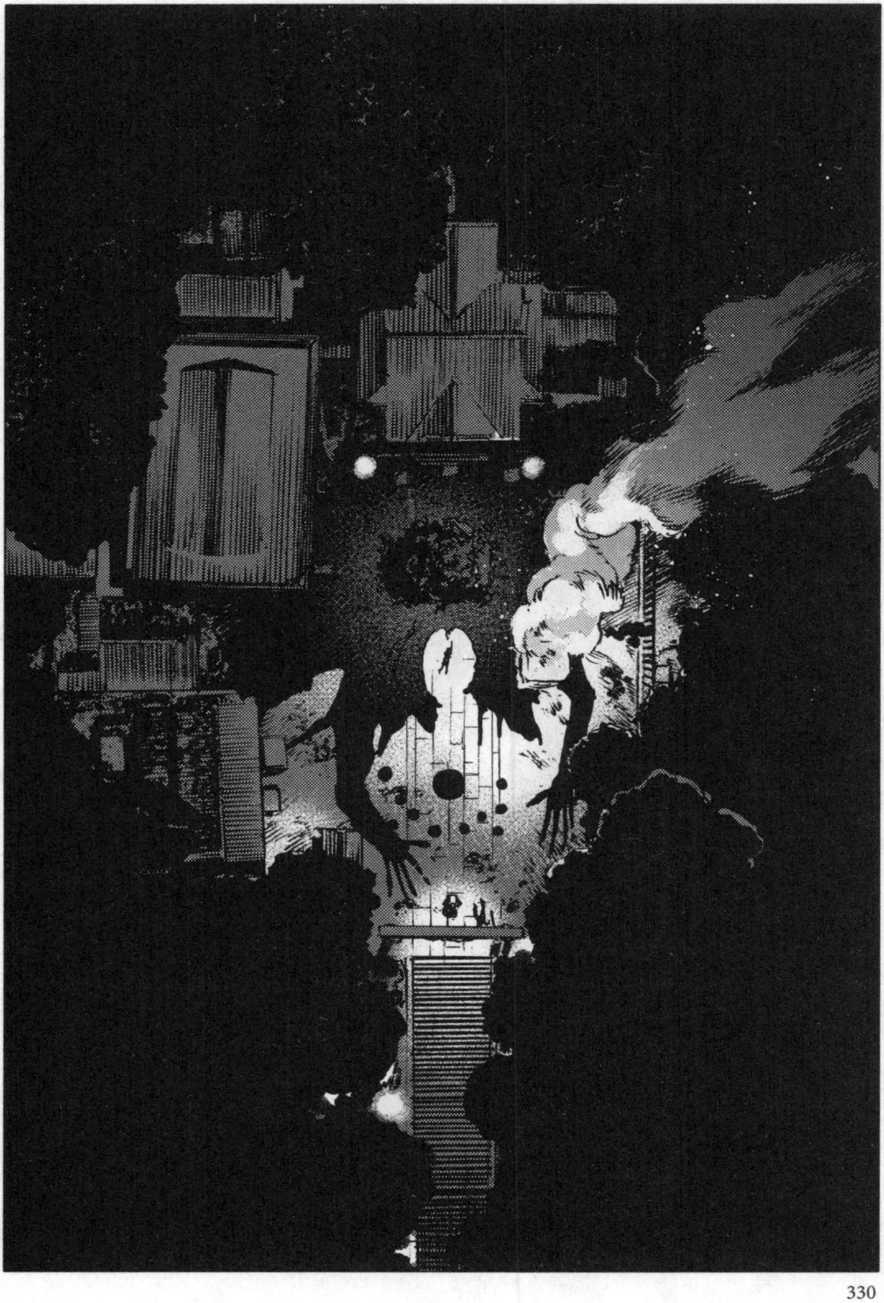

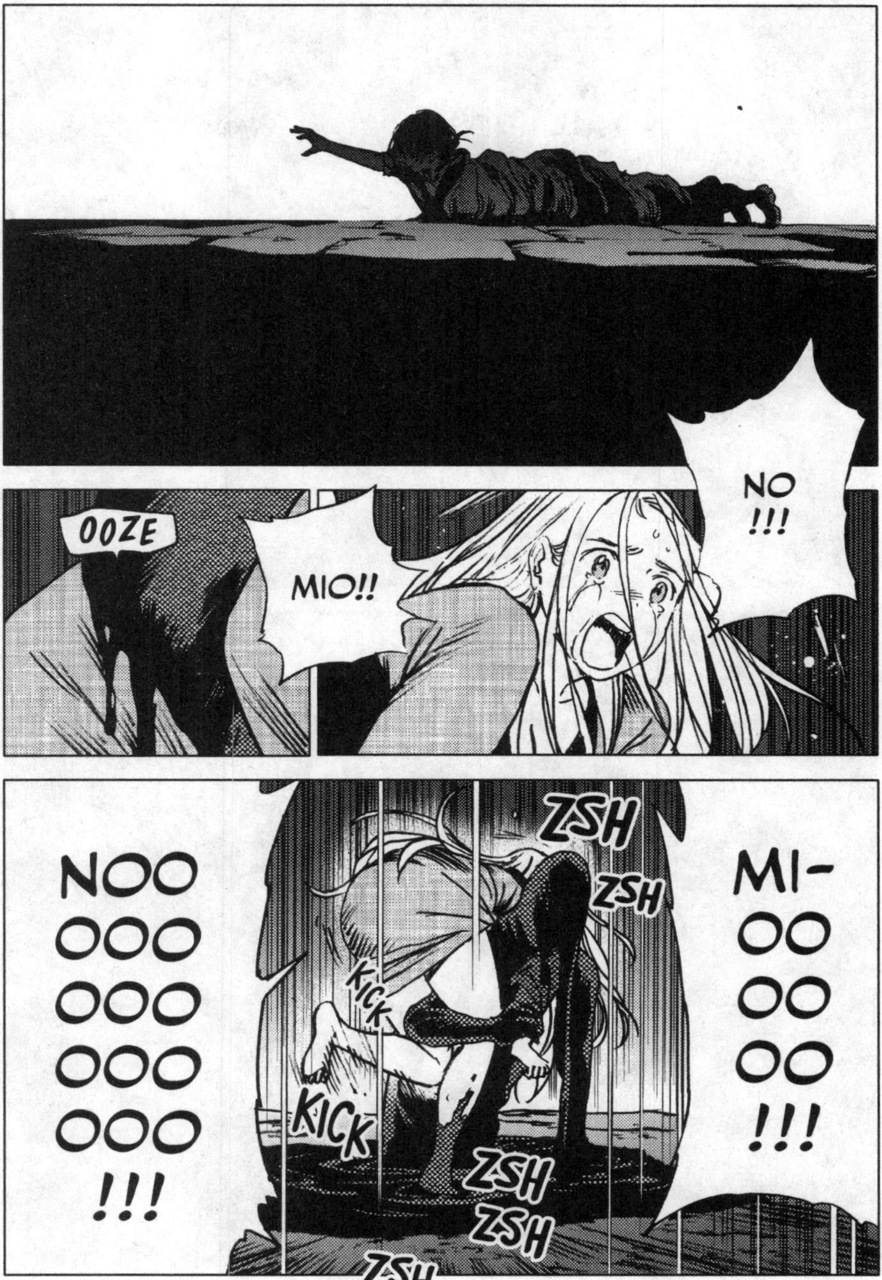
NO !!!
MIO!!
OOZE
MI- OO OO OO !!!
ZSH
ZSH
KICK
KICK
ZSH
ZSH
ZSH
NOO OOO OOO OOO OOO !!!

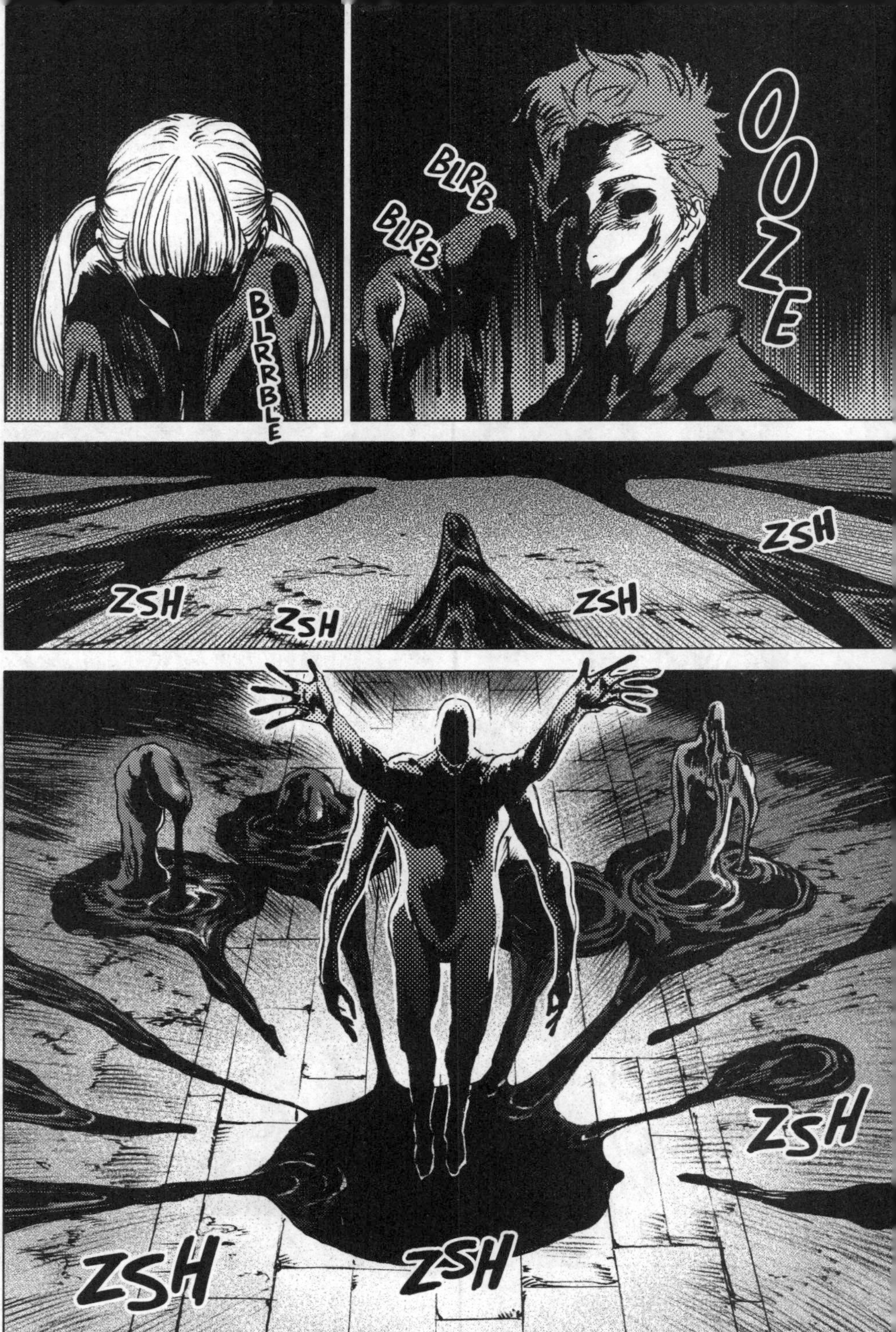
OOZE
BLRB
BLRB
BLRRBLE
ZSH
ZSH
ZSH
ZSH
ZSH
ZSH
ZSH

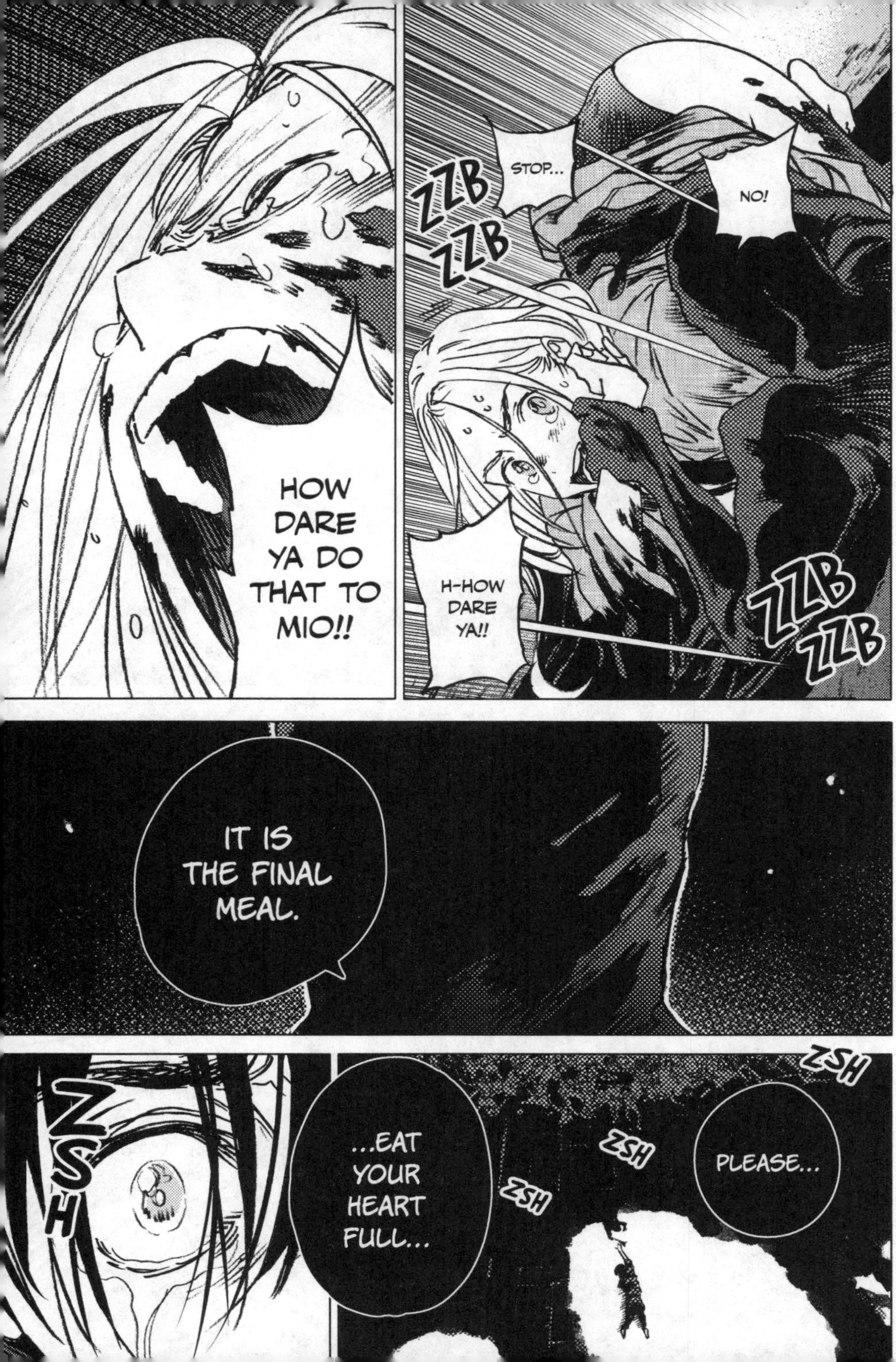
NO!
STOP...
ZZB ZZB
ZZB ZZB
H-HOW DARE YA!!
HOW DARE YA DO THAT TO MIO!!
IT IS THE FINAL MEAL.
ZSH
PLEASE...
ZSH
ZSH
...EAT YOUR HEART FULL...
ZSH

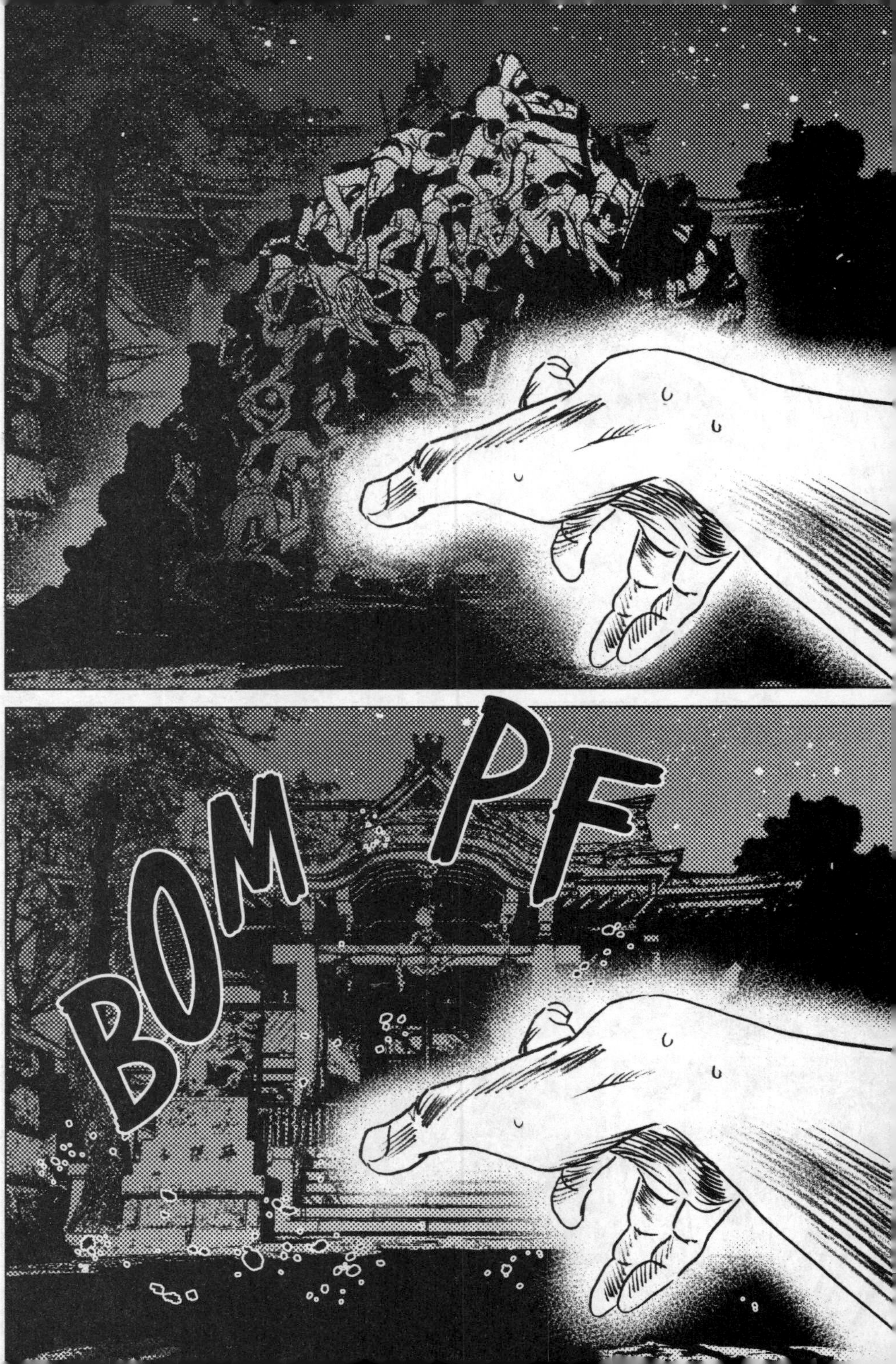
BOMPF

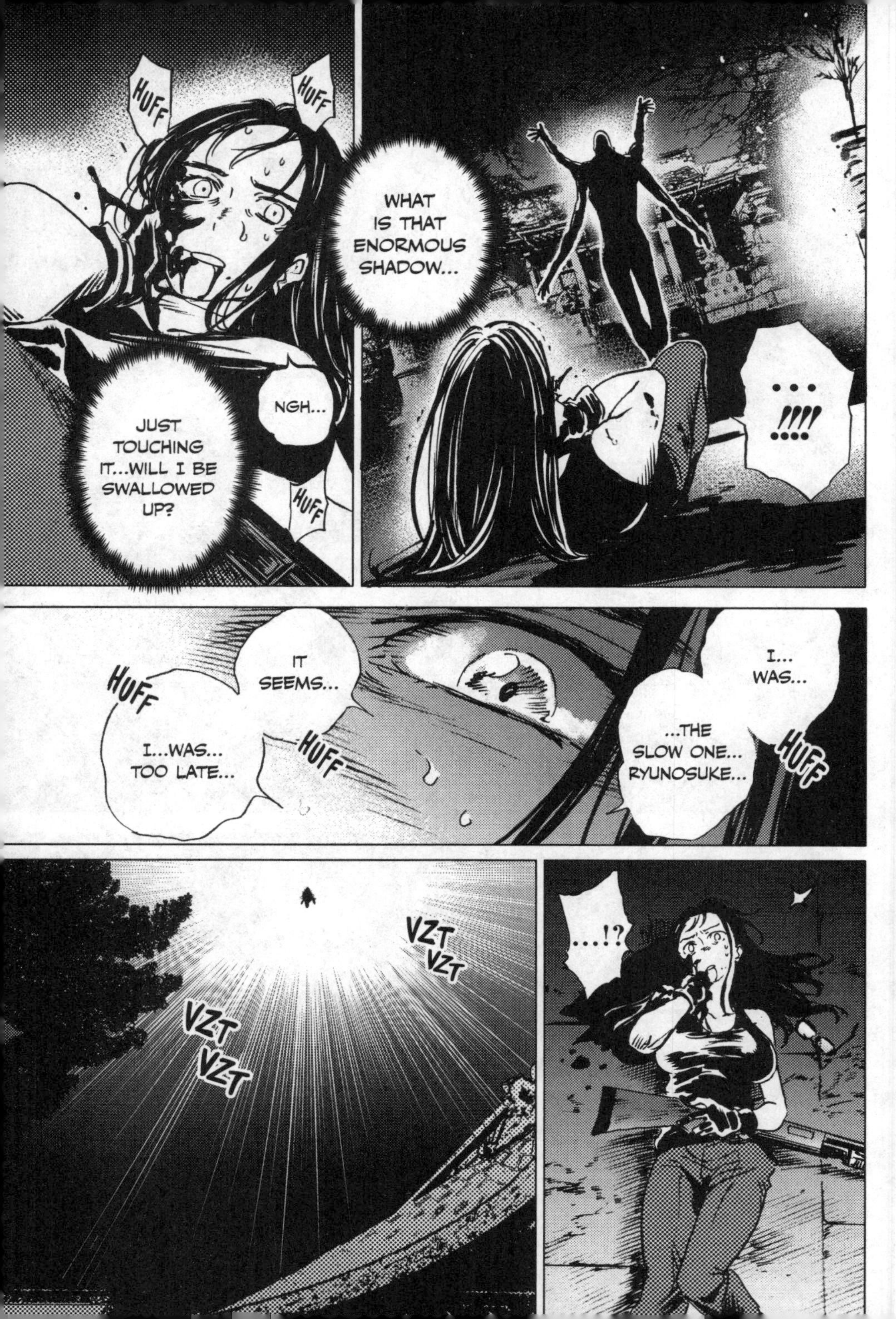
WHAT IS THAT ENORMOUS SHADOW...
...!!!!
HUFF
HUFF
NGH...
JUST TOUCHING IT...WILL I BE SWALLOWED UP?
HUFF
I... WAS...
...THE SLOW ONE... RYUNOSUKE...
HUFF
IT SEEMS...
HUFF
I...WAS... TOO LATE...
HUFF
...!?
VZT
VZT
VZT
VZT

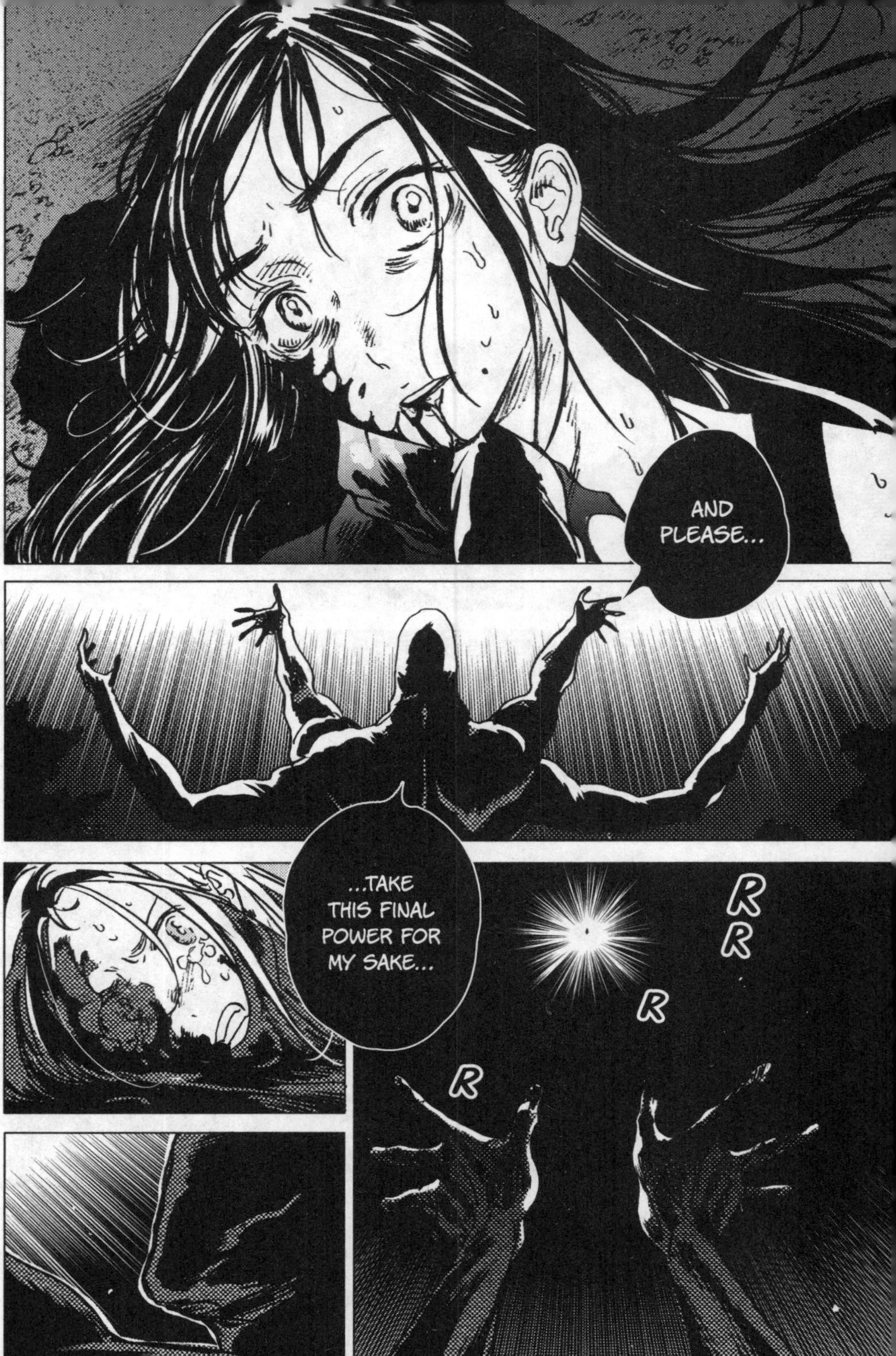
AND PLEASE...
...TAKE THIS FINAL POWER FOR MY SAKE...
R
R
R
R

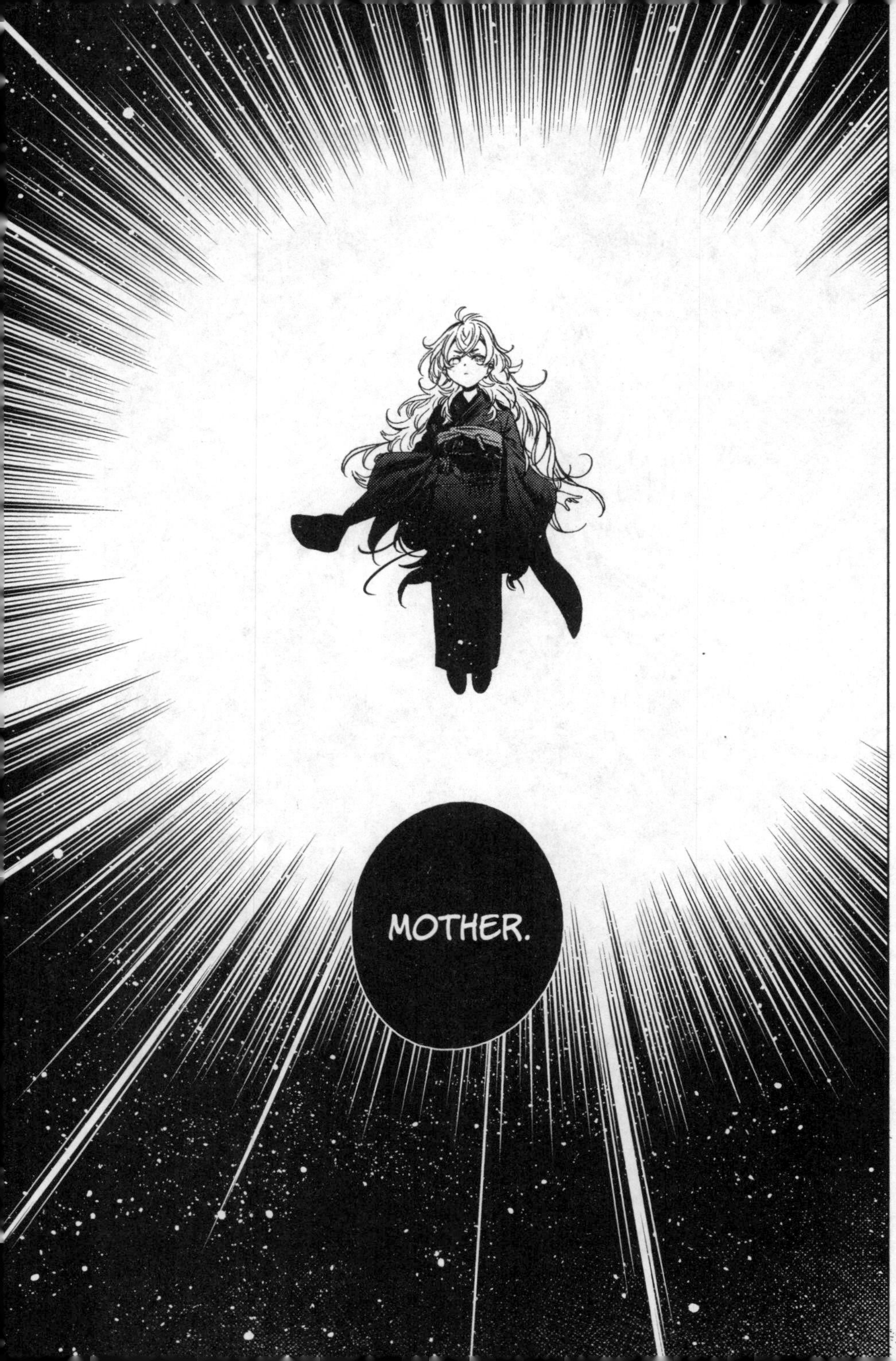
MOTHER.

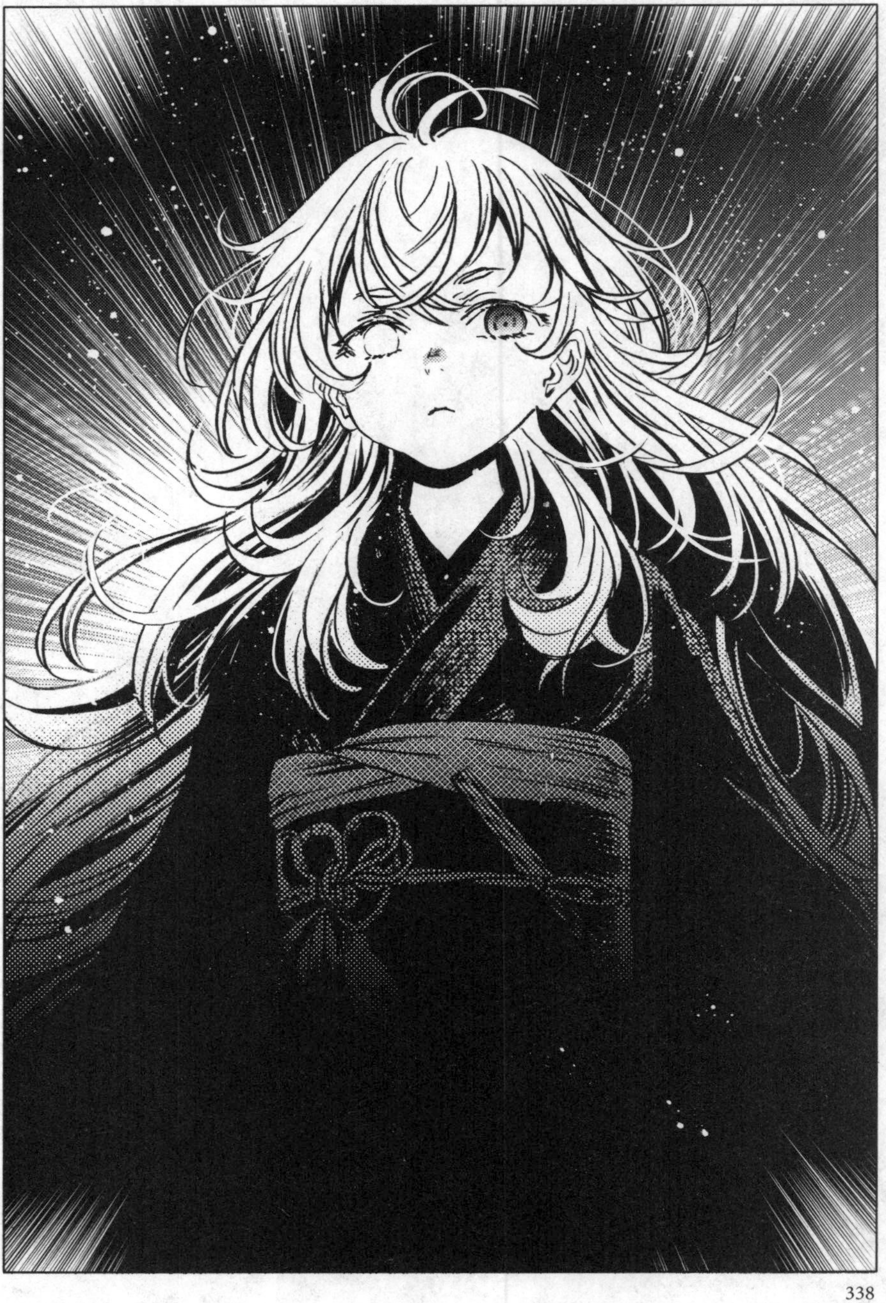

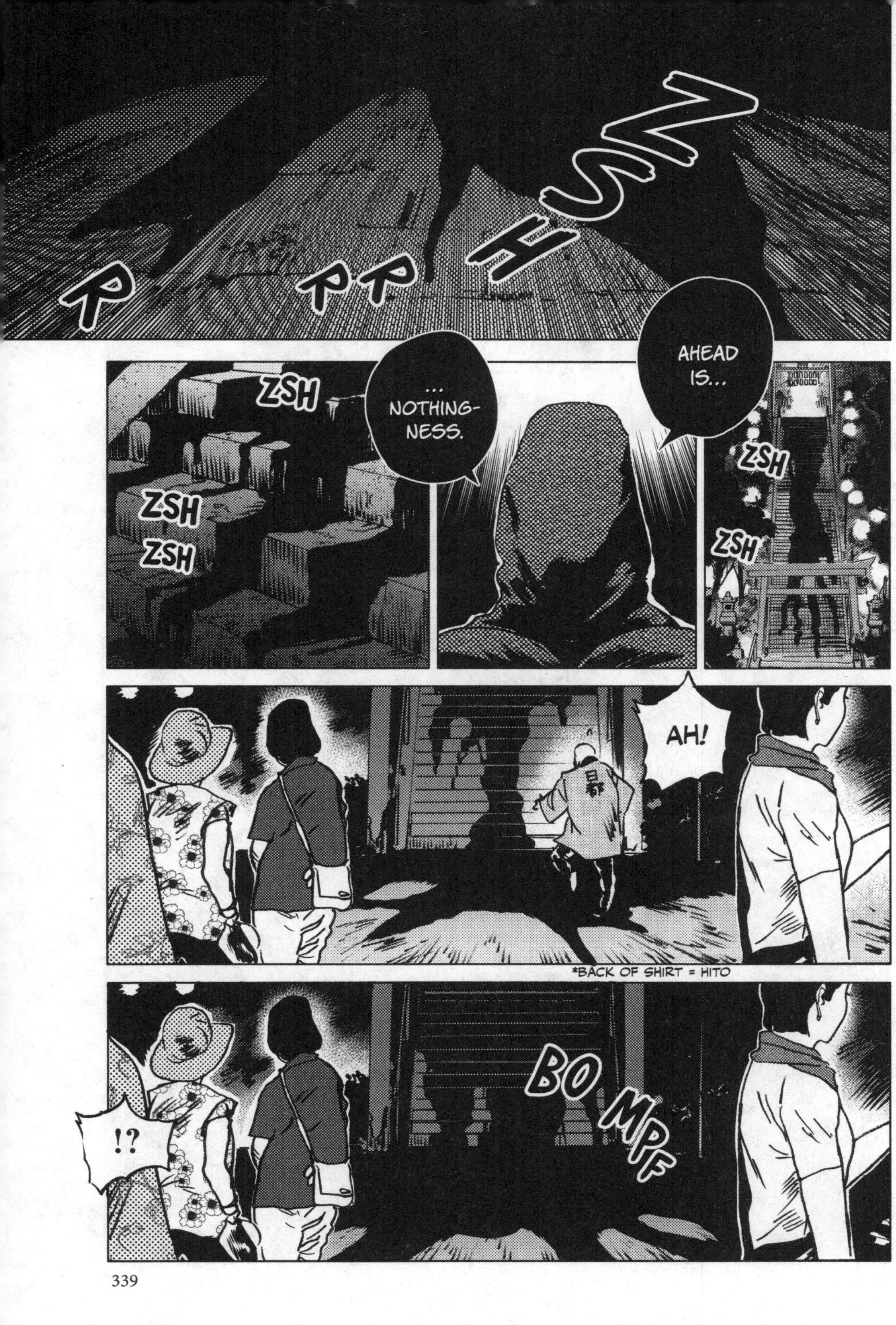
R RP RP H S N Z
ZSH
ZSH
AHEAD IS...
... NOTHING-NESS.
ZSH
ZSH
ZSH
AH!
*BACK OF SHIRT = HITO
BO MPF
!?

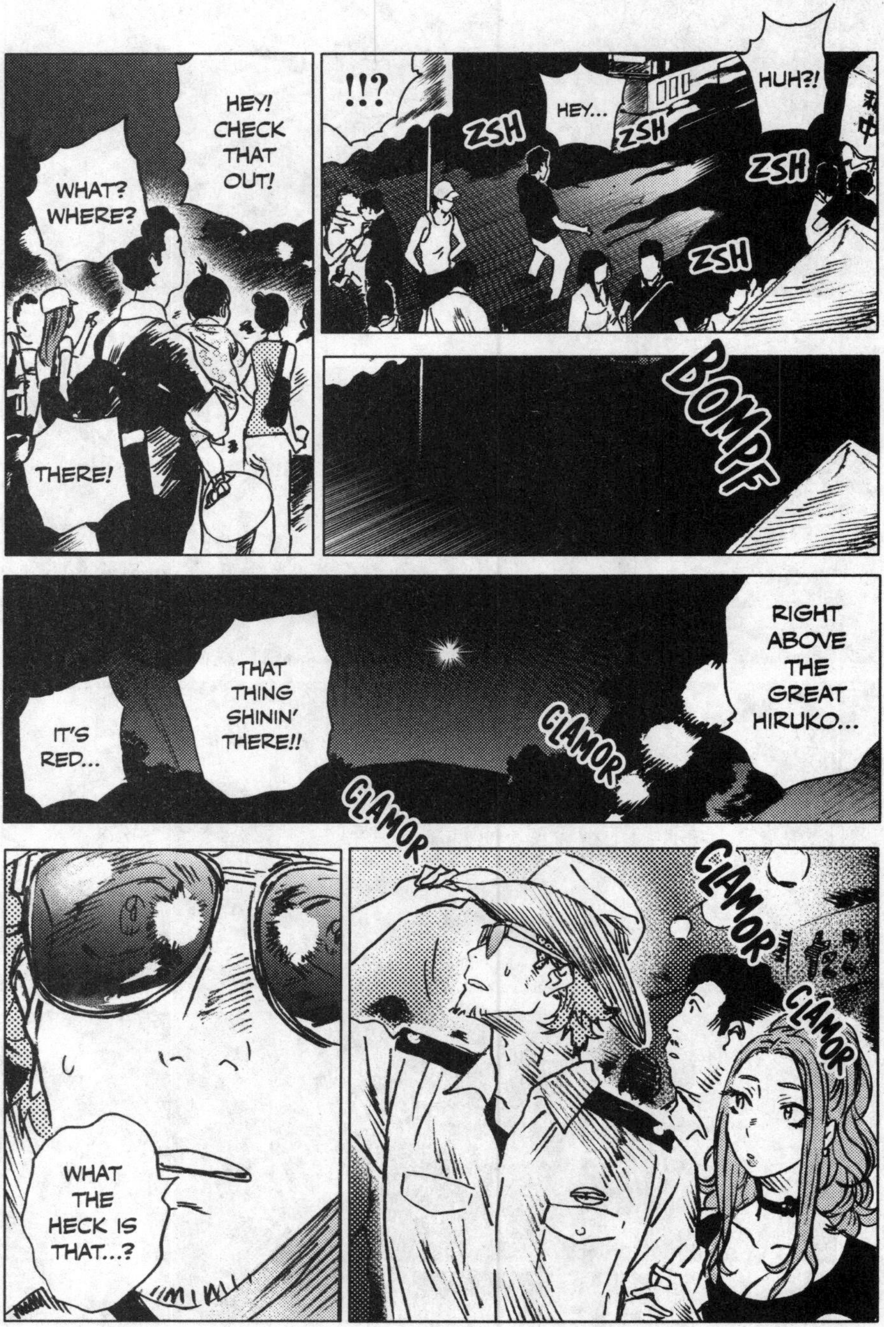
HUH?!
ZSH
HEY...
ZSH
ZSH
!!?
ZSH
BOMPF
HEY! CHECK THAT OUT!
WHAT? WHERE?
THERE!
RIGHT ABOVE THE GREAT HIRUKO...
CLAMOR
THAT THING SHININ' THERE!!
IT'S RED...
CLAMOR
CLAMOR
CLAMOR
CLAMOR
CLAMOR
WHAT THE HECK IS THAT...?

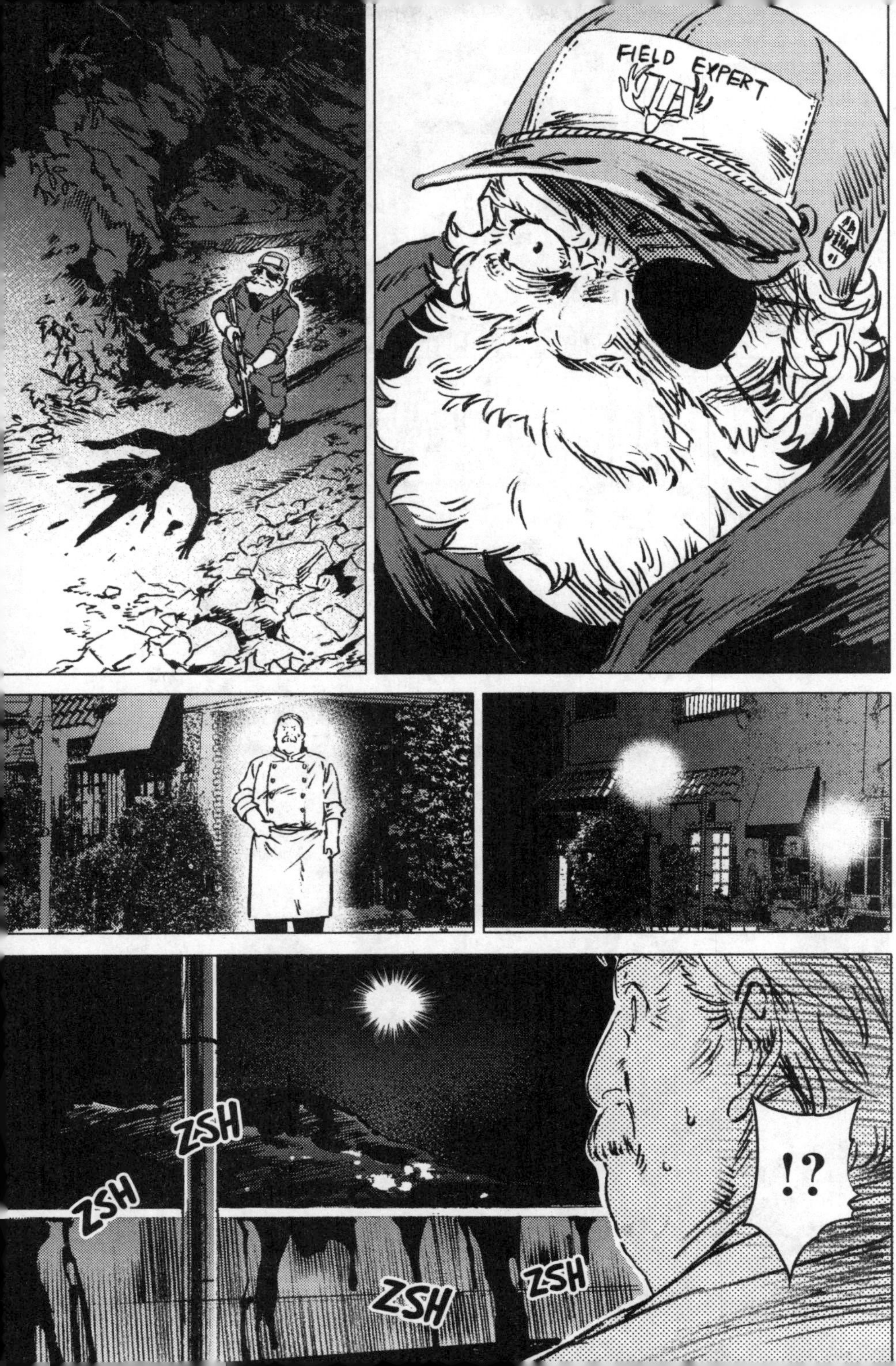
FIELD EXPERT
!?
ZSH
ZSH
ZSH
ZSH

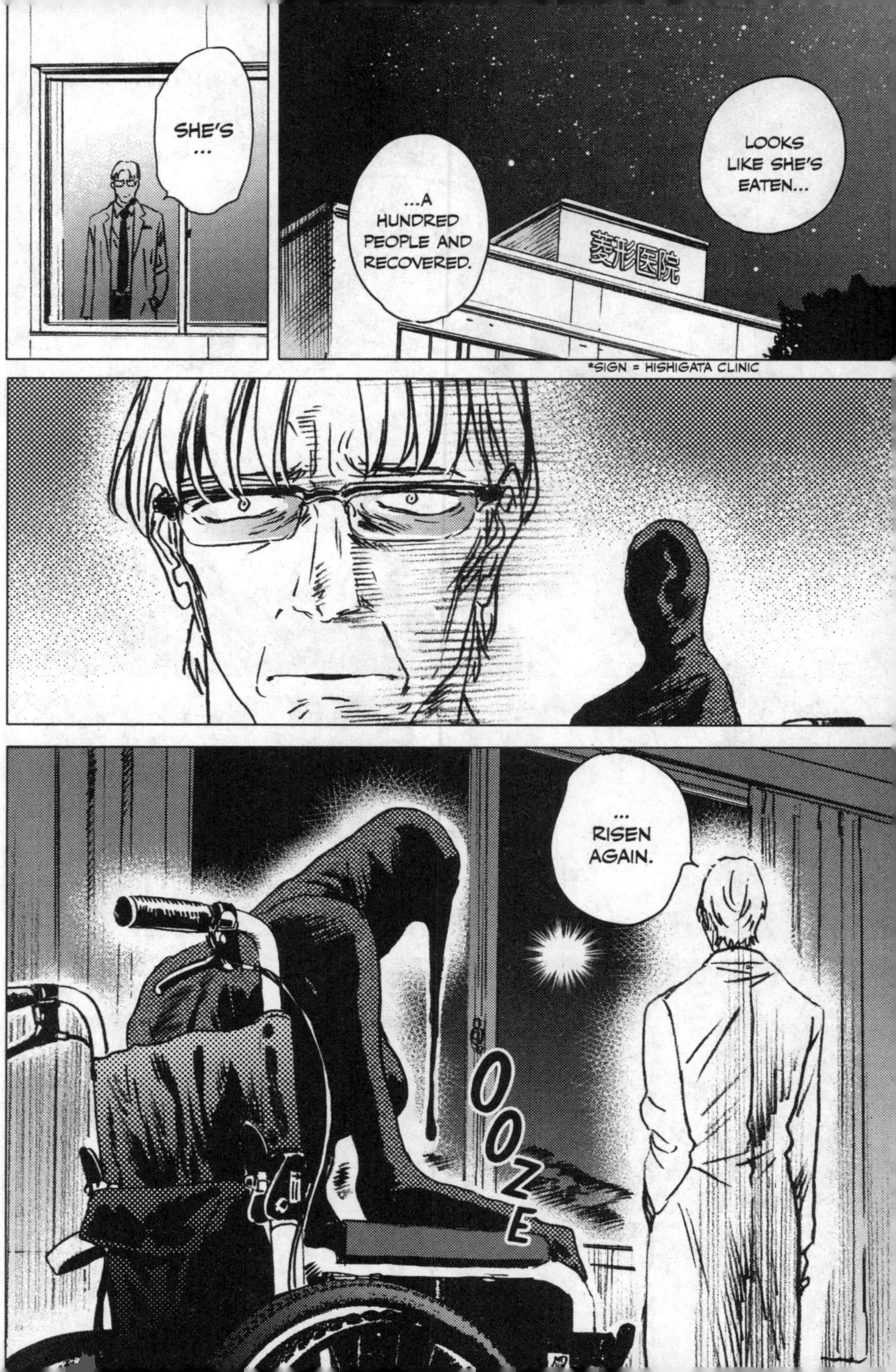
LOOKS LIKE SHE'S EATEN...
...A HUNDRED PEOPLE AND RECOVERED.
菱形医院
SHE'S ...
*SIGN = HISHIGATA CLINIC
... RISEN AGAIN.
OOZE

... BEING SWALLOWED UP BY SHADOWS.

THE ISLAND'S ...

ZSH ZSH ZSH ZSH

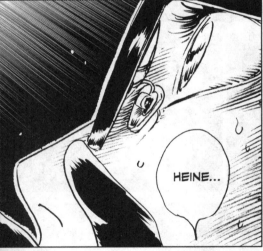

HEINE...

LICK

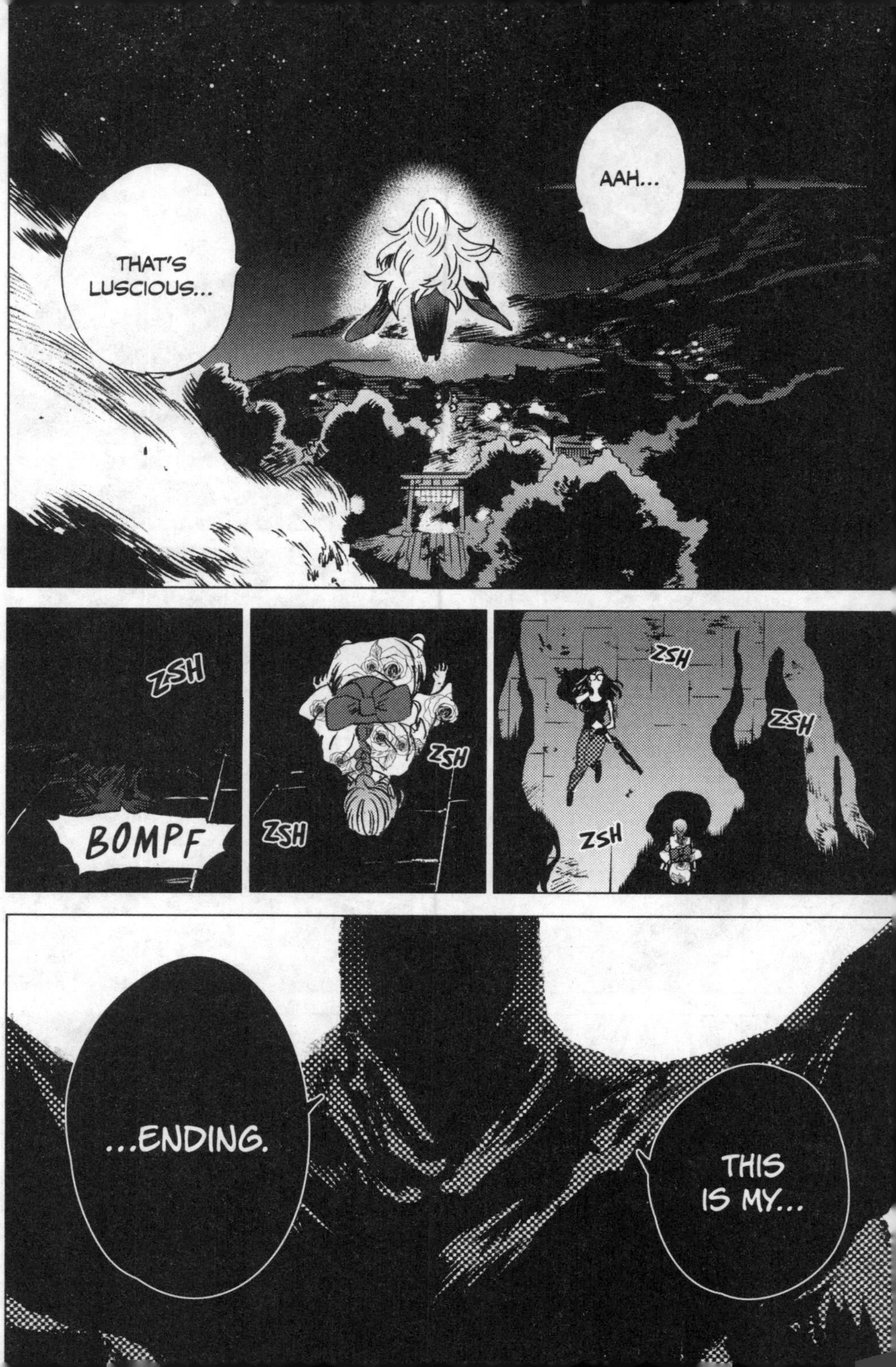
AAH...
THAT'S LUSCIOUS...
ZSH
ZSH
ZSH
ZSH
ZSH
ZSH
BOMPF
THIS IS MY...
...ENDING.

ZSH ZSH ZSH

I...

I'M SORRY...

MIO!!

IF I'D ONLY...

...BELIEVED THAT MESSAGE SOONER...

HUFF HUFF

SORRY...

SHINPEI...

EVERY-ONE...

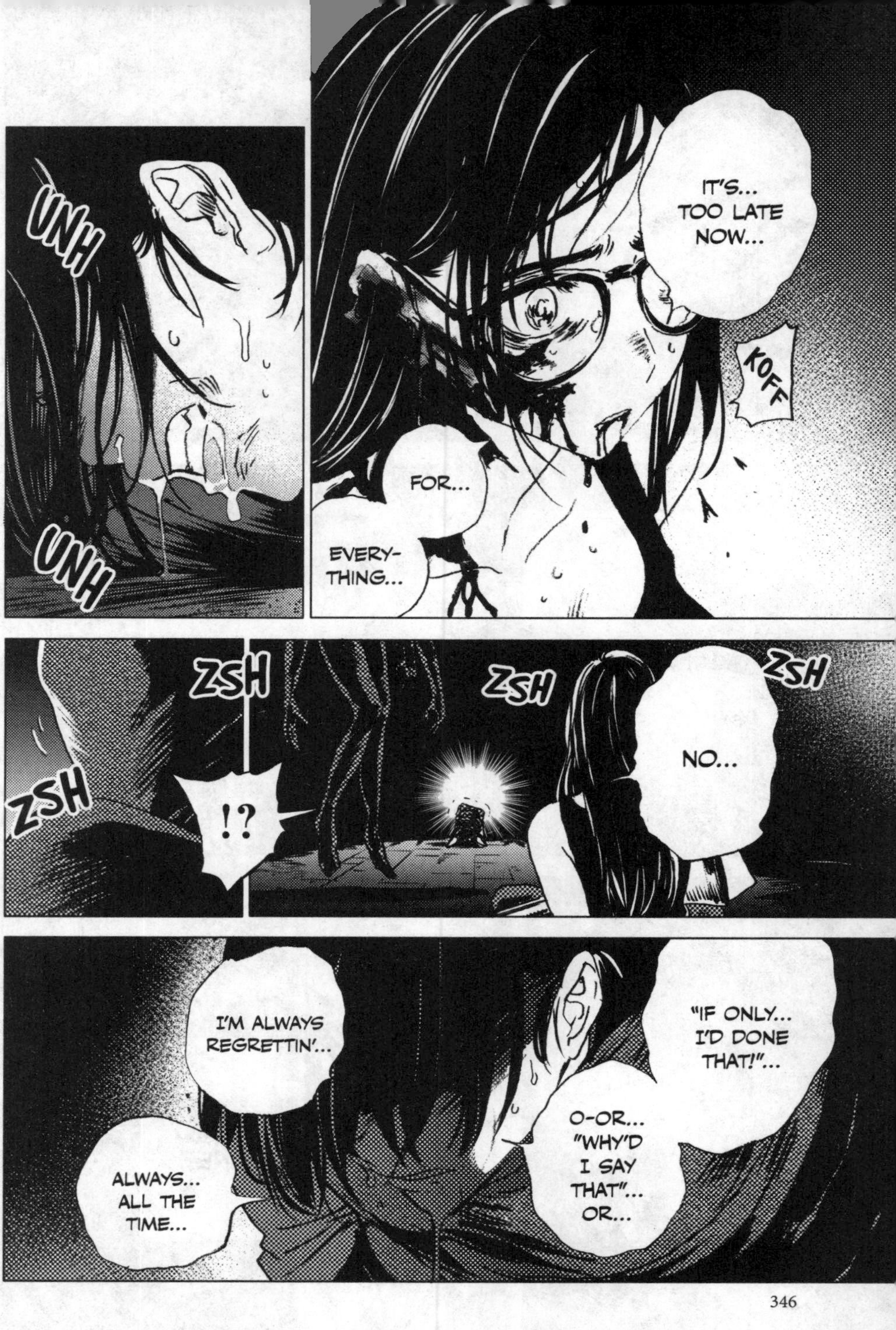
IT'S... TOO LATE NOW...
KOFF
FOR...
EVERY-THING...
UNH
UNH
ZSH
ZSH
NO...
ZSH
ZSH
!?
"IF ONLY... I'D DONE THAT!"...
O-OR... "WHY'D I SAY THAT"... OR...
I'M ALWAYS REGRETTIN'...
ALWAYS... ALL THE TIME...

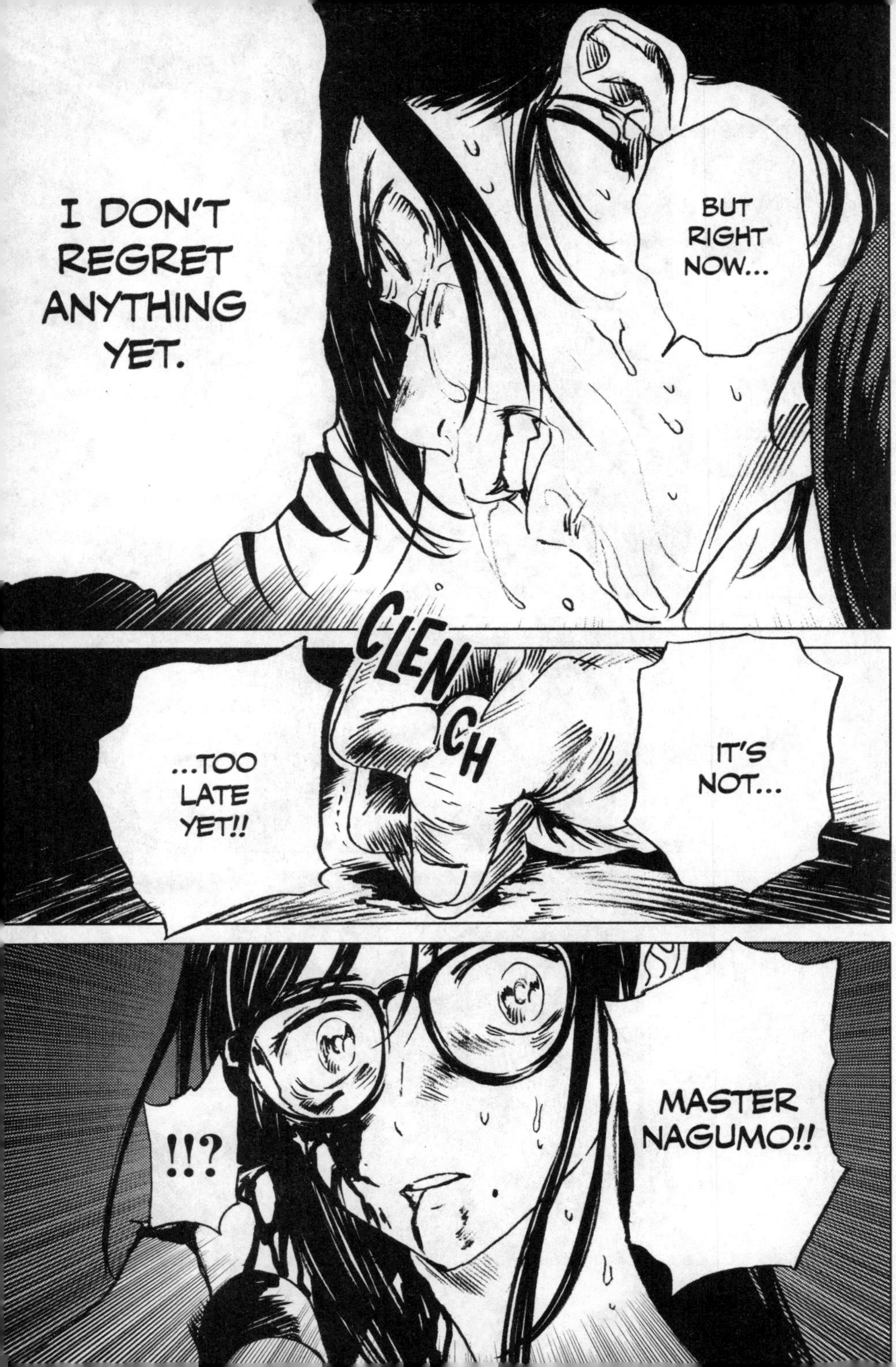
BUT RIGHT NOW...
I DON'T REGRET ANYTHING YET.
CLENCH
IT'S NOT...
...TOO LATE YET!!
MASTER NAGUMO!!
!!?

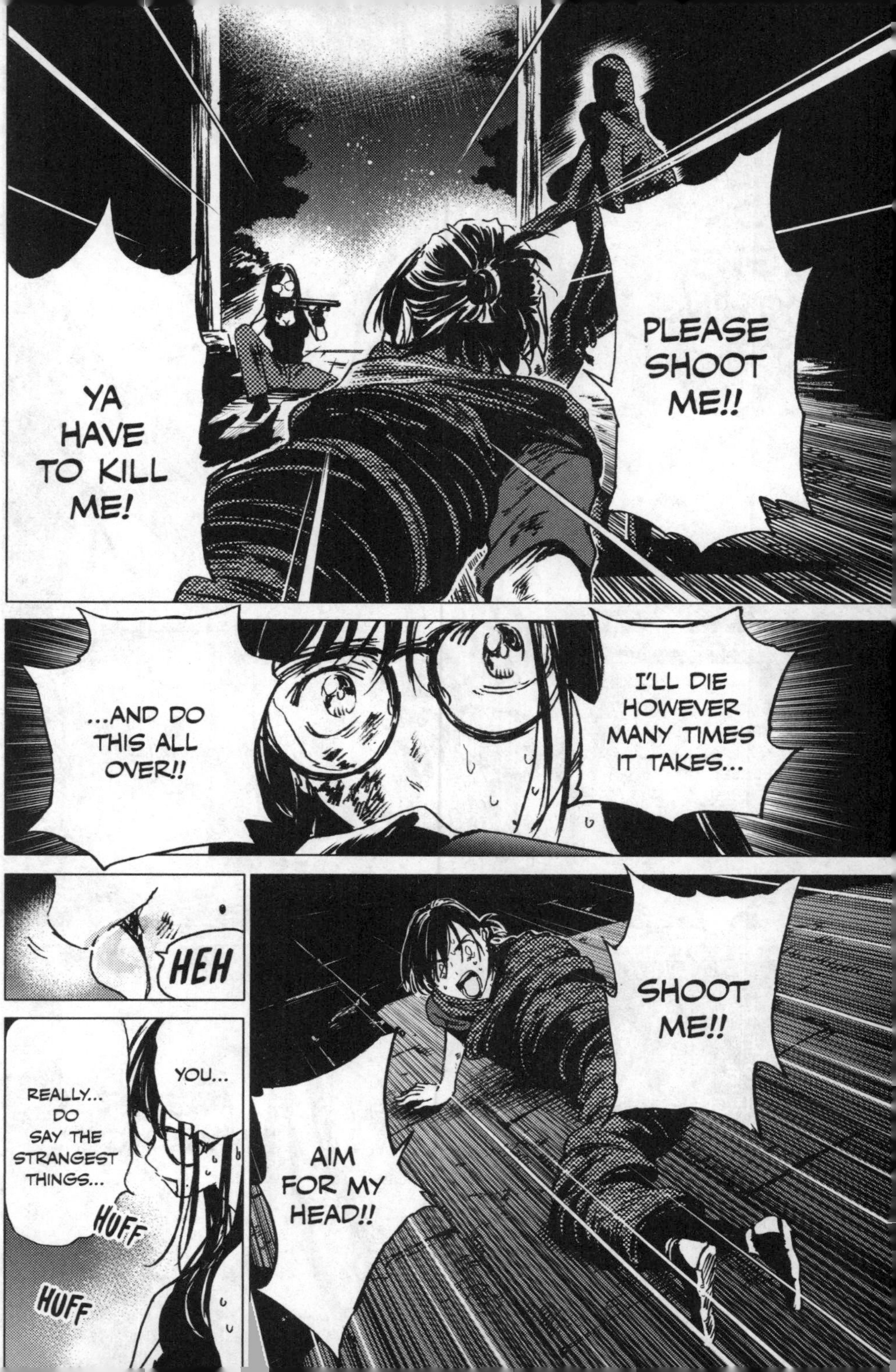
PLEASE SHOOT ME!!
YA HAVE TO KILL ME!
I'LL DIE HOWEVER MANY TIMES IT TAKES...
...AND DO THIS ALL OVER!!
SHOOT ME!!
AIM FOR MY HEAD!!
HEH
YOU...
REALLY... DO SAY THE STRANGEST THINGS...
HUFF
HUFF

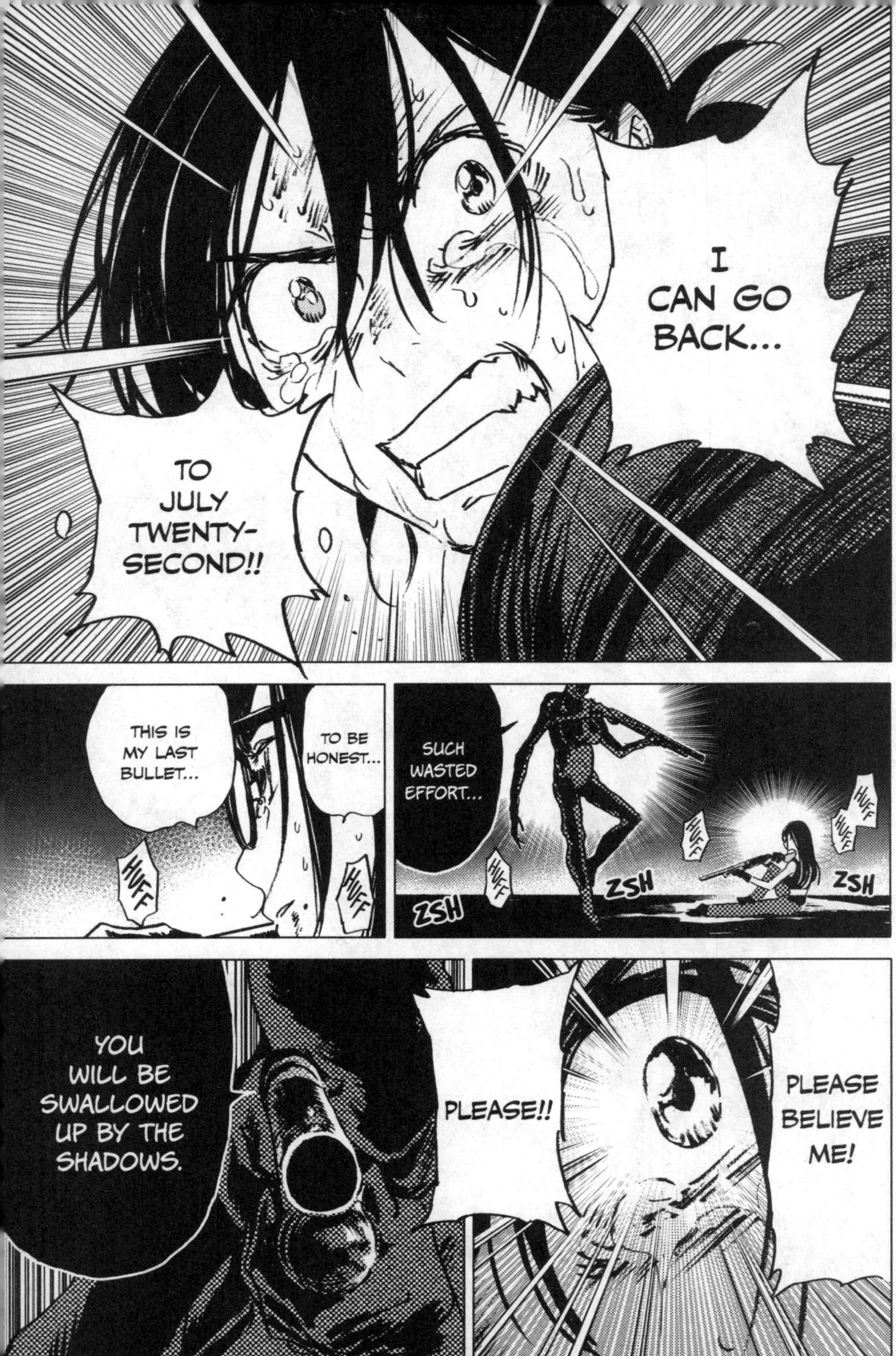
I CAN GO BACK...
TO JULY TWENTY-SECOND!!
SUCH WASTED EFFORT...
HUFF
HUFF
HUFF
ZSH
ZSH
HUFF
ZSH
TO BE HONEST...
THIS IS MY LAST BULLET...
HUFF
HUFF
PLEASE BELIEVE ME!
PLEASE!!
YOU WILL BE SWALLOWED UP BY THE SHADOWS.

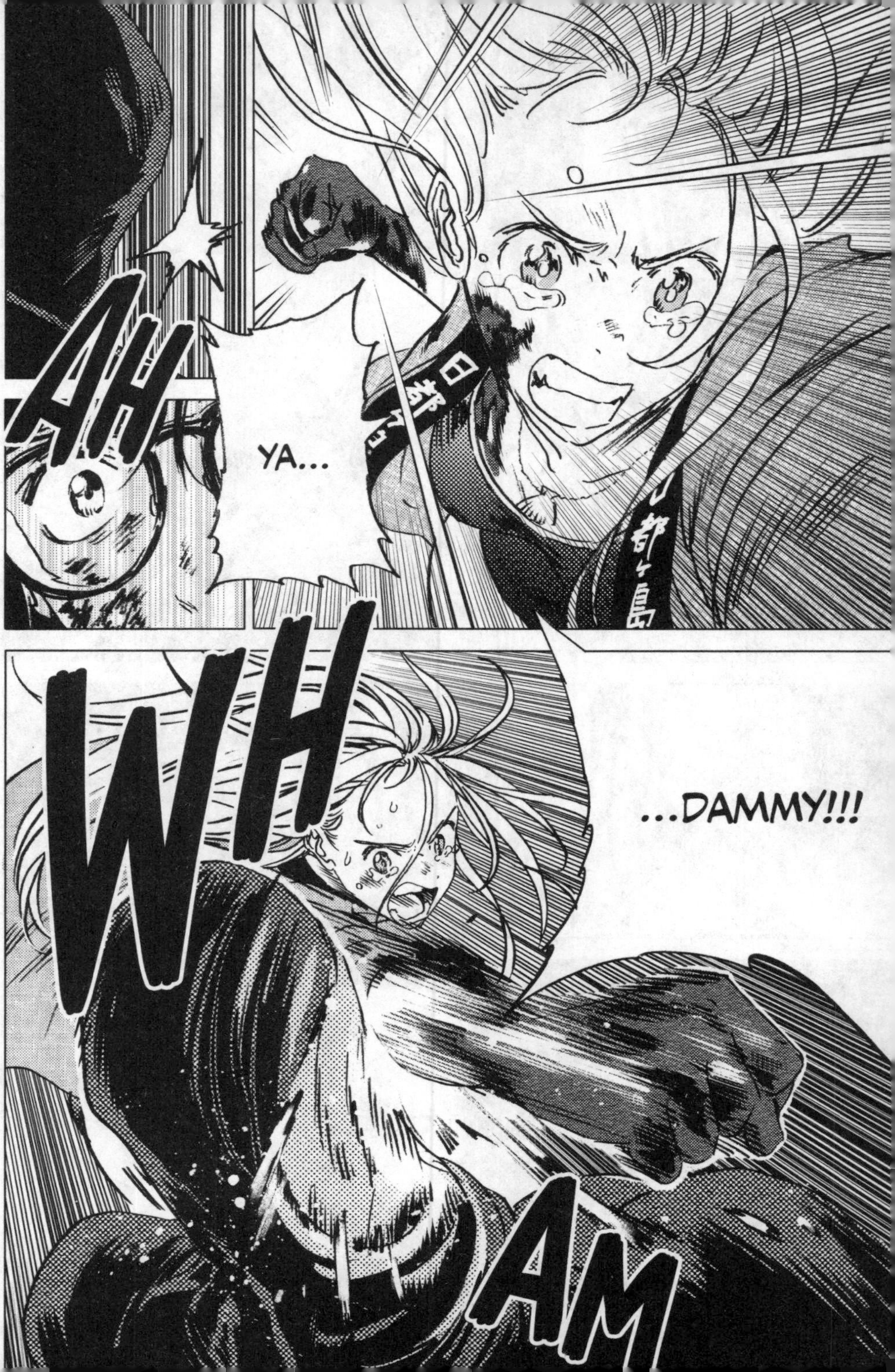
AH
YA...
...DAMMY!!!
WH
AM

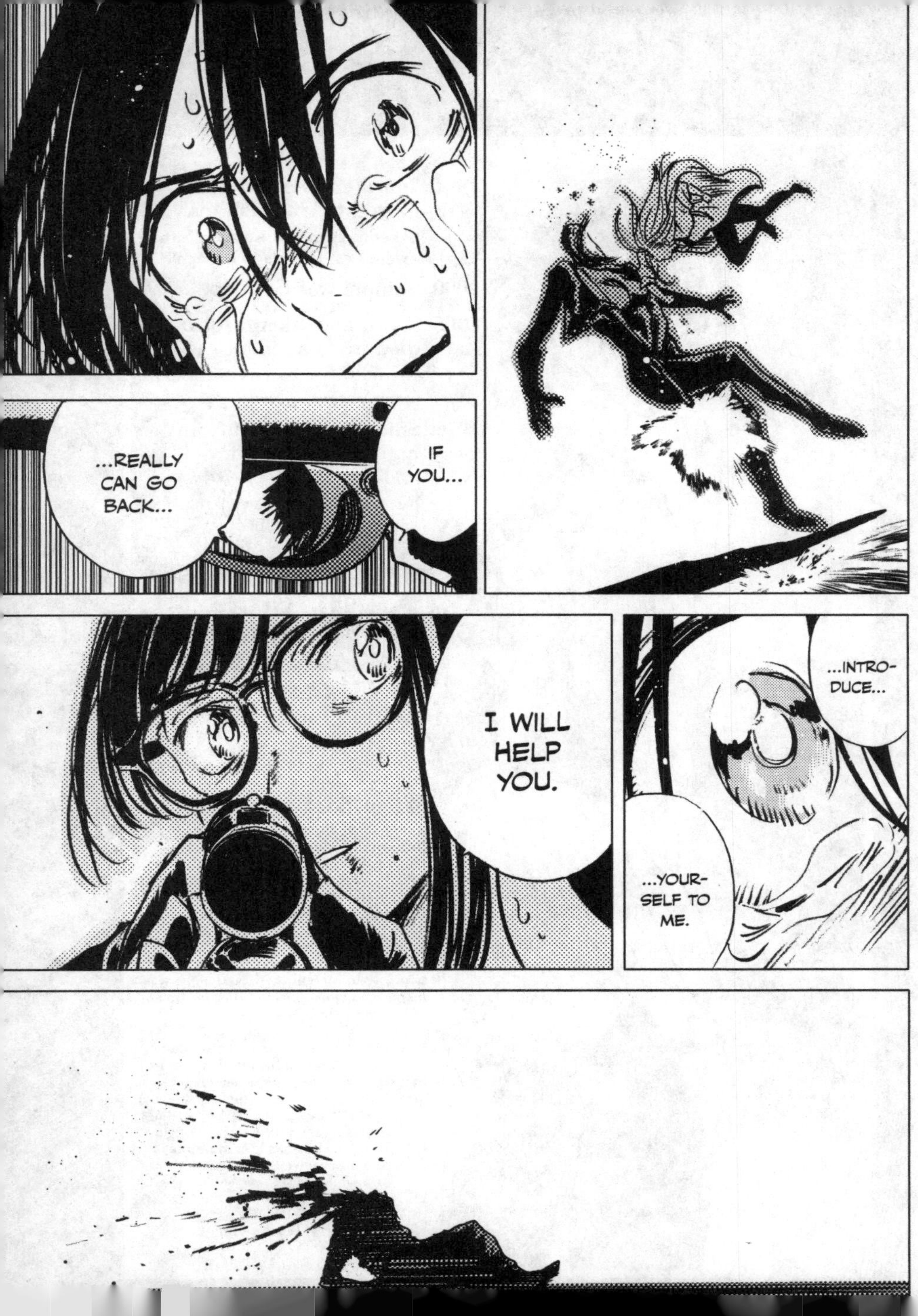
IF YOU...
...REALLY CAN GO BACK...
...INTRO-DUCE...
...YOUR-SELF TO ME.
I WILL HELP YOU.

1994 Tooru and Akemi Ajiro
     moved to Hitogashima.
     (Akemi Ajiro and Kotoko Kofune
     were best friends in college).

2000 Shinpei was born.

2008 Tooru and Akemi Ajiro
     died in an accident.
     Alain Kofune became Shinpei's
     foster parent.

2016 Shinpei graduated from
     high school and moved
     to Tokyo.
     He started going to a cooking
     school to get his GED.

SHINPEI AJIRO (AGE 18)

Date of Birth: May 8th   Blood Type: O

Favorite Food: Chicken Wings,
              Bell Peppers, Green Soft.

171cm/58kg

- Influenced by his father who loved reading, Shinpei has loved to read books since he was a little child. He likes mystery and Sci-fi stories. His favorite author is Ryunosuke Nagumo.

- Because of Alain's influence, he started cooking. Thanks to people (Ushio and Mio) who love to eat Shinpei's cooking, he was inspired to work hard to fulfill his dream to become a chef.

- Panicking causes him to make another version of himself in his mind and from that standpoint he has the tendency to view himself objectively. (Bird's Eye View)

- Understanding the process of cooking and his love of mystery has helped Shinpei develop his objective thinking self.

- He loved Ushio Kofune.

- He hates water. He can't swim.

1991 - Hitogashima born Kotoko Kofune (age 20 at that time) went to study in France and met Alain (age 32 at that time).

1994 - Kotoko and Alain moved to Hitogashima.
Same year, they got married and opened the restaurant "Bistro Kofune".

2000 - Ushio Kofune was born.

2002 - Mio Kofune was born.
Kotoko died due to complications during postpartum confinement.

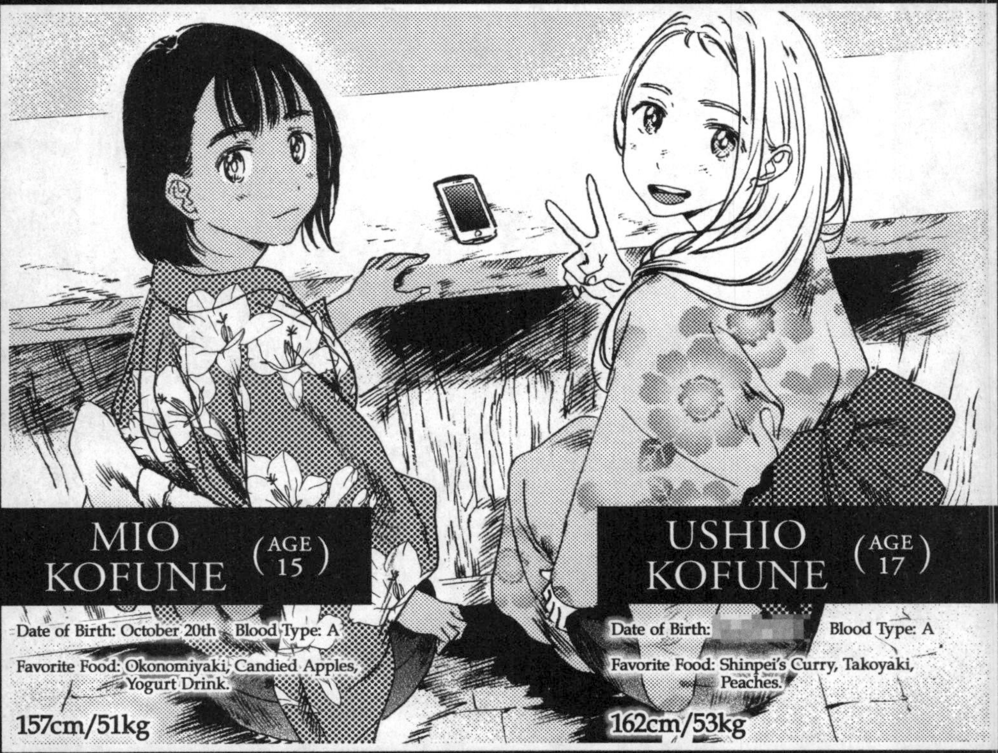
MIO KOFUNE (AGE 15)
Date of Birth: October 20th Blood Type: A
Favorite Food: Okonomiyaki, Candied Apples, Yogurt Drink.
157cm/51kg
USHIO KOFUNE (AGE 17)
Date of Birth: [redacted] Blood Type: A
Favorite Food: Shinpei's Curry, Takoyaki, Peaches.
162cm/53kg

- Ushio's younger sister.
- She has black hair and sun-tanned skin, which she took after her mother. She looks just like her mother when she was her age.
- She goes to the same high school as her big sister. She is good at playing sports. She is good at swimming and is on the swimming team.
- She loves to eat, but not good at holding knives. She has an aversion to cooking.
- She thinks her sister is the most beautiful person in the world.
- She thinks herself as the opposite of her sister.

AS THE HUMAN "USHIO" ---

- She is attending third year at a local high school.
- She got picked on when she was in her elementary school because of her blonde hair color which she took after her French father.
- She loves festivals and she was always looking forward to going to the Hitogashima's summer festival.

AS THE SHADOW "USHIOH" ---

- She doesn't recognize herself as a shadow and she thinks she is human.
- When Ushio Kofune was dying in a state of confusion her strong feelings for Shinpei clearly remained.

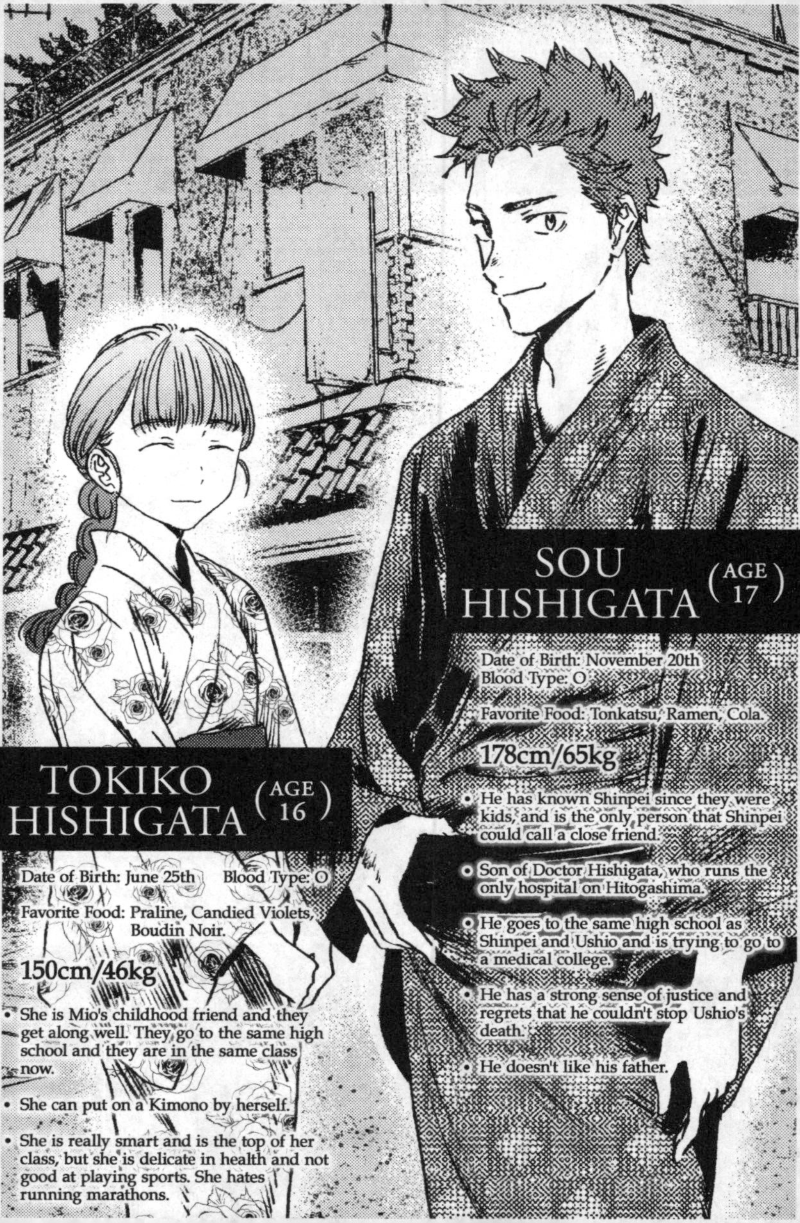

TOKIKO HISHIGATA (AGE 16)

Date of Birth: June 25th Blood Type: O

Favorite Food: Praline, Candied Violets, Boudin Noir.

150cm/46kg

- She is Mio's childhood friend and they get along well. They go to the same high school and they are in the same class now.
- She can put on a Kimono by herself.
- She is really smart and is the top of her class, but she is delicate in health and not good at playing sports. She hates running marathons.

SOU HISHIGATA (AGE 17)

Date of Birth: November 20th
Blood Type: O

Favorite Food: Tonkatsu, Ramen, Cola.

178cm/65kg

- He has known Shinpei since they were kids, and is the only person that Shinpei could call a close friend.
- Son of Doctor Hishigata, who runs the only hospital on Hitogashima.
- He goes to the same high school as Shinpei and Ushio and is trying to go to a medical college.
- He has a strong sense of justice and regrets that he couldn't stop Ushio's death.
- He doesn't like his father.

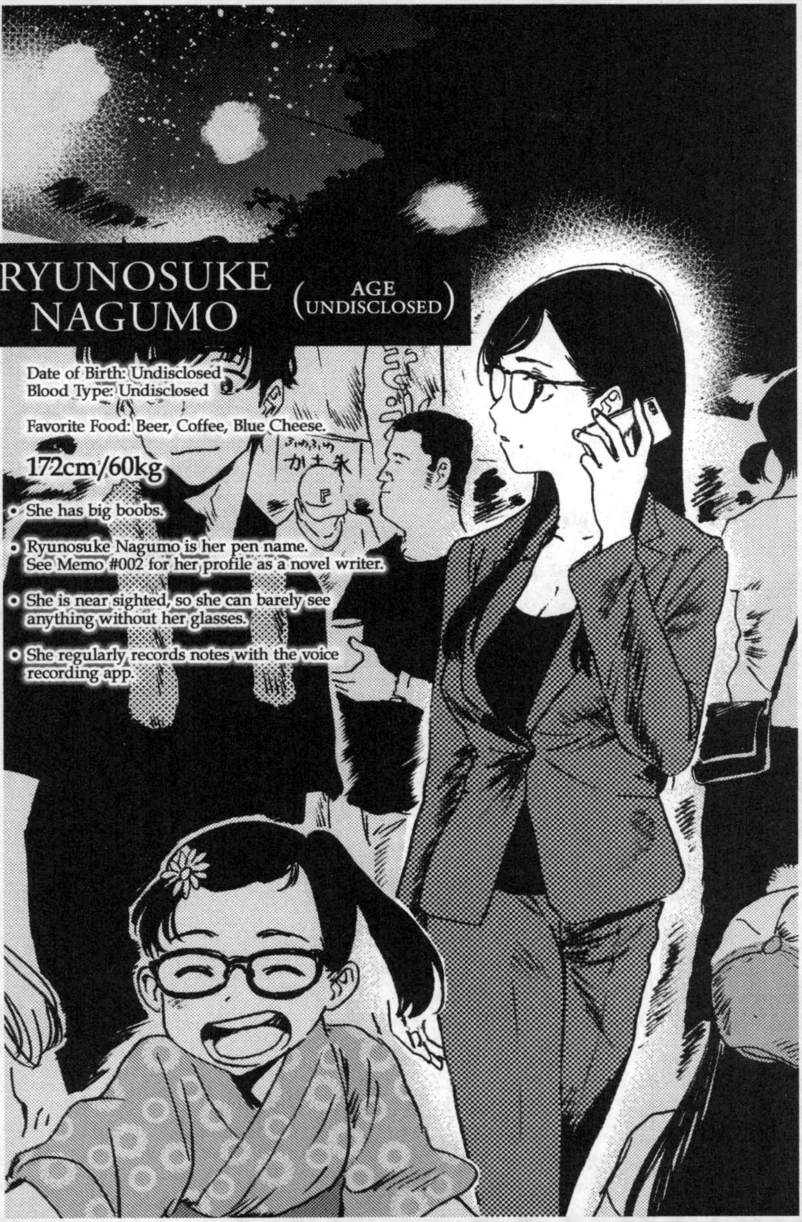
RYUNOSUKE NAGUMO
(AGE UNDISCLOSED)
Date of Birth: Undisclosed
Blood Type: Undisclosed
Favorite Food: Beer, Coffee, Blue Cheese.
172cm/60kg
• She has big boobs.
• Ryunosuke Nagumo is her pen name. See Memo #002 for her profile as a novel writer.
• She is near sighted, so she can barely see anything without her glasses.
• She regularly records notes with the voice recording app.

7月18日 水曜日 天気 晴れ

今日から夏休みです。みんなで万年青浜のゴミひろいに行きました。とうだいくんとはまじくんが、ゴミをひろわなくて、カニをつかまえてあそんでいて いくらちゅういしても、聞いてくれませんでした。帰り道で、うしおおねえちゃんたちと、海水よくに行くやくそくをしました。うしおおねえちゃんに、かげについて聞かれました。わたしが見たわたしそっくりの女の子のことです。今日は見てないけど、いつもどこからか見られてる気がします。とてもこわいです。

7月19日 木曜日 天気 雨

今日は大雨でした。雷がゴロゴロなっています。どこにもいけないので、うちで店番をしました。おきゃくさんがあまりこないのでお父さんとテレビでゲームをしてあそびました。ゲームをしているときに、おきゃくさんがきて、わたしのことを、さっきヒルコさまで見かけたと言いました。へんです。わたしは今日、ずっと家にいました。

Today, on my way home, I felt like someone was following me. When I turned to look back, there was no one there, but I think it was that girl. Big sis Ushio and Mio were at the store, so I told them about the girl that looks just like me. Tomorrow I will go to the garbage picking event at Omotohama beach with the two of them. My teacher said that since there's more tourists, there's more garbage.

July 18th, Wednesday - Weather: Sunny

It is summer vacation from today. We all went to the garbage picking event at Omotohama beach. Todai and Hamaji were not picking garbage but were playing around catching crabs, and did not listen to me no matter how much I told them to stop. On our way home, I made a promise to go swimming in the ocean with big sis Ushio and others. Ushio asked me about the shadow. It is about that girl that looks just like me. I hadn't seen her today, but I always feel like she's watching me. It is very scary.

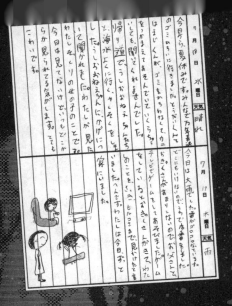

July 19th, Thursday - Weather: Rainy

It was raining heavily today. The thunder was rumbling. I couldn't go anywhere, so I stayed at the store. There were not many customers, so my daddy and I played video games. When we were playing the games, a customer came in and said that they had just seen me at the Great Hiruko. It's weird. I stayed home all day today.

7月20日 金曜日 天気 くもり

明日は朝から、うしおおねえちゃんたちといっしょに、海であそびます。学校のうらの、プライベートビーチに行きます。きょ年の水ぎが入らなくなったので、今日お母さんと本土に買いに行きました。わたしはおよぎが苦手だけど、みおおねえちゃんが教えてくれます。みおおねえちゃんは水えいぶでおよぐのがとてもじょうずです。けど、プライベートビーチにはカが多いのでいやです。家の店においている虫よけスプレーをもっていこうと思います。明日は晴れてほしいです。

July 20th, Friday - Weather: Cloudy

Tomorrow I will go play all day at the ocean with big sis Ushio and others. We will go to the private beach behind the school. I couldn't fit in my swimsuit from last year, so my mommy and I went to the mainland today to buy one. I am not good at swimming, but big sis Mio will teach me. Mio is a member of the swimming club and is very good at swimming. But I don't like it that there's a lot of mosquitos at the private beach. I think I will take the bug spray we have at our store. I hope it will be sunny tomorrow

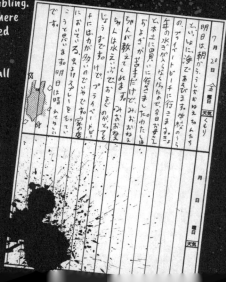

MEMO#001

DIARY OF SHIORI KOBAYAKAWA (EXCERPTS)

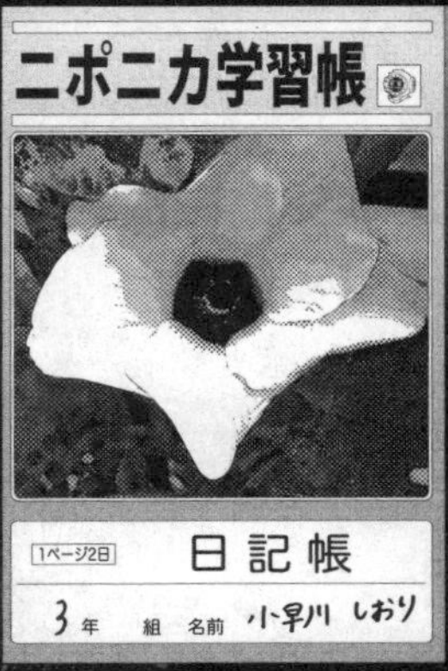
ニポニカ学習帳
1ページ2日
日記帳
3年 組 名前 小早川 しおり

THE NOTEBOOK USED AS THE DIARY OF SHIORI KOBAYAKAWA (THIRD GRADE)

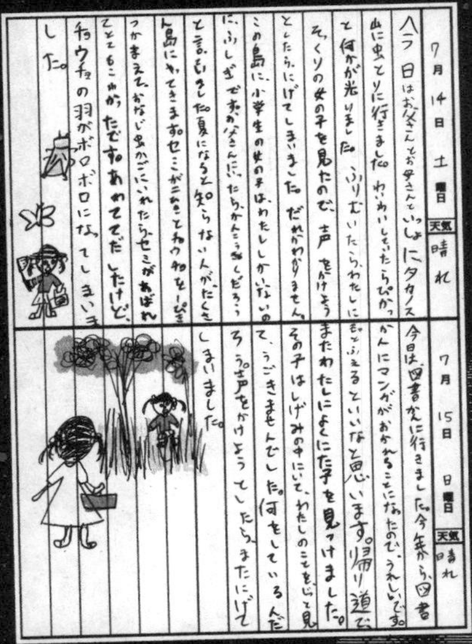

7月14日 土曜日 天気 晴れ

今日はお父さんとお母さんといっしょにタカノス山に虫とりに行きました。わいわいしていたらぴかっと何かが光りました。ふりむいたらわたしにそっくりの女の子を見たので、声をかけようとしたらにげてしまいました。だれかわかりません。この島に、小学生の女の子はわたししかいないのに、ふしぎでお父さんにいったらかんこうきゃくだろうと言いました。夏になると知らない人がたくさん島にやってきます。セミが二ひきとチョウチョを一ぴきつかまえて、おなじ虫かごにいれたらセミがあばれてとてもこわかったです。あわててだしたけど、チョウチョの羽がボロボロになってしまいました。

7月15日 日曜日 天気 晴れ

今日は図書かんに行きました。今年から図書かんにマンガがおかれることになったので、うれしいです。もっとふえるといいなと思います。帰り道で、またわたしによくにた子を見つけました。その子はしげみの中にいて、わたしのことをじっと見て、うごきませんでした。何をしているんだろう。声をかけようとしたら、またにげてしまいました。

July 14th, Saturday – Weather: Sunny

Today I went to Mt. Takanosu to go bug catching with my daddy and mommy. We were having fun then suddenly there was a flash. When I looked back, there was a girl that looked just like me, so I tried to greet her, but she ran away. I don't know who she is. I am the only elementary school aged girl on this island, so it is weird, but when I told my daddy he said she is probably a tourist. When summer comes, a lot of people I don't know come to the island. We caught two cicadas and one butterfly, but when I put them in the same bug cage, the cicada went crazy and tore around, and I was very scared. I hurried to let it out, but the butterfly's feathers were all damaged.

July 15th, Sunday – Weather: Sunny

Today I went to the library. I'm happy because from this year they have comic books. On my way home, I found a girl that looks a lot like me again. She was in the bushes, quietly looking at me, not moving. I wondered what she was doing. When I tried to greet her, she ran away again.

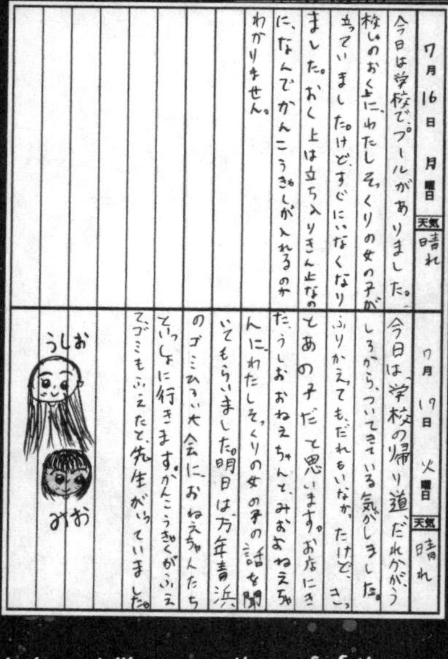

7月16日 月曜日 天気 晴れ

今日は学校でプールがありました。校しゃのおく上に、わたしそっくりの女の子が立っていました。けど、すぐにいなくなりました。おく上は立ち入りきん止なのに、なんでかんこうきゃくが入れるのかわかりません。

7月17日 火曜日 天気 晴れ

今日は学校の帰り道、だれかがうしろから、ついてきている気がしました。さっとふりかえっても、だれもいなかったけど、きっとあの子だと思います。おなにきた、うしおおねえちゃんと、みおおねえちゃんに、わたしそっくりの女の子の話を聞いてもらいました。明日は方年青浜のゴミひろい大会に、おねえちゃんたちといっしょに行きます。かんこうきゃくがふえてゴミもふえたと、先生がいっていました。

うしお
みお

July 16th, Monday – Weather: Sunny

Today, there was a pool class at school. I saw that girl that looks just like me on the roof of the school building. But she was soon gone. It is prohibited to go on the roof, so I don't know how a

★★☆☆☆ Hmmmmm.
By dorisan on February 14, 2017

There are many positive and highly rated reviews so I gave it a try, but honestly I couldn't see what is so interesting.

There aren't any characters that really stand out, and from the very beginning the narrative of "I" goes on and on and on, it's extremely boring.

The mysterious girl who appeared from the middle section was a character that drew me in, so I was like, gee, bring her out earlier.

In my opinion, if you can improve on the composition, the pacing and reading quality will improve, and you could probably shorten the book by at least 200 pages. Maybe try giving the main character some special power, or something like that.

The development at the end is also a little forced, and lacks persuasive power.

3 people found this review helpful.

★★★★☆ Not for Nagumo beginners
By Gilliam Terry on October 24, 2015

Compared to Nagumo's previous works, this one has a very different feel. Since the story is set in the author's birthplace, I got the impression that it was more like an I-novel than a mystery. If you read it expecting a classic whodunit like the Hijiri series,

you may not be satisfied.

If you have never read Nagumo's work before, I don't recommend starting with this book. Begin with something like the so-called Hijiri series in which detective Hijiri Aruhiko plays an active part, or the previous work "Hotel Necropolitan", or the debut work "Shadow Ball" which has even become a movie.

11 people found this review helpful.

★★★★★ Idiot
By Passive Nihilism on June 4, 2018

The main character doesn't stand out? Give some special power?

Who cares about such crap! Are you an idiot? There's no need to add unnecessary character personalities to a mystery. If you want to read stuff like that, pick up a Jump magazine.

1 person found this review helpful.

★★★☆☆ Masterpiece~!
By Hellzapoppin Seedbed on September 1, 2017

Perhaps because I like mysteries and read them often I could see where the story was going to be honest, but even so, the foreshadowing techniques and psychological depictions were truly impressive and I could feel the author's skills.

It's not outstanding compared to previous works,

but if you like the author, it's a great work that you won't want to miss.

5 people found this review helpful.

★★★★★ This was AMAZING…
By Sand on November 10, 2015

Towards the end, I was so amazed with how the secrets unfold, hitting me right in the heart… so much so that it made me mutter "OMG…!"

I highly recommend this.

10 people found this review helpful.

★★★☆☆ It's both good, and bad?
By World Eater on January 1, 2018

I wonder if this can be called a mystery. Finding the criminal and revealing the tricks are the important factors in this book (although saying this may be misleading), so for some people it may be unsatisfying.

However, the author still has a neat writing style, and hats off to the technique for appropriately depicting the particular eeriness and gloomy feelings that provincial towns hold.

The reading experience is something you can't really get with other books, and I would like to recommend it to people who are a little bit tired of typical mysteries.

3 people found this review helpful.

★☆☆☆☆ I was deeply moved
By Pillar of Salt on December 24, 2015

I could not hold my tears when I read the last scene, where the main character sinks into the blast furnace with his thumbs up. I would recommend it to everyone.

3 people found this review helpful.

★★★★★ Greatest work!!!
By Byakuranhime on September 22, 2015

I myself has read… every work by Ryunosuke Nagumo… including the short story "Did you just say angel?"… which hasn't been collected in a book yet! Even among them… I think… this work… is the best masterpiece! Wonderful feeling… after reading it. Super impressed! This is… the best book I've read… this year!

What is, "I"?

I feel like…I've been thrown a question…again… about the issue of self-identity… which has been the theme for Nagumo-sensei since debut!

6 people found this review helpful.

★★★★☆ Frightening
By Masapon on March 3, 2018

I thought it would be convenient if I had a copy-human of myself, because I could have it attend a class, a drinking party, or a part-time job that I

didn't want to go to, but it's scary to think that it would come to kill me to have to take over my life. And even if my life is taken over, no one can tell the difference.

I can't say much because it's a spoiler, but a person in the middle of the novel tells how to distinguish between a copied human and the real person, but even though I read to the end, I still couldn't understand it after all. I wished it had been made clearer.

38 people found this review helpful.

★★★★★ To those who have not yet read
By Shin on July 18, 2018

This book is strictly prohibited from spoilers!

This contradicts itself, but you should not be reading reviews here.

Don't think anymore, press the buy button, and close your browser now.

Was this review helpful?

REVIEWS OF RYUNOSUKE NAGUMO'S SWAMP MAN

Ryunosuke Nagumo

Swamp Man

★★★★☆ (221)

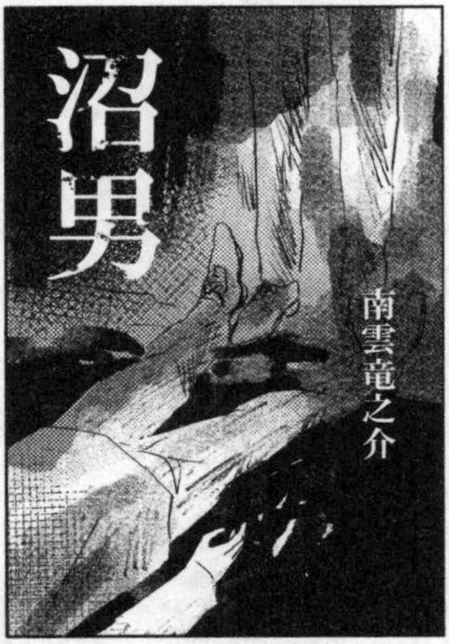
沼男
南雲竜之介

Publisher: Yorunotobari Sha
Publication date: September 15, 2015

Format: Hard Cover

Price: ¥ 1,808

Only 2 left in stock
(more on the way)

Add to Cart

Story

In the summer of my second year of middle school,
I was killed by me —

Hizuru Sagimori is obsessed with the delusion that her family and friends are being replaced by another person who looks exactly like them. One summer day, a girl who looks just like Hizuru herself appears in front of her. As was expected, the girl gently puts her hands on Hizuru's neck.

What is "I"...? Ryunosuke Nagumo's latest compilation, raises questions about self-identity.

About the Author

Ryunosuke Nagumo

Born in Hito town, Wakayama City, Wakayama Prefecture.

Real name, gender, date of birth, educational background, and work history not disclosed.

The author is a masked writer and was absent from the Yumemizogawa Doppo Award Ceremony. In the 63 years since the award was established, Nagumo is the only no-show winner of the award. In 2010, the author made their debut as a novelist by winning the 32nd Detective Novel Newcomer Award for "Shadow Ball", and attracted attention as a talented young writer of classic whodunit. They specialize in the technique of incorporating Sci-Fi and fantasy elements into classic subjects with a slipstream manner and reconstructing them from a modern perspective. This novel was made into a movie in 2014.

There are rumors that the author may be a woman because of the literary style and unique touch. [citation needed]

Customers who bought this item also bought

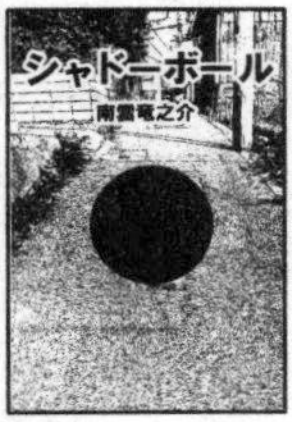
シャドーボール
南雲竜之介

Shadow Ball

★★★★½ 343

¥ 1,618

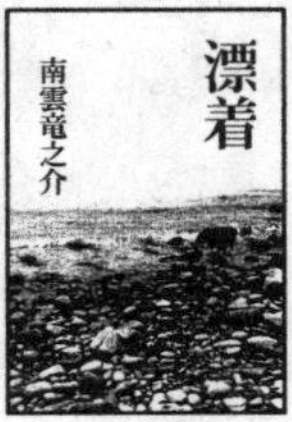
漂着
南雲竜之介

Drifting

★★★★☆ 172

¥ 1,752

AFTERWORDS

ORIGINALLY PUBLISHED IN VOL. 1 OF THE JAPANESE EDITION.

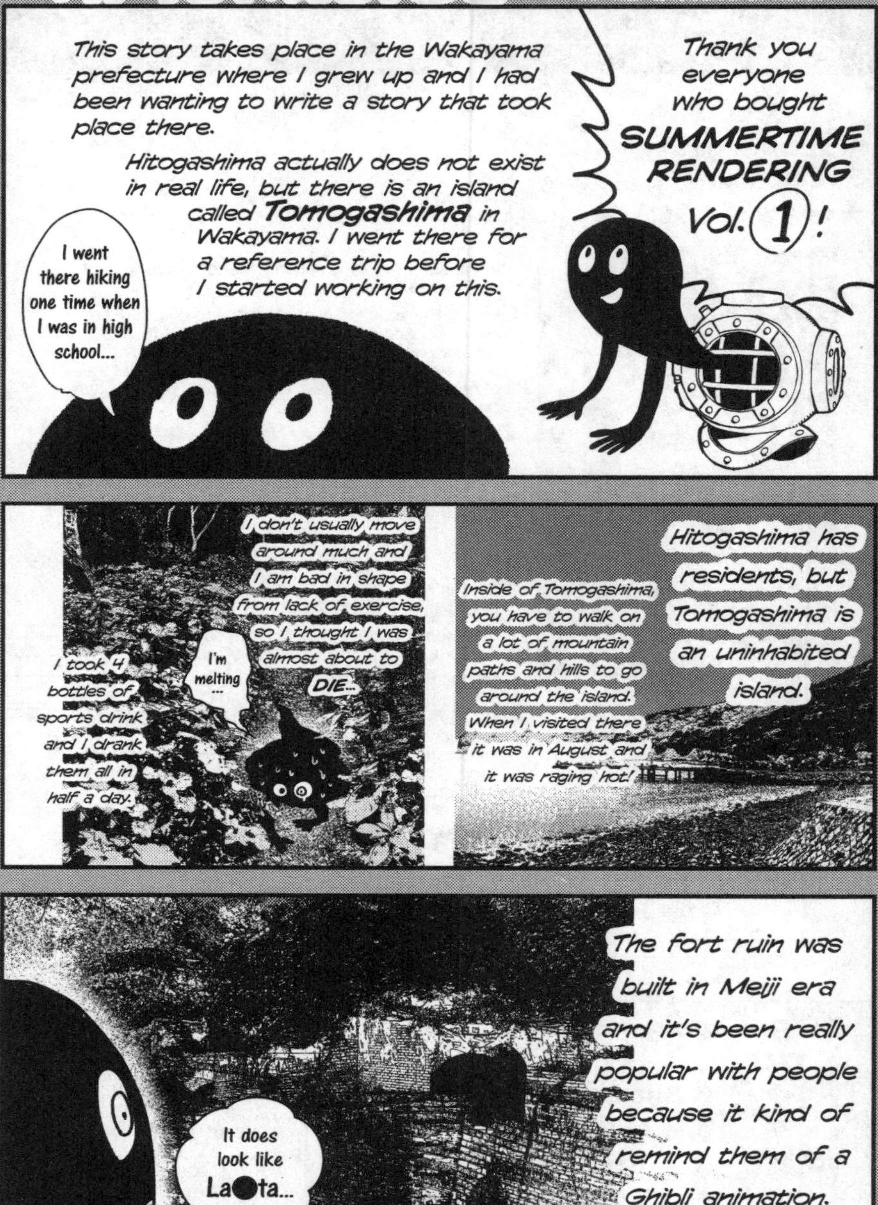

Thank you everyone who bought SUMMERTIME RENDERING Vol. 1!
This story takes place in the Wakayama prefecture where I grew up and I had been wanting to write a story that took place there.
Hitogashima actually does not exist in real life, but there is an island called Tomogashima in Wakayama. I went there for a reference trip before I started working on this.
I went there hiking one time when I was in high school...
Hitogashima has residents, but Tomogashima is an uninhabited island.
Inside of Tomogashima, you have to walk on a lot of mountain paths and hills to go around the island. When I visited there it was in August and it was raging hot!
I don't usually move around much and I am bad in shape from lack of exercise, so I thought I was almost about to DIE...
I'm melting...
I took 4 bottles of sports drink and I drank them all in half a day.
The fort ruin was built in Meiji era and it's been really popular with people because it kind of remind them of a Ghibli animation.
It does look like La●ta...

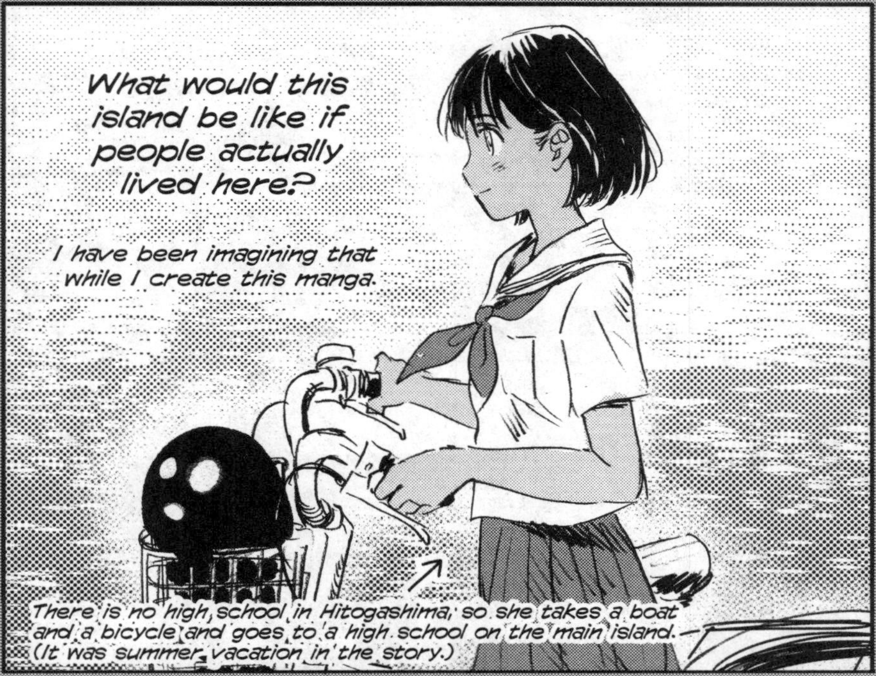
What would this island be like if people actually lived here?
I have been imagining that while I create this manga.
There is no high school in Hitogashima, so she takes a boat and a bicycle and goes to a high school on the main island.
(It was summer vacation in the story.)

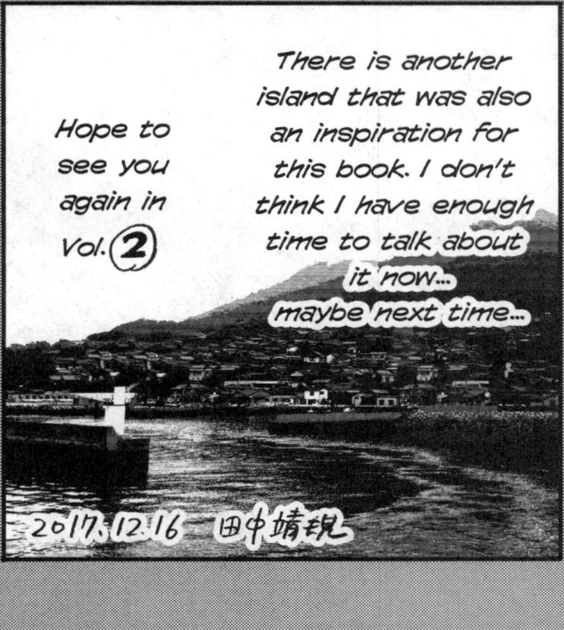
There is another island that was also an inspiration for this book. I don't think I have enough time to talk about it now... maybe next time...
Hope to see you again in Vol. 2
2017.12.16 田中靖規

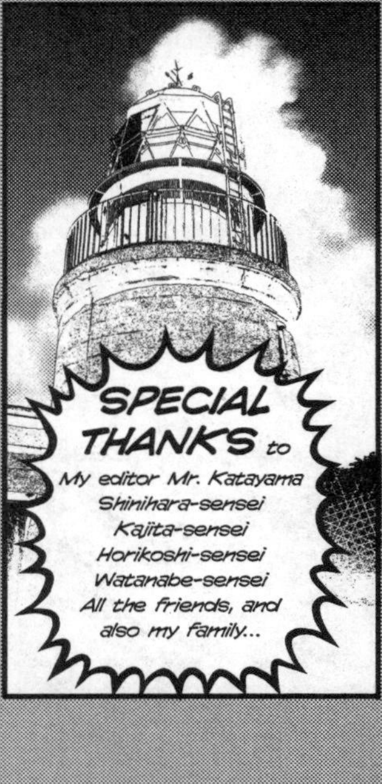
SPECIAL THANKS to
My editor Mr. Katayama
Shinihara-sensei
Kajita-sensei
Horikoshi-sensei
Watanabe-sensei
All the friends, and also my family...

AFTERWORDS

ORIGINALLY PUBLISHED IN VOL. 2 OF THE JAPANESE EDITION.

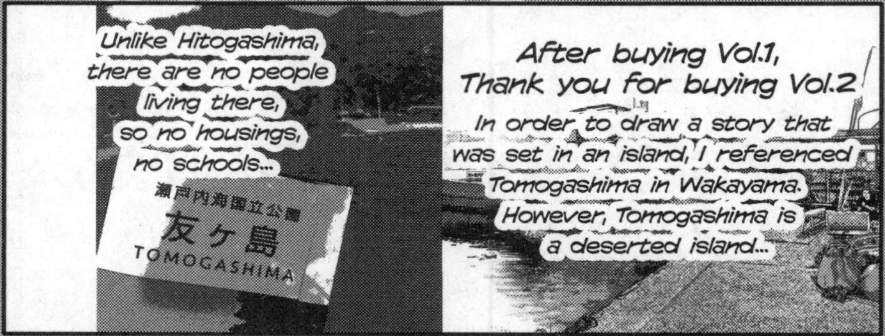

After buying Vol.1, Thank you for buying Vol.2
In order to draw a story that was set in an island, I referenced Tomogashima in Wakayama. However, Tomogashima is a deserted island...
Unlike Hitogashima, there are no people living there, so no housings, no schools...
瀬戸内海国立公園
友ヶ島
TOMOGASHIMA

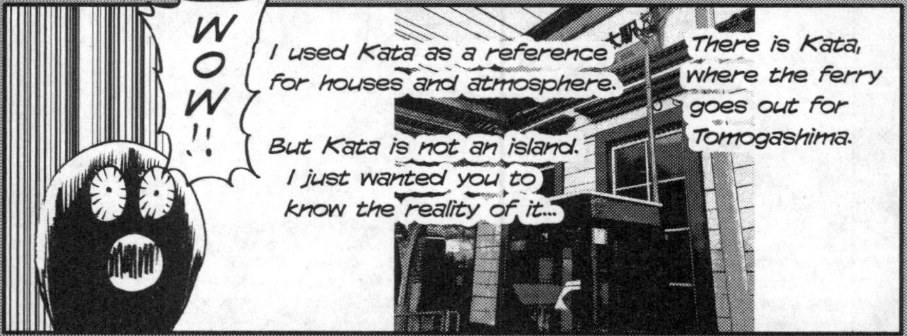

There is Kata, where the ferry goes out for Tomogashima.
I used Kata as a reference for houses and atmosphere.
But Kata is not an island. I just wanted you to know the reality of it...
WOW!!

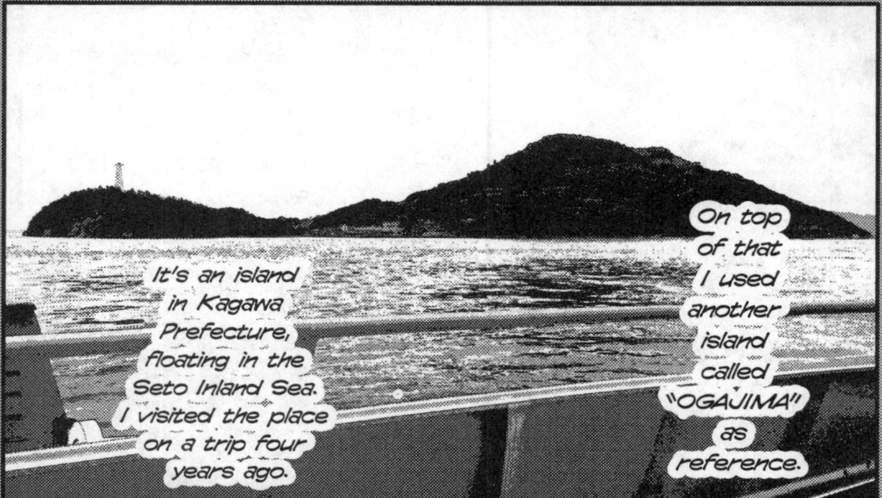

On top of that I used another island called "OGAJIMA" as reference.
It's an island in Kagawa Prefecture, floating in the Seto Inland Sea. I visited the place on a trip four years ago.

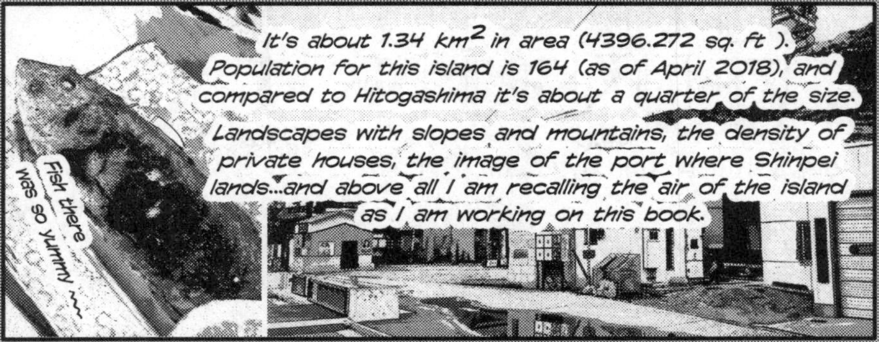
It's about 1.34 km² in area (4396.272 sq. ft).
Population for this island is 164 (as of April 2018), and compared to Hitogashima it's about a quarter of the size.
Landscapes with slopes and mountains, the density of private houses, the image of the port where Shinpei lands...and above all I am recalling the air of the island as I am working on this book.
Fish there was so yummy ~~

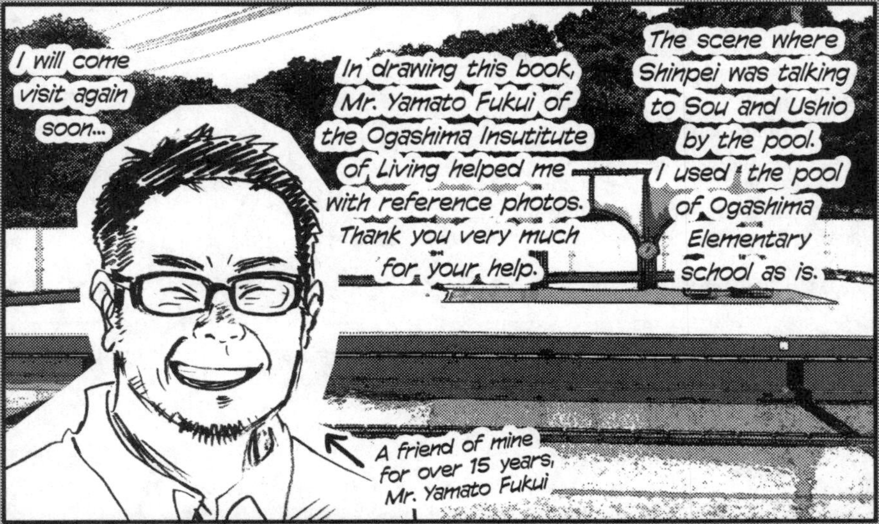
The scene where Shinpei was talking to Sou and Ushio by the pool. I used the pool of Ogashima Elementary school as is.
In drawing this book, Mr. Yamato Fukui of the Ogashima Insutitute of Living helped me with reference photos. Thank you very much for your help.
I will come visit again soon...
A friend of mine for over 15 years, Mr. Yamato Fukui

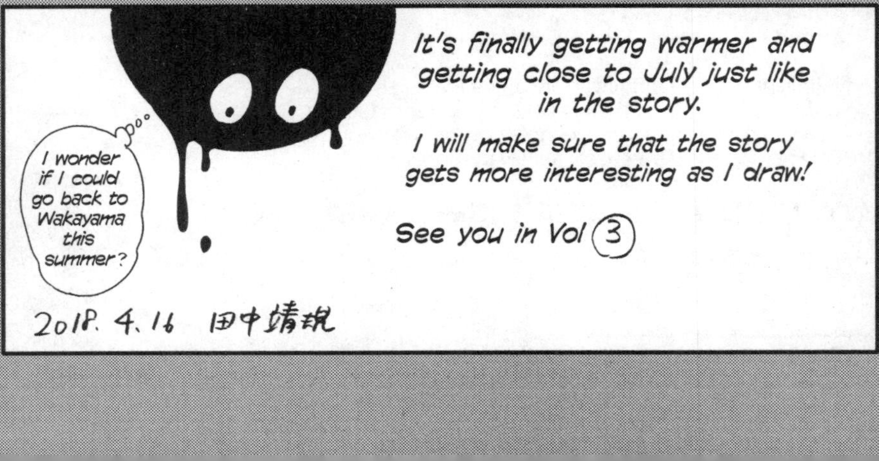
It's finally getting warmer and getting close to July just like in the story.
I will make sure that the story gets more interesting as I draw!
See you in Vol ③
I wonder if I could go back to Wakayama this summer?
2018. 4. 16 田中靖規

SUMMERTIME RENDERING 1

Story & Illustration by: Yasuki Tanaka

English Edition
Translation: Jocelyne Allen
Additional Translation: Megumi Cummings & Anna Kawashima
Lettering: Janice Leung
Sound Effects & Touch Up: Phil Christie & Jeannie Lee
Copy Editor: Claudia McGivney
Associate Editor: M. Chandler
Graphic & Cover Design: W.T. Francis

UDON Staff
Chief of Operations: Erik Ko
Director of Publishing: Matt Moylan
VP of Business Development: Cory Casoni
Director of Marketing: Megan Maiden
Japanese Liaisons: Steven Cummings & Anna Kawashima

SUMMER TIME RENDER
©2017 by Yasuki Tanaka
All rights reserved.
First published in Japan in 2017 by SHUEISHA Inc., Tokyo.
English translation rights arranged by SHUEISHA Inc.
through Tohan Corporation, Tokyo.

This volume contains contents originally published in サマータイムレンダ 1, 2.

English language version published by UDON Entertainment Inc.
118 Tower Hill Road, C1, PO Box 20008
RIchmond Hill, Ontario, L4K 0K0, Canada

www.UDONentertainment.com

First printing: October 2022
Hard Cover ISBN: 978-1-772942-38-5

Printed in Canada

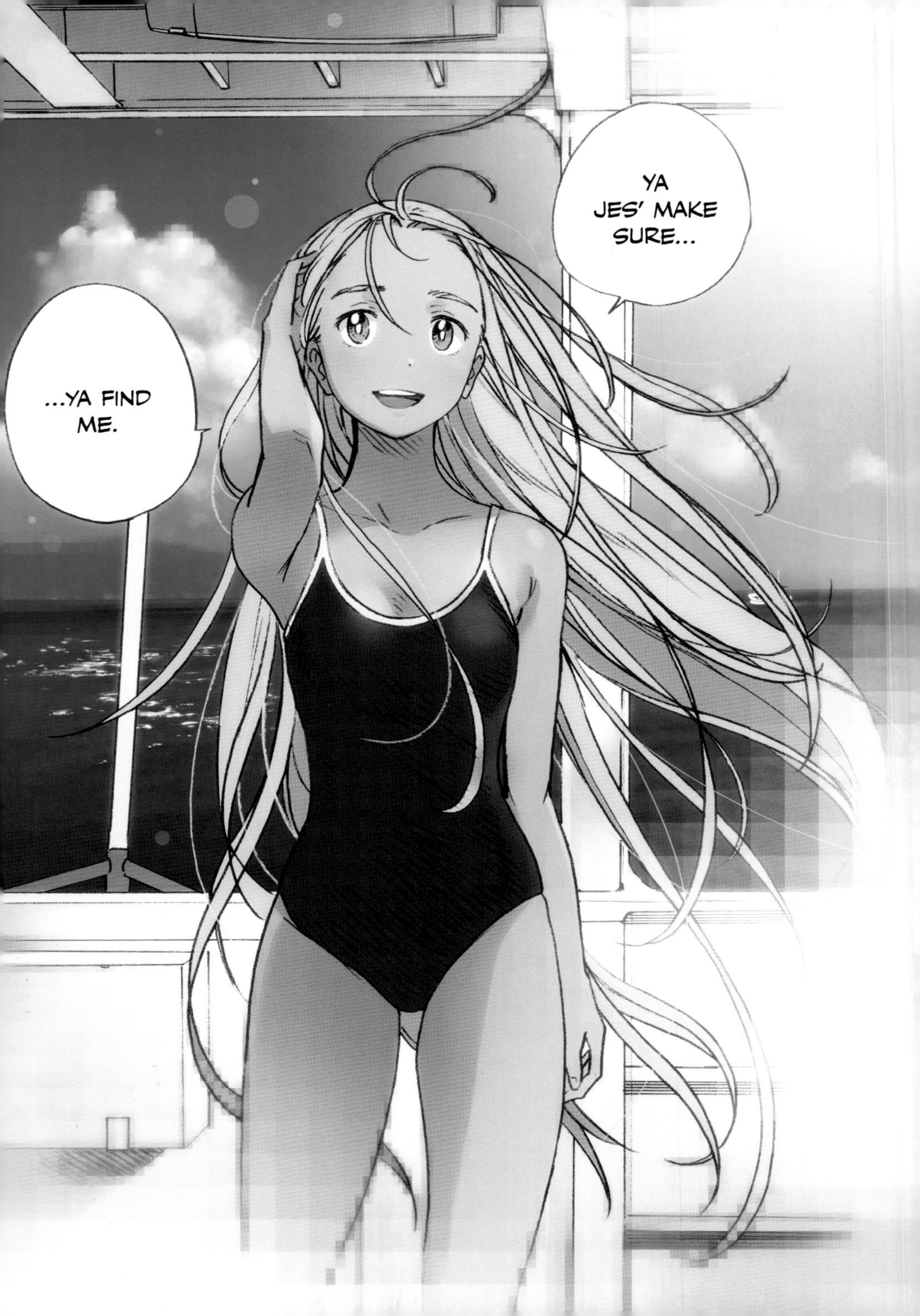
YA JES' MAKE SURE...
...YA FIND ME.

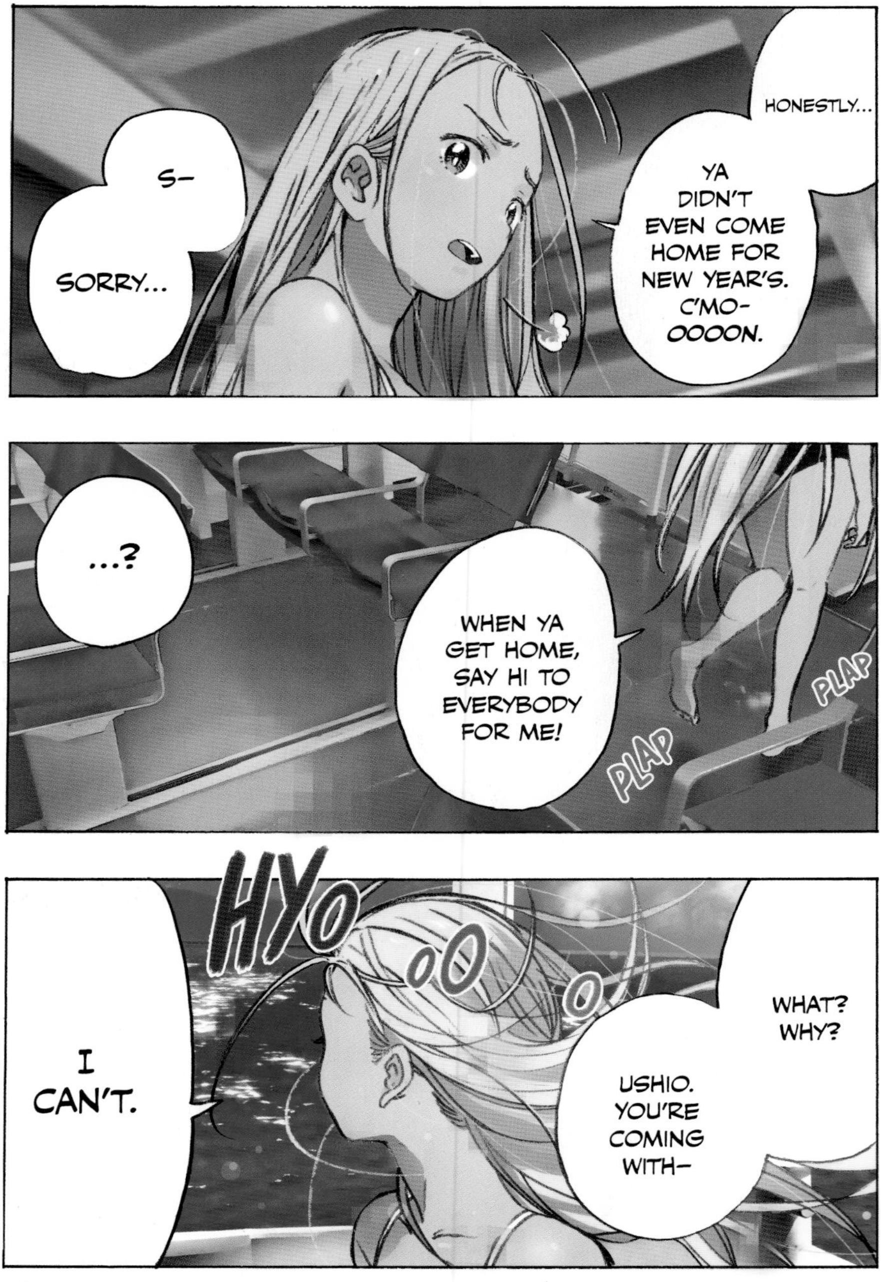
HONESTLY...
YA DIDN'T EVEN COME HOME FOR NEW YEAR'S. C'MO-OOOON.
S–
SORRY...
WHEN YA GET HOME, SAY HI TO EVERYBODY FOR ME!
PLAP
PLAP
...?
WHAT? WHY?
USHIO. YOU'RE COMING WITH–
HYOoOo
I CAN'T.

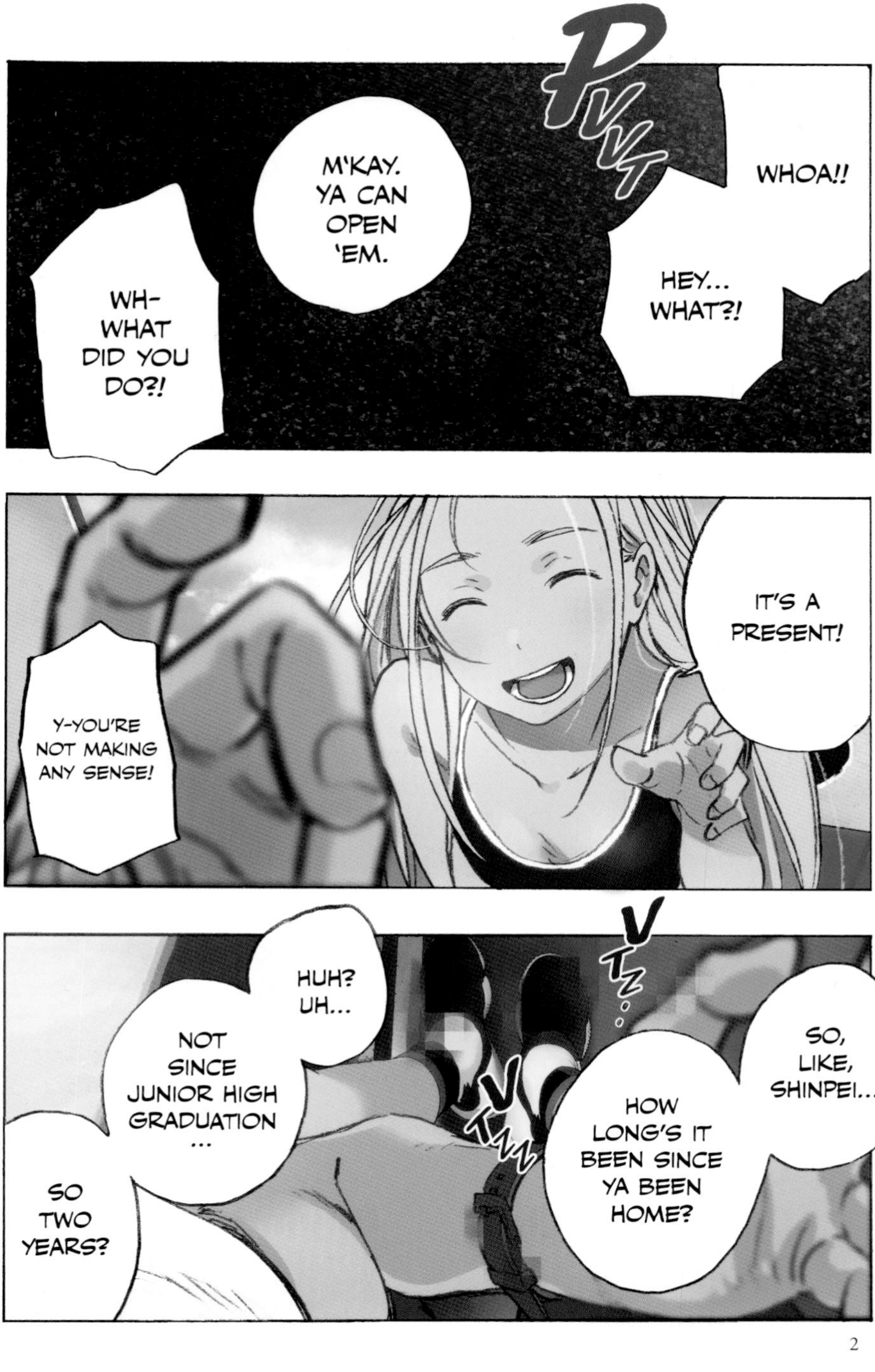
PVVT
WHOA!!
HEY... WHAT?!
M'KAY. YA CAN OPEN 'EM.
WH- WHAT DID YOU DO?!
IT'S A PRESENT!
Y-YOU'RE NOT MAKING ANY SENSE!
VTZ...
SO, LIKE, SHINPEI...
HOW LONG'S IT BEEN SINCE YA BEEN HOME?
VTNN
HUH? UH...
NOT SINCE JUNIOR HIGH GRADUATION ...
SO TWO YEARS?

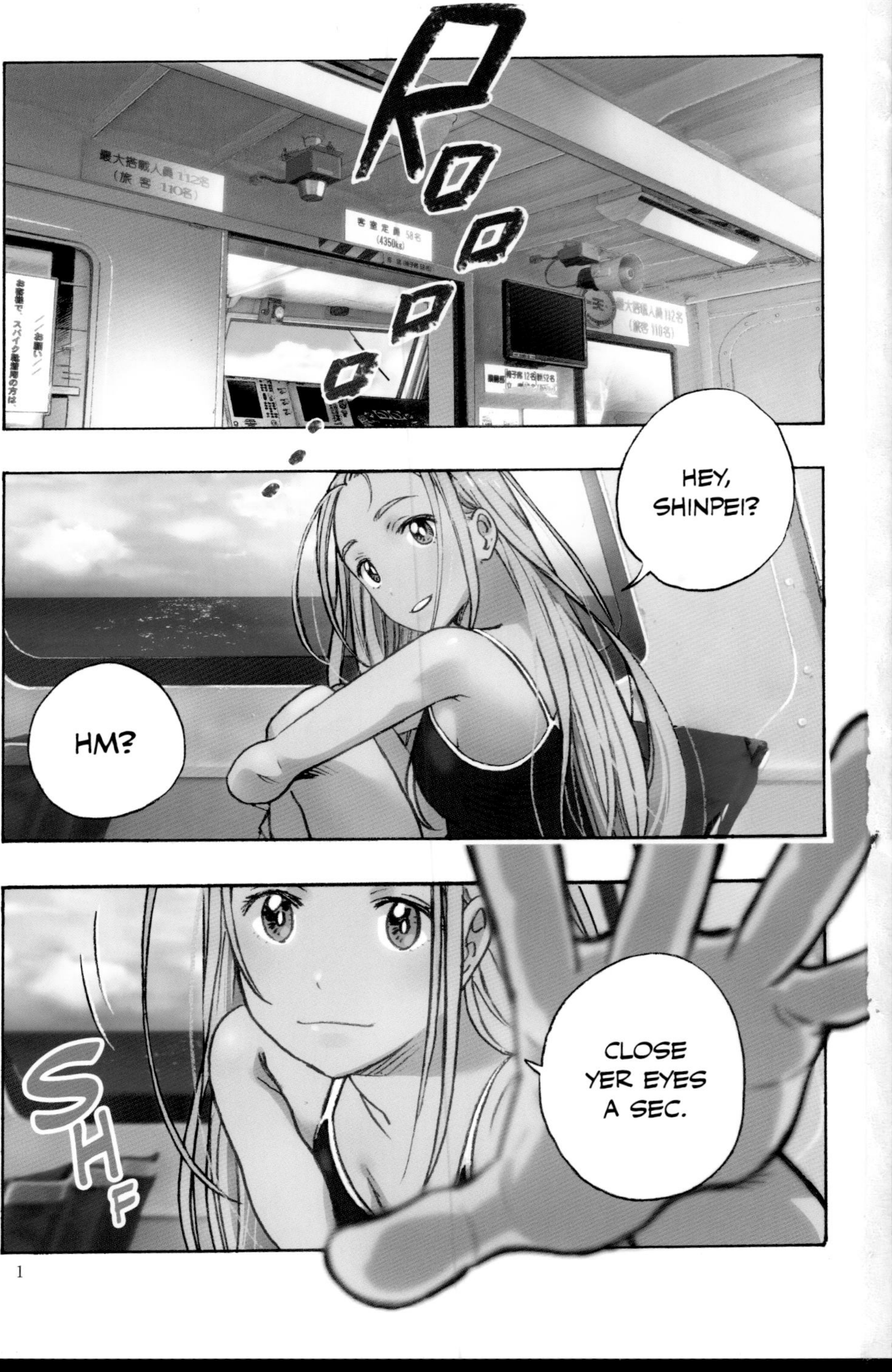
ROOOO
最大搭載人員112名
(旅客110名)
客室定員58名
(4350kg)
お願い
お客様で、スパイク靴着用の方は、
HEY, SHINPEI?
HM?
CLOSE YER EYES A SEC.
SHF